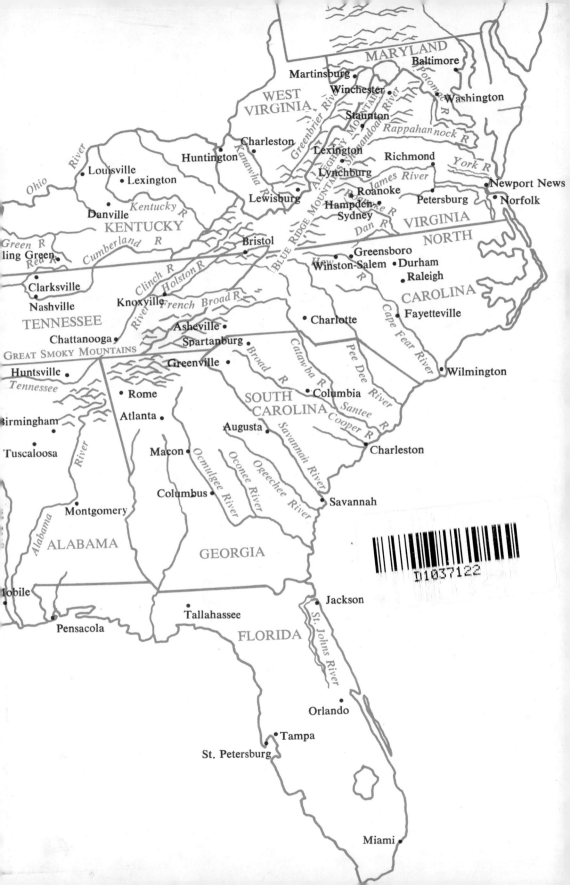

MARYLAND

Martinsburg

Baltimore

WEST
VIRGINIA

Winchester

Washington

Staunton

Charleston

Lexington

Richmond

Huntington

Lynchburg

Louisville

Lexington

Roanoke

Petersburg

Newport News

Lewisburg

Hampden-
Sydney

Norfolk

Danville

KENTUCKY

VIRGINIA

NORTH

Bristol

Greensboro

Clarksville

Winston-Salem

Durham

Raleigh

Nashville

CAROLINA

Knoxville

Fayetteville

TENNESSEE

Charlotte

Chattanooga

Asheville

GREAT SMOKY MOUNTAINS

Spartanburg

Huntsville

Greenville

Wilmington

Rome

SOUTH
CAROLINA

Columbia

Birmingham

Atlanta

Charleston

Tuscaloosa

Augusta

Macon

Columbus

Savannah

Montgomery

ALABAMA

GEORGIA

D1037122

Mobile

Jackson

Tallahassee

Pensacola

FLORIDA

Orlando

Tampa

St. Petersburg

Miami

Ohio River
Green R
ling Green
Red R
Kentucky R
Cumberland R
Clinch R
Holston R
French Broad R
River
Tennessee
River
Alabama River
Ocmulgee River
Oconee River
Ogeechee River
Savannah River
Broad R
Catawba R
Santee
Cooper R
Pee Dee River
Cape Fear River
New
Dan R
Roanoke R
James River
York R
Rappahannock R
Shenandoah River
ALLEGHENY MOUNTAIN
Greenbrier River
Kanawha R
BLUE RIDGE MOUNTAINS
St. Johns River

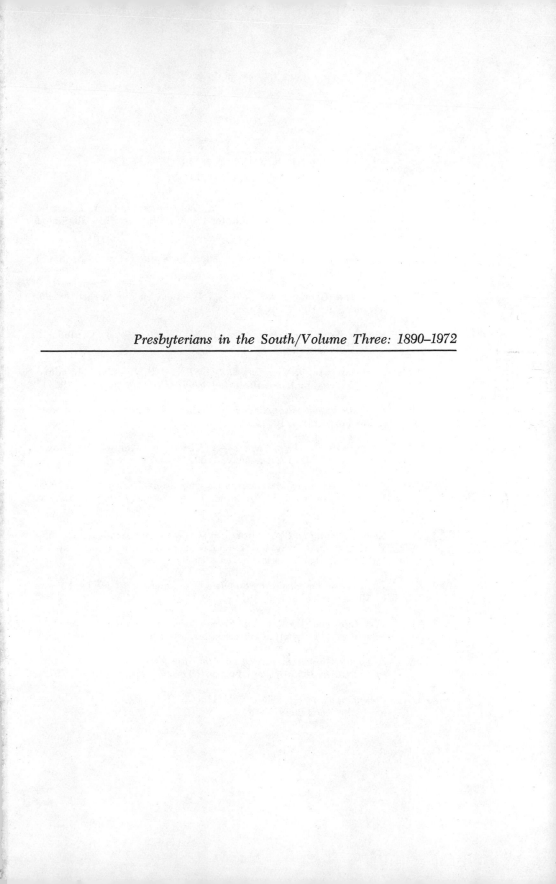

Presbyterians in the South/Volume Three: 1890–1972

PRESBYTERIAN HISTORICAL SOCIETY
PUBLICATION SERIES

* Out of print

ERNEST TRICE THOMPSON

PRESBYTERIANS IN THE SOUTH

VOLUME THREE: 1890-1972

JOHN KNOX PRESS, *Richmond, Virginia*

285
T

Library of Congress Cataloging in Publication Data
Thompson, Ernest Trice, 1894-
    Presbyterians in the South.

    Includes bibliographies.
    CONTENTS: v. 1. 1607-1861.—v. 2. 1861-1890.—v. 3.
1890-1972.
        1. Presbyterian Church in the U.S.—History.
        2. Presbyterian Church in the Southern States.
I. Title.
BX8941.T5   285.175   63-19121
ISBN 0-8042-0998-7

V. 3

The publication of this volume
has been made possible through support
from a number of sources, including the
Marietta McNeill Morgan and Samuel Tate Morgan, Jr., Memorial Fund
(First and Merchants National Bank of Richmond, Virginia, Trustee),
the Cameron D. Deans memorial fund,
and the Walter Lingle fund.

Contents

Foreword

For 150 years Presbyterians in the South were members of a denomination recognizing its obligation to carry the gospel to the nation as a whole. Civil War brought separation from their brethren in the North. In announcing to the world the organization of "The Presbyterian Church in the Confederate States of America," the General Assembly pled in partial justification the desirability that "each nation should contain a separate and independent church." When the Confederacy collapsed and the seceding states returned to the Union, the Southern body chose deliberately a new name without sectional connotations—"The Presbyterian Church in the United States"—in the hope that the "distinctive" principle—"the spirituality of the church"—characterizing the denomination might attract wide support in the North. There were indeed some border accessions, but by the end of the Reconstruction period it had become clear that the Presbyterian Church in the United States had become and would remain a sectional church, what might truly be termed a *Southern* Presbyterian Church, whose history and outlook would be closely intertwined with the history and outlook of its particular region.

Around the turn of the century, however, the dead hand of the past began to lose its grip; a new generation that "knew not Joseph" was arriving on the scene.

Since World War I the church has been buffeted by winds of change—theological, ethical, and ecumenical. At first hesitantly, and then—particularly after World War II—more decidedly, the church, despite strain and stress, has begun to move out of the backwaters into the mainstream of American Christianity.

This movement—the issues faced, the tensions created, the uncertainties that remain—has meaning, we believe, not only for Southern Presbyterians, but also for others interested in the working of the religious mind and in the role of the church in our modern society.

Part 1

OUT OF THE BACKWATERS

I

The "New" South

During the period now under review (roughly 1890-1930) the South remained primarily agricultural. Rice culture declined in the Carolina and Georgia coastlands but found favorable growing conditions in Louisiana and Texas and in portions of Arkansas. Sugarcane continued to be grown in Louisiana. Truckers found a profitable outlet for their vegetables in the growing urban centers of the Northeast, and their farms multiplied in the coastal areas from Delaware southward to the Rio Grande. Apples became a major product in Virginia, peaches in the Carolinas, and citrus fruits in Florida. Corn remained the most widely grown Southern crop. In 1930 every Southeastern state gave to it at least one fourth of its cultivated acreage. The legumes—soybeans, velvet beans, peanuts (a major crop in portions of Virginia and North Carolina), and cowpeas—were grown almost as widely.

Despite these variations, however, Southern agriculture remained dependent in most areas upon its single crop system—either cotton or tobacco. By 1930 cotton was the major crop in a broad crescent of land, 125 to 500 miles wide and extending 1,600 miles from eastern North Carolina southwesterly into Texas and Oklahoma, with fingers reaching into Tennessee, Arkansas, and one or two counties in Missouri. Tobacco, the second distinctive crop of the South, was grown principally in the two Carolinas, Kentucky, Tennessee, Georgia, and Virginia. Like cotton it required many hours of back-breaking labor, and like cotton it put a premium on family labor—women and children as well as men. By 1900 the amount of tobacco produced was almost twice that of the prewar period. The rapid expansion of the tobacco acreage after that time was due to the much higher consumption of tobacco products, particularly cigarettes, both at home and abroad. The new tenant, sharecropper, tax-lien system, which had developed after the Civil War and on which both cotton and tobacco had come to depend, attracted not only the Negroes but also the poor white farmers who, hitherto, had lived very precariously on the outer fringes of the cotton kingdom. Gradually the white tenants came to outnumber the black (by two to one in 1940), and the number and proportion of both increased year after year, decade after decade. In 1880 30 percent of all Southern farmers were tenants, working the land of others. By 1930 the ratio had risen to 68 percent and among farmers who raised cotton it was approximately 80 percent.

> These farmers had little opportunity for advancement. They were un-trained in the better techniques of farming and, since they moved frequently, were interested only in the existing crop. The tenant farm had no orchard, few gardens, and few animals except for work. Further-more, the sharecroppers were "kept" men, in a sense, dependent upon the local merchants or their landlords for food and clothing. Without their consent diversification of output was impossible, for they insisted that labor and borrowed capital be devoted to the old staples. Moving on the average of once every two years, these migrant farmers had no interest in keeping up their houses and barns or engaging in soil con-servation. Children were not properly schooled or personal property accumulated. The standard of living of both white and black was pitiably low, and the environment played havoc with home life, citizen-ship, and the instinct normally associated with inherited ownership of the land. In short, tenancy led many Southerners into a situation much akin to that of the lowest European peasantry.[1]

A study carried out by the U.S. Department of Agriculture into the living conditions of white cotton farmers in a Piedmont county in Georgia (1924-1926) revealed that the average family of five lived on a farm valued at less than $2,000; received a cash income of $424; consumed for family living goods valued at $687.14; lived in unscreened houses, built in many cases out of a single thickness of lumber; spent only $24 a year on books, magazines, recreation, amusements, and religion combined; spent $15 a year for snuff and tobacco, their only luxury; and attended churches whose min-isters were farmers like themselves and served practically without remuneration.

Most of the tenants and sharecroppers in the beginning belonged to the Baptist and Methodist churches. Beginning in the 1880's newer emotional sects, some stressing the gift of tongues, some shouting and rolling on the floor, began to replace both of these as the churches of the poor. Presbyterians made little or no appeal to this portion of the population.

I. THE INDUSTRIAL REVOLUTION[2]

In the antebellum South, life had centered about the plantations and their needs. Towns existed mainly to serve the countryside. There were industries of course. But the South lagged far behind the North in industrial development and was almost entirely dependent on other regions for the tools and machines needed to maintain industrial production. The number of workingmen employed by manufacturing firms in the North was six times the number employed in the South, and the value of what they produced was five and a half times as great.

The outcome of the war convinced some Southern leaders that they must develop a different type of economy, that their region could no longer live "by cotton alone." Many of the South's manufacturing plants had been destroyed by the holocaust of war, and there was little capital with which to rebuild. For some time it was hoped that financial aid and also a supply of skilled labor might be forthcoming from the North, but neither of these hopes materialized. Without much aid from the outside, the South gradually rebuilt the plants destroyed by the war; but industry in the North, meanwhile, had developed by leaps and bounds, and, comparatively, the South was farther behind than before.

By 1880 some Southern capital had been accumulated, and a group of able leaders had arisen—merchants, editors, political leaders, and even ministers—who were convinced that the South could recover its prosperity only through the development of industry. The movement came to have all the enthusiasm and drive of a great political revolution, the fervor of a religious revival. The necessary capital was contributed in the beginning largely by the Southern people themselves and included the small investments of hundreds and thousands of individuals.

This industrial revival developed most rapidly in the Piedmont, where some cotton mills had been erected before the war and where water power was easily accessible. The South has the nation's most abundant rainfall, well distributed through the year, and this water rushes down the Appalachian Mountains toward the sea. Before the Civil War, it was the power of falling water which cut the lumber, ground the grain, and spun the yarn for the South. The earliest factories were built at spots where the numerous rivers in Virginia, the Carolinas, Georgia, and Alabama dropped from one level to the other. After the war, water power was succeeded by steam as the prime source of energy, and most of the old water mills fell into disuse. Steam continued to turn the wheels of the Piedmont factories until about 1900, when a new use was discovered for the rapidly falling streams of the Southeast—the manufacture of electricity, generated hitherto by steam through the use of coal.

The first hydroelectric power zone to emerge in the Southern Piedmont was in the Catawba Valley of North and South Carolina. Here is found the maximum water power capacity of the Southeast, a capacity exceeded only by that of the Tennessee Valley system on the western slope of the Appalachians. With its source on the flanks of Mount Mitchell, which rears its crest 6,684 feet above sea level and is the highest peak east of the Mississippi, the Catawba River drops to the easy flow of the coastal plains in less than 200 miles. In 1900 the valley had no plants operated by electricity, compared with a three percent electrification, for the rest of the state. Four years later the Southern Power Company was organized (since replaced by the Duke Power Company), and the great Catawba Valley, including 15 industrial counties of the two Carolinas, quickly took the lead in electrification and therefore in industrialization.

The Catawba-Wateree was only one river system whose potentialities were developed. Other full-length river systems utilized for the generation of hydroelectricity in this area were the Dan-Roanoke, the Yadkin-Pee Dee, the Santee, the Savannah, and the Chattahoochee-Appalachicola.

It was along these river systems that the power empire of the South developed and that the first real break with the agrarian tradition occurred. This great industrial area of the South "stretches in crescent from its southernmost tip at Birmingham, Alabama, to its northern end near Danville, Virginia. It passes through Alabama, Georgia, South Carolina, North Carolina and Virginia. For its southern and eastern boundary it hugs the fall line, for its northern and western boundary it encroaches on the southern highlands. Its total area may be estimated at 50,000 square miles."[3]

Though it was water power which determined the general area in which Southern industry first developed, hydroelectric power can be transmitted along high tension wires for a considerable distance from its source; as the various power systems became more closely integrated, electric power could be delivered at practically any point where the convergence of labor, raw materials, and markets made the construction of a factory advantageous. By 1930 these high voltage lines stretched for over 3,500 miles and served an area of 120,000 square miles, more than double the territory included in the Piedmont. As a result the industry of this area was from the beginning decentralized—not thickly clustered in an urban industrial area as in the older cities of the Northeast, but spread out through the countryside and distributed along a number of smaller towns. In the whole Piedmont, where most industry was concentrated, there were no large cities except Atlanta and Birmingham, for whose growth there are other explanations. But there were an unusually large number of thriving towns (in 1930 there were 160 industrial communities in the Carolinas alone, besides many isolated mills and factories), linked together, particularly in North Carolina by a system of modern highways, so that one community almost merged into the next.

The first industry to rise in the Southern Piedmont was the textile industry. Its roots, as we have seen, stretched back into the antebellum period. But while some mills below the dams along the streams wove the cotton into cloth, most of the South's great crop was shipped either to England or to New England, and the enhanced value of its manufactured product passed into other hands. By 1870 the South had rebuilt the mills destroyed by the war, but these mills for the most part carried out only the more elementary processes, while the yarn, which was their chief product, continued to be sent to New England to be woven into the finished product.

In the 1880's textile mills began to multiply rapidly in the Piedmont, and by 1900 cotton spindles (a measure of productive capacity) had mounted to 23 percent of the nation's total. Meanwhile, the migration of Northern mills to the South (attracted in part by the cheap and abundant Southern labor supply) had begun. By 1920 more than half the active spindles in the nation were to be found in this area, and by 1930 the proportion had come to be 73 percent. The leading textile states were North Carolina, South Carolina, and Georgia. In textile factories were employed more than half the people with factory jobs in all the South.

The rayon industry, regarded originally as an appendage of cotton textiles, quickly became a giant in its own right. The first rayon mill in the South was opened in Roanoke, Virginia, in 1917; by 1940 two-thirds of the rayon in the nation was manufactured in this region.

The labor supply for the mills was drawn at the outset from the poor whites on the neighboring farms and in the nearby mountains and was seemingly inexhaustible. "These folk eagerly sought industrial employment as a means of improving their low economic status. The hiring of women and children was hailed as a boon not only by the mill owners but by those to whom it gave a livelihood."[4]

The workers in the mills came to live for the most part in homes furnished by the mill owners and in villages which they controlled. They also operated the stores, provided the schools and churches, hired the teachers, ministers, and police, and in general furnished the same paternalistic oversight which had characterized the plantation.

This arrangement was a natural outgrowth of conditions, and there can be little doubt that "it was well meant."[5] The homes, furnished by the mills, were better than those to which the majority of the workers—drawn almost entirely from the poorest classes of whites—had been accustomed, and they preferred the social contacts of the villages to the isolation of backward rural communities. Still, the mill villages were drab, and the people came to regard themselves and to be regarded by others as a people apart.

Tobacco, cotton's great rival as a cash crop, came to have even greater value for the South as a manufactured product. In the 1880's, when the textile mills were springing up so rapidly through the Piedmont, tobacco factories were also doubling their productive capacities. From its first usage tobacco had been smoked in pipes; plug tobacco for chewing reached the height of its popularity in the 1890's; cigars reached their highest point of favor between 1870 and 1905. The cigarette was introduced into America about 1860 and became popular in the South during the period of the Civil War. Their manufacture in unlimited quantities became possible in 1884, when James Duke acquired the rights to the first cigarette machine. Six years later Duke consolidated the five largest companies into the powerful American Tobacco Company, which was dissolved in 1911 into its component parts. Since then the manufacture of cigarettes has increased at a rapid rate—twentyfold between 1900 and 1924. The First World War made the use of cigarettes almost universal among the male population, and their use by women was to become almost as common. It was the tobacco industry which produced the first great fortunes in the South.

Durham and Winston-Salem in North Carolina, Richmond, Virginia, and Louisville, Kentucky, became the centers of the new industry, which remains almost a Southern monopoly. But factories were processing tobacco in one way or another (cigars, pipe tobacco, chewing tobacco, snuff, or cigarettes) in almost every Southern state. In 1929 Winston-Salem had the largest tobacco factories in the world, and North Carolina produced nearly half the nation's total. In the textile mills the labor force was almost entirely white; in the cigarette factory Negro labor, which worked for lower wages, was extensively used.

Industries tend to concentrate in typical clusters. So the textile industry was only the entering wedge for many other industries, which entered first the Catawba Valley and then scattered through the Piedmont.

One of the most important of these industries was timber and its products. The quantity of timber taken from the Southern forests more than doubled between 1880 and 1890, giving the South first rank as the source of the nation's lumber. For a time, after 1900, lumbering became the largest industry in the region, employing one of every three wage earners and producing half the nation's total. In 1930 the proportion was 47 percent. Though the region had wasted many of its timberlands through failure to replant, it still had the nation's largest forest reserves (stretching from Maryland to Texas), and these were much nearer the great markets than the vast tracts of Canada, Alaska, and the West. In addition, the South had one asset which no other region possessed: it could replace its forests, especially its pines, useful for paper pulp, at a much more rapid rate than any other section. Greater attention was directed to forest conservation, and the South began to realize that with proper care its pine forests could replenish themselves indefinitely.

Furniture, the most important of the many products of wood, began to be manufactured at High Point, North Carolina, in 1888; its manufacture spread quickly into other communities of that state and into Virginia and Tennessee. By 1928 North Carolina led all other states in production of lumber used to manufacture furniture, and one-third of the furniture manufactured in the nation came from the South.

Hosiery mills tended to rise in the vicinity of the furniture factories—a good illustration of how one industry is apt to attract another. The furniture and hosiery mills supplemented one another admirably, for furniture requires male operatives and hosiery female operatives. So work became available for the whole family.

The industries hitherto mentioned were found in greatest strength in or near the Piedmont crescent, which curves about the Appalachian Highlands. At the southern tip of this industrial crescent, where the hills slope gradually to the level coastal plain of Alabama, coal and iron, on which the heavy industry of America depends, are found in great abundance and are easily accessible; along with them are the dolomite and limestone needed for the fluxing of the iron. It was here, in the lower tip of the Piedmont, from Chattanooga southward, that the Southern iron and steel industry developed. Birmingham, the site of a cotton field in 1869, produced its first pig iron in 1876, and in 1888 put its first ton of steel through the furnaces. By the turn of the century the South was producing 1,965,000 tons of pig iron, compared to 212,000 tons 20 years earlier, and was employing about one fifth of the total workers in the nation's blast furnaces. Birmingham, the Pittsburgh of the South, ranked fifth in production of iron and steel.[6]

It was in the 1880's, that critical decade in which Southern industry first began to expand, that modern methods of exploitation were first applied to the Southern coal fields. The output increased from six million tons in 1880 to 26 million tons in 1890, to twice that amount in 1900 (54 million tons), and to almost four times this latter amount in 1930. West Virginia and Alabama were the primary centers, followed by Tennessee, Virginia, and Kentucky, with smaller deposits in Arkansas, Oklahoma, and Texas.

Other minerals, less important than iron and coal—diamonds in Arkansas; small amounts of gold and silver in Georgia, North Carolina, and Texas; sulphur in the Gulf Coast area; granite and marble in Georgia and Tennessee; lead, manganese, mineral clays, and gravel—added to the South's wealth. All in all, by 1930 this region was responsible for a fourth of the mineral output of the United States.

Oil was discovered in Pennsylvania in 1859, and by 1883 was flowing in West Virginia, Kentucky, and Tennessee. In 1901 the famed Spindle Top Pool near Beaumont, Texas, blew in with a ten-day gusher that opened the great Gulf field, and made Texas one of the great industrial and manufacturing states of the Union. Five years later a wildcatter discovered the Glenn field near Tulsa, Oklahoma, and opened the immense mid-continent field for the Southwest. Tulsa, which had been a small trading post, became a great city of 100,000 people, almost within a decade. One boom succeeded another in rapid succession. Towns grew up almost overnight in the sparsely settled areas of Texas and Oklahoma. By 1930 the Southwest was the greatest oil-producing area in the United States, and its 150 oil refineries processed about 40 percent of the nation's crude petroleum.

Meanwhile, railroads had expanded their lines; by 1930 the South had 82,000 miles of tracks, about one-third of the nation's total, and was as well supplied in this regard as was any other region.

New industries were developed to make use of the once rejected cottonseed. Oil pressed from the seed was utilized as a cheap substitute for such expensive items as olive oil, lard, and butter, and as a basic ingredient in soap, cosmetics, and other oil-based products. The cake or meal from which the oil is pressed was valued as fertilizer and food for cattle. By 1880 45 mills were producing 7,000,000 gallons of cottonseed oil for export alone. Twenty years later Texas and Georgia ranked first and second in an industry of 353 factories which by 1914 were producing over $200,000,000 in products.

Fertilizer was also made from phosphate rock, discovered in rich abundance in South Carolina, Florida, and Tennessee. By 1930 the South was producing and making use of more than half of the nation's supply.

With the growth of industry and the extension of the railroads came increased urban development.

The cotton mills, rising so rapidly in the Piedmont, produced no large cities but stimulated the growth of a number of small towns, particularly in the Carolinas, about which the mill villages were clustered as their natural centers. Within the 17 counties of the North Carolina Piedmont there were by 1945 some 88 cities, towns, and villages closely knit together by the South's first system of modern highways. The most important of these Piedmont towns were Winston-Salem, Greensboro, and Charlotte in North Carolina; Greenville and Spartanburg in South Carolina.

The rising tobacco industry brought some towns to birth and stimulated the growth of others. Winston-Salem and Durham in North Carolina, Richmond, Virginia, and Louisville, Kentucky, became centers of the new cigarette industry; Tampa, Florida, with its large Latin quarter, Ybor City, became the center of the cigar industry. Birmingham, as we have seen, became the South's largest purely industrial city because the availability of coal, iron ore, and limestone made it a natural center for the production of pig iron. About it were a number of important industrial suburbs.

Population increases in the Southern Appalachians in the opening decades of the present century were chiefly in counties where coal mining and manufacturing were expanding. Population decreases occurred for the most part in counties where such industrial development had not taken place. Chemical industries were attracted to the Kanawha Valley in West Virginia, and Charleston and Huntington became the centers of a triangle of thickly clustered industrial communities. The timber and mineral resources of Eastern Tennessee, along with the native rural people from whom abundant labor supplies could be drawn stimulated the growth of a number of industrial communities, including Bristol, Johnson City (the commercial hub), Greenville, Jonesboro, and Kingsport, whose rapid growth in 1930 had barely begun. Knoxville and Chattanooga, farther west, were larger cities, whose growth in recent years has been stimulated by the TVA.

The petroleum industry, as we have seen, gave rise to many boom towns in the great Southwest. Oklahoma City, for example, had a population of 4,000 in 1890 and of 185,000 in 1930, an increase of more than 4,000 a year for 40 years. Tulsa, meanwhile, had grown from a mere 1,400 inhabitants to a city one hundred times as large. Along the Gulf Coast of Texas arose a great chemical industry, based particularly on petroleum and its products. Houston, at the center of this industrial development, became one of the nation's busiest ports. From it were shipped the greater part of the petroleum products of the whole Southwest and most of its vast cotton crop. The population jumped from 78,000 in 1910 to 292,000 in 1930.

As industry grew and agricultural products increased, important trade centers developed. Some of these were in land cities where important railroads connected or great trucking routes converged, like Memphis, Louisville, Richmond, and Charlotte. In the Southwest there were Dallas, San Antonio, Fort Worth, and El Paso. One of the fastest growing towns in this category was Atlanta. Through its network of railroads this city, after the Civil War, became the chief distribution center of the Southeast—"the wrist of a hand whose fingers reach the five principal ports of the Gulf and Atlantic coast," as General William T. Sherman put it.

New Orleans, the largest wholly Southern city (St. Louis, Baltimore, and Washington had larger populations but were border cities, only partially Southern) remained the most important port in the South and the second largest in the nation. But the Norfolk–Portsmouth–Newport News area in Virginia was beginning its period of rapid growth.

Industry accounted for the growth of many of the Southern cities; trade and government for others. In Florida the attraction was mainly sunshine and climate. Semitropical Florida increased in population from 752,619 in 1910 to 1,265,549 in 1925. Miami, during the same period, rose from 5,471 to 69,654; five years later the population, despite the bursting of the speculation bubble, was 110,632.

After 1900, cities in the South had grown more rapidly on the whole than those in other parts of the nation. The ones which had lagged behind were chiefly the South Atlantic ports of Wilmington, Charleston, and Savannah, and such interior places as Lynchburg, Petersburg, Danville, Fayetteville, Augusta, Natchez, and Lexington (Kentucky). The primary cause in all these cases was diversion of trade to other centers by railroads.

Yet, despite the growth of its cities, the South remained basically rural, far more so than the nation as a whole. Thus in 1930 the U.S.

Census revealed that 56 individuals out of 100 lived in communities which had a population of more than 2,500; in the South the proportion was 32.1 percent.

As the 19th century drew to an end, the *Southwestern Presbyterian* looked exultantly toward the future. The Civil War, though legally justified, it declared, had proved to be a blessing in disguise—"the occasion of untold profit to the Southern section of our common country." Before emancipation the South, it was pointed out, had been almost exclusively an agricultural country. It continued to hold its agricultural prestige, but free men raised more of the staple crops than ever before, and to these staples had been added other agricultural pursuits and crops which had added untold millions to Southern wealth. Then there was the output of sawmills and coal mines, with the manufacturing interests of every kind multiplying so fast that it was difficult to keep the run of them. "One stands amazed," said the editor, "at the amount of good which through Providence has grown out of the War." Thoughtful men, he declared, were convinced that the South had only begun to enter upon the era of increased prosperity. And meanwhile population was pouring into this favored section at the rate of 100,000 a year.[7]

The South had indeed made amazing progress in agriculture, as recognized by the *Southwestern Presbyterian*, but particularly in the rise of its industries. In the 20-year period between 1880 and 1900 the total capital invested in its manufacturing enterprises had nearly quintupled, the number of employees had trebled, and the value of its products had more than trebled. Its proportion of the nation's wage earners had advanced from eight to 13 percent and the value of its manufactures from six to eight percent. Progress continued during the next three decades. During this period the total increase of gainful workers in manufacturing and mechanical industries was 99.1 percent for the United States as a whole and 147.8 percent for the Southeast. In the 20-year period, 1909-1929, the South's share of the industrial output rose from 12 to 14 percent. In 1900 the total wealth of the South was only 17 billion dollars; in 1922 it was 70 billion.

And yet in spite of this encouraging increase, the South was still industrially retarded. As one Southern historian remarks, the South had seemingly passed out of the vale of poverty caused by the Civil War, and yet it continued to be the poorest section of the nation— "the most glaring illustration of Henry George's paradox of poverty existing amid progress."[8]

In the 1938 report of the National Emergency Council to Presi-

dent Roosevelt on *Economic Conditions of the South,* this region
was designated as "the nation's economic problem number one."
Figures and facts were presented to sustain the conclusion. As summarized by F. B. Simkins:

> In 1929 the South, with approximately the same population as the
> states of the Northeast had less than half the gross wealth of that group
> of commonwealths. In per capita wealth certain Southern states ranged
> between one and two thousand dollars as compared with four to six
> thousand dollars in favored Northern states . . . Average cash farm
> incomes of many Southern states were under $1,000 as opposed to Cal-
> ifornia's average $4,000. The Southeastern states, with 13.2 per cent
> of the wage earners in the nation's factories, received only 8.4 per cent
> of the wages, or $844.00 per person as against $1,364 for the Northeast
> . . . These material deficiencies were inevitably reflected in living con-
> ditions. The South was no exception to the universal rule that poverty
> breeds ignorance and slovenliness, indicated by an unintelligent use of
> meagre resources. The depressing slums of all Southern cities seemed
> practically unlimited . . . Either from necessity or choice, millions of
> Southerners continued to subsist on the three M's—meal, meat and
> molasses. Human happiness and life itself were needlessly sacrificed to
> pellagra, tuberculosis, rickets, anemia, and other diseases resulting from
> dietary deficiencies. The death rate, especially from malaria, typhoid
> fever, childbirth, and pellagra, was much higher among Southern
> whites than among Northerners, and still more appalling among the
> Negroes.[9]

In spite of its great forward strides, the Southeast produced only
six percent of the nation's industrial output compared with 42 percent for the Northeast and 36 percent for the Middle states (and
much of the South's industry was owned by Northern capital, which
drained off its profits). Its per capita income for the decade 1930-
1940 was still less than half that of the North ($276 compared with
$567).

This great disparity between the industrial opportunities in the
North and South was one of the factors which led the Southern
states to lose nearly three and a half million of their population to
the North between 1900 and 1930. "Southern states spent more than
$2,000 to nurture each of its young people only to have millions of
them, upon reaching maturity, move elsewhere to expand their productive energies and take along their inheritances."[10] Sociologists
estimated that in the process the South lost from five to ten billion
dollars. Losses in intellectual, moral, and spiritual resources would
be more difficult to estimate.

Cities in the South had grown, along with its industries, and yet
"the region . . . remained essentially rural and agricultural in economy and in patterns of thought, with only a veneer of industrialism."[11]

II. THE NEGRO IN THE SOUTH

Reconstruction in the South had ended with the withdrawal of Federal troops and the overthrow of the carpetbag governments. Negroes retained the right to vote which had been granted to them after the war, and which the North regarded as the guarantee of other rights. Southern political leaders gave assurances that no wholesale disfranchisement was intended. They were determined, however, to restrict the Negro vote and to prevent the Negro from playing a decisive role in Southern affairs. To accomplish the end, a fourfold policy emerged: to appease the North (more and more content to wash its hands of the matter), to solidify the white vote for the Democrats, to encourage the Negro to vote the Democratic ticket, and to diminish or nullify the vote of those who supported the Republican party. This policy was justified on the ground that the Negro vote was ignorant and corrupt and that it must be held in check for the best interests of both black and white.

For some time the Negroes continued to vote in sizable numbers and to run and to be elected to minor political offices—in a few states they continued for a time to hold the balance of power. Various expedients, however, were employed to restrict Negro participation at the polls, some of them legal and some, many of them, extra-legal. When such measures brought the threat of Federal intervention, first Mississippi (1890), then South Carolina (1895)—two states in which the Negroes outnumbered the whites—followed shortly thereafter by the other Southern states, moved to disfranchise the Negro by constitutional means. As Carter Glass of Virginia, more forthright than most Southern leaders, frankly acknowledged, the purpose was to eliminate "every Negro voter who can be gotten rid of legally, without materially impairing the numerical strength of the white electorate."[12] This policy was justified and accepted by "good men," both North and South on the grounds that the Negro was politically irresponsible. White supremacy in the South was now generally accepted as inevitable. By 1910 Negro disfranchisement in the South, which meanwhile had received the Supreme Court's stamp of approval, was virtually complete. The means employed to this end included literacy tests, which could be applied quite unequally; poll taxes, which discouraged the indigent voters, both black and white; and the all-white primary, which excluded the Negro from the only elections in the South which had any real significance.

Along with this drive to isolate the Negro politically came the effort to segregate him socially and economically as well. There had

been no need for segregation laws before the Civil War, and none
were adopted in the Reconstruction period and for some time afterward. As Professor Ezell indicates, the post-war leadership, "although
believing the Negroes to be inferior, saw no essential connection between white supremacy and the need to humiliate the Negroes publicly."[13]

Negroes, however, had withdrawn, as we have seen, from the
white churches, where segregation in seating was the custom and
where only white leadership was available; there had been no mix-
ture of the races in the public schools; and in personal relations, where
freedom of choice was involved, there was likewise little mingling
of whites and blacks. The move to separate the two races in railroads and other forms of public transports began in 1887. Legal
sanction was given to this and other segregation measures in 1896 by
the Supreme Court decision in *Plessy* v. *Ferguson,* which upheld
the policy of "equal but separate accommodations." Shortly thereafter, coinciding with the all-out effort for political disfranchisement, came the all-Southern drive for thoroughgoing segregation—
in penal and charitable institutions, in recreational facilities, in public
accommodations, in residential areas—in short, nearly everywhere except in the stores and on the streets. Such separation was defended
on the grounds that the Negro was inherently inferior to the white
man and that amalgamation of the races, the inevitable results of
any lowering of the social barriers, must be avoided at all costs.

Political disfranchisement, along with segregation, which despite the Supreme Court ruling led to separate but not equal facilities, placed additional obstacles in the way of the Negroes' economic advancement, in both the city and the country, in both
skilled and unskilled labor fields. Booker T. Washington, a graduate
of Hampton Normal and Industrial Institute and founder of Tuske-
gee Institute in Alabama, became the most influential Negro leader
and spokesman, equally acceptable to the whites both North and
South, and remained such until his death in 1915. He urged the Negroes to abandon all ideas of social equality and to interest themselves in educational and economic improvement, holding that other
benefits would follow in due time as a consequence.

Opposition to Washington's philosophy came from some Negro
intellectuals, notably W. E. Burghardt Du Bois. In 1910, he with
other Negro and white leaders, combined to form the National
Association for the Advancement of the Colored People (NAACP),
which in 1919 issued a pamphlet setting forth its objectives as follows:

(1) To abolish legal injustices against Negroes; (2) To stamp out race discriminations; (3) To prevent lynchings, burnings, and torturing of black people; (4) To assure every citizen of color the common rights of American citizenship; (5) To compel equal accommodations in rail-road travel, irrespective of color; (6) To secure colored children an equal opportunity to public school education through a fair apportionment of public educational funds; (7) To emancipate in fact as well as in name, a race of nearly 12,000,000 American-born citizens.

Other individuals and organizations were now working for the betterment of race relations in a variety of ways.

The Negro's effort to improve his lot met with some success. "In fact," writes John Samuel Ezell,

one of the most outstanding developments in American history was the progress made by the Negro race in the period before 1930. Despite ignorance, poverty and caste discriminations, by 1900 one in every five Negroes owned his home and their farms were valued at nearly $500,000,000. That they had taken advantage of their educational opportunities was evident in the rise of their literacy rate from nearly zero to 56 percent. This increased knowledge was also reflected in a slow but steady improvement in morals and family relations. One room cabins were being replaced by two or even three room houses. In 1915, although they existed to serve their own people, Negroes in the South could boast of owning 30,000 businesses, including 1,000 millinery and 7,000 grocery stores, 100 drug stores, 200 sawmills, 50 banks, and 120 insurance companies. Some 34,000 Negroes were employed as teachers.[14]

But there had also been serious disappointments.

The Negroes' hopes, raised by their participation in a war "to make the world safe for democracy," were not realized; they did not receive the better understanding, the larger opportunities which they now thought to be their due. Instead there were increased fears and suspicions, embodied in a revived Ku Klux Klan and in a new wave of lynchings and race riots. The increased prosperity which came after the First World War did not include the Negroes in due proportion. "When the crash came in October, 1929, Negroes already knew their own depression. Yet despite such setbacks, it can be truthfully said that never before had any race made such great progress in so short a period as had the Negroes in the South."[15]

II

The Growth of the Church

With the recovery of economic prosperity in the South there came an increase in population, the filling out of empty spaces, the settlement of new regions, the growth of great cities, a rise in foreign immigration, and the formation of alien communities in the midst of a hitherto homogeneous South—each of these aspects with its own peculiar challenge to the missionary forces of the church.

The most rapid growth was in the area's borders. The United States census revealed that in the decade of the 1880's, for example, the increase of population had been as follows:

Virginia	9.0%
Kentucky	12.5%
Mississippi	13.6%
Tennessee	14.3%
South Carolina	15.2%
North Carolina	15.5%
Georgia	18.9%
Alabama	19.5%

In all of these the rate was less than 20 percent. On the northern frontier, the rate was:

West Virginia	22.8%
Missouri	24.0%

and on the southwestern border, and in the southeastern extremity, the increase was two or three times as rapid:

Arkansas	40.0%
Texas	40.2%
Florida	44.9%

And yet, as the Home Missions Committee reminded the Assembly in 1889:

It is a great mistake to suppose that our missionary field lies only in

Texas, Arkansas, the Mississippi bottom and in the state of Florida. In
the Synod of Kentucky . . . a vast field has been presented . . . In West
Virginia the sturdy, settled population is increasing, and a large number
of miners and foreigners are found. In the Valley of Virginia the increase
of population is constantly giving to our church new and inviting fields.
The same is true in a very marked degree in the Southwestern part of
Virginia, where new railroads, new mining and other enterprises are constantly increasing the population . . . East Tennessee and Missouri are
fields as good as those of West and Southwest Virginia. In the Presbytery
of North Alabama there has been an influx of population of perhaps
125,000 people within the past two years. . . . In one word, almost the
whole country in the Southern States presents an inviting, promising field
for the aggressive work of God's people . . .[1]

To raise the funds necessary for the conduct of its Home Missions the General Assembly had adopted in 1866 a Preferred Plan
and an Optional Plan. According to the Preferred Plan all Home Mission funds were to be sent to the executive committee and were to be
allocated to the presbyteries according to their needs. In practice
this meant that each presbytery was allowed to, and often did, draw
out as much as its churches contributed. According to the Optional
Plan a presbytery could manage its own funds, provided a collection was taken during the year for the benefit of the Assembly's committee.

Practically all the presbyteries came to follow the Preferred Plan
for a while, and the number of churches which contributed to the
work of the committee, less than one-fifth in 1866, gradually increased. The amount left in the hands of the executive committee,
however, for the growing edges of the church was utterly inadequate
for the task in hand. In 1891-1892, for example, nine synods contributed to the central committee in Atlanta larger sums for the
evangelical fund than they received back. Their net contribution this
year was as follows[2]:

Virginia	$3,207
Missouri	$1,342
Georgia	$1,038
Kentucky	$747
Nashville	$535
South Carolina	$404
Florida	$193
North Carolina	$135
Memphis	$10

The 1866 plans had provided that the aggressive work of Home
Missions be carried on by the presbyteries; no responsibility was put
upon the synods, which some of the leaders of the church argued
had no constitutional right to engage in such activities.

The entrance of the synods into the field of Home Missions came through the vision and drive of a few far-seeing men in the Synod of Kentucky. For more than 40 years Presbyterianism in this state, in relation to population, had barely held its own, and the church was confined by narrower limits in 1880 than it had been in 1840. The blue grass region comprising about 10,000 square miles, one-fourth of the state, was reasonably well supplied with self-sustaining congregations. In the western, eastern, and southeastern portions there had been a virtual extinction of Presbyterianism, and the organization of a new church was not only unusual but practically unknown. Dr. Stuart Robinson, who had labored to arouse the church, became convinced that the synod itself must assume responsibility for the work if there was to be real evangelistic advance. He died on October 5, 1881, with his project unrealized.

The Synod of Kentucky met a few days later. Toward the end of the meeting great excitement was aroused by a member of the body rising with a telegram in his hand from two gentlemen in Louisville, neither officers in the church (Colonel Bennett H. Young, son-in-law of Dr. Robinson, and the Honorable R. S. Veech), offering to double any amount between $2,500 and $5,000 which might be raised by the synod for evangelistic labor within its bounds.

Synod, thrilled with the offer, appointed an executive committee to take charge of the work and apportioned the entire amount among the churches. More than $11,000 was raised the first year, at a time when the entire church with its 120,000 members raised only $15,000 for evangelistic work and only $32,000 for sustentation. Five evangelists were put into the field at the outset, two as general evangelists, and three appointed to serve particular presbyteries. The synod's evangelists had three duties: to preach the gospel to vacant and feeble churches; to organize churches in destitute places where the way was clear; to group churches and aid them in securing the stated services of ministers. Five years later there were 25 evangelists supported by the synod. And in spite of the large amount of money raised for the synodical enterprise, a larger amount than before was left in the hands of the Assembly's committee for the work of the church as a whole. Within ten years, 65 churches had been organized, and half as many resuscitated; 50 new buildings had been erected; and more than 10,000 members had been received on confession of their faith in Christ. The Presbyterian banner had been planted in 20 new counties, most of which had suffered from extreme religious neglect, and an interest in mountain missions had been aroused which was to awaken the entire church to this neglected area at its own backdoor.

In 1889 the Synod of North Carolina, inspired by Kentucky's example, adopted a plan of synodical evangelization; and Virginia was the third state to develop a synodical program. Dr. Egbert W. Smith pointed out that there were vast areas within the bounds of every synod in which the seeds of Presbyterianism had never been planted; for example, in ten of the most fertile and populous counties in Alabama, 30 in Kentucky, 48 in Georgia, 64 in Missouri, 125 in Texas, in one-third of the Synod of Mississippi, in one-half of Tennessee, and in two-thirds of Arkansas. In each of these states there were many other counties where there was no more than one lone Presbyterian church. The influence of the Presbyterian Church, Dr. Smith estimated, was practically unfelt in one-half of Alabama, more than one-half of Kentucky, two-thirds of Tennessee, Georgia, and Arkansas, and in three-fourths of Missouri. "What we do we must do quickly," he wrote. "The South is entering upon a career of un-precedented development."[3] Within a few years all of the synods had entered upon some plan of synodical Home Missions, though there was a variety of plans in actual operation.

As synodical missions developed, the plan of work adopted by the General Assembly of 1866 became increasingly unsatisfactory. More and more presbyteries preferred the Optional Plan (raising and re-taining their own funds); some switched from one plan to the other, or cooperated in one area and worked separately in others. Presbyteries which conducted their own work through local treasurers rarely gave the annual collection for which the Assembly had called. Instead, they generally proposed to give a percentage of their collections for the General Assembly's committee. But too often the percentage was never given. Funds contributed to the General Assembly's committee therefore varied from year to year, and the amount left in the hands of the executive committee for the aid of the needy presbyteries in the Southwest was utterly inadequate.

As a result of these various factors, the General Assembly in 1893 abandoned the plan for Home Missions which it had approved in 1866 and adopted a new plan which it thought might avoid the weaknesses of the old. It now urged both synods and presbyteries to handle their own funds (raised by collections taken in the churches during the months of February, June, and August) and to prosecute the work within their own bounds to the extent of their ability. Funds for Assembly's Home Missions were to be secured by two annual collections taken in all the churches in the months of January and September. The committee was instructed, other things being equal, to apply these funds to the development of the work in the weaker portions of the church.

According to this plan, the Executive Committee on Home Missions was made almost exclusively an aggressive agency for evangelizing the frontier. The older and stronger presbyteries were encouraged to prosecute the work within their limits; in an older synod, when some of the presbyteries were weak, opportunity was given to the stronger presbyteries to aid the weaker.

There had been a time when Home Missions was mostly pioneer work. Home missionaries camped on the trail of Presbyterian folk in the western migrations, and shared their hardships and fortunes, while the executive committee strained itself to support them and to erect chapels and churches for homeless congregations. But now the frontier was beginning to return upon itself. The economic development of the country which produced new towns left other sections depleted of their population and destitute of religious ministrations. At the same time it created new communities, whose needs could not be met by the presbyteries in whose bounds they were located. The South could no longer be looked on as a rural section, the *Christian Observer* pointed out. The vast industrial development of nearly every section of the South increased the urban and often decreased the rural population. Factories and furnaces, mills and warehouses, were everywhere turning villages into towns, and towns into cities. Side by side with the problems of the city rose the problem of the country sections. The latter was depleted to fill the former. Consequently, the old country church declined and had difficulty in sustaining the means of grace. These two problems just taking definite shape in the South gave immense importance to the work of Home Missions. In bygone days it was mainly a matter of the frontier. Now it was largely a question of city evangelization and the sustaining of weak churches. There was frontier work in Texas, Arkansas, Oklahoma, and the Indian Territory to be pushed, but there was also the growing city, with its teeming multitudes, and the mountain sections with their scattered population and the weakened country churches. There were also the needs of the growing industrial communities to be met.[4]

As the churches in the old frontier region approached self-support and as these new needs appeared in the older portions of the church, feeling arose that the Home Mission plan of the church should again be revised. In 1903 the General Assembly launched a new plan. Once more it urged all of its synods and presbyteries to prosecute the work of Home Missions within their bounds. But the Assembly's committee was instructed to aid the work in any presbytery where it was shown to the satisfaction of the committee that the said presbytery was unable to compass the work.

Though the Assembly's committee continued for a good many years to spend the bulk of its funds on the western and southern frontier, it gradually assumed obligations in the older synods as well, until every synod in the church enjoyed its needed ministrations.

In a hotly contested election in the General Assembly, Dr. Samuel L. Morris of Macon, Georgia, had been elected Executive Secretary of Home Missions two years before the adoption of the new plan. The votes were taken by roll call, and seesawed back and forth. The Moderator announced a tie and inquired if anyone had failed to vote. Up sprang a "colored brother," the Reverend R. H. Alston of New Orleans. "Morris" was all he said, but it was enough. His vote carried the election. So the Home Mission cause received a forceful executive, responsible for expanding the church's missionary activities in the home field for the next three decades.

The aid which the Assembly had extended, and which it now extended more widely through the church as a whole, came under three heads: evangelism, church erection, and sustentation.

Logically, as well as historically, evangelism was the first task of Home Missions; but when an evangelist had gathered a new congregation it had to be housed, and in many cases, if a structure was to be reared, some assistance had to be given by the church at large.

Such assistance was extended by the Presbyterian Church as early as 1733, and from the origin of the Home Mission Board in 1816 the matter was brought constantly to the attention of the General Assembly which urged its churches to contribute to this particular cause. In 1844 the Board of Domestic Missions of the Old School Assembly erected a Committee on Church Extension, which became a distinct and separate agency in 1855, and whose purpose was to extend aid to feeble churches in the erection of church edifices, or in relieving their property from debt.

The first Assembly of the Southern Church recognized the services of this committee and the importance of continuing to extend aid to feeble churches in erecting church buildings and assigned its duties to the Committee on Domestic Missions. When the Civil War was ended and the General Assembly met to take stock of the situation, it instructed the Committee on Domestic Missions, first of all, to make provisions for the support of the gospel in the churches that had been impoverished by the war and, second, to aid in repairing or rebuilding church edifices injured or destroyed in the conflict.

For several years help continued to be given to repair or to rebuild, and when that task was completed aid was given each to a few churches—a dozen more or less—to erect needed houses of worship. By 1898 aid had been extended to 649 buildings, 238 of these being in Florida, Arkansas, Texas, and the Indian Territory.

In 1892 Mr. William A. Moore, an elder in the First Presbyterian Church of Atlanta, for years a member of the Home Mission Committee, left a fund of $5,000 to be established as a low-interest loan fund for church erection. Within a generation or so, churches built with the aid of this fund had passed the hundred mark; they were scattered from Maryland to New Mexico, from Missouri to Florida.

In 1911 the Southern Presbyterian Church set out to raise a semicentennial building fund of $100,000. After six years $20,000 was raised, which, with the Moore Fund and a small manse fund, gave the committee a working capital of $31,000. At this time the Northern Presbyterians had a permanent loan fund of more than $4,000,000; the Northern Methodists a fund of $11,000,000; Southern Methodists, $800,000; Southern Baptists had $160,000 and were endeavoring to raise it to a million. Slowly the semi-centennial fund grew till at last in 1923 the full amount was realized.

In addition to the Assembly's Church Loan Fund some synods and presbyteries developed church and manse building funds of their own.

But though the money invested in this cause paid splendid returns, the field was not greatly cultivated. "Church erection is 'the neglected continent' of Home Missions," said Dr. Morris in 1925. "The insistent demands of forty dependent presbyteries for appropriations, each seriously claiming to be 'the neediest section in the whole Church', leaves the Home Mission Committee practically no funds for erecting new churches." As a result in many communities the Southern Presbyterian Church had passed its day of opportunity.

A congregation is collected, a house of worship is erected, and ordinarily the new church must be aided for a time by stronger churches or it will languish and die. Any full program of Home Missions must therefore include not only evangelism and church erection but also sustentation. The vast majority of our churches, and those of every denomination, received in their early stages grants-in-aid from the mission boards of the church.

When a new church was organized the expectation was that it would grow, along with its community, and that mission aid would gradually diminish until the church was able to assume the burden of its own support and to contribute to the benevolent program of the church. In many cases this was indeed the result.

But two sorts of conditions gradually emerged in the history of Home Missions and became frequent enough to be regarded as characteristic.

The first was that the older settled, rural communities in very many cases began to decline in population and wealth. Such a tendency very early appeared in many parts of the older settled east, weakened by successive migrations westward and by the movements to the cities.

Thus, churches which had gone through the initial process of missionary promotion and had become self-supporting found themselves enfeebled and unable to provide for their own support. Furthermore, many of these older communities began to change in character. Their original populations were replaced by new types of population not so congenial to the existing churches. So churches found themselves partly stranded.

By 1930 this had become a familiar occurrence in the older sections of many cities.

A second condition was that in many sections, particularly in the west, the anticipated growth in population and in wealth never materialized, or at least was much less than expected. Therefore in such communities very many churches never were able to make the progress that was expected of them and never passed out of the stage which required assistance from the outside.

Both of these conditions were accentuated by the lack of interdenominational planning, and by the fact that in many communities of both sorts there were too many churches.

Later on a third condition was faced which, while not so widely characteristic, was nevertheless frequent enough to become a definite factor in Home Mission policy. This was that many churches were established for special types of population, as for Indians, or for foreign-language groups. From the outset special factors retarded the development of these churches in numbers and in financial strength, so that it was not possible to set a fixed term for the withdrawal from them of missionary aid.[5]

The simplest remedy for this state of affairs was to group a number of churches into a single pastoral charge and this was very generally done. But in many cases subsidies or grants-in-aid were still necessary if the church or combination of churches was to enjoy the advantages of pastoral care, and so it came to be that in the presbytery, in the synod, and in the General Assembly sustentation became the most characteristic feature of Home Missions and the department which absorbed the largest part of its funds. "New churches are continually reaching self-support," said Dr. Morris in 1910 "but our missionaries are aggressively pushing into newer territory and churches are being organized faster than others reach self-support. Thus the burden of sustaining a larger work grows with the growth of the Church. In small towns or scattered destitute communities it could not be expected that self-support would be easily or speedily obtained. The Executive Committee encourages every effort in that direction, but much work of this character will be purely benevolent and missionary for years to come."[6]

By 1930 half of the churches in the denomination were mission churches, receiving aid from either presbytery or Assembly.

Home Missions had begun with evangelism. In the Colonial period and also in the antebellum South the primary function, for a while almost the sole function, of Home Missions was to follow the pioneer westward with the gospel, to preach and gather congregations in new communities and states that were destitute of gospel privileges.

In the period of the Civil War and of Reconstruction, when the whole efforts of the church were centered on sustentation, the larger goal was not lost to sight. The executive committee was specifically instructed to promote the preaching of the gospel in the more destitute portions of the country, and the Assembly enjoined every presbytery to seek out and set apart a minister to do the work of an evangelist within its own bounds.

In 1872 a special collection began to be taken for evangelism, and after 1874 the collection was administered as a special fund. This fund and the number of contributing churches grew steadily until in 1887 the Assembly aided in the support of 61 evangelists in 38 different presbyteries. Presbyteries which did not employ "evangelists" sought to spread the gospel through the agency of pastors sent out to hold meetings in unreached territory. By such means 450 new churches were organized in the decade ending 1891.

In 1893 the revised plan of Home Missions work was adopted. Presbyteries and synods became responsible for their own work; collections were taken in the churches specifically for presbyterial and synodical Home Missions and were sent directly to presbyterial and synodical treasuries; the General Assembly confined its attention for ten full years almost entirely to the growing states on the southern and western frontiers.

Under this plan about 15 or 20 evangelists were aided each year by the Assembly's committee in Texas, Arkansas, Oklahoma, and Florida. A much larger number could have been used, with larger results in proportion, except for the fact that the bulk of the Home Missionary funds were required as heretofore to sustain feeble churches already formed. The same situation prevailed in presbyteries and synods throughout the church.

After 1903 when the Home Missions plan was again modified, the Assembly's committee began to support evangelists not only along the frontier, but once more throughout the church, where there was need which the presbyteries could not meet alone, in synods where synodical evangelists were desired and the synod was weak, and among special classes for whom the General Assembly had assumed a special responsibility.*

The evangelists on whom presbyteries, synods, and General Assembly depended so largely for their advance work during the period, traveled, before the advent of the automobile, mostly by horseback. In the Ozark Mountains one minister in 12 years traveled thus by actual estimation 25,000 miles, a distance sufficient to belt the globe. Many of the evangelists rode from 5,000 to 10,000 miles annually. "One travels all day on horseback in a driving snowstorm among the Ozarks without alighting from his saddle. Heat, dust, cold and wet, hunger and painful waking and waiting, fatigue and the privations of home life, make up a good part of any live preacher's experience, and especially that of the missionary and evangelist."[7]

Toward the close of World War I the Synod of Virginia began to recognize the need of better transportation for its workers: "A Ford car at 20 to 25 miles an hour, instead of a slow horse at 5 to 7 miles an hour!"[8]

During the decades of the 1880's Moody and Sankey, popular evangelists, then at the height of their influence, held successful revivals in a number of Southern cities, including Richmond, New Orleans, and Louisville. Success of these campaigns stimulated revivals throughout the South, in rural and urban areas, in towns small and great, and on many college campuses. At Davidson College it was reported in 1884 that nearly every college student attended prayer meeting and that every non-Christian among the students had been to inquiry meetings.[9] Sixteen hundred members were added in one year to the Presbyterian roll in Kentucky through the labors of synodical evangelists. In 1886 all of the presbyteries in the Synod of Nashville reported revivals within their bounds. "God's Spirit has been manifestly present in many of the churches," ran the Narrative, "and unusual numbers have been added to their membership."[10] Rev. J. W. Hoyte, M.D., evangelist, reported conversions in various towns throughout the Southwest—114, 104, 47, 55, 32, 25, 31, 58, and 44. During the year he had had 828 conversions. Rev. Joseph Bingham Mack, D.D., who served for some years as an evangelist in North Carolina, Georgia and Alabama, was said to have seen 8,150 souls added to the church and to have been instrumental in leading about 100 young men into the ministry.[11]

---

* Gradually "evangelists" in presbytery and synod gave way to Home Mission Superintendents.

Revivals continued to make headlines in the decade of the nineties. The reports came from almost every part of the country. "More persons have been added to the churches than for many years before," reported the *Central Presbyterian* in early 1894. "In some cases the revival has been confined to a single church or a single religious denomination, but generally all the churches and ministers in a single town or city have united and cooperated in the work. These union meetings have been, for the most part, but not always, under the conduct of a noted evangelist, invited for the occasion, and expected to do the preaching."[12] When Dwight L. Moody returned to Richmond this same year it was realized that the Armory would no longer suffice to accommodate the crowds, so a special tabernacle, seating 6,000, was erected. It proved too small. Overflow meetings were held, and still the multitudes were not fully accommodated.[13]

Other popular revivalists were coming to the fore, some utilizing high pressure techniques that would be worked out more fully in the colorful career of Rev. William A. (Billy) Sunday, reaching its climax in the years preceding World War I.

The editor of the *Central Presbyterian* protested against the growing number of these professional revivalists. "A vast and growing horde of irresponsible men," he charged, "are traveling the country, welcomed into our pulpits and pastorates, many of them the exponents of doctrines we disapprove and the advocates of methods we do not endorse . . ." Too many communities, he complained, had been brought to look upon the revivalist as the instrument for building up the church; they were insensibly led to discount the regular, stated means of grace, and to depend too much upon the periodical visit of the revivalist.[14]

But the *Central Presbyterian* did not oppose revivals as such. It gloried in the fact that remarkable revivals had recently occurred throughout the state of Virginia—in Petersburg, Abingdon, Staunton, and Rocky Spring (a small country church in the western part of Augusta County) for example—not conducted by evangelists, but by the pastors, assisted by some neighboring minister or ministers invited for the occasion. At the Rocky Spring Church, which had only 85 members, there had been 64 conversions, of whom 53 were added to the church, almost doubling the membership. "The revivals which we report from such churches week after week," said the editor, "are quite as remarkable as those resulting from the great meetings which attract more attention. A very large proportion of our smaller churches have been blessed in this way."[15]

The protracted meetings, held every summer now in the rural areas, said the *Southern Presbyterian*, are wonderfully beneficial to the church in reclaiming backsliders, upbuilding the saints in grace, and bringing sinners to a conviction of their sins and their need of the grace of God in Christ.[16] During the closing years of the 19th century, there was a period of religious declension. Worldliness prevailed, the *Christian Observer* recalled. Coldness, not spiritual warmth, was the rule through the churches. There was a diminution in the numbers uniting with the church; there were fewer candidates for the ministry; the growth of the church was slower than it had been for many years.[17] But this period proved to be the darkness that preceded the dawn.

New evangelists were now coming to the fore. One of the greatest of these, whose influence was strongly felt in the Southern Presbyterian Church, was Dr. J. Wilbur Chapman, who in the early 1900's had been elected chairman and chief agent of a committee to stimulate interest in evangelism in the Presbyterian Church U.S.A. Dr. Chapman soon discovered that the effective work in this area must be interdenominational. He and his associates conducted a series of highly effective campaigns, beginning October 1904 in Atlanta and closing May 1905 in Seattle. In this same season Torrey and Alexander were carrying on a remarkable series of meetings in England, and an unprecedented revival was under way in Wales. By many these were taken as signs of a sweeping revival which might well become worldwide. Dr. Chapman's plans for the following year took in 11 cities, including Roanoke, Austin, and Dallas. In 1909, he came to Richmond, teamed now with his revivalist singer Charles M. Alexander. It was the first time in the memory of the oldest inhabitant that all the evangelical churches had united in a revival effort. The central meetings were held in a big building, formerly a market, converted into an auditorium for these meetings by the City Council at a cost of $10,000. Two hundred cottage prayer meetings held in homes throughout the city prepared the way for the meetings. A chorus of 700 voices sang gospel hymns and led many to Christ. When Dr. Chapman preached, hundreds would frequently be in tears. The interest was so intense that many who were unable to enter the auditorium waited outside and were at length admitted to the after-meeting. Perhaps the most notable meetings of the series were those for men only. Great numbers professed conversion.

The following year Chapman and Alexander went on world tour, the most extensive undertaken up to this time by modern evangelists. They traveled 36,000 miles, and held 1,000 services, attended by 1,200,000 people. The gospel was preached in Australia, Korea, Japan, China, Hawaii, Fiji, and other islands of the South Pacific.

The *Presbyterian Standard,* in the course of a later series of meetings held in Charlotte, North Carolina, described Dr. Chapman as a man "after our own heart. He is always the dignified Christian gentleman, on fire with his message, with a heart melting with love for sinners . . . There is in his preaching nothing sensational, no clap-trap or striving for effect . . . Instead of weakening the influence of the resident minister, he does everything to exalt it, so that he always leaves the churches stronger by his coming."[18]

A new star was now rising on the horizon, Rev. William A. (Billy) Sunday, like Chapman, a minister in the Presbyterian Church U.S.A., but a preacher of a very different type, in whose highly organized campaigns the high-pressure methods developed earlier by B. Fay Mills now reached their ultimate perfection. A converted big league baseball player, Sunday brought slang and dramatic acrobatic action into his tabernacle campaigns that offended the fastidious but attracted the largest crowds and led to the largest number of "conversions" that the revival technique had yet witnessed. When Sunday first attracted attention in the Southern Presbyterian press he was dismissed as an evangelist run amuck.[19] Leaders of the church remained critical, but—impressed by his sincerity, his orthodoxy, his success, and the acceptability of his labors to community leaders in every city in which he campaigned—finally accepted him as he was.

As the *Presbyterian of the South* commented after Billy Sunday's 1919 campaign in Richmond: Mr. Sunday is a unique man. In his preaching he holds up sin in all of its blackness and heinousness. He has no patience with hypocrites. He has no sympathy with anyone who questions the inspiration of the Scriptures, the divinity of Christ, the atonement, man's total depravity, or any of the other great fundamental doctrines of the Christian religion as held by the Presbyterian Church. As a result of his preaching hundreds were led to profess their acceptance of Christ as their Savior and many more to reconsecrate themselves to the service of God. As to the permanent results it is too soon to pass judgment, but one thing is evident. Religion of the highest type has never occupied as high a place in the thoughts and lives of the people of this city as it now does.[20]

In this period, the opening decades of the twentieth century, the Southern Presbyterian Church became more evangelistic minded than ever before, and evangelism, the "winning of souls," came to be widely accepted as the primary, and sometimes it almost seemed, as enthusiasts at times claimed it to be, the sole mission of the church.

In 1905 the General Assembly was overtured to set up a committee on evangelism similar to that erected four years earlier in the Northern Church. The Assembly saw no need for additional machinery but urged pastors to engage more frequently in evangelistic services in their own fields and to call to their aid as far as practicable their own brethren in the ministry. It urged that the coming year be signalized by aggressive work for the winning of souls and recommended that each church by special services or otherwise take definite and systematic measures to that end.

In 1906 a voluntary "Association of Evangelistic Missions" came into being, for the purpose of forwarding a conservative evangelism, particularly within the bounds of the Southern Presbyterian Church. It had the support of leading ministers in the church and looked to Dr. Chapman for counsel and aid.

About this time Dr. Melton Clark indicated the nature of the revival message. It must, he wrote, "declare and expose sin and it must show clearly that the paths of sin . . . inevitably lead to perdition . . . It must be a precious message *about the Savior* . . . [The preacher] must tell of Christ's death, and proclaim his shed blood—the grounds of the sinner's justification, but he must also tell of the Risen Christ and the more abundant life he gives through his victory over sin and death . . . The message should emphasize service. As the Christ through love has saved men from sin, so the Savior demands the wholehearted, loving service of the saved sinner."[21]

In 1902 the General Assembly appointed a Permanent Committee on Evangelism "to organize and direct the distinctly evangelistic work of the church." Presbyteries and synods were encouraged to appoint similar committees, and this became the pattern widely accepted throughout the church.

Meanwhile, Dr. J. Ernest Thacker, pastor of the Second Presbyterian Church of Norfolk, had been called into the evangelistic service of the church. He entered at once upon what was destined to be a series of notable campaigns, held throughout the church. The first year there were 1,124 professions of faith in his meetings. The figure rarely went below this in the following years; by 1921, when evangelism in the Southern Presbyterian Church (and in the Protestant churches generally) reached its peak, there were in his meetings 1,498 professions of faith. Notable in these meetings held by Dr. Thacker were the large number of young men who chose as a result of them to give their lives to the gospel ministry.

The Assembly planned to increase the number of its evangelists, and at the same time urged every synod to secure synodical evangelists who might be able to supplement the work of the presbyterial evangelists. In 1914 Rev. W. H. Miley of Louisville became superintendent of evangelism, in connection with and under the direction of the Assembly's Committee on Home Missions, with the hope and expectation that this special work would be supported by voluntary offerings and subscriptions.

In the four years that Dr. Miley served the church in this capacity, a rising interest in evangelism was discerned, an increasing number of presbyteries appointed committees on evangelism and adopted definite evangelistic programs, conferences on evangelism were held at the summer conferences, and simultaneous evangelistic campaigns were held throughout the church. The older evangelism had sought out "destitute regions" and looked toward the establishment of new churches; sought now was an intense evangelistic effort in every individual church. In two years there was a decrease of 23 percent in the number of churches failing to report converts, an increase of 35 percent in the number of additions on profession.

And yet there were straws, which indicated that the wind was shifting. In a symposium on revivals published in the *Union Seminary Magazine* on the eve of World War I, a contributor wrote:

> The Church proclaims a message but the unchurched are not coming to church to hear . . . and there are influences at work which militate more and more against church attendance. The Sabbath day as a day of meditation, prayer, public and private devotions is rapidly slipping away from us. The Sunday newspaper is the largest of the week and the one most generally read. Because of its advertising feature it has made the Sabbath a day of unusual activity in rental and real estate operations and this at the very hour of church services. The street railway does its largest business on Sunday, employing thousands of men. Many of our stores are open the whole of the Lord's Day. On Sunday night the theatres are crowded and the churches are all but empty . . . To get the ear of the unchurched today it is necessary to go after them in a determination to be heard and that for a protracted season [in other words, through revival services].[22]

But the protracted services, which the churches were expected to hold annually, no longer drew as once they did. According to the *Presbyterian of the South* they had fallen into "innocuous desuetude." In the towns and the cities, reported the editor, it is getting to be increasingly difficult to secure an audience. One of the most aggressive pastors was quoted as saying, "I am ashamed to ask a fellow minister to hold a meeting for me; the people *will not* come out during the week." Perhaps, he suggested, the protracted meeting had been exploited by the professional evangelist. Too much dependence had been put on the special effort—the church going to sleep for the rest of the year.[23]

The special Department of Evangelism with its own superintendent was abolished in 1918 because the voluntary support which had been expected failed to materialize. The Reverend William A. Sunday held a number of successful campaigns in various Southern cities after World War I, but his popularity had begun to wane, and would soon precipitously decline. An Assembly-wide evangelistic campaign carefully planned and energetically promoted in the early 1930's proved disappointing.

Professional revivalism had become discredited in the minds of the general public; revivals in Presbyterian churches generally, whether conducted by the pastors or by guest ministers, invited in for the occasion, had had their day.

Throughout this period the General Assembly's committee had utilized the most of the funds left at its disposal for the advancement of the gospel on the Southern and Western frontiers. What had been achieved?

In Texas This state had been regarded as the land of opportunity ever since the General Assembly inaugurated its aggressive Home Mission policy in the early seventies. Each year it received the largest surplus of the Home Mission funds—all that could be spared.

In 1897 the committee reported that the population was increasing with great rapidity: "Whole colonies of people from other states as well as foreigners are moving into its vast acres."[24]

At this time Texas had a population of 3,250,000 of whom only 16,000, a mere pittance, were Southern Presbyterians. There were 250 towns in Texas, with a population ranging from 300 to 2,500, which had not been touched, as well as a vast number of rural neighborhoods with little or no religious advantages. One of the Assembly's evangelists, who had ten Texas counties to cover, described the situation in a few words: "The country is being developed, settled with people. The circuit rider comes along and organizes a society with a class leader in charge, and Presbyterians are invited to join with them until a Presbyterian church can be organized. The Presbyterian evangelist does not come, and the children of those families strengthen a sister denomination."[25]

An evangelist in Western Texas reported during this period that he had organized 15 churches in 15 months, and would organize 12 more in the next 12. But the Assembly could not sustain the churches and the zeal of the evangelist had to be restrained. In many localities growth of a newly planted church was slowed by the presence of another Presbyterian church where there was room for only one. Rivalry between Northern and Southern Presbyterian Churches was intensified after the Union of the Cumberland Presbyterian Church with the Presbyterian Church in the U.S.A.*

One critic complained that the Presbyterian minister could not endure hardship as did ministers of other denominations. In the seven years required for his preparation for the ministry he had neglected his body. He came to Texas pretty well equipped in mind, but with a body disqualified from enduring a long ride or any unusual strain.[26]

With limited forces Presbyterians had almost uniformly occupied the villages and towns. With only feeble roots in the open country, churches in town did not grow as otherwise they would have done.

During the decade of the nineties the population of Texas increased at the rate of 80,000 per annum; within the next few years it became 100,000 a year. The people were pouring into East Texas to engage in fruit and vegetable growing; in Southeast Texas, rice culture as well as the oil industries were attracting thousands; in West Texas, the large ranches were being divided and sold into small farms.

In 1912 Dr. Morris prophesied: "Owing to its new lands opened up, new towns being built, and its ever increasing population, [Texas] is compelled to accept aid from the Church. The East is pouring its sons and daughters into Texas and must bear a part of the burden of their support. The time will come when Texas will lead all the Synods in membership and will pour its money into the Treasury of the church for the evangelization of every destitute section."[27]

In 1930 these words were approaching fulfillment. Texas, after having received Home Mission aid for more than 50 years, during

---

* In 1907 Texas Synod, continuing the original U.S.A. Synod, reported to the General Assembly 3 presbyteries, 40 ministers, and 60 churches, with a total membership of 4,077. Texas Synod, representing the Cumberland contingent received, but as yet unmerged, reported 21 presbyteries, 245 ministers, 580 churches, and a total of 24,373 members. The following year, when the merger had been completed, the single Synod of Texas reported to the Assembly 12 presbyteries, 263 ministers, 461 churches, and 21,884 members. In this same year the Synod of Texas in the Southern Church reported 12 presbyteries, covering approximately the same territory as the similar number in the combined U.S.A. Synod, 221 ministers, 475 churches, and 26,508 members. It will be observed that the two synods were now approximately the same size, with the same number of presbyteries, and with approximately the same boundaries. There were more ministers in the U.S.A. Synod, but the U.S. Synod had the larger number of churches and more members. Its subsequent growth has been the more rapid.

the largest part of which it was the chief beneficiary of the Home
Mission funds of the General Assembly, had approximately 50,000
members, had become the third largest synod in the church, and
had contributed the third largest amount to the benevolences of the
church.

> The changing scenery of a half century ago [wrote Dr. Morris]
> revealed limitless plains, innocent of plow or grain, covered with herds
> of cattle, while the wild beasts and the adventurous cowboy fought
> for supremacy. Then the picture changed rapidly as locomotives
> swept across the plains, leaving towns and villages in their wake, and
> in the field of vision farms appeared dotting the prairie, and wild
> nature fled before the face of advancing civilization. It now became a
> race between the church with its Home Mission forces and paganism
> with its ungodly ideals as to which would permanently organize and
> consolidate the territory. It was originally "No man's land." The
> whirling kaleidoscope moves more rapidly today and we can scarcely
> fix one picture in our mental vision before others displace it, and in
> the maze, cities, oil wells and derricks mix inextricably. The struggle
> for possession is still an unsettled question.[28]

In Oklahoma   White people began to press into the Indian Territory
at a very early date, some as traders, some refugees from justice, an
increasing number as settlers. Though they were not permitted to
become citizens of the Territory, they were allowed to settle upon the
payment of a small tax, and many rented farms from the Indians who
owned but did not wish to utilize the land. Missionaries reported
in 1888 that the population of the Territory was rapidly changing.

H. H. Read and F. H. Wright, missionaries to the Indians, held
meetings in some of these white communities and a considerable
number professed their faith in Christ. Mr. Wright said: "The Lord
was with us and the Spirit's presence was marked in most places, especially on Red River at the mouth of the Washita. This place had
the worst of reputations, and murder, drunkenness and other crimes
abounded. Preaching was rare, and the people were demoralized. At
our services there were, as we hope, several conversions and at times
it would seem that the people were melted by the Spirit's power."[29]

Oklahoma Territory was a part of the Louisiana Purchase and
was included in the "unorganized or Indian Country" set apart by
Congress in 1834. After the Civil War the Creeks and Seminoles who
had sympathized with the Confederacy were forced to cede back a
large part of their land to the government. A number of Western
tribes were located on a part of this land, but a large portion of it
remained unoccupied. White settlers had to be restrained from entering by troops. Finally in 1889 the government opened the first

strip for occupation. On the appointed day exactly at twelve o'clock a gun was fired and the expectant settlers began their mad rush for land. Four years later the Cherokee strip was opened in the same manner, amid still wilder scenes, and 200,000 eager men and women fought and struggled at the risk of life and limb for "a claim" in this new country. The southern section was opened in 1901, only in this case townsites were sold at public auction and quarter sections were drawn by lottery.

Settlers flowed into this new region at an unprecedented rate. Thus between 1890 and 1900 the population advanced from 61,834 to 389,245, a gain of 500 percent, "surpassing all other records for the decade, and probably any decade in the history of American settlement."

As the population poured into Oklahoma Territory, Congregationalists, Northern Presbyterians, Methodists, Baptists, and Episcopalians followed with their religious ministrations; Southern Presbyterians took little notice, and as in previous cases a majority of their sons and daughters who moved into the area were lost to other denominations.

The white immigration which was pouring into Oklahoma began to spill over into Indian Territory. As railroads penetrated the country, towns began to spring up, from which the Red Men were characteristically absent. In 1901 Dr. S. L. Morris wrote in the *Christian Observer*: "The Indian Territory is Indian only in name. It is true that it contains fifty thousand Indians, but it contains a population of over four hundred thousand; nearly ten whites to every Indian. It is a white man's country. No section of the country is more thoroughly white and the people are still pouring in."[30]

A few months earlier, Dr. Morris had been elected Secretary of the Executive Committee of Home Missions; the General Assembly passed at the same time a resolution "that Oklahoma be included in our Home Mission field, and that the Executive Committee be directed to make such an investigation as will enable it to undertake work intelligently in that territory."[31]

Dr. Morris had hastened to Oklahoma to make his investigation. As he described his trip:

> The Secretary hurried down into Southern Oklahoma, just opening up, hoping to secure that territory. Lawton was found to be a city six weeks old, containing eight thousand people and eighty barrooms. But the Northern Presbyterian preacher was there and had organized a strong church, largely of Southern Presbyterian people. So our Church is practically shut out of its own territory and de-

barred from utilizing its own material . . . Not only has the northern section of the Indian Territory and almost all of Oklahoma been lost, but even in the southern section our church has made the costly mistake of spending nearly all its money on the Indians. It is a grand work which has been done among the Indians, but they constitute such a small percentage of the population. The church has neglected the whites who are in the vast majority . . .[32]

Indian Presbytery at this time was connected with the Synod of Texas and only one of its eight ministers served the rapidly growing white population of Indian Territory. To minister to this latter group the services of an evangelist, C. E. Paxson, was now secured. At the same time Rev. H. S. Davidson was sent to investigate the possibilities of venturing into Southern Oklahoma. As the Home Missions Committee had no funds at its disposal, his salary and expenses were secured from private sources. The first church was organized at Mangum, with about 15 members. Several others were organized shortly thereafter. The committee did not have the means, however, to make a vigorous campaign in this rapidly developing section. Most of its attention was directed instead to Indian Territory. Twelve churches were organized in this section in a little over 12 months, and men were secured for them as fast as organized.

In 1901 when Dr. Morris assumed responsibility there were 24 churches in Indian Territory, all Indian except half a dozen. Four years later there were 47 churches in the Territory, the majority being white. The ministers in charge of these churches were at first members of Indian Presbytery. But the Indian work was concentrated in the southeastern corner of the territory where there were no railroads, and one could go to St. Louis quicker than he could to a meeting of presbytery when it met, as it generally did, in this section. The Indians were never in a hurry. They called presbytery "big meeting," and expected to stay for a week. They wanted much preaching, three or four sermons a day, each of which needed to be preached, then interpreted. Business was carried on in both English and Choctaw. The elders of the white churches were businessmen, professional men, and farmers who could not spare so long a time for presbytery. By common consent there was a division, and on May 2, 1903, Durant Presbytery was organized with seven ministers and 26 churches, embracing the ministers working among the white population in Indian and Oklahoma Territory. The presbytery grew slowly year after year with the help of the Home Missions Committee and through the evangelistic labors of its missionary pastors.

It was easy to organize churches but impossible, for lack of funds, to man them. Presbyterian evangelists sowed the seeds but were unable to reap the harvest. In 1907 Superintendent Matthews reported: "growth and development are limited only by the number of men and the amount of money at our command for its prosecution. . . . During the entire year there have been only six churches organized. It is not because of the lack of opportunity for organizing more, but because of the lack of men to care for those already organized."[33]

This same year Oklahoma Territory and Indian Territory were united and accepted into the Union as the state of Oklahoma. No state east of the Mississippi compared with it in size. Its population had reached one and a half million, about equal to South Carolina and more than three times the population of Florida. Fifty thousand people were said to have entered the state in a single year. Its cities had sprung into existence like magic. Lawton was a prairie one day and the next day its town lots sold for $600,000, and about 10,000 people began their sojourn within the beginning of a town. Durant, Guthrie, Enid, and other towns had each about 10,000 people. Shawnee, Tulsa, Muskogee, and others varied from 20,000 to 25,000, while Oklahoma City, a mere village ten years earlier, contained about 50,000 inhabitants.

The Presbyterian Church, meanwhile, in the past five years had increased its membership from 800 to 1,300, its ministers from 9 to 26, its churches from 22 to 52. In 1908, one year after the state of Oklahoma came into being, the Synod of Oklahoma was organized, including three presbyteries, Indian, Durant (in the old Indian Territory), and Mangum (in the old Oklahoma Territory). Three years later the Assembly's committee suggested that its evangelists cease organizing new churches in Oklahoma, giving the church time to catch up and properly equip the work already organized.

With the exception of Snedecor Memorial, a Negro Synod, the Synod of Oklahoma was by 1930 the weakest and neediest in the church. In 1926, when a United States religious census was taken, the adult population of the state was estimated to be 1,461,408, and only 35 percent of this number were members of any church; this was the lowest ratio for any of the states in the territory of the Southern Presbyterian Church. In material resources the state was one of the wealthiest in the Union. Few of the churches in the synod, however, were self-supporting, and the synod remained dependent upon the Home Missions Committee for aid.

In Arkansas   The frontier which the Assembly's Home Missions Committee endeavored to serve after the Civil War included not only Texas and Oklahoma, but also Arkansas and Florida. At the end of the war, Arkansas was still very much of a wilderness; Presbyterians were only a tiny handful, approximately 1,200 members and 13 ministers, not all of whom were actively engaged in preaching.

Home missionaries testified that in large sections of the state no true gospel was preached; the people, they claimed, were in the most grievous ignorance, and those who thought on eternal things at all were deluded, fanatical, and misguided. One of the most judicious and efficient ministers in Arkansas wrote: "The religious condition of the country is painful to contemplate; Brazil can scarcely need a pure Gospel worse. Many neighborhoods have no preaching of any kind; many have preaching only occasionally. And very much of the preaching so called is worse than none."

No doubt these remarks were overstated. Pioneer conditions, however, continued to exist in Arkansas for some time after the Civil War and did not begin to pass away till about 1872 with the advent of the railroads. Five times between 1865 and 1880 the synod was unable to meet because of a lack of a quorum.

In 1889 the Home Missions Committee reported that the increase of population in Arkansas was numbered by many scores, if not by hundreds of thousands annually. "The great Mississippi bottom," it said, "is being opened up year by year."[34] But the great tide of population flowing into the Southwest poured into Texas and Oklahoma, and Arkansas was sometimes described as "The State which is passed by." There was much malarial country in Arkansas and the hazards to health in the state were exaggerated, as was its reputation for lawlessness. Not till later did its fertile land and unrecognized opportunities attract public attention.

As a consequence, the Home Missions Committee spent most of its resources on the territory further west. Up to 1885, indeed, Arkansas never received more than a few hundred dollars in outside aid. After this time appropriations were increased. At the turn of the century, the Home Missions Committee was giving aid to 71 ministers in Texas, 19 in Florida, 16 in Arkansas, two in Indian Territory, and one in Tennessee. For 30 years after the Civil War, the average number of ministers in Arkansas was less than 29, and there never was a time when that number was actively engaged in ministerial labor. Meanwhile the membership in the Southern Presbyterian Church increased slowly, until by 1900 it was a little more than 5,000. The population of the state at this time was about a million and a half. During the next 20 years, through lack of funds and workers, over half of the churches lost ground, only a few made definite progress, many grew weak, dissolved, and disappeared. Meanwhile the material resources of the state were being developed; railroads were being extended; new towns were being built; and there was a large influx of population, composed of farmers and artisans, from the Northern and Western states. Many of these were Presbyterians and were being lost to other denominations. According to one Presbyterian minister, one of the great obstacles to Presbyterian growth in this state was the narrow and bigoted sectarianism of some of the denominations. In some places, he charged, Presbyterianism was dragged in where no Presbyterian members were to be found and where there had never been a Presbyterian minister to be "the red flag for the bull."[35]

In 1920 the synod embarked on an aggressive campaign of state-wide synodical Home Missions. Traveling evangelists moved through the state; churches were organized where there were definite needs that were unmet and where adequate support was assured; sustentation aid came from the Executive Committee on Home Missions, which returned $1.50 for every $1.00 that was received from churches within the synod. In seven years 17 churches were organized or resuscitated or received from other denominations, and more than 10,000 members were added to the church rolls, 1,600 more than the total membership at the beginning of the synodical campaign.

At this time there were still 22 counties not entered by the Southern Pesbyterian Church; half the adult population (estimated at 1,176,054) was outside of any church. Only one out of 120 was a Presbyterian; Methodists were 12 times, Baptists 13 times, as numerous.

Arkansas lies in the very heart of the great Mississippi Valley. It is cleft by great rivers, whose bottom lands are as fertile as the delta of the Mississippi, and crossed by the Ozark Mountains, some of whose peaks are 2,500 feet high. Thus it has a wide variety of climate and soil and is capable of producing the most diversified crops. One of the weakest of the synods, it remained in 1930 one of the neediest of Home Mission states.

In Florida Florida, the second largest state east of the Mississippi received Home Mission aid steadily from the time of the Civil War. Evangelistic work carried on through the state by the Presbytery of St. Johns, with the aid of the Assembly's committee, made possible the organization of the Synod of Florida in 1891. Ten years later one-half of its 32 ministers were still being aided by the Assembly's committee, and no more than 12 out of its 74 churches were entirely self-sustaining.

The great influx of population into Florida which began about 1900 was due to improving economic conditions and the growing popularity of the state as a winter resort. During the next 15 years or more it grew more rapidly than any state in the South with the exception of Oklahoma. It even surpassed Texas, which gained 27 percent from 1900 to 1910, while Florida increased 42 percent during the same period. Towns seemed to spring up out of the palmetto scrubs overnight.

A large percentage of this immigration came from the North and included more than the usual number of Presbyterians. The Home Missions Committee took advantage of this opportunity and through its aid churches were organized more rapidly in Florida than in any other state in the South.

William H. Dodge, whose ministry was inseparably interwoven with the development of the church in Florida, wrote in 1915: "The growth of the state has been great compared with the majority of the Southern states, but the progress of the Presbyterian Church has so far surpassed that of the state as to be nothing short of phenomenal. . . . Much of this marvelous growth has been due directly to Home Mission effort, and Florida presbytery is indebted very largely to the generous support which the Executive Committee has rendered. Except for this help many important towns would not be occupied by our flourishing and active churches."[36]

But great as was the growth of the Presbyterian Church in Florida, its membership remained small compared with that of Methodists and Baptists. In 1930 one-half of the church membership of the state belonged to the former and two-thirds of the remainder to the latter. These two popular denominations continued to reap the rewards of their extensive missionary sowing at the beginning of the national era.

In 1924 the great Florida boom developed. According to Rev. T. P. Walton, superintendent of St. John's Presbytery: "No one but those who have actually been on the ground can have an adequate idea of the wonderful development going on in the southern part of Florida. . . . Whole sections, thousands of acres, are laid off into town sites; splendid buildings, hotels, apartment houses, stores, bank buildings, palatial residences are constructed and people move into them and settle down to the serious business of making a living."[37]

The next year Dr. J. G. Anderson wrote: "The roads from California to Maine are almost clogged with automobiles going to Florida. Steamships are doubling their numbers and booked up weeks ahead. Railroads are double tracking and double-scheduling and embargoing some freight at the present time with berths taken far in advance. Every mode of conveyance is burdened with passengers . . ."38

The very next year economic difficulties began to develop, and it was not long before the boom had exploded. Churches were impoverished as well as individuals, but the marvelous resources of Florida remained, and tourists and permanent residents continued to be attracted.

New Mexico, Arizona, and Southern California might have been claimed by the Southern Presbyterian Church. Population was pressing into them as into other parts of the West; towns without churches were springing into existence. "Being a part of our own Southland," said Dr. Morris, "there is a tremendous obligation upon us to give this vast section the Gospel."39 A few missionaries were actually sent into New Mexico, beginning in 1894, and met with some success. But funds were insufficient and the work could not be pushed. By 1930 there were three small churches in New Mexico, none in Arizona, and none in California.

The church was growing meanwhile in the older synods along the Atlantic seaboard. Kentucky, as we have seen, embarked upon a program of synodical missions in 1882. The next synod to assume responsibility for its Home Mission work was North Carolina.

Presbyterians had been early in this state—Scotch Highlanders moving up the Cape Fear River and settling around what is now Fayetteville, beginning about 1735, and Scotch-Irish pioneers settling thickly in the western area of the state from 1740 on. But Presbyterians had not reached out to claim other areas in the state. In 1860 there were in the synod about 92 ministers, 185 churches, and less than 16,000 members, divided among the three original presbyteries: Orange, stretching from the Yadkin River to the Atlantic; Concord, from the Yadkin west to the limits of the state; and Fayetteville, embracing the whole southern part of the state, from the Yadkin to the ocean. In more than half the state the name "Presbyterian" was hardly known. During the war years the church gained eight ministers and five churches, but lost more than 2,000 of its communicant members, these latter consisting in large degree of its young men who had fallen in battle, or had died in prison, or from diseases and exposure. In 1868 Wilmington Presbytery was erected, in hope that it might stimulate the evangelization of the southern part of the eastern portion of the state—despite the protests of influential men in the presbytery, who argued that it was a waste of men and money. For 40 years, they said, evangelists had been sent and nothing had been accomplished. The following year Mecklenburg was formed out of Concord for more efficient work in the west. In spite of the new interest now being taken in evangelization, there were in 1880 29 counties (out of 94) in which there was no Presbyterian church (20 of these were east of the Atlantic Coast Line Railway) and 24 more which had only one Presbyterian church each. Seventeen years later, Presbyterian churches outside the original Scottish and Scotch-Irish settlement areas still were few and far between.[40]

In 1888 a memorial to the synod from Orange Presbytery called attention to the fact that its Home Mission field was twice as large as that of the other four presbyteries put together. Its energies were exhausted in keeping four or five evangelists in the field, and as many more were badly needed. The presbytery expressed the hope that some way might be found for "removing the disproportionate and unequal burden of the presbyteries and so further the more effective prosecution of the great work of state evangelization."

Next year after strenuous debate and strong opposition to the plan of synodical Home Missions, the synod, following the lead of a group of its younger ministers, erected a permanent Committee of Home Missions, and declared that the responsibility for evangelizing its territory lay upon the synod itself as well as upon its presbyteries. The first synodical evangelist was appointed the same year.

This beginning of synodical Home Missions ushered in a period of expansion, which continued for the next 40 years and more. Twenty years after the inauguration of the plan, nearly 200 churches had been organized, the unoccupied counties had been reduced by half, the membership of the synod had doubled. For the 40 years preceding 1888 there was an average addition of 300 communicants per year to the synod; for the next 25 years there was an annual increase of 900. From 1910 to 1920 the population of North Carolina increased 16 percent, the Methodist population 31.6 percent, the Baptist 37 percent, the Presbyterian 40 percent. By 1930 the Synod of North Carolina had become the strongest synod in the General Assembly, its comparative strength due in large measures to its aggressive plan of synodical Home Missions begun in 1888. Superintendent of synod's Home Missions during the larger part of this period was Rev. Ernest Eugene Gillespie. The most successful evangelist in the field, and the one who also served for the longest period, was Rev. William Black. In a typical year, the 29th of his career as synod's evangelist, Dr. Black reported 950 professions of faith and 456 additions to the church. He was well known all over the state, and beyond, for his vigorous style of preaching, "evangelical to the core," and conservative. He remained to the end of his life (1928) passionately opposed to the doctrine of evolution. Needed financial help for North Carolina's Home Mission effort during this period came from the personal generosity of Mr. William Henry Belk, and from the J. M. Belk fund, to which each unit of the widely distributed Belk Bros. Company made annual contributions.

Presbyterian strength in Virginia after the Civil War was in the Valley centered about Staunton where the Scotch-Irish immigrants had settled. Presbyterians were also found on a wide swath through the Piedmont, where there were numerous small churches (West Hanover Presbytery, now Appomattox), and on to Petersburg and Richmond (East Hanover), where some strong city churches were to be found. The three Valley presbyteries—Winchester, Lexington and Montgomery—carried on vigorous mission work in the territory to the West, in Abingdon, Greenbrier, and later Kanawha presbyteries. In eastern Virginia, Washington south to Norfolk, the church had little strength; in 1870 for example, there were only 436 members in the whole of Norfolk Presbytery. In the generation following the war many new churches were organized, and membership in all the presbyteries more than doubled. Many of the churches however had not grown; in four of the weaker presbyteries half of the churches had no regular ministry because of shortage of funds, and Home Mission activity had come to a standstill. In 1890 Virginia became the third synod to adopt a plan of synodical Home Missions. Dr. J. E. Booker became chairman of the committee in 1895 and shortly thereafter Superintendent of Home Missions, a position which he retained for the next 35 years. The synodical plan enabled the stronger presbyteries to come to the aid of the weaker ones, and in 1929 when Dr. Booker retired as superintendent most of the fields were supplied with ministers. There had been another period of substantial growth. In 1860 less than one person out of 100 in Virginia was a Presbyterian; in 1930 the proportion was nearly three out of 100.

In 1895 Virginia remained largely rural. At that time there were 260 ministers in the synod, and of these only about 30 were pastors of city churches. In 1930 West Hanover, Winchester, Lexington, and Montgomery were still largely rural. In Lexington Presbytery, the largest in the synod, there was only one town with a population of more than 10,000 and only two with a population of over 5,000; in West Hanover, 38 of the 48 churches were assisted by Home Missions. The rural population was now flocking to the cities, and in the next generation the growth would be in the Norfolk, Washington, and Richmond areas.

Greenbrier Presbytery had been organized out of Lexington Presbytery in 1838 and was the only presbytery in the present state of West Virginia until well after the Civil War; it extended to the banks of the Ohio River and included most of the territory now in the synod. In 1869 there were 23 churches, 14 ministers, and 1,587 members, a few score less than there were before the war. In 1888 the number had grown to 45 churches, 21 ministers, and 2,861 members. Kanawha Presbytery was set off from Greenbrier in 1895, with seven ministers, 19 churches, and 1,831 members. Tygart Valley Presbytery was organized in 1912, mostly out of mission churches founded and supported by Lexington and Winchester presbyteries. In 1914 these three presbyteries were detached from the Synod of Virginia and organized as the Synod of West Virginia. There were unique Home Mission opportunities within the state, and it was felt that only as the work was unified could these opportunities be adequately met. With the organization of the synod began a new era in the history of Presbyterianism in this portion of the South. In 1930 the three presbyteries, rearranged in 1928, had strength as follows:

Presbyteries	Ministers	Churches	Members
Bluestone	21	24	3,892
Greenbrier	36	55	5,794
Kanawha	26	31	8,392

West Virginia was one of the fastest growing synods in the church. It may be recalled at this point that when Tygart Valley Presbytery was organized in 1912, the Parkersburg division of the Baltimore and Ohio Railroad was accepted as the dividing line between the two major Presbyterian churches in West Virginia, an agreement which has continued to be faithfully observed by both bodies. It may also be recalled that when the Synod of West Virginia was organized, certain churches in the Eastern panhandle remained within the Synod of Virginia.

South Carolina, because of constitutional objections, was the last synod to undertake any type of synodical missions. Its goal up to the year 1896, when it finally fell into line, was for each presbytery to carry on its own Home Mission activities with the aid of an evangelist. Under this plan of operations its growth was steady, but slow. The claim was made that in proportion to the number of its white population, South Carolina had more Presbyterians than any state in the South. According to the census of 1890, it was pointed out, the state had a white population of 462,000 and a Presbyterian membership of 16,112, an average of one to every 28 of the white population. North Carolina meanwhile had 1,055,442 whites and 25,189 Presbyterians, an average of one Presbyterian to every 40 white inhabitants. Virginia had a white population of 1,020,122 with 27,400 members, an average of one to every 41 white people in the state. And these three it was noted were by all odds relatively the strongest Presbyterian states in the South.[41]

In South Carolina, as in other Southern states, Presbyterianism was very unevenly distributed. In 1896 there were 12,190 communicant members north of Columbia, the capital and center of the state, and only 5,981 south of this center. Outside of Charleston there were eight counties in the lower part of the state covered by Charleston Presbytery, in which there were 22 churches with a total membership of 820; whereas four counties in the northeastern part of the state, comprising Bethel Presbytery, reported 50 churches with a communicant membership of 5,653. The difference, as in the case of North Carolina and Virginia, was found in the fact that it was in the northwestern portion of the state that the Scotch-Irish immigrants had settled.

In 1896, when the synod finally approved a plan of synodical evangelism, only one presbytery had an evangelist at its disposal, though another had been recently elected. The three presbyteries in the lower part of the states lacked resources to take advantage of their opportunities—one was actually losing ground, while the upper tier of presbyteries were relatively strong in numbers and resources. It was some years however before an effective plan was developed, one which had the full support of all the presbyteries. Synodical evangelists succeeded in organizing a number of new churches and adding many members to the rolls. Particularly successful was Dr. W. H. Miley, who came to the synod after terminating his work with the Assembly. In one year his meetings added 662 to the church rolls on profession of faith and 136 by letter.

In 1925 Presbyterian strength was as follows:

Presbyteries	Ministers	Churches	Members
Bethel	27	46	7,087
Charleston	17	27	2,538
Congaree	18	30	4,111
Enoree	34	43	6,280
Harmony	16	32	3,839
PeeDee	22	39	4,469
Piedmont	15	32	3,564
South Carolina	22	43	5,119

While the synod as a whole had grown, efforts to plan churches among the many new mill villages had not proved successful. In 1892 the synod had taken note of these cotton mill towns "rapidly springing up within our bounds" and observed that vigorous efforts were being made to organize churches in such villages. A second effort was made in 1903. In four mill towns in Aiken County, Charleston Presbytery, there was a population of 7,000, about one in eight being a member of some church. There were just 27 Presbyterians in the area. After three years labor the missionary withdrew without being able to accomplish more than to discover the needs of the work and reveal to the synod the conditions that have to be met in such work.[42] Later unsuccessful efforts were made to open work among the cotton mill operatives around Spartanburg.[43] The failure of the Presbyterian efforts among the mill hands will be considered later in another connection.

Presbyterianism in Georgia grew a little more rapidly than in South Carolina, a little less rapidly than in North Carolina. It more than doubled in three decades, 1870-1900, and nearly doubled again in the three following decades. For some time church extension was left in the hands of the presbyteries, which at times employed evangelists to look after the weaker churches and sought to organize new churches in the "waste places" where there was an opportunity. In 1890 a synodical evangelist, Dr. J. B. Mack, was employed. Of the 137 counties in Georgia at this time, about 55 more than a third, were without a Presbyterian church; in many other counties there was only a single church.

In the next eight years Dr. Mack participated in the organization or reorganization of 44 churches, most of which had been provided with church buildings.[44] But why had the Presbyterian Church not grown more rapidly? Is the fault in our ministry asked Dr. Mack? No, he replied, for they are as pious, as learned, as able, and as active as either the Methodists or the Baptists. And so with the church membership. Is the fault then in our Confession of Faith? Dr. Mack concluded that it was.

I found, he reported, that not one out of 20 of our elders or deacons had ever read the Confession through. How then could they advocate its doctrines or defend them when assailed? The charge constantly made, for example, that Presbyterians taught that there were infants in hell "not even a span long." "When I realized," wrote Dr. Mack, "that our Confession was so bulky in its volume, so metaphysical in its distinctions, and so philosophical in its statements, that all our elders would not read it—when I also realized that the people thought our Confession had a God who delighted to create the wicked in order to damn them, and who was well pleased in feeding the flames of hell with little babies—then I was not surprised at our comparative failure."[45]

Dr. Mack was not advocating an abandonment of the Confession; rather, he advocated its restatement in language that men could be induced to read. But Dr. Mack's proposal met with no response. The church was not yet prepared to acknowledge that its faith could be presented in more appropriate dress.

Despite its Confession of Faith, the Presbyterian Church in Georgia was now growing more rapidly than the population as a whole, in a 60-year span (1840-1900) twice as fast.

After 1901 evangelistic activities were for a time in the hands of the presbyteries, but in 1914, after many efforts, the synod once again took over evangelistic responsibility.

Six years later it was claimed that only two synods had experienced a larger net growth during the period. The last year had been the best yet, and all presbyteries were beginning to occupy new territory. There was need. Methodists in Georgia at this time numbered 275,000; Baptists 375,000; Presbyterians had less than 30,000 resident members. Employed now was the synodical superintendent, along with five presbyterial evangelists, three of whom were partially supported by the synod's committee. Laymen were being used increasingly to supply vacant churches. Synod's goal approved by the General Assembly, was a special evangelistic campaign in every congregation, and at least one evangelistic service by every pastor. Young women, employed by the synod in conjunction with the Executive Committee on Religious Education, organized mission Sunday schools, with the hopes that in time they might become independent churches.

In 1926 an ad interim committee appointed to study the workings of the synod's Work Committee, which had taken over responsibility for the total work of the synod including Home Missions, reported that more progress had been made under the current synodical Home Mission plan than any yet tried. The largest growth during this decade was in the presbytery of Atlanta.

The older synods along the Atlantic seaboard made substantial gains in membership during the 50-year period of 1880-1930; gains in the border states west of the Alleghanies, meanwhile, were not so marked. The synodical plan of Home Missions, as we have seen, had its birth in Kentucky, and within a 20-year period

(1880-1900) the membership of the synod had more than doubled. Then the growth suddenly ceased. In the next decade membership in the synod actually declined, as it did also in the following decade. In the 1920's there was a small increase. Over a period of 30 years membership in the synod had gained only 1,417 members—creeping from 20,504 in 1900 to 21,922 in 1930. From 1879-1889 there had been a gain of 63 percent; from 1889-1899 a gain of 32 percent, after which there was little or no growth at all.[46] Meanwhile in a ten-year period the number of communicants in the city of Louisville had increased 50 percent. The lack of growth had been in the rural areas and in the mountains. Many of the Home Mission churches founded in the period of advance had failed to grow and became a burden on the benevolent funds of presbytery and synod; money formerly employed for evangelism now had to be used for sustentation. And the amounts required for sustentation left the church less free to advance in the growing cities.

The Independent Synod of Missouri, representing the majority of the original synod withdrawing from the Presbyterian Church in the U.S.A. after the war, came into the Southern Church in 1874. Its total communicant membership in 1880 was 7,376, a thousand less than the Synod of Kentucky. A report made to synod the following year revealed that its churches were found in only 47 of the 114 counties in the state, and in 14 of these 47 counties there was only a single church, generally weak and small. A third of its 128 churches were pastorless, and half of these had less than 10 members.

In 1885 synod assumed responsibility for Home Mission activity, which it continued to direct through the rest of the period. For five years there was one general evangelist in the field almost continuously and another for a portion of the time. After 1890 five or more evangelists were employed. Within nine years 29 churches had been organized by the evangelists with between 500 to 600 members, and 32 church buildings had been erected. In the decade of the 1880's and again in that of the 1890's, growth of the synod was approximately 28 percent. It dropped during the next two decades, and in 1930 the synod reported fewer members than it had ten years earlier. Many of the churches founded earlier in the Ozark regions had perished. In one presbytery (Palmyra), wholly rural, there was only one church with as many as 300 members, and only three churches with a full-time minister. In St. Louis Presbytery there were 24 churches, only eight of which were self-supporting and two of these were on half-time basis. The total membership of the 16 Home Mission churches was 622, an average of 39. With the rural communities now declining

in population, and many of them now over-churched, it was recognized, in some quarters at least, that the church's future lay in
the cities.

The Synod of Tennessee was organized in 1901, including two
presbyteries (Memphis and Western District) formerly belonging to
the Synod of Memphis, and four presbyteries (Holston, Knoxville,
Nashville, and Columbia) formerly belonging to the Synod of Nashville. The boundaries of the synod were now for a short time made
coterminous with those of the state. Few new churches had been
organized within the state during a 50-year period, but there were
a number of churches in the four larger cities in the state (at the
time of the synod's organization—three in Knoxville, five in Chattanooga, ten in Nashville, and seven in Memphis). In these four
cities were 5,790 members, almost a third of the synod.

The First Church, Nashville, had a membership of 1,074; the
Second Church, Memphis, a membership of 770. Three other
churches in the synod had a membership above the 500 mark—large
for the times. In 1915 Knoxville and Holston presbyteries (East Tennessee) were detached from the Synod of Tennessee to enter into
the newly organized Synod of Appalachia, leaving the Synod of
Tennessee (now with three presbyteries, Memphis, Columbia, and
Nashville) claiming the central and western portions of the state.
Despite the lack of any aggressive Home Mission endeavor, the presbyteries of Nashville and Memphis made steady gains after 1901;
the Presbytery of Columbia, with no large city within its bounds
lost in membership. In 1926 a little more than half of the synod's total
membership resided in Memphis and Nashville, and a good part of
the remainder in five of the synod's larger towns. It was an urban
synod, and becoming increasingly more so.

The Synod of Appalachia, drawing from the mountain areas of
five states—Virginia, West Virginia, North Carolina, Kentucky and
Tennessee (14 counties in Virginia, one in West Virginia, 15 in
North Carolina, 7 in Kentucky, and 30 in Tennessee)—was organized in 1915, on the suggestion of Dr. R. F. Campbell, pastor
of the First Presbyterian Church of Asheville, North Carolina, who
emphasized the impetus given to Home Mission work in North Carolina by synod's policy of erecting new presbyteries where there was
territory of considerable extent requiring more thorough evangelization. It had been the policy of synod to create a new presbytery
and to unite the older presbyteries in an earnest effort to evangelize
the needy field through the agency of synod's Home Missions. He
suggested that, along the same line, the Synod of Appalachia be

constituted within the territory of the Appalachian Mountains. Within the bounds of the new synod were a large number of towns and cities (Knoxville, Chattanooga, Bristol, and Asheville, for example), but mountain slopes occupied 90 percent of the area, and within the mountain coves were many people isolated from the main currents of American life.

The new synod and its constituent presbyteries entered upon an aggressive plan of Home Missions. In Holston Presbytery the most effective work was done perhaps by community and Sunday school workers; the average number being employed was about 15. In Knoxville Presbytery little mountain schools, supplementing the meager provision made by the state, and in some cases giving boys and girls their first oportunity for an education, opened the way for evangelistic efforts. In the cities much of the advance came through congregational Home Missions, the work being conducted by a particular church or its members in mission Sunday schools and chapels. In the territory included in the four presbyteries of the synod, growth was as follows[47]:

	1896	1906	1916	1926
Ministers	56	74	84	125
Churches	132	158	161	174
Members	8,835	11,405	15,523	24,077

At the outbreak of the Civil War there were less than 6,000 Presbyterians in the whole state of Alabama. The Civil War, followed by Reconstruction and depression, brought losses. In 1870, five years after the war's end, many pulpits were vacant, and there were 750 fewer members than there had been ten years earlier. By the end of another decade the total number of members was still not up to what it had been in 1860, but the number of ministers had increased and most of the pulpits were now supplied. In the 1880's a tide of immigration and prosperity began to set in, and the spirit of missions was revived. New churches were organized, and there was a considerable jump in membership, from 5,804 in 1880, to 9,803 in 1890. In 1883 the Presbytery of North Alabama, till then attached to the Synod of Memphis because of poor transportation facilities with the rest of the state, was incorporated into the Synod of Alabama, thus bringing the entire state into the synod. Growth of the church, though at a less rapid rate, continued in the decade of the 1890's. Many of the churches found in this area later had to be dissolved. Presbyterians had little strength in the rural sections. In 1909 Dr.

A. A. Little pointed out that there was not one self-sustaining country church in the entire synod, and so far as he was aware there were only two self-supporting groups of country churches. In the past 15 years Baptists had organized about 15 new churches in Tuscaloosa County, the Presbyterians had organized one. The same condition he stated, prevailed in Mississippi and in Georgia and in nearly every other state in the far South. The Presbyterian Church, he went on to state, was made up almost altogether of ex-slaveholders and their descendants.[48]

For a few years the synod carried on a plan of synodical evangelism, for the rest of the time it was left in the hands of the presbyteries, most of which for most of the time employed presbyterial evangelists. All churches were urged to hold evangelistic services annually; all ministers were requested to volunteer their services for a week of evangelistic services. In 1914 an evangelistic campaign with the voluntary help of ministers and laymen was reported to have been "very successful." Eighty-six meetings had been held through the synod, resulting in 600 additions to the church. The next year 145 evangelistic services were reported, with 891 additions to the church. In 1916 there were 109 campaigns held in churches both large and small, rural and urban—and there were 1,565 conversions claimed. In 1929 a two-year evangelistic movement was planned. There were plans for evangelistic committees in every church, covenant prayer bands, personal workers' groups, systematic lists of prospects, evangelistic services held by the pastor or a visiting minister. But the great Depression intervened, and the elaborate plans were never put into effect.

Growth of the synod was slow, but steady, particularly in the cities. As in other Southern states Presbyterians lagged far behind Baptists and Methodists in numbers. In 1916 they claimed approximately two percent of the total church membership. But the higher economic status of their membership, or we might say the smaller appeal made to the lower economic classes in city and country, along with their educated ministry, gave them greater influence than their numbers would indicate.

The Synod of Mississippi to the end of the century contained the whole of Louisiana and three-fifths of Mississippi within its bounds (the remaining two-fifths was attached to the Synod of Memphis). The synod, like Alabama, recovered slowly from the War and Reconstruction. A prime weakness was lack of ministers. In 1860 there were 85 ministers on the roll; in 1870, only 80; in 1880, 79; and in 1890 only three more than there had been 30 years earlier. In 1862 there had been 132 churches in the synod, and perhaps a score more belonging to the United Synod of the South (New School). In 1875 the combined bodies had only 160 churches and only four more in 1880. The next decade there was more growth and the synod enrolled 210 churches, a large number to be served by only 88 pastors. Church membership meanwhile had increased much more rapidly. There had been a dip in membership in the 1860's, but in the next 20 years membership in the church increased nearly 80 percent (from 6,613 to 11,871), in a period when population of the area had increased an estimated 60 percent.

In 1890 Mississippi followed the lead of North Carolina, Virginia, and other synods in emphasizing synodical evangelism. Four years later there had been 1,231 additions to the rolls, 17 new churches organized, and a number of half-dead congregations rehabilitated. The end of the decade revealed advance all along the line, an increase in the number of ministers (from 88 to 115), churches (from 210 to 257), and members (from 11,871 to 15,625).

In 1901 Louisiana and Mississippi became distinct synods, each organized along state lines.

The growth of the Synod of Mississippi during the next three decades was steady, though not spectacular. The fact that year by year churches were dissolved as well as organized suggests that in Mississippi, as in other states, congregations were hastily organized which the synod was unable to keep supplied with ministers. Numerous small churches survived, making heavy drains on available Home Mission funds. The synod for a time made good use of elders, who spoke in the home churches while their pastors preached in the vacancies. Experience showed that if the vacant churches could be supplied as often as once a month the congregation could be held together and a pastor more readily secured.

In the 1920's a new "Mississippi plan" developed. Rev. O. G. Jones, superintendent and evangelist, directed the labors of a group of young women, graduates of the General Assembly's Training School, who served as Sunday School Extension workers, and aided in the organization of new churches in both urban and rural areas.

The Synod of Louisiana, when organized, was one of the weakest synods in the church—possessing only 30 active ministers, approximately the size of the young Synod of Florida. In the next three decades there was a gain of only 14 churches (from 90 to 104), but six churches had been dismissed to the Synod of Mississippi, about five to Snedercor Memorial, and a number of churches had been lost to the Presbyterian Church in the U.S.A. The number of ministers in the synod meanwhile had nearly doubled, and membership had increased more than 100 percent.

Impetus was given to the growth of Presbyterianism in Northern Louisiana by organization of the Laymen's Association of Red River Presbytery. Rev. B. C. Bell, pastor of the First Presbyterian Church in McComb, Mississippi, was secured as laymen's evangelist. In 1922 he added the superintendency of Home Missions to his responsibility as evangelist. Under his leadership a dozen new churches were organized within the bounds of presbytery. In the first decade of his labor in the presbytery there was a net gain of 2,288 church members as compared to an increase of 46 in the pervious ten years. "The stimulus he gave to Presbyterians fired them with vision and courage and was a major factor in the growth of the churches."[49]

Twelve ministers and 28 churches (six of which were shortly thereafter transferred to the Synod of Mississippi) were affiliated with Louisiana Presbytery in 1901 when it became part of the Synod of Louisiana. Its churches, except for those in the vicinity of Baton Rouge, were scattered, and the interval between pastorates in the smaller and somewhat isolated churches were sometimes so extended that it was difficult to maintain them. The First Presbyterian Church in Lake Charles, organized in 1888, became a strong organization and provided a pivot for Presbyterianism in Southwest Louisiana. A foothold was established among the French-speaking people in South Louisiana, a work hitherto neglected. Reorganization of the First Presbyterian Church in Alexandria (1891) gave an impetus to the church in Central Louisiana. In 1930 the presbytery enrolled only 25 churches, three less than the number originally enrolled in 1901, but there had been a fair increase in the number of ministers, and membership in the churches had more than doubled.

The Presbytery of New Orleans was the strongest of the three presbyteries in the newly organized Synod of Louisiana; in the three decades that followed, its growth was very limited. In a 20-year period, the number of churches increased by one and, in a 30-year period, there was a gain of only nine. Increase in membership lagged far behind that of the other two presbyteries. Growth of the synod picked up in the 1930's and early 1940's.

During the 50-year period of 1880-1930 proportionate growth of the church was as follows:

States	Multiplied Times
Florida	20
Texas	10

West Virginia	8
Virginia	5 and more
North Carolina	4
Georgia	4
Louisiana	4
Arkansas	4
South Carolina	3
Alabama	3
Mississippi	3
Tennessee	3
Kentucky	2½
Missouri	2

The largest aggregate gains for the period were in North Carolina, 61,000; in Virginia, 55,000; and in Texas, 45,000. The smallest aggregate gains were in Missouri, 9,000; in Louisiana, 10,000; and in Arkansas, 11,000.

Looking at growth by sections it will be observed that the largest gains were made on the frontier, where aggressive Home Missions was conducted, Arkansas and Oklahoma being neglected for Florida and Texas; substantial gains were made in the older synods along the Atlantic seaboard: Virginia (West Virginia), North Carolina, and Georgia, with South Carolina faltering; smaller gains were made in the deep South: Alabama, Louisiana, and Mississippi; the smallest gains were registered in the border states: Tennessee, Kentucky, and Missouri, where Presbyterianism, once strong, had been badly torn by dissension.

During this period, particularly after the turn of the century, growth of the Presbyterian Church compared favorably with that of the much larger Baptist and Methodist churches. In the first decade of the twentieth century, for example, it was estimated that Southern Presbyterians gained 25½ percent, which equaled the record of the Southern Baptist churches and surpassed that of the Southern Methodists. According to statistics compiled for the Home Mission Board of the Southern Baptist Convention the Southern Presbyterian Church led all denominations in the percentage of growth for the ten years between 1906 and 1916. Methodist growth during this period was estimated to be 28 percent, Baptist growth 31 percent, while Southern Presbyterian growth was 34 percent.[50]

The growth in this period as noted was mostly in the cities. The population movement from rural to urban areas led to an inevitable decline in the rural church. Concern over this development was expressed in the early 1890's. "The villages and towns that have sprung up in the South during the past thirty years," wrote Rev.

J. S. Watkins, "do not owe their origin to foreign immigration. They are filling up with annual additions from the surrounding country with families seeking greater educational, religious and social advantages. Farmers . . . have never been as restless, as discontented with country life as they are today . . . The removal of the wealthier farmers has left the country poor. Downright poverty is one cause of the decline of our rural churches. The people are poor." The older, more settled population, he might have added, had been largely replaced by tenants, who sank few roots, and moved frequently. "It is more difficult," continued Dr. Watkins, "for the Presbyterian churches in the country to obtain ministerial supply than for some other denominations, because we have a high standard for the ministry and therefore send out fewer ministers. Men who have spent a great deal of time and money upon their education are, as a rule, not so content to live on small salaries as those who are more ignorant and uncultivated . . . Again the drain to which many of these churches have been subjected has left them without good lay material for officers . . . Some of them have only one elder, others are 'manned' entirely by women." And then there are "the ravages of death. The valuable old members pass away, and the younger members of the families . . . are wanting in spiritual force as well as in financial ability to help."[51]

The only sections in which Southern Presbyterians had ever held and now retained strong roots in the country were in those areas settled by Scots and Scotch-Irish—the Valley of Virginia, the Piedmont and Cape Fear sections of North Carolina, and upper South Carolina, and here too there was the inevitable erosion.

Concern over the plight of the country church grew, until in 1925 the General Assembly elected its first director of country church work, Dr. Henry W. McLaughlin, an eminently successful country pastor, whose name for the next generation would be almost synonomous with that of the country church.

In town and countryside, meanwhile, there were numerous small churches which continued to absorb an undue proportion of the church's mission funds. In 1893 a correspondent estimated that the average membership of the 2,652 churches in the General Assembly was 71. There were 131 churches in the Assembly the number of whose members could be given with a single digit. Only 86 churches had more than 300 members; 20 of these were in Virginia, 10 in North Carolina, 12 in Kentucky, 7 each in South Carolina, Nashville, and Texas.

In 1886 there was one church (the Nashville First) with more than

1,000 members, and 8 with more than 500. A decade later there was still one church with more than 1,000 members, and 25 with more than 500; in 1912 there were four churches with more than 1,000 members, and 73 with more than 500 members; ten years later there were 27 churches with more than 1,000 members.

In the 30-year period of 1880-1910 Presbyterian church membership in typical Southern cities had grown more rapidly proportionately than had the cities themselves.

1880-1910 Percentage	Population Growth	Membership Growth
Atlanta	314	400
Richmond	100	149
Louisville	81	240
Nashville	155	234
Norfolk	208	185
St. Louis	93	120
Birmingham	4,183	2,560
Houston	377	670

The strongest Presbyterian centers in 1916 were the following:

Cities	Members	Cities	Members
Atlanta	5,719	New Orleans	3,744
Louisville	5,126	Houston	3,463
Richmond	4,630	Birmingham	2,976
Nashville	4,244	Dallas	2,683
Memphis	4,165	Charleston, W. Va.	2,309
Charlotte	4,165	Norfolk	2,233

The average church membership in 1930 was about 125. More than half of the churches in the Assembly had less than 75 members and these churches contained more than a fourth of the total membership. Approximately one-half of the church received Home Mission aid. They absorbed perhaps an undue proportion of the church's mission funds, money which might have been spent to better advantage in the expanding cities. But from these churches came a disproportionate number of ministers and missionaries for the church at home and abroad.

Church membership in the cities had increased, but so also had the number of the unchurched.

The city, itself, as a mission field, perhaps the mission field of the future, began to attract attention around the turn of the century. Rev. A. B. Currie wrote:

In speaking of the Home Mission field, one's thought is apt to turn first to the destitute and frontier country districts, but it is well to remember that this field lies partly and largely in our cities. It is a well-known and often remarked fact that the trend of population in our republic is toward the cities, steadily and increasingly so. . . . The cities are becoming the centers of influence, commercially, politically, socially and religiously; this influence is for good or evil, too often the latter; and one of the most serious and difficult problems now confronting the church is the evangelization of the modern city; for, notwithstanding our city pastorates, a large portion of every modern city is mission ground, where thousands of people are outside the pale of gospel influence . . . The president of a labor organization, in a not large Southern city, stated some months ago, that there were a thousand men in his organization alone indifferent or hostile to the church. We are not however to suppose that the mission field in our cities is composed only of the poor, or even of the laboring classes . . . This field is composed in part of the wealthy classes, habituees of clubs, hotels, boarding houses, bachelors' apartments, and not infrequently palatial homes . . . [These last] are the most difficult of all classes to reach with the gospel, because of their complete self-satisfaction. And so we have in the cities the neglected rich, as well as the neglected poor, and these two classes are the weakness and despair of our city religious life.[52]

How was this situation to be met? Dr. J. M. Spencer, Southern Presbyterian pastor in St. Louis, pointed out that the combined church membership of all Protestant churches in his city was only 33,833 out of a total population of 500,000. It is evident, he wrote, that the masses are unreached by present methods of church work. The only solution of the problem, he claimed, was the establishment of institutional churches among the masses—"that is, church, in connection with which *everything* that is *lawful* and that has a tendency to elevate people along industrial, social, intellectual, moral and religious lines shall be provided." He offered as examples churches in Boston, New York, and Philadelphia, as well as overseas (the McAll missions in France). He himself opened a Peoples' Church in St. Louis, which developed some of the "best features" of such an institutional church. It was open for two services a day throughout the year. Drunkards, prostitutes, and criminals were numbered among the reclaimed and saved.[53]

No objection could be raised to the idea of a city mission, in which the gospel was preached to the down and out. This expedient was being attempted in a number of Southern towns. The *Union Seminary Magazine,* which carried a regular missionary column, carried an article commending the idea for the first time in 1897.[54]

There were strong objections, however, to the idea of an institutional church. Such an approach, wrote Dr. R. Q. Mallard, editor of the *Southwestern Presbyterian*, tended to secularize the church, turning it aside from the obligation resting upon every Christian to be in his or her sphere a messenger of tidings to lost men. "It puts the chief emphasis where Christ and the apostles do not put it, namely on human misery and not on human guilt . . . It reverses the gospel method of saving the sinner and society." The gospel method is from center to circumference; the method of the institutional church is from circumference to center. The former "saves the individual first, and through him betters the masses"; the latter seeks to better the earthly conditions of the masses as the first step toward the spiritual salvation of the individual.[55]

Dr. Mallard was greatly disturbed the following year over a volume commending the institutional church and bearing the imprimatur of the Executive Committee on Publication. Among the so-called "improvements upon the New Testament model" which Dr. Mallard decried were men's clubs, athletics, libraries, reading rooms, entertainment courses, boy's clubs, industrial classes, day nurseries, kindergartens, beneficiary and loan associations, and so forth. Methods more antagonistic to Presbyterian views, he insisted, could hardly be devised. He was somewhat relieved that in the page of commendations he could not find the name of a single minister south of the Potomac.[56]

The *Christian Observer* agreed with Dr. Josiah Strong, a strong advocate of the institutional church, whose writings had done much to arouse interest in the problem of the city, that the churches should not desert the downtown sections, but should rather adapt their methods of work—within proper limits—to the new conditions which existed in the cities. But the paper was not yet ready to approve the idea of an institutional church. The "gospel alone can save," wrote the editor.[57]

A year later the editor returned to the subject. Something must be done, he insisted, lest the poorer people in urban centers drift or feel driven away from the ordinances of religion. This could be done, he suggested, in either of two ways: one, provide for such services as the poor people will attend; two, have mission buildings where there are regular religious services and where other provisions are made for the temporal and religious welfare of the classes of people who cannot be induced to go to one of the elaborate churches. "In many cases, this is, perhaps, the only way by which the lapsed city masses can be reached.—Whilst we cannot approve of some things in what is called 'the institutional church,' yet there are certain features in it which seem to have good promise . . . How far each city church should be made a center of institutional church work must be decided by each church for itself.—Old methods seem inadequate . . ."[58]

The time would come when certain features of institutional church work would be generally acceptable within the Southern Church; but opposition to recreational and other social activities within the church facilities continued for another generation and more. In 1926, for example, Rev. S. B. MacLean read a paper before the Presbyterian Ministers' Association of Charlotte, North Carolina, in which he complained that churches, instead of being holy temples, were becoming community centers, social resorts, and places of entertainment, and even amusement. He recognized that pastimes in the larger churches were generally carried on in the basement, but pointed out that in the smaller churches, encroachment was made upon that part of the building dedicated to the worship of God. "When banquets, smokers, concerts, minstrels, etc.," he wrote, "are being carried on in adjacent and communicating rooms, the spirit of levity and even revelry is so often present" that being in another part of the building does not prevent "desecration of the Holy of Holies." Even in the larger buildings, he objected to the sounds and odors issuing from elaborate kitchens, and to the hilarity and smoke fumes which arose from the banqueting hall. From present indications, he predicted, an expert chef and staff of waiters would become a regular requirement of all first-class church dining rooms. What precedents, he asked, are to be found in God's Word, for the sanction of such ideas and usages?[59]

More serious was the question raised earlier by Dr. Mallard. Is the church concerned only with the salvation of the individual, or is it concerned, must it be concerned, also with improving the material conditions under which the mass of the people lived? If the latter is correct, how are the two to be related? That question remained for the time unanswered and still continues to be debated.

III

Wards of the South

Presbyterian missionary efforts in the South have been concerned largely with carrying the gospel to the descendants of the original Presbyterian settlers and into the main currents of Southern life. But from early times the church has recognized a responsibility to two particular groups—Indians and Negroes—and later to other needy groups within its bounds—Mexicans, other foreign-speaking groups, Highlanders, Jews, workers in industry, for example. We are concerned in this chapter with Presbyterian missions for the earliest wards of the area—the Indians, whom the white man displaced in America, and the Negroes whom he had transplanted to America.

I. THE INDIANS[1]

The decade ending with 1870 saw the passing of the veterans who had, under God, made a civilized Christian people out of certain primitive Indian tribes. It also saw the work crippled and reduced by the ravages of the war, by the weakness of the church in the Reconstruction period, and by the increased difficulty of reaching the Indians with the gospel.

Nonetheless the two decades which saw a general revival of Home Missions activity in the Southern Presbyterian Church witnessed fresh interest in the mission to the Indians. Gradually, though with some difficulty, new missionaries were secured to replace the notable leaders who had dropped by the way.

The great missionaries after the war were W. J. B. Lloyd among the Choctaws and J. J. Read among the Chickasaws, but there were others who came a little later, whose influence was almost as great. J. P. Gibbons came to the Choctaw country in 1884 though he was almost 34 years of age. "Like all the other great missionaries to the

Indians," says Professor W. B. Morrison, "Mr. Gibbons gave his entire
life to the work with no thought of reward other than the good he
could do. At no time during the thirty-four years of his ministry did he
receive a salary of more than fifty dollars per month, and yet through
the help of a loyal wife and his own labor on the little mission farm, he
was able to give all his children a college education."[2] He was vitally
interested in every phase of Indian education and was instrumental in
the establishment of Goodland Orphanage. Mrs. J. P. Gibbons (neé
Bella Callum), who married Mr. Gibbons in 1902 and who had been
serving the Goodland Orphanage as a teacher or treasurer since coming there in 1898, was chosen by the Oklahoma Memorial Association
in 1933 as one of the ten most eminent citizens of the commonwealth.

Charles E. Hotchkin, son of the pioneer missionary Ebenezer
Hotchkin, with that command of the language which comes from early
familiarity, preached with good success to the Choctaws from 1884 to
his death in 1905. Rev. Calvin J. Ralston left the pastorate to take
charge of Armstrong Academy in 1890 and identified his life with
that of the Indians till his death in 1929.

By 1889 the Southern Presbyterian Church had 13 missionaries
(ten natives and three whites) in the field with 22 churches under
its care. But the field was too large for this small force to cultivate. The
Northern Presbyterian Church was working in the contiguous territory and had greater funds at its disposal. In this year four of the native preachers, with the churches under their care, and 332 members
withdrew from the Southern Presbyterian Mission and joined that
of the Northern Presbyterians. Nine ministers, 13 churches, and 638
communicants remained in the Southern connection. Two years later
the Indian missions were transferred from the Executive Committee
on Foreign Missions to the Executive Committee on Home Missions, to
which they had come more naturally to belong.

Before the Civil War, the American Board, through
whom the Presbyterians had worked at the start, and later the Presbyterian Board, had sustained a notable educational work among the
Indians. Southern Presbyterians were not able to sustain this work
during the war and finally abandoned education altogether for evangelism. When at last the church was ready to resume the educational
task, many of the old stations and much of the opportunity had passed
into other hands.

Spencer Academy, which had been the Choctaws' largest boarding
school for boys before the war and which had helped to train almost
every man of prominence and usefulness in the Choctaw Nation, was

reopened in 1871 under the charge of J. H. Colton. J. J. Read rendered faithful service in this institution and molded the character of outstanding native preachers like Henry Wilson and Silas L. Bacon. But in 1881 the Indians failed to renew their contract with the Presbyterians because of the school's inadequate support by the church.

Armstrong Academy, which had been another important school for boys among the Choctaws before the war, was operated by the Presbyterians from 1873 to 1894. Under the management first of W. J. B. Lloyd and later of C. J. Ralston, it rendered splendid service to the Indian people and to the Presbyterian Church. But, in the last year mentioned, the Choctaws canceled all of their educational contracts and began to operate their own schools without missionary aid.

The Southern Presbyterian Church, then, along with other churches working in Indian Territory, established Neighborhood Schools in strategic centers, which ministered not only to Indian children but also to the white children whose parents were crowding into the territory in ever-increasing numbers. In 1903 eleven of these schools were supported by the Home Missions Committee; and 23 teachers gave over 1,200 scholars instruction in secular subjects, along with the Bible and the Shorter Catechism. The majority of the schools were self-supporting; for a number of years the church's only aid came through the offerings of the children in the Sunday school.

The Home Missions Committee embarked upon this educational program in Indian Territory because it was urgently needed. Indian children were able to attend public schools for a few months in the year, but there was no guarantee of any religious instruction. The children of the poor white people in the territory had no school advantages at all, except those afforded by the mission schools. In 1904 the Commissioners of Indian Affairs reported to the government that there were 119,000 white children in the Territory for whose education no provision had been made.

Oklahoma Presbyterian College for Girls began in 1894 as a primary school for Indians. The first building was only a small log cabin, with its desks and seats cut from rough logs, and with a tiny window sawed in the walls of the cabin. It was named Calvin Institute, in memory of the little son of Rev. C. J. Ralston. The lad was accidently drowned when he was just four years old, and the grief-stricken parents had given $200, which they had saved for the boy's education, to the Home Missions Committee to establish the new school. Mary Semple Hotchkin, the last of the pre-war missionary teachers, a cultured young society girl, who had come to Indian Territory by boat and wagon train in 1856 at the age of 19, was placed in charge.

The school was operated by the Home Missions Committee as a

primary school for Indians until 1902, when, aided by a contract system with the Indians and by generous gifts of the people of Durant, a
large substantial brick building was erected in the heart of the town
and Durant Presbyterian College came into existence. For eight
years the "College" gave a creditable high school education to boys
and girls, both Indians and whites.

At the end of that time a new building was erected on the out-
skirts of Durant; the name was changed to Oklahoma Presbyterian
College for Girls, and the high school became a junior college. New
buildings were added in the years that followed, a burdensome debt
that threatened to wreck the school was paid off, and a small endowment raised. The Bible department was endowed by the Auxiliary
Birthday Offering in 1926.

For some time Oklahoma Presbyterian College was the only high
grade institution in Southern Oklahoma. Its moral and spiritual
influence was felt throughout the entire region. Later Southeastern
Teachers' College, one of Oklahoma's largest normal schools, was located at Durant. A cooperative arrangement between the two schools
made it possible for a girl to remain under the influence of the church
college while completing her work for a degree at the state school.
In 1932 there were 162 girls in the school, 97 of whom were Indians.
The college, however, was on the brink of financial collapse. The
great Depression had reduced its income by 65 percent.

To meet the emergency the school wisely sent its students to the
neighboring Teachers' College for their academic work and became
a "home," offering courses in Bible and Christian Education for Indian
girls who otherwise could not have received a college education.
Within a short time the institution became co-educational, open to
students from other backgrounds—Mexican, Chinese, and Anglo-
Americans, as well as Indians, who were not attracted in the same
numbers as formerly. The "College" had served its purpose, and in the
1960's its long and honorable history came to an end.

Goodland Indian Orphanage and School was the second neighborhood school to survive through the period. Its roots ran into the past
and were intertwined with the history of the Indian mission. The
station at Goodland was opened in 1859 by Rev. O. P. Stark. There was
no money for a teacher, so Mrs. Stark, who had three small children
of her own, gathered the Indian children of the neighborhood in a
side room of the log manse (the main room served as living room,
bedroom, dining room, and kitchen) and opened and taught the first
school at Goodland. The labor was too much for Mrs. Stark and she
died a few months later with her newborn babe in her arms.

Other teachers paid by the Foreign Mission Board continued the work until the Civil War. The school received no mission funds from 1866 to 1890, but was kept alive and taught year after year by some member of the Goodland Church. "Special credit," says Professor Morrison, "should be given to Mrs. Carrie LeFlore, wife of the Choctaw Chief, Basil LeFlore, who supervised the school for a number of years. She was a woman of culture and refinement as well as a splendid Christian character, and exercised a remarkable influence not only upon the people of the Goodland neighborhood, but upon the entire Choctaw nation."[3]

The school came under the influence of our mission again in 1890 when Rev. J. P. Gibbons took over the work at Goodland. The strenuous life of farming, teaching, and preaching was too much for Mr. Gibbon's health, and after three years he was forced to abandon the school. It was reopened the next year with four or five white children, and all the Indian children in the neighborhood. In addition a number of orphans were cared for, at first in the homes of Mr. Gibbons and the members of the church, and then later in a small log dormitory; support for the orphans came from the members of the Goodland Church. For four years they supplied their wants out of their own scanty resources; at the end of that time a series of scanty crops compelled them to end the experiment. The school continued, however, as a day school under Miss Bella Callum, who later became the wife of Mr. Gibbons.

Through the efforts of Mr. and Mrs. Gibbons, and the renewed interest in Indian missions which came with the appointment of Dr. S. L. Morris as secretary of Assembly's Home Missions, Goodland became at last a "contract" school, aided by the Choctaw tribal funds. The boarding department was reopened and the orphanage was reestablished under the direction of one of the most eminent of the Choctaw Christians, Rev. S. L. Bacon. Mr. and Mrs. Bacon gave over their home to the use of the orphanage, and until their death in 1922 these devoted Indians gave every moment of their time to the youth of their people; at death they willed their entire property to the orphanage. "If Indian Missions had produced no other Christian character than Silas Bacon," wrote Professor Morrison, "it would have been worth all it has cost."[4]

Rapid progress was made under the care of Mr. and Mrs. Bacon. New buildings were erected; the material assets were improved through gifts of the Indians themselves—some in the church, some out of the church. The Choctaw legislature finally voted to appropriate $10,000 from their tribal funds for the school. In order that the school might receive this gift, the Home Missions Committee recommended that it be turned over to a Board of Trustees elected by the Indian Presbytery. This was done in 1913 and Goodland Indian Orphanage came under the control of an independent Board of Trustees, most of whom continued to be Indians and members of the Presbyterian Church. In 1930 there were approximately 250 Indian children in the school, and each year hundreds of applications were refused. Young people left the institution to find places for themselves in all walks of life, and this they have continued to do until the present time.

In the 1960's the Goodland Indian Orphanage, which had come under the ownership and control of the Synod of Oklahoma and had also greatly improved its facilities, became the Goodland Presbyterian Children's Home—one of the better such homes under the care of the Southern Presbyterian Church.

In addition to the work carried on among the Choctaws and the Chickasaws the Southern Presbyterian Church also developed an interesting work among the Alabamas. These Indians were a branch of the Choctaws and lived originally in the state whose name they bore. They were pressed westward by the advancing whites across the Mississippi and over the Red River, until they settled down at last near the Trinity River in Polk County, Texas.

Back in 1880, Dr. S. F. Tenney got lost in the woods and was discovered by an Alabama Indian who gave him shelter in his own home. When Dr. Tenney discovered that none of the Indian's tribe had any knowledge of Jesus Christ, he interested himself in their behalf. The next year the Presbytery of East Texas employed Rev. L. W. Currie of North Carolina to settle among them. After great difficulty, and in spite of much opposition on the part of white men, Mr. and Mrs. Currie established a church and a school. The house of worship was burned down; the work was interrupted and for a time suspended by outlaws. Mr. Currie gave up the work and went as a missionary to Alaska. Mrs. Currie returned after her husband's death and taught with faithfulness and efficiency until 1899.

From March 1890 till his death in 1899 Rev. W. A. Jones labored among them for a part of his time and received a few members into the Presbyterian Church.

Rev. C. W. Chambers and his wife moved into the village in May 1900 and remained there as preacher and teacher until his honorable retirement from the ministry in 1936; they were faithful, uncomplaining workers, with meager support and for much of the time with poor equipment.

When missionary work was begun among them, the Alabamas were still following the "chase" for a livelihood; wearing blankets, leather breeches, and feathers for clothing; drinking as much whisky as they could get. Presbyterian missionaries transformed them from a band of savages, illiterate and pagan, to a civilized Christian community.

In the 1930's there were about 332,397 Indians within the borders of the United States; approximately one-third of this number lived in Oklahoma, remnants of about 100 different tribes from every section of the United States. The bulk of the population was composed of Cherokees, Choctaws, Chickasaws, and Seminoles—four of the "five civilized tribes"—among whom Presbyterians had worked from the start.

But though the number of Indians in Oklahoma was increasing, the number of church members was decreasing. Thus in 1894 there were 786 churches and 28,600 members among the "five civilized tribes," while in 1931 there were only 200 churches with about 8,700 members. Membership in the Southern Methodist Church declined in this period from 9,683 to 2,687; in the Southern Baptist Church from 9,147 to 4,791. Southern Presbyterians had 1,800 members before the war, 686 in 1875, and only 550 in 1933.

The Indian is by nature a religious person, a worshiper of the Great Spirit; yet after more than 100 years of missionary effort, he had not been won in great numbers to the Christian religion. What was the explanation?

As pointed out by Herman N. Morse in *Home Missions: Today and Tomorrow*: "There are some very obvious reasons for this limited result. Many things have militated against the success of Indian missions. From the very beginning the Indian has been the victim of conquest, international strife and war, and exploitation at the hands of the white man. Our treatment of the Indian makes the blackest page of American history. No wonder he is slow to accept the white man's religion."[5]

But there were also other reasons. It had been difficult, for example, to secure ministers for the Indian churches. This, according to Dr. Homer McMillan, Secretary of the Assembly's committee, had been the supreme need and the great lack through the ages. Perhaps it was true, as Dr. T. C. Johnson had charged a generation earlier, that the work among the Indians had not been done in a way to make them strong enough to take care of themselves; that insufficient attention had been paid to the training of pastors, teachers, and sessions.[6] In 1930 R. N. Firebaugh, Superintendent of Indian Missions, said: "Our task today is to care for a growing work with fewer workers. One man today is doing the work where five men used to be and where there ought to be ten." A few years earlier there had been six white ministers devoting their whole time to the work in addition to the Indian ministers. At the time Mr. Firebaugh was the only white minister, and there were six native ministers, only two of whom could preach in English.

Native ministers had rendered faithful service, but it had been impossible to secure thoroughly equipped natives, who were able to appeal to the rising generation, trained and educated in modern American ways. As early as 1894 Rev. Allen Wright marked the new attitude of the younger generation. The break with the older generation was subsequently intensified by the government schools, which trained annually 30,000 Indian students. As the Home Missions Council pointed out in 1924, no longer were these students

> . . . tolerant of anything less than that which they see demanded by white boys and girls. Moving pictures, automobiles, radio machines, lectures, contact with student movements of the world—all have been of infinite influence in shaping their ideas and ideals. The girls bob their hair and the boys press their clothes in the latest fashion of movie stars; they hear great music, and they have seen on the screen life in other places from reservations. They know what other young people are doing and are eager to imitate them, even in the extremes. They also know what other young people are longing to do, and they too have all the ambitions and enthusiasm of youth to be leaders.
>
> It is not to be wondered at that when these stylishly dressed girls and boys return to the reservation they are strangers in a strange land. Frequently they do not respect or understand the methods and teachings of the uneducated native or white missionaries and are even intolerant of the splendid, self sacrificing older missionaries who, because of their isolation, know far less of the present world and its ways than these Indian boys and girls have experienced. Hence the returned students are not "at home" in the missions, nor the missionaries "at home" with them.[7]

Another difficulty stemmed from denominational rivalries. Such competition did not exist when the Presbyterian missions were established but developed after the Civil War. In 1889 missionaries began to mention the tendency of the Indians to divide into denominational factions. There were instances where different denominations, in one case as many as four, were struggling for the ascendency in little communities which, taken together, would barely suffice to support a single church. Mr. Hotchkin, speaking of denominational rivalries in his own field, said, "It takes a great deal of forbearance and Christian charity to keep the peace." Writing of the situation in Oklahoma at the end of the period, George W. Hinman said: "Present conditions of Christian work among Indians of Eastern

Oklahoma are not encouraging. Neglect and indifference of white Christian neighbors, the rivalry of sects, the perpetuation of pre-war denominational divisions, the dominance of reactionary religious bodies, jealousies and competition, give little hope for immediate spiritual revival."[8]

Another difficulty came from the presence of the white man. Before Oklahoma was opened for settlement, unprincipled white men were drifting into Indian Territory. Many were indifferent to religious ministrations; others were ungodly: they intermarried with the Indians, sold them whiskey, and in many other ways made the work of the missionary more difficult. When Oklahoma was opened for settlement and became a state, the Indians were soon outnumbered by 20 to one and too often there was neglect and indifference on the part of Christian neighbors. In 1922 Mrs. Gibbons wrote: "The Indian is fast becoming civilized, but the conditions which surround him are more deplorable than they were fifty years ago. Then the missionaries had only to fight the traditions, superstitutions and customs of the Indians. Now the greatest battle the missionary has is to keep the Indian from falling into the vices of the white man."

In 1924 Rev. R. M. Firebaugh, who had served since 1912 as a missionary and who was now Superintendent of Indian Missions wrote:

> The great problem of the Indian work from its very beginning has been to keep up with the changed conditions—changes over which we had no control—and which were in the main good, but inevitably brought disastrous results for the time being to well developed religious growth. Since we began work among them a hundred years ago, there has been an exodus from Mississippi to a wilderness— Indian Territory—accomplished with considerable pain and hardships . . . Here in Indian Territory they vacillated for a time between what civilization they had attained to and things primordial and finally established themselves as a pastoral people. Then came the shift from tribal government to statehood, from settlement to rural life, from communism to individual property rights. These changes have come so fast and so insistently that even the white race in Oklahoma has been unable to keep pace; and it would be unreasonable to expect that the Indian, who loves to hold on to the old until the new has become quite ancient, should be able to do anything more than mark time. The changed conditions incident to the World War that have been felt over the whole nation are only a faint illustration of the quick-silver state that has been among the Indians for the last five generations.[9]

But Mr. Firebaugh was not discouraged. There were Indians who held on to their religion, homes which preserved the family altars, sessions which kept wise oversight of their flocks, Sunday schools in which the Word was studied. Young people were being reached more effectively than in the past; two Choctaws were preparing for the ministry in a theological seminary.

There had been many eminent Indians among those trained by the Presbyterian missionaries: the Folsom brothers and their descendants; Allen Wright and his son, Frank Hall Wright, the Indian evangelist and singer who converted thousands of Indians and whites to Christ throughout the United States and Canada; Silas Bacon, who gave his property and his life to the Goodland Orphanage; Jonas Wolf, a chief of the Chickasaws; William A. Durant, "prominent and forceful in Choctaw politics before statehood and in Oklahoma ever since"; William F. Semple, graduate of Washington and Lee University and later chief of the Choctaw nation; and many others.

But the success of the Indian missions is gauged not only by the eminent men won to the service of Christ but by a host of humbler men and women in every walk of life. At a meeting of Indian Presbytery, Rev. Silas Bacon once said: "It is often asked what has become of the money spent on Indian missions. If you will come with me to yon cemetery, I will show you the graves of hundreds of sainted dead. Is the money wasted that filled those graves with Christians instead of heathen?"

World War II ushered in a new period for the Indian mission in Oklahoma. Young men were drawn into the armed forces; some returned to settle in the areas from which they had come; many did not. The Indian churches were in rural areas, among a people of small means, at some distance from any urban community. The young people, educated in government schools, were drawn off to the towns where there was an opportunity to make more money, or, as it was reported to the General Assembly, forced to go elsewhere to make a livelihood. Only the older people remained behind. Ministers died off and there were few replacements. Inevitably the Indian churches declined in strength.

In 1957 boundary lines of presbyteries within the Synod of Oklahoma were redrawn. Indian Presbytery retained its name, but the lines were now geographic rather than ethnic. Five years later Raymond B. Spivey, Superintendent of Church Extension in the synod, reported:

> For generations our missionaries have labored toward the day when Indians of Southeastern Oklahoma would take their places in the general society in our church on a basis equal with all others . . . among the Chickasaws and the Choctaws this has in large measure now been achieved . . . As with members in general many of our In-

dian members seeking work move into areas in which we have no churches and often enter into other denominations.

The effectiveness of our Church's work and the search for challenging work for which the church and the public school have prepared them have led to the present situation which finds only a half dozen small congregations of Chickasaw and Choctaw people, totaling about 75 members, in the Presbyterian Church in the United States in Oklahoma. Almost every church in the Synod has members of Indian ancestry.

For the benefit primarily of the older members in our Indian churches we also have a supplemental program, including biannual meetings of three days each, while cooperating with other presbyterian groups and occasionally through the Oklahoma Protestant Indian Council with other denominations. Some of these older members cannot see clearly the victory of the church for the anguish it brings them to know that their time as a separate people is practically at an end. And though their churches are at times moved by this sadness they would not wish to turn back the pages of time for themselves.[10]

Meanwhile there had been a somewhat similar development among the Alabama Indians in Polk County, Texas. Here, however, the Indian community was more in contact with the outside world and was approaching economic independence. Many of the more progressive Indians wanted their children to participate in the opportunities of full American citizenship. In 1955 Malcolm L. Purcell, Executive Secretary of Church Extension in Brazos Presbytery, wrote: "Most of the youth are now graduating from a nearby consolidated school . . . about a dozen have already graduated from college, and others are in college now. This is leading to a quest for jobs away from the reservation. A number are seeking work in the industries around Houston. This of course depletes local leadership and poses problems of adjustment to city life."[11]

Two years later there were reports of a program of integration with city churches in whose territory some of the Indians from the reservation were now living, and in 1964 Mr. Landry wrote: "In many respects this community is becoming more like a typical rural community. We are now a feeder community of the city church."

The parent church on the reservation, out of Livingston, remains a strong church with more than 100 members, retaining the allegiance of most of the Indians in the community.

II. THE NEGROES

Elected in 1898 to succeed Dr. A. L. Phillips as Secretary of the Committee on Colored Evangelization was a young minister, D. Clay Lilly, only five years out of the seminary and pastor of the church in Tuscaloosa, who retained his pastorate and gave his services to the committee without remuneration. Two years later, after the death of O. B. Wilson, Mr. Lilly resigned his pastorate and accepted a full-time job as Executive Secretary of the Committee on Colored Evangelization and Superintendent and Professor of Theology in Stillman Institute. He was now "the overseer of plowing, digging and building," professor not only of Theology but also of Church History and Polity, Exegesis and Homiletics, at Stillman Institute; agent for the cause of colored evangelization before the church at large; shepherd and bishop of the infant African Presbyterian Church, which only recently had been launched on its independent career.

Mr. Lilly's first report to the church was encouraging. Sunday schools were being organized. The debt on Stillman had been liquidated. There were ten students in the academic department, and 12 in the theological department.

Other educational efforts were now encouraged by the church. One of these, Ferguson-Williams Industrial College, at Abbeville, South Carolina, offering academic work with industrial features, was aided by the committee and finally in 1903 taken over by the Assembly. It was fairly prosperous at one time, with 110 boarders and a total enrollment of 240. Gradually, however, the work began to drag; the school was embarrassed by debt, inadequate equipment, and the inability of the executive committee to render any substantial aid. In 1920 the institution was finally liquidated, and its funds invested in the enlarged program of Stillman Institute.

The North Wilkesboro Industral Institute at North Wilkesboro, North Carolina, was transferred from the Synod of North Carolina to the Assembly in 1900. The next year aid began to be given to the J. H. Alexander Academy at Vicksburg, Mississippi. The two latter instiutions were parochial schools offering some industrial features and were taught by Negro ministers in connection with their regular church work.

In 1903 there were 500 pupils in these four schools operated by the Southern Presbyterian Church. The committee, with the sanction of the General Assembly, was seeking to encourage at this time the establishment of additional parochial schools among the Negroes and hoped to open up several boarding and industrial schools as soon as the means were put into its hands. But the funds which the committee hoped to receive did not materialize and its aid was soon restricted to Stillman Institute. Though help from the Assembly was lacking,

some of the more energetic pastors maintained for a while parochial schools, as at Texarkana, Selma, Montgomery, Milton, Thomasville, and Florence. In 1933 six pastors still operated schools in connection with their churches; these schools had a total enrollment of
approximately 800.

Colored evangelization, however, was "not succeeding," as Mr. Lilly
candidly declared. After 25 years of labor, there had not been developed one self-supporting church. Financial support remained very
meager—in the year ending May 1902 the total contributed was less
than $6,500. Only two churches had contributed as much as $100
each, and only four presbyteries gave more than $200. Forty-eight
presbyteries gave less than $100. Dr. Thornton Whaling, pastor at
Lexington, Virginia, wrote eloquently in support of the work. The
existence of nine million colored people in the Southern states, he
argued, imposes upon us a duty which we cannot evade, not only
because they are a part of the world for which Christ died, but also
because we thereby preserve the safety and the prosperity of our own
institutions and life. "If a large proportion of these people are to remain ignorant, superstitious, immoral and irreligious it must react
injuriously upon the interests of our entire section of country."

He pointed out that it remained the mature and settled policy of
the church to organize an independent African Presbyterian Church
and to train for the service of this church and for the reaching of the
unevangelized Negroes a native, colored ministry:

> Against this policy [he added] not a word can be said; it does not
> raise the spectre of either social or ecclesiastical equality. . . . Mean-
> time, the preparation by us, in our own Colored Theological Seminary,
> of a competent and trained colored ministry provides this African
> Church with ministers who have no racial prejudices to overcome [he
> meant, it may be presumed, Negro ministers who accepted the doctrine
> of white superiority] and who can be supported at a comparatively
> small cost. . . . It is wonderful how cheaply these ministers can live.
> Some years the appropriations have not averaged over forty dollars a
> year. They could be well sustained by appropriations averaging one
> hundred dollars each.[12]

A few months after the appearance of this article, Dr. Lilly, finding
the burdens of his office and the nervous strain arising from the indifference of the church and its lack of support for the work too
heavy for his strength, resigned his position and was succeeded by
the Reverend J. G. Snedecor of Birmingham.

James George Snedecor, whose name was henceforth to be closely
intertwined with work for Negroes in the Southern Presbyterian
Church, was born on a Mississippi plantation, June 21, 1855. A grad-

uate of the University of Mississippi, he carried on post-graduate
studies (in journalism) at Cornell University, and later read law
at Washington University in St. Louis. He edited for a short time
the leading paper in Oxford, Mississippi, practiced law for a few
years in Memphis, and then took over a farm in Florida. Here, in
debt and with five children to support, he underwent a deeply religious experience and felt called to preach, a decision never regretted. He served churches in Florida and Alabama, and for some
years served as district superintendent of the American Bible Society.

> In September, 1903, came a call to his life work among the neglected
> people of the South, the Negro. For thirteen years he gave himself un-
> reservedly to this call for service: he traveled from Virginia to Texas,
> from Missouri to Florida, calling upon the Christian people of the
> Southern Presbyterian Church to help this needy people "at their own
> doorstep", to teach them and to help them to walk in the right way
> [wrote his wife in a sketch intended for her children]. Nearly always he
> faced an unsympathetic audience, but always rejoiced over the few
> that came asking what they could do to help. He always tried to give
> the ministers, and especially the younger ones, a vision of their re-
> sponsibility to the ignorant, "poor men at their gate."[13]

The work grew, but slowly. In 1892, when the Committee on
Colored Evangelization was established, there were 56 colored
churches and about 1,600 members; in 1910 when the committee, for
lack of financial support, was finally discontinued, there were only
69 churches and 2,355 members. The committee acknowledged that
the work was discouraging, and that "few of our pastors and evangelists present satisfactory reports." At the same time it pointed out that
due allowance must be made for the extraordinary obstacles that
confronted the Negro missionaries.

First and foremost (as the committee saw it) the field had been
largely occupied. While the Presbyterian Church attempted to hold
its Negro members in the same status they had occupied before the
war, the independent Negro churches (Baptist and Methodist) had
practically preempted the field. Negroes attached to the Presbyterian churches in the South before the war seceded and found their
way for the most part into the Northern Church, as did many of the
churches organized by Southern Presbyterians after the war.

Second, when the Presbyterian Church attempted to build an
independent Negro church it aroused the active opposition of the
other churches. There are many references to the jealousy, the opposition of the colored pastors. Thus Dr. Snedecor reported: "The
meager results reported by [our] pastors may be explained when we
remember the difficult material upon which they labor, the fierce op-

position of other ignorant and envious preachers, and the higher standards of church life demanded by our people."

In one case at least the opposition took violent form and came from whites rather than Negroes.

The work at Street, Mississippi, Dr. Snedecor reported to the executive committee, was in a very prosperous way under the care of the Reverend L. L. Wells, when men of evil mind, known as "white cappers" ran Wells out of the community and dispersed his congregation by threats of bodily harm. Upon inquiry it was learned that Wells was the only Negro preacher disturbed, and it was distinctly understood that this was done because he made some pretensions to respectability, and was better educated than the poor class of whites who comprised the "white cappers."[14]

"The feeling of our people on this whole subject is undergoing a change; for quiet indifference is hardening into steady aversion, and in some cases open opposition and hostility," reported the Committee on Colored Evangelization to the Synod of Louisiana, citing the Street incident as an example. "Now at every step we take in this work we must face a glittering phalanx of Southern feeling, which has taken alarm, on account of present conditions."[15]

There were other reasons as suggested in other comments here and there. O. B. Wilson's efforts to establish Sunday schools taught by whites in Atlanta were not welcomed by many of the Negro ministers in the city. To allow colored children to be taught by white teachers, they said, was to admit the inferiority of the Negro and to educate him to think he could not himself become a teacher. Again, for white people to offer to teach Negroes while they did not grant them justice was hypocrisy. They needed teaching themselves; let them look after their own neglected. They have much more to do than they are doing or can do.[16] In an article entitled "Our Church and Our Negroes," the Reverend R. R. Howison charged that the sad failure of the church in the evangelization of the Negroes was traceable to only two causes. One, the apathy and indifference of the church on the subject; the other—the strongest and most to be deplored—is the fact that the Negroes have developed an aversion toward the Southern Presbyterian Church. Some, he recognized, would indignantly deny this but the facts, he insisted, were too strong for doubt, and the reason was plain. His reference was to the continuing justification of slavery, set forth from time to time in the religious newspapers, articles deeply offensive and deterrent in their effect on the Negroes.[17]

He might have gone further. The fear of social intermingling, even in the courts of the church, the many subtle, and not so subtle, reminders that the Negro was an inferior human being are quite sufficient to explain the very apparent unpopularity of Presbyterianism among the masses of the colored people. It should be noted, however, that attitudes toward Negro commissioners in the church courts was beginning to moderate. Negro commissioners now attended the General Assembly, where they sat together in a pew toward the front of the church —as they would continue to do for many a year—and were given all the rights and privileges of commissioners. They were called upon to lead in prayer and were given an opportunity to speak from the platform. They ate, however, apart from the white commissioners and were separately housed.

In 1907 an indignant correspondent called attention to the fact that important issues before the recent General Assembly had been carried by the small black vote. "Our church," he complained, "is confronted with a menace in this humiliating fact that these vital questions so pregnant with serious and far-reaching effects should not be settled by the deliberate and mature white thought, but the immature, and volatile black thought."[18]

A third recognized and quite patent explanation of the failure of the Southern Church's evangelistic endeavor among the Negroes was the church's indifference and apathy in the matter. Dr. Phillips reported in 1892, "There is a serious lack of information and of interest in the Colored Work"; next year, "We do not feel that we had the proper support of the presbyteries."[19] The Reverend O. B. Wilson reported in 1898 that there was "much prejudice against the work," and "a great indifference toward it."[20] In 1905 Dr. Snedecor wrote:

> This is not a popular cause. . . . It is worthy of notice that two classes of our church membership are steadily devoted to it; the elderly people, whose memories run back to slavery times and the missionaries. The latter class get the viewpoint of the foreign shore. They have traveled thousands of miles to help the heathen and they are constantly reminded of the heathens at home. Of the former class, it may be said, this cause finds itself poorer each year by the loss of many of the dear old saints who are falling on sleep. May the prayer of the Church be raised to God in our behalf. "Help, Lord, for the godly man ceaseth; for the faithful fall from among the children of men."[21]

In 1906 he reiterated: "The Church seems apathetic, many good people are prejudiced against this enterprise."[22]

Four years later: "We can safely report a steadily growing conviction that the efforts of this committee to spread good morals and true religion among the Negroes should be more generally supported by the Church. This conviction makes headway slowly against a very prevalent prejudice and against much misconception of what we have been appointed to do."[23]

Dr. S. L. Morris in *The Romance of Home Missions* recalled the experiences of the men who set out to serve the Negro. Dr. Stillman began teaching a class of Negroes in preparation for the ministry without funds and with but little sympathy from his brethren. The Reverend James G. Snedecor, a man of noble blood, of wealth, of scholarly distinction, felt keenly the loneliness of his position, the lack of sympathy and support of the church.[24] The Reverend O. B. Wilson was subjected to many humiliating experiences. The Reverend S. F. Tenney and his family suffered reproach and public obloquy for their efforts on behalf of the colored people. Someone remarked facetiously and yet with much truth that when one went to Africa as a missionary to evangelize the Negro he was canonized; when he stayed home to teach the Negro he was ostracized.

The indifference of the church reflected itself in the meager support given to the cause of colored evangelization. The income of the committee was never large enough to support the work in any adequate fashion. Most of the colored ministers had to support themselves by farming, teaching, or some other occupation.

"I can't do my duty when fixed as I am," wrote one preacher. "My nights are often spent in my kitchen, my days in the schoolroom—I am trying to do three things—baking, teaching and preaching. I don't want to join the Northern Church and don't expect to, but I must support my family."

A minister wrote from Alabama: "I am here working as hard as a man can work,—minister or not,—and getting no pay scarcely from the people. . . . I taught nearly twenty scholars during March and received for it so far, the sum of fifty cents. Now, how can I get on at this? Yet I am not going to quit. I am determined, God helping me, to go on, if I don't get a cent from the people here."[25]

As the work of the Executive Committee on Colored Evangelization had failed to secure the substantial support of the church, its work was transferred by the 1910 General Assembly to the Executive Committee on Home Missions, despite a fear openly expressed on the floor of the Assembly that prejudice against working among Negroes might cause a drop in the funds of this important committee. As a result of the change, colored evangelization received a somewhat larger appropriation, but the amount remained totally inadequate and the transfer made little practical difference. Dr. Snedecor, none too happy at the change, remained in charge of the Department of

Colored Work until 1916, when he resigned because of failing health.[26]

After the resignation of Dr. Snedecor, there was no Superintendent of Colored Work until 1922 when the Reverend R. A. Brown was chosen to the position, one which he continued to hold till his death in 1931. Dr. Brown was "a man with a fine mind and an understanding heart. He loved the Negroes and had a real sympathy for them in their limited and restricted lives. The Negroes loved Dr. Brown and thought of him not only as their Superintendent, but as their friend." No successor was sought for Dr. Brown because of the committee's lack of funds.

The independent Afro-American Synod, meanwhile, had not prospered. There is no indication that the Negroes themselves had ever really desired it. The Birmingham Convention called at the instance of the Executive Committee on Colored Evangelization to promote the organization of the independent Afro-American Synod was composed mostly of delegates from the two presbyteries (Central Alabama and Ethel) attached to the Southern Church; the independent presbyteries sent only three representatives. The decision to form the synod came at the instance of the white ministers in attendance and came only because there was assurance of continued financial support from the General Assembly. But Central Alabama Presbytery and Ethel Presbytery proved unwilling to withdraw from the Southern Church. As Dr. R. C. Reed wrote in 1905, "Strong arguments cannot shake them loose, neither can soft arts beguile them into turning loose. They think they know which side of the bread has the butter on it."[27]

The General Assembly finally (in 1901) gave over its protracted efforts to get the two presbyteries into the Independent Synod. Little financial help was ever given to this body. Dr. Reed referred to it as "a small tin cup on the end of a long pole, by means of which we hand over to our colored mendicants our little dole of charity."[28]

He recalled the fire and force, the mingled wit and wisdom, with which Dr. Phillips had gone up and down among the churches in his effort to secure the minimum amount required to put the work on a firm basis—without success; the Reverend D. Clay Lilly had consecrated his splendid gifts and the strength of his young manhood to the same task—likewise without success; Dr. J. G. Snedecor, with a brave heart and the spirit of a martyr, had undertaken the same hopeless task—and there had been some advance, but it was pitifully small.

Dr. Snedecor had pointed out that the setting apart of the Afro-

American Synod was supposed to be a panacea for prejudice and a lifter of the floodgates of liberality. Nothing came of it except a great deal of advice to the Northern Church to do as the Southern Church had done. The Assembly's committee then went almost bankrupt and Dr. Phillips resigned. "But both he and Dr. Lilly, while failing to receive the financial support of the Church, did not fail in advancing the arrangements and facilities for carrying on the work. They made heartbreaking experiments and spent sleepless nights in praying and planning and much of the equipment we now have is the result of their painful labors."[29]

As time passed it became increasingly difficult for the independent Afro-American Synod to secure a quorum. Finally, in 1915, the Executive Committee on Home Missions proposed to revitalize the synod by having its presbyteries become an integral part of the Southern Assembly. The proposal was approved at a conference held in May 1916, which was attended by practically all the Negro ministers in the church. In accordance with the decision, the Presbytery of North and South Carolina, which had been a part of the synod, the Presbyteries of Ethel and Central Alabama, which had remained organically connected with the Southern Church, and the Presbytery of Central Louisiana, which was formed in 1916, were constituted as a new Afro-American Synod connected with the General Assembly, and with its presbyteries represented in the Assembly on the same basis as those of any other synod. The name of the new synod was soon changed to Snedecor Memorial Synod, in honor of the great man who had given so much of his life to the evangelization of the Negroes. Theoretically the goal of the church continued to be the establishment of an independent Negro church; practically, Snedecor Memorial Synod had become a constituent and a permanent part of the Assembly.

In the years that followed, the synod added each year a fair number to its rolls, but the net growth remained very small. In 1918 there were 1,492 members and in 1933 there were 1,847, only a few hundred more than in 1892, and considerably less than the Presbyterian churches in the South had before the war. None of the 51 churches were at this time self-supporting. Yet very little aid was given by the executive committee. In 1927, before the financial debacle, the average salary of the Negro minister in the church was $50 a month, of which about $40 came from the executive committee; only in rare cases was there a manse. "I have heard of no complaint," said Superintendent Brown, "though they have to give up many of the necessities of life to continue in this service."

The great Depression was particularly hard upon the Negroes; they received less aid from the government than did the whites; it was more difficult for them to support their churches, and the support of the executive committee had fallen off. Yet the work continued.

The Negro churches had remained small and few in number, and yet out of them had come some eminent Christians—among them the Reverend William H. Sheppard, a graduate of Stillman, who, with Samuel N. Lapsley, laid the foundation of our mission in the Congo, and whose discoveries in Africa were recognized by his election as a Fellow of the Royal Geographic Society in London; Maria Fearing, who, at the age of 56, sold her home and possessions and went to Africa at her own expense that she might have the privilege of ministering to her own people*; the Reverend H. P. Hawkins, a graduate of Stillman, who also went as a missionary to the Congo; Sam Daly, who founded the Daly Reformatory for Boys; Charles Birthright, born a slave, who died with an estate valued at between $40,000 and $50,-000, all of which he bequeathed to the Stillman Institute to support the training of colored youths for the ministry—the largest amount which up to this time the school had ever received; the Reverend W. A. Young, consecrated evangelist, eloquent preacher; Althea Edmiston, who went as a missionary to the Congo and wrote a grammar and dictionary of the Bushonga language, besides several smaller volumes; and the Reverend A. M. Plant of Texarkana, who in addition to his pastorate, served as principal of one of the city schools and wielded public influence as an educator.

Work among Negroes in the Southern Church continued to revolve around Stillman Institute. The school had been founded for the purpose of training a godly ministry especially for the Presbyterian Church. The number trained was comparatively small, something over 500 by 1933, but graduates of the school had gone into the Home and Foreign Mission fields (seven to Africa), into the ministry of the Southern Church, and a good many more into the ministry of the Methodist and Baptist Churches. The training given was far below that given to white ministers, but it helped in raising, if only for a little, the standards of the Negro ministry as a whole.

But the small divinity school at Tuscaloosa had developed gradually through the years into an educational plant for Negro youth in general, its aim being to provide a practical industrial, as well as academic and Christian, training for both boys and girls. By 1916 the

---

* Not until she had proved her worth on the mission field was she engaged as a regular missionary.

school, according to its prospects, had come to embrace the following
departments:

Theological (three-year course)—based on a thorough knowledge of
the English Bible
Academic—including high school and junior college
Normal—an up-to-date practice school for prospective teachers
Home Economics—including cooking, sewing, and laundry
Mechanical Arts—including carpentry, blacksmithing, and automobile
repair
Agriculture—including stock raising, poultry, and hogs

In 1929, through the gifts of the Women's Auxiliary Birthday Offering and other friends of Home Missions, there was opened the
"Estes Snedecor Memorial Training School for Negro Nurses."

The physical plant at this time included dormitories, recitation
rooms, professors' homes, model dining room, mechanic's shop, nurses'
training building with 20 standard hospital beds and an operating
room completely equipped with all modern appliances, an agricultural farm of more than a hundred acres, a small canning plant with
a cooling box for meats and vegetables.

In 1933 the total number of students in the Institute was 148,
eight of whom were taking theological training, preparatory for the
ministry. There was a faculty of 12 members, six white and six colored,
who had their degree or its equivalent from a standard college.

One reason why Stillman Institute had won a secure place in the
affections of the church was that it took care not to offend Southern
susceptibilities. The *Central Presbyterian* quoted with approval a
statement of Dr. Snedecor as he began his labors as Secretary of
Colored Evangelization: "I am spending no time studying the so-
called race problem, but I am going on energetically to prosecute
the work of our church as aligned by the General Assembly."[30] The
church received more positive assurance. "There is a constant effort
[at Stillman]," reported Dr. Snedecor, "to prevent the students from
imbibing along with book knowledge any impossible notions of their
position in society."[31] But a rebellion against the paternalistic attitude
which had characterized the Negro work as a whole would not be long
in coming. This attitude had rendered the evangelistic effort ineffec-
tive, and it would shortly bring the educational effort to the verge
of collapse.

Difficulties meanwhile had begun to appear in the once promising
Sunday school movement.

In 1905 Dr. Snedecor wrote:

We still regard . . . Sunday Schools as a most efficient and practical agency for the uplift of the colored people. It is a matter of common remark that the younger generation of negroes is more neglected than any that has preceded them. Parental authority exerted for proper ends is almost unknown. The Sunday Schools of their own churches are rarely efficient and are not generally attended. While the importance and possibility of reaching these neglected children by the establishment of Sunday Schools is acknowledged, it is becoming more difficult to find teachers and superintendents for them. The arduous nature of the work, the apparent paucity of results, the indifference of the whites, and the jealousy of the colored pastors are some of the reasons given for the failure to persevere in this noble effort.[32]

Christian men and women continued to teach in Negro Sunday schools in their own communities on Sunday afternoon, but as a general agency of colored evangelization the movement soon ceased to figure except in the slum section of a few of the larger cities. Here, however, the movement was to bear notable fruit. For example, one of the most successful missions for Negroes in the entire country was the Sunday school begun at Louisville, Kentucky, in 1898 by the Reverend John Little.

This noble servant of God, pioneer and apostle of Negro institutional work in the South, was born in Tuscaloosa, Alabama. His father, representative of a distinguished Southern family, was treasurer and trustee of Stillman Institute, so that his son imbibed an interest in Negro missions from his infancy. He came to Louisville as a student in the theological seminary. One Sunday in February he and a few other students set out to organize a Sunday school in one of the crowded Negro sections of the city. "We believed that some effort should be made to teach the Gospel to the 40,000 Negro people living in Louisville," said Mr. Little, "and we could not find any effort being made by the church to which we belonged." A Sunday school with 23 Negro children as charter members was organized in an old building which had formerly been a lottery office. Mr. Little continues: "We soon found there were hundreds, even thousands, of colored people lying within sound of the church bells of both white and colored churches who never attended any church. Not a member of my class knew anything about Jesus Christ." On Sundays and Wednesday evenings the six students took turns in preaching. The interest was so great that the Sunday school was continued through the summer by volunteer teachers from the churches of Louisville. When the students returned in the fall they persuaded these teachers to retain their classes, while they went out and secured additional pupils for new classes. At the request of a Negro boy, another mission was opened in April by the Students' Missionary Society in "Smoke Town," a mile away.

The enrollment of the two missions grew from 23 to nearly 2,000 in the 1930's. The doors were opened by this time seven days a week, morning and evening. There were classes in sewing, cooking, shoe repairing, and carpentry; recreation clubs for boys and girls, a bath house, a playground, a Daily Vacation Bible School, together with Sunday school and preaching services, were distinct features in the yearly program.

Each of the various activities of the mission was begun to meet a particular and definite need.

Some of the girls in the Sunday school asked to be taught sewing —the teachers recognized that this could be made a useful supplement to the Sunday school. A woman volunteered to come on Saturday morning and teach those who were interested. Eleven girls assembled as pupils and 18 cents was invested in materials. The boys, seeing the girls with extra classes, made a request and a class in basketry was organized; this later developed into a carpenter's shop.

Another consecrated woman, realizing the importance of proper nutrition, offered her services to teach a class in cooking. A cheap shed was built for the class; the teacher bought dishes and cooking utensils; and this department, soon the most popular in the mission, was begun.

Realizing the need for recreational facilities, playgrounds were opened in the side yards of the two missions; they were the first playgrounds for Negro children in Louisville—a few swings, bean bags, jumping ropes, and sand boxes being all the equipment provided at the start.

When announcement was made that a bath house with showers and bathtubs was to be established, one mother said, "I am glad to hear this, for I am tired of carrying water on Saturday. My whole family will be present each week." And she kept her word. This was the only bath house open at this time to colored people in the east end of Louisville.

The teachers visited the pupils regularly in their homes. Many were found to be sick, with no competent medical advice. Prominent physicians volunteered their services, and a visiting nurse was provided. In cases of extreme destitution nourishing food and medicine were provided.

So the work grew. "The first aim of all of our teachers," said Dr. Little, "is to give the Gospel to the colored man. In giving him the Gospel we believe that it is wise to use as auxiliary means such things

as will help him to help himself. . . . It has been demonstrated that our
industrial work, our clubs and playgrounds have a strong spiritual
influence. Most of the boys who have united with the church have
come from our classes in carpentry and our boys' clubs."

Seven years after the Sunday school was opened, a church was
organized with seven members. A quarter of a century later the
church had nearly 200 members, and many more attended the services. A majority of the Sunday school pupils went into churches of
their own choice.

For twelve years the work was conducted in two old dilapidated
store rooms rented for the purpose. About 1915 the missions moved into
better quarters. In 1929 these quarters were overgrown; a successful
campaign was put on for funds and a new plant was erected at a cost
of over $100,000.

In 1932 attendance on the two missions was 13,200 more than the
preceding year; the total attendance was 108,713; the following year it
was 4,000 more. One hundred and fifty white men and women volunteered their services that the work might be carried on. Most of the
financial support for the work came from Louisville, some from
churches, more from individuals; aid was also given by the Presbyterian Church in the U.S., the Presbyterian Church in the U.S.A., the
Associate Reformed Presbyterian Church, and the Reformed Church
in the U.S.

Meanwhile, successful Negro missions had been developed in
Richmond, Atlanta, and New Orleans. The colored mission in Richmond was organized by two students of Union Theological Seminary in
1911. Seeking the worst and toughest Negro section in the city, they
were directed to "Hell's Bottom," a district bordering on an open sewer
creek east of Richmond. The students rented an old building and
began the Seventeenth Street Mission, with a purely religious program (though students from the seminary and the General Assembly's
Training School visited regularly in the neighborhood). No church
was organized here, however, until after World War II when the
church took a new look at its total Negro work.

The colored mission in Atlanta embraced two centers, one in the
Pittsburgh section of Atlanta, the other in Decatur. The Pittsburgh
mission originated about 1900 in a mission Sunday school of the Central Presbyterian Church. In 1918 it was decided to enlarge the work,
and with the aid of the Executive Committee on Home Missions, the
colored mission of Atlanta was organized. The section chosen for the
mission was a destitute churchless section. The mission was opened
along institutional lines, with a full-time superintendent and a corps

of volunteer workers from the Atlanta churches. A church was organized in connection with the mission and placed under the charge of a
Negro minister. The Decatur Negro mission, with a smaller program,
was opened in 1927. A medical clinic ministered to hundreds of
Negroes each month.

The last of the church's successful colored missions, "The Berean
Center" in New Orleans, was opened in 1929, under the leadership of
Dr. U. D. Mooney, who resigned the pastorate of Napoleon Avenue
Church to lead in this endeavor. The center was located in the midst
of 130,000 Negroes, probably the largest Negro urban population of the
South. The program of the mission, carried on by a paid staff, with the
aid of 50 white volunteers, included a number of clubs and classes, a
free baby clinic, and the services of a visiting nurse.

Another type of work among the Negroes was represented by the
Colored Women's Conferences conducted by the Woman's Auxiliary.
The conferences were inaugurated by Mrs. Hattie Winsborough, and
were first held at Stillman Institute, beginning in 1916; they were
said to be the first conferences of their kind in the South. As their
popularity grew they were transferred to Synodicals, most all of which
came to hold their own annual conference. About 1,000 selected Negro
women were enrolled in them each year for Bible study, Missions,
Church Activities, Health and Sanitation. Leaders in interracial work
testified that these conferences of the Presbyterian Church for colored
women were of inestimable service in promoting better understanding
between the races.

This need for better understanding was growing. The Negro
revolution was already knocking at the door.

IV

New Responsibilities of the South

The Southern Presbyterian Church had attempted from the outset to discharge its responsibility to the population advancing westward and also, to some extent at least, to the Indians and the Negroes. In "the New South" it began to recognize its debt to other needy classes.

I. THE HIGHLANDERS

The Southern Highlands include two distinct but, in some ways, similar sections: the Appalachian Mountains in the East and the Ozark Mountains in the West.

The Appalachian Mountain chain extends along the Atlantic Coast from the Gulf of St. Lawrence to the low-lying lands on the Gulf of Mexico. It is cut almost in half by two rivers, the Potomac and the Monongahela. The southern half of this mountain country extends into the heart of the South east of the Mississippi and divides it into two approximately equal divisions. This whole mountain area is about 650 miles long and 200 miles wide; it includes the western part of Maryland, Virginia, and North Carolina; the whole of West Virginia; the eastern parts of Kentucky and Tennessee; and a portion of the northern end of South Carolina, Georgia, and Alabama.

The region has three zones running the long way of the barrier. On the east stand the Blue Ridge Mountains, a narrow chain at the northern end, but widening to the south into a complicated maze of peaks and ranges. On the west lies the Alleghany-Cumberland Plateau, for the most part deeply furrowed by water courses and declining slowly westward. Between the two rugged sections lies the Great Valley, which itself is some hundreds of feet higher than the general level beyond the bordering mountains. It is literally a succession of valleys [the most famous of which are the Shenandoah and the Holston], in which lie the upper course of many rivers, which pass out of the long trench either at the end or through gaps in the mountain walls. On the east in North Carolina and westward in West Virginia, broad and fertile river valleys extend up among the hills.[1]

In this mountainous district thriving cities and fertile farms, particularly in the Great Valley, were to be found, but this was not characteristic of the Southern Highlands as a whole. Mountain slopes occupied 90 percent of the total area. Not more than a fourth of the land was under cultivation. As one observer wrote, there were more mountains in Appalachia, the valleys were deeper and more frequent, the surface rougher, and the trails steeper than in any other section of the country. Another described a characteristic section:

> The mountains come down to a point like the letter V. Down this crease brawls a pretty river; leading into this from a smaller valley will be a creek; into the creek a branch, and into the branch a fork. Each settlement is a shoestring along one of these water courses and constitutes a world within itself, for it is insulated from its neighbors by one or two thousand feet of steep wooded ridge. The only wagon trails lie in the bed of a stream which you may need to ford twenty times in a mile.[2]

The Ozarks penetrate and divide the southern territory west of the Misissippi just as the Appalachian Mountains divide it in the east. They are a smaller replica of the Eastern Highlands, covering about 70,000 square miles to the latter's 108,000 square miles, and occupying a good-sized portion of three states, Arkansas, Missouri, and Oklahoma.

The total population of the Appalachian Highlands in 1930 was 6,750,000 and of the Ozark region, 1,850,000.

The Reverend Dr. R. F. Campbell, of Asheville, North Carolina, who did much to arouse the interest of the church in the Appalachian area, divided the natives of these sections into three classes: (1) those whose ancestors settled in the broad, rich valleys, or on extensive plateaus, where prosperous towns surrounded by fertile farms were to be found, such towns as Staunton, Lexington, Roanoke, Salem, and Abingdon in Virginia; Morganton and Asheville in North Carolina; and Bristol, Knoxville, and Chattanooga in Tennessee. The inhabitants of these towns and the regions round about compared favorably with any population.

(2) Radiating from these valleys and plateaus were ranges of mountains growing more and more rugged and inaccessible, among which were to be found two other grades of mountain people. The higher grade were hardy, hospitable, honest and intelligent, but too far from the highways of civilization to have kept pace with their

more fortunate kinsmen in education and the conveniences of modern life. In native force, however, they were in no way inferior, but rather superior to many more highly favored representatives of the same race. As Dr. Campbell declared: "They only need an introduction to civilization to prove themselves equal to any men in the world."

(3) People of the third class, according to Dr. Campbell, were shiftless, ignorant, and apparently without aspirations. They haunted the fringes of the better communities in narrow coves, or far up on the mountain sides, though in some instances they were not so isolated, but were gathered in settlements which were homogeneously bad. "The mountains as well as the cities have their slums," wrote Dr. Campbell. "Many of those who have written about the 'mountain whites' have made the mistake of describing this class as representative of the general condition of the Southern Appalachians."[3]

The native Highlanders were for the most part descendants of those early groups who settled the American colonies and who, pushing westward, remained for one reason or another in the broad river valleys or in the narrow mountain coves.

The three main stocks represented were: first, the English, earliest and most important settlers of the Atlantic seaboard; second, the Scotch-Irish; and third, the German. These last two groups came in great numbers, especially to Pennsylvania, in the 18th century. In addition there were a few Huguenots and some of the Highland Scots.

Colonists from these various strains entered the Valley of Virginia and began gradually to penetrate the mountain regions about 1730. Germans settled thickly in the regions about the lower end of the Shenandoah; the Scotch-Irish pushed on boldly into the regions beyond. Settlement of the Highlands continued during the Revolutionary War and at an increasing speed after its end until about 1790. After this time there was some change in the character of the immigration. The movement of Germans and Scotch-Irish up the valley from Pennsylvania slowed down. There was a greater migration to the Highlands and, through the Highlands, to territory farther west by the earlier colonists from eastern Virginia and North Carolina. "In judging those who stayed in the Highlands," wrote Miss Hooker, "it must be remembered that there was less difference than today between the Highlands and neighboring areas. Everywhere roads were poor, the forests were only partly cleared away, institutions had not been developed. And no one knew that the Highlands were to stand still for generations, cut off from the rest of the world."[4]

But so it happened. "After 1850 the westward migration through the Highlands practically ceased; and while neighboring territory gradually acquired turnpikes and railroads, these improvements did not come to the Highlands. The people left behind were pretty much forgotten by the world outside."[5]

Isolation from the outside world, ignorance due to lack of schools or to inadequate schooling and extreme poverty had come to characterize thousands of the Highlanders. The civilization of America had developed all about them and left them stranded in the fastnesses of the mountains.

The religious institutions of the Highlands, as might be expected, were relics of the early religious history of America, modified by the characteristics just mentioned. Presbyterian churches in this area were isolated and found it impossible to secure qualified ministers. In many sections Primitive Baptists, who opposed Sunday schools and an educated ministry and carried their belief in predestination almost to the point of fatalism, became the dominant group. Around the turn of the century various Holiness and Pentecostal groups began to make headway in the mountains. As described by a careful observor in the early thirties, the standard religious experience for the Highlanders is a sudden emotional conversion rather than the gradual development of character. To bring about the conversion of sinners and the renewal of religious emotion in those previously converted, the protracted meeting is almost universally considered an important part of the church year. Aside from the protracted meeting the indigenous churches throughout the Highlands have a very simple program. Preaching services, usually held only once a month, and weekly Sunday School sessions, with here and there a prayer meeting, are about all there is to it. No form of community service is undertaken by the churches, the sole function of which is believed to consist in the preparation of individuals for happiness in a world beyond the grave. The ministers, or rather the preachers, for their duties in relation to their congregations are conceived to be fulfilled almost entirely through preaching, are in large measure untrained men who earn their living wholly or partly through other occupations, and who receive very little compensation from their churches, of which they usually serve from two to five.[6]

Some of the mountain people enjoyed no religious ministrations; many others heard only a caricature of the gospel; an increasing number of the young people were dissatisfied and could not be reached by the ignorant, uninstructed preachers to whom they were accustomed. For all these reasons the Appalachian Mountains came to be recognized as one of the great mission fields of the South. The chief problems were lack of economic opportunity and consequent poverty; lack of adequate medical and hospital facilities and of schools and consequent illiteracy; lack of good roads and adequate transportation facilities and consequent isolation and retardation; lack of strong churches with educated leadership and consequent weakness of religous life. Housing and social life presented important related problems.

The situation in the Ozarks was similar to that in the Appalachians. Population here came chiefly from the Southern Highlands with the Scotch-Irish in the lead, 1820-1840 being the period of greatest migration. Unlike the Appalachians, however, there had been a continuous but fluctuating migration to the Ozarks since the first settlement. Religious destitution here was even greater. Only about a fourth of the population were members of any church. No county in the area had more than half of its population in the membership of the Protestant churches. In the Arkansas section seven counties out of the 34 had less than 20 percent of the population in church membership; only one had over 40 percent. In Oklahoma 11 out of 14 counties had less than 20 percent of the population in the church, and none had more than 24 percent. Though the need here was greater, the Ozark mountain region had never made such an appeal to the general philanthropic interest of the country as had the Appalachian region and had not attracted anything like the same degree of public and private philanthropic effort.

The Presbyterian Church in the U.S.A. began its missionary operations in the Southern Highlands as early as 1879, establishing a mission school near Concord, North Carolina. Gradually its work spread over the mountain region of North Carolina, Tennessee, Kentucky, and West Virginia. By the end of the century there were 31 churches and 37 mission schools under the control of its Home Mission Board. Other churches followed the lead of the Northern Presbyterians and developed both educational institutions and evangelistic work throughout the Southern Highlands—Congregationalists in 1884, Episcopalians in 1889, and Northern Methodists in 1891.

First of the Southern denominations to begin missionary activities in the mountains was the Presbyterian Church in the U.S. Their work, as that of other Southern demoninations, was at first evangelistic and only later educational. The man who awoke the Southern Presbyterian Church to the need of the mountains and who laid the foundation for its subsequent work in the Highlands was Dr. E. O. Guerrant of Kentucky.

According to Dr. Guerrant's own account, his interest in the Highlanders went back to his early career as a soldier in the Civil War and to his subsequent labors as a physician:

> I was brought up in a village of churches [he said] and thought all people this side of China were equally blessed. . . . When a young man I went to Virginia, the land of my fathers, to join the army and rode more than one hundred miles across the Cumberland Mountains. Although not looking for churches or preachers, I do not remember seeing a single one. During the year I crossed those mountains several times and still found no churches.—After the war I became a physician and frequently rode through those mountains, visiting the sick, and still found only a church or two in many miles, though here were thousands of people with souls.[7]

Dr. Guerrant finally abandoned the practice of medicine and entered Union Theological Seminary, with the intention of devoting his life to preaching the gospel to the poor. As pastor of churches near the Highlands and then of the First Presbyterian Church of Louisville, Kentucky, he reminded the synod repeatedly of the destitution of the mountains and spoke of the culpable neglect of the church in not sending the gospel into this area.

When the Synod of Kentucky embarked upon its plan of synodical Home Missions in 1881, Dr. Guerrant resigned his comfortable pastorate in Louisville to become one of the first synodical evangelists. He was assigned the eastern part of the state, including the mountain country. "I thought I had some idea of the vast destitution of the mountain regions," he wrote, "but when I entered the work I was amazed to find a region as large as the German Empire practically without churches, Sabbath Schools or qualified teachers; whole counties with tens of thousands of people who had never seen a church or heard a gospel sermon they could understand."[8]

For almost four years Dr. Guerrant labored as a synodical evangelist, most of the time in the mountain section where no Presbyterian churches were to be found, and where few churches of any denomination were to be seen. "In the glory of his splendid prime, he passed like a veritable tongue of flame through the narrow valleys and along the tortuous waterways of [the] mountain country, bringing light and heat to many a dark cold abode." And the people responded. Twelve churches were founded in this brief period. One of these was the first church to be founded in Breathitt County.

After four years of such labors, Dr. Guerrant was forced by broken health to return to his pastorate; he continued, however, to serve the Highlanders to the extent of his strength.

Finally, in 1897 he organized a Society of Soul Winners to support more extensive work among the mountains than his own denomination had been able to support. "After fifty years' knowledge of this people, and twenty-five years' labor among them as a minister," he said, "I was convinced that all agencies now employed or available by neighboring churches would never reach them in this generation or maybe in a dozen generations. So I appealed to all Christian people who loved their own countrymen to help save them. The response was such as only God could inspire. From every branch of the Church and every section of our country and beyond it, even from China and the Sandwich Islands God has raised up loving hearts and liberal hands to help."[9]

The society began with $360 and one missionary. For 12 years it raised $12,000 a year, maintained as many as 70 workers, and established scores of churches in the mountain sections of Kentucky, Tennessee, Virginia, and North Carolina.

"By this time Dr. Guerrant had become convinced that lasting religious results could not be obtained without training up leaders through teaching the young. He therefore introduced primary schools, many of which began their sessions in a log schoolhouse, in a tent or under a tree."[10] The annual report of the Society of Soul Winners for 1910 enumerated 59 day schools, 1,343 pupils, and 239 teachers. Many of these schools were small and were held only in summer; but some developed into boarding schools of considerable size.

Dr. Guerrant continued to conduct this widespread mountain work through the Society of Soul Winners, "on faith," without the backing of any church or patron till finally in 1911, burdened with years and infirmities, he turned it over to other agencies, mostly to the Home Missions Committee of the Southern Presbyterian Church.

Meanwhile, mountain work had begun to be developed in other parts of the church. North Carolina began its synodical missions in 1888. Wherever a pioneer evangelist went in the mountains he was likely to start a day school in connection with his work, and some of these schools, taught by consecrated women, developed into useful institutions of learning.

Mountain missions were pushed more aggressively in North Carolina after the founding of Asheville Presbytery in 1896. Two years after the presbytery was set up, it commissioned two evangelists to investigate the conditions in its own territory, including seven of the westernmost counties in the state. The investigators were directed to leave the railroads and the larger villages and to seek out the secluded coves and the highlands. They found a number of homes without a lamp, a candle, a comb, a brush, a looking glass or similar articles of civilized life. Many of the people had never seen a town. A buggy was an object of curiosity. The food was coarse, half-cooked, sometimes served on pieces of dishes black with dirt. The beds were often offensive to smell and inhabited by insects. There were families, none of whose members could read, and in whose home there was not one word of print. Many other families had no Bible. In one thickly settled district, 150 square miles, in which there were 400 children of school age there was neither school, Sunday school, nor church. In other sections the religious leaders were ignorant and sometimes immoral.[11]

Under such circumstances Asheville Presbytery developed a program which included both evangelism and education. By 1903 there were five mission schools within its bounds. In this same year, the General Assembly's committee began its work in the mountains. Through the gift of a Christian philanthropist, Nacoochee Institute in north Georgia was opened; the capacity of Lees-McRae Institute in Concord Presbytery, North Carolina, was doubled; financial assistance was given to the five schools in Asheville Presbytery.

This aid was continued for a number of years, being extended gradually to a large number of institutions through private gifts, without calling on the regular funds of the church. Regular Home Mission help was also given to some of the mountain presbyteries: Asheville and Concord Presbyteries in North Carolina, Athens Presbytery in Georgia, Knoxville Presbytery in Tennessee, Ebenezer and Transylvania in Kentucky.

In 1911 the General Assembly took over the extensive work developed by Dr. Guerrant, largely in the mountains of Kentucky. Included were 50 missionaries, operating 18 mission centers; 17 schools, including such outstanding ones as Highland Institute and Stuart Robinson; and an orphanage—34 buildings in all.

To take charge of its greatly increased obligation in mountain missions, the executive committee elected in 1911 its first mountain superintendent, the Reverend William E. Hudson, who was succeeded in 1914 by the Reverend J. W. Tyler, and on his death in 1924 by the Reverend E. V. Tadlock.

Five years after the Assembly had taken over the work of the Guerrant Inland Mission, mountain missions had become its most extensive work, requiring more of its income than all the vast territory beyond the Mississippi, once its sole missionary responsibility. Though the executive committee supported a Superintendent of

Mountain Missions who gave himself largely to evangelistic work, and though it aided the mountain presbyteries in their evangelistic labors, the bulk of its support was given to the mission schools. At this time the Congregationalists supported five schools in the Southern Highlands; the United Presbyterians, eight; the Disciples, ten; Southern Methodists, 14; Presbyterians U.S.A., 15; Southern Baptists, 34; Southern Presbyterians, 45.

Further impetus was given to the progress of mountain missions in 1915 by the formation of the Synod of Appalachia, including sections out of the four synods of Virginia, North Carolina, Tennessee, and Kentucky. The formation of these presbyteries, with their common interests and common problems, into a separate synod lifted the mountain sections of the church out of the background and gave them a church-wide prominence. The churches of the mountain presbyteries, having the same educational and religious needs, were able to develop their own resources, train their own leaders, build their own educational institutions, and carry out the programs best adapted to their needs.

In 1933 an Interim Committee reported to the General Assembly: "The record of this youngest synod of the Assembly reveals a phenomenal growth. Within the sixteen years of her short life, she has made an increase in membership of nearly eighty per cent. The record shows she is leading the other synods in every department of church work. Further, we find in this young synod an enthusiasm, a zeal, a synodical consciousness, a solidarity of mind, heart and purpose that is unprecedented."[12]

The most distinctive and most valued work in the mountains was that done by the mission schools. After 1911, when the work of the Society of Soul Winners was transferred to the General Assembly, some of these schools were supported wholly by the executive committee; others were supported by presbytery or synod, in most cases, with aid from the Assembly's committee.

In 1927, before the Depression began to affect the mountain work, there were 12 schools with 64 teachers and 1,222 pupils supported entirely by the Assembly's committee and under the immediate supervision of the Mountain Department of the executive committee. There were 21 schools, with 116 teachers and 2,081 pupils, that received financial aid from the Assembly's committee, but that were under the immediate supervision of presbytery or synod.

Seven of the 12 schools supported by the Assembly were in Kentucky; two were in Tennessee; there was one each in North Carolina, Virginia, and West Virginia. The largest schools in this group were

Stuart Robinson at Blackey, Kentucky, with 18 teachers and 400 pupils; Highland Institute at Guerrant, Kentucky, with 15 teachers and 200 pupils; Madison Synodical School at Madison, West Virginia, with eight teachers and 117 pupils; and Blue Ridge Academy at the Hollow, Virginia, with six teachers and 109 pupils.

The Stuart Robinison School, founded in 1914, was the last enterprise undertaken by Dr. Guerrant. It was located by him in Letcher County, Kentucky, which held the record for the largest percentage of unchurched people in the United States, 97 percent being out of the church altogether, and most of the rest being Primitive Baptists opposed to missions, Sunday schools, and other forms of church activity. Opposition to the Presbyterians was at first intense and active, but was gradually overcome as the work of the school became better known. Within a few years this school had become the largest Home Mission school in the General Assembly and, next to Davidson College, educated more young people annually than any other school in the Presbyterian Church. Its curriculum included the grades and the work of an accredited high school, with courses in agriculture, home economics, Bible, music, and typing.

Highland Institute, founded by Dr. Guerrant in Breathitt County in 1908, included for a time an orphanage, a hospital with resident physician and nurse, a farm, and a church. The medical work in the Kentucky Highlands developed out of the practice of Dr. E. O. Guerrant in taking physicians and surgeons to various places in the mountains for the benefit of those who were destitute of medical services. After his death, doctors were employed to look after the health of workers in the various schools and missions. This attention was extended to the pupils in the schools, and then clinics were held for the people residing in the communities adjacent to the schools. Finally, a resident physician came to take charge of the hospital at Highland, and from Highland to carry his healing services throughout the mountain country.

Some of the largest and best equipped mountain missions schools were those conducted by presbyteries and synods in cooperation with the General Assembly, among them, Rabun Gap–Nacoochee School in Georgia; Lees-McRae College in North Carolina; Grundy in Virginia; Caddo Valley in Arkansas; and the School of the Ozarks in Missouri.

Lees-McRae College represented the lifework of Edgar Tufts, who carried on summer work at Banner Elk, North Carolina, while a student at Union Theological Seminary, and on graduation accepted a call to take charge of this inviting field. A little handful of children were being taught during a part of the summer by mission workers to supplement the brief and inadequate session of the public school. Mr. Tufts began to aid in the instruction of some of the more advanced pupils. The monotony and isolation of their lives, particularly the lives of the mountain girls, depressed him and fired him with a mighty resolve to give them the normal opportunities of youth, to build them "a boarding school right here in Banner Elk." In the fall of 1898 he laid the matter before his little congregation. Subscriptions were received from them and from the people of the community to the value of $250 in lumber and work. After months of hard labor, during which no debts were ever incurred, the dormitory and a two-room school building were ready for use. Additional buildings were erected as needs developed; the course of study was expanded, and the faculty enlarged. In 1905 the boys' department was established at Plumtree; to the original purchase of land Tufts added gardens and orchards along the river; a beautiful church was erected. There were hundreds of neglected orphan children in the mountains. Moved by their need and aided by the small gifts of many friends, Mr. Tufts bought a farm and established the Grandfather Orphanage. There was no doctor near to take care of the children or to minister to the people of the neighborhood, so an old building was converted into a hospital and dispensary for the care of the people. On June 1, 1924, a modern hospital and dispensary was opened, made possible through the generous gift of a friend in New York. And so the work continued to expand.

Edgar Tufts, frail of body, but large of soul and far-ranging in his vision, whose sympathy for the neglected mountain folk had taken permanent form in one of the greatest works of the church, died January 6, 1923. The mission schools at Banner Elk and Plumtree (later combined in Lees-McRae College at Banner Elk), Grandfather Orphanage, and Grace Hospital were incorporated the next year as the Edgar Tufts Memorial Association. Each project retained its own administrative head, but was part of a larger whole controlled by the Board of Trustees of the Memorial Association.

Most of the mountain schools were in the Appalachians. The Synod of Missouri developed a splendid school, the School of the Ozarks, at Point Lookout. In the early thirties, the school had 200 students, 12 teachers, and 12 other members on its staff. It was an accredited high school, offering vocational and spiritual training, as did all the mountain schools. In one year 1,000 were turned away because of lack of room.

So each of the mountain schools had its own history; each was an attempt to meet some specific need in the name of Jesus, the Savior of all men, the friend of youth. In every school, instruction in the Bible went along with secular education; in most of them, industrial and agricultural instruction for the boys and domestic science for girls was included. The attempt was made not to educate the young people away from the mountains, but to fit them for life in the mountains. Workers in the mountains were not only evangelists and educators, but social and community workers as well. They visited in the homes, offered sympathetic suggestions along lines of sanitation and domestic science; cared for the sick; endeavored to meet every need in the spirit of Christ.

But conditions in the mountains were changing. The rapid extension of an improved highway system had opened them to the world and made the former isolation a thing of the past. The gradual improvement of the public schools had removed in many cases the necessity for the mountain schools. State and philanthropic agencies had conducted campaigns against poor sanitation and disease. The introduction of industries, the development of natural resources, and the ingress of population from the outside had provided in places money and facilities for better living. These and other changes had imparted to the Highlanders a widening life. At the same time they had brought new problems, dangers, and temptations. The new conditions in the Highlands did not therefore end the need for missions; it only changed them.

In 1929, the executive committee took notice of the changing situation in the mountains and emphasized its policy not to compete with the public schools, but to pass the responsibility for education to the state whenever it was possible.

Two years later the Assembly adopted a report offered by an Ad Interim Committee which acknowledged that mission schools had been planted too promiscuously and sometimes were poorly located. It approved the recommendation of the committee which declared that the ultimate aim of all mission schools should be evangelistic; that the church would not plant or continue mission schools where the state provided adequate schools; that no graded or high school would be continued unless it were needed for some special forms of training which was not provided by the state, and which was necessary to the permanence and progress of the church in the regions served.

In accordance with this policy, but partly because of greatly diminished resources, the number of mission schools was gradually decreased. Thus, in 1925, 14 mountain schools were maintained by the Assembly's Home Mission Committee. A few years later the committee controlled only Stuart Robinson School, Highland Institute, and Brooks Memorial Academy, all in Kentucky. In similar fashion, institutions controlled by presbyteries and synods had decreased in number.

Some of the schools with a record of distinguished service changed their purpose to meet the changing times. Thus Grundy Presbyterian School at Grundy, Virginia, which for 25 years had given Christian training to more than 100 pupils each year, assumed care for a small number of orphans and furnished a home for students from remote sections of Buchanan County who otherwise would have received no high school education. In somewhat similar fashion, Bachman Memorial School and Home, supported by the Presbytery of Knoxville, became a home for mountain children, particularly orphans. It turned its children over to the state for their secular education and gave such supplementary training to the public curriculum as might be conducive to the development of a well-balanced character.

The Highlands were now entering a period of transition. Good roads were built; public services extended; buses penetrated the mountain coves and transported the children to newly erected consolidated schools. The need for mission schools under such circumstances diminished. In 1955 the Board of Church Extension maintained only the Stuart Robinson School, with which Highland Institute had been consolidated, at Blackey, Kentucky. Other institutions controlled by synods or presbyteries were Lees-McRae College at Banner Elk, North Carolina; Glade Valley High School, also in North Carolina; Rabun Gap–Nacoochee School in Georgia; the School of the Ozarks at Point Lookout, Missouri; and Caddo Valley Academy at Norman, Arkansas.

Every presbytery with territory within the Appalachian or Ozark Mountains sought to provide a more adequate spiritual ministry by organizing Sunday schools and establishing churches. Guerrant Presbytery, for which the Assembly's board retained particular responsibility, was in the heart of the Cumberland Mountains in Eastern Kentucky. Its 19 counties covered an area almost as large as the state of Connecticut, and contained a population of more than half a million. This region was said to have the highest birthrate and the lowest church membership of any region in the United States. In 1946 the Synod of Kentucky and the Assembly's board joined hands in a determined effort to remedy this situation. Presbytery's Superintendent of Home Missions, D. C. Amick, succeeded in enlisting an unusually able and consecrated group of workers, some of whom literally devoted their lives to this particular undertaking. New churches were established, outpost preaching points maintained, and a variety of services rendered.

Coal mining was the area's single industry, on which the well-being of miners, merchants, mechanics, doctors, lawyers, truck-drivers, and teachers all depended. For a time there seemed to be hope. Then came the decline—coal lost its markets; mechanization lessened the need for workers; strip mines completed their operations and departed, leaving hideous scars and ravaged landscapes. Seventy-five percent of the young people completed their schooling and went elsewhere to earn a living. Guerrant Presbytery was ministering to one of the neediest areas in the Appalachians, whose plight had attracted the attention of the nation. Aided by a birthday gift from the Women of the Church the Board of National Ministries (succeeding the Board of Church Extension, formerly the Executive Committee on Home Missions) launched in 1966 an extensive program of training and service, which it was hoped would supplement the government's program and offer constructive relief for a people with whose total welfare it had been so long concerned.

II. FOREIGN-SPEAKING MISSIONS

Immigrants came to America in ever increasing numbers through the 19th century and up to the eve of World War I. The following table indicates the average number coming annually in the indicated decades:

1820-1830	14,000
1830-1840	60,000
1840-1850	171,000
1850-1860	260,000
1860-1870	231,000
1870-1880	281,000
1880-1890	525,000
1890-1900	384,000
1900-1910	880,000

The high-watermark was reached in 1907, when the number of immigrants was 1,285,000, though these figures were nearly duplicated again in the year ending June 30, 1914, at the outbreak of World War I. At this time one-third of the people living in the United States were either foreign-born or the sons of foreign-born.

An important change in the character of this immigration occurred about 1890. Arrivals before this time were largely from the north and west of Europe, and the stock was similar to that of the original settlers; it could be assimilated, therefore, fairly easily into American culture. After 1890 immigration began to come more largely from the south and east of Europe; it included Italians, Greeks, Poles, Russians, and emigrants from the various Balkan states. Springing from a different stock than that of the original Americans and representing on the whole a lower culture, they were not immediately assimilated into American life.

The vast majority of the immigrants settled in the large cities, the great industrial centers of the East. But with the returning prosperity of the South, the rise of new industries, the development of coal mines in West Virginia, steel mills around Birmingham, oil wells in Texas, and the like, an increasing number, especially after the turn of the century, began to push into the South. In three years 15,000 foreigners came to live in Norfolk, Virginia. In 1910 there were 15,000 Cubans and 10,000 Italians in Tampa, Florida, and a large polyglot population running into much higher figures in New Orleans.

Some of these immigrants attracted to the South, Czechs and Hungarians, for example, were Protestants in the old country, but found here no church to minister to them. The vast majority came from Roman or Greek Catholic lands, but many had become indifferent to the Catholic Church; others were frankly hostile, some to all religion.

Missions among these immigrants began through the interest of a few individuals, ministers or laymen, in the neglected foreign element of their own communities. The churches were aroused later. In fact, the great denominations did not seriously attempt to carry on work among the immigrants from southern Europe until about 1908. After that date the needs of the foreign-born assumed a commanding position, especially in the work of the larger Northern denominations. Professor T. F. Abel, in his survey, *Protestant Home Missions to Catholic Immigrants,* discovered among the four major racial groups— the Slavic, Italian, Magyar, and Mexican—2,082 Protestant foreign-language churches and missions with more than 184,000 members. Lutherans had over 1,000 of these centers; Northern Baptists, 247; Presbyterian U.S.A., 236; Northern Methodists, 122.

The Southern denominations, with a smaller foreign population in their midst and with smaller resources, developed their foreign work later and on a smaller scale. At the time of Dr. Abel's survey, Southern Methodists operated 68 centers; Southern Baptists, 56; and Southern Presbyterians, 49.

The oldest work developed by the Southern Presbyterian Church, and its largest in this area, was among the Mexicans who were constantly crossing and recrossing our Southern border. Not all the Mexicans in the United States, however, were immigrants. Texas and the southwestern portion of the United States belonged originally to Mexico and when this territory was annexed to the United States, the Mexican residents, the earliest residents, became citizens of the United States. Among the Spanish-speaking inhabitants of the United States, therefore, there was a large native element.

Mexicans, however, continued to come into the United States after annexation, because of troubled political conditions at home or because they hoped to improve their economic conditions. After 1890 immigration became more rapid; in 1894 there were 75,000 Mexicans in the United States; in 1910 more than 200,000. During World War I there was a great demand for unskilled labor and Mexicans crossed over the boundary in larger numbers, completely displacing the Negro in many sections of the Southwest. In a region 60 miles wide on the Texas side of the Rio Grande, it was estimated that there were ten or 20 Mexicans to every American of other stock. In many towns English was rarely spoken; Mexican customs prevailed and the Roman Catholic religion was the only religion. San Antonio and El Paso in particular became great Mexican centers. In 1930 the census showed 1,422,533 Mexicans in the United States, about half of these in Texas, an increase of more than a 100 percent since 1920.

Nominally, the Mexicans who came to the United States were Roman Catholics. But a strong movement away from the Roman Catholic Church had developed in Mexico, and thousands of the immigrants were in revolt against the only church that they knew.

Southern Presbyterian work among this people began in the closing years of the 1870's when the two Graybill brothers went out from Virginia under the auspices of the Executive Committee on Foreign Missions: one (J. W.) pressed on into Mexico; the other (A. T.) remained in Brownsville, Texas. Under the faithful ministry of Dr. A. T. Graybill, the church at Brownsville became the mother church of all the mission work which the Southern Presbyterian Church has done for the Mexicans in Mexico.

Home mission work among the Mexicans was an indirect product of the Brownsville church. It had its origin in a humble Mexican Christian named Jose Maria Botello who was converted to Christianity through reading a religious tract. He joined the Mexican church in Brownsville and later became an elder.

In 1883 Senor Botello moved with his family from Brownsville to San Marcos in the interior of the state. "Being a sincere Christian and a loyal Presbyterian," wrote evangelist W. S. Scott, "Botello did not hide his candle under a bushel. He and his family held daily prayers and gospel services on the Sabbath. This brought on petty persecutions, but the Lord sustained them and gave them the victory. It was not long before they began to have inquirers. . . . In less than half a year Botello had ten or twelve converts ready to accept the gospel and make public profession of their faith in Christ."

On July 13, 1884, ten of these converts were received into the First Presbyterian Church of San Marcos, then supplied by the Reverend J. B. French. Three years more and the Mexican Presbyterian Church of San Marcos was organized with 26 members, two ruling elders, and two deacons, the church being under the charge of a Mexican, Juan C. Hernandez.

On the same day that this church was organized a young man with whom the Mexican work in Texas would long be identified was taken under the care of Western Texas Presbytery as a candidate for the gospel ministry. This young man, Walter S. Scott, was born of Scotch parents who moved to Mexico during the Civil War. Reared among the Mexicans, he spoke the language with the ease and fluency of a native. He had intended to return to Mexico as a missionary, but was persuaded by older missionaries to work among the Mexicans in the United States, assured that if they could be brought to Christ they would become in turn a power in the work among their own countrymen.

On April 17, 1892, Scott was put in charge of the San Marcos Church, which he had visited repeatedly during the preceding years, and was also appointed as an evangelist to the Mexicans in Texas.

In a few years there were five churches in the neighborhood of San Marcos and four more which Scott had developed in the Uvalde field 143 miles away. With the aid of native elders, he cared for both of these groups of churches, worked at ten or 12 other points, and had charge of all the territory embraced by the Presbytery of West Texas. He organized churches at Bexar, Laredo, Corpus Christi, Beeville, Clareville, Victoria, Gonzales, San Antonio—15 churches in his first 16 years, 25 churches by 1924.

To the assistance of Mr. Scott in 1894 came Dr. H. B. Pratt, formerly a missionary in South America. Dr. Pratt was an outstanding scholar; he had given the Spanish-speaking people a translation of the Bible in their language and written a commentary on the Pentateuch. He now rendered valuable assistance as evangelist and pastor among the Mexicans at Laredo; his greatest service, however, was to train several young Mexicans for the ministry, men needed for the waiting fields.

When Dr. Pratt had to leave Texas in 1899, the Reverend R. D. Campbell, who had been a missionary in Mexico, come to take his place. He took charge of the work at Laredo and Corpus Christi. As a result of the combined labors of Scott and Campbell and the native missionaries trained by Dr. Pratt, preaching points increased and believers multiplied.

On July 30, 1908, at the request of the Mexican pastors, the first Mexican presbytery, Texas-Mexican, was formed with 17 churches and four ministers, W. S. Scott, R. D. Campbell, Reynoldo Avila, and E. Trevino. The new presbytery extended over a territory 400 miles long and 300 miles wide and included 70 or more counties. Headquarters for the presbytery were at Austin, residence of Dr. R. D. Campbell, who, in addition to his pastorate, was the wise counselor and trusted friend of his Mexican brethren.

The Mexicans who had at first congregated in a strip along the border spread gradually throughout Texas, and Mexican colonies sprang up in the central and northern parts of the state. With the passion of a pioneer W. S. Scott sought them out, and in 1918 the advance field covering roughly the northern half of the state was organized as a mission field by the Synod of Texas, with Mr. Scott as evangelist-in-chief.

There were difficulties in carrying the gospel to the Mexicans. For one thing, they were constantly on the move. Few owned their own homes. Many were tenant farmers. Some rode the cattle ranges. Great numbers were manual laborers on railroads and farms and in mines. "In addition to the difficulties common to all mission work," wrote R. D. Campbell, "we encounter those peculiar to the stranger in a strange land, with its attendant poverty, ignorance, especially of our language and customs, and consequently hard working conditions and ever-increasing search for something better." Illiteracy, wretched housing conditions, unstable support, poverty, and a general low standard of living everywhere prevailed.

In spite of the difficulties, the work grew steadily and was as successful as any mission conducted among foreign-speaking people. Statistics are an inadequate indication of work accomplished. A large number of the converts moved on beyond reach; many returned with the gospel to their native lands.

Yet, with all that was done, the Protestant churches as a whole had hardly touched the fringe of the problem. In all the missions there were less than 38,000 Protestants.

If Mexicans in Texas were to be won for Christ, it must be done ultimately by the Texas-Mexicans themselves. Realization of this fact led to the establishment of two schools for Mexican youth—the Texas-Mexican Industrial Institute for Boys at Kingsville, and the Presbyterian School for Mexican girls at Taft, Texas.

"Tex-Mex," as the former school was affectionately termed, opened its doors October 1, 1912, under the direction of Dr. J. W. Skinner. The school possessed at the time 660 acres of uncleared land, a two-story frame house, a mule barn used for a classroom, and a feed shed converted into a dormitory. A Gulf storm blew down the school building in 1916 and a tornado wrecked buildings again in 1920. But in spite of such mishaps the school grew steadily in equipment and in usefulness. The curriculum included primary grades through the high school. Industrial features were included so that the pupils might be enabled to serve their own people and if need be to make a living with their own hands. By 1930 graduates of the school were holding important positions in secular and religious affairs both in Mexico and in the United States.

The women of the church sensed the fact that girls as well as boys must be trained if there were to be Christian homes and, through them, Christian leaders among the Mexicans in Texas. Most of the Mexican girls in the Presbyterian Church could neither read nor write. Though naturally bright, they had little chance to learn. A few progressed as far as the high school, but almost none graduated. Language was one serious difficulty, poverty another, race prejudice another. So the women of the Texas synodical secured funds for a school which opened its doors in 1924 with 24 girls. Academic work continued through high school. Industrial features were included, and self-help required as in the school for boys. Students were chosen by the various churches and mission centers so that the girls entered the school as the chosen representatives of their communities.

Dr. J. W. Skinner, founder and for 19 years President of Texas-Mexican Industrial Institute, died October 24, 1931. He had resigned his pastorate in Colorado and come to Texas to salvage a shaky financial investment. There he was drafted into the service of the Southern Presbyterian Church and of the Mexicans in Texas. In reporting his death to the General Assembly, Dr. McMillan described him as one of the foremost ministers of the Presbyterian Church and a pioneer in Christian industrial education for Mexican youth:

> This splendid school for Mexican boys, known far and wide as a model of its kind [declared Dr. McMillan] is a monument to his faith and vision and perserverance. When the companion school for Mexican

girls at Taft, Texas was organized, he gave generously of his assistance in providing material equipment and in outlining practical courses of study. These two mission schools are visible symbols of Dr. Skinner's work. Yet his greatest monument is inscribed in the hearts and lives of the boys and girls who through the years he lived with them, caught a vision of the beauty of a life of Christian service. Preacher, Scholar, Scientist, Moderator of the General Assembly, Dr. Skinner considered it his greatest honor to be a Home Missionary . . .[13]

The prestige of Tex-Mex continued to mount under Dr. Skinner's successor, his former associate, Rev. S. Brooks McLane, D.D. Dr. McLane retired in 1955 because of ill health, after 41 years of service to the school, now a fully accredited high school. During his regime selected students were encouraged to remain at Tex-Mex as counselors and tutors in English, while they completed their own education in the neighboring A. and I. College. Ninety-five percent of the student body came from Mexico (where church-sponsored education was forbidden) and planned to return to their native land.

Re-evaluation of the Latin-American work in Texas led to the merging of the two schools—Texas-Mexican for boys and Presbyterian-Mexican for girls—at Kingsville. In 1957 the campus of the new Presbyterian Pan-American School began to take shape, as the first step in a two million dollar development campaign. Elected President was Sherwood H. Reisner, who had served as a UPUSA missionary in Mexico and as pastor of the National Mexican Church in Brownsville, Texas. For the first time students were selected for ability (particularly leadership potentiality) as well as for need. They came now from other Latin-American countries as well as from Mexico, and a few Anglo-American students were accepted; approximately half of the student body was drawn from the Mexican churches in Texas. Every student had to be sponsored by the session of a Presbyterian Church.

The school flourished under its new leadership, but not the Presbyterian churches among the Mexican-Americans in Texas. From 1908 till 1954 there were about 30 churches included in the Texas-Mexican Presbytery. During this period there was little contact between the Latin pastors and the Anglo ministers. To remedy this situation, and for other reasons, the Mexican presbytery was dissolved in 1954 and its churches distributed among the presbyteries within whose bounds they were located. In the years that followed existing churches were aided; their structures improved, rebuilt or relocated; a few were brought to self-support. Little new work, however, was developed.* In 1965 there were only 36 Mexican churches in the synod, and about

---

* From 1930 to 1951 there was a gain of only 160 new members.

20 ministers; the majority of these were over 40 years of age; one candidate was expected to finish his training the following year. Of all ministers on the field only four had college and seminary degrees.

The Mexican-American population—perhaps 15 percent of the total Texas population—was growing. Every year 50,000 Mexicans crossed the border, legally, to become permanent residents in the United States, most of these in Texas. Eighty percent of this nominally (cultural) Roman Catholic population was said to be without spiritual roots. The Presbyterian Church (PCUS and UPUSA), despite the efforts of consecrated men, had not succeeded in breaking through the barriers of language and culture. In the large cities a few Mexican-Americans identified themselves with the Anglo churches, but not many. In McAllen, Texas, two congregations, one Anglo, the other Mexican, joined hands in a church ministry with common means, program, and staff. The success of this experiment offered at least a ray of hope. Some Latin-American leaders, however, convinced that the Spanish language and the Mexican culture should be preserved, did not see amalgamation with Anglos as the solution. The outlook for the future was uncertain.

In addition to the work carried on among Mexican-Americans (in connection with the Synod of Texas) the Executive Committee on Home Missions attempted, in a smaller way, to aid various presbyteries in carrying the gospel to other foreign groups in the South.

This aid began to be given and a specific department of foreign work was established in the executive committee in 1909. In that year help was given to the French and Italian work, which had been conducted for years in the Presbytery of New Orleans, and to evangelistic work which was being carried on among Italians in Birmingham and among Czechs in Virginia. Independent work was being carried on at the same time among Italians in Kansas City, and work was being planned among Cubans in Tampa, Florida. In a few years the General Assembly was taking an active part in preaching the gospel to a dozen different nationalities.

The synod which had the largest foreign problem on its hands was the Synod of Louisiana. There were approximately 400,000 French-speaking people in its bounds, descendants for the most part of the original settlers who occupied the country about New Orleans before the Louisiana Purchase, or of the early arrivals in the "Evangeline Country"—refugees from the French provinces which Great Britain conquered in Canada. The intervening years had not served to assimilate them wholly into American life; French was the native tongue of whole sections of the state, and Roman Catholicism was the only religion.

In addition to the French, there were in Louisiana approximately 50,000 Italians, great numbers of Germans, some 10,000 Spanish-speaking people, 1,000 or more Syrians, a colony of Hungarians, and numbers of Chinese passing in and out of New Orleans.

The Presbytery of New Orleans, in which the most of this need lay, had begun work among the foreign groups as early as 1882, but found it difficult to carry the work alone. Presbyterians were the strongest Protestant denomination in New Orleans, but they numbered less than 5,000, while the city contained 200,000 Roman Catholics. The Synod of Louisiana was one of the weakest of the synods. Most of its churches were small. It was only natural that when the General Assembly developed its foreign-speaking work aid should be given to this faithful and over-burdened presbytery.

In 1911 the presbytery, with the aid of the General Assembly, employed two missionaries among the Germans, two among the Syrians, one among the Spanish-speaking people, one among the Chinese, two among the Hungarians, two among the Italians, and four among the French. In 1915, 22 missionaries were ministering to the foreign-speaking people in the state.

The two German missions quickly became self-supporting. In the Depression years other missions were discontinued, some for lack of funds, others for lack of workers.

A Sunday school begun by a group of young people in 1882 led two years later to the opening of a mission for the Chinese. It was, in general, a wayside ministry to those in need and became known as such to every Chinese immigrant who shipped for New Orleans. If any Chinese was sick or in trouble, help was always available. Preaching services were held and a Sunday school conducted in a building owned by the presbytery. Converts of the mission joined white churches of New Orleans, and many carried their newfound faith to other cities in America and back to their native land. In 1957 a Chinese church was organized, and five years later an attractive building, with aid from the Women of the Church's annual birthday gift, was erected. This was the one church ministering to the Chinese scattered through the city. There was thought to be a greater percentage of Christians among this community than could be found among the Chinese in any other part of the world.

Most numerous by far of the immigrants who came to American shores in this period were the Italians, a "familiar and omnipresent part of the American scene." According to the 1930 census there were four and a half million of them in the United States. Missions for the Italians sprang up in many parts of the country. One of the most successful of these was the Italian Institute and Central Chapel at Kansas City, Missouri. The mission had a long history. In 1897 Central Presbyterian Church started a Sunday school which was known as "Little Italy," intended for native Americans as well as foreign born. But as Italians moved in and the older Americans moved out, attention of the mission became directed almost entirely to the former. There were 6,000 of them, mostly from Southern Italy, congregated in a section of the city in which most of the saloons were located and which contained the city's segregated vice district.

A native minister was called; a fine plant costing about $16,000 was erected by Central Church. The Reverend J. B. Bisceglia in 1918 took charge of the mission to which he was to devote the rest of his active ministry. A little later a branch mission was opened in the northwest district of the city, into which a large number of the Italians were moving.

The principal aim of the mission was always to win souls for Jesus Christ, and the main emphasis continued to be placed on the religious work, but to attract people who otherwise would fail to come to the place of worship and to improve the minds and the bodies as well as the souls of these new Americans, settlement features were used from the beginning with great success. In the early 1930's its varied program reached 5,000 or more individuals, approximately one-half of the Italian population of Kansas City.

In the following generation the character of the neighborhood changed. Christ Church was relocated in a better neighborhood to which many of its members had moved. The old neighborhood became a low-rent, inner-city area, 80 percent Catholic, among whom there was no Protestant church. Here, on the old mission site, presbytery began a new ministry, the Northside Community Presbyterian Church, attempting as its predecessor had done to serve both the social and the spiritual needs of the community.

Birmingham, as one of the great industrial centers of the South, attracted an unusually large number of immigrants. Forty-one different nationalities were listed by the United States census, the largest single group being the Italians. Thirty thousand were estimated to live in or around Birmingham in 1925, and they were particularly numerous in the town of Ensley. Work was opened here in 1909 and continued here for several years with an Italian pastor in charge. When World War I came, however, the Italians were scattered and the work declined. The Italian mission in New Orleans was abandoned for the same reason after a successful service of 35 years.

The only indigenous Protestants in Italy are the heroic and often martyred Waldensians, tracing their lineage back to Peter Waldo in the 12th century. They have belonged to the Reformed or Presbyterian branch of the church since the early Reformation. Aid was extended to a few colonies of these Waldensians in the South, one at Valdese, North Carolina, others at Wolf Ridge and at Galveston in Texas.

The census of 1930 reported two million foreign-born Slavs in America. In this conglomerate of racial groups or nationalities were included Russians, Bulgarians, and Serbians, who belonged predominantly to the Greek Orthodox Church, and Czechs, Slovaks, Poles, and Slovenes, who were predominantly Roman Catholics. The Czechs, or Bohemians, constituted about one-tenth of the Slavic group in the United States. A few thousand of them, Protestants, Reformed, or Presbyterian in their background, settled in Prince George County in Virginia, where they came to own a large proportion of the farms. A group of these was organized into a church by East Hanover Presbytery. A work was begun among the Bohemians in Texas in 1910 but was transferred the next year to the Presbyterian Church in the U.S.A., who had developed a very extensive and successful mission among this particular folk.

Most of the foreign-speaking population of Florida lived either in Key West or in that portion of Tampa known as Ybor City and was made up chiefly of Cubans, Spaniards, and Italians. Around 1925 there were about 7,000 Cubans and Spaniards in Key West and about 17,000 in Tampa, most of them employed in the manufacture of cigars.

The Cubans spoke their native tongue almost exclusively, making little effort to learn the English language. The Roman Catholic Church had largely lost its hold upon them. Not one percent, it was estimated, ever entered their original church, and very few had been reached by an evangelical church. In 1923 a church was organized in Key West with 25 Anglo-American members and 22 Cubans. Southern Presbyterians began work in Ybor City in 1909, and organized a church in 1915, which in the 1930's came to have a membership of 47. In the years that followed, it became one of the most successful of the church's foreign-speaking missions, rivaling in its influence the Italian mission in Kansas City.

A gift from the Women of the Church in 1956 led to the erection of St. John's Presbyterian Church and Community Center in West Tampa, into which many of the people who had prospered in Ybor City were now moving. As more people moved in, membership of the church grew. Work of the Ybor City mission, with its seven-day program serving the spiritual and social needs of the people, was continued under the guidance of the session of St. John's Church and its pastor, Walter B. Passiglia. In the 1960's the mission found new opportunities of service among the Cuban refugees, thousands of whom were now living in Ybor City. Interested churches in the Presbytery of Everglades, meanwhile, had established a Latin-American mission for the Spanish-speaking population of Miami.

Of special interest to Presbyterians were the quarter-million or more Magyars (Hungarians) in the United States. This sturdy race, which migrated from Asia and with their flocks and herds occupied the fertile plains of Hungary in the ninth century, played an important role in the history of Europe and its religious life for more than 1,000 years. About a fourth of this group, both in Europe and America, were Protestant, and the most of these were Presbyterian or Reformed.

In the early 1900's several thousands of these Magyars, along with Italians and Slavs, were employed in the vast coal and coke industry centering around Norton in southwestern Virginia and spilling over into the mining areas of West Virginia. For some time no work was done for them by any denomination, except the Roman Catholic, which sent them an occasional itinerant priest. Southern Presbyterians somewhat later developed a successful work among the Hungarians which continued for a number of years. A Hungarian church supported at Hammond, Louisiana, was more enduring.

For many years, beginning in 1920, the Southern Presbyterian Church cooperated with the Presbyterian Church U.S.A. in a joint mission carried on in Baltimore in the heart of a Jewish settlement of about 45,000, many of whom were recent immigrants to America.

For a number of years a work for a large Syrian colony in Atlanta was conducted with varying success. During World War I religious work was carried on for a short period among colonies of Russians and Japanese. During the course of the war many who had come from other lands returned to their native countries. Some of the Southern Presbyterian missions for foreign-speaking people were depleted by such movement. Others were hopelessly crippled by the Depression, or closed because it was impossible to secure acceptable workers. Here and there a church and its people, as in Prince George County, Virginia, or the Waldensian Church in Valdese, North Carolina, became completely assimilated into the life of its new denomination. In two of the most successful missions, the Italian mission in Kansas City and the Latin American mission in Ybor City, members of the church prospered and moved into more affluent suburbs where they entered into the mainstream of American life. The flourishing mission in Ybor City, the recently organized mission among the Cubans in Miami, the fully organized and attractively housed Chinese church in New Orleans, the score or more Mexican-American churches in Texas—little else remained of the small, but highly publicized, work once carried on among the foreign-speaking people of the South.

V

Expanding Overseas

The time came (1884) when Dr. J. Leighton Wilson, who more than any other had awakened Southern Presbyterians to a recognition of their responsibilities for carrying the gospel to other lands, requested that he be relieved of his office as Secretary of the Executive Committee on Foreign Missions. "It is not a little gratifying," he wrote, "to be permitted to withdraw from this work at a time when it combines within itself all the essential elements of hope and prosperity. The cause of Foreign Missions now holds no doubtful place in the heart of the Southern Presbyterian Church. Its claims are well nigh universally admitted. More than this. The cause has enthroned itself in the affections of the great body of our Christian people to remain there as long as we have any claims to be regarded as a true Church of the Lord Jesus Christ. . . ."[1]

"Foreign" Missions at this time were being conducted in Indian Territory (transferred five years later to the Executive Committee on Home Missions), and in China, Brazil, and Mexico. A large proportion of the churches gave nothing at all to the cause, and per capita giving of the church as a whole to this enterprise was only 50 cents a year, but this was more than was being given by other Southern denominations or by many of those in the North.*

---

* The table of comparative per capita giving as printed in *Central Presbyterian* for August 12, 1885, was:
  1. Moravians, leading with $4.47
  2. Congregationalists, second with $1.39
  3. Reformed Presbyterian Church $1.36
  4. Presbyterians USA $1.12
  5. Presbyterians US $0.50
  6. Northern Baptists $0.49
  7. Episcopalians $0.35
  8. Southern Methodists $0.22
  9. Northern Methodists $0.21
  10. Southern Baptists $0.08

Elected as Dr. Wilson's successor was Dr. Matthew Hale Houston, then at home on sick leave after 20 years of service in China.

During his administration (1885-1893) two new mission fields were entered—Japan and the Congo. The Japanese mission was opened in 1885, at a time when Christianity was riding a brief wave of popularity in a land which had been long closed to all Western influence. The pioneers in this undertaking were Rev. Randolph Bryan G. Grinnan, a Virginian, and Rev. Robert Eugenius McAlpine, from Alabama; some of the latter's descendants have continued to labor in Japan until the present time. The two were assigned a post in Kochi, where a small but enthusiastic band of believers warmly welcomed them, and the mission prospered from the outset. Rev. William B. McIlwaine, founder of another missionary dynasty, who was to play an influential role in the life of the Japanese mission for the next 43 years, arrived in 1889. Four years after the opening of the mission there were 16 missionaries in Japan, occupying four important stations.

Southern Presbyterians had long felt that Africa was a mission field peculiarly appropriate for them to enter and had looked forward to the time when they could send missionaries (under white supervision) from the African race within their own bounds. Dr. C. A. Stillman heartily approved the project, hoping that Negroes carrying the gospel to Africa would soften prejudice against the Negro among members in the home church.[2] The opportunity came in 1889, when the Assembly was informed that a white licentiate was prepared to enter upon the work in company with a patiently waiting graduate of Stillman Institute.

The next year two young ministers, Samuel N. Lapsley, born in a cultured Southern home in Selma, Alabama—his father, later Moderator of the General Assembly, was a judge—and William H. Sheppard, a Negro, whose father was a barber and whose mother was a maid in Waynesboro, Virginia, were sent to Africa as pioneers to determine the most appropriate site for a mission to the people on the Congo River—an area recently opened up by the explorations of Henry M. Stanley. A dangerous trip far into the interior led to the choice of a site, Luebo, in the heart of the African jungle. A year later, Lapsley, stricken with fever, died, leaving Sheppard for a time to carry on the work alone.

The hopes of the mission board had been to reinforce the mission chiefly with colored men and more of them volunteered than the executive committee was able to send;[3] white men, however, were necessary, to carry on negotiations with the state and these were slow to offer—perhaps because of the overall policy just mentioned. For a time it seemed as though the work of the mission would have to be suspended. Then finally two white men responded to Dr. Chester's plea—S. P. Verner and W. M. Morrison, the second of whom was to become the dynamic leader of the mission, and the one who more than any other was responsible for its final success. Missionary recruitment however remained slow; racism, perhaps, remained a factor, but there were others—the unhealthy climate, for example. The situation remained critical until 1912 when Rev. Motte Martin on furlough made an impassioned plea, stirring deeply the Laymen's Missionary Movement, meeting that year in Chattanooga. Twenty-eight delegates volunteered on the spot, and 12 of them were immediately appointed to the Congo.

Eleven Negro missionaries altogether were dispatched to the African field, the last of them being sent out in 1906, after which time Belgium ceased to welcome black missionaries from abroad. Negroes already appointed however were permitted to remain until retirement or death. Mr. Sheppard, the earliest volunteer for the Congo, continued in the field for many years. He retained the respect of his colleagues, and to the Congolese became something of a demigod. He was honored in London and Brussels as one of the greatest of African missionaries and was the only one of the Presbyterian mission to be honored with a fellowship in the Royal Geographic Society of London. Dr. S. H. Chester described him to Elihu Root, then Secretary of State, as "perhaps the most distinguished minister of the Presbyterian Church South."[4]

The African mission was established at a time when the Negro in the United States was being disfranchised politically and when segregation—by custom and law—was being extended into every area of Southern life. The mission, in contrast, was integrated from the outset. Every member had an equal voice in mission affairs, and each of them received the same salary.

One of the vital questions which arose at this time was what was the relationship of missionaries to the native church. The policy of all Presbyterian missions up to the year 1875 had been to organize presbyteries composed of missionaries and natives in organic connection with the home churches. On this basis a presbytery had been organized in Southern Brazil and another in Central China. After a year of this experiment the Presbytery of Hang Chow, under the leadership of Dr. Houston, overtured the Assembly asking to be dissolved. In granting this request the Assembly declared that it had no constitutional right to organize presbyteries at home or abroad and that it was inexpedient for the missionaries to become voting members of church courts in mission lands. Churches growing out of our mission work, said the General Assembly "are free born, and have the inherent right of self-government, through rulers whom the Lord authorizes them to select."[5]

"This action of the Assembly," wrote Dr. S. H. Chester, Dr. Houston's successor as Secretary of Foreign Missions," placed our church in a position of leadership in the establishment of this principle of administration which has now come to be accepted with practical unanimity by the Presbyterian group of churches, and to a large extent also, so far as the principle is concerned, among the other Protestant denominations. Stated as a formula the principle is that all foreign mission work is pioneer and preliminary, having as to its objective the establishment of self-governing, self-supporting and self-propagating native churches, on which the chief responsibility for evangelizing all non-Christian lands must ultimately fall."[6]

The principle that it was inexpedient for missionaries to become voting members of church courts in mission lands was included in the first missionary manual drawn up under the leadership of Dr. Houston in 1887. A later revision of the manual, however, permitted missionaries to become voting members of these courts under exceptional circumstances. The majority of missionaries in Brazil and China ultimately became voting members of the native courts under the plausible assumption that by so doing they could guide the development of these courts. As the native churches grew in strength, this policy inevitably aroused resentment. In 1917 the Brazilian General Assembly adopted a plan of cooperation with the mission under which no new missionaries coming to the field could have voting membership in the native presbyteries, except those called to special forms of labor by the Brazilian church itself. Most of the older missionaries voluntarily transferred their membership back to their home presbyteries. In the Church of Christ in Japan from the beginning the missionaries usually held only associate and advisory relations to the native presbytery except when employed by the presbytery in some special work.[7]

Dr. Houston was the Southern Church's pioneer in cooperative missions. Presbyterian mission boards united from the start to build up a united Church of Christ in Japan. In response to memorials from several of its missionaries, the General Assembly in 1887 approved the formation of an independent Brazilian synod with four presbyteries including churches organized by both major branches of the Presbyterian Church in the United States.

During the eight years in which Dr. Houston served as secretary the missionary giving of Southern Presbyterians almost doubled, from $72,500 to $137,500. Per capita giving increased from 50¢ in 1885 to 69¢ ten years later. Per capita giving of other churches during this year was

Congregationalists $1.29
Presbyterians U.S.A. 94¢
Northern Baptists 61¢
Protestant Episcopals 42¢
Northern Methodists 41¢
Southern Baptists 8¢

Dr. Houston was a man of strong convictions which at times aroused antagonisms. To resolve differences which had arisen between the secretary and the members of the executive committee the General Assembly shifted the committee's site from Baltimore to Nashville, where it has since remained. Difficulties continued and in 1893 Dr. Houston resigned,[8] and returned to the land where he had first labored as a missionary.

Back in China, Dr. Houston came to believe in the possibility of sinless perfection; he taught that the Lord's Supper was a household as well as a church ordinance and that as such it could be rightfully administered by the head of a Christian family, and that there were no distinctions between ruling and teaching elders—that every ruling elder could perform all the functions of the minister or pastor. His mission advised that he place his novel doctrines before Louisville Presbytery, his home presbytery, which he proceeded to do. The presbytery, finding him out of accord with the Westminster Confession of Faith on these matters, divested him of his office without censure[9] and advised that he not be returned to the mission field. Dr. Houston thereupon withdrew from the ministry and spent the rest of his life in semiretirement.

Dr. S. H. Chester, elected to succeed Dr. Houston in 1894, took over the administration of the foreign missionary enterprise in a difficult period. The country was in the midst of a severe depression. A false sense of economy on the part of the Executive Committee left him without needed office aid. Ministers for the most part he discovered to be without vital missionary interest. The only organization outside his office for the promotion of the work was the old-fashioned Women's Missionary Society which existed in only about half of the churches and which usually included only a small proportion of the women of the church. It was their interest and their contributions which finally, he felt, saved the day.[10] But the first seven years were trying ones.

The break came in 1902 with the Forward Movement, which with brief recessions continued till the onslaught of the great Depression following the First World War. The Forward Movement in its beginning was a plan for the assumption by churches, societies, and individuals of definite responsibility for definite parts of the work, such as the salaries of missionaries or shares in the work of a station, based on individual pledges taken in an every member canvass. The plan was pushed by three young missionaries (J. Leighton Stuart, Lacy Moffett, and Fairman Preston) under appointment but detained at home for lack of funds. In two years they succeeded in enlisting 300 churches and 30 individuals in the movement; the foreign mission income increased during the same period from $165,000 to $236,000. In 1905 Dr. James O. Reavis came in to labor with Dr. Chester as Coordinate Secretary. When he retired six years later on account of broken health the number of missionaries had increased from 113 to 297 and the income from $236,000 to $452,000. More important than the statistical increase, as Dr. Chester saw it, was the inauguration of methods and plans of organization and missionary education that insured the continued progress of the work.

It was during this period that the women's societies began to organize themselves into presbyterials and synodicals and finally into a Women's Auxiliary, which came to be the most efficient educational agency—insofar as the work of the church was concerned—which had yet been developed. In this period also the laymen's missionary movement was born, which in its brief existence had great success in educating and enlisting the interest of men in the work of the church.*

The most important single development, in the estimation of

---

* The average receipts of the church for Foreign Missions for the two years 1901-1902 preceding the Forward Movement amount to $133,250. For five years after the Forward Movement began the average receipts were $193,752. For the seven years following the inauguration of the Laymen's Missionary Movement, 1908-1915, the average receipts for Foreign Missions were $471,830 (CO [August 11, 1915] p. 1).

By 1910 Presbyterian and Reformed Churches had assumed the lead in missionary giving in the United States. Per capita gifts were reported this year as follows:

United Presbyterians	$2.56 per member
Dutch Reformed Church	$1.76
Presbyterian U.S.	$1.53
Presbyterian U.S.A.	$1.13

Other leading denominations were far behind (CO [May 18, 1910]).

Dr. Chester, was the adoption by the Birmingham Assembly in 1907 of a missionary platform in which the church solemnly assumed the responsibility for giving the gospel to the people in definite areas within seven foreign countries (China, Japan, and Korea in the Far East; the Congo in Africa; Brazil, Mexico, and Cuba in Latin America), estimated at that time to contain a population of 25 million. The allocation of territory had been approved by the Annual Conference of Mission Boards of the United States and Canada, with which Southern Presbyterians had cooperated since its formation in 1892; the first suggestion of possible division of territorial responsibility was made to the conference by Dr. Chester in 1896, and the Southern Church was the first of the cooperating bodies to act on the proposal. "As a business proposition," Dr. Chester recalled, "the Platform stabilized our work by giving us a definite goal to work for. It immediately strengthened our appeal by adding to all other considerations the force of acknowledged responsibility."[11]

Comity and cooperation between the major mission boards was further stimulated by the New York Ecumenical Conference of 1900, the Edinburgh Missionary Conference of 1910 (out of which grew the modern ecumenical movement), and two great Latin American Conferences—the one held in Panama in 1916 and the other in Montevideo, in Uruguay, in 1925—in all of which Southern Presbyterians participated. As a result of these conferences, cooperative schools, hospitals, and other forms of institutional work were developed in almost every mission field in a large and efficient way that could have been conducted by single denominations only in a small way or not at all.[12]

An illustration of comity at work comes from Mexico. In the year 1919 there were missions of the Southern Presbyterians, the Southern Methodists, the Disciples of Christ, and the Society of Friends congested and competing with each other in a territory in northern Mexico containing about half a million people. As a consequence of two interdenominational conferences, the Southern Presbyterian Mission transferred its entire force to southern Mexico, the Disciples transferred theirs to one of the central states, leaving the Friends, whose mission was a very small one, and the Southern Methodists in sole charge of the territory in the north.[13]

One of the more troublesome and annoying episodes to arise during Dr. Chester's incumbency was the protracted discussion regarding the legitimacy of receiving into the church by baptism a man with more than one wife. The question was raised when Rev. M. B. Grier was charged with baptizing a Chinese convert having a second wife, and then Dr. W. M. Morrison in the Congo baptized several with plural wives (on condition that there would be no additional mar riages). Dr. S. S. Laws, a resident of Washington, D. C., regarding this practice as a shameful compromise with evil, brought Morrison's case before the Synod of Virginia, carried it on complaint to the General Assembly, and finally framed an indictment against Mr. Grier before the Presbytery of South Carolina. His views were developed at length and put before the church in a large pamphlet or booklet of 212 pages. Dr. Laws was sustained in his campaign against the acceptance of polygamists into the church by the influential church periodicals—the *Central Presbyterian*, the *Southern Presbyterian*, and the *Presbyterian Standard*. In the judgment of this group a convert should be required to put away all wives subsequent to the first. It was the contention of the missionaries, supported by the executive committee, that this would in many cases involve injustice and cruelty to the secondary wife and her children, inflicting on them the humiliation and disgrace of an outcast position. Dr. Motte Martin stated that in Africa in the case of tribal chiefs, most of whom had many wives who were the daughters of other chiefs, the putting away of their wives would be taken as a mortal insult by the tribes from which they came and might bring on bloody tribal wars. Dr. A. W. Pitzer of Washington insisted that the Word of God could be searched in vain for authority to enact the rule requiring a wholesale divorce of wives at the missionaries' dictation as a condition of baptism and the Lord's Supper. Altogether the matter was before three General Assemblies, two synods, and several presbyteries. The Presbytery of South Carolina declined to indict Mr. Grier and was sustained in this action by the Synod of South Carolina; the Synod of Virginia and the General Assembly steadfastly declined to take the action against Dr. Morrison desired by Dr. Laws, thus leaving the matter in the hands of the missionaries. They were affectionately enjoined however to be careful not to compromise the honor of the church or any of the principles of its holy religion and not to pursue any policy that would fail to make it plain that such customs and practices were to be condemned as contrary to the law of Christ, as revealed in the Scriptures.[14]

As a consequence, the African mission, in which for a time a few converted polygamists had been baptized, decided to discontinue the practice and to retain such converts in the position of permanent catechumens.[15] The conversion of tribal chiefs (whose status and relationships with other tribes were dependent on their wives), as well as others, was thereby rendered more difficult. Some missionaries have continued to maintain that this was mistaken policy—in part because the lot of unmarried women in the Congo is so very difficult.

During Dr. Chester's incumbency Southern Presbyterian missionaries attracted international attention and support in their struggles against two of the most firmly entrenched evils of their times—the opium trade in China and the exploitation of the Congo natives by King Leopold II of Belgium. The one man above all others responsible for the final suppression of the opium traffic was Rev. Hampden C. DuBose, who arrived in China in 1872, and continued to labor there, in the city of Soochow, until his death in 1910. Dr. DuBose was primarily an evangelist, a popular preacher to the Chinese masses. He was also a prolific writer, both in English and in Chinese. His great fight against the opium traffic developed during the last 15 years of his life.

When Dr. DuBose arrived in China the opium trade had been legalized for 14 years and was rapidly becoming a national vice. Of the one hundred million adult males in China, one tenth, it was estimated, had become addicted to opium. The Indian government (then British-controlled) sent into China annually between 5,000 to 6,000 tons of the stuff and almost a third of the revenue of the Chinese Imperial Customs was derived from this source; deprived of this income, the Chinese government would face bankruptcy. In India the manufacture of opium was one of the chief sources of state income. The British government in India was the largest manufacturer of opium in the world, and it was the British government which had imposed the opium traffic on China.

Dr. DuBose's first step was to study the opium curse from every point of view, to get the facts. His second step was the stirring of public opinion among the missionaries and the Chinese, Christians and non-Christians. It was in this second step that he was subjected to the most ridicule—some of it coming from his fellow missionaries, who felt that he had undertaken a hopeless task. His third step was to organize his forces for the final struggle. In January 1896, 24 years after landing in China, he organized the National Anti-Opium League of China, of which he was elected president annually for the remaining 15 years of his life. Under the leadership of Dr. DuBose, the League, enlisting the aid of other organizations, brought facts and figures regarding the opium traffic to international attention. President Theodore Roosevelt was persuaded to put the American consuls in China behind the propaganda effort; the British Parliament was led on May 30, 1906, to adopt a memorable resolution branding the Indo-Chinese opium trade as morally indefensible, and requesting the government to bring it to a speedy close. At the great missionary conference at Shanghai in 1907 a cablegram concerning opium suppression was sent to The Hague. This was one of the causes which brought about the meeting of the International Commission against Opium in June 1913, when representatives of practically every great nation condemned the opium traffic.

Although the League accomplished much directly and indirectly through this international campaign, its greatest and most difficult efforts were in China itself. Hundreds of missionaries, inspired by Dr. DuBose, spoke publicly against the evil. Thousands of anti-opium leaflets were distributed. The aid of China's growing press was enlisted. Year by year the number of those opposed to the opium curse increased. Finally at long last came a breakthrough among the official governing class. The Viceroy in Nanking suggested that Dr. DuBose draw up a formal anti-opium memorial signed by the missionaries, which he might present to the throne. Attached to this memorial were the signatures of 1,333 American and British missionaries. On September 20, 1906, an imperial edict which sounded the death knoll of the opium trade in China was issued—practically a verbatim copy of the memorial written by Dr. DuBose. Imperial edicts in the past had failed to get results. With the aid and encouragement now of the Premier, the most powerful man in the Empire, Dr. DuBose traveled through the provinces enlisting the aid of the local officials. The campaign increased in power and momentum, and before Dr. DuBose's death the triumph of the great crusade was assured.[16] To him more than to any other the ultimate destruction of the opium trade was due.

World attention was drawn to the Congo atrocities by Rev. William McCutchon Morrison and Rev. William H. Sheppard.

The Congo Free State, created by 14 signatory powers in 1885, with King Leopold of Belgium at its head, had been organized "to seek the moral and material regeneration of the Congo natives," and the nations which brought it into being bound themselves "to watch over and care for the native tribes." All control however was exercised by the Belgian government, in effect by Leopold himself, who reigned as an absolute monarch. Pledges concerning freedom of trade and the humane treatment of the natives were disregarded. All the land except that actually occupied by the natives was taken over by the state, that is, by Leopold. The licenses of all the small concessionaires were revoked and in their stead large monopolies, in which the government, that is King Leopold, owned 50 percent of the stock, were given exclusive control over large areas of land. All competition was thus eliminated, and the companies fixed their own price for the rubber and ivory which the natives were compelled to bring in. Required to labor for long hours, cruelly punished for any infractions of the rules, they became virtual slaves in what was "the most cruel and brutal regime of exploitation to which any conquered people were ever subjected."[17]

Reports had begun to circulate regarding the inhumane treatment of the natives, but it was Dr. W. M. Morrison who, by letters to officials, by articles in periodicals, and by publications in the *Kasai Herald*, the organ of the mission, became recognized as the foremost champion of the oppressed Congo people. Two years after his arrival in the Congo he wrote articles protesting atrocities, evidence for which had been uncovered by William H. Sheppard. The enormities had been perpetrated in the course of raids made by the notorious cannibal tribes of the Zappo Zaps, who were employed by agents of the state to collect tribute from a number of the tribes who did not acknowledge the sovereignty of the government. The 1900 General Assembly adopted resolutions approving the steps taken by the Executive Committee on Foreign Missions to bring to the attention of the King of Belgium and other civil authorities the brutal conduct of the Zappo Zaps, for which Morrison held the Congo authorities directly responsible.

On his first furlough, returning home after a stopover in Europe, Dr. Morrison stepped up his attack. He called public attention to the flagrant violations of the treaty by which the Congo State had been erected, the wanton vandalism and destruction of the country's resources, and the horrible cruelties practiced upon the natives. In Belgium an ineffectual effort was made to have an audience with the king. In England leading newspapers and magazines were open to him. He addressed the Aborigines Protection Society, citing several instances of oppression and intimidation witnessed by members of the mission in the ten-year period of 1892 through 1902. Public sentiment was aroused and Parliament passed a resolution which impeached King Leopold before the bar of Christendom for his high crimes and misdemeanors against humanity, and particularly for his violation of the provisions of the international act setting up the Congo Free State in 1884-1885. Arriving in America, Dr. Morrison continued his efforts to arouse public sentiment for the Congolese. In May he made a notable address before the PCUS General Assembly. He spoke first of the remarkable success of the Southern Presbyterian Mission at Luebo: in 1895 the first converts had been won; by 1903 the number had increased to nearly 2,000. Morrison then went on to emphasize the cruelty and abominations practiced by the government of the Congo Free State under King Leopold of Belgium, its absolute monarch—the natives reduced to slavery, 15,000 people hiding in the forests to escape such fate. Missionary Sheppard, he reported, had viewed 81 hands cut off from slain natives, and seen 45 bodies whose flesh had been partly eaten by cannibal soldiers of the government. The Assembly appointed a committee to prepare a memorial and present it to the President of the United States. Realizing that public sentiment must be aroused before our government could be induced to take a stand, Morrison continued to keep the subject prominently before the public through leading magazines and newspapers. He also addressed large audiences through the country, pleading for the emancipation of the Congolese.

A lengthy communication signed by three of the Southern Presbyterian missionaries to the Congo (W. H. Sheppard, L. C. Vass, and W. M. Morrison) gave further details—the natives, stripped of their ancestral lands and transported to distant parts of the country, were compelled at gun point to bring in rubber required as tribute. The missionaries described outrages which they had seen with their own eyes: "mangled bodies, severed hands, devastated villages, terrorized districts, cars loaded with government slaves, men captured and carried away right under our own eyes . . . truly a harrowing tale . . . all . . . done for gold."[18]

The interest of leading United States Senators was aroused, and for their use Morrison prepared a memorial, signed by 40 missionaries, representing nearly all the American Protestant bodies working in the Congo.

Though failing to secure the interposition of the Federal government, the pressure of public sentiment in the United States, in Great Britain, and in Belgium itself had its effect. A Belgian commission was appointed, whose findings supported the charges of the missionaries. The Congo was wrested from King Leopold's personal rule, and pledges of reform were given. But the promises given were not fulfilled, and the reforms were limited. As Dr. Morrison wrote to Dr. Chester: "I need only say that we are not now suffering from the old forms of outrage so much—hand cutting, slave raiding, murdering, etc., but I am sorry to say that I believe the sum total of suffering is much more than it was formerly."[19] Dr. Morrison's continued exposure of conditions led the British government to have their consul make an extended tour through the country to investigate complaints now coming from all quarters. The consul's published report confirmed charges made by Morrison and other missionaries. Publication of this report aroused more public indignation and the stock of the Kasai Rubber Company suffered a severe slump. Unable to proceed against the British consul the rubber company now brought suit against the missionaries responsible for the agitation, assuming no doubt that their conviction would help to disapprove their allegations.

In January 1908, Mr. W. H. Sheppard had written for the *Kasai Herald*, a magazine published by the mission and for which Dr. Morrison bore the responsibility of editor, an account of a trip through the Bakuba country, describing the wretched condition to which the natives had been reduced by the robbery and oppression of the rubber company, a government monopoly. The corroborating report of the British consul was published in September 1908. In February 1909 the two missionaries found themselves confronted with a suit for punitive damages to the amount of 80,000 francs ($16,000) for injury done to the business of the company by Sheppard's article and for libeling the government. They were ordered to appear for trial at Leopoldville and notified that if they failed to appear judgment would be given against them by default. As the date set was in the dry season when the mission steamer could not navigate the river and as Leopoldville was 900 miles from Luebo and more than 1,000 miles from the place from which native witnesses would have to be brought, the meeting of this summons was a physical impossibility, and, as was evidently intended, the missionaries would be condemned without a hearing.

The Southern General Assembly, after debate, adopted resolutions expressing their confidence in the two missionaries, and urging the President of the United States through the State Department to use his influence with the Belgian government to have the trial postponed and to see that the missionaries were properly represented. Rev. A. M. Fraser and Rev. R. C. Reed, strong advocates of the "spirituality of the church," protested this resolution on the grounds that it contradicted the historic position of the church. Said Dr. Fraser: "We ought to take our appeal to the King of Heaven and leave it there."[20] Dr. Chester fortunately urged the State Department to act; the trial was postponed (for a variety of reasons), and when the time came the two missionaries were defended by one of the leading trial lawyers (a non-believer) in Belgium. The charge against Dr. Morrison was dropped on technical grounds, and Mr. Sheppard was acquitted in a face-saving decision, which left the rubber company free of blame for the long continued exploitation of the Congo. In October 1909 King Leopold died and was succeeded by his nephew, Albert, a man of quite another stripe. "Under his benign and just admiration the reforms that had previously been attempted in vain were gradually put into effect."²¹*

Most widely known as a champion of the oppressed, Dr. Morrison was also a linguist of exceptional ability; he reduced to writing the Baluba and Lalua dialects, wrote a grammar and dictionary, and began a translation of the Bible which was completed under the supervision of his biographer and collaborator, Rev. T. C. Vinson. In addition, he was far-seeing as a missionary executive. To him more than any other was due the success of the Congo mission. When he began work at Luebo the native Christians were less than 50; when death halted his career, at the height of his influence, at the age of 50 (1918), there were 17,268 on the roll, more than a third of all the Protestants in the Congo—surprising when it is recalled that the Southern Presbyterian missionaries represented only 11 percent of the Protestant missionaries in the area. The educational work had been equally successful, and missionary stations had increased from five to 450. Informed missionaries, representing other denominations, regarded it as one of the most successful missions in all of Africa.²²

Growth of the mission was caused by a number of factors: the choice of a site in the midst of a numerous people, all speaking the same language and open, as others were not, to the gospel; the determination, dedication, and resourcefulness of the Southern missionaries of both races working together for the common good; the wide use of well-trained native evangelists left in charge of outpost stations (a method in which the Congo mission pioneered);²³ and, last, but certainly not least, the struggle of the mission for an overhaul of the Congo administration, looking toward a fuller measure of justice for the overly exploited Congolese. "Nothing was more important," comments Shaloff, "in winning the respect and loyalty of the people . . ."²⁴ "Perhaps the mission enjoyed the growth that it did," he concludes, "because the evangelists followed [Morrison's] advice to 'remember first and last that the natives should be treated as kindly and courteously as white people. We should always keep in mind that we are their servants and not their masters. Under their black skins they have feelings and responsibilities similar to ours,

---

* After 20 years in the Congo mission, Sheppard was invalided home; he recovered sufficiently to come to the aid of Rev. John Little in his work among the colored people of Louisville and, upon the organization of the Grace Church, became its pastor. His labors were ended by a stroke of paralysis in 1926; his death followed a year later. Funeral services, held in the Second Presbyterian Church of Louisville, were crowded with both white and colored friends; hundreds were denied admittance.

which ought to be respected. If we laugh at their customs, appearances or fetishes, we destroy their confidence in us and repel them.' The Presbyterian missionaries were not always able to adhere to this high standard," comments Shaloff, "but they tried."[25]

In 1911, Dr. Egbert W. Smith was elected as Co-ordinate Secretary, and, in 1912, Executive Secretary of Foreign Missions, a position retained for the next 20 years.* The outlook for world missions as reflected in reports from the fields never seemed brighter. Every nation in the world, including Tibet, was open to missionary work, and missionaries on the field were "full of faith and courage." Korea had begun its remarkable campaign for a million souls. The church in Japan was rapidly approaching self-support. A revolution in China appeared promising for the church as well as for the nation. "Now is the time" was the cry. In the Congo delegations from neighboring tribes were beseeching the missionaries to send teachers who might lead them into the light. New commercial relations were being forged between the United States and Latin American lands. In one year 33 new missionaries had been sent out, and 14 more were under appointment to go. Missionary giving meanwhile had reached a new high.

Dr. Smith, a popular and inspiring speaker, devoted his pre-eminent ability and tireless energy to the administration and promotion of the work. A Department of Missionary Education was established. The Presbyterian Progressive Program, which linked up the educational and spiritual development of the church with the practice of stewardship, expanded the committee's financial resources. In the six-year period following World War I income doubled.[26] Expansion over a 30-year period was as follows[27]:

	1894	1924
Home Income	$143,000	$1,390,000
Field Income	6,000	370,000
Foreign Workers	135	517
Native Workers	140	3,600
Organized Churches	37	275
Communing Membership	2,700	50,000

Fields occupied at this time, with date of opening, were China (1867), Brazil (1869), Mexico (1874), Japan (1885), Africa (1891),

---

* Dr. Chester remained with the committee as Secretary of Foreign Correspondence until his retirement in 1926.

and Korea (1892). In four fields work had been begun, but later discontinued: Italy, Colombia, Greece, and Cuba. The earliest missionaries, Dr. Donald W. Richardson later recalled:

> went out into strange lands. Before them were great unexplored geographical areas and all around them were vast stretches of territory upon which the messages of Christ had never yet trod. There was the lure and adventure of going out into great distances and among great dangers.
>
> The great distances have been done away with. The world has been drawn closer together. We are in a less romantic period, but the hindrances are just as great . . . The perils have not all passed away. Within the last five years one of our most beloved missionaries has met with martyrdom [John Walker Vinson, killed by bandits in China] . . . The representatives of our church have preached the Gospel of God's redeeming love. They have made the teaching of Christ to be understood and to become operative in the lives of many. Through them the people in other lands have learned of religious and political liberty, social righteousness, international justice, racial unity and human brotherhood. Through their efforts the worst of the social and moral evils in at least some sections of society have been driven into denial or shamed into concealment. They have helped to elevate the status of women and create new conditions for childhood. They have established orphanages and asylums and places of refuge and healing for lepers. They have reduced languages to writing and put up printing presses for the distribution of the Word of God and the production of literature. They have built hospitals and carried the ministry of healing to the sick. They have established institutions of learning, all the way from the kindergarten to the college and industrial school and theological seminary.—During the 74 years of our church's history she has sent to the foreign fields more than a thousand missionaries: 340 to China, 173 to Korea, 152 to Africa, 135 to Brazil, 102 to Japan, 49 to the Indians [before 1889], 48 to Mexico, 30 to Cuba, 10 to Greece, 4 to Colombia, and 3 to Italy . . .[28]

In Brazil, Mexico, and Japan, the Presbyterian churches, built up by Presbyterians U. S. and U.S.A., were the largest Protestant bodies in the land, and in Korea the Presbyterian Church was larger than all the other denominations together.

But the church was now entering upon a new era in its missionary work. In 1931, as effects of the First World War and the subsequent Depression were beginning to be felt, a Congress on World Missions of the Presbyterian Church in the U. S. was held in Chattanooga. It was built around the reports of six commissions which brought to the Congress the fruits of a year of study on various phases of the work.

"Since the World War," read one report:

> new movements have been under way among the nations, and vast new forces have been set in operation, movements and forces which have

shattered the tradition of white race supremacy, and reacted powerfully upon the progress of mission work in many ways and in many lands. The tremendous growth and spread of nationalism in various countries has issued in upheavals which tend to challenge and in some cases to restrict the efforts of the missionary. Churches established by missionaries on foreign fields are coming to full consciousness. They have become articulate, and are claiming new privileges and assuming new responsibilities. Many in our Church here at home seem to have suffered from post-war disillusionment and from the spirit of secularism, and have lost their former fervor and enthusiasm. Many are questioning the necessity and urgency of the Gospel message and are doubtful of its results when it is brought to bear on non-Christian people and non-Christian cultures. . . .[29]

The Report of Commission I, chaired by Dr. Walter L. Lingle, President of Davidson College, recognized that "while the essential features of the Gospel message are unchanging, there is still abundant room for the Christian worker and for the Church to make such adjustments in emphasis, in approach, in statement, and in methods as any particular age, country or circumstances may require in an ever changing world. In fact," it was emphasized, "it is vitally important that such adjustments should be made."[30]

The report continued:

It is not enough to preach what is usually called the spiritual message for the non-Christian world. If we are going to preach Jesus Christ and Him crucified, we must preach and practice these great social teachings which he taught and which he translated so perfectly into life. The social problems in our own country are great enough, but in non-Christian lands they are simply appalling. The problems created by poverty, ignorance, superstition, vice, disease, oppression and a thousand and one other ills are overwhelming. Industrial problems are looming large in countries like Japan. They are growing larger every year in such countries as China and India. The problems of nationalism, racial honor and racial relationships are growing in every part of the non-Christian world. . . .

The Gospel of Jesus Christ, including his social teachings, is the only remedy. . . . To recover the sense of missionary obligation, we need to learn that we are in danger not only of the wrath of God hereafter, but that here and now a world without Christ faces immediate disaster in its economic, social and international relationships. Our age is not primarily interested in what it conceives to be a mere figment of the theological imagination, but it is vitally concerned in present losses and disasters. It is this loss of a mighty conviction about salvation and of both a present and a future disaster to the soul and to modern civilization without Christ that has cut the nerve of missionary obligation and enthusiasm.[31]

The congress endorsed the report of this commission as a whole but emphasized, to avoid misunderstanding, that the real mission

or missionary motive "is still to save men from a peril—from hell."
And added, "Only this message can restore the sense of urgency, of
immediate danger, of crisis in salvation."[32]

The Jerusalem Missionary Council, meeting a few years earlier,
had recognized that the world missionary enterprise must be concerned with both individual conversion and with necessary social
change. Only in the report of the first commission at the Southern
Presbyterian congress was there any awareness of this double obligation, and the indications are that in this respect it spoke neither
to nor for the church. Commission VI, reporting on the "kind of
missionaries needed today," emphasized among other things the
need for courage, perseverance, a sense of humor, convictions, and
consecration—all desirable qualities—but gave no hint that a missionary must also be concerned with the bearing of the gospel upon
distressing conditions about which masses of the people were more
and more concerned.

"Our missionaries on all our fields," said Commission II, "should
place the great emphasis on direct evangelism, the preaching and
teaching of the Gospel and the seeking to win converts to the Lord
Jesus Christ."[33] The schools and hospitals controlled by the missions
should have this as their primary aim, it was asserted. As quickly
as possible the missions should turn over the fruits of their labors
to the younger churches on the various fields, releasing the
missionary forces and funds for evangelistic work on the frontiers.
"The control of the work begun by the missionaries," it was held,
"must pass from the mission to the church as rapidly as the developing ability of the church to direct this work makes possible. Where
the Church desires such a relationship, the missionary should identify
himself with the younger church and be subject to the jurisdiction
of its courts working where and how the church may appoint."[34]
Missions in the different fields, it was further indicated, "should
affiliate with and heartily aid all national co-operative movements
which are evangelical in spirit and aim, and which purpose to unite
separate Christian groups into one larger federation and promote
the growth of a common Christian consciousness."[35] "Native Christians," it was added, "should in all our mission fields be associated
with the missionaries in the direction of all schools, hospitals and
other institutions which have been established for furthering the advance of the Kingdom of Christ."[36]

The congress took note of the fact that with the turn of the century
there had dawned a new era in Foreign Missions—the beginning
of a great forward movement, which, with an interruption during

the war period, had continued for two decades. In 1920 Southern
Presbyterians were giving to the cause of Foreign Missions nearly
seven times as much as they were giving in 1902, 18 years before
($1,115,345). In the third decade the advance had been arrested.
Total receipts were somewhat greater in 1930 than they had been
ten years earlier, but membership of the church had increased,
and per capita giving had declined. Meanwhile costs had greatly increased, and there had been a steady curtailment of the church's
foreign force and work. In 1925 there had been 517 missionaries.
In 1930 the number had been reduced to 427.[37] There was no lack
of missionaries ready to go—in fact it was pointed out that the church
had never lacked for prospective missionaries—lacking was only the
money to send them. The congress adjourned with a new call to
missionary commitment and advance. It did not realize that the full
force of the Depression was about to fall upon the missionary enterprise and that another generation would pass before it recovered its
former strength.

Meanwhile rifts had appeared within the missionary force—a consequence of the modernistic-fundamentalist controversy rising in the
Northern churches in the United States and observed with growing
concern in the more conservative South—rifts which would seriously threaten the Southern Presbyterian commitment to full cooperation with other evangelical forces on the foreign field.

VI

Advances in Religious Education

Dr. James K. Hazen, who had succeeded Dr. Baird as Secretary of Publication in 1877, died in 1903. "Caution and conservatism" were said to have been the marks of his administration. And that, it was pointed out, was understandable, for he had taken office when the former secretary of the committee by unwise or unfortunate management had wrecked its affairs and shaken the confidence of the church from center to circumference.

> Caution and conservatism were the maxims of his business life, the foundation principles of his business methods, the warp and woof of his business character [commented Dr. R. C. Reed]. Caution and conservatism breathed in all his business correspondence, his business reports, in his business addresses . . . He was the very embodiment, the incarnation of caution and conservatism.
>
> The result was that he had not been secretary very long until the business was put on a safe basis and the confidence of the church was thoroughly re-established.

For this outcome of his policy of caution and conservatism Dr. Hazen deserved great praise. But all the time he was growing older, "and growing age is not likely to grow less cautious and conservative. [And so] he pursued persistently and relentlessly the policy with which he began [to the very end]. He made no ventures, he took no risks, he suffered no innovations. Perhaps [concluded the writer] this was well. Perhaps his term of office was not too long to secure the best results from caution and conservatism, but it was sufficiently long for the purpose."[1]

The call now, it was generally agreed, was for a more aggressive policy, and this, it was hoped, would occur under the new leadership. According to the new plan, drawn up largely by Dr. A. L. Phillips and accepted before Dr. Hazen's death, the Executive Committee of Publication and Sunday Schools, as it was now called, was to have editorial, Sunday school, and business departments. Mr. R. E. Magill, a businessman of Nashville, Tennessee, was elected Secretary and head of the business department; Dr. Phillips remained as head of the Sunday school department; and Dr. R. A. Lapsley became head of the editorial department. Dr. R. C. Reed, who had decried the long-continued policy of "caution and conservatism," rejoiced that the right men had taken over—all of them young, bold, and bouyant. With these men in the lead, he predicted, a forward movement in publication work was inevitable. Mr. Magill and Dr. Lapsley were to remain in their posts for a full generation and more and were in large measure to determine the educational program of the church during this period. Under their leadership the work of publication and Sabbath schools expanded, but theologically and ideologically the policy remained one of "caution and conservatism."

When Mr. Magill assumed office (in 1903) a series of seven periodicals with a total circulation of about three million copies was being issued, and a book store for the distribution of religious books was maintained. A staff of three editors and three clerks was operating the periodical and book departments. The total business reported to the General Assembly the previous year was $40,000. During Mr. Magill's tenure (1903-1934) the series of Sunday school periodicals increased from seven to 28 and 12 full-time and contributing editors were associated in the work. The circulation had grown from three million single copies to about 18 million per year. Colporteurs had been replaced by field workers, who distributed far more literature on a donation basis in one year than was done in five years under the old plan. The book department had likewise expanded.* The volume of business had grown from $40,000 in 1902 to over $600,000 per annum. One building had been erected and outgrown, then a second, in Richmond, Virginia, and a branch office had been opened in Texarkana, Texas.

The greatest expansion had been in the Sunday school area. Sunday schools did not become a universal adjunct of the churches

* During a 25-year period [1903-1928] 47 books of a theological character were published, most of them selling not more than 1,000 or 2,000 volumes. Among the best sellers were *Creed of Presbyterians* by Egbert W. Smith (18,700 copies), *Presbyterianism: A Challenge and a Heritage* by W. L. Lingle (13,000 copies), and *Presbyterianism* by S. L. Morris (13,000 copies). Thirteen biographical and historical works appeared, including lives of R. L. Dabney and B. M. Palmer, none of which sold more than 1,000 copies. Twenty thousand copies of M. R. Turnbull's studies in Genesis, Exodus, Leviticus, and Hebrews were sold; also a million and a half copies of the Shorter Catechism (Grant M. Stoltzfus, "Survey of the History and Present Publishing Program of the Presbyterian Church of the United States," term paper, Union Theological Seminary in Virginia, 1955).

until the early years of the 20th century. Until then the record was uneven. Thus, Lexington Presbytery, a progressive presbytery, with many strong rural churches, reported to the Synod of Virginia in 1871 that it had within its bounds 41 churches and 41 Sunday schools. About the same time (1879) the Synod of Kentucky reported 138 churches, 60 of which had no Sunday schools; the Synod of Missouri, this same year, reported Sunday schools in only 48 of its 132 churches; three years later the Synod of South Carolina stated that many flourishing Sabbath schools were to be found within its bounds; it greatly feared, however, that the greater number of churches had no school at all or one that had only a name to live and was actually dead. In 1895, out of 2,713 Presbyterian churches in the South, 900 reported no Sunday schools. In the Synod of Virginia, 133 out of 511 churches reported no Sunday schools as late as 1912. In many of the rural churches Sunday schools still operated only in the summer months, which led some to wonder why day schools could operate but not the Sunday schools.

Until 1875 the Publication Committee prepared its own Sunday school curriculum. Bible and catechisms composed the textbooks. Question books were prepared covering various books of the Bible. Pupils were expected to memorize the answers to these questions, and the Sunday school hour was used mainly in hearing the pupils recite.

The executive committee opposed at the outset the introduction of the New International Lesson series, but yielded finally to pressure which came from the churches. The new series, proposing to cover the whole Bible in the course of seven years, was warmly welcomed by the church at large. Sunday school helps now became readily available for teachers; religious journals set aside a column for the discussion of the lessons. Material presented was adaptable to both younger and older pupils. Normal classes for training teachers were introduced, and methods of instruction developed in the secular schools were brought over into the Sunday schools. Presbyteries were encouraged to hold Sabbath school conferences and teachers' institutes. In 1888 the General Assembly suggested that "wherever it is practicable, separate classrooms should be provided for the very young children, and also for the advanced classes."[2] Unfortunately, as instruction in the Sunday schools improved and became almost universal, home training diminished—or so the church courts began to complain. In 1890 it was reported to the General Assembly that accessions to the churches from the Sunday school exceeded those of the previous year by nearly 50 percent, though not more than one school in 20 reported any special religious interest, i.e., religious revival.

Agitation was now rising for the appointment of a General Sunday School Superintendent. Approximately one-fifth of the churches, it was pointed out, still had no Sunday schools, a proportion which had not significantly changed for a number of years. The Sunday school, it was alleged, was not being used as an evangelistic agency of the church, as it might be, particularly in view of the fact that one-half of the children in five states of the South (Arkansas, Kentucky, Louisiana, Mississippi, and Texas), and one-third in four others (Alabama, Missouri, Tennessee, and West Virginia), were in no evangelical Sunday schools. Critics lamented the Sunday school's "manifestly imperfect organization, its sadly defective teaching, and its imperfect organization in the face of its magnificent possibilities,"[3] and charged that there had been little progress of any sort in recent years. Other progressive branches of the church, it was pointed out, had appointed general superintendents with encouraging success, notably the Southern Baptists, the Southern Methodists, the Cumberland Presbyterians, and the Northern Presbyterians. Most commonly heard objections to the appointment of a General Superintendent were that the plan involved an unwarranted intrusion into the work of the pastors and sessions, charged under the Presbyterian system with the organization and conduct of the Sunday schools; that it was unwise and unsafe to multiply general officers; and that the church could not afford the added expense of such an office.

There were also those, like Dr. T. D. Witherspoon, professor in Louisville Presbyterian Theological Seminary and a former Moderator of the church, who lashed out at the so-called "new education" which ridiculed the old question-and-answer method of instruction and suggested the use of scissors and paste—kindergarten methods for young children. The idea of chairs of pedagogy in theological seminaries, and of training schools in pedagogy for Sunday school teachers, Dr. Witherspoon dismissed as utopian and visionary.[4]

In 1901, ten years after the idea had first been broached, Dr. A. L. Phillips, characterized as "the long-sought-for storage battery," became the first General Superintendent of Sabbath Schools and Young People's Work in the Southern Presbyterian Church. Born in Chapel Hill, North Carolina, two years before the Civil War, a graduate of the University of North Carolina, without formal theological training, he served pastorates in North Carolina and Alabama, became first a field secretary, and then Executive Secretary of the Committee of Colored Evangelization. Under his enthusiastic leadership the Afro-American Synod had been organized. Dr. Phillips returned to the pastorate for two years and then came to his new post in the Executive Committee of Christian Education.

The new Sunday school movement, on which the church after considerable hesitation had now embarked under the dynamic leadership of Dr. Phillips, included:

1. A graded system of lessons (prepared largely under Dr. Phillips' direction).

2. A careful and complete organization of the school, accomplished by division of the school into departments according to grade, by careful classification of the pupils in the different grades, by reports to the parents, by promotions and rewards.

3. Trained teachers, furnished by normal classes and institutes.

4. Separate classrooms. Regarded as a necessity in the public schools, they were now deemed equally important for the Sabbath schools.[5]

To forward his program Mr. Magill recalled that Dr. Phillips had to overcome traditional conservatism, indifference, pure ignorance, and all the forces which conspire against constructive forward-moving Christian enterprises—and, according to Mr. Magill, "right valiantly did he fight."[6]

During this period many organized Sunday school classes began to function as if they were churches. Using fixed orders of worship, men's Bible classes duplicated many features of the eleven o'clock service of worship. Emphasis was placed upon singing and music. Offerings were received and disbursed according to budgets prepared by class officers. "Many of these Bible classes had a strong evangelistic program and appeal. In some cities, after nationally known evangelists conducted lengthy revivals, independent or non-denominational Bible classes were established. These were not related to the church and usually were promoted by laymen who wished to perpetuate the activities of the revival. Too often, members of those large Bible classes had no further connection with the church. After Sunday school was over, the men went their own way."[7]

In 1908 the International Sunday School Association began preparation of a series of graded Bible lessons in addition to the Uniform Lessons. The Assembly, urged by its Executive Committee of Christian Education, opposed these graded lessons on the grounds that they contained erroneous views concerning regeneration, the inspiration of the Scriptures, and other important doctrines. But the demand of the church became so insistent that on January 1, 1915, the committee began publication of departmental graded lessons "wholly biblical, and distinctively evangelical" prepared in cooperation with the Presbyterian and Reformed Sabbath school agencies in the United States and Canada.[8] By 1929 these departmental graded lessons had a circulation almost as large as that of the Uniform Series. The junior and primary materials had been revised in accordance with the then current goals of religious education. "These goals represented a shifting of emphasis from a body of materials to be studied to a growing person whose spiritual needs were to be met."[9]

When Dr. Phillips died early in 1915 there had been marked progress: the number of schools had increased, more pupils were enrolled, modern methods of grading and instruction had been widely accepted, more than 3,600 teachers had fitted themselves for more efficient service by taking teachers' training courses. Through Dr. Phillips' efforts Sunday school committees in presbyteries had come to life, and the interests of the young people had come to have a large place on presbytery dockets. One of his last great visions and ambitions was the establishment of a Training School for Lay Workers where lay men and women might prepare themselves to become pastors' assistants, Sunday school superintendents, and workers in the mission fields at home and abroad.[10]

"Possessed of an optimistic temperament which bubbled over with enthusiasm and unfailing good humor [Dr. Phillips] was bold and fearless in his attack on laziness and indifference . . . a man with the vision of a seer, a doer of deeds . . . [of] boundless faith and simple life. . . ."[11] So he was recalled by his friends and associates.

Dr. Phillips was succeeded as Superintendent of Sunday Schools and Young People's Work by Dr. Gilbert Glass, pastor of the Presbyterian church at Johnson City, Tennessee, who remained in this position until 1924, when he became editor-in-chief of Sunday school publications. A few years earlier, he had mentioned as three recent developments in religious education: (1) cooperative leadership training schools offered all evangelical denominations by the International Sunday School Association; (2) the daily vacation Bible school which was being utilized more and more by the churches; and (3) the growing recognition of the home as the most fertile field for the religious instruction and training of childhood and youth—along with the hopes that it might be wrought into the practical educational program of the church.[12]

Success of the daily vacation Bible schools inspired more thoroughgoing programs of weekday religious education. In Chattanooga, largely under Presbyterian leadership, plans were worked out which long served as a model for other cities in the South. Protestant church-men, with Southern Presbyterians largely in the lead, formed a gen-eral education committee and succeeded in getting regular courses in daily Bible study in connection with both the high schools and the grade schools of the city. The church people of the city provided the salaries and employed the Bible teachers (acceptable to the school authorities) who taught credit courses in the high schools on school time.

In 1920 the Assembly's committee recommended that synods elect Superintendents of Sunday Schools and Young People's Work, offer-ing to pay their salaries if the synod would carry the expenses. Among the first to respond promptly was the Synod of Mississippi. Most of its superintendent's time (R. L. Landis) was given to the super-vision of the Sunday school work and the young people's societies, to conferences and training schools in the local churches, to the setting up and direction of summer conferences, and to the supervision of the work of the religious directors in the synod's schools.[13]

The plan quickly commended itself to other synods and by 1928 most of them had their own directors in the field. Their influence was quickly felt in the whole field of religious education.

The growth of young people's organizations was one of the most amazing developments in the decade of the '80's and '90's, con-tinuing through the first quarter of the 20th century.

Impetus to the development of this movement came in 1881 through the organization of a Society of Christian Endeavor by the Reverend F. E. Clark in his church in Portland, Maine. Eight months later another society was formed in Newburyport, Massachusetts. Gradually the number of societies increased, and then suddenly began to boom. The societies spread from denomination to denomi-nation, from state to state, and province to territory, and from nation to nation, "until now," reported the *Southern Presbyterian* of July 7, 1892, "there is scarcely a land on the face of the earth without its societies of *Christian Endeavor*. The last year has been the year of greatest growth in the history of the movement. Almost every evangelical denomination in America has either adopted the society as its own or allows its existence without any opposition. There are now at least 22,000 societies with a million and a quarter members in all parts of the world."

The purpose of Christian Endeavor was to encourage and train young people to participate in the life of the church. Each member pledged himself not only to attend but also to participate in the Sunday evening meeting—either leading in prayer or joining in the discussion of the topic of the evening; social gatherings were included on the agenda. Program materials came from the Boston headquarters of the international society. Each local society was subject to the authority of its local church, but regional, national and international gatherings, cutting across denomination lines, stirred interest, enthusiasm—and opposition.

The *Christian Observer* took notice of this rapidly growing movement and urged the church to be on its guard. It was important, it warned, that sessions assume control, particularly to prevent young women participating with young men in the public exercise of religion, a practice encouraged by Christian Endeavor, but clearly forbidden in the Word of God.[14] The *Southwestern Presbyterian* pointed out that Christian Endeavor was directed by Northern men, under no ecclesiastical control, and that heresy was bound sooner or later to intrude itself into a professedly creedless organization. It called upon the General Assembly to take hold of the matter and to organize these "warmhearted, fiery young soldiers under the blue banner of conservative Presbyterians."[15] The *St. Louis Presbyterian*, with similar concerns, pointed out that Methodists and Baptists had sought to protect their young people by organizing Epworth Leagues and Baptist Young People's Societies, and that Northern Presbyterians were beginning to form Westminster Leagues. To prove that he was neither bigoted nor an alarmist the editor called attention to a recent letter by Mr. Clark, accepting the presidency of the society, in which he insisted that Christian Endeavor Societies should advocate moral reforms and philanthropic measures, "which things, however they may properly enlist the individual Christian, are not," the editor insisted, "within the province of the church."[16]

The following year (1892) two overtures came up to the General Assembly from Texas, one from the synod, the other from the Presbytery of Brazos, requesting the Assembly to devise some plan of its own to enlist the activity and secure the cooperation of young people in church work. The Assembly encouraged the formation of such societies by the sessions of the church and under their care, and appointed an ad interim committee to report back to the Assembly.[17]

The movement among the young people, the committee reported, was the most distinctive and conspicuous feature in the life of the church. All evangelical churches, it noted, were hastening to define their attitude toward it. Methodists, Baptists, and Episcopalians had formed their own denominational bodies. The most popular and aggressive of the interdenominational organizations was the Young People's Society of Christian Endeavor, "Finding a home in all the evangelical churches, and planting itself in every land where a Christian church exists, it challenges the attention of all who are concerned for the coming of the Kingdom of God."[18]

The ad interim committee felt that it was unwise to suggest any special form of organization or to prescribe any method of work. It recommended only that all young people's organizations be under the full and exclusive control of the session, that the sessions maintain careful oversight of any inter-denominational affiliations into which the young people entered, and that "in societies which are constituted of both sexes, sessions should take care that the women and girls do not transgress the limitations of Scripture by conducting meetings or by engaging in public prayer and exhortation."[19] These proposals were held over for another year, heatedly debated, and then adopted.

Sentiment for a purely denominational organization was growing and the following year the Assembly approved a plan for such organization to be composed of "Westminster Leagues." No reference was made in this plan to the propriety of girls speaking or leading in prayer; the Assembly, however, reaffirmed its previous position on the issue, insisting that women and girls should not transgress the limitations of Scripture by conducting meetings or by engaging in public prayer or exhortation. The Assembly also warned against the danger to which young and inexperienced persons were exposed in attendance upon large and "promiscuous" conventions not under ecclesiastical control. Though Christian Endeavor was not named, it was this body which the Assembly primarily had in mind. It was, recalled Mrs. Winsborough, later to become Secretary of Women's Work, a victory for the conservatives.[20]

By 1903 there were nearly 1,000 young people's societies, operating under about 60 different names, without standardized programs, and with no instruction regarding the work of their own church. But the trend was definitely toward Christian Endeavor.

Despite continuing criticism, this movement grew until by 1917 there were 650 Christian Endeavor Societies in the church and only 61 Westminister Leagues.[21] In this year the General Assembly commended the organization of Christian Endeavor societies in all churches. The society, it was noted, had been richly blessed of God for 36 years. "It possesses sufficient flexibility for all varieties of circumstances and exercises no authority over the separate organizations incompatible with its control by sessions."[22] The Westminster League, though modeled after Christian Endeavor, had lost out to its interdenominational rival, after a long struggle on the part of conservatives to preserve it—in part, because the latter gave full scope to the participation of girls in its program and work, and, in part, according the *Christian Observer,* because the Westminster Leagues "lacked the inspiration that comes from concerted work with other churches of the community."[23]

In the early days of the young people's organizations there had been decided opposition to large gatherings of young people, and especially across denominational lines. The first "College Students' Summer School for Bible Study" was conducted by Dwight L. Moody at Northfield, Massachusetts, in July 1886. "The idea of the summer student conference," Clarence P. Sledd later wrote, "has been the most creative, contagious and kindling idea that has come out of the life of the Intercollegiate Young Men's Christian Association. It has spread not merely through all the student movements of the world but into many different sections of the life of the Christian church, and has become the pattern for the multitude of summer conferences for young people held under the auspices of the many branches of the Christian church in every land in recent years."[24]

In 1892 the summer conference idea was extended into the South. The conferences were held first at Knoxville, then near Black Mountain, North Carolina, in what later became the well-known Blue Ridge Conference. Conferences for young people began to be held at Asheville, North Carolina, under the auspices of the Young People's Missionary Movement in 1903. Five years later representatives came from nine denominations and 17 states—home and foreign volunteer movements were represented. Somewhat before this time the Reverend D. Clay Lilly, D.D., who would continue to guide the church in progressive ways in the generation ahead, wrote of impressions which had come to him at a young people's conference in Charlotte, North Carolina, and at a conference of theological seminary students in Richmond, Virginia. He confessed that his former lukewarmness toward such conferences had vanished, and that he had become alive to their tremendous possibilities for good. He suggested that it was time for the church to revise its "unwritten creed" regarding conferences, conventions, institutes, and other such meetings of Christian people.[25]

The church was, however slowly, then in process of revising its unwritten creed in such matters. In 1917 conferences for young people, sponsored by the four executive agencies of the church, having General Assembly endorsement, began to be held at Montreat.[26] This same year Texas young people were organized at Kerrville into the Texas Federation of Presbyterian Young People.[27] Oklahoma was the second synod to provide a young people's conference (1918), followed a year later by the synods of North Carolina and Georgia. Virginia, Kentucky, Mississippi, and Tennessee quickly followed suit, with the remaining synods not far behind. The *Christian Observer* termed these conferences the most helpful indication of progress in the church.[28] In the Synod of Virginia there were 188 young people registered the first year, 395 the second year, 545 the third year, and by 1925 the number had climbed to 641.

In 1925 the Synod of Mississippi held a conference for Intermediates. The idea spread quickly to Virginia and other synods. The success of the synod-wide conferences inspired conferences for both Intermediates and Seniors on the presbytery level.

Summer conferences for Christian workers of every sort were now being promoted throughout the Assembly. Montreat, 17 miles from Asheville, became the focus of Assembly effort. The Mountain Retreat Association had been formed by the Reverend John C. Collins, a Congregational minister of New Haven, Connecticut, in the 1890's. Most of the lots were bought by Northern people, several of whom built permanent homes and formed the town of Montreat. A few Southern people became interested and built summer cottages. A number of religious assemblies were held during the succeeding summers, though they were never largely attended. Mr. John S. Huyler, a candy merchant, whose life had been greatly influenced by Dwight L. Moody, became interested and built a hotel at his own expense to enable the Association to accommodate its summer visitors. Dr. E. O. Guerrant described it in the summer of 1900 as "a delightful resort for those who seek rest and recreation away from the heat and dust of cities and lowlands."[29] He spoke of it as the "Southern Northfield" for the annual conferences of Christian workers during the summer months. Thirty cottages had been built by this time, and "a commodious hotel" was being erected. The Reverend J. R. Howerton, pastor of the First Presbyterian Church of Charlotte, North Carolina (1896-1906), became interested in Montreat and made it the summer home of his family during nearly the whole of his pastorate. In 1905 he secured an option to buy the property from Mr. Huyler, who had been forced to take over the property because of its debts, provided he could secure the backing of the Presbyterian Church. Approved by the Synod of North Carolina, the stock was over-subscribed, and on November 21, 1906, the property (including 4,000 acres of land) passed into the hands of a new association, of which Dr. Howerton was the president and treasurer. Dr. Howerton wished Montreat to be a place where the various causes of the Assembly could be presented to general audiences, where Sunday school conventions and young people's missionary societies could be held. He wished "to make it something of a Chautauqua, something of a Lake Winona, something of a Northfield, something more than any of these."[30]

Conferences were held in the summer of 1907. The *Christian Observer* rhapsodized: "Montreat is a little Palestine in its geographical location. It is in the midst of our busy and noisy world, yet shut off so as to be a secluded and ideal retreat. It ought to become like Palestine, the center of spiritual and missionary force, the fountain of new and life-giving streams of holy influence in our church."[31] An ad interim committee appointed by the 1906 General Assembly reported that the Montreat project was exceedingly opportune and most important to the welfare and progress of the church, which needed just such provision for the theological freshening up on the part of ministers, the exploiting of the departments of Christian work as conducted by the executive agencies of the church, the promotion of Sabbath school and young people's work, and the ventilation of other plans of Christian service. In 1916 the majority of the common stock of the Mountain Retreat Association was transferred to a board under a declaration of trust designed to guarantee church control of the Association for all time without direct ownership. The total value of the property at this time was estimated to be approximately $200,000. Already Montreat was tending to become the heart and center of the church's life, a rallying point where leaders of the church were able to gather and meet for at least a portion of the summer. Under the dynamic leadership of the Reverend R. C. Anderson, who became president, treasurer, and manager of the Mountain Retreat Association in 1911, its influence and place in the life of the church would continue to grow in the years ahead. The General Assembly from time to time expressed appreciation for the services rendered to the church by the Mountain Retreat Association, and in 1919 endorsed a campaign throughout the church by the Association to raise $200,000 for the proper equipment of Montreat; two years later it apportioned to Montreat the sum of $200,000 out of the General Equipment Fund being raised throughout the church.

The question was now being raised regarding the Assembly's relation to Montreat, to which the church was contributing funds, and whose annual summer conferences were becoming more and more vital to the welfare of the church. An ad interim committee appointed in 1920 recommended that the amount promised from the General Equipment Fund not be made available to the Association until absolute ownership of the property of the Mountain Retreat Association be given to the "Trustees of the General Assembly," a corporation controlled by the General Assembly. The Assembly adopted instead a minority report which stated that the direct control of "Montreat" through the "Trustees of the General Assembly" would be neither wise nor practicable; and that the present control and ownership was solely in the interest of and for the advancement of the Presbyterian Church in the United States and of Presbyterianism in general; and that there was no apparent danger, nor could any remote conditions be foreseen to induce or incite fear that the control and management of Montreat would ever be otherwise.[32] So the question was settled for the time.

Since 1907 Montreat had been to all intents and purposes the Assembly's conference grounds. Other centers were sponsored by various synods; thus in 1908 the General Assembly commended not only the "summer school" to be held in Montreat, but also synodical schools in Crystal Springs, Mississippi; Kerrville, Texas; Searcy, Arkansas; and Nacoochee Institute, Georgia. The two additional conferences which would come to have a permanent place in the life of the church were those in Kerrville (later Mo-Ranch, near Hunt), Texas, and at Massanetta, Virginia.

The Westminster encampment for religious instruction and inspiration was organized at Kerrville in 1906 by a committee of the Presbytery of West Texas. At first it was simply a gathering place for the Presbyterians of western Texas. By 1914 it had become in effect a synodical enterprise, and six years later the synod had assumed full control. The attendance had risen from 60 in 1906 to 1,143 in 1920, including visitors from Texas, Oklahoma, Arkansas, and Louisiana. By 1932 the value of the property was estimated to be around $70,000. In addition to a dining hall and an auditorium there was a two-story roominghouse and 40 cottages available for rent; 48 other cottages, privately owned, had been built on property belonging to the encampment.[33]

The Synod of Virginia held its first conference at Massanetta Springs in 1921. The following year the hotel and other property of the resort, situated in the beautiful Valley of Virginia, and once a favorite watering place, came into the possession of the synod. Five conferences were held the second year—a young people's conference, a standard training school for church and Sunday school workers, a women's summer school of missions, a men's conference, and a Bible conference. The Massanetta board reported to the synod that the summer program had been a phenomenal success, largely attended, and financially profitable. Additional property was gradually

added, coming by 1930 to a total of 101 acres. The Young People's
Conferences at Massanetta continued to draw huge crowds through
the 1930's (one year there were 565 at the Intermediate Conference,
and 500 at the Young People's Conference), as did the Women's
Conferences, and the weekend conferences for men. The season
came to a climax in a two-week Bible Conference, with as many as
17 speakers appearing on the platform, including nationally and inter-
nationally known Bible lecturers, drawing large crowds representing
many denominations. The success of Massanetta was due largely to
Dr. William E. Hudson, who served as its manager for 25 years,
from 1922 to 1947. With an old straw hat in his hand, and a speech
that, like the hat, seldom changed, he welcomed a full generation
of youth and adults to summer conferences that helped to mold the
life of the church.[34]

In the decade of the 1920's, and for some thereafter, Christian
Endeavor remained the dominant youth organization. The Westminster Leagues, the Covenanters for boys, and the Miriams for girls, were
all dying out.* The ideal of one inclusive organization of and by all
the young people of the local church persisted, however, and to
accomplish this end the executive committee now (1916-1923)
promoted a plan for an organized class and department in the Sunday school that would perform all the functions of a young people's
society. The General Assembly accepted the plan as an alternative to
Christian Endeavor, but, influenced no doubt by Christian Endeavor
enthusiasts, declined to add its endorsement.[35] The number of organized classes increased, but the new plan as a whole made little
headway.

All efforts to muzzle girls in the youth organizations had now
been abandoned, though in some individual churches—for example,
the First Presbyterian Church in Staunton, Virginia—they could not
participate freely until an old and beloved minister was removed by
death.

A turning point in young people's work came in 1923. In this year
the General Assembly instructed its committee to employ a director
of the young people's division of Sunday schools and young people's
societies, whose duty it should be to promote the organization of
new societies where needed, to bind existing societies more closely
to the churches, and to enlist them more fully in the denominational
program. Rev. Walter Getty, elected to this post early the following

* In 1920 there were reported 1,125 Christian Endeavor societies with 32,929
members; and only 15 Westminster leagues, 15 Covenanter companies, and 24
Miriam chapters, with a combined membership of 1,059.

year, developed a comprehensive plan, enthusiastically endorsed by the General Assembly, covering youth activities in synod, presbytery, presbyterial district, and local church. With regard to the local church the plan was to take whatever organization the local church might have and bring to it a larger program of activity by having five committees corresponding to the five departments of the Presbyterian Progressive Program. It was also suggested that in each church there be a young people's council to act as a clearing house for all young people's activities.[36]

Mr. Getty hoped to incorporate the Christian Endeavor Societies into this overall program. "Everywhere I have gone over the denomination," he reported in 1926, "I have found an interest in Christian Endeavor that cannot be put down, an interest that has to be recognized . . . The difficulty," he continued, "has been that Christian Endeavor has not been serving the denomination as it should."[37] Mr. Getty was hopeful that a way would be found out of this difficulty, but it was this failure of Christian Endeavor to sense adequately the situation existing in its participating denominations that led little by little to its replacement by a denominational organization.

In 1926, a year after taking office, Mr. Getty promoted a Young People's Conference in Montreat, making large use of discussion groups—a procedure which had been followed for some time in Y.M.C.A. conferences, but which had no precedent within PCUS. The discussions revolved around three themes: Young People and Social Life, Young People and the Church, and Young People and World Fellowship. The young men and the young women met in separate groups, with leaders of their own sex, but came together finally to discuss findings of the various groups in open session. Topics discussed were those in which young people then had particular interest—among them dancing, petting, boy and girl relations, movies, auto-riding, cards, smoking, drinking, and the race question. The findings, to a later generation appear remarkably conservative. Regarding dancing, for example, the majority of the conference felt that this amusement should be considered with an open-minded desire to understand and appreciate real conditions and to carefully evaluate the various features of dancing by Christian criteria. A minority thought that dancing could be carried on constructively without sacrifice of Christian principles; the majority concluded otherwise. Petting was unanimously disapproved. A majority felt that it was proper for young people to attend the better class of movies. There was a diversity of opinions regarding "cards." The majority believed that there was no inherent wrong in the cards themselves, but that young people would be better Christians if they refrained from playing; a minority believed that they could without loss of Christian principles. There was general agreement that smoking, by both boys and girls, was physically and mentally detrimental, economically wasteful, and spiritually harmful. Drinking was disapproved by all, as detrimental to both character and influence. The conference agreed that the treatment of the Negro was a supreme test of Christianity in the South. They felt that the Negroes should be treated justly by the courts, that the state should provide equal—though not necessarily identical—opportunities for education, that separate churches served the best interest of both races. They commended heartily the work of the Inter-racial Commission. "This is the first time discussion groups of this nature have been conducted at the Young People's Conference," they concluded. "We believe that they have started the Young People to thinking on many vital questions which they have never seriously considered before . . ."[38]

Sharp criticisms had been voiced at the beginning of the open forums, and the conference was hardly over before the storm broke furiously over Mr. Getty's head. Mr. McGill, Executive Secretary of the Publication Committee, wrote a severe letter of condemnation. It was "a frightful error," he held, for the leader to call continually for expressions of the minority viewpoint, "in other words, from the radical element . . ." "The Montreat Conference," he continued, "has been held up as a model for the conferences of the whole church, and if the amazing findings issued today ever get abroad the Young People's work of our Church will be subject to an attack the like of which we have never seen through these past years of stress and difficulty. The function of the church," he insisted, "is to instruct its young people, not to encourage them to follow the lead of bolshevistic crowds, which have been gathering under other auspices. From the beginning of the open forums," he continued, "I began to hear sharp criticisms . . . of the amazing subjects the Young People were permitted to discuss in mixed meetings . . . subjects . . . which have always been beyond the pale in good society in the South . . ." Synodical leaders of young people, wrote Mr. McGill, were strong in their condemnation and had expressed the hope that the discussion method would never again find a place in a young people's conference. The Montreat management, he stated, would not consent to the holding of another conference of young people which would end with such a paper as the one just adopted.[39] The Young People's Advisory Council (composed of adult leaders, representing the various synods), took prompt action leading to the discontinuance of the

Montreat Young People's Conference on the grounds that it was no longer needed.

There were those, in positions of prominence, who defended the discussion method which had been followed in the conference and the findings to which it had given rise—Dr. Egbert W. Smith, Secretary of the Executive Committee of Foreign Missions; Dr. W. Taliaferro Thompson, Professor of Religious Education in Union Theological Seminary; Mr. Edward D. Grant, then Educational Secretary of the Foreign Missions Committee; and others. Wrote Mrs. John Bratton, a leader among Presbyterian women: "I can very well see why criticism would come from some people, and if [the findings] are published the criticisms will pile mountain high. But we might as well 'face the music'. We cannot fit these young people into the same molds which developed us. These young people are thinking, really thinking today as they did not in my generation. I am afraid my sympathies are with the young people . . . the church . . . [must] be allowed to change if it would come nearer meeting the needs of the younger generation . . ."[40]

The executive committee, however, thought otherwise, and took prompt action by relieving Mr. Getty of his position. Two years later (in 1929) Dr. John L. Fairley, a Wilmington, North Carolina, pastor, was elected Co-ordinate Secretary of the Executive Committee of Religious Education and Publication with "exclusive charge of the Department of Religious Education under the direction of the Executive Committee." The following year the Young People's Advisory Council expressed the judgment that the time had come to set up a denominational young people's organization and recommended that steps be taken in this direction. As Dr. Wallace M. Alston, looking back, commented: "A new turn in the road . . . had been made. A denominational program was being demanded. Christian Endeavor's absolute sway over our young people's work was definitely waning."[41] The felt need was for a more unified organization and for a program based on the total program of the church. Dr. Fairley was elected because it was felt that he could develop such a program.

It came a year later, entitled "The Kingdom Highways," "an inclusive educational program, built on the basis of the program of the church" and with a unified form of organization. The now seven departments were those of the Presbyterian Progressive Program— Spiritual Life and Evangelism, Foreign Missions, Home Missions, Christian Education and Ministerial Relief, Religious Education and Publication, Stewardship of Possessions, and Christian Social Service. The young people's offerings were to go to the support of the total program of the church. The program was intended to function through the church services, the Sunday school, the young people's vesper services, through-the-week meetings, the personal devotional life, the home, the daily vacation Bible schools, the weekday church school, young people's conferences, and intermediate camps. Provision was made for use by groups which wished to retain their Christian Endeavor affiliation. Topics recommended for the evening program at the outset and for some time thereafter were of the pietistic type —as they were in the Christian Endeavor program—such as Trust, Adoration, Prayer, Loving by Service, Guidance, Joy, Courage, the Great Commission. Topics dealing with the particular problems of youth, or with burning social issues confronting the nation or the region, were conspicuous by their absence.

Christian Endeavor did not yield to the new set-up without a struggle—its partisans offered a spirited defense, insisting that denominational objectives could be obtained through the Christian Endeavor framework, and that it offered in addition advantages of a broader worldwide fellowship.[42] Their societies continued in the church for many years but with steadily diminishing support.

Meanwhile Young People's Leagues, under the guidance of Young People's Councils, had been organized in presbyteries and synods. In 1931 as the capstone there was erected the Young People's Council of the General Assembly, composed of the presidents of the Young People's Leagues of the various synods. The following year, on recommendation of the council, the Young People's Advisory Council composed of adult leaders of the young people was disbanded. The Young People's Council elected three adult advisers to serve as full members with voting power, but the indication was clear—youth was assuming the leadership of its own movement.

VII

Toward a Sound Educational System

Public school systems were established in all Southern states after the Civil War, but standards remained low and popular support was not enlisted until after the turn of the century.* Boys and girls were prepared for college by private schools and academies, usually having poor equipment and a temporary existence.

Under these circumstances, some education-minded Presbyterians, with returning prosperity, reaffirmed their traditional ideal, never realized in practice: a college in every synod, an academy or high school in every presbytery, a parochial school under the control of every session.

The Synod of North Carolina, in 1888, for example, "urged its churches to establish wherever practicable or convenient one or more primary schools for the younger children under twelve years of age in which shall be taught reading, writing, the four primary rules of arithmetic, with primary geography, etc., and also the Bible and the Catechisms of our Church; said schools to be *free* to all the poor of our Church, and if practical *free* to all."[1] It also recommended that in every church or in each suitable group of contiguous churches steps be taken to establish a classical or high school as preparatory to the college or university.

---

* Before 1900 there were a few real high schools in some of the cities. In 1903-1904 27.7 percent of the male population of voting age in 11 Southern States were illiterate and of these 12.3 percent were white. The length of the school term was only 170 days for both white and colored schools. The average funds expended for each child in the South was only $3.89 as against an average for the whole United States of $11.20. Florida and Texas were the only states expending half the latter amount. Children in Alabama attended schools an average of 73 days (Charles William Dabney, *Universal Education in the South* [Chapel Hill: University of North Carolina Press, 1936], Vol. II, pp. 78, 397).

Seven years later synod's Committee on Church and Christian Education reported that Davidson College was more prosperous and Peace Institute for Young Ladies was better equipped than ever before. In secondary education much progress had been made. The older preparatory schools were never more prosperous; a number of new ones had been founded—some exclusively for boys, others for both boys and girls. Mebane High School, sponsored by Orange Presbytery, received particular commendation. Fayetteville Presbytery, it was noted, had accepted a proposition to locate a female school at Red Springs (to become Flora MacDonald). Concord and Mecklenburg Presbyteries had taken joint action to form a school for girls (to become Queens College). Parochial schools were said to be growing in favor, more ardently advocated than for many years past. Some of these were supplementary to the public schools, and nowhere, according to the committee, was there any friction between the two.* J. B. Shearer, chairman of the committee, pointed out in this connection that in the rural areas and in many of the small towns and villages the sessions of the public school were brief and inadequate. Many of the children were needed for work in the fields or in the factories; but there were many others not so employed, who ought to be in school, and others who would be spared for schools if there were proper facilities.[2]

In 1895 the synod reported that parochial schools were growing in favor and were more ardently advocated than for many years past. The number of such schools, it stated, had greatly increased.[3]

"The free or public schools in our country districts by reason of limited funds and constant change of teachers," explained Orange Presbytery, "are very imperfect and inadequate—a very poor substitute for the parochial or church schools of former years. Yet they are the only schools available in many sections."

"Let us return to the system of our fathers," the presbytery urged, "and plant the school house by the side of the church and give to the children of our churches and of their neighborhood an elementary as well as a liberal Christian education."[4]

In other areas also numerous secondary schools were being es-

---

* "Our public and graded schools . . . are admirable and are doing great good," wrote Rev. Dr. J. Henry Smith, "but they utterly ignore the study of Greek . . . and all our candidates who have attended no other schools than these, go to the college sadly deficient . . . This makes a special appeal to every Presbyterian minister and church to favor and patronize [the denominational] schools" (NCP [December 27, 1894]).

tablished under private auspices, with the blessing of the church, some coming for a time at least under its control.*

Encouragement for the establishment of a male high school was given, for example, in a report to the Synod of Memphis: "We find," the ad interim committee stated:

> that there is a public school system in operation throughout your territory—that is, in both the states of Tennessee and Mississippi—schools which are sustained by state and county and in some instances municipal funds, and of which the tuition is free, or of a merely nominal rate. We find further that in Mississippi the free schools teach only the primary grades, i.e. the first five grades of the ordinary graded schools. In Tennessee the course runs up three grades higher. In some cases where the state and county fund is supplemented by the municipal corporation there is provided a course that is almost a complete preparation for college studies. But in most cases, if not all, there is between the most advanced grade of these schools and the lowest college course an unoccupied space, a space for which the high school provides.
>
> We find that there is a class of people which is not entirely satisfied with the state schools, notwithstanding the advantages of free tuition. The several considerations—that the text books are chosen by state authority, that the teachers of these schools in some cases are not Christians, and that in these schools children of all sorts, good, bad and indifferent are gathered, when taken together form such a decidedly strong objection to the free schools that a class of well-to-do people prefer to patronize the private or church school when this can be conveniently done.[5]

Next year it was reported that hopes for a synodical female college and a high school for boys had not materialized, but that Chickasaw Presbytery was endeavoring to carry forward the work at Pontotoc; North Mississippi was doing good work with the well-established Female College at Holly Springs; Western District was beginning work at Bethel Springs and Union City. "We cannot but hope," said the synod, "that those are the beginnings of greater things."[6]

In 1898 East Hanover Presbytery overtured the General Assembly to appoint an ad interim committee to consider the whole matter

---

* Among the latter were: Cluster Springs Academy, Hoge Academy, and Stonewall Jackson Institute in Virginia; Lewisburg Female Institute in West Virginia; Red Springs Seminary, Peace Institute, Sprunt Institute, Banner Elk, and McRae Institute in North Carolina; high schools in Florence and Columbia, South Carolina; Donald Fraser High School, Euharlee Academy, and Blackshear Academy in Georgia; Chamberlain-Hunt Academy and French Camp Academy in Mississippi; Silliman Female Institute in Louisiana; Searcy Female Institute in Arkansas; Stuart Academy in Texas; Elizabeth Aull Female College and Elmwood Female College in Missouri.

of the systematic education of the young. In support of the overture, Dr. R. P. Kerr pointed out that "even the reading of a passage from the Bible" was rapidly disappearing from the daily exercises of the public schools. "The nation," he said, "is trying an experiment fraught with momentous consequences, of educating the children in secular learning, to the neglect and exclusion of the moral." Such godless education, argued Dr. Kerr, "only makes [man] more powerful for evil. It is putting a rifle in the hands of a wild Indian and teaching him to use it, before he has become civilized and moral." The whole system of public education, in Dr. Kerr's opinion, was wrong, "and it is time that the Church and parents awoke to their responsibility for the proper education of children."[7]

Rev. R. R. Howison, D.D., in opposing Dr. Kerr's proposal on the floor of presbytery, pointed out that "the central and fatal error of his position and argument is his denial that it is the proper duty and function of a state or nation to educate, in such secular learning as will properly fit them for duty as citizens, the children and young people who are unable by poverty or otherwise, to attend schools in which money is charged for tuition. In other words, his effort is to overthrow the whole 'common school' system of the United States.—He objects to any measures to be adopted by the civil government for educating the children by a system of common schools on the ground that such measures would be what he calls 'paternalism' . . ."[8]

The report of the ad interim committee, appointed in response to the overture from East Hanover and other presbyteries, set off an extended debate in the 1899 General Assembly, in which the relations of church and state and their functions with respect to education were discussed at length. Dr. Kerr, supporting the committee's recommendation, pled for the development of a parochial school system, in which Bible and catechisms were taught, under the control of trustees, appointed by the various church courts. Dr. J. W. Walden proposed, as a substitute, Christian schools at the various levels, supported by Christians as individuals. "The common school system," said Judge W. K. James, in support of the substitute, "is an example of the evil tendency of paternalism in the State, and Church education is an example of ecclesiastical paternalism, the tendency of which is only evil." Dr. James Woodrow, leading the debate against the committee's report, denied that education was the business of the church at all. There are three divine institutions, he affirmed: family, church, and state. "The state has police power and that only. The principal that the state has a right to educate, is socialistic; it has just as much right to feed and clothe its citizens." He acknowledged that the church had a right to educate its own ministers, but that was all. "The mission of the church is the preaching of the Gospel." Education is the business of the family. "The scheme of church education is a usurpation of the rights of the head of the family to whom it is left to say how and where his children shall be educated."[9]

Woodrow and Walden weakened their case by acknowledging that their principles demolished the public schools as well as the church schools.

The ad interim committee report, which was overwhelmingly approved, declared, "The General Assembly does not consider it safe for any church to turn over to any other parties, either religious or civil, the entire education of her sons and daughters." It hailed with delight "the unmistakable signs of a re-awakening, not in our church only, but in all the evangelical churches, to the great importance of Christian education." It recorded its satisfaction with the increasing prosperity, success, and usefulness of the higher institutions of learning, male and female, under direct church control and denominational influence, and rejoiced in the increasing number of high schools, academies, grammar schools, and mission schools, which had more or less direct church control. It recommended that synods, presbyteries, and church sessions undertake whatever was practicable in the furtherance of this cause. Guidelines were laid down for "Westminster" schools, to be founded by one or more local congregations. The Assembly appointed a Permanent Committee on Church and Christian Education, and urged synods and presbyteries to do likewise, in order that this matter might be kept constantly before the church.[10]

Synods and presbyteries responded to this plea and renewed their efforts to build schools, with a Bible-oriented religion, on all three levels: primary, secondary, and collegiate.

The same year in which the General Assembly hailed the new interest in education which was being manifested by Presbyterians and called upon the church to enlarge the enterprise with even greater vigor, an educational conference sponsored by clergymen met in Capon Springs, West Virginia. The original idea was to cultivate more favorable sentiment in the South toward better education facilities for the underprivileged groups, both Negro and white, but as the meetings progressed, the broader idea developed of an improved system of public education for all.[11] Other conferences followed. Distinguished scholars, philanthropists, and publicists from the New England, Middle, South Atlantic, and Gulf states were present and participated in the discussions, which embraced all branches of school work from the kindergarten to the university.

The idea caught fire and spread. The long-awaited renaissance of Southern education had begun—a fervor for public schools matching that in advanced states preceding the Civil War.[12] Improvements followed, not only in the graded schools, but also in the high schools, whose numbers until now had been severely limited.*

There were some who feared the growth of a secular education, and looked upon its growth as an even greater challenge to the church to found schools where proper training in the Bible might be given. There were some also who looked upon the rise of a system of state schools as a danger to the struggling schools of the church.

In general, however, what has been said of North Carolina could be said of other Southern states: "The relationships between church and state in the realm of elementary and secondary education were friendly and cooperative. Church and private schools occupied the field until 1840, when the state came in to supplement the work already being done. The state took over much of the spirit, purpose, and materials of the church institutions. When, after the Civil War, the state system of public schools broke down, it was the churches which kept alive interest in education. And when the economic and political conditions of the commonwealth regained their equilibrium, the churches threw the full weight of their influence back of a movement for a state-supported system of common schools. In general, the church institutions retired as the state advanced to occupy the field."[13] New schools were opened by the church, for the most part, now only in remote sections where state schools had not yet been opened or where they remained inadequate.

The gradual withdrawal of the church from the field of both primary and secondary education was eased by the fact that it was never financially able to maintain such schools in any number, that education in the state schools was not yet completely secularized (Bible reading and prayer remained the general practice), and perhaps even more by the fact that Presbyterians had traditionally given strong support to all efforts to extend public education to the masses.

It may be observed in this connection that the first State Superintendent of Education, elected by popular vote under Virginia's new constitution adopted in 1902, was Joseph D. Eggleston, a deeply religious Presbyterian elder, later President of V.P.I. and of Hampden-Sydney College. The public schools in this state had made little

---

* Churches and private agencies supplied practically all secondary education in North Carolina prior to the 20th century. In Virginia the 74 public high schools reported in 1905-1906 had increased to 218 in the session 1906-1907. See Buck, *op. cit.*, p. 143; Gobbel, *op. cit.*, p. 201.

progress in the ten-year period following the resignation of Dr. W. H. Ruffner. It was Dr. Eggleston who redeemed the system from political interference and brought Dr. Ruffner's well-conceived plan to fruition. In a commencement address delivered at V.P.I. in 1941, Dr. Jackson Davis, one of Eggleston's associates in the crusade for better public schools, said:

> The spread of education to all the people, the dream of Thomas Jefferson, was the epic achievement of the South in the first part of the Twentieth Century, and one of the most valiant captains in that fight was—Dr. J. D. Eggleston . . . When Dr. Eggleston became Superintendent of Public Instruction, we used to hear about the public free schools with a sort of connotation of public charity on the word "free." Under his zeal and irresistible energy the people of the state in many counties were soon taxing themselves to the constitutional limit and then going down in their pockets to make up funds enough to build high schools, put on school buses, and extend the school term. The term "free school" was forgotten. People everywhere talked with the pride of ownership of "our schools" and they learned that this was the most profitable investment they had ever made.[14]

While the Presbyterian Church slacked its efforts to build primary and secondary schools; its struggle to maintain institutions of higher education remained—with final success for a time in doubt.

The *Southern Presbyterian* reviewed the situation as it existed at the close of the century. In Virginia, said the editor, there is Washington and Lee University, which is patronized by Presbyterians and has a sort of Presbyterian strain in its blood, but which cannot be called a Presbyterian school. There is old Hampden-Sydney, Presbyterian, but not owned by any of its courts. Then there is King College, just across the Virginia line in Bristol, Tennessee. It is Presbyterian and is owned by presbyteries. Financially, it is the weakest of the three, but has done a wonderful work for the church. Its men are filling prominent pulpits all over the South. In North Carolina, Presbyterianism is honored by stately old Davidson. It is grounds for rejoicing that we have at least one really strong Presbyterian college between Maryland and Texas on the Atlantic and Gulf coast which is not pitifully weak. Yet Davidson could advantageously absorb several hundred thousand dollars. In South Carolina 20,000 well-to-do Presbyterians rejoice in a perfect paralysis of educational interests. Some are Davidson supporters, but Davidson does not seem to be very much the gainer thereby, either in men or in money. Some are South

Carolina State College supporters. They pay their taxes and call this supporting the college. The Presbyterian College of South Carolina at Clinton is almost of age. Nearly 21 years ago it was founded in poverty, and there it remains. It has friends who helped it in a small way, so that it has grown slowly, but, oh, how slowly.

We had hoped much from the last meeting of the Synod of Georgia, continued the editor. We thought Donald Fraser High School would bloom into a full-fledged college with the united support of all the men and means of the great Synod of Georgia. We were disappointed. How much longer Georgia intends to wait before it establishes a Presbyterian College for boys we do not know. They say, Agnes Scott is to have a large endowment. We hope she will get a million, but unless the synod educates a few boys, where will husbands come from to match those beautiful and cultured Agnes Scott girls? Florida Synod does not have a college, male or female, nor a seminary, no, nor so far as we know, even a high school within her bounds. There are not many Presbyterians in Florida, but surely something can be done for a high school, if nothing more. In Alabama there is no college for boys, nor in Mississippi, nor in Louisiana. There are two in Texas, Austin and Daniel Baker, but they are very poor in this world's goods. Arkansas has Arkansas College, with good men and promising students, but with inadequate buildings and almost no endowment. Tennessee rejoices in the Southwestern University at Clarksville, which fortunately has a wealthy patron in New York, which saves the pocketbooks of Tennessee Presbyterians. King College, at Bristol, on the eastern edge of the state, has been mentioned. Missouri has Westminster College at Fulton. Kentucky has Central University at Richmond. Both are excellent institutions, ranking with Davidson and Southwestern to make them the four strongest Southern colleges owned by Presbyterians. It is pleasant to have some grounds for congratulation in the existence of a few strong colleges, but it is sad they are so few. We have plenty and to spare of so-called female colleges, but they all need endowments in order to enable them to educate those who are lacking in means.[15]

The 1900 General Assembly received an overture from the Presbytery of Louisville asking that a fund of $1,000,000 be raised for the permanent work of the church to be known as the 20th-Century Fund. The Assembly approved the request, stating that the object of the fund would be to promote and put upon a surer basis the cause of Christian education, to endow and more fully equip theological seminaries, schools, colleges, and other institutions of learning both for males and females, and to found such new institutions of similar character as may seem advisable. Each synod or presbytery or division of the church cooperating in the movement was to employ such agencies as it deemed wise, choose the institution or institutions for which its funds should be raised, and have entire control and direction of such funds.[16]

The church papers welcomed this step, pointing out that it coincided with movements already rising within the synods:

> If there ever existed a church which needs a million dollars for education [commented the *Southern Presbyterian*] it is ours. Leaders in demanding an educated ministry, we are laggards in developing educational institutions. We have relied upon state and private institutions and institutions of other denominations to educate our sons to such an extent that we are now far behind denominations which have never paraded their interest in education as we have. Once the banner denomination in pushing the development of educational interests we are now bringing up the rear. Our glory as an educational denomination has departed. We are proud of the fact that our Assembly is waking up and that we are to vie with our Methodist brethren in the cause of education.[17]

Five years later, on the basis of the partial reports submitted to it, the committee estimated that the following amounts had been raised:

Synod of Texas	$250,000
Synod of North Carolina	$111,199
Synod of Missouri	$ 85,000
Synod of Alabama	$ 75,000
Synod of Virginia	$ 75,000
Synod of Georgia (Agnes Scott)	$ 35,000

Unfortunately not all of the amount pledged was paid; a number of schools had been aided, but far more needed to be done if Presbyterian schools were to be maintained on a level comparable with those of other denominations.

Prior to 1900 the General Assembly had accepted no responsibility for higher education and except for theological education had given little direction or aid. There had been no well-defined plans and no unity of action. In 1899 a step in this direction was taken by the erection of a permanent committee (but without a full-time secretary) on the Church and Christian Education, which at least served to bring the subject regularly before the Assembly. Neither the Assembly nor its committee assumed any responsibility for the raising of the 20th-Century Fund. Need for greater effort was revealed in the fact that not a single Presbyterian college was on the accredited list of the newly founded Southern Association of Schools and Colleges.

True [reported Professor H. B. Arbuckle of Agnes Scott], Washington and Lee has an honored place there, but we cannot as a church lay claim to Washington and Lee, though we recognize the fine work it has done for us, and we value its influence as Presbyterian. I have reason to believe that Davidson College will at an early date fall in line . . . We . . . hope to see it a member of the Association next year. Still, it remains that we have not a single member now and we have not a college that has sufficient endowment to insure its future success . . . The Methodists have four colleges on the list, the Episcopalians one, the Baptists one, and the other institutions are our most strongly endowed state universities [Vanderbilt, the University of North Carolina, the University of the South, the University of Mississippi, the University of Tennessee, the University of Alabama, the University of Missouri, the University of Texas].[18]

The General Assembly in 1906 went a step further and established an Executive Committee of Schools and Colleges, instructing it "to make a thorough study of present conditions and movements in our educational work, and a similar study of the conditions and movements in educational work in general, and put the results of their investigations in such form as will make them practically available for the information of our people. . . ."[19] In 1909 the Reverend William E. Boggs, D.D. was made secretary and succeeded in launching a loan fund, from which any boy or girl of approved character and aim in life might secure a loan of $100 a year while taking the four-year course in one of the church's colleges. The following year the Executive Committee of Schools and Colleges was consolidated with the Executive Committee of Ministerial Education and Relief, of which Dr. Henry H. Sweets was Executive Secretary, and the committee was renamed "The Executive Committee of Christian Education and Ministerial Relief." Dr. Sweets, sole secretary after June 1912, was the man who, for the next generation, would provide leadership and direction for the total educational program of the church.

The times were ripe. The Synod of Texas and the Synod of South Carolina, which had recently made successful canvasses for much needed funds, were now planning statewide educational systems. North Carolina, Missouri, Mississippi, and Kentucky were thinking in similar terms.

In the summer of 1913, under the chairmanship of Dr. Sweets, a conference was held in Montreat, attended by representatives of the synods along with representatives of the various schools and colleges throughout the Assembly. "When I saw the number, the wisdom, and the enthusiasm of these men," wrote Dr. Walter L. Lingle, "and saw them organized for the first time for a definite campaign, whose purpose it is to usher in a revival of Christian Education, I felt the hour had struck."[20] It was indeed the beginning of a new era of educational advance.

Similar conferences held the next two years led to agreement on standards for Presbyterian institutions; to the erection of a permanent advisory committee on education with the Executive Secretary of Christian Education and Ministerial Relief as chairman and composed of one member from each synod; to the formation of a Presbyterian Educational Association of the South meeting annually for the purpose of advancing the cause of Christian education within the bounds of the church; to an elaborate campaign of education, calling upon Presbyterians to resume the sadly neglected educational task in which they had once been pioneers; and, finally, to a systematic effort to aid the synods in raising essential financial support. A "field force," at first under the capable leadership of Dr. M. E. Melvin and then of Mr. S. W. McGill, moved into one synod after another to raise a stipulated sum, a million dollars, more or less, according to the strength of the synod and its needs. Within a period of eight years (1918-1926) the entire Assembly was covered. In practically all synods, the campaign was counted a success. They had gone "over the top"—so far as pledges were concerned. Collection, as hard times approached, proved another matter.

When the campaign began, the colleges were indeed in imminent peril. Costs were mounting and conditions were changing; what could be done a generation earlier, with limited equipment, and meager endowment, was no longer possible. "Had it not been for the liberal response in recent campaigns for equipment and endowment," Dr. Sweets reported in 1923, "not one of our colleges would be recognized as of standard grade."[21]

In 1925 the Executive Committee of Christian Education and Ministerial Relief reported progress made on the 12-point program which it had proposed and which the General Assembly had approved ten years earlier:

1. "To complete the organization of educational forces in each of the synods." Before 1916 there was much confusion. Some synods had synodical plans; others had none. Now almost every educational institution had been brought under its own synod's control, and the place, needs, and opportunities of each institution were given careful consideration in the light of the total synodical responsibility.

2. "To awaken our people to the vast importance of Christian Education." Once more the Presbyterian Church is awake and alive to the vital importance of the teaching function of the church, said the

executive committee. It noted in this connection that more than 86,000 individuals had contributed to the educational movement in the various synods, and that this was probably more than 100 times as many as had contributed in the previous 30 years.

3. "To inform all Presbyterian parents of the advantages of education under Christian auspices." In 1915 the General Assembly had directed the executive committee to study the place and use of the Bible in public schools and the care of Presbyterian youth in state institutions. The committee reported some progress in this direction.

4. "To increase the enrollment of our Presbyterian schools, colleges and theological seminaries." The enrollment in the church institutions, it was claimed, had kept pace with the marvelous growth of other educational institutions. Since 1916 there had been an increase in the attendance of all the church's schools and colleges of 4,895.

5. "To increase the physical equipment and endowment of all institutions to standard requirements." Much progress had been made, the committee declared, calling attention to the $11,500,000 raised in cash and pledges by the educational movement, but much remained to be done. Not one of the Presbyterian colleges for women had yet received recognition as a standard college from the Association of Colleges and Secondary Schools of the Southern States. Agnes Scott, an affiliated Presbyterian College, partly controlled by the synods of Georgia and Alabama, was the only member of the Association.

6. "To assist in solving urgent local problems for our institutions." Here, it was noted, that the charters of several leading colleges had been changed, linking them as securely as possible to the Presbyterian Church.

7. "To provide fully endowed professorships for Bible and other subjects of applied Christianity in all our colleges." There had been progress here, and some colleges were also making provisions for a Department of Bible and Religion.

8. "To increase the Student Loan Fund." In 1916 it was $20,503. Now it was more than ten times as much. It had helped 685 young men and 440 young women to attend Southern Presbyterian colleges.

9. "To cooperate with other evangelical bodies." Little had been done along this line.

10. "To promote well-directed and carefully planned Bible study and evangelistic campaigns in all our educational institutions." Efforts had been made to identify students with the local church.

11. "To cooperate in the religious culture of Presbyterian students at the state universities." Great progress, it was felt, had been made in this field. Local churches, synods, and the executive committee were cooperating to met the spiritual needs of the more than 11,500 students in 80 of these institutions.

12. "To devise means for securing better support for our self-denying and too-often overtaxed teachers." Some progress, it was said, had been made here, but larger resources were needed to provide properly for these men and women.[22]

This year there were listed the following Presbyterian institutions: four theological seminaries, one training school for lay workers, two training schools for Negroes, 18 Presbyterian colleges, one affiliated Presbyterian college (Agnes Scott), ten junior colleges, 13 Presbyterian secondary schools, 16 mountain secondary schools, 14 Presbyterian homes and schools.

The following year, 1926, the report contained only one significant item. It was suggested that it might be well for the synods to evaluate afresh their efforts in education. "Some," said the committee, "may be attempting too ambitious a program."[23] Signs of financial strain were appearing. The great Depression was just around the corner.

In the Synod of Virginia at this time were two colleges, Hampden-Sydney for men and Mary Baldwin for women, and a secondary school, Danville Military Institute. When Dr. R. M. McIlwaine succeeded Dr. Atkinson as president of Hampden-Sydney College in 1884, the section of Virginia in which it was located "was still red with the stripes of war and reconstruction. It was poverty-stricken. The college lacked the equipment of a modern high school."[24]

During Dr. McIlwaine's administration (1885-1904) the physical equipment of Hampden-Sydney was greatly improved, bringing it in line with its more favored sisters, it was claimed. Forty thousand dollars had been added to the endowment. The average student enrollment was 116, the highwater mark being reached in 1892 when the number climbed to 155. Six or eight protracted services had been held in the chapel during this administration, most of them conducted by Dr. McIlwaine himself; all but one were fruitful in the conversion of souls among both students and community. The most serious blow that befell the college during this period was the removal of Union Theological Seminary from Hampden-Sydney to Richmond. To justify this removal "it was thought necessary," so Dr. McIlwaine recalled, "to villify and abuse its location and surroundings. This, of course," in his estimation, "reacted on the college."[25]

The Reverend Dr. J. Gray McAllister, who served as president for one brief year, in 1908 advocated removal of the college to Lexington, Virginia, and merger with Washington and Lee. For this, Hampden-Sydney was not ready; the effort failed; Dr. McAllister resigned; and the college remained in its original location.

Throughout its history, Hampden-Sydney had regarded itself as Presbyterian, even though the constitution of Virginia did not permit it to come under direct ecclesiastical control. A change in the state constitution altered the situation, and in 1918 the college became a synodical institution. It had at this time property worth about $200,000, and an endowment of $225,000.

There were eight members on the faculty and 89 students. "The student body was small, the salaries of the professors were very low [that of a full professor was $1545], the equipment in the various departments was extremely meager, especially in the science department; two of the buildings . . . were lighted with acetylene gas, while all the other buildings had no lighting system except oil lamps; there was not a properly equipped college building or residence on the campus and nearly all the buildings were in serious need of repairs."[26] At this time Hampden-Sydney had the lowest endowment of any standard college in the United States.

A "million-dollar campaign" conducted in 1920 for the benefit of the synod's educational institutions brought needed financial relief, and in 1928 the college was finally free from debt. Ten years after synod had assumed control, President Eggleston was able to report appreciable progress toward the board's four-point program: improvements of the physical plant, steady increase in salaries of the professors, expansion of the faculty to meet a growing student body, and broadening of the course of study to meet modern demands. In 1933 the college enrollment was 333, the largest number of students in its history (and many had been turned away).

Mary Baldwin Seminary, then operating as a junior college, had come under synod's control in 1922. It, like Hampden-Sydney, had been Presbyterian from the outset. The preparatory department was dropped in 1929, and three years later Mary Baldwin became a fully accredited class A college. In 1935 there was a faculty of 24, and a student body of 308.[27]

Danville Military Institute had been organized by citizens of Danville, Virginia, about 1890. It was turned over to the Synod of Virginia without debt in 1921, and for a time seemed to have a promising future. In the aftermath of World War I the synod adopted a declaration in harmony with a recent General Assembly declaration against military training in church schools and directing the institute to work out some system of discipline other than military training. Attendance dropped, deficits increased, and the institution was finally compelled to close its doors.

West Virginia, which became a separate synod in 1914, had in its territory Davis and Elkins College at Elkins and Greenbrier College for Women at Lewisburg. Davis and Elkins, founded in 1904, was under the joint control of the two synods of West Virginia, Presbyterian U. S. and U.S.A. The Southern synod hoped in time to make its junior college for women a four-year institution. The Depression brought mounting debts, and the college passed finally into private ownership.

The Synod of Appalachia, including parts of Virginia, West Virginia, North Carolina, and Tennessee, at its opening meeting in 1915 recognized 24 schools and colleges within its bounds—a total of 1,365 pupils, served by 58 teachers. The school year varied from four months in the little mountain mission schools in Knoxville Presbytery to nine months in most of the other institutions. Work began with the first grade and extended through high school and college. Some of the schools were controlled by the Assembly's Committee of Home Missions, some by individual presbyteries, and others by presbyteries jointly. King College and Stonewall Jackson were adopted as synodical colleges for boys and girls respectively. Rogersville Synodical Institute, closed since 1913, was leased to the high school of Rogersville. The growing effectiveness of the public schools led to the gradual closing of most of the mission schools. The three institutions at Banner Elk, Lees-McRae College, Grace Hospital, and Grandfather Orphanage, serving the isolated mountain regions, were administered by the Edgar Tufts Memorial Association under the control of Holston (Synod of Appalachia) and Concord (Synod of North Carolina) presbyteries. By 1931 Lees-McRae had become a fully accredited junior college. Mounting debts led to the closing of Stonewall Jackson during the Depression years. The same year King College, the synod's one remaining institution, opened its doors to women, thus insuring a balanced educational program for the synod. Throughout its history King College had waged a constant struggle against poverty but had continued to educate young men who would have found it difficult to secure an education elsewhere. Over the years it had educated some of the most eminent ministers in the church, among them R. C. Reed, professor in Columbia Theological

Seminary; James I. Vance, pastor of the First Church of Nashville; and J. S. Sprole Lyons, pastor of the First Church, Atlanta, Georgia.

The Synod of North Carolina had by 1925 the broadest system of denominational schools: three colleges—Davidson for men, Flora MacDonald and Queens for women—along with two junior colleges— Mitchell at Statesville and Peace in Raleigh.

In 1876-1877 the University of North Carolina was reopened and drew a number of Davidson students; the registration of the latter institution was reduced to 88, and did not reach the hundred mark again until 1879-1880, after which there was small annual increase. The most striking feature during this period, as recalled by Professor William Waller Carson, "was the lack of money, so evident at every turn. The impression was not of shiftlessness or neglect, but rather this—that everything in the way of improvement or of repairs had run up against one and the same question, 'Can it wait?' "[28]

Dr. Walter Lee Lingle, who entered Davidson as a freshman in 1888, has left us a picture of Davidson at this time. The dormitory rooms were not furnished by the college, and the boys made out with dilapidated, secondhand furniture secured in the village or handed down from one generation of students to the next. Kerosene lights furnished illumination; practically all rooms had grates, though a few had stoves; students bought wood and chopped it to fit their particular grate; there was no pumped water, and the students drew all water for their own purposes from wells. Water was heated for baths, which were taken in portable tin tubs. Wooden privies were located in the rear of the buildings. Classrooms were as primitive as the dormitories, dingy, not well lighted or ventilated. They were heated by stoves, "sometimes underheated, and at other times overheated." There were no desks. "Those were primitive days," Dr. Lingle recalled, "but we loved them . . . If you are inclined to find fault with those who are responsible for the well-being of the college, remember that we were not far removed from the War between the States, which had impoverished the college and the whole South. Remember too that we had a great faculty, and nothing else mattered much."[29]

In 1888 the Reverend J. B. Shearer, D.D., LL.D of Clarksville, Tennessee, a professor in Southwestern Presbyterian University, was elected President of Davidson College, continuing to serve in this capacity until 1901, and thereafter until 1918 as Professor of Biblical Instruction. During Dr. Shearer's regime student enrollment increased from 86 in 1888 to 171 in 1901. In 1898 Dr. Shearer reported to the board: "In response to the continued importunity of the students, the faculty conceded to them the permission to engage in inter-collegi-

ate athletics to the extent of playing two games of football away from
Davidson, under the oversight and control of a member of the faculty.
This was granted as an experiment without any promise as to the
future."[30]

The most distinctive thing Dr. Shearer did for Davidson, in Dr.
Lingle's opinion, was to introduce courses in the English Bible, covering three full years, and to raise these courses to a college level.
The Bible had been taught at Davidson from the beginning, but the
courses were very much of the nature of Sunday school lessons, and
very few of these were required. Dr. Shearer's influence resulted in
the introduction of courses in English Bible in a number of church-
related colleges.

Dr. Shearer's method of teaching, according to Dr. Lingle, was
dogmatic, and sometimes he substituted ridicule and sarcasm for
argument. This was especially true, Dr. Lingle recalled, when he came
to the subject of higher criticism, which was just then being brought
into the popular ken.

In 1901 Dr. Henry Louis Smith succeeded Dr. Shearer as President of the college, and a period of expansion set in which has continued to the present day. Smith was the first layman to serve as
President of the college; he was 41 years of age when elected, one
of the youngest men to hold the office, a scholarly, energetic, enthusiastic man, full of plans and ideas. First of all there was a vigorous and successful campaign for students. The enrollment shot up
from 173 in 1900-1901 to 323 in 1911-1912. The increased student
body called for new buildings and equipment, and for a larger faculty,
which in turn led to the raising of a large endowment. In addition the
curriculum was broadened, and the college standards considerably
raised.

In 1912 Dr. Smith became President of Washington and Lee
University, and was succeeded as President of Davidson by William Joseph Martin, who had served the institution as Professor of
Chemistry. Under his administration, progress was marked and steady.
Enrollment increased from 323 in 1911-1912 to 627 in 1924-1925.
North Carolina's "million-dollar campaign" added half a million
dollars to Davidson's assets and was followed by another successful
campaign for $200,000. The burning of the Old Chamber's Building
led to still another campaign for $600,000. In 1924 announcement
came, out of the blue, that Mr. James Buchanan Duke, a Methodist,
had set up an endowment of $40,000,000 and that Davidson was
to receive five percent of the annual income from this endowment.
From a financial point of view it was the biggest event by far in the

history of the college. "When the income from Duke endowment began to arrive in amounts ranging from sixty to seventy thousand dollars a year," wrote Dr. Lingle, "it was apparent that Davidson had reached a new era . . ."[31]

In 1916 the Synod of North Carolina appointed an Executive Committee of Education to have general oversight of its various schools and colleges. The "million-dollar campaign," it reported in 1920, had saved the day for many, but increased costs and debts had consumed a great part of the proceeds of the campaign, and the amounts were inadequate to meet the needs and challenges now facing them all.

In 1928 the synod accepted an offer to take over a Methodist junior college in Maxton, North Carolina, and establish it as a junior college for boys. Flora MacDonald College, founded at Red Springs by Fayetteville Presbytery in 1896, and Queens College in Charlotte, purchased about the same time by the Presbyteries of Mecklenburg and Concord (known originally as the Presbyterian College for Women), were at this time four-year colleges for women, supported, the one by presbyteries in the eastern portion of the state, the other by presbyteries in the western portion. Peace Institute, purchased by the First Presbyterian Church of Raleigh in 1908 had come under the control of synod and was now operated as a junior college, as was Mitchell, under the control of Concord Presbytery. All six colleges (including Davidson), were accredited by the North Carolina State Board of Education. There was as yet no unified synod-controlled system of education.

In South Carolina the influence of Dr. Thornwell prevented the synod from entering upon an early venture in education. In 1880, however, Dr. William Plumer Jacobs induced the Presbyterian Church at Clinton to found a college (with the usual high school curriculum) which became in time the Presbyterian College of South Carolina. In 1904 it passed from local control and management into the possession of the presbyteries composing the Synod of South Carolina. Real growth of the college began in 1911, under the presidency of the Reverend Davison McDowell Douglass. Within five years the student body had grown from 85 to more than 200, modern buildings had been erected, the faculty relieved of the indignity of small and uncertain salaries. Generous gifts had been secured outside the state from foundations and individuals, and help from within the state through a partially successful million-dollar campaign. In 1922, the college which six years earlier had come under synodical control was a fully accredited member of the Association of Colleges and

Secondary Schools in the Southern States. When Dr. Douglass resigned in 1926 to become President of the University of South Carolina, Presbyterian College "had a good reputation, held the confidence of the public, was the pride of the [Synod], and had the esteem of educators . . ."

Meanwhile the synod had become interested in a college for women. Chicora College, which up to this time had been privately conducted, came under the ownership and control of the South Carolina presbyteries in 1906. The "million-dollar campaign" conducted in 1921-1922 had seemed for a time to be a glorious success, with the full amount oversubscribed. But the subscriptions were made when prosperity prevailed in an unparalleled degree and, before the subscriptions became due, adversity befell the state in an unprecedented degree. A considerable portion of the amount pledged was never received. Debts on the synod's education institutions totaled almost $900,000. Presbyterian College was "plunging so rapidly down into the abyss of debt that only the most vigorous measures can save its existence . . . The experience seems to indicate that the Synod has undertaken a heavier educational load than its people" were able to carry.[32] A staggering amount would be required to bring the synod's related institutions up to standard. Meanwhile the requirements for standard colleges were being raised rather than lowered, making the peril of the colleges even more acute. To avoid catastrophe the synod took over control of Chicora College, arranged its merger with Queens College in Charlotte, which became Queens–Chicora, and made plans to liquidate the remaining debt.

In the 1890's the Synod of Georgia revived the idea of a Presbyterian university to be located in the deep South, preferably in Atlanta. The idea gathered new momentum after the turn of the century when citizens of Atlanta raised "the large sum of $250,000" which they were prepared to give if the seven concerned synods would agree to bring together, and locate in Atlanta with a combined endowment of $500,000, the two institutions under their control, Southwestern University at Clarksville, Tennessee, and the Theological Seminary at Columbia, South Carolina. The movement, which appeared promising for a time, collapsed when the Supreme Court of Tennessee ruled that Southwestern could not be moved from Clarksville, and when the General Assembly of 1905 declined to give the project its formal endorsement. Some believed that the times were not ripe for such an enterprise; others had grave doubts as to whether the church should, under existing conditions, engage in the training of civil engineers, lawyers, doctors, and scientists.

The Synod of Georgia then toyed with the idea of establishing a synodical college but soon abandoned this project and adopted a recommendation calling for the establishment of presbyterial high schools and the better equipment of those already in existence. Two years later Thornwell Jacobs, minister and journalist, a son of William Plumer Jacobs, launched an ambitious program to revive Oglethorpe University, which, before the Civil War, had been a significant influence in the Southern educational world, and to make it the greatly needed and long desired Southern Presbyterian University. Won to the idea and serving on the executive committee of the perspective university were some of the most influential ministers in the General Assembly and some of its most influential and generous laymen. Traveling widely through the Assembly, appealing for contributions to this grandiose project, Dr. Jacobs raised a sizable amount of money and for a time seemed to be on the road to success. The General Assembly of 1915 heard Dr. Jacobs and prayed that God would bestow his blessing upon the new institutions, but declined to take further responsibility. The next year it appointed an ad interim committee to see if it were possible to come to some agreement as to the relationship of Oglethorpe University to the Presbyterian Church U. S. The institution, a university as yet only in name, opened its doors in the fall of the year with four professors and a freshman class of 48 (later rising to about 60). The Synod of Georgia expressed its pleasure in Dr. Jacobs' remarkable success in securing subscriptions which aggregated more than $700,000, and in completing ". . . one of the largest and finest fireproof college buildings in the South, and in selecting a faculty conspicuous for scholarship and Christian character, and in attracting [a] remarkably large freshman class of choice young men . . ."[33]

It expressed the hope that other synods would follow its own example in the endowment of synodical professorships "in this great Presbyterian University."

The ad interim committee reported to the 1917 General Assembly that there was an irreconcilable difference of opinion in the church regarding the control of the proposed university:

> As we study the recent actions of Assemblies, Synods, Presbyteries, and of the Assembly's Executive and Advisory Committees of Christian Education, we are convinced that the Presbyterian Church in the United States believes that educational institutions, built by the Church's money, and using the Church's name and influence, should be owned by the Church and governed by trustees appointed by the proper courts of the Church. . . .

On the other hand . . . those in charge of the Oglethorpe movement believe that their institution should be owned and controlled by a self-perpetuating board, independent of all Church courts . . .[34]

Oglethorpe, it was pointed out, could hardly recede from this view, since it had been written into the very warp and woof of its charter, and contributions had been made with this understanding.

Involved in the long and sharp debate that followed was the question as to whether or not the church should sponsor a university. One opponent, Dr. C. M. Richards, then pastor of the College Church at Davidson, claimed that universities were notoriously centers of heresy and infidelity and that it would be dangerous for the Southern Presbyterian Church to have one.[35] But the real point at issue was indicated by the *Presbyterian Standard*: "Dr. Jacobs . . . is one of the most magnetic speakers in the church. He can win over a set of hard headed preachers, as well as draw from the pockets of close-fisted Scotchmen money by the thousands of dollars. He has done a wonderful work at Oglethorpe, and the pity is he did not do it in a way that would disarm criticism and opposition, but as it is, the pledge of money given will ever prevent the Church from having full control, and that is the main ground of the opposition."[36]

In the end the Assembly adopted the recommendations of its ad interim committee. It commended the zeal and energy of those responsible for Oglethorpe University and wished them great success in building up their institution, but declined to adopt the university or to commend it to the churches for their contributions. Instead presbyteries and synods were urged to increase diligence in building up and maintaining their own schools and colleges.[37]

So ended the dream of a great Presbyterian university first proposed by Dr. Lyon in 1861 and often subsequently revived. Oglethorpe insisted that it would continue its growth "as a great Southern Presbyterian University, not under the control of any ecclesiastical court, but strictly and completely under Presbyterian control."[38] But as Dr. Jacobs later wrote: the terms of the Assembly's actions "were so clear-cut as effectively to end solicitation of funds for Oglethorpe as a church-wide Southern Presbyterian University."[39] The Synod of Georgia continued its interest in the Oglethorpe institution for a time, but failing in its efforts to effect "closer relations" with the institution finally dropped it from its list of schools. In 1927 Dr. Jacobs published a book entitled *The New Science and the Old Religion*. The review notices were kind, according to Dr. Jacobs, "but the book listed me in ministerial circles, definitely, among the heretics. From that day on, I had to swim upstream in the river Jordan."[40] As a suspected evolutionist, pulpits hitherto opened to him were now closed.

For a time Oglethorpe University prospered, but the great Depression brought financial difficulties. Dr. Jacob's refusal to seek accreditation aroused opposition within his own board, and in 1943 he was forced out of the institution, which he almost single-handedly had brought into being. Oglethorpe carried on as a small college but had long since ceased to be regarded as Presbyterian.

The one college of which the Synod of Georgia could be justifiably proud was Agnes Scott. Its success from the outset was regarded as "little short of phenomenal."[41] In the summer of 1889, a few members of the Decatur Presbyterian Church, under the leadership of its pastor, the Reverend F. H. Gaines, determined to supply what they conceived to be a great need in the Synod of Georgia by founding a distinctively Presbyterian school for the higher Christian education of young ladies. Its original name, Decatur Female Seminary, was changed to Agnes Scott Institute after the mother of Colonel George W. Scott, who provided a convenient site of land and made a generous donation, enabling the school to erect "one of the most completely appointed and admirably adapted college buildings in the South."[42] According to the *Southwestern Presbyterian*: " 'The new woman,' in the offensive sense of the term, will be no product of her training; but the making of the new woman, in a good sense, the sister, the daughter, wife, mother, who, without sacrificing one particle of her charming femininity, will be the intellectual peer of her life-long companions of the rougher sex, is her aim and crowning glory."[43]

The school prospered from the start. In 1908 it reached the standard required by the Southern Association of Colleges and passed from the class of secondary schools to the class of colleges. It had at that time an attendance of 274 with about 25 turned away. In 1922 the Synod of Georgia recognized Agnes Scott as in a special sense the synod's college, recommending it to the support and patronage of its people and assuming a share in its control. As defined by the General Assembly it became and has remained an "associated Presbyterian College."

The Synod of Florida took a deep interest in Palmer College, at De Funiak Springs, which was organized in 1906, and for some years controlled by the Presbytery of Florida. When the synod finally assumed control, in 1927, the institution operated on three levels—elementary, secondary, and junior college. The Depression brought financial difficulties, and in 1936 the college was closed.

Efforts of the Synod of Alabama to support a college for men at Anniston and one for women at Talladega came to nought, and the synod by 1925 concentrated its efforts on Southwestern University, located now at Memphis, Tennessee, and controlled by the synods of Tennessee, Alabama, Louisiana, and Mississippi. In addition to Southwestern, the Synod of Mississippi supported Belhaven, a four-year college for girls, two junior colleges for women—Chickasaw at Pontotoc and Mississippi Synodical College at Holly Springs—and two academies—Chamberlain-Hunt at Port Gibson and French Camp at the town of the same name in Mississippi. The hard times preceding the great Depression cut down funds which might otherwise have been received from the "million-dollar campaign"; mounting debts led to the closing of Chickasaw College in 1932, and consolidation of Mississippi Synodical College with Belhaven in 1939.

Belhaven College had its beginning in 1893 in the city of Jackson as a private institution for young women. It took "high rank" among the educational institutions of the state, and numbered among its patrons a large number of "the best people" of the state. In 1910 the college buildings were destroyed by fire and Dr. Preston, the President and a Presbyterian elder, offered the name and goodwill of the college to the Presbytery of Central Mississippi. Dr. J. B. Hutton, pastor of the First Church, Jackson, enlisted the cooperation of Central Mississippi and Mississippi Presbyteries in the building of the new Belhaven. The latter presbytery had conducted for some years a small school at McComb City, called the McComb City Female Institute. This school was merged with the new college to be built at Jackson, and Dr. R. V. Lancaster, the moving spirit at McComb, called to the presidency of Belhaven. The new college opened its doors in September 1911. In 1913 the Synod of Mississippi adopted a plan for the correlation of all of its schools, and the two presbyteries owning Belhaven transferred their interest to the synod. The college weathered the financial storm, became fully accredited in 1934, and by 1939 had retired its bonded debt.

Louisiana, united with its neighboring synods in the control and support of Southwestern University, voted in 1919 to accept as a synodical institution Silliman Institute, a Junior College, located at Clinton, and since its founding in 1866, under the care of the Presbytery of Louisiana. In 1925, with 39 students in the college department, 9 in the high school, 16 in the primary grades, and 8 special, the college was reported to be in financial difficulties. It was closed at the end of the 1926-1927 session, briefly reopened, and again closed in 1931.

Southwestern, styled a university and with aspirations to become one in fact, in 1885 added to its academic department a school of divinity which for a generation and more trained some of the leading clergymen of the church. Efforts to add departments of law and medicine failed to materialize, and mounting financial difficulties led to the suspension of the School of Divinity in 1917. Sometime earlier realization had dawned that Southwestern, on the northernmost border of the territory of the four cooperating synods, was badly located with reference to its territory, and agitation for removal had developed. In 1903 came an invitation to move to Atlanta with an offer of generous financial aid. To block the Synod of Tennessee's acceptance of this offer, the Board of Directors instituted a suit, which was finally settled by a decree of the Supreme Court of Tennessee in 1914, upholding the authority of the Board of Directors and ruling that the institution must remain at Clarksville.

In 1917, Dr. Charles E. Diehl, pastor of the First Presbyterian Church of Clarksville, a scholar deeply interested in education, was elected President of the "University." The dire straits into which the school had fallen soon convinced Dr. Diehl and his board that some move must be made. Successful financial campaigns and a new court decision opened the way for removal to Memphis, and in September 1925 Southwestern (the misleading term "University" having been dropped), now coeducational, began its 51st session with magnificent buildings of the collegiate gothic type, an able faculty, and a new and distinctive character. Under Dr. Diehl's leadership the college accepted some of the ideals of the great English universities, Oxford and Cambridge—particularly their tutorial method of instruction. An imposing array of former Rhodes Scholars, familiar with the Oxford system, were secured for the faculty with this in mind.

> In 1931, with a liberal grant received from the Carnegie Corporation for this purpose, the tutorial method was applied to all departments of the college, and a plan worked out which has attracted widespread interest and commendation throughout the educational world. The chief purposes of this plan are the individualizing of instruction, the avoiding of mass production methods in education, and the provision of means whereby a student may go beyond the scope of a class course, both in the kind of work done and in the kind of interests pursued. The method is that of extensive reading under guidance, and individual conferences with the tutor on the material read.[44]

Dr. Diehl wished the study of the Bible to remain at Southwestern as the capstone of its educational system, and to be taught in the same scholarly fashion as were courses in Shakespeare, mathematics, and the sciences. In the fundamentalist atmosphere of the late 1920's and early 1930's suspicion developed regarding Dr. Diehl's orthodoxy. In 1930 a petition filed with the Board of Directors and signed by the ministers of ten of the Presbyterian churches in Memphis charged that he was "not what may be called sound in the Faith." A memorial from the Presbytery of Central Mississippi, received by the board in April 1931, asked the board "to seriously consider the advisability of retaining as President of the school one who is unacceptable to a large portion of the constituency of the school and of the controlling Synods." At Dr. Diehl's own request the Board of Directors of Southwestern and Nashville Presbytery, of which he was a member, investigated carefully these and other charges and completely exonerated him.[45] But the widespread charges made more difficult the raising of a permanent endowment and necessary funds for the building of Southwestern's magnificent plant and for the operation of the colleges. For a time it appeared that Southwestern might have to close. Generous friends came to the college's aid, and in 1930 Southwestern's total mortgage indebtedness of $700,000 was retired and the future of the college assured.

At the meeting of the Board of Directors of Southwestern in February 1931 a tribute to Dr. Diehl was adopted, which read in part:

> At this first meeting of the Board of Directors of Southwestern since paying off the great mortgage, it is fitting that the Board express its appreciation of the magnificent work done by President Charles Edward Diehl in building the new College, in administering its affairs, and finally as leader in paying off the mortgage . . . It took manliness, it took courage, it took faith, it took persistence, it took industry, it took brain with artistic ability and business acumen, it took a heart devoted to Christ . . . to build, to equip, and to pay for Southwestern as it stands today, and that with opposition without and at times within . . .[46]

It was a tribute richly deserved.

The Synod of Arkansas and the Synod of Texas, once united in support of Southwestern, had withdrawn to develop their own synodical institutions. The Synod of Arkansas so acted in 1895 in order that its "united energy and undivided moral and financial support" might "be concentrated in the support of Arkansas College."[47] Efforts to establish a Synodical College for Women failed, and Arkansas College became coeducational in 1910. It weathered the financial crisis of the great Depression, and while not yet fully accredited was accepted as a four-year college by the state educational association.

The Synod of Texas, itself growing, and in a rapidly growing state, developed an ambitious educational program. Austin College, after its removal to Sherman and adoption by the synod (in 1885), for a time seemed to prosper. Daniel Baker College, founded and operated by members of the Presbyterian Church U.S.A. in Brownwood, was taken over by Central Texas Presbytery of the Southern Church in 1893, and came under the control of the synod in 1902. It grew from a junior college to a four-year, class A (coeducational) institution; from 143 students to 228; from a local to interstate and international patronage.[48] Meanwhile, the synod had opened at Milford a Synodical State College for Women, later named Texas Presbyterian College. A generous bequest of Captain Charles Schreiner (a non-Presbyterian) led to the opening of Schreiner Institute as a junior college at Kerrville. In addition, the synod was endeavoring to maintain a theological seminary in Austin. Increasing indebtedness, particularly of the three senior colleges, led to appointment of a survey committee, which in 1928 gave a sobering report which reflected the problem of the church as a whole. It pointed out that the synod had assumed responsibility for a theological seminary; three senior colleges; one junior college; two mission schools (Tex-Mex and Pres-Mex); and one school for children, Southwestern Presbyterian Home and School for Orphans. It was the three senior colleges that formed the acute problem for the synod. While Presbyterians with 46,112 members sought to support three colleges, Baptists with 477,683 members had four, and the Southern Methodists with 379,155 had only two. And meanwhile there were at least 1,280 Southern Presbyterian students in state institutions for which nothing was being done.

Within a period of ten years the synod had launched two big financial drives for funds to pay the debts and to provide for enlargement of its schools. Close to two million dollars had been subscribed in these campaigns and approximately one and a quarter million of it paid; yet the institutions were not free from debt, and their enlargement was still in prospect. During the latter part of the decade the educational work had been given a place in the synod's budget, but the amount received from this source had steadily declined.

What was to be done? Another drive was out of the question, and in the meantime the institutions were drifting toward bankruptcy. As seen by the committee there were three possible procedures.

One, to maintain the status quo, which meant an endless wrestle with deficit and debt. Such procedure was dismissed as out of the question.

Two, to withdraw altogether from the field of secular education. "Giants" in the past (Dr. James H. Thornwell, Dr. Robert L. Dabney) had argued that the church had no business entering the field of secular education. The church had not heeded them; rather, it had launched an ambitious scheme which sought to provide a thorough education for its children, one calling for parochial schools for the local congregations, an academy for the presbytery, and a college for the synod. The plan collapsed because there were not sufficient funds to meet the cost. Public schools crowded out their parochial competitors; high schools supplanted the academies. And many were now predicting a like fate for the church colleges, the only remnant that still remained of a once proud structure. Sentiment for abandonment of church colleges was indeed rapidly growing within the synod. And there were good arguments to support this position.

(1) Modern education called for vast outlays of money, and the church could no longer keep pace with the state in this field. In addition it should be remembered that the church had originally built schools because there was no one else to do it, not because it could do it better.

(2) Presbyterians, taxed to support the state schools, and then called to dig deeper to support church schools doing the same work, but often not doing it as well, felt needlessly burdened.

(3) Both the patronage and financial support of the church schools were declining. About seven-eighths of the Presbyterian young people were already in the state schools. And there were cogent reasons why they were there: for example, "We cannot honestly promise them the facilities the state school is prepared to furnish; we cannot give them an education at so low a cost as does the state, and with most of our people who have children to educate, cost is an item which they cannot overlook."

(4) Withdrawal from this portion of the field of education would relieve the church of a tremendous financial burden, one that grows heavier with every passing year.

(5) Withdrawal from this portion of the field of education would not mean that the synod had withdrawn from the whole field of education. It might mean that the synod, no longer burdened with the program of general education, would be free to perfect a plan for the religious training of its hundreds of young people already in the state schools and the increasing hundreds yet to come.

The third possibility recognized by the ad interim committee was to remain in the field of higher education, but, by means of necessary and even drastic consolidation, to remake its system. It was this plan which the committee recommended, recognizing correctly that the synod was not prepared to abandon the field as long as there remained any possibility of holding it.[49]

In accordance with its committee's recommendation, the synod voted to consolidate its three major colleges into one and to confine its efforts henceforth to building up Austin College at Sherman. Even so a crippling debt remained on the college, and annual deficits continued through the Depression years. Not until 1934 was the Standing Committee able to report: "The uncertainty about the future of the institution appears to be gradually disappearing. . . ."[50]

Oklahoma, one of the weakest synods in the church, at its first meeting in 1908 accepted Durant, later Oklahoma Presbyterian College, as a ward of the synod, and in 1923 agreed to take responsibility for Goodland Industrial School and Orphanage. Both actually were Home Mission projects and largely supported by Assembly funds. Goodland served only Indians; O.P.C. was a junior college for girls, white or Indian. In addition, the Synod of Oklahoma joined in the support of Austin College and Austin Theological Seminary. In 1933 the trustees of Oklahoma Presbyterian College, in view of increasing indebtedness, suspended all teaching in the junior college. Five teachers offered to serve without obligation except as to board and room on condition that junior college instruction be revived, and their offer was accepted. "So far," it was reported to synod, "they are not discouraged, having received $28 each from free will offerings."[51] In 1934 synod was informed that both Oklahoma Presbyterian College and Goodland Industrial School and Orphanage continued to serve synod in a most important and helpful way. "Struggling against seemingly insurmountable difficulties these two institutions have passed successfully through most trying circumstances."[52]

The Synod of Missouri controlled Westminster College for Men (jointly with the Northern Synod) and Synodical College for Women, both at Fulton. In 1907 it was reported that one-third of the ministers in the synod were sons of Westminster. The college remained one of the stronger schools in the church, and in 1934 was able to report a balanced budget and the largest enrollment (322) in its history. Synodical College did not fare as well. For some years its work was carried on in the name of the synod, but in reality as a private enterprise. In 1906 synod again assumed direct control, but debts mounted, and in 1928 the college was forced to close its doors.

Central University with its law department in Richmond, Kentucky, flourished for a time, along with its medical department—the Hospital College of Medicine and the College of Dentistry in Louisville—and its collegiate schools at Jackson, Elizabethton, and Middlesborough. But, as pointed out by the *Christian Observer,* educational conditions had changed in Kentucky as elsewhere. The large endowments of state universities and the increasing income of other great universities in various parts of the country had rendered the task assigned to Central University (Presbyterian U. S.) and Centre College (Presbyterian U.S.A.) more and more difficult from year to year. Presbyterianism, with its forces divided, could no longer maintain the type of institution that both bodies desired. The mission of the church, it had become clear, could be best fulfilled by the consolidation of the synods' respective institutions into one completely unified scheme: academic, collegiate, professional, and theological.[53]

To attain this objective, the two synods agreed to consolidate their theological schools in Louisville and their collegiate work under the name Central University in Danville. The university might continue as it deemed expedient the departments of medicine and dentistry established at Louisville and the department of law established by Centre College in Danville. The collegiate schools—S. P. Lees Collegiate Institute at Jackson, the Hardin Collegiate Institute at Elizabethton, and the Middlesborough University School at Middlesborough—were to be organized as separate and independent corporate bodies under the charge of the Southern synod. In 1907 the charter of the university was changed to permit government by a self-perpetuating Board of Trustees, the determining factor being the university's desire to qualify for aid from the Carnegie Foundation. In 1921 Centre College, having dropped its pretensions of being a university, once more came under the direct control of the two Presbyterian synods, which agreed at this time to unite their forces and to concentrate their combined energy and strength in the development of their theological seminary in Louisville, Centre College in Danville, and a standard class A college for women, which, it was agreed, should be the Kentucky College for Women, then a junior college, located at Danville. Sayre College, which the Southern synod had adopted in 1917, now became a secondary school, Sayre Institute, under the sole control of the Southern synod. Efforts to develop an accredited college for women failed, and in 1926 Kentucky College for Women became the Women's Department of Centre College. In 1930 Centre had an enrollment of 396, 112 of these being women, the largest enrollment in its history. This same year it was reported that 3.28 percent of the alumni of the college were listed in *Who's Who,* which gave Centre the rank of 14th in the nation, and second in the South.

The fact that Presbyterian synods, both U. S. and U.S.A., were now united in support of educational institutions in three of the border synods—Missouri, Kentucky, and West Virginia—was significant. As reported to the Synod of Kentucky: "The hope of the future is with the followers of Christ; and the torn world needs nothing more than the healing which comes when men are one in Christ Jesus. Unless Christians can unite to do, in a Christian spirit, what they cannot do separately, time may prove they were not equal to the great responsibility that was theirs . . . Some think denominations must soon unite to meet the strain; how dull of mind we must be if we sense not the dangers and unworthy, if we seek not to meet them. It is Christian statesmanship that moves us to unite as Presbyterians U. S. and U.S.A. in a common effort. . . ."[54]

In the course of the numerous synodical campaigns it had become evident that a new apologetic for the church's educational institutions needed to be developed. Originally church schools had been established because otherwise for large numbers an education was unavailable. Now with state institutions multiplying, providing a good education at less cost, this was no longer the case. The Synod of South Carolina, which for long had declined to accept educational responsibility, now presented the case:

> . . . an attempt to suggest future lines for our educational policy must begin with appreciation of the splendid work of the past . . . But manifestly the church faces a new educational situation. Some of the reasons that were adduced in a former day for the building up of church colleges no longer exist. It cannot be said that without these institutions gifted and aspiring youth would be denied an opportunity for a higher learning. It cannot be convincingly urged that the church has a peculiar duty to provide such education for the sons and daughters of the poor . . . Has the church college then a present and permanent reason for being? . . . This Committee hastens to express its profound conviction that the church positively has a permanent and definite mission in the sphere of college education, and that the elimination of the church college would be a stupendous disaster both to the life of the church itself and to the nation . . .

The church has a mission, the committee went on to claim,

> . . . to illustrate and provide a distinctive type of higher education . . . in which spiritual culture accompanies and crowns intellectual culture —in which Christian character is no less a goal than sound scholarship —in which devotion to Jesus Christ and loyalty to his kingdom are the dominant motives. . . . The Christian college is a necessary training school for the church's own leaders. . . . The best guarantee of Christian ideals in state institutions is to maintain alongside of these institutions colleges whose Christian standards are guaranteed by the church of the Lord Jesus Christ.[55]

Laboring under this conviction, Presbyterians in the South struggled manfully through the Depression years to maintain their institutions of higher learning; they had meanwhile come to feel increasing responsibility for ministering to Presbyterian students now crowding the state institutions.*

> The drift of Presbyterian students to the state universities and to undenominational colleges [reported the *Christian Observer* in 1909] is steadily increasing. This seems to be due, not to any particular decline in loyalty to the church, but rather to the superior advantages of the other institutions. This superiority consists largely in better buildings, better equipment and more varied courses of instruction. Presbyterian homes compare favorably with the average home in the comforts of life. And it is inevitable that parents who have reared their children in such homes should hesitate to send them to some of the cheerless and comfortless buildings in which our schools are housed. This is especially true of schools for young women.
> The Presbyterian families are furnishing their due proportion of the large and increasing corps of teachers, engineers, electricians, chemists, and specialists in scientific work. These young aspirants for distinction in their chosen line of work naturally seek those institutions where they can receive the special training which they desire. And they are attracted by the variety of courses and the opportunities for laboratory work which schools outside the church can offer . . . The large independent colleges like Princeton and Yale and [others], offering all sorts of courses but charging high tuition . . . tempt and secure the sons and daughters of prosperous families who do not need to consider very carefully the matter of expense. While the State universities, offering equally wide and varied courses . . . bring the cost of living down to the level of the poor. . . .[56]

The new importance of the state schools created a problem for the church. All possible expedients, Dr. Thomas W. Currie recalled, were tried by one or another branch of the church, varying from an effort to turn the students back to our church colleges on the part of some, to an effort to control the election of presidents and professors in these schools on the part of others. These efforts, as he indicated, failed. Then the idea of a student pastor was tried, the first denomination to try this expedient being the Presbyterian Church in the U.S.A. The first university pastor was placed by this church at the University of Michigan in 1893. The experiment worked and was taken up by other denominations.

To the student pastor, continued Dr. Currie, has now been added the University Church; the Westminster Hall (or the like), used for

---

* Not until the beginning of the century did attendance of students at the state institutions surpass that of the private and denominational schools. The startling increase of students at state institutions of higher learning came after World War I.

dormitory and social purposes; the Bible chair; Bible courses and affiliated courses given by the church on the outside and accorded credit on university degrees on the inside.[57]

The first work of this kind done by the Southern Presbyterian Church was at Blacksburg, Virginia, the seat of Virginia Polytechnic Institute. The Synod of Virginia in 1901 became deeply interested in providing here a suitable church building. The following year the Y.M.C.A. placed at V.P.I. the first full-time Christian worker among students in the South. Shortly thereafter the Synod of Virginia began to supplement the salary of the Presbyterian pastor at Blacksburg that he might give more time to a ministry to the students. Aid was also extended to other college pastors.

In 1905 the Synod of South Carolina gave financial assistance that the Fort Hill Church might secure a resident pastor to work among the students at Clemson College; the Synod of Alabama did the same for the church at Auburn. The Synod of Missouri heard this year an address by Dr. J. C. Jones, acting President of the University of Missouri, who asked the synod to cooperate with the Northern synod in establishing some means for taking care of the religious interests of the Presbyterian students of the university. He emphasized the fact that the attitude of the universities had materially changed in recent years. While many of their faculties formerly were largely non-Christian and partly infidel, they were now largely Christian and were turning to the churches for help.[58]

Three years later the General Assembly urged all the synods to follow the good examples of the synods of Alabama, North Carolina, South Carolina, and Virginia in making special provision for the spiritual interests of young people from Presbyterian homes who were students in state institutions and directed the executive committee to continue its work of presenting to them the claims of the gospel ministry. Most of the synods responded immediately, and within a few years religious work among the students of private and state supported institutions became one of the vital interests of them all.[59]

New impetus was given to the work in 1925 when the Reverend Robert Miles, who had been signally blessed in his work at Auburn, Alabama, was called to become the first University Secretary of the Board of Christian Education. It was estimated at this time that one out of every seven or eight students in the state institutions came from Presbyterian homes. In 1915 the church was advised to work in cooperation with existing religious agencies on the college campuses, notably the Y.M.C.A. and the Y.W.C.A;[60] after the First World War denominational organizations came to be more common. One of the

most successful churches in its student work at this time was the
First Church at Columbia, Missouri, under the pastorate of John
M. Alexander. Work among students, under the control of a joint
committee of Presbyterians U. S. and U.S.A., was carried on in a
student center equipped by the Columbia Church. On the campus
there was a Presbyterian Student Association federated with other
groups in a Students' Religious Council. United efforts were made
by the churches of Columbia for affiliate membership among the
students. Evening services were turned over to students who had
their own elders and deacons (elected, though not ordained). Efforts made to secure a full-time student pastor proved successful.[61]

As more and more young people received their education in state-
controlled schools, Southern Presbyterians became concerned not only
with maintaining their own institutions of higher learning and not
only providing a ministry to students on the campuses of state institutions, but also with safeguarding the true faith as it was taught or
affected by instruction offered in the tax-supported institutions.

In a discussion on the floor of the Synod of South Carolina on
the eve of the educational renaissance, President Reverend Dr. James
Woodrow and Chaplain Dr. J. W. Flinn pointed out that Christianity
was distinctly recognized in the organization of South Carolina College, the very constitution requiring faith in the sacred Scriptures as
an indispensable qualification for holding the office of President, that
it was daily and systematically observed and taught in the chapel
and classrooms, that it dominated and controlled the government and
conduct of the student body. They went on to point out that the same
was true in general of all schools and colleges, both male and female,
private and public, in the state. The synod rejoiced that education
throughout its bounds was so nearly universally under direct Christian influence, whether conducted by the church, the state, or by private persons and corporations. "We trust," concluded the synod, "that
it may continue so to be."[62]

To the Reverend Dr. N. M. Woods, prominent pastor and retiring Moderator of the General Assembly, the picture a few years
later did not seem so bright. He warned the Assembly that if the various denominations did not rally their forces they would see "this
so-called Christian land practically paganized, largely by means of
the anti-Christian institutions from which all religious instruction
and worship has been eliminated, and in which an overwhelming
majority of the youth of America are now receiving training for their
life work."[63]

The General Assembly, two years later, counseled its members to be diligent in their duties as citizens in guarding the purity and elevating the character of the public schools of the country. "The Christian citizens of a state owe it to themselves, their children, the State, and their Lord," it stated, "to be faithful in protecting public schools from the evil of influences unfriendly to Christianity, in the studies, the teachers, or the directors of the public schools in which the large majority of the children of the land are taught." It gratefully recognized that public education on all levels in the South was in general friendly to religious faith and life. "Let our people, as citizens," it urged, "see to it that Christian influences in all state schools are constantly maintained in purity and power."[64]

Church courts on occasion endorsed the practice of a daily reading of Scriptures in the public schools.[65] The Synod of Kentucky in 1913 expressed its profound concern at efforts being made "to exclude the reading of the Bible from the public schools," regarding "such influences as hostile to the stability and usefulness of the American public school system and at variance with the fundamental principle of religious and civil liberty upon which the life and institutions of this nation are founded."[66] "Whether or not the Bible shall be a text book in all our schools is now a living question," wrote the editor of the *Presbyterian Standard*. "That it will be, ere long, one of burning interest to the country admits of no doubt. . . . The really American people [*sic*] are more and more insistent upon the use of the Bible in their schools. . . . The day comes on apace when there must be a decisive and powerful conflict between the two contending parties."[67]

In response to such sentiment, the Virginia State Board of Education, in 1916, appointed a committee of seven, one of whom was the Reverend Dwight M. Chalmers, pastor of the First Presbyterian Church of Charlottesville, to prepare courses in Bible study for the public schools in the state of Virginia. Among the members of the committee were representatives of the Jewish, Roman Catholic, and Protestant faiths. Under their sponsorship two courses of study on the Old Testament and one on the New Testament were prepared and accepted for use in the state schools. Public funds were not to be used for teaching the courses, and responsibility of pupils for engaging in the courses remained with the parents.[68]

In North Carolina there were numerous experiments in moral and religious instruction in the public schools and also in the state university.[69] As summarized by Luther L. Gobbel:

Some of the denominational leaders, particularly Presbyterians, have insisted that the Bible should be used as a textbook. Widespread disagreement among the churches on this issue [particularly the opposition of the Baptists], however, has resulted in its elimination from the regular curriculum, except under special experimental arrangements. One arrangement, worked out by the several co-operating denominations and the local school boards, permits pastors or other teachers representing the churches to go to the public high school once each week for a period of teaching. A modification of this plan permits the pupil to use public school time in which to go to their respective churches for religious instruction. In some cases, high school credit is given; in others, it is not. In some places local churches have united to pay the salary of one or more teachers of Bible in the public schools, and the local board of education furnishes the room. In a number of places instruction in Bible, ethics and morals has been given "in connection with other courses." In a few places public-school credit has been allowed for work done in the Sunday School.

The University of North Carolina and most of the denominations of the state, moreover, cooperated for two years in maintaining a chair of Bible at the University. The financial support was provided by the churches.[70]

After two years the experiment was discontinued. The university, however, subsequently established a full-fledged curriculum in "the history and literature of religion," including studies in the Bible.

In most Southern states, religion, with Presbyterian support, has continued to have some place in public education, at least on the primary and secondary levels.

At times Presbyterians protested against particular textbooks used in the public schools. Thus in 1910 the Synod of Texas sent a protest to state authorities regarding the use of such books as Meyer's *Ancient History* (a textbook used in many high schools and colleges) whose effect, according to the synod, "must be to impair or undermine the faith of the young in the supernatural inspiration of the Holy Scriptures."[71] Copies of the memorial were sent to all of the Methodist Conferences, to the Baptist State Conventions, to the U.S.A. and Cumberland synods; it was published also in the *Dallas News* and the *Houston Post*. The synod of Alabama in 1917 condemned the use of a specified textbook, widely used in the public school, which, it claimed, denied the authenticity and historicity of portions of the Word of God.[72]

A few years earlier the editor of the *Presbyterian of the South* had called attention to an article in *Cosmopolitan* entitled "Blasting at the Rock of Ages," describing the teaching which was going on in many of the universities and colleges in the departments of sociology, ethics, and religion. A prefatory note by the editor was quoted as saying:

"Out of the curricula of American colleges a dynamic movement is upheaving ancient foundations and promising a way for revolutionary thought and life. Those who are not in close touch with the great colleges of the country will be astonished to learn the trends being fostered . . . In hundreds of classrooms it is being taught daily that the Decalogue is no more sacred than a syllabus; that the home as an institution is doomed; that there are no absolute evils; that immorality is simply an act in contravention of society's accepted standard; that democracy is a failure . . ."[73]

In the South the battle over such dangerous trends in the educational institutions would soon be joined—directed specifically against the teaching of evolution.

VIII

Maintaining the Faith

The earlier theological seminaries—Union in Virginia and Columbia in South Carolina—had been established, as was natural, by the older and stronger synods along the Atlantic seaboard. On these two institutions the church largely depended for the training of its ministers from early days until the end of the 19th century. As the Western synods grew in strength, however, it was inevitable that efforts would be made to build theological seminaries west of the Alleghenies.

Isaac Jasper Long, first President of Arkansas College in Batesville, explained the beginning of theological education in his state:

> So far as the movement in Arkansas College is concerned we were waked up on this point as far back as 1871. Previous to that date, so far as I could find, only one man who was brought up in the state entered the ministry of our church, and he was lost to the much needed work in his own state in consequence of having to be sent to the Atlantic States to receive his literary and then his theological training. Since the founding of the college in 1872, including those now in the institution, fifteen from the state have been and are now [1884] being trained for the ministry. We incorporated into our college course what ought to belong to the curriculum of every college claiming to be Christian, the English Bible, ecclesiastical history and the exegetical study of the New Testament in Greek. When students reach graduation if they enter the ministry they need only additional training in the same course, some more systematic instruction in theology proper, together with the elements of Hebrew. After a protracted struggle of at least fifteen years we are just getting where we can more fully develop what has been aimed at from the beginning. We earnestly desire a good Presbyterian institution *in every Synod* west of the Mississippi River as can furnish a Christian education to all, and appropriate theological training to those who enter the ministry. The idea advocated by Dr. W[itherspoon] of a richly endowed seminary is just what many of us would oppose to the last. We sadly need town and country preachers. Men well versed in the Bible, Confession of Faith, Shorter Catechism, who can read their Greek New Testament . . . who can lay foundations and

abide the day of small things, men who are trained in full view of the field . . . After . . . 18 years on the ground the writer is fully convinced that we will never obtain the men we need from richly endowed theological seminaries located in cities of the older states.[1]

The following year the Synod of Arkansas approved the establishment of a theological department in the college, for the specific purpose of training candidates for the ministry.

The Divinity School, opened in Southwestern University at Clarksville, Tennessee in 1885, was more enduring and made a far more significant contribution to the life of the church. Some of the church's most eminent scholars served on its faculty and among its graduates were many of the leading ministers in the church. In 1893 the Divinity School reported a faculty of five—comparable to that of other theological schools—and a student body of 33. But financial resources proved inadequate, and the school was suspended, as we have seen, in 1917 and not reopened.

The Synod of Texas, struggling against great odds, had succeeded meanwhile in establishing its theological seminary at Austin.

The first steps were taken when Dr. Robert L. Dabney came to Austin as Professor of Mental and Moral Philosophy in the newly opened University of Texas. Within a year he and Dr. Richmond K. Smoot, pastor of the Free (later the First Southern) Presbyterian Church, had conferred about the mutual concern which they and others felt for establishing a school of theology in the rapidly growing Southwest. As Evangelist C. H. Dobbs explained: "We saw that our young men who went East were alienated from us, and many of them never returned. We did not think the semimonastic life of our theological seminaries fitted them for the pioneer life of our destitute regions. We find it costly to send them so far and utilize their labors during the summer months. We felt the need of a school in our own midst, where our young men would get in sympathy with the people and with the peculiarities of Texas work, where they would be known to our churches."[2]

On October 27, 1884, the Presbytery of Central Texas formally acted to establish a School of Theology at Austin, an enterprise endorsed a little later by the Presbyteries of Eastern and Western Texas, and then by the Synod of Texas. The first classes met in the Free Presbyterian Church with Dr. Smoot as the teacher and in Dr. Dabney's study. By the spring of 1889 a lecture room and library, two blocks west of the university, had been erected. The school finally closed in 1895, due, among other things, to Dr. Dabney's advanced age and failing sight, his forced retirement from the university, the failure of

Central Texas Presbytery to pay the salary of the student assistant, and the unwillingness of the synod to assume support. During the 11 years of its existence the school had sent 27 licentiates into the gospel ministry in the Southwest; during the same period Dr. Dabney estimated that only three of the Texas candidates who had gone "to Seminaries across the rim" had returned to labor in the state.[3]

It was indeed becoming clear that if the synod was to retain its native sons, or fill its vacant pulpits, it must establish a "trans-Mississippi Seminary." Trustees were appointed, a president, Thorton Rogers Sampson, elected, and on October 1, 1902, Austin Presbyterian Theological Seminary formally opened its doors, with six students, and a faculty of four. Dr. Sampson saw the new seminary meeting the needs not only of Texas but of Arkansas, Indian Territory, Mexico, and New Mexico—the entire Southwest, now growing rapidly, and with many unmet needs. Dr. Sampson resigned the presidency of the seminary in 1905, and was succeeded three years later by Rev. Dr. Robert E. Vinson. In the interim the Synod of Arkansas and the Synod of Oklahoma had joined Texas in control and support of the seminary. Dr. Vinson resigned in 1916 to become President of the University of Texas. Dr. Neal L. Anderson, elected to succeed him, discovered that trust funds, including endowment, had been spent to erect buildings and to pay the running expenses of the institution. The seminary faced bankruptcy. The desperate financial situation, along with the reduced enrollment occasioned by the First World War, led to the temporary closing of the institution. Only Dr. Thomas W. Currie, Chairman of the Faculty (later elected President), remained to look after the seminary property.

A three-year breather permitted funds to grow and friends to rally to the seminary's support. A new faculty was gathered, and in September 1921 the institution opened its doors, with seven students in attendance and a faculty of four. There were still difficult days, especially during the Depression years, when President Currie to save expenses doubled as stated supply for Highland Park Church in Dallas. But the student body increased, and the seminary was soon established on a firm financial basis.

Dr. Dabney and his colleague Dr. Smoot had been unyielding Calvinists, leaders of the more conservative and isolationist wing of the church, adamantly opposed to any closer relations with Northern Presbyterians. A broader point of view became characteristic of the seminary under the leadership of Dr. Currie. He himself emerged as one of the leaders of the movement looking toward cooperation and union with the Presbyterian Church in the U.S.A.

The seminary continued its closer relationship with the University of Texas, which had begun with its founding by Dr. Dabney. Dr. D. A. Penick, Professor in the Department of Classical Languages, and a Presbyterian elder, made it possible in the early days for the seminary students to receive their instruction in Biblical Greek in the University. Professors in the seminary taught Bible courses in the University. The correspondence course in Bible offered by the Extension Department of the University was prepared by Dr. Currie.

Presbyterians in Kentucky were among the first to feel the need of a theological seminary in the Mississippi Valley. In antebellum days it seemed for a brief moment as though their dreams might be realized. The General Assembly of the then united church established in 1853 a seminary at Danville, Kentucky, to serve the western synods. For eight years the seminary prospered; then came the Civil War. Attendance dropped, and in 1866 when the Synod of Kentucky divided, the seminary passed into the hands of the loyalist faction which remained within the Presbyterian Church in the U.S.A. Having lost the support of its major constituency, the seminary barely managed to hold its head above the waters. For three years indeed there was only a single professor, retained to instruct any students who chose to matriculate. Efforts of the two synods, Northern and Southern, to agree on some plan of joint occupancy in 1883 failed to materialize, and the seminary, strengthened somewhat in its faculty, continued its operations, as an institution of the Northern Church, until the merger of 1901.

When the Supreme Court rendered its decision awarding the two educational institutions of Kentucky Presbyterianism—Centre College and Danville Seminary—to the loyalist minority, friends of the Southern synod organized promptly to provide educational institutions replacing those which had been lost. The charter and constitution of the new Central University provided for a number of colleges, including a College of Philosophy, Literature, and Science; a College of Theology; a College of Law; a College of Medicine; a College of Dentistry; and also six preparatory schools.

The first of these colleges opened in Richmond, Kentucky, in 1874, but the way did not seem clear to undertake the establishment of the College of Theology until 1889, when the synod began systematic efforts to raise funds for the undertaking. Two years later the synod invited its sister synods in the Mississippi Valley to join it in this endeavor. A number of these were now committed to Southwestern University, with its theological department, at Clarksville. Only one, the Synod of Missouri, responded to the invitation of the Synod of Kentucky. On October 2, 1893, the Louisville Presbyterian Theological Seminary, jointly owned and operated by these two synods, began its first session with a faculty of six professors and with 31 students in attendance. This was a larger enrollment than the most sanguine had anticipated. "No seminary has ever started under more favorable conditions,"[4] it was reported to the General Assembly. It was the first theological institution in the Southern Church to be located in a large city, a step which both Union and Columbia would soon feel compelled to follow. The enrollment at Louisville increased to a total of 67 in the fourth year. The average attendance for the first eight years was 47, and in this period there were 91 graduates.

It became increasingly clear, however, that divided Presbyterianism in Kentucky could not adequately support competing institutions. As a result of a number of unofficial conferences of mutual friends of the two synods of Kentucky an agreement was reached by the governing boards of the Louisville Presbyterian Theological Seminary and the Danville Theological Seminary, and the governing boards of Central University and Centre College, for the consolidation of the two seminaries under the name of the Presbyterian Theological Seminary of Kentucky, with location in Louisville, and for the consolidation of the two colleges under the name of the Central University of Kentucky, with location in Danville. In the spring of 1901 this consolidation was effected, and for the first time synods of the two main branches of Presbyterianism in the nation joined in support of a theological seminary that would train ministers for both.

There was intense opposition to this move on the part of a few within the Southern Synod of Kentucky and more opposition came from the church at large. As the *Central Presbyterian* reported when the news broke: "The proposed consolidation of the Theological Seminary at Danville of the U.S.A. Church and of our Seminary at Louisville is one of profound concern to the whole church." A party within the Northern Church, it was observed, was clamoring for a modification of the doctrinal standards of the church; and, until it became clear that the church as a whole had not drifted from its moorings, one seminary could not be expected to train ministers for both branches of the church.[5] Without announcement or submission to the General Assembly, the editor complained, a scheme has been adopted both by the board and the Synod of Kentucky which merges this theological seminary into one which is not a seminary of our church, but something else. "To negotiate a consolidation of a theological seminary with another outside of our church's jurisdiction without the consent of the Assembly previously obtained, and literally without announcement to the Church, was something beyond the moral right of any Board or Synod to accomplish . . ."

"We regret to say," concluded the editorial, "that the movement seems to us to be one that if established will seriously compromise the Southern Church, and bring us into entanglements that will prove to be embarrassing in the extreme. We can see nothing for the Assembly to do but to decline courteously any participation in it."[6]

The issue was heatedly debated before the General Assembly. A majority committee report recommended that approval not be given, among other reasons because "the basis on which it is proposed to unite the two seminaries naturally and logically leads to organic union between the two churches." Dr. S. L. Morris, chairman of the committee, argued for the majority that the two churches were divided on questions of basic principle. They had different views and practices on the woman question, the Negro question, and others. He held that in the event of consolidation the Northern idea would be taught and not the Southern and graduates would naturally preach organic union of the two churches. Professor Thomas Cary Johnson of Union Theological Seminary in Virginia opposed the union of the two seminaries because of the difference in the distinctive principles of the two churches. The Northern Church, he charged, does not confine itself to spiritual matters, nor does it respect the Standards. Union of the seminaries would commit us to the latitudinarian broad-church view of the Northern Church. To say that we have the same Standards seemed to him a huge joke. "If our brethren in Kentucky associate with these U.S.A. men," he inquired rhetorically, "how long will they remain sound?"

Proponents of union replied that the seminary was by the plan of consolidation literally nailed to the Confession of Faith and the common Standards of the two churches and so its orthodoxy was more fully guaranteed than that of any other seminary; that the Kentucky brethren did not desire organic union, and that all agitation on that subject would be given the quietus if the present plans were adopted; and that unless increased endowments and larger patronage were secured the Presbyterian schools in Kentucky would be forced into the background and finally strangled.[7]

After prolonged debate the Assembly by a sizable majority adopted a substitute resolution: "That while the Assembly may not wholly approve the wisdom of the consolidation of the two seminaries yet in view of the fact that there was practical unanimity in the Synods of Kentucky and Missouri as to the measure, and because of the safeguards thrown about the contract, this court hereby interposes no bar to such consolidation but gives its assent thereto, leaving the entire responsibility thereof to the Synods of Kentucky and Missouri."

But the apprehensions of many in the church had not been assuaged. "The exposition of the embarrassments likely to be introduced into its teachings, and the evils which might ensue from a compact, combining Northern and Southern Presbyterians, controlled by a Directory, made up equally of men of both churches, and taught by a faculty taken from bodies not homogeneous," declared the *Southwestern Presbyterian* after the issue had been raised again the following year, "did not appear to us exaggerated . . . We can only hope and pray that the safeguards may prove effective."[8]

The fears aroused by the consolidation soon vanished, though it must be admitted that the joint educational program conducted by the Synod of Kentucky and the Synod of Missouri stimulated the growing sentiment for union which continued to appear in this portion of the Assembly.

The Synod of Appalachia joined in the support of Louisville Seminary in 1918, as did the Synod of Tennessee in 1924. These were years of solid growth. Dr. Vander Meulen, retiring from the presidency of the seminary in 1930, noted that during the ten years of his incumbency endowment had increased from $757,402 to $1,362,320, the faculty from five chairs to eight, the student body from 38 to 96. Two permanent lectureships had been endowed; six fellowships had been provided.

In 1884 there came to Union Theological Seminary in Virginia the man who was to become in effect the second founder of the institution, Rev. Walter W. Moore, Adjunct-Professor of Oriental Literature. The seminary was located at this time at Hampden-Sydney, adjacent to the college of the same name, in what had been before the Civil War a prosperous countryside. Friends of the seminary, especially those closely connected with its work, had recognized for many years that changed conditions would sooner or later require the institution to move to a more central location.

In 1892 Dr. Moore reported to the Board of Trustees that among the difficulties he had encountered in attempting to raise money for the seminary "was the widespread dissatisfaction with the location of the Seminary, and the consequent indisposition to contribute to the erection of any more buildings in the wrong place. Many of our private members, as well as many of our ministers and ruling elders," he continued, seem to think that the officers of the Seminary have been blind to the changed conditions of the country since the war and have not recognized the vital importance of planting our principal training school for ministers in some center of population and business influence, where its property would accumulate and increase rapidly in value, where its accessibility and metropolitan advantages would commend a much larger patronage, where the best methods of Christian work could be seen in actual operation, and where the contingent of picked men reinforcing the pastors in their Sunday Schools and mission would make Presbyterianism a colossus instead of a pigmy among the Christian denominations of the future.[9]

"The Protestant idea of a divinity school," Dr. Moore continued to insist, "is not monasticism but ministry, not monkish seclusion from the world, but genial, helpful, Christlike mingling with one's fellowmen."[10]

The loss of 12 men in one year and of eight in the next—men who stated that they would have gone to Union but for its unfavorable location—added weight to Dr. Moore's argument. Ultimately, he stressed, it was a question as to whether the synod would educate its candidates at its own institution, within its own bounds, or whether they should go to Louisville, McCormick, or Princeton.

Louisville Seminary, sensing its opportunity, invited Dr. Moore to accept a chair in their new institution. Convinced that Union had no future in its isolated location, Dr. Moore accepted and was retained at Union only because of an overlooked clause in his contract which would not permit him to leave Union for another year.

The board could now no longer delay. In 1894 it announced that it was prepared to consider offers for a new site in the state. The most appealing offer came from Richmond, and on October 18, 1895, the board voted to accept the offer and requested the controlling synods to approve the removal. The Synod of North Carolina voted almost unanimously in favor of the move; in the Synod of Virginia there was a hard-fought battle. Opponents of removal, friends of Hampden-Sydney, argued that the synod should let well enough alone; that to remove would be a betrayal of trust to the donors, a reflection on the wisdom of the founding fathers, and a serious blow to the college. The seminary, it was further pointed out, would leave unsalable $150,000 worth of excellent property. Populous places, it was added, are not the best places for theological training. In a rural location there is a greater concentration on the studies of the seminary and less temptation to spend the evening in that which merely entertains. The Rev. T. P. Epes, President of Hope Academy and pastor of Blackstone Church, developed an extensive argument to

show that the city originates heresy, while the country perpetuates orthodoxy. To the argument that some students would be drawn away
from a seminary in the country to the rich Northern seminaries, Dr.
R. L. Dabney replied in a long article in the *Central Presbyterian*:
Let them go. We should be well quit of them. "These self-indulgent
men are not fit for the work. To my apprehension there is no manifestation of character more contemptible than this, to see a young
fellow, most probably poor and plainly raised, demanding these
luxuries, as essential to his wants, while professing to enlist in the
hard and rough warfare of Christ." He feared that the softness of city
life would unfit men for rural churches and the mission field. "She [the
church] has taught each young minister to say: 'I am bound to have
my streetcar conveniences, my hydrant water, my bathtub and my
city luxuries; and I can't go where these are not.' . . . How much
good," he asked, "will one of these clerical dudes ever do, with his exclusive luxuries, among plain farmers . . . and laboring men who do
not and cannot have them?"[11]

The synod met in Charleston, West Virginia, in 1895 and, after a
very hard and sometimes bitter debate, voted 100 to 67 for removal.
Three years later the seminary began work in its new location, and in
1904 Dr. Moore, who more than others had been responsible for the
removal to Richmond and who had developed unmistakable gifts of
leadership, was elected as the first president of the institution. He
labored now with renewed zeal to increase the endowment, enlarge
the faculty, improve the plant, adapt the curriculum to the needs of
the age, and to win for the seminary the full and undivided support of
the church.

The average number of students attending the seminary per annum for the 25 years preceding the move to Richmond was 43, and at
the end of the period there was a decided drift to other institutions
more advantageously located. The first year after removal, 88 students
were in attendance—an all-time high. From this time on there was a
steady increase in the number of students, except for two short periods, one at the turn of the century, when there was a slump in the
number of candidates for all denominations, and the other during
World War I. In 1926, the year when Dr. Moore resigned his office,
158 students were registered—a new high for Southern Presbyterian
seminaries. The faculty meanwhile had increased from five to eight.
New courses had been developed to keep the seminary abreast with
the best that was being offered elsewhere: training in the use of the
voice, courses in "sociology" (the very word frightening some tradi-
tionalists within the church), a chair of Christian education (some of

the older members of the faculty were a little fearful that *emphasis* on psychology might lead to a depreciation of the Holy Spirit), and a chair of Christian missions. A lectureship had been established, bringing annually three distinguished scholars to the campus. Under Dr. Moore's guidance, and prompted by his suggestion, the faculty organized in 1915-1916 courses of advanced postgraduate study leading to the degree of Doctor of Divinity (later changed to Th.D.). An annual midwinter course was introduced for the benefit of ministers who could return for short intensive studies that would help to keep them abreast of advancing theological knowledge. Fellowships for graduate study were created. In 1912 Mission Court was established, offering a temporary home for missionaries on furlough, enabling them to benefit from, and themselves to benefit, the seminary community. In 1908 members of the faculty began to offer a two-year course, without charge, to young women who wished to prepare themselves for mission work at home and abroad. At one time 23 of these enrolled in this course and were soon at work, some in Korea, China, and Africa; others in various parts of the home field from Virginia to Oklahoma. Requests for this sort of preparation multiplied. A separate organization developed and grew into the General Assembly's Training School for Lay Workers (now the Presbyterian School of Christian Education) located, largely through the efforts of Dr. Moore, in Richmond, in close proximity to the seminary, on which in the early years it remained largely dependent.

Before the move to Richmond, Dr. Moore had been largely responsible for the publication of the *Union Seminary Magazine*, which after a few years became the only serious theological publication within the church.

At the time of the removal fear had been expressed that the conveniences of modern life furnished at Richmond might unfit students for bearing hardship in the field. Students' acceptance of calls to difficult and dangerous fields at home and abroad quickly showed this to be a delusion. In fact the larger opportunities at Richmond (so at Louisville, at Austin, and later at Atlanta) for active service, for clinical work, for the practice—hand in hand with the principles of ecclesiastical therapeutics—gave the students much better training for the cure of souls in mission fields both at home and abroad.

The increase in the numbers of student body and faculty, the expanding services of the seminary to its own constituency and to the church at large, was necessarily accompanied and made possible by a corresponding increase in resources and facilities.

During Dr. Moore's lifetime Union Seminary, with larger resources, usually set the pace, and pioneered in areas where it was followed more or less quickly by its sister institutions.

Columbia Seminary struggled for a time to maintain itself in its original location at Columbia, South Carolina. Closed in 1886-1887 as a consequence of the Woodrow crisis, the school reopened in 1887 with 14 students in attendance. The enrollment increased to a peak of 53 in 1894, by which time Louisville Seminary was in operation and Union was looking toward Richmond; then declined to a low of 19 in 1905, after which there was a new rise, cresting in the early days of World War I when there were 64 in attendance. Suggestions came repeatedly during this period that the seminary move to Atlanta, but all came to nought.

It became increasingly clear, however, that Columbia could not receive adequate support in its present location. The number of students was increasing, but with them came increasing costs, along with mounting deficits, and no new legacies. More serious was the lack of equipment. There had been no new building in the last 50 years. The refectory was a dilapidated wooden structure, the floor of which was none too solid. The chapel building had been intended for a stable. An old residence had been converted into an administration building, providing classrooms, offices, and library; the dormitories were old and entirely inadequate.[12]

Dr. John M. Wells, who succeeded Dr. Thornton Whaling as President in 1921, proposed consolidation with Union Seminary in Richmond.

Three of the supporting synods—South Carolina, Florida, and Alabama—approved a proposition submitted by the Board of Trustees to move the seminary to Atlanta or some other place within their bounds or, failing in that, to merge with Union Seminary in Richmond. The Synod of Georgia held out against removal to Virginia. The Board then agreed to move to Atlanta provided that the synod put on a campaign for half a million dollars, of which at least $250,000 was to be raised by Atlanta Presbytery for buildings, and that a suitable site be provided within the bounds of this presbytery.

The offer was accepted. Dr. Wells, feeling that he was not the proper one to lead in the move to Atlanta, resigned as President and was succeeded in this office by Dr. Richard T. Gillespie, under whose leadership the removal and subsequent rebuilding in Decatur, just out of Atlanta, took place. Work in the new location began on September 14, 1927. The Synod of Mississippi meanwhile had become one of the controlling synods. The seminary now served a territory stretch-

ing from the Mississippi River to the Atlantic Ocean and from the
North Carolina line to Key West, about 600 miles each way. It was
situated upon a beautiful campus of some 60 acres, near the center
of its territory and adjacent to one of the most important and rapidly
growing cities in the South.

The new President was:

> a man of action, and a leader who compelled cooperation by his un-
> selfish devotion and winsome personality. He literally poured out his
> life into the new Columbia Seminary. Said the member of the Board
> who had been chairman of the building committee: "I see him now as
> he stood at the beginning of his Presidency . . . a young man with a
> strong, agile and alert body, and a quick and steady step; with a clear,
> keen and logical mind, with a vision that was brilliant with the richest
> hopes; and an enthusiasm that was freely fed from the exuberance of
> youth . . . I see him as he called me to the rear of the chapel, just
> after the graduating exercises of this Seminary [six years later] in 1930,
> and threw his head on my shoulders and poured out the inner feeling
> of his heart to me. His task was done and he had sacrificed all for his
> ideals and he stood like a wounded veteran! In less than a month he
> was dead."[13]

Succeeding Dr. Gillespie in 1932 as President was Rev. Dr. J.
McDowell Richards, former Rhodes Scholar, then pastor of the
church at Thomasville, Georgia, under whom the seminary would
write a new chapter in its long history of service to the church.

The Presbyterian Church had long set high qualifications for its
ministers, including four years of college and three years of seminary
education. But provision had always been made for exceptional cases.
Throughout the 19th century there were ministers who had been
privately guided in their study of theology. As late as 1900 there were
complaints that some students omitted the third year of seminary
instruction, with the encouragement of the churches which called
them, and the approval of their presbyteries.[14]

In the early 1900's a new effort was made to delete the requirement of a Latin thesis for ministerial ordination. Lead in the effort
was taken by Rev. W. L. Lingle, described by Dr. Russell Cecil, as
"one of our clever and accomplished young ministers, of whom we
expected better things." According to Mr. Lingle the typical thesis
consisted of copious quotations of Turretine and the Vulgate bound
together with a few sentences of dog Latin. The requirement to him
had become "a farce, a delusion, a snare, and a weariness to the
flesh." Once, when students studied their theology from a Latin text,
the requirement had significance; but that day was now gone.

Opponents argued that the Latin thesis was necessary to uphold the standard of a liberal classical education ("If Latin goes, the study of Greek and Hebrew will be seriously affected"). "The gravest objection to this change," wrote one minister, "is that it will be a change . . . We are too much given to change."

The Assembly had declined to eliminate the Latin thesis requirement in 1891, 1892, and 1894; it declined to do so again by overwhelming vote in 1903. Ten years later there came another and more successful effort. An amendment to the Book of Church Order was adopted (1914) which permitted presbyteries to accept a certificate from an approved college in lieu of the examination on academic studies, and from the theological seminaries on the original languages of Scripture and church history. The thesis might now be in either English or Latin at the discretion of the presbytery. It was invariably the former.[15]

The seminaries continued through this period to receive students who had not completed their full college course. In one entering class, 13 out of 25 students lacked a college degree. For those unable to complete their language requirements there was granted a diploma without degree.

By 1930 the four theological institutions on which the church depended for the training of its ministers had improved their plants and had begun to enrich their curriculums, to raise their standards, and to enlarge their services to the church. There had been as yet however no pronounced shift in theological perspective. A "new theology" was making headway in the North; the "critical" study of the Scripture was gaining acceptance in scholarly circles and being popularized through the mass media; but the South as a whole, including the Southern Presbyterian Church and its theological seminaries, remained a bastion of conservatism.

The theology which had shaped Old School Presbyterianism, both North and South, was largely "a reproduction of the Calvinism of the 17th century, as it is formulated in the Westminster Confession and the Consensus Helveticus, and as it was elucidated by [the Swiss theologian] F. Turretine in his *Theologia Elenctica*."[16] Dr. Robert L. Dabney, Professor of Theology at Union from 1853 through 1883, and co-founder and Professor of Theology in the Austin School of Theology from 1884 through 1895, made use of Turretine (in Latin) as a textbook. His *Syllabus and Notes of the Course of Systematic and Polemic Theology* taught at Union was published in 1871, revised and reissued in 1878, and in all went through six editions, the last one dated 1927. Through his teaching, his students, and his textbook, Dr. Dabney probably did more to mold theological thinking in the Southern Presbyterian Church than any other person.

Dr. Dabney was succeeded as Professor of Theology in Union by Dr. Thomas E. Peck (1883-1893), who taught the theology of Thornwell (under whom he had studied) though he had also absorbed much from Dabney. He held that "every *word* of Scripture is the word of God; just as much so as if spoken in an audible voice from the throne, without the instrumentality of man or angel."[17]

Regarding the divine sovereignty he wrote: "God must control *all* things in order to control *any* thing; he must determine the *least* thing in order *to determine* the greatest."[18] For him, the sovereign grace of God included both his sovereign choice or election and also this sovereign application of the gospel to the elect by effectual calling. He sought to bring every opinion to the test of Scripture.[19] The chief element of his power, according to one who knew him, was his doubtlessness.

Dr. Clement Read Vaughan (1893-1896), who succeeded Peck, was a follower of Dabney, as was Givens Brown Strickler (1896-1913) and Thomas Cary Johnson (1913-1930); the latter followed Dabney's *Syllabus* slavishly and drilled it into successive generations of students paragraph by paragraph. For him Calvinism was the biblical system of religion and the student needed to know no other. The student at Union, through the early 1920's, underwent his preparations for the ministry without really hearing the name of Schleiermacher, Ritschl, and other great theologians who were so profoundly influencing the thought of the age. Dr. Johnson held that "the writers of Holy Scripture were so superintended by the Holy Ghost that their writings as a whole and in every part, are the word of God to us—that the original *autographs* of these writings were absolutely infallible when taken in the sense intended."[20] In 1924 when the evolution controversy was at its height the Presbyterian Committee of Publication published a small volume by Dr. Johnson entitled "God's Answer to Evolution." God's teachings in his Holy Word, Dr. Johnson held, proved that man could not have come into existence by chance or by any possible development of natural selection. Dr. Johnson taught as did his predecessors *jure divino* Presbyterianism. "The distinctive features of Presbyterianism, as a polity," he insisted, "are biblical . . . every essential feature of that polity is biblical . . . the whole system, with the exception of the circumstantial details, is revealed in the word of God and bound on the conscience with the authority of law."[21]

In 1894, Dr. Johnson, then Professor of Church History, wrote *A History of the Southern Presbyterian Church*, which appeared in the American Church History Series, and remained the sole history of the denomination until a brief centennial history appeared in 1961. In the preface of his book Dr. Johnson explained that he wrote, in part at least, "to furnish materials for answer to three specific questions, viz: why did the Southern Presbyterian Church come into separate existence? Why has it continued till the present a separate existence? Are there sufficient reasons why it should continue for a longer time to maintain a separate existence?"[22] This last question was answered emphatically in the affirmative. The Southern Church came into existence and must continue its independent existence to maintain the true conception of the non-secular, or purely spiritual, mission of the church—a doctrine, he charged, which Northern Presbyterians, both Old and New School, had finally abandoned in 1861.

The *Central Presbyterian* regretted, as did others, the harsh language and the partisan spirit of the book but approved, as did others, its substance, and gloried in its "noble vindication of the non-secular character of the Southern Presbyterian Church as one of its most distinguishing features."[23] The *Southwestern Presbyterian* expressed the hope that "this noble little book" might have a wide circulation, North as well as South.[24] Dr. W. McF. Alexander, one of the influential younger ministers of the church, later to be elected Moderator of the General Assembly, reviewing the volume in the *Presbyterian Quarterly*, wrote "No Southern Presbyterian can afford to be ignorant of the glorious position his church took . . . for the headship of Jesus Christ—for Christ and his crown . . . He who will look at the FACTS and 'call a spade a spade' will see that God brought our beloved Southern church into existence to conserve the truth, to bear witness to the fact that Christ Jesus is alone the Head of his church and that it is not to be prostituted to Caesar." He rejoiced to know that the book had been adopted as a textbook at Union Seminary and the Southwestern Presbyterian University, and expressed the hope that Louisville Seminary, Columbia, and Austin would do likewise.[25]

Inerrant inspiration, rigid Calvinism, *jure divino* Presbyterianism, and the non-secular mission of the church continued to be taught at Union Seminary, chief training grounds for the church's ministers, by Dr. Johnson until his death in 1930.

So it was also at Columbia Seminary, where Thornwell's theological lectures and Hodge's Theology (the Princeton School), in general agreement with Robert L. Dabney at Union Seminary, remained the basis for theological instruction. Thornwell's most dis-

tinctive contribution to Southern Presbyterian thought had been in
the field of ecclesiology. The church, he taught, should not add anything to its theology, its polity, or its worship that is not specifically or
by good and necessary inference derived from Scripture. ". . . the
silence of Scripture," he insisted, "is as real a prohibition as a positive
injunction to abstain. Where God has not commanded, the Church has
no jurisdiction."[26] He, more than any other, had developed the
theory of the non-secular character of the church, now firmly em-
bedded in the church's tradition.

John Lafayette Girardeau, Columbia's most important theologian
(1876-1895) after Thornwell, whose published works are critical
and apologetic rather than constructive, was in the Thornwellian
succession. Inspiration he defined as "an immediate, supernatural influence of the Holy Ghost upon the mind, objectively communicating
to it such truth as God wills to impart, effecting the infallible communication to others of their truth, and attested by miraculous proof."[27]

In a series of popular lectures, subsequently published, Dr. Girardeau strongly defended orthodox Calvinism as against evangelical
Arminianism on the disputed doctrines—total depravity, unconditional election, limited atonement, irresistible grace, perseverance of
the saints. Election and reprobation were justified on the grounds of
the end sought, which is glorification of divine grace in the salvation
of sinners and glorification of God's justice in the punishment of
sinners. In Calvinism, he held, this end is certainly and efficaciously
accomplished. In Arminianism, it would be uncertain if any would be
saved.[28]

In the evolution controversy Dr. Girardeau took the position that
"professors were debarred by their subscription from inculcating
contra-confessional views; that the Standards were the impregnable
ramparts against error; that to teach what is contrary to any statement
of the doctrinal standards was to teach what is contrary to some statement of doctrine in the Scriptures."[29]

Professors of Theology following Girardeau—William T. Hall
(1895-1911), Thornton Whaling (1911-1921),[30] and James B. Green
(1921-1950)—taught the Thornwell-Girardeau theology, using Thornwell and/or Hodge as texts, though in his latter years Dr. Green
dropped Hodge and used the equally conservative one-volume work
of Louis Berkhof on *Systematic Theology*. There was no departure
here from the traditional theology, though Dr. Green came to feel
that the language about reprobation was too strong, and in the 1940's
defended modifications in the extreme language of the Confession of
Faith against his colleague in the field of historical theology, William
Childs Robinson.[31]

Professor Francis R. Beattie, Professor of Apologetics at Columbia (1888-1893) and Professor of Systematic Theology and Apologetics in the newly organized Louisville Presbyterian Seminary (1893-1906), was a Canadian by birth, who came to Columbia Theological Seminary in 1888 to fill the chair once occupied by Professor James Woodrow. Dr. R. A. Webb, a graduate of Columbia Theological Seminary, and in its theological tradition, then Professor of Theology and Dean of Southwestern University School of Theology, described Dr. Beattie as "clear and conservative in his exposition of evangelical truth . . . thoroughly and conscientiously out of sympathy with all radicalism in criticism, in science, in philosophy, in theology, in apologetics . . . He is a Calvinist," continued Dr. Webb, "of the school of the Hodges . . . His theological alignment is with the federalists . . . He stands in with our own matchless Thornwell."[32]

In 1909 Dr. Webb succeeded Dr. Beattie as Professor of Theology in the Louisville Seminary, a position which he held for the next ten years. "Recent events and discussions," wrote Dr. Webb, "emphasize the imperative importance of our Protestantism, reminding its adherents that some questions are closed and removed from the storms of debate." Among such questions he counted "the genuineness, authenticity, verbal inspiration and inerrancy of the Scriptures," along with "the contents of the denominational creed." "Creeds," said he, "are a covenant of fellowship voluntarily subscribed to, and covenant fidelity closes their contents against all destructive criticism within the fellowship. For purposes of self-protection, for the sake of internal peace and undivided co-operation, each denomination exacts of all its officers a solemn oath that they will in no point contravene that confessional bond of fellowship . . . Denominational infidelity is perjury . . ."[33]

Drs. Dabney and Smoot, co-founders of the Austin School of Theology, laid a conservative base on which their successors continued to build. Dr. Samuel Alexander King, Professor of Theology and senior member in the new Austin Presbyterian Seminary (1903-1918), was a disciple of Hodge and taught the five disputed points of Calvinism, along with the Federal Theology, in full accord with the Westminster Standards.

Dr. King had no reservation regarding the plenary verbal inspiration of the Bible. "All the books are inspired," he wrote, "and every part of each book is the inspired Word of God . . . inspiration extends not only to all the books, but also to the words."[34]

Dr. Arthur Gray Jones, who accepted the chair of theology after the reopening of the seminary (1921-1927), was a Calvinist, without apparent reservations, and like his predecessor used Hodge as his text.

He was however "first of all a pastor and an evangelist. The emerging trends in theology held for him no special fascination. He was concerned [rather] for the vital relation of a sinner and his Savior."[35]

But the time was approaching when the emerging trends in theology, ignored or too easily dismissed not only in Austin but also in the other seminaries, must be taken into account. And so with the new approach to the Scriptures.

In January 1892 Dr. William M. McPheeters, Professor of Old Testament in Columbia Seminary, noted: "The views of the 'Higher Critics' are being rapidly popularized and propagated among all the more intelligent people of our churches." He recognized that this might be more true of the churches of the North than of those in the South, but predicted "we will make a sad, possibly a fatal mistake, if we flatter ourselves that we will not have to face these issues."[36]

Scholars of the church were well aware of the danger. But too many sought to parry its threat by ridicule or by a dangerous argument that could be too easily turned against them—that acceptance of the critical conclusions destroyed not only the inspiration of the Bible but also the very foundations of the Christian faith.

Dr. Walter W. Moore, Professor of Old Testament and first President of Union Seminary, was one of those who keenly regretted "the violent and abusive tone" in which so much of the conservative reaction to the "higher criticism" was expressed.[37] He insisted, however, that Dr. Cheyne was wrong in ascribing the 110th Psalm to a post-exilic origin, and gave, as the strongest reason of all, the fact that "Our Lord says that 'David himself' was the author of this psalm."[38] Archaeological evidence, he claimed, helped to establish the historicity of Jonah,[39] undermined the anti-supernatural interpretation of the early Hebrew history,[40] bolstered traditional views regarding the authorship of Daniel and Isaiah.[41] The documentary view of the Hexateuch he considered "a passing phase of criticism."[42]

Dr. Edward Mack, who followed Dr. Moore in the Old Testament chair (1915-1938), remained to the end an eloquent foe of the higher criticism which rejected the Mosaic authorship of the Pentateuch and accepted the theory of the two Isaiahs. He ended his teaching career insisting that the most recent scholarship had rendered the findings of the higher critics untenable.

Dr. R. C. Reed, Professor in Columbia Theological Seminary (1898-1925), an Associate Editor of the *Presbyterian Quarterly* (1902-1904) and of the *Presbyterian Standard* (1905-1925), sought to discredit the critical reconstruction of the Old Testament by pointing out that it originated in Germany as a "pastime of German professors," who "had no more reverence for the Bible than for Homer," and by calling attention to its consequences: "The results of this criticism are such that they cannot but impair one's faith in the authority and inspiration of the Bible." It "tells us [that] much which purports to be history is not history"; "the final effect of the higher criticism, should it prevail, can be nothing less than the total destruction of the whole Bible as a divine book." He agreed with the *New York Sun*: "They try to make themselves and others believe that they are only putting the authority of the Bible on a more rational basis, when in truth they are utterly destroying it, and along with it the supernatural basis of all theology and religion."[43]

Dr. W. M. McPheeters, a colleague of Dr. Reed on the faculty of Columbia Seminary, in a memorial bulletin, recalled that the years of his ministry (1875-1925) was a period when "the tumult of those who had risen against Jehovah and against his anointed" had increased until it became a "deafening hurricane." The spirit which had emanated from these hostile forces, Dr. McPheeters identified as humanism, which he defined as the apotheosis, the deification of man. Many of its progeny—democracy, feminism, evolutionism, the radical criticism, and all the movements seeking to substitute a mere external union of the churches for the true unity of the faith—bore like Satan, he charged, the outward mien and semblance of angels of light. In such an atmosphere, he pointed out, Dr. Reed had borne his witness for the truth—not particular doctrines only, such as the irremediable and everlasting punishment of the finally impenitent, but also Calvinism in its entirety, "all of which is an abomination to the aggressive humanism of our day." Of particular significance here, he claimed, was the scriptural doctrine of the church, which had never received adequate exposition and formulation until it was expounded and formulated by the founding fathers of the Southern Presbyterian Church.

In formulating this scriptural doctrine of the church, Dr. McPheeters claimed, God bestowed upon James Henley Thornwell and those associated with him "an honor comparable to that granted Athanasius, who in the fourth century was used of God for the formulation of the Scripture doctrine of the Godhead; comparable to that granted Augustine, who in the fifth century was used to formulate the doctrines of sin and grace; comparable to that granted Luther and Calvin, who in the sixteenth century were instrumental in formulating the doctrine of salvation by grace through faith." According to this doctrine, Dr. McPheeters explained, the church could speak only what Christ commissioned it to speak; it was exclusively a spiritual organization; its mission was to promote the glory of God and the salvation of men from the curse of the law; it had nothing to do with the voluntary associations for men for civil and social purposes. To these and similar propositions regarding the nature and mission of the church, Dr. McPheeters recalled, Dr. Reed had given his cordial assent. To them he had witnessed on the floor of the various courts of the church, and in the press. To them, for 27 years as Professor of Church History and Ecclesiastical Polity, he had witnessed ceaselessly in his classroom, seeking to commend them to every student's understanding and conscience in the fear of God.[44]

In so writing Dr. McPheeters described himself as well as Dr. Reed, though for him it was an even longer battle, a period of 44 years (1888-1932). Dr. McPheeters began his teaching career at a time when traditional views of Scripture were being seriously challenged by the so-called higher criticism, which, as he viewed it, *"in the name and interests of religion* subjects the written word to treatment not one whit less ignominious and degrading than that to which Pilate's minions subjected the incarnate Word."[45] "It is upon this foundation—the integrity, authenticity, genuineness, supernatural origin and divine authority of the Bible—that the church needs to center her most serious attention," he wrote.[46] To a defense of the traditional views of Scripture and of the Reformed faith as embodied in the Westminster Confession of Faith, Dr. McPheeters gave his life. He countered attacks from without and sought to stem any defection from within. To the author of this volume, some of whose views he opposed, Dr. McPheeters wrote that no teacher in one of the theological seminaries of the church had any right to teach anything that was contrary to the Confession of Faith or to the traditional interpretations of that Confession (the view which in the 1880's had been urged against Dr. Woodrow). "For his actions," wrote Rev. S. C. Byrd, Vice President of Queens–Chicora College, in a memorial bulletin issued by Columbia Theological Seminary, "he was regarded by some as a meddler and criticized by others as a heresy hunter. But in spirit and in purpose he was not either merely. His efforts and his zeal were for truth's sake, and so he was undeterred by criticism, censure and rebuff. He was of the spirit of which martyrs are made . . ."[47]

Professor Francis R. Beattie, Professor of Systematic Theology and Apologetics in Louisville Seminary (1893-1906), wrote a series of articles in the *Christian Observer*, which was later published under the title *Radical Criticism: An Exposition and Examination of the Radical Critical Theory Concerning the Literature and Religious*

System of the Old Testament Scriptures. According to an unsigned review in the *Union Seminary Magazine*: "No work from the pen of any southern Presbyterian writer since the war has been received more cordially or referred to more respectfully by all kinds of literary and religious journals inside and outside our bounds."[48]

In the first part of his book Dr. Beattie defined higher criticism and sharply discriminated between higher criticism as a legitimate biblical discipline and radical higher criticism with its vast and unfounded assumptions, its questionable principles, its uncritical methods, and its unproved—if not unprovable—assumptions. In the second part he traced the history of the radical movement, revealing its intimate connections historically and logically with a philosophical denial of the supernatural. In the third part he examined the philosophical presuppositions of the various schools of radical higher criticism as related to the doctrine of inspiration. A true doctrine of inspiration, he indicated, must be determined by the claim which the Scripture makes for itself and by the facts which the sacred record actually contains. This once ascertained, our whole study of the questions which higher criticism handles should be pursued mindful of the fact that Scripture actually possesses the peculiar quality which inspiration denotes. To adopt critical methods and results which shut out inspiration, he charged, is the great danger to which advanced criticism is exposed.[49]

Dr. Beattie saw no middle course between the radical critical theory and the historical conservative view of the national and religious life of Israel. Ministers who accepted the radical views, he was convinced, must be disciplined.[50]

In Austin Presbyterian Theological Seminary Dr. Robert F. Gribble, Professor of Old Testament (1923-1960), became the protagonist for the strict interpretation of the Standards of the church.[51] He warned his students to the very end to beware of the inroads of the documentary theory of the Pentateuch.[52]

At the close of the 19th century the Southern Presbyterian Church seemed solidly conservative, strongly Calvinistic, distinctly sectional, and remarkably homogenous in outlook and belief. Articles, pamphlets, and books expounded and defended the disputed points of Calvinism. The editor of the *Southwestern Presbyterian* was convinced that all the main fruits and fundamental principles of the Bible had long since been discovered and set forth in systematic form and that they could not be affected by subsequent discoveries of biblical truth. "We need not look, then," he concluded, "for Scriptural theology to advance beyond or contradict any of the five points of Calvinism."[53] The Southern Church watched apprehensively efforts being made in the Northern Church to amend its Confession of Faith. "A great many," reported the *Christian Observer*, "are recording their votes in favor of maintaining the system of doctrine in the Standards and yet of adopting certain amendments such as will really destroy its consistency as a system of doctrine . . . The sequel will be that when under this enfeebled doctrine men of laxer views have been ordained they will want to eliminate all Calvinism from the Creed and our church will have lost its charm."[54] To make it doubly certain that no changes would be made in its own Confessional Standards the requirement that two-thirds of the presbyteries must approve was altered in 1894 to read three-fourths.

Editors, scholarly ministers, and faculties of colleges and theological seminaries joined hands in repudiating the "new theology." The spiritual welfare of millions of our people in the vast future, declared the *Central Presbyterian* in 1890, depends upon our firm adherence to the essentials of that old theology which lies enshrined in the sacred pages of the Holy Scriptures. These essentials include the fall and total depravity of man, universal guilt and condemnation to death, need of pardon through the atoning sacrifice of a divine and human substitute, and regeneration by the almighty power of God, the Holy Ghost. "A theology that assails any one of these fundamentals, directly or indirectly, is too new for an honest Presbyterian Christian."[55]

A decade later, Dr. Eugene Daniel asked, what is the attitude of our church toward the modern theology? Our attitude, he replied, is not one of ignorance; not one of indifference; not one of arrogant intolerance or of uncharitable malice; not one of opposition to sanctified scholarship; not one of stolid narrowness. "The attitude of our Church toward the Regenerated Theology is that of thoughtful, intelligent, positive and, I believe, unanimous rejection and antagonism."[56]

To Southern Presbyterians the burning issue at stake in the theological debates of the 1890's was the inspiration of the Scriptures. The Christian faith, it was claimed, depended on the absolute inerrancy of the original autographs. To those who offered any other view of inspiration Henry C. Alexander, recently retired Professor of New Testament in Union Seminary, applied "the remorseless maxim, falsus in uni, falsus in omnibus [false in one point, false in all]; the witness discredited in court on the score of his veracity as to one part of his evidence stands discredited as to the whole of it.

If God's word contains error on any subject whatever, how can it be any more accepted as ... God's word?"[57]

Any conclusions of biblical scholars ignoring or threatening this basic position were accordingly dismissed out of hand. A clinching argument was the witness of Jesus. As the *Christian Observer* pointed out, Jesus had occasion to refer over and over again to the very books in which the would-be critics professed to have found errors, and he always found them entirely trustworthy. "Our modern critics find them not so. Are these men," queried the editor, "so much superior to Jesus in their knowledge of science that they can discover in Genesis, scientific errors which he never perceived?"[58]

According to Rev. Dr. George D. Armstrong, the inspiration of Scripture as plenary and verbal extended beyond moral and religious truths to all statement of facts, whether scientific, historical, or geographical. "Where there is a conflict between a truth or doctrine clearly taught in Scripture and the generally accepted conclusions of science," he claimed, "sound logic requires that we accept the former, and reject the latter. God cannot err; science may err, in the present, as it often has in the past."[59]

In accordance with this belief Dr. Armstrong held to the historicity of the flood, and to the creation of woman out of a rib taken from Adam's side. He was ready to acknowledge, however, that the seven days of Genesis referred to periods of indefinite length.[60] Evolution was dismissed by Dr. Armstrong, and by Southern Presbyterians generally, as unproven theory, and contrary to the Scriptures.

The editor of the *North Carolina Presbyterian* agreed with "one of the acknowledged leaders of the church" who expressed the belief that there was not a Presbyterian Church on the face of the earth so completely united as the Southern Church. The questions which are raised, he continued, "are more surface questions—they concern matters of administration chiefly—they do not go down to the roots of doctrinal belief, or touch the fundamentals of faith ..."[61]

Rev. Dr. R. Q. Mallard, editor of the *Southwestern Presbyterian* and retiring Moderator at the 1897 General Assembly, closed his sermon by giving some of the distinctive emphases of the Southern Presbyterian Church: (1) a positive, written creed, resting upon the bedrock of the Scriptures alone, subscribed ex anima by all its officers; (2) utter, entire, everlasting separation of church and state; (3) its rulers, permanent, educated, divinely ordained ruling and teaching elders of the male sex. According to one qualified observer at this Assembly no group of men more thoroughly representative of the distinctive principles of the Southern Church had ever gathered in one body since 1861. The trusted leaders, the men whom the church most delighted to honor, were there in force. It was an old men's Assembly. The great event was the celebration of the 250th anniversary of the Westminster Standards. In honor of the occasion there was a series of addresses—later gathered into book form. "Every address," wrote Dr. W. McF. Alexander of Memphis, "was conservative, and praised our historic standards. The Assembly was heart and soul with every speaker. It was Calvinistic first, Presbyterian next, and proud of its glorious record in the past. The Southern Church is absolutely satisfied with her historic symbols of faith, and she believes that the antidote to the new theology and the moral laxness of the age is to be found wrapped up in the Westminster Standards."[62]

The succeeding Assembly was perhaps even more significant. It gathered in New Orleans. Dr. B. M. Palmer, who had preached at the opening Assembly in 1861 and was now drawing close to the end of his earthly career, preached the Communion sermon. Rev. Joseph R. Wilson, D.D., LL.D., who had served the church first as permanent clerk and now for many years as stated clerk, was constrained by growing feebleness and the weight of years to tender his resignation—the older generation, the founding fathers were passing from the scene, but the younger generation, or so it seemed to a perceptive observer, walked in the footsteps of the fathers. "These younger brethren," he exulted, "have drunk at the fountain of testimony the fathers of 1861 gave to the world, and have imbibed their faith. The Church has not swerved from the moorings where these sought to anchor her . . . Today," continued the writer, "peace prevails throughout our borders. Our church is rent by no divisive matter of doctrine, policy or sentiment. No disturbing questions agitate its bosom. Fraternal confidence, a community of ideas and unity of worship characterize its life and membership. . . ."[63]

The Assembly itself recognized this unanimity. In a pastoral letter addressed to all its members it stated:

It is a fact, calling for sincere thanksgiving to the great Head of the Church, that while religious error, in many plausible and dangerous forms, pervades our country, it has not yet succeeded in making its way into our ministry and churches. So far as is known, it may safely be said that our denomination, amidst all the defections of the time, still stands with entire and sincere unanimity for all the great essential doctrines of the Gospel so clearly and scripturally expressed in the standards of our faith. And as to the future, it is a source of great satisfaction that all our Seminaries, in which our future ministry is being trained, are schools, which while encouraging the widest and freest investigation in every department of sacred learning, as fully and as firmly as ever before hold fast to every article of "the faith once delivered to the saints."[64]

This homogeneity continued through the first and on into the second decade of the 20th century.

In the summer of 1907, the "new theology" was blasted time and again "in masterful addresses" at Montreat. "We are profoundly thankful," said the *Presbyterian Standard*, "that this theology has no sympathy among teachers in Southern theological seminaries."[65] The *Central Presbyterian* was struck by the continuing unity of conviction. Recalling recent General Assemblies, the editor commented:

Nowhere in the world, we believe, can be found a body of men from such widely distributed localities, organized in deliberative council, of such homogeneous and at the same time lofty ideals of life and symbols of faith. When you have heard the opinion of one of these men on the authority of the Bible, the sovereignty of Christ, the necessity and efficiency of the atonement, the essential nature of the church, and its relation to its great Head, you have virtually heard the opinions of all. Men who never saw each other before, reared, the one in the new West, and the other in the historic East, are as united and sympathetic in faith and zeal as though from childhood to manhood they had been trained in the great truths and principles of life until of one dominating mind.[66]

In the judgment of the *Presbyterian Standard* genuine Calvinism was dead in all the world except in the Southern states and in Ulster County, Ireland. "The surpassing purity of Presbyterianism in the Southern States," the *Standard* claimed, was a blessing to the whole world. It was the distinctive mission of the Southern Church, "to wave the blue banner proudly, for an ideal to Presbyterians in all lands and throughout successive generations."[67]

The only theological question to arouse controversy during this period in the Southern Church was one regarding the elect infant clause (Chap. X—now XII—in the Confession of Faith). According to this article elect infants, dying before they reach the age of discretion, are saved through the grace of God. For 100 years and more Cumberland Presbyterians and others had aroused strong feeling against the Presbyterian Church on the ground that this clause taught that non-elect infants were eternally lost. This Presbyterians denied, claiming that the Confession of Faith based on Scripture could go no further than the Scriptures went—and that on the fate of non-elect infants Scripture was silent. Current efforts of the Presbyterian Church U.S.A. to revise its Confession of Faith reopened the question.

An overture to the Southern Assembly asking for an amendment declaring that all infants dying in infancy are elect was declined on the ground that "the present language of the Confession cannot, by any fair interpretation, be construed to teach that any of those who die in infancy are lost." A resolution that the Publication Committee be directed to attach a footnote to the Confession of Faith explaining this action of the Assembly was then adopted—without debate.[68]

The action of the General Assembly in ordering the printing of the footnote brought strong protests from Benjamin M. Palmer, Thomas Cary Johnson of Union Seminary, Francis R. Beattie of Louisville Seminary, other leading theologians of the church, and from all the church papers, except the *Presbyterian Standard,* edited for a brief period by the brilliant and in some respects forward-looking Alexander J. McKelway. Opposition was not so much to the matter of the footnote. Few Presbyterians, if any, believed that any children dying in infancy were eternally damned, and it was generally denied that any such doctrine was taught in the Confession. The footnote was opposed through fear that if the Confession were amended, by so much as a footnote, it would involve other parts of the Confession and result in attempts at revision, such as had developed in the Northern Church. The Confession in its present form, it was argued, said as much as the Bible explicitly declared and no more.[69] Advocates of change argued that if Presbyterians did not believe in infant damnation why not say so, and thus remove one of the great obstacles that had hindered the progress of Calvinism through the years.

Overtures from six synods and 29 presbyteries came to the 1901 General Assembly, asking in various terms that the action of the previous year be rescinded, and this the General Assembly proceeded to do by nearly unanimous vote, declaring, however, that this action was not intended to modify the answer made to the overture by the Assembly of 1900. Two overtures asking that amendments to the Confession clarifying the church's belief as to the salvation of infants were rejected on the ground that it was unwise to initiate at this time agitation of the question among the people, because the Confession in this section did not teach the damnation of any infant dying in infancy, and "because, while we have a well grounded hope, founded on Scripture, that all infants dying in infancy are saved, yet the Confession of Faith goes as far as the Scriptures to justify a positive creedal statement upon the subject."[70]

The 1902 Assembly received 11 overtures, all expressing more or less dissatisfaction with some parts of the action taken by the 1901 Assembly touching the question of infant salvation and expressing the desire that the church authorize some positive statement as the certainty of the salvation of all infants dying in infancy. A proposed amendment to the Confession with this end in view was defeated by a close vote (92 to 85); the Assembly however repealed the final reason (quoted above) given by the previous Assembly for declining to adopt an amendment on the subject and adopted in its stead a positive statement—"we are persuaded that the Holy Scriptures, when fairly interpreted, amply warrant us in believing that all infants who die in infancy are included in the election of grace, and are regenerated and saved by Christ through the Spirit."[71]

This remained the final action of the General Assembly—there was no amendment to the Confession, no explanatory footnote as had been adopted earlier by the Presbyterian Church U.S.A., only a positive statement of what Presbyterians generally had come to believe regarding the salvation of all children dying in infancy— buried in the Minutes of the Assembly. But it was not for the want of effort. For a full decade it had remained the most debated theological issue before the church. Overtures to amend the Confession, to approve a footnote, to add a declaratory statement, to appoint a committee to study and report, had been brought before successive Assemblies and as regularly defeated. The 1908 Assembly, taking note of the widespread difference of opinion as to the necessity of changes of some sort in the Confession of Faith on this topic asked the presbyteries for an expression of opinion—"Shall any change be made . . . ?" Twenty-four presbyteries answered this question in the negative, and 44 in the affirmative. Many of these latter submitted overtures as to what the change should be, and these suggestions were varied and diverse. An ad interim committee was appointed to consider these and other suggestions and to frame a proper amendment for submission to the presbyteries. Amendments were submitted for three successive years; each received the favorable votes of a majority of the presbyteries (the last vote being 55 presbyteries in favor, 22 opposed) but none secured the requisite three-fourths vote. The 1913 Assembly declined to send down still another amendment in view of the fact that the question had been before the church for 13 years and that during this period the church had been unable to reach agreement and in view of the further fact "that the Assembly of 1902 declared that the Holy Scriptures amply warrant us in believing that all infants who die in infancy are included in the election of grace and are regenerated and saved by Christ through the Spirit, which declaration we would here reaffirm . . ." Here for the time the matter rested. Those who opposed any tampering with the Confession on the grounds that once begun the desire for change might get out of hand had won the day, but presbyteries by a vote of more than two to one had registered dissatisfaction with the wording of one of the more provocative sections.

There were other signs of dissatisfaction. Before the 1912 General Assembly came "a startling overture"[72] from the Presbytery of Panhandle (Synod of Texas) asking the General Assembly to appoint a committee of 15 to write a new Confession of Faith based on the doctrines of the present Confession. This overture was greeted with a burst of "derisive laughter,"[73] whereupon a young minister from West Texas took the floor and explained some of the difficulties faced by a Home Mission worker unprepared, as he and others were, to defend the Confession against the frequent and fierce assaults made upon it. He pled for a plain and simple statement of doctrine that could be easily understood and easily defended. "This pathetic speech," reported the Presbyterian Standard, "created no little sympathy, and at once there was an extensive bombardment of the old Confession as a document unsuited to our age and a serious handicap to our progress."[74]

A motion offered by Dr. James I. Vance, influential pastor of the First Church, Nashville, that an ad interim committee be appointed to prepare a brief popular statement* for submission to the next General Assembly was approved by a small majority. The statement so prepared was approved by the 1913 General Assembly for general information and distribution as a tract. In 1931 and again in 1939 the Assembly ordered it bound and published along with the Standards of the Church. This earlier "brief statement" was finally replaced by that of 1962. Neither statement however has become a part of the church's official Standards.

Popular theology was beginning to replace the older Calvinism in the pulpits, if not yet in the classrooms. The Synod of Missouri in 1901 had commented on the growth of the non-denominational spirit which made it increasingly difficult for preachers to set forth doctrines from the pulpit and which had in large measure driven doctrinal instruction out of the Sunday school.[75] Dr. Richard McIlwaine referred to two Christian men of high intelligence and

* The Presbyterian Church, U.S.A., had adopted a brief popular statement in 1902.

character, both personally known to him, who had declined election to the eldership in their respective churches, because they could not subscribe to the Confession of Faith in all of its teachings. "I have heard within a short time," he added, "of two strong churches . . . in each of which several reputable Christian men elected to the eldership, declined to qualify . . . Such declinatures are new to me, as I suppose they are to the church."[76]

The *Christian Observer* detected a doctrinal drift in the church. "We have not drifted so rapidly or so far as other bodies," it declared. "But it is stated again and again that in some of our prominent pulpits the truth is either suppressed or perverted, and that pastors are sustained by their congregations and tolerated by their presbyteries, when they are known to be decidedly out of harmony with our confessional position . . . The present crisis in the life of the Presbyterian Church at large calls for serious thought, and above all for very earnest and constant prayer."[77]

Some years earlier the Presbyterian Committee of Publication had printed in tract form a sermon on predestination preached by James I. Vance, popular preacher of the First Church, Nashville. A reviewer in the *Presbyterian Quarterly* complained that the predestination set forth would satisfy neither Calvinist nor Arminian—it offered little more than man has sinned; God has provided an escape; the plan is offered for man's acceptance or rejection.[78] As a pulpit orator Dr. Vance was unexcelled, but in other respects typical of a new generation of preachers—little concerned with the niceties of Calvinistic dogmatics, greatly concerned with God's redemptive love, freely offered to all mankind through Jesus Christ.

Twenty years after Dr. Vance's sermon on predestination, Dr. E. C. Caldwell, Professor of New Testament in Union Theological Seminary, favorably reviewed the latest book by Dr. Vance, now the outstanding pulpiteer in the Southern Presbyterian Church. The *Presbyterian Standard,* edited by Dr. James R. Bridges, was not surprised at Dr. Vance's "milk and water" theology, of which, it was noted, he had given previous evidence. It was surprised, however, to hear a professor in Union Seminary pray for the speedy coming of the day when many of our Christian denominations should agree to suppress all formal statements of dogma and unite on a basis that does not contain enough Christianity to feed a baby. True," stated the editor, "we had a little forewarning of what was coming when the reviewer said, 'It is hard at times to tell whether Dr. Vance is a Calvinist or an Arminian, but that does not matter.' . . . To us," concluded Dr. Bridges, "it matters amazingly."[79]

Dr. E. C. Caldwell, a professor first in Austin Theological Seminary and then in Union, was little concerned with upholding the Calvinistic system; he was profoundly concerned with enabling students to discover the true meaning of the Scripture. He shared his own independent convictions quite fearlessly with his students and compelled them to think for themselves. He widened the horizons of a generation of students and was responsible for some of the new currents of thought that soon made themselves felt within the church. A more open attitude toward new truth, a greater readiness to re-examine old traditions, in fact an increasing determination to throw off the dead hand of the past, had begun to appear in both student body and faculty, and increasingly among the ministry, throughout the church.

The *Central Presbyterian* perceived evidences of polarization in the 1906 General Assembly. "To a thoughtful observer," wrote the editor, "it was clearly evident that there were two distinct parties in the Assembly that appeared again and again as particular subjects presented themselves for consideration. They were lined up with but slight variations on a number of issues . . . Our church may as well recognize that she has a 'liberal' element of a milder type within her own fold, whether for her advancement or her embarrassment, and adjust herself to the new conditions."[80] Eight years later the *Presbyterian of the South* (which had absorbed the *Central Presbyterian,* the *Southern Presbyterian,* and the *Southwestern Presbyterian*), expressed its unhappiness over the marked discrimination made at the Assembly of this year between those "who assumed the title of progressives and those who were set down as ultra-conservatives, stand-patters, reactionaries and the like."[81] Lines of cleavage would soon become more apparent.

IX

What Does the Lord Require?

As the church moved out of the old century and into the new, pulpit, church courts, and press emphasized, as they had always done, the threefold obligation of Micah's great text— "what doth the LORD require of thee, but to do justly, and to love mercy, and to walk humbly with thy God?"—but the application in each case remained largely in the personal realm and within the framework of the existing social order.

The dangers most frequently recognized and castigated by the church courts were Sabbath desecration, worldly amusements, gambling, and liquor.

Sabbath desecration was particularly abhorrent because it was thought to undermine both religion and morality, and therefore the stability of the nation itself.

Railroads, operating seven days a week, compelled some to labor and encouraged others to travel on the Sabbath. Church courts therefore repeatedly urged their members to stay off the Sunday trains. Since the transportation of the mail was the chief cause and support of the Sunday train, the Synod of South Carolina in 1897 petitioned the Federal government to forbid the transmission of any mails on Sunday and to order the closing of all post offices on this day through the United States.[1] In 1907-1908 representatives of the Synod of Virginia supported a bill which eliminated Sunday excursions and the reduced Sunday fares that made them more appealing and which restricted unnecessary operation of freight trains on the Sabbath.[2] The Synod of Texas about the same time declined to approve the use of the streetcar in attending church on the grounds, among others, that if it did so it could not consistently enjoin its ministers against use of the train to reach their appointments.³ Some students at Union Theological Seminary continued to walk three or four miles to their mission appointments rather than ride the trolley on the Sabbath, as late as the 1920's.

Sunday newspapers were declared by the General Assembly in 1890 to be eminent influences of evil and only evil. "They employ their operatives on God's day, thus allowing no rest on the Sabbath; they flood the land with promiscuous literature; they send it forth on the Sabbath and for Sabbath reading." Members of the church, said the Assembly, should give them neither countenance nor support.⁴ Forty years later there were still Presbyterian homes in which this injunction was observed.

The Puritan tradition against Sabbath amusements lingered on. The *Southwestern Presbyterian* opposed even the playing of Sunday Bible games with children.⁵ A proposal to open the 1893 World's Fair in Chicago on Sunday, and to keep it open every Sunday thereafter, brought forth a chorus of protests from evangelical churches throughout the nation. The General Assembly of the Presbyterian Church in the U. S. for three successive years appealed to the Fair authorities to change their announced plans, as did most of the synods. Congress was asked to take legislative action in the matter. In 1909 the Synod of Oklahoma complained that the Sabbath baseball and golf were viewed by many as allowable on the Sabbath, and confessed with shame that some Presbyterians participated in these forms of Sabbath desecration.⁶ By 1920 new forms of desecration had come into being, and were listed—among them, moving picture theaters and joyriding in automobiles.⁷

In response to an overture from Fayetteville Presbytery, the General Assembly this year reaffirmed its loyal adherence to the time-honored standards of the church, and reminded its people that "The Sabbath is to be sanctified by a holy resting all that day, even from such worldly employments and recreations as are lawful on other days; and spending the whole time in the public and private exercises of God's worship, except so much as is to be taken up in the works of necessity and mercy."⁸ As late as 1934 the Assembly in its restatement of "The Origin and Purpose of the Sabbath" called for "a complete separation from the distracting demands of material things, whether of toil or pleasure."⁹

To safeguard the Sabbath for its proper ends, the church relied on preaching from the pulpits, on instruction in the Sabbath school, and on the good example of its faithful members. At times it appealed to corporation heads, and on occasion it addressed "humble" petitions to the proper legislative body. It also exhorted its members to take proper action as citizens to secure needed legislative enactment and enforcement. Thus in 1912 the Assembly recommended that its people continue their efforts to secure the closing of post offices and carriers' windows on the Sabbath day and that they use their influence, as Christian citizens, to have the authorities enforce all civil laws enacted for the purpose of making the Sabbath a rest day, such as the closing of places of business, drugstores, soda fountains, ice-cream parlors, cigar stands and baseball games on the Sabbath, that the sanctity of the day might be preserved.[10]

To ensure more effective action, the church courts urged its members to support voluntary agencies organized for the direct political action on which Southern Presbyterians did not believe that the church as such should rely.

In the 1870's the Southern Assembly had taken the initiative and urged other evangelical bodies to join with it in forming such an organization, but this effort had proved premature. Ten years later the Methodist Episcopal Church launched a similar effort and with greater success. "Never before," according to the General Assembly, had "a popular movement taken hold so *quickly* and so extensively upon the hearts and consciences of all classes of our people. The general and deep interest in this matter is evidenced by the astonishing fact that, in the brief space of one year, there have gone up to the Congress of the United States the petitions of more than ten millions of people, praying Congress to give to our toiling millions the relief they desire from the enforced labor of seven days in the week."[11]

The purpose of this organization, the American Sabbath Union, was fourfold:

1. To work up a wholesome sentiment among the great mass of the people in regard to Sabbath observance. . . .
2. To bring this wholesome public sentiment to aid in the enforcement of Sabbath laws.
3. To present the subject of Sabbath reform to the individual members of our National and State Legislatures, and secure such legislation as will guarantee to all who are directly or indirectly in the employment of our government their constitutional right to a weekly Sabbath rest.
4. To promote, by lawful means, any other needed Sabbath reformation.[12]

The Assembly appointed its representatives to the Union and commended its literature and work until the end of the century; in 1921 it entered into close working relations with the Lord's Day

Alliance, successor organization to the American Sabbath Union, a partnership which has continued to the present time.

There were some, of course, who opposed such direct or indirect efforts to secure legislation for the protection of the Sabbath, insisting, in the Thornwellian tradition, that the mission of the church was purely spiritual. The majority attitude was expressed by an editorial appearing in the *Central Presbyterian*. Said the editor:

> The Sunday laws which the state may rightfully enforce are not religious laws, or for the purpose of enforcing religion, or for the perfection of religion. They belong to the same class of protective legislation as laws for the protection of health, laws which secure education, forbid gambling, protect the home, preserve morality and encourage patriotism. They are not fences to restrict liberty, but bulwarks to uphold liberty . . . They rest upon the natural law of the need of rest, the protection of the working man and the poor against the demands of greed and selfishness . . . The Sunday laws rest upon such broad foundations that they should have the support of all citizens, of all religions and of no religion . . .[13]

Efforts of the churches to secure or maintain legislation safeguarding the Sabbath as a day of rest from unnecessary labor were largely successful, and such laws upheld by the Supreme Court on non-religious grounds remain on the statute books until the present day, but efforts to preserve the traditional Puritan Sabbath from all encroachments proved unavailing.

In 1892 the Permanent Committee on the Sabbath presented a discouraging report to the General Assembly:

> The constant influx of a foreign element into our population, coupled with the wider dissemination of European sentiments, is making its impress both seen and felt upon the Sabbath, as well as upon all our American institutions. Sunday travel, under the stimulus of cheap rates offered by many railroad companies, is on the increase, becoming more and more common, even on the part of many professing Christians. The Sunday newspaper, that insidious foe of religion and the church, is still sought with the same and perhaps greater avidity than ever. The practice of social Sunday visiting likewise seems to be getting more and more fashionable, especially with the young. In many of the States, freight trains run regularly on the Lord's Day as on any other . . .[14]

In 1906 the Permanent Committee on the Sabbath reported to the Synod of Tennessee that "the current evils such as the Sunday Press (with its comic supplements), concerts, amusements and traffic are not now confined to the cities," but have been extended to the rural communities as well. "A score or so of miles from the populous centers are parks and watering places, where gather mixed multitudes to hear so-called 'sacred concerts', to witness vaudeville displays and engage in games. At some of these places the conduct is riotous and indecent."[15]

The remaining dykes crumbled quickly in the aftermath of the First World War. A mighty current has been unloosed, said the 1921 Assembly, before which "we find ourselves almost helpless." Unloosing of the flood was traced:

1. To the unwillingness or tardiness of communities and individuals to rid themselves of the abnormally free and easy practices which were brought in by the Sunday sports and the recreation halls of war camps and communities.

2. To the unholy efforts of commercialized amusements (under whose pressure the remaining so-called blue laws were gradually removed from the statute books).

3. To the general tide of worldliness which came with easy money and the rise of the irresponsible rich.

4. To an alarming lack of knowledge and appreciation of what the Sabbath and family religion meant both to Christian faith and to the nation.[16]

Resolutions looking back to the old ideal continued to be adopted, but any real effort to recover the Puritan Sabbath, or to reenact the old blue laws were ended. In 1958 the General Assembly adopted a lengthy report offered by an ad interim committee to study the biblical teaching and the proper use of the Lord's Day in which emphasis was put on the positive values of the day. The Sabbath, said the Assembly, was intended to be a day for the worship of God, a day of instruction, a day of rededication, a family day. It was intended to be a happy day, which might well include "playing games" and "even serving special refreshments"; also a day of rest, but not necessarily a day of physical activity. "For many," it was recognized, "exercise can be a means of rest." Finally it was recognized to be a day of Christian service, and a day of rejoicing.[17]

Efforts of the church to enforce its oft-repeated protests against "worldly amusements" by discipline collapsed after the celebrated Block case in 1879.[18] The General Assembly, followed by the lower courts, made it clear at this time and later that former deliverances against such forms of worldliness had not been repealed. Disciplinary action, however, was left in the hands of the session, and sessions generally chose not to act; they "do not dare to attempt to remove this evil," charged the *Christian Observer*, "or else do not care."[19] In some quarters it began to be claimed that the Presbyterian

Church had abandoned its former position of condemnation of the worldly amusements. Pastors stated that when they remonstrated with young people about these things they were met with the answer that the church no longer condemned them.[20]

To resolve this uncertainty the Assembly in 1900 addressed a pastoral letter to its members which declared: "There is dancing which is innocent in itself, there are plays that are not immoral, and card-playing without gambling cannot be called a sin." On the other hand, it pointed out, there were forms of all three which were undoubtedly evil, and against which the church had repeatedly warned. The question then arises, "May not Christians freely indulge in such forms of worldly amusements as are not sinful in themselves?" The Assembly in reply urged its people to refrain altogether from these amusements as a matter of Christian prudence, example, and out of regard for the honor of Christ.[21]

Another pastoral letter was issued in 1911 and still another in 1912. Church members were urged to abstain from the theater, from dancing, and from card playing—also from the secular Sunday paper, from travel, and from social visiting on the Sabbath.[22] Ministers were requested to preach on the subject of worldliness at least once during the ensuing year.

The silence of the pulpit in regard to worldly amusements is often misunderstood, said the *Presbyterian Standard*, which then went on to explain that it is not because the ministers have changed their mind regarding the evil, but only because they think sermons will do no good. Dancing, for example, is one of the evils which the church has denounced for ages. But nothing has been gained. "Old and young, elders and deacons, saints and sinners, have all patronized the dance, and by so doing they have undone all their pastor could do." The *Standard* rejoiced under these circumstances that one well-known minister had recently preached to a crowded house on this great evil which he declared to be "the seed of the social evils that are cursing our land." "All honor," cried the editor, "to the brave pastor who is willing to lead a forlorn hope."[23]

Church papers continued to inveigh against the various forms of worldliness after the pastors on the whole had apparently given up the battle. There was an unending series of editorials and contributed articles continuing on into the post-war years. In 1920 the *Presbyterian of the South* complained that the older and less objectionable forms of dancing had practically been discarded and warned against the vulgar cheap jazz that was running riot through the land.[24] The ban on dancing held longest at some of the denominational colleges. Synods dominated by ministers and elders from the rural churches were largely responsible. So the Synod of South Carolina instructed its Board of Trustees not to permit dancing on college-owned property in 1932, and again in 1934. Dancing was not permitted in the town of Davidson, controlled by the college of that name, until 1944.

Moving pictures, which attracted notice of the church bodies from 1910 on, were never opposed as completely as the theater had been to this time, but there were repeated objections to the type of movies, and a call for censorship.

The church has designated as worldly, especially card playing, dancing, theater-going, the *Presbyterian Standard* reminded its readers in 1911, and added: "Obviously the attempted restraints of the Church have not been effective. One who claims to have wide observation in all parts of the country says that at least eighty per cent of Christians take part in one or more of these amusements."[25]

Whatever the percentage, it increased after the First World War. In a vain effort to roll back the advancing tide the 1921 General Assembly reaffirmed all past deliverances on the question of worldly amusements.[26] Finally, in 1930, came the first official change of attitude. The Assembly this year did not repeat its customary condemnation of particular amusements, but declared instead that "the personal decision in such matters is to be made by a scripturally enlightened conscience under the guidance of the Holy Spirit . . ."[27]

Fifteen years later the Assembly was asked to reaffirm the older deliverance adopted in 1900, singling out dancing for particular condemnation. This the Assembly declined to do, stating that it would be quite impossible to condemn dancing per se from the teachings of Scripture:

> The amusements usually listed as worldly—dancing, theatre going, and card playing—are not inherently evil [continued the Assembly], nor do they always lead to evil. To condemn them therefore as "worldly amusements" is to give young people and others a false and distorted view of the Christian life; it would be better for the Church to warn against over-indulgence in, and abuse of these and other amusements, and to encourage positively all wholesome recreation and fun. Instead of condemning amusements which may be innocent, we should rather condemn these evil motives which sometimes pervert them. The "principles and practices that mar Christian character and influence" have their roots in the heart and may be, and often are, manifested as dangerously in business, politics, race relations and in national selfishness and isolationism, as in amusements.[28]

The real objection to card playing had been the inducement it offered to gambling, and against gambling in any form the church had been and remained vehemently opposed. Its mightiest effort in this field was directed against the notorious Louisiana Lottery. Lotteries were forbidden in the constitutions of Louisiana adopted in 1845 and again in 1852, but this prohibition was repealed in the constitution forced on the people of Louisiana in 1868. The carpetbag legislature of this year proceeded as one of its first acts to charter the Louisiana Lottery (controlled by a syndicate of gamblers, formed in New York in 1863) and to give it a monopoly of drawing lotteries in the state for 25 years. The Democratic legislature in 1879 repealed the charter of the lottery company and make it a penal offense to buy or sell lottery tickets in the state. The repealed charter, without its state monopoly features, was reinserted however in a new constitution, which provided that after January 1, 1895, all lotteries should cease.

But with this new lease of life came a new lease of power and almost incredible prosperity. The legislature, through gifts of money, was induced to grant no other lotteries. The market share of stock in the Louisiana Lottery rose from $35 a share in 1879 to $1,200 per share in 1890; its capital by this time was more than double the whole banking capital of the state. The aggregate of its daily, monthly, and semiannual drawings mounted to nearly 50 million dollars. There were more than 100 policy shops in New Orleans alone, where policies or bets on the number of daily drawings were sold with a percentage of from 22 to 41 percent in favor of the lottery. The octopus obtained control of a large portion of the organized capital of the state. It captured three-fourths of the press. Its evil influence, sapping the foundations of both private and public integrity, was felt and recognized not only in Louisiana but throughout the nation.

Four years before the charter of the Louisiana Lottery expired, the company began its fight to extend and renew the charter. The venal legislature passed a bill submitting a constitutional amendment to be voted on in 1892 giving the Lottery Company practically exclusive lottery privileges for another 25 years. The Governor vetoed the bill. The house voted to overrule the Governor's vote, and a similar effort barely failed in the senate. The lottery company resorted to the courts, which ruled that the people must be allowed to vote on the constitutional amendment.

The anti-lottery fight was begun and largely waged by the church forces in Louisiana, though other allies joined as the struggle grew in intensity. The *Southwestern Presbyterian* gave valiant aid, week after week, month after month, year after year, exposing the evils of the system, charging bad faith and corruption. Rev. T. R. Markham, D.D., pastor of the Lafayette Street Church, New Orleans, flayed the Supreme Court of the state from his pulpit for its "open and flagrant affront" to the moral and religious forces of its citizens;[29] all ministers in the city joined in an open memorial to the Congress of the United States on the subject. The Presbytery of New Orleans adopted a resolution offered by Dr. Palmer calling upon "the Christians under its jurisdiction not to relax their opposition to this injurious and corrupting institution."[30] The Synod of Mississippi emphatically condemned the Louisiana State Lottery Company and warned its people against all complicity with it in any shape or form.[31]

The General Assembly, responding to a communication addressed to it by the Anti-Lottery League of Louisiana, adopted the following year a strong paper, condemning the whole lottery scheme, charging that representatives of the system "have with brazen effrontery entered the halls of legislation, and have sought to bribe our lawmakers in the interests of their nefarious traffic," and expressing heartfelt sympathy with all lawful and proper efforts to secure the enactment of such laws, by the state legislatures and by the Congress of the United States, as will suppress every lottery scheme in the land.[32] Similar resolutions were adopted by various synods.

On June 25, 1891, the Anti-Lottery League sponsored a great mass meeting in New Orleans, at which the major address was offered by Dr. B. M. Palmer. In the judgment of many it was his oration which, more than any other single thing, determined the final outcome—rejection of the proposed amendment to the constitution by the people of Louisiana at the ballot box in the spring of the following year. A few months earlier the Congress of the United States had passed a law excluding the lottery from the mails. The Lottery Company attempted to carry on its business, operating out of Honduras, with a distributing center for its literature in Tampa, Florida. A new law passed by Congress in 1895, with Southern Presbyterian endorsement, gave the Louisiana Lottery its finishing blow.[33]

The church's objection to gambling in any form was repeatedly voiced. Church members were urged to refrain from making small bets—in a game of bridge, for example—and as citizens to take necessary action to "break up the gambling hells that have been flaunting their lawlessness in the face of the . . . people."[34] "The gambling mania is in the air," declared the Synod of Mississippi in 1907. "This acquisition of great and sudden riches by any method, however mean or crooked, the system among the highest commercial circles called 'frenzied finance' is claiming its victims all over our land by the thousands. One day it is the suicide of some poor dupe who has lost his last cent on the races or a game of cards. Another day it is the disgrace of some trusted employee who has stolen his employer's money to repair his losses at roulette . . ." There followed an indictment of the gambling "mania" in all of its forms, including the greatest curse of all—stock gambling.[35] The Synod of Kentucky fought a losing battle against pari-mutual betting at the race tracks and continued to urge its people to use their influence and their ballots "to break the chains that bind Kentucky to this shameful partnership and put an end to this gigantic gambling monopoly that disorganizes society, demoralizes business, debauches the electorate, and is fatal also to the liberties, the economic welfare, the moral and best life of our people."[36]

The General Assembly in 1936 urged its members to discourage all forms of gambling in their community and especially to help in the removal of all public forms of gambling and gambling devices from public places.[37]

A fourth evil to which the church remained steadfastly opposed was the liquor traffic. In 1891 the General Assembly, in accordance with former deliverances on the subject, bore its testimony against the traffic in intoxicating liquors as a fruitful source of abounding iniquity and misery; urged its people to use all means, which might be approved by their Christian conscience and judgment, to remedy this evil; and particularly urged its members to abstain from the use of intoxicating liquors as a beverage.[38] This was to remain the basic position of the church for the next half-century and beyond.

The proposition that the saloon is a public nuisance is one that has united the people, observed the *Central Presbyterian*. "It is not any extreme view as to temperance, or any disposition to interfere with personal liberties, but the righteous indignation of the public against a nuisance, destructive of all things good in the community."[39] Ministers, with rare exceptions, the same paper indicated, are enemies of the liquor traffic and their reasons for it are overwhelming. As pastors they have occasion and opportunity for seeing the evil effects of the drink habit to an unusual degree.[40]

As the prohibition movement gained in strength, the W.C.T.U. and other organizations urged the various courts of the church to endorse this particular solution of the liquor problem; the Anti-

Saloon League repeatedly sought the official support of the church. The General Assembly in 1897 informed the Prohibition Party in the state of North Carolina that "uniform practice and constitution" both forbade it—"to intermeddle with political parties or questions."[41] This was the position which on the whole it continued to maintain. Presbyteries and synods took a similar stand. As the Synod of Missouri declared in 1907: ". . . the officers and members of the churches connected with this Synod are as citizens generally disposed to cooperate with all well-considered movements looking to the restraint and if practicable the abolition of the traffic in alcoholic liquors. At the same time the Synod is constrained to say that as a body of Presbyters, sitting as a court of Jesus Christ, they have no authority to dictate to the ministers and people under their jurisdiction what their views must be as to state prohibition, nor to instruct their ministers what to preach on this subject."[42]

As the Anti-Saloon League extended its legislative victories and popular enthusiasm mounted, it became more and more difficult for the church to maintain this line. The church papers, one after the other, threw their support to the Anti-Saloon League, and enlisted in the struggle for prohibition. The Synod of Alabama in 1906 expressed its sympathy with the work of the Anti-Saloon League and bade it Godspeed in its efforts to redeem the state from the evils of the traffic in intoxicating liquors.[43] The following year the Synod of North Carolina gave thanks for the rapid progress which prohibition was making in the state, and expressed earnest hope that the traffic in intoxicating liquors would soon be driven from the state.[44] Fayetteville Presbytery urged adoption of proposed legislation designed to close every saloon and dispensary within the state.[45] More positive action was taken by the Presbytery of North Alabama. During the course of a very heated campaign on the question of the adoption of a constitutional amendment prohibiting the manufacture and sale of intoxicating liquors in the state, Rev. W. I. Sinnott, Stated Clerk of the Synod of Alabama and of North Alabama Presbytery, printed or allowed to be printed communications over his name in the daily press of the state opposing the principle of prohibition in general and the provisions of the constitutional amendment in particular. These communications were seized on by the opponents of the amendment and broadcast over the state, to which the presbytery claimed was its great embarrassment and hurt. To remove misunderstanding the presbytery in 1909 adopted resolutions urging its people to vote for the proposed amendment to the state constitution. It was the first time a court of the church had explicitly endorsed a specific legislative proposal in this disputed area. A complaint of Mr. Sinnott against this action came before a Commission of the General Assembly, which dismissed the complaint and upheld the action of North Alabama Presbytery on the grounds that endorsing a legislative proposal drawn up by the state, independently from the church, did not breach the church's historic position of non-intrusion into civil affairs but was in line with the oft-repeated instruction of the General Assembly to "use all legitimate means" to banish the liquor traffic from the land. The Commission went on to condemn the action, language, and spirit of Mr. Sinnott, the complainant, as highly unbecoming in a minister of the gospel. This action of the Commission, which became the action of the Assembly, was strongly protested by a minority which held that it contravened constitutional provisions regarding separation of church and state.[46]

This decision stirred discussion which continued in the church for a full decade. The 1911 Assembly rejected Mr. Sinnott's petition to reopen the case on the grounds that the judicial deliverances of one General Assembly are not reviewable by a subsequent General Assembly. In response to a series of overtures it reaffirmed constitutional provisions regarding the relations of church and state, but added that the "cases extraordinary" in which its right to petition the state was recognized were to be decided according to the nature of each case, and that when the General Assembly had determined that question in any concrete case it was not competent for any subsequent Assembly to question such decision by a rehearing of the case.[47]

The prohibition movement was now rapidly extending its gains. In 1913 the Anti-Saloon League launched its campaign for national prohibition. The following May, the General Assembly, in response to a communication from the W.C.T.U., resolved "that we are in hearty favor of National Constitutional Prohibition, and will do all properly within our power to secure the adoption of an amendment to the Constitution forever prohibiting the sale, manufacture for sale, transportation for sale, importation for sale, and exportation for sale, of intoxicating liquors for beverage purposes in the United States."[48]

This action, so opposed to the Thornwellian principles usually upheld by the Assembly, seems to have been taken, one observer explained, in response to a very general feeling that the time had come for the church, as representative of the great moral forces of the world, to take a clear-cut stand against the evils of alcohol.[49]

A protest against Assembly's action was signed by 40 commissioners on the grounds that it was a deliverance upon a political question and hence a violation of the scriptural function of the church of God and contrary to the historic position of the church. This protest was echoed widely throughout the church. The church as a whole was not prepared to abandon its long accepted understanding of the church's purely spiritual mission, but the actions of the Commission of the Assembly in 1910 and of the Assembly itself in 1914 had opened breaches which it would be difficult to close.

Quite properly pastors, press, and church courts called for observance and enforcement of the Prohibition Amendment as finally adopted—with no endorsement of the specific measures approved by the Anti-Saloon League, and courts here and there joined the church press later on in opposing repeal of the prohibition amendment.[50]

The church continued during this period to recognize only two grounds for divorce—adultery and irremedial desertion—this in accord with its legalistic interpretation of Scripture. The privilege of remarriage was permitted to only the innocent party. Only rarely it appears did Presbyterian pastors disregard this law of the church. But in 1901 there occurred a cause célèbre. The Florida legislature had passed a bill permitting divorce and remarriage of a person whose spouse had been insane for the past four years. Mr. H. M. Flagler, a Presbyterian elder, past 70 years of age, a citizen of Florida and one of the wealthiest men in the nation, for whose benefit the law had apparently been passed, now divorced his insane wife, and remarried. His new wife was likewise a Presbyterian. The marriage ceremony was performed in North Carolina by Dr. Peyton H. Hoge, an honored Presbyterian minister, long in the Southern Church, now a minister in the Presbyterian Church U.S.A., who had known Mr. Flagler for the past two years and his bride from early youth. The *Presbyterian Standard* made its indignant protest: "In the name of our Southland whose pride has been humbled, in the name of the Church whose righteousness has been made a laughing stock and whose testimony against wickedness when veneered by wealth had been made a mockery . . . in the name of common decency and morality, to say nothing of the loftier ideals of the Christian faith, we denounce the divorce of Henry M. Flagler from his insane wife and his remarriage as an indefensible wrong against all."[51] In response, Dr. Hoge rejected the legalistic interpretation of Scripture as embodied in the Presbyterian tradition and insisted that a minister had a responsibility to decide each case presented to him on its own merits in the light of the facts and of the Word of God—and this, he insisted, he had done.

In 1912 an effort was made to revise the Confessional statements regarding divorce and remarriage. Some wished to make the law more strict, allowing only one ground for divorce—that of unfaithfulness; others wished the rights of remarriage to be liberalized on one or more grounds. The Assembly voted to leave the law unchanged, and this continued to be its position until the year 1959, when, as we shall see, the principle for which Dr. Hoge had contended was finally written into the constitution.

II

Sabbath desecration, worldly amusements, gambling, liquor, divorce—these were evils which the church had always opposed, and for which it had warrant from Scripture and the Confession of Faith to speak. But new problems were now emerging for which the church found no answer in Scripture, as interpreted in the Confession of Faith, problems therefore on which it did not feel that it could officially speak, in accordance with its doctrine of the spirituality of the church.

One of the most pressing of these problems was that of capital and labor. The first serious labor disturbances leading to riot and bloodshed had occurred, as we have seen, in the 1870's. A second series of conflicts developed in the 1880's, including strikes against railroads in the Gould system, and culminating in the tragic Haymarket affair, in which eight anarchists were convicted on very flimsy evidence of conspiring to throw a bomb which took the lives of seven policemen. The Knights of Labor which had been the most militant and successful labor organization declined rapidly after this event; the newly organized American Federation of Labor slowly gained strength among the skilled trades. In 1892 a battle broke out between strikers and Pinkerton guards hired by the steel mills at Homestead, Pennsylvania. The panic of 1893 was followed by the Pullman strike of 1894, accompanied by serious damage to railroad property. The strike was finally broken by the intervention of Federal troops.

During this period Southern Presbyterian papers published occasional editorials and articles recognizing the need of labor unions, the justice of their cause, and their right to strike. The resort to violence, however, was universally deplored.

The *Southwestern Presbyterian* in 1877 approved the words of Judge Drummond of the Federal Court at Indianapolis in sentencing 15 railroad rioters to three months imprisonment. His position was that wages are subject to the strict law of supply and demand, and should be fixed by common bargain and agreement.[52] In the 1880's the editor had thought a little more deeply on the matter. "It will hardly be questioned," he wrote, "that some of the strikes which have occurred during the past year had justice on their side . . . selfishness and injustice on the part of the employers . . . [have] compelled laborers . . . to form unions . . . for self protection. Properly managed, such institutions serve a good purpose. They serve to protect the laborer against that aggressiveness of capital, which manifests itself in the constant tendency to enforce a reduction of wages. . . . In many instances, however, these organizations have so reversed the condition of things that corporations and employees are at their mercy . . . And often they are not only unjust, but cruel and reckless. The labor riots in Pittsburgh form a case in point. . . ." As a possible solution the editor, Dr. H. M. Smith, suggested a remedy which he pointed out had worked well in France—the cooperative system, by which all employees become, to a certain extent, partners in the concern, and partners in the profits.[53]

The following year, when railroad strikes broke out, particularly against the Gould system, Dr. Smith declared that the old proverb "Corporations have no souls" aptly described the spirit of monopolists toward their employees. "If public opinion is not egregiously mistaken about Gould and his imitators," he added, "employees have been driven to the walls . . . Public sentiment is on the side of the strikers. The time has come when the avarice of the corporations should be checked."[54]

After the Homestead riot, Dr. R. Q. Mallard, who had succeeded Dr. Smith as editor of the *Southwestern Presbyterian*, condemned lawlessness on the part of labor and also the "employment of Pinkerton Janissaries" on the part of management. "We have no justification for the rich," he wrote, "who in their selfish greed for accumulation cry in the face of the poor." He called for a return to the guiding principles of the Word of God, and commended the proposed organization by the government of a Board of Conciliation and of Arbitration.[55] "Let capital," he wrote again, "recognize labor unions, and arbitrate the differences; above all let the rising scale of wages be as common in prosperity, as the falling scale is in unprosperous times and at least discontent will in part be allayed and the temptations to the drastic remedy lessened."[56] Two years later, disturbed over the ever-deepening chasm between capital and labor, each preparing for what both regarded as an unavoidable war, Dr. Mallard expressed his hope "for a peaceful revolution which will, in orderly way, reduce the distance between American citizens and make it impossible for a millionaire, because he can afford it, to monopolize for 'Lord Money Bags' the whole upper deck of a common carrier, seagoing vessel, and condemn his neighbor, because a wage earner, to keep below decks."[57]

The *Southwestern Presbyterian* did not stand alone in its condemnation of irresponsible wealth. Dr. Robert L. Dabney took issue with the *Central Presbyterian* which had approved of Andrew Carnegie's use of his wealth by way of liberal benefactions. "Ought there to be any grand millionaires in a republican country?" asked Dr. Dabney. "Has any honest citizen any right to get these surplus millions?" His own answer was an emphatic "no." He insisted that in a democratic country like ours such vast riches could not be honestly acquired. The larger part of them must necessarily be the fruits of overt or concealed extortion and plunder. "These millionaires," he concluded, "are dishonors, and not honors to the Church of Christ."[58]

In the decade of the 1890's the *Christian Observer* printed a number of articles dealing with the responsibility of the church and its ministry under such conditions. One of these, by A. C. Houston, called attention to the growing disposition on the part of the struggling masses to part company with the church, charging that where it was not passive, it was decidedly hostile to the well-being of the people. Mr. Houston denied that this was the case, but was forced to admit that the weight of the ministers' influence served to retard rather than to advance movements concerned with political and socio-economic reformation. This he held was due to their ignorance of the workers' situation, due in turn to the fact that such information was not available in the sources of information on which they relied. The ministry, he argued, had a responsibility to become better informed and, once informed, to speak. "It cannot be . . . a matter of little moment . . ." he exclaimed, "that a governmental policy . . . enables one class of citizens to rob and plunder, under the forms of law, another class equally deserving. It cannot be . . . a matter of little moment to God's ministers that a financial policy is inaugurated, and relentlessly pursued by the money powers of the earth, that tends to enslave the laborer, to make of him 'a soulless machine of toil,' and to destroy homes and to ruin souls." He was dismayed by "an awful thought"—the possibility that the world might "move into [a] new era with the church lagging behind, and with estrangement between the people and their religious leaders."[59]

A little later the *Christian Observer* published an article by Count A. Bernstoff of Berlin which noted that in this age the laboring classes were struggling for political and social emancipation. The question, which would be carried over into the 20th century, he prophesied, was: would it be possible to achieve this in the peaceful way of reform or would bloodshed and fire be unavoidable? If the church cannot espouse the cause of the working man, insisted Count Bernstoff, she certainly must not make herself a defender of the status quo. She must show practically that she does not bow before the almighty dollar, that the soul of the working man is just as valuable to her as that of the wealthy merchant.[60]

Rev. Alexander J. McKelway, brilliant young editor of the *Presbyterian Standard* (successor to the *North Carolina Presbyterian*), wrote an editorial, "Murder for Gain," in which he called attention to needless sacrifices of human life in legitimate businesses—all because it is cheaper to kill than to prevent the destruction of life. He gave concrete illustrations—freight trains, lacking of safety devices; glass blowers, dying unnecessarily from lead poisoning; sweat shops in the great cities; child labor in Southern mills. His suggested remedy was pressure for laws, recognizing that life is more sacred than luxury and that the conveniences of the many cannot be purchased by the sufferings of the few.[61] He welcomed some advance toward the Christian socialism foreshadowed in the second chapter of Acts, and pointed to Germany where workingmen were insured against sickness, accident, weakness, and old age as an example "of a beneficent socialism."[62]

In 1906 Dr. McKelway, as retiring Moderator of Mecklenburg Presbytery, preached a stirring sermon, later published at the request of presbytery, on God and money. His indictment was strong and specific: Gould, "a man . . . who lied and cheated and over-reached his neighbors, wrecking railroads and pocketing them"; the first president of the Billion Dollar Steel Trust, who had forfeited the confidence of the people by trying to steal a few millions more in the organization of a ship-building trust; an "open and shameless effort [recently] of certain rich railroad corporations to control the policy of a Southern paper." Every department of the government—the legislature, the executive, and even the judicial—he stated, had been more or less corrupted by the monied interests. The whole organization of the business world, he further charged, operated along two lines which were equally violations of the golden rule—either the line of competition, in which every man's hand is turned against his neighbor, the very law of the jungle; or the line of combination, which is another name for the monopoly that extorts and oppresses and grinds the face of the poor.[63]

Dr. McKelway was a new type of editor in the Southern Presbyterian Church. Some of his brethren thought him wanting in delicate consideration for those whose opinion he controverted. He was accused of dealing somewhat freely in ridicule and sarcasm "and with concerning himself little with the corns on the toes on which he trod."[64]

But Dr. McKelway did not stand alone in recognizing a possible affinity between Scripture and some forms of socialism. The *Christian Observer* questioned the claim that socialism was inevitably anti-Christian and that the doctrine of private property is a teaching of Holy Scripture.[65] "The very essence of Christianity," declared the *Central Presbyterian,* "is self-surrender to Christ and generous devotion to the welfare of others, and if modern socialism could limit and adjust itself to this principle it would be essentially and eminently Christian. It may be," the editor continued, "that two mighty forces starting from separate origins, but working toward each other, will finally combine to work out a form of socialism that will approximate the ideal of Christian life."[66]

Editors of both these two papers warned that the rapid drift toward a more radical and undesirable socialism would continue unless there was more economic justice. "Crying evils must be redressed, great wrongs must be remedied, man as man must receive due recognition," warned the *Christian Observer,* "or the pent-up stream will burst its bounds and develope into a deluge, which will sweep all before it."[67] The paper quoted the exclamation of the chancellor of an Eastern University: "What is all [this] cry about the poor wage earner? The wage earners get enough for what they do and a great many of them get more." "Utterances such as these," retorted the *Christian Observer,* "are doing more to foster a spirit of anarchy and build up a sentiment in favor of socialism than all the clubs of foreign anarchists and all the socialistic sheets in the land."[68] The injustice of the existing division of the profits of industry," said the *Central Presbyterian,* "is enough to agitate a whole nation and summon the people to remedial action. That one class should sow the seeds and cultivate the growing product, while another class gathers the harvest, is a condition which a free and intelligent social order will not persistently allow."[69]

In this period—the first decade of the 20th century—the great issue in the South came to be that of child labor. Leader of the struggle against this issue within the Southern Presbyterian Church, and later one of the leaders in the struggle North and South, was Rev. A. J. McKelway, fighting editor of the *Presbyterian Standard* (1898-1905). Dr. McKelway had hoped originally that the North Carolina mill owners would honor their pledge, in lieu of legislation, voluntarily to cease employment of children under 12. When he discovered that their promises could not be trusted, he led the fight for the necessary laws. The children in the mill, he wrote, "are slaves, made to work when they should be at play, made to work when they should be sleeping the deep sleep of childhood, hired into slavery under masters that are not always the kindest, for the sake of the pittance that they can earn and upon which they have no claim . . ."[70] Seventy-five percent of the spinners in the state, he pointed out, were children between the ages of 12 and 14, and according to the laws of the state they could be worked 12 hours a day—or night.[71] Dr. McKelway carried on his fight against the opposition of many of the state's newspapers and of the *Manufacturer's Record,* which insisted that child labor was necessary for the industrial development of the South. He pled the cause of the children in the columns of the *Presbyterian Standard* and in the *Charlotte Evening News,* which he also edited simultaneously for three years; he proclaimed his crusade in the pulpit and out of the pulpit. In 1906 he resigned as editor to become Secretary of the National Child Labor Committee, a position he continued to hold until his death 12 years later; by which time his influence had become nationwide.

The only resolution adopted by the General Assembly for the guidance of its people in the realm of capital and labor in this entire period was one regarding child labor. Christian employers and parents were exhorted in 1908 to obey the laws that had been enacted on this subject "and to strive after more effective laws to the end that the exploitation of childhood within our borders shall be ended."[72]

A second moral issue which began to trouble the conscience of the American people during this period and on which Southern Presbyterians could not remain entirely silent was the question of war and peace.

In the 1890's a Southern Presbyterian minister initiated a movement for compulsory arbitration that gathered worldwide support and aroused brief hopes that mankind was indeed moving toward enduring peace. Rev. William A. Campbell, D.D., some-time evangelist and for 27 years Stated Clerk of East Hanover Presbytery, had long talked with friends about the possibilities of getting churches throughout the world to send in petitions for the abolition of war and the settlement of all international disputes through arbitration. His plan was approved by the Presbyterian ministers of Richmond in the spring of 1890 and a little later, through overture, by the General

Assembly of the Southern Church.[73] An address drawn up by Dr. Campbell was adopted, inviting Christian churches in all lands to appoint delegates to meet at a designated time and place for this purpose. In 1891 a conference attended by representatives from leading churches in America met in response to Dr. Campbell's efforts in New York and arranged to prosecute the matter further before all the leading ecclesiastical bodies of Christendom. Two years later a similar meeting was held in Chicago. The address and petition were translated into the languages of 32 different countries and sent to representatives of all the great churches of Christendom—Roman Catholic and Orthodox as well as Protestant. In the estimation of the *Richmond* [Virginia] *Times* this effort on which Dr. Campbell had labored unstintedly without compensation did more than any other single thing to arouse public sentiment in favor of arbitration and to bring about the preparation of a treaty embodying this principle between Great Britain and the United States (the Olney-Pauncefote Treaty), which it was hoped would lead to similar treaties between other nations. The British Parliament promptly approved the treaty, and President Cleveland sent it to the Senate on January 11, 1897, with his strong approval. The following summer Southern Presbyterians, with others, warmly welcomed Czar Alexander's proposal regarding disarmament and peace by universal consent. In December 1898 a delegation composed of representatives of the four major Presbyterian and Reformed bodies in the United States presented to the President of the United States two petitions, one signed by representatives of 146 churches on six continents, asking for the reduction of the heavy armaments maintained by Christian nations "ready upon provocation to go to war and settle their disputations by bloodshed" and requesting the influence of the government of the United States in favor of international arbitration as a substitute for war; the other, from the Pan Presbyterian Alliance including 80 Reformed and Presbyterian churches throughout the world, endorsing the first petition, and requesting a permanent and peaceful method for the settlement of all controversies arising between the peoples of the British Empire and the Republic of the United States of America.[74]

Dr. Campbell did not live to witness this outcome of his dream, nor to know the disappointment that followed. President McKinley endorsed the Olney-Pauncefote Treaty, as had his predecessor, but the United States Senate failed to ratify it. And meanwhile war with Spain, to free Cuba from Spanish oppression, had come with the enthusiastic support of the American people.

The General Assembly of the Southern Presbyterian Church, meeting shortly after the declaration of hostilities, adopted resolutions calling attention to the church's historic position on matters of secular concern, and urged ministers to proclaim from their pulpits nothing but the glorious gospel. In its own devotional meetings there were prayers for army and navy and for a righteous issue of the conflict and for a speedy peace, but "no unseemly references to the war, no loud professions of patriotism, and no public meetings of a political nature."[75] This example of the Assembly was followed generally by lower church courts, as well as by pastors in their pulpits.

The church papers, on this as on other issues, permitted themselves more freedom, reflecting apparently the feelings of Southern Presbyterians and of the American people as a whole. "If it be jingoism to sympathize with the dying, to pity the starving, to detest and even hate the inhumanity of the Spanish government," wrote Dr. J. Ferdinand Jacobs, editor of the *Southern Presbyterian*, "then we confess with some pride that we believe in jingoism. It is credible to our people that they cannot rest quietly when such horrors exist at our very doors."[76]

There was general approval of the successive steps taken by the government, including the final declaration of war. Whatever doubts some may have entertained, prior to the declaration of war, declared the *Southern Presbyterian*, are now to be suppressed.[77] The rapid victories of the American forces were looked upon as providential, what the *Southwestern Presbyterian* termed "an overruling Providence . . . favoring the cause of justice, freedom and humanity."[78] "To doubt that God is on our side," rhapsodized the *North Carolina Presbyterian* after the great naval victory at Santiago, "is to doubt the truth of the revelation he has given us of himself."[79] The end of hostilities was welcomed as was the humanity and generosity which the Army and Navy had shown toward their enemies, feeding the hungry, nursing the wounded and sick.[80]

There was not the same support for the continuation of the war, after the surrender of Spain, in the Philippines. The *Christian Observer* saw no justification for America's attempt to overcome the Filipino insurgents.[81] The *Southern Presbyterian* opposed annexation. "Even if the government established by the natives was but semi-civilized, the faults of the government would be chargeable to the natives themselves. We cannot help believing that even barbarous people have the right to self-government."[82] The conquest of the Philippines and of Puerto Rico, according to this paper, had arisen out of a newly developed sentiment fostered by military and naval success, the spirit of conquest.[83] A year later it remained convinced that the government had made a very great mistake in attempting to possess the Philippines without the natives' consent. Southern papers, it claimed, were almost a unit against this oppression.[84]

James Power Smith, who had been an aide-de-camp of Stonewall Jackson and was now editor of the *Central Presbyterian*, pointed out that a great change had come over the people of the United States. The war with Spain had awakened them to a consciousness of wealth and power and of their standing among the nations. With this change came peril, enormous and fearful peril—America tempted to new and dangerous departures from honored American principles; confident in its material strength, assuming a new role in the affairs of the nations.[85]

The church papers reported progress of the First World War when it broke, but refrained, in accordance with President Wilson's request, from taking a strong partisan position. When, however, the war had raged for two full years and a longing for peace had begun to manifest itself, the *Presbyterian Standard* agreed with a statement drawn up and signed by a number of leading men, college presidents, editors, judges, and ministers, earnestly deprecating peace "at the present time." "War is horrible," wrote the editor, "yet like the surgeon's knife, it is sometimes necessary to cure certain ills. To stop before its end is attained is not wise . . ."[86]

When America's entry into the war became a certainty, the paper admitted that it was unable to sympathize with those who would have peace at any price. Defensive war is justifiable, declared the editor, and if there were ever a way that was justifiable this would be it.[87] A year later the paper reprinted an article from *The Presbyterian* which stated, "More and more people are awakening to the conviction that this war is not merely a conflict between civil powers for the mastery . . . It is a conflict between the power of darkness and evil on the one hand and the powers of light and righteousness on the other."[88]

Similar views were expressed by the *Christian Observer* and by the *Presbyterian of the South*. This was indeed the general feeling of Southern Presbyterians, as of the American people as a whole. The General Assembly, however, along with its lower courts, adhered to its traditional position regarding the spirituality of the church and made little reference to the war. The 1917 Assembly, recalling the long service President Woodrow Wilson's father had rendered the church, informed the son that they had united in earnest prayer that he and those associated with him in authority might be given divine guidance and strength.[89] The people were exhorted to be much in prayer, to turn with repentance and confession of sin unto God, to avoid passion and bitterness.[90] That was all.

The 1918 General Assembly set aside an hour to be observed as a time of confession and prayer to God, supplicating his pardon for sin and the manifestation of his power in bringing about a righteous peace; asking also that he would bless and keep the men who were fighting in the battle for the world's freedom. A telegram was dispatched to President Wilson commending him to the God of all grace, and declaring that they were confidently relying on him as the spokesman for the moral forces of the work to carry on his gigantic task to a righteous consummation.[91] Dr. W. M. McPheeters, ever on the watch for the slightest infraction of the church's historic position on the spirituality of the church, objected that the Assembly here overstepped its bounds; he found, however, little support for his position.

Synods for the most part followed the lead of the Assembly, as did the presbyteries. All pledged their support to the government's plans for food conservation; all supported plans looking to the moral welfare of the young men in the army. Endorsement of the war and its aims where found was indirect. The Synod of Arkansas in 1917 heard a lecture by Rev. Hay Watson Smith on "The German Menace and How to Meet It." In 1918, after hostilities had ended, it pledged to the President its loyal support in his constructive program for enduring peace. The Synod of Florida spoke of "our nation" as having joined forces with England, France, and other allied nations to defend our national honor and in behalf of downtrodden and outraged humanity—but this was included only in a series of "whereases" looking toward the waste of grain in the manufacture of alcoholic beverages.[92] The Synod of Texas adopted similar resolutions, looking toward the conservation of food supplies.[93]

It was generally agreed that it was improper for ministers to preach patriotism, and to a very large extent this self-imposed ban was observed. As a citizen I am ready to do my bit for my country, wrote Dr. Edward R. Leyburn, pastor of the First Church in Durham, North Carolina, to speak for my country on any day except Sunday in any public hall or suitable place, to speak in the church on Sunday in behalf of the work of the Red Cross or Y.M.C.A. and other religious and relief work among the soldiers. I am ready to enlist as a chaplain, if I can better serve God than by remaining here. I am ready if our country should be invaded, to shoulder a gun and as a private soldier go into the army, "but God being my helper, so long as I am in the pulpit, it shall not be used for waving of flags and delivering of patriotic declamations and denunciations of the enemy or praises to the President, but in preaching the simple gospel of the blessed Son of God."[94]

Dr. Leyburn spoke here for the mass of Southern Presbyterian ministers.

There were, however, pleas from the pulpit regarding food conservation. Many churches, perhaps a majority of them, found a place for the American flag, usually on the pulpit; some protested the impropriety of such action. The church aided in the sale of war bonds. Dr. J. R. Bridges wrote an editorial in the *Presbyterian Standard* on Liberty Bonds as a means of grace. We are faced with alternatives, he declared. It is liberty or slavery. In order to secure liberty we must lend our money to the government. To do so, develops unselfishness and is therefore a means of grace.[95] Members of the churches opened their homes to soldiers and manned or provided places of entertainment. But the church's doctrine of the spirituality of the church held it back from the extremes to which ministers in some other churches were carried and which in some areas tended to turn the war into a crusade.

Work of the church for soldiers in the camps was directed by a War Work Council, which supported camp pastors, and organized and stimulated the work of pastors and churches in cities contiguous to the camps. When the war was ended, the Assembly noted "with patriotic pride and gratitude to God that in the supreme crisis, when all things worth having were at stake, Presbyterians of the South bore their part. They bore it as enlisted men and in organizations devoted to the enlisted men's care, physically, socially and morally." This effort was continued during the days of demobilization. Six volumes containing the War Statistics of the Churches as gathered by the Council were presented to Union Theological Seminary to be kept by that institution and to be accessible for purposes of reference.[96]

The *Christian Observer* rejoiced when President Wilson offered his plan for a League of Nations. It is an absolute necessity, it declared, if the world is not to be cursed again with international wars. When provisions for the League were finally included in the Treaty of Peace, the editor predicted that it would ensure the peace of the world for many generations, if not forever. "Christian principles," he declared, "have triumphed over the unbelief and false philosophy taught in Germany for more than a generation. Civilization is saved and God has vindicated the right."

The *Presbyterian of the South,* convinced that Wilson had done more for the world politically than any man who ever lived, reminded its readers, however, that the League was a political project with which the church as such had nothing to do. The General Assembly apparently agreed. Southern Presbyterians as a whole were strongly in favor of the League, and warm supporters of the President, a devout son of the church. But on this great issue of the day the church had nothing officially to say.

In 1918 it had expressed its hopes that President Wilson would carry on his gigantic task to its righteous consummation, and three years later it felicitated him on completing his eight years as President under conditions of unparalleled importance. It congratulated him on his great achievements in behalf of peace and for the relief of the war-stricken peoples on the earth; on his fidelity to duty and "for persistently holding aloft Christian standards and ideals in this age of turmoil and unrest."[97] But at no time did it give explicit endorsement to his efforts to form a League of Nations. In 1927, replying to requests from the Federal Council of Churches for deliverances on matters of international peace, the Assembly stated: "While we believe in peace, good will and love between man and man, nation and nation, and race and race, throughout the world, while we believe that war is a curse absolutely out of harmony with the Christian religion . . . still we cannot approve the methods recommended . . . We believe that peace, good will and love in a warless world are not to be achieved by passing resolutions . . . but rather by the regeneration of the hearts of men." It then proceeded to request its ministers to hold up before its people the ideas of worldwide peace and to encourage all its people to work and pray for this same glorious end.[98]

The pacifist wave that spread through the American churches as a whole in the aftermath of the war stirred brief ripples in the Southern Presbyterian Church. Under the proddings of a few pacifists and more near-pacifists, the Assembly agreed in 1929 that the church should never again bless a war or be used as an instrument in the promotion of war. Two years later it reaffirmed this position, and expressed its judgment that no church-owned or church-controlled school should make compulsory military training a part of its curriculum. Synods and presbyteries owning or controlling such schools were urged to make such training optional as soon as possible.[99]

X

The Church and Its Mission

The great problem which the South faced as it emerged from the Reconstruction period was a new phase of the same problem it had faced ever since slaves were first introduced into Virginia. That problem as seen by the white South was first to recover and then to maintain political supremacy which had been lost to the alliance of Republicans and Negroes in the course of Reconstruction. The battle entered a new phase with the withdrawal of Federal troops in 1877. Negroes retained the right to vote granted them by the post-war amendments to the Constitution and for some time were permitted to exercise that right, and even at times to hold office. But the right to vote and to hold office was kept within limits, by cajolery, manipulation, bribery, intimidation, and fraud.[1]

Such methods had their drawbacks and toward the close of the century a new solution to the old problem grew rapidly in favor. It was a two-pronged solution—disfranchisement, on the one hand; segregation, on the other. Disfranchisement, that is, of the Negro in such a way that there would be little or no disfranchisement of whites.

Mississippi pointed the way in its new constitution adopted in 1890. The two chief reliances were a poll tax and a requirement that the voter must be able to give "a reasonable interpretation" of a passage of the state constitution chosen by the registration board. Since there was no provision for bipartisan and biracial representation on the registration boards, discrimination was easy—and inevitable. South Carolina in 1895 adopted a new constitution with similar requirements, and the remaining Southern states quickly followed. The decisive role played by Negro ballots in the Populist revolt of the 1890's had gained the support of both Southern liberals and conservatives for this restrictive movement, which gained such momentum that Republican parties in the various states disavowed their Negro supporters and took on the "lily-white complexion," which they largely

have retained to the present time. By 1910 the Negro disfranchisement movement was virtually complete.

Along with the drive to isolate the Negroes politically came an
effort to segregate them socially and economically.[2]

There had been no segregation of the races prior to the Civil War,
though Negroes worshiping in the church were isolated in the bal-
conies. After the war, Negroes, as we have seen, withdrew from the
white churches, against the latter's desires. Attempts to establish integrated schools met with complete failure. By the end of the Reconstruction period there was therefore a voluntary separation of the races
in both schools and churches. But there was no rigid segregation
elsewhere. "Negroes were admitted to theaters, at least in most cities,
and were served at bars, soda fountains, ice-cream parlors, and general merchandise stores. Parks and public buildings were usually
open without discrimination, and the practice of using a common
cemetery continued for many years. They rode street cars and were
unrestricted on the railroads except by the custom which barred
them from 'ladies' cars except in the capacity of servants. Some
Negroes served on juries, and they continued to work with whites on
political committees and sit in political conventions. There were no
strenuous efforts at geographical residential segregation. Only in hotels was discrimination likely to be encountered, and this lacked the
force of law."[3]

The drive for the separation of the two races—by law—on railroads and in other forms of public transportation began, as we have
seen, in 1887, and for thoroughgoing segregation in all areas, mostly
after 1900.

There were Southern conservatives, convinced of Negro inferiority, who did not wish the Negro to be segregated or publicly humiliated; there were Southern radicals—the populists—who sought to
integrate them into their political faction; there were Southern liberals—George Washington Cable, the Louisiana author, for example—
who fought discrimination and opposed segregation—but segregation
first as custom and then as law spread from west to east and such
resistance as appeared quickly crumbled. The triumph of racism,
enforced by law, sanctioned by religion, supported by custom, and, if
needed, by social ostracism was complete. It extended to churches,
schools, housing, jobs, eating, drinking; eventually to all forms of
public transportation, sports, recreations, hospitals, orphanages, pris-
ons and asylums, funeral homes, morgues, and cemeteries. It did not
apply to certain areas where Negro inferiority was distinctly recog-

nized but had particular force where there was any intimation of "social equality."

The Southern Presbyterian Church, in accord with its "distinctive" doctrine of the "spirituality of the church" remained silent as disfranchisement proceeded, and as segregation became first the practice and then the law of the various states. But its silence gave consent, and such voices as appeared gave religious sanction to the legal enactment.

The church papers—the *Central Presbyterian*, the *Presbyterian Standard*, the *Southern Presbyterian*, the *Southwestern Presbyterian*, the *Christian Observer*—all, without exception, approved legislation disfranchising the Negro, though disapproving at times the means by which it had been accomplished. The *Presbyterian Standard* and the *Southern Presbyterian* both contended that the disqualifying clauses in the state constitutions should apply equally to both black and white, that there should be no discrimination on the ground of race. This was the position taken by Dr. Richard McIlwaine, President of Hampden-Sydney College, before the Virginia Constitutional Convention; and it was the position for which ex-Governor McCorkle of West Virginia, later a Presbyterian elder, argued before a Southern Conference convened at Montgomery, Alabama, to consider the race question before the South. All speakers at this conference, the first of its kind to be held in the South, agreed, however, that Negro suffrage must be limited, and that the domination of whites by Negroes, however great the Negro majority, would never be tolerated in any Southern community.[4]

Justification for this position was found in the abuse of black power in the Reconstruction days—what the *Christian Observer* called the $213,000,000 robbery[5] of the Southern people—and in the unhealthy state of Southern politics, due to Negro voting power, since that day. The franchise is not the right of the Negro, declared Rev. J. R. Howerton, D.D., Professor of Philosophy at Washington and Lee University, in his sermon as retiring Moderator of the General Assembly; intrinsically, he stated, it is not the right of any man. If the Negro will forgo theoretical rights (like the franchise) and claim only practical rights, continued the speaker, there can be harmony between the races.[6]

The *Central Presbyterian*, in agreement with Dr. Howerton, insisted over and over again that the withdrawal of Negroes from politics, voluntarily or involuntarily, was for the best interests of both blacks and whites. "The southern states restrict the franchise," wrote the editor, Rev. James Power Smith, a Civil War veteran, "that they may have an honest ballot [it was generally agreed that whites resorted to bribery and stuffed the ballot boxes to offset Negro votes], that all local government may be in the hands of the intelligent and the upright, that the Negro may be delivered from politics which has been his bane, that the Southern people may give consideration to other things than the possibility of Negro domination, and that there may be peace and order in each community and section where the Negro in politics has been the source of untold evil to whites and blacks, bringing alarm and violence and bloodshed."

"The new constitution of Virginia, in its limitation of suffrage," wrote Dr. Smith, "offers a continued reward for education and economy and thrift and good behavior . . . We believe that nothing has ever been done for the Negroes of the South that promises as much for their protection and improvement as the constitutional restriction of suffrage, and time will prove it so."[7] The *Presbyterian Standard* quoted approvingly an editorial by Lyman Abbott, editor of *The Outlook*, a Northerner who had been converted to this point of view.[8]

Support for the Southern position was found in the widely publicized admission of Booker T. Washington that bestowing the franchise prematurely upon the rank and file of the colored people in the South had been a mistake.[9]

The Southern white man, it was generally agreed, was the Negro's best friend, and there was a naïve assumption that the Negro, stripped of political power, could rely upon the unselfishness of the whites to see that his real welfare would not be neglected.

The most enlightened churchmen, it may be observed at this point, agreed with Southerners generally, and also with the view that prevailed in the North, that the Negro was inherently inferior to the white man. "He is not the equal of the white man, either mentally or morally," declared Rev. D. Clay Lilly, who had served as secretary of the Assembly's Committee on Colored Evangelization and was now pastor of the First Presbyterian Church, Winston-Salem, North Carolina.[10] The science of ethnology puts the white race at the top, the black race at the bottom, of the five great divisions of mankind, claimed Rev. Egbert W. Smith, Louisville pastor, soon to become Secretary of the Executive Committee of Foreign Missions.[11]

Admittedly there were Negroes of superior attainments, like Booker T. Washington, but this, it was explained, was due to an infusion of white blood. That there had been serious deterioration in the Negro's moral character since the Civil War days, all agreed. Evidence for this was found in the growing crime rate among Negroes. Especially alarming was the rape of white women, once almost unheard of, now increasingly common—300 cases, so it was charged, in a three-month period during the year 1893. Mobs took the punishment of the accused into their hands and lynching, which was in the 1880's confined mostly to the Western frontier, became increasingly a Southern phenomenon. In the decade of the 1890's the annual average was 154, most, though not all, being in the South. After 1901 there was a slow, but irregular decline, but lynching remained a blot on the South until comparatively recent times, and has indeed been revived under other forms, and for different reasons, during the recent civil rights disturbances.

There could be and there was no defense of such barbarity. The *Southern Presbyterian* and the *Southwestern Presbyterian*, the two papers published in the deep South where lynching was more common, did at times attempt to explain, though not to condone, the resort to lynch law or, rather, lack of law. Thus, Dr. R. Q. Mallard, editor of the *Southwestern Presbyterian*, commented:

> It is useless to reason about "letting the law take its course" when the Negro commits a certain crime, it matters not what white community is the scene of the outrage. All the knightly instinct in our Southern people which prompts protection of woman's honor . . . prompts to retribution swift and terrible. The unprotected condition of wives and daughters in farming communities where the Negro population is in excess and the younger generation unprincipled and many of them not only insolent, but idle and vicious, and the universal alarm created by the commission of such a crime as that recently so frightfully punished, impel a panic stricken community to the belief that the only safety lies in making a terrible example of the miscreant.[12]

But as Dr. Mallard went on to point out, lynching did not seem to have a deterrent effect, and "the irregular justice is not only becoming more irregular, but Judge Lynch has enlarged the scope of his court, and now the murderer, white or black, must be strung up by the mob without judge or jury."[13] Lynchings, too, it was pointed out, were resorted to for lesser offense than rape.* And one death no longer satiated the lynchers. There must be several deaths, and sometimes even more than death—tortures, as fiendish as those charged against the savage Indians. Many of those so destroyed had not been proved guilty; some were demonstrably innocent. Failure to protect mob victims or to punish those who took the law into their own hands, in the judgment of Dr. James Ferdinand Jacobs, was due not to the weakness of the law, but to the fact that officers of the law sympathized with the mob and were sustained in this attitude by both legislature and courts.

---

* Rape was the cause of approximately one-fifth of the total number of lynchings in a 40-year period, 1895-1935.

"All good men in the South are agreed," said Dr. J. W. Stagg, pastor in Charlotte, N. C., addressing a New England audience, "that lynching is barbaric, anarchic and wrong."[14] Because this could be taken for granted, it may be, and because the Assembly was not accustomed to speak on "secular" issues, the highest court of the church did not warn its own constituency or the Southern people in general regarding the danger of mob violence, and for the most part this was true also of the lower courts.*

Replying to an appeal from the North for some deliverance by the Southern Assembly on the subject, the *Southern Presbyterian* in the 1890's replied somewhat facetiously: "This is not the way we do things down here. We first adjourn, then meet as a 'committee of citizens' and pass resolutions, not as presbyters in an organized capacity, but as private gentlemen, and this keeps our church records clear of political . . . deliverances, or letting off steam for our excited feelings. Seriously speaking we think our Northern Brethren would do well to imitate us in keeping the passions and the opinions of politics as far as possible out of church courts."[15]

A strong resolution, expressing the church's utter condemnation of lynching, introduced into Atlanta Presbytery, which was regarded as one of the church's more progressive presbyteries, failed to pass in 1916 on the grounds that the church has nothing to do with lynching.

There are occasional references to sermons on the subject. Rev. W. C. Alexander, a North Carolina pastor, walked by the side of two mob-condemned men, and amid the cries and curses of the crowd pled in vain for their release. Dr. W. C. Campbell, pastor of the First Church, Roanoke, Virginia, had undergone a similar experience, some years earlier, at some risk to his own life. But these were isolated examples. The church press, here as elsewhere, were the spokesmen for the church, and they continued without letup on what Dr. Mallard, in the *Southwestern Presbyterian,* referred to as "a damnable plot on our civilization and an ominious menace to civil liberty."[16]

Churchmen in the South had shared in the general fear from Emancipation onward, that "social equality" led to amalgamation of the two races and that this spelled the end of Southern culture. On these grounds they had opposed racial intermixture in the church and in the schools, indeed, opposed all social intermingling. Rev. D. O. Davies, D.D., a Kentucky pastor, who had served churches both North and South, and in both branches of the church, argued that the

---

* There were exceptions; for example, the Synod of Nashville in 1893 and the Synod of Georgia in 1916.

colored people should have separate churches, separate schools, and, as far as possible, separate workshops as well. "Let there be as little commingling of the races," he urged, "as may be consistent with all the duties of life . . . Give the colored people all possible help," he continued, "instruct them, counsel them, sympathize with them . . . give them all possible help, but—KEEP THEM BY THEMSELVES. Every step toward miscegenation, and everything that makes the first, least step possible, should be avoided as the touch of death itself."[17]

Rev. J. Ferdinand Jacobs blamed education, holding out to Negroes the possibility of privileges which were beyond their reach, for the rising crime rate among Negroes, and particularly for the increasing number of rapes, which led in turn to the mounting lynch horrors which he and all responsible Southerners deplored. "The social law," contended Dr. Jacobs, was unalterable, and must be obeyed. To disregard it meant the extermination of one or the other of the races.[18]

Rev. John W. Stagg, D.D., pastor of the Second Church, Charlotte, N. C., delivered an address on the "Race Problem in the South" before the Unity Club of New Bedford, Mass., in which he argued that "there is a barrier in the race itself that prevents anything like the approach to social equality in the South." There is nothing that Southerners would not do to help Negroes as Negroes, he added, "but if they arrogate to themselves equality of race, that moment life is jeopardized. There is a boundary beyond which he cannot pass."[19]

Booker T. Washington's acceptance of President Theodore Roosevelt's invitation to dine in the White House was deeply resented in the South as an effort to transcend these necessary bounds. "When we were hoping that alienations were being allayed, the old-time sympathies revived, and generous purposes moved, this unhappy incident comes to throw us back a long way," wrote one editor. "It stirs the mistaken social ambition of some of the Negro race, and arouses the alarm of a great body of whites. Suspicions and animosities spring up which we hoped were dying out. Crimes are committed, stirred by race ambition and hatreds, which are met by other hideous crimes and vengeance . . ."

"The separation, social and racial, is not one of prejudice," the editor insisted. He claimed in fact that there was less prejudice in the South against the Negro than anywhere else. "But there is a difference in the races so real and most distinctly understood by the people of the South, who know the Negro from close contact, that the conviction of the necessity of entire separation is simply universal and beyond consideration."[20]

Dr. J. R. Bridges, a Southern gentleman of the old school, now editor of the *Presbyterian Standard*, tried to explain the Southern attitude for the benefit of puzzled Northerners. A Southern lady, he said, would ride in a buggy on the same seat with a Negro driver who was in her employ, but would not do so if he came as her equal. A white man would not lift his hat to a Negro woman or call her "Mrs.," but would put himself out to do her a favor. Our Northern friends, wrote the editor, will have to take us as we are. They will never understand us or our relation to the Negro. We are persuaded that the Negro has no better friend than the better class of Southern whites. We have educated Negroes among us, and they are respected and treated with respect; nothing could be pleasanter than the relation existing between them and the whites. While we may be a bit remiss in respect to social recognition, we make it up in things that are of more practical value.

"The Southerner always has before him the sad example of the countries where races have mixed, and in his endeavor to avoid this constant danger, he feels that he must resist the beginnings, and in order to do so, he has to do many things that in the eyes of those who cannot appreciate his fears, seem foolish and inconsistent. One of the strongest proofs that he is not far wrong is found in the fact that those who criticise these things, when they live among us any length of time, do as we do and sometimes even more so."[21]

This editorial is a fair representation of the Southern point of view, of the view then prevailing in the Presbyterian Church in the United States. It also reflects the blindness of the average Southerner of goodwill to the injustices which had multiplied under this paternalistic point of view; blindness also to the fact that a new generation of Negro youth, many of whom had fought to make the world safe for democracy, was coming into being who would not be content with things as they were; blindness likewise to a new ferment arising within the church itself.

Churchmen had always recognized the changed attitude the gospel might work in the Negro; slowly they came to realize that the gospel also required more effort at understanding, and some changed attitudes on the part of the white man, if the steadily worsening race problem in the South was to approach solution.

At the beginning of the century a conference for the discussion of the problem met in Montgomery, Alabama, under the auspices of the Society for the Promotion of the Study of Race Conditions and Problems in the South, of which the Rev. Neal Anderson, pastor of the Presbyterian Church in Montgomery, was the president. According to its sponsors it marked an epoch in the attitude of the South toward the race problem, being the first open parliament ever to meet for "the consideration of the greatest problem any people" ever faced.[22]

Speakers at the conference representing various shades of opinion agreed on limitation of Negro voting privileges and approved overwhelmingly the value of industrial education, but developed no new remedy for what was generally recognized as a deteriorating situation. Commented the *Central Presbyterian*: "We can conceive no question so completely beyond the reach of human wisdom. It looks like one of those extreme cases that God alone can deal with . . . Prayer is our only hope."[23]

Four years later Rev. Dr. D. Clay Lilly, pastor of the First Presbyterian Church, Winston-Salem, addressing a regional Y.M.C.A. conference on "The Attitude of the South to the Colored People," began by emphasizing the common assumption that the Negro is not the equal of the white man, either mentally or morally. The general attitude of the Southern people to the Negro, he insisted, was kindly. Industrially—the white people of the South had not abridged the Negro's right to earn his daily bread in any direction of human interest or of honest effort. Civilly—no injustice had ever been done him in the courts of law. Politically—unrestricted Negro suffrage had proved to be a colossal mistake, and the South had moved in an orderly way to keep government in the hands of the superior race. Socially—the racial integrity of both races must be preserved, and "It is kinder to make the line of separation plain and to observe it strictly than to dally with it." Educationally—the Southern people with practical unanimity endorsed an elementary education for the whole race; higher education for those who had the capacity—its future leaders; industrial education of the highest type for those who could receive and use it. Religiously—the Negroe's greatest need was for the gospel, and it was on this point that Dr. Lilly spoke at greatest length.[24]

The beginning of a more enlightened approach to the race question came after World War I in which Negroes had fought side by side with whites "to make the world safe for democracy." It was becoming clear to all who had eyes to see that returning Negro veterans would not settle down quietly into the old patterns of acknowledged inferiority. In 1919, a crucial year, when "what little interracial contact and more there was seemed about to dissolve in violence," Mr. John H. Eagan, a Presbyterian elder and one of the South's leading industrialists, helped to organize a Commission on Interracial Cooperation, which five years after the war had established

branches in every Southern state and in some 800 counties. The efforts
of these groups were directed toward the removal of race antagonism
and the substitution of friendly and helpful relations, through conference and cooperation, between representative leaders of the two
races. They sought to demonstrate the possibility of two diverse
races living side by side in mutual goodwill, justice, and racial integrity.[25]

The General Assembly in 1920 commended the labors of this
commission "led by Southern men." Again, the following year, it
urged its people "with the greatest possible earnestness" to encourage
the work in their local communities; particularly did it urge cooperation between white and colored ministers.[26] Presbyteries and synods
added their endorsement and appointed committees to cooperate
with the commission in promoting better relations between the races.

More influential probably were the interracial committees appointed by the women's organizations of various Southern denominations, which cooperated with the Commission on Interracial Cooperation generally and labored for the establishment of Women's
Interracial Committees in every community. In 1920 a Woman's
Interracial Conference was held in Memphis, Tennessee. The conference called for remedial measures in the field of domestic service,
child welfare, sanitation and housing, education ("a more equitable
distribution of funds," "steps taken to create mutual respect in the
hearts of children"), travel and accommodations, lynching (to be
prevented at all costs), and justice (competent legal assistance for
Negroes).[27]

The Women's Auxiliary of the Southern Presbyterian Church,
participating fully in these endeavors, developed a unique work—
conferences for colored women, which came to be held in various
synods. In 1924 Mrs. W. C. Winsborough, Executive Secretary of
the Women's Auxiliary, at a meeting of the Executive Committee of
the Federal Council of Churches, delivered an address, "How Can
the Churches Join in a Larger Service to the Movement for Interracial Cooperation and Goodwill." Her indictment of the Ku Klux
Klan, which, under the guise of patriotism, was sowing seeds of race
hatred, lawlessness, and anarchy and which, if not checked, she
charged, would strike at the very heart of the nation's life, received
tremendous applause. Mrs. Winsborough urged that the Interracial
Commission of the Federal Council (organized in 1921), which
worked in close harmony with the Southern movement, establish a
publicity department in which information concerning the whole
subject of interracial cooperation and especially concerning the prog-

ress and present achievement of the Negro race might be widely disseminated throughout the church.[28]

Exposition of the Sunday school lessons in the *Presbyterian Standard* for some time now had invited readers to consider concrete injustices in the light of Scriptural truth. One practice here questioned was the segregation of Negro commissioners to the General Assembly. In 1929 it was noted that these commissioners attending the Assembly at Montreat, the "church's home," had been compelled to eat apart from the white commissioners—in the kitchen.[29] Two years later Rev. William Crowe, Jr., writing in the *Union Seminary Review*, flayed the unreasonable race prejudice of the South, and pointed specifically to the backwardness of Negro education in this region, to the terrifying economic ills to which he was subjected, to the many injustices he faced at the courts and in the polling booth.[30]

Further impetus to the movement would come with the great Depression. But already it was becoming clear that the younger generation of ministers—post-World War I—would not share the racial attitudes of their fathers or be content for the church to remain silent on other issues. On the eve of the great Depression, A. J. McKelway, Jr., pastor of the church at Laurel Hill, North Carolina, wrote on "Labor's Judgment on the Church." He said:

> The main and all-embracing contention of labor is that the church has failed to give the causes for which organized labor is struggling, that moral and active support which it has the right to expect of organized Christianity. . . . Believing that the church should emphasize its protest against social injustice in all its forms, [labor] finds itself impatient with the repeated emphasis on the sort of message that might be described as calculated to lull the laborer in his temporal misery with promises of eternal bliss . . . Labor marvels at the silence of the church on questions of legislation, for the protection of women and children or the betterment of intolerable living conditions and the adjustment of pitifully inadequate wage scales. . . . Do we dare wonder why the church does not draw the multitudes as Jesus, the laborer, having compassion on them, drew them to himself?[31]

The problems of war, industry, and race, aggravated by the great Depression, which churchmen could no longer avoid, led the church in this period to reexamine its "distinctive" doctrine—the spirituality of the church.

In the closing decades of the 19th century and in the opening decades of the 20th century this doctrine seemed firmly entrenched in the life and thought of the church. What is meant by the spirituality of the church? asked Robert P. Farris, veteran editor of the *St. Louis*

Presbyterian and Permanent Clerk of the General Assembly. First, that the mission of the church is not to reform men or to correct the evils of society or to advance civilization, he replied. And, second, that the mission of the church is to save sinners, to beseech them, through Christ, to be reconciled to God.[32]

Did this mean that the church had nothing to say on the larger social issues before the American people? It could teach general duties set forth in Scripture but not- their specific applications, explained Dr. C. R. Vaughan, later to become a professor in Union Theological Seminary.[33] The attempt to teach anything beyond what the Scriptures teach would only beget confusion, wrote D.C.I. in his critical examination of Richard P. Ely's small volume entitled *The Social Aspects of Christianity*. More than this, he continued, it is not the business of the preacher in his official ministrations to discuss such questions. Christ's method of establishing his Kingdom is the very reverse of the author's. Make the tree good and its fruit good is the law of Christ. All true and lasting reformation begins with the individual soul by renewing it after the image of God, and all social reformation must be the product of that gospel which is working for the world's regeneration.[34]

In 1894, as previously observed, there appeared a history of the Southern Presbyterian Church written by Thomas Cary Johnson, then Professor of Church History in Union Theological Seminary, later to become its Professor of Systematic Theology (1913-1930). In this volume Dr. Johnson justified the organization of the Southern Presbyterian Church and argued for its continued independent existence on the grounds that Northern Presbyterians had repudiated, and that Southern Presbyterians alone preserved, the true doctrine of the church and its non-secular mission. William M. McPheeters, longtime professor in Columbia Theological Seminary (1888-1932), decried every departure from the strictest construction of the traditional Thornwellian doctrine. According to Dr. McPheeters, the church had been assigned by Christ a perfectly definite mission which is to bring men to the cross and to reconcile them to God through the blood of the Lamb. The church is not at liberty to substitute for this any other end; the church is not at liberty to associate it with any other end; it is not at liberty to seek the attainment of this end by the use of any other means than those appointed by Christ. While designed to be the source of innumerable and incalculable moral and ethico-economic blessings to mankind, the church is not authorized to address itself directly to the securing of these benefits to them.[35]

This had been the view of the founding fathers; it remained the general view of the church in the opening decades of the 20th century. But it was a view that became increasingly difficult to defend.

Dr. B. M. Palmer, one of the earliest and one of the most persistent champions of the doctrine, as we have seen, supported secession in 1861 and in the 1890's fought violently against the Louisiana Lottery. But—and this distinction was for him, and others, an important one—he acted in both instances as a citizen, not as a pastor. He denounced the lottery evil, not from his pulpit, but before a mass meeting of citizens in the municipal opera house. Dr. R. C. Reed, stalwart defender of the doctrine in the next generation, preached "pretty often about the evil of liquor selling," recalled Rev. A. J. McKelway. But he did not advocate prohibition. He expelled from his church men who persisted in liquor selling. "But to have suggested from his pulpit that there ought to be a law to protect men from the evils of the liquor traffic would have been a crime, while even the preaching he did would have been unlawful if he had thought that it would eventually have 'called for legislation.' As a citizen he appeared before the county judge to urge that liquor licenses be not granted. But not as a minister." To Dr. McKelway this seemed a very finespun distinction. Dr. Reed retorted: "When a man cannot see, and cannot be made to see the essential distinction between the functions of an ambassador of Christ and the functions of a citizen of the commonwealth, he is beyond the reach of logic."[36]

The Westminster Confession recognizes the right of synods and councils to handle affairs which concern the Commonwealth "by way of humble petition in cases extraordinary," and on rare occasions the General Assembly availed itself of this constitutional privilege—in 1890, for example, when it adopted a memorial containing a petition to be addressed to Christian nations around the world regarding the arbitration of international disputes; in 1908, when it urged adoption of more effective child labor laws; and, in 1914, when it approved the Prohibition Amendment to the Federal Constitution—three scattered incidents over a period of years. The Assembly's first two uses of this constitutional privilege did not attract much attention—approval of the Prohibition Amendment, on the other hand, brought a storm of protest. Dr. W. M. McPheeters also opposed the mild telegram which the Assembly dispatched to President Wilson in 1919, declaring among other things, "We are confidently relying upon you . . . to carry on your gigantic task to a righteous consummation," but on this occasion Dr. McPheeters stood almost alone.

Synods too occasionally availed themselves of their constitutional right to send in their "humble petitions" to the government. In 1899, for example, the Synod of Alabama, protested the seating of a Mormon by the Congress of the United States; in 1895, the Synod of Georgia appointed a committee to appear before the state legislature protesting a bill legalizing Sunday freight trains; two years later the Synod of South Carolina forwarded petition to the Postmaster General to stop Sunday mail. Dr. McPheeters protested this action, insisting that the church could not recognize state officials as such and that state officials could not recognize the church as such. Dr. Palmer likewise disapproved the resolution but was forced to admit that it was permitted by the "humble petition" clause of the Westminster Confession, which both he and Dr. McPheeters would like to have seen excised from the Constitution.[37] A storm of criticism broke, as we have seen, when the Presbytery of North Alabama gave its approval to a state prohibition law, and when the Assembly declined to accept Mr. Sinnott's complaint against this action.

Rev. Charles M. Parkhurst, Presbyterian pastor in New York City, drew headlines in newspapers throughout the country by his crusade for civic righteousness in New York City. Southern Presbyterians generally disapproved this sensational preaching. But in the *Union Seminary Magazine,* edited at this time by students, there was a new note sounded. Wrote the editor:

> One of the distinctive principles of the Southern Presbyterian church . . . is that the Church and State are entirely separate, and that there is no place whatever in the pulpit for politics. We believe heartily in the soundness of this principle . . . Let us beware, however, lest in our fear of touching political issues, we neglect to fight the great evils of our day . . . If our city governments are rotten . . . must the minister thank God that he has nothing to do with public morality, and leave these cesspools of iniquity untouched for fear of preaching politics . . . We do not approve of all Dr. Parkhurst's sayings and doings, but we glory in the work he has done and is doing for New York City. He believes that a commission to preach Christ's gospel is a commission to fight sin and vice in every place he finds it . . . We are glad to note that others are beginning to follow his example . . . Let us do our part.[38]

Other voices were beginning to question the church's silence on pressing moral issues. "It still remains an open question," wrote A. C. Houston in the *Christian Observer,* "to what extent and in what manner the clergy of the land should . . . make their influence felt for the triumph of the right. One duty is plain . . . that the man of God, being a citizen, should . . . find where truth lies and there in the discharge of his duties as a citizen stand bravely up . . . for that which is right."[39]

The principle of the spirituality of the church, complained William S. Bean, is pressed to such an extent as to make one wonder whether the Southern Presbyterian Church is not made up altogether of disembodied spirits. "Let us not forget that Christ came to save men, body and soul."[40] There are two extremes, wrote J. R. Howerton, pastor of the First Church, Charlotte. Some think there is no limit— preachers are licensed to treat every subject under the sun. Others think the preacher must confine himself to proclaiming the conditions of salvation in another world, but resent the application of religion to this life, to business, and to politics. Many who think they are objecting to politics being brought into the pulpit are really resenting the application of religion to politics. "They want their political consciences left undisturbed . . . Perhaps preachers in our church are in more danger of this latter extreme than the other."[41]

It was Rev. A. J. McKelway, editor of the *Presbyterian Standard,* however, who first seriously challenged the traditional Southern Presbyterian view of the church and its mission. In tough, hard-hitting editorials he fought for racial justice, for civic reform, for child labor laws. He called attention to moral issues before the state legislature which demanded the support of Christian people. "What the minister should do in the affairs of his city," he wrote, "is a mooted question. But there is certainly no more effective way of building up the Kingdom of God than by tearing down the opposing kingdom of Satan. And we believe that many a man of God is hampered by tradition from taking hold of a civic evil that is the worst enemy of his church . . ."[42] "The extreme view of the historic position of the Southern Church," he wrote again, "has prevented our ministers from entering a most fruitful and useful field of study, that of social science, in which the principles of the Gospel may be applied to the solution of social problems. If our ministers fail to lead our people along ethical lines in the solution of these problems, who shall do it?"[43]

He rejected the commonly held idea that the church should not handle political issues, pointing out that the constitution stated that the church should handle nothing but that which is ecclesiastical, which is an entirely different proposition. "When a matter concerns the church as well as the state," he insisted, "it is the duty of each to handle it in the manner appropriate for each. No minister will ever obey the injunctions of 'Preach the Word,' if he is forever afraid of trenching upon the political sphere. And the church can never be a faithful witness to the truth if she is to be limited in her testimony by fear that something she should advocate or oppose may perhaps become a subject for legislative action. To be silent when the truth should be spoken, because good men may differ, is to be indolent in the search after truth, or cowardly in proclaiming it."[44]

More influential in the long run in reshaping the mind of the Southern Presbyterian Church on this point was Rev. Walter Lee Lingle, who came to Union Theological Seminary as a permanent member of its faculty in 1911. He had recently read Walter Rauschenbusch's *Christianity and the Social Crisis*. The book, he confessed, "almost startled" him. "There were so many new ideas and suggestions that were new to me."[45] He read it again a second time, and a third time, and when he came to the seminary he began to teach a brief course on Christian Sociology, followed by a study of Francis Peabody's *Jesus and the Social Question*. This series of lectures, the first on social ethics in any Southern Presbyterian Seminary, had great influence on successive generation of students, some of whom, like the author of this volume, had been profoundly influenced by Walter Rauschenbusch before coming to the seminary. Most of the younger ministers who led in the social awakening of the church had been students of Dr. Lingle. As popular lecturer and columnist, first in the *Presbyterian of the South* and then in the *Christian Observer*, he was never so far in advance of the church that he could not gain a hearing, but always far enough to broaden the church's viewpoint on this, as on numerous other fronts. In 1929, at the request of the students, Dr. Lingle delivered the annual Sprunt Lectures at Union Theological Seminary on the Bible and social problems. Published in book form at a critical period in the church's life, they added impetus to a growing movement.

Meanwhile other voices were being heard, laymen as well as ministers.

Mr. A. W. McAllister, prominent businessman, a ruling elder and retiring Moderator of Orange Presbytery, for example, opened its 1914 spring meeting with an address, later published at presbytery's request, in which he insisted that the church had placed too exclusive emphasis upon the individual aspects of religion. "The workingman," said he, "is deaf to [the church's] pleading for righteousness because the church has been deaf to its cries for justice. The poor, the unfortunate, no longer hear her voice, because she preaches to them afar off and does not go down to help them. The world gives little heed to them because she has cut herself off from and has placed herself out of sympathy with the world. . . . This lingering monasticism in the church, this withdrawing from the world, this traditional conception of a religious life separate and apart from the world and everyday life, this mischievous distinction between things sacred and things secular, this making of the unity of life into a confusing duality," he insisted, "is responsible for much misunderstanding between the Church and the world, for much of their lack of sympathy."[46]

In the spring of this same year, Rev. Stonewall J. McMurray of Austin, Texas, speaking to the alumni of Austin Seminary, held that the church could not look with indifference upon the great ethical problems of the day, inequality and injustice in wealth and wages, for example. The current social unrest, he indicated, was the church's opportunity.[47] The Honorable A. M. Scales, ruling elder in Greensboro, N. C., and a former governor of the state, agreed. "If the church," he said, "would more clearly show to the world the whole mind of the Master, and would to a greater degree use social service, as he so frequently did, as a means of approach and a point of contact, we would have more success in bringing the unchurched millions in our country to the feet of their Lord."[48]

The growing interest of the church at large, and of individual Southern Presbyterians here and there, in the so-called social gospel, led to renewed defense of the church's traditional doctrine of the spirituality of the church, which grew more intense after the Federal Council of Churches began to address itself to specific issues which Southern Presbyterians felt were beyond the church's province. The *Presbyterian Standard,* under editors succeeding Dr. McKelway, and the *Presbyterian of the South* (formed in 1909 through a merger of the *Central Presbyterian,* the *Southern Presbyterian,* and the *Southwestern Presbyterian*), assisted by such men as McPheeters and Reed of Columbia Theological Seminary, kept up a constant drumfire against any departure from the traditional doctrine. The only sure way for improved social conditions, said the *Presbyterian Standard,* is better men. "Make the tree good and the fruit cannot be evil . . . Is not this the one all-inclusive mission of the church? Christian citizens can give themselves heart and soul to all manner of moral reforms, but the church in its corporate capacity is God's witness, and its business is to get men's relations right with God."[49]

Rev. Dr. J. R. Howerton, Professor of Philosophy at Washington and Lee University, and one of the more liberal voices in the church, wrote a book entitled *The Church and Social Reform,* upholding this point of view. "The Church . . . as an organization," he wrote, "cannot and ought not to engage in secular reforms, political or economic. She always makes mischief when she does so. She turns aside from her own proper mission, and, at the same time, violates the freedom of conscience of her members. The only real good the Church has ever done in promoting such reforms is by her influence in forming the character, the principles and the motives of men and women whose real business in life is to engage in such services to business, to society and the state. She can reform law by reforming the lawyers . . . she can reform politics by reforming the politicians . . . and in no other way."[50]

The Federal Council of Churches of Christ in America, around which much of the argument over the church and its mission would henceforth swirl, had been organized a few years earlier (1908). Its purpose was "to manifest the essential oneness of the Christian Churches of America in Jesus Christ as their divine Lord and Savior, and to promote the spirit of fellowship, service and cooperation among them for the prosecution of work that can be better done in unison."

The Presbyterian Church in the U. S. declined, without giving much consideration to the matter, to participate in the initial shaping of the organization, one of the few major denominations that did so. "We adopted the policy of 'magnificent isolation,'" commented editor McKelway in the *Presbyterian Standard*. "But we could not maintain our isolation. There were others on the outside and we were grouped with them. Catholics . . . could not affiliate, Unitarians . . . were not allowed to participate, Universalists were not invited . . . The Southern Presbyterians held aloof, so that the outsiders were composed of 'us four and no more.' "[51]

The feeling grew that the church could not remain out of the mainstream of American Protestantism, and, after representatives of the 34 participating churches had completed their plans, the Presbyterian Church in the U. S. belatedly accepted the invitation to participate. But not without opposition. The *Southwestern Presbyterian*, maintaining the tradition of Thornwell and Palmer, had scented danger at the outset. The proposed organization, it had warned, will take up such problems as labor, capital, the money power, trusts, divorce, child labor, international arbitration, the saloon, and so forth—all important questions, deserving serious attention, but none of them falling within the province of the church. "Her mission is spiritual . . . her governing principles should be to preach Christ and His Gospel."[52]

Once in the Council this was the point on which opponents persistently hammered. The organization of a Social Service Commission, the adoption of a "Social Creed," were taken as indications that the Council misconceived the mission of the church. The church has no right to have a social program of any sort, insisted Dr. Mc-

Pheeters. In his estimation the prophets of the Old Testament set no precedent for the church. "Our Lord had no social program," he insisted, "and neither he or his apostles outlined a social program for the church."[53]

A special committee of the Council, looking into the great steel strike in South Bethlehem, Pennsylvania, stated—among other things—that "A twelve-hour day and a seven-day week are alike a disgrace to civilization." "Is this their idea of a Kingdom whose King said, 'It is not of this world?'" asked the *Presbyterian Standard*.[54]

The following May the General Assembly, for what it deemed "sufficient reasons," withdrew from the Council, affirming however that it stood ready at all times to cooperate with the Council "in any work which, in our judgment, is vital to the interests of the Kingdom of Christ."[55]

This return to isolationism pained many ministers and laymen in the church and in the following Assembly the issue was squarely faced. Advocates of "the spirituality of the church" were concerned that the Council in its recent meeting had favored the obligatory arbitration of international differences which could not be settled by diplomacy and by the fact that it had sent a representative to a recent meeting of the American Federation of Labor.[56] Dr. R. C. Reed argued before the Assembly that the Southern Church should not ally itself with churches concerned with things political in character. Dr. R. A. Webb (Louisville Theological Seminary) insisted that it was wise to withdraw from associations and surroundings "which lead us to depart from the truth."[57] The counter-argument that testimony to the truth could better be born in dialogue with others than off in a corner by ourselves seemed to carry greater weight, and the Assembly voted to resume its formal relationships with the Council.

Two years later the Assembly adopted a report drawn up by a joint committee representing the Presbyterian Churches U. S. and U.S.A., the United Presbyterian Church, and the Associate Reformed Presbyterian Church on the relation of the Christian faith and the Presbyterian Church to social reform and social service. The report recognized that the church had a distinctive work to do in bettering the social relations of men in the present world and that this function of the church needed to be emphasized at the present time. This mission could be carried out, it was indicated, first, by inspiring its members to put into practice the Christian principles of love, justice, and truth in all their social relations—economic, industrial, or political; second, by encouraging voluntary organizations for the betterment of social conditions, urging their members to cooperate in them, leaving private judgment to decide what means or methods, or what organizations were best adapted to promote these desirable ends. The report also recognized and encouraged the Federal Council of Churches as affording a common ground where all who loved and served Jesus Christ could meet for conference and cooperation "in the vast and holy enterprise of Christian Society Service." The *Presbyterian Standard* pointed out that the report recommended nothing which the church was not already doing; the church had always encouraged its members to work as citizens for human betterment. Dr. R. C. Reed, however, took violent exception to the confidence which the Assembly had expressed in the Federal Council. Its ends were worthy, but the means it employed to achieve those ends breached Southern Presbyterians' much vaunted doctrine of separation of church and state.[58]

In 1915 and again in 1916 the General Assembly entered its solemn protests against various actions of the Federal Council which "do violence to the historic and scriptural position of our church." It emphasized the need to guard carefully "against the age tendencies which are turning the forces of the church into so many side channels and so weakening the force of her supreme call to save men for time and eternity."[59]

Grounds for the continuing opposition to the Council were basically two: first, theological. In the early years two men, in particular, regarded as dangerous liberals, were chosen to serve as President of the Council, Dr. Shailer Mathews (a Northern Baptist) and Dr. Parkes S. Cadman (a Congregationalist), described as "a well-known advocate of destructive higher criticism." The Assembly declined to withdraw because of the theology of these two men for several reasons: among others because the Council was composed of denominations representing evangelical Christianity, and was itself committed to belief in the deity of Christ. Subsequent presidents of the Council did not draw the same fire.

Objection continued however to be raised to some of the radio preachers who appeared under the auspices of the Council, particularly Dr. Harry Emerson Fosdick, the most popular radio preacher of his day, long the whipping boy of the "fundamentalists." More and more came to identify the Council with modernistic theology.

The second and chief objection to the Council, however, continued to be, as it had been from the beginning, to deliverances of the Council itself; or of its Commission on Church and Social Services; or of special commissions set up by the Council on some particular issues, deliverances which the objectors could not reconcile with the denomination's distinctive doctrine of the spirituality of the church. Most of these early deliverances were in the field of industry and of international relations.

Only a few months after the Assembly had reentered the Council, the *Presbyterian of the South* complained that it had placed on its social program, "the abolition of child labor, old age pensions, a minimum wage, a free Sunday, and reduction of labor hours." It was not that the editor was necessarily opposed to any of these objectives. He held, erroneously, that the influence of the church was uniformly favorable to a righteous cause. The church, he insisted, should pray and exert its spiritual influence in these and other important departments of civil legislation as a matter of course, but when it attempted to shape specific acts of civil legislation, it was, he warned, on dangerous ground.[60]

Dr. A. W. Pitzer of Washington, in advance of his church in other areas, shared here the difficulties of his more cautious brethren. When the Council "undertakes to reconstruct human society, to eliminate all the evils of man's simple estate, to prepare this present world for man's eternal home," he declared, "then I am forced to withstand them to their face . . ."[61]

Shortly after the close of World War I, Dr. W. M. McPheeters cried out in protest. "For the first time in American history," he noted, "moderators and chief officers of a number of denominations [including PCUS] had united in a joint appeal to the nation on a great public issue." It was an appeal for "some rational and pacific method for the settlement of international disputes," to which Dr. McPheeters could hardly have been adverse. But he saw it as an entering wedge—an invasion of church members' constitutional rights and Christian liberties.[62]

Always in the background there was the great question which had done so much to shape the church's doctrine of "the spirituality of the church" from the outset, the matter of race. The first article in the Council's Social Creed was a stand "for equal rights and equal justice to all men in all stations of life." The *Presbyterian of the South* observed that the Council was concerned with the plight of the Orientals on the West Coast, and in the East of immigrants from Europe, and in the South with "the awful blight of Negro enfranchisement." "The Church," insisted the editor, "has no right to be dealing with such a question."[63]

Year after year protests against the Council's deliverances and activities on these and other subjects were made to the General Assembly, in the General Assembly, and by the Assembly to the Council. The Council patiently explained, as would need to be done again and again, that "In a body like the Federal Council, which unites thirty-one denominations, it would be too much to expect that every particular action taken should express the unanimous judgment of these bodies in every case" and that it was for this reason that wise provision had been made that no action taken by the Council was binding on the various denominations unless approved by them.[64]

In 1922 numerous presbyteries sent up overtures to the General Assembly among them were 13 requesting the Assembly to withdraw the whole or a part of its small appropriation to the Council; nine requesting to withdraw from the Council; and 13 approving the Federal Council and its appropriation. The Assembly adopted the following resolution: "In view of the fact that the Federal Council is the only organization which unifies Protestant Christianity in the United States of America; furnishes a medium of accomplishing certain desirable things which we as a church are debarred from undertaking; and makes it possible for use to combine our efforts with the thirty other constituent bodies in such work as general evangelism, restoration of devastated churches in Europe, relief of distress caused by famine, solving race problems, and other matters of similar nature, [the church does] not withdraw from the Federal Council." The church's representatives, however, were instructed to protest against any action of the Council that did not jealously guard the spirituality of the church and recognize as its supreme mission the preaching of the gospel.[65]

Overtures to withdraw from the Council continued to be received year after year, and were declined—almost as a matter of routine— because, as the 1922 General Assembly declared, there was so much of the Council's work of which the church, its boards, and agencies approved, and which could not be accomplished in any other way; because protests against actions of which the church disapproved could accomplish more within the Council than without; because of what Dr. J. Sproul Lyons termed "the danger of isolation—not merely unseemliness, but danger—danger of loss of vision, danger of service refused." "All a man has to do to become a pygmy," said Dr. Lyons, "is to shut himself away in a pitiful isolation."[66]

There were also some who were ready to defend the Council's right to speak on social issues. Among the first to do so were prominent laymen in the church, among them the Honorable A. M. Scales, who argued that there was need for the ethical emphasis of the Federal Council, and A. W. McAlister, who defended the Council's concern for the laboring man. "The Church cannot hold a commanding place in the lives of men," said he, "if she loses touch with their aspirations. She cannot be a reactionary without the reactionary's inevitable fate."[67]

Unfortunately, as time went on, proponents of the Council assumed a preponderantly defensive attitude. On the eve of the great Depression, which would constitute a watershed in the church's thinking, Dr. Walter L. Lingle stressed this point. Usually, he recalled, defenders of the Federal Council assumed a somewhat apologetic attitude, intimating that the Council's concern for social issues was a evil which must be put up with in light of the Council's undeniably positive values. He was impressed by the fact that Dr. Harris E. Kirk, retiring Moderator of the 1929 General Assembly, had defended the Council's right to investigate such things as the coal strike and the steel situation. "They are injustices which need investigating," said Dr. Kirk, "and who can do it better than the Council?"[68]

The church's decision to remain in the Council by this time seemed to be firmly established. In 1928, 1929, and 1930, the customary motion to withdraw was defeated by heavy majorities—in 1928, without debate; in 1929 by a vote of 132 to 66; in 1930 by a vote of 179 to 32. The next year, however, unexpectedly the Assembly voted to withdraw by a top-heavy vote of 175 to 79.

New issues which precipitated this unexpected action were twofold.

(1) A charge of Communism. It was the period following World War I when the rise of Bolshevism had aroused anti-Communist hysteria in America. For many the social concern of the Federal Council now took on a red coloration. Two books, *Tainted Contacts* and *The Red Net Work* (both later discredited), charging that the Federal Council of Churches was infiltrated by Communist sympathizers, were widely circulated and believed. On the basis of information supplied by such unreliable "authorities," some commissioners were swayed to vote against the Council.

(2) The question of birth control, which was now beginning to attract public attention. A report on marriage and the home drawn up by a commission of the Council had been printed and distributed for examination and study. A majority of the commission approved the practice of birth control under some circumstances; a minority of two, one being a Southern Presbyterian, disapproved. The report had aroused strong feelings in many quarters. "This matter of birth control is only another phase of modernism," charged the *Presbyterian Standard*. "May God spare our communion the mess of divorce, free

love, neglected children, and the murder of unborn generations which birth control means."[69] Eleven overtures came to the Assembly complaining of the actions of the Council, the majority of them asking that the Assembly sever its relations with the Council—the birth control resolution was highlighted as a major cause of dissatisfaction. The General Assembly this year was a conservative one, as indicated by its choice of a Moderator. In the debate over the Federal Council it was the birth control issue which proved to be the decisive issue, and which in the judgment of those present explained the final vote, reversing the trend of previous years.

To the next Assembly came 16 overtures, nine requesting reentry into the Council, seven urging otherwise. On the floor of the Assembly charges of Communism, free love, and Unitarianism were bandied about, and still carried weight. The vote to reenter the Council was lost by a vote of 68 to 168.[70]

Fundamentalists, who a few years earlier had committed the church to a continuing struggle against evolution, seemed to have won the struggle also against the church's freedom to deal with the pressing social issues of the day. But in this case, as in the other, it proved to be the darkness that precedes the dawn.

XI

Presbyterians North and South

The question of the reunion of Presbyterians North and South, which opponents had hoped was settled forever by the negative vote of 1895, was kept alive, among other reasons, by the fact that the two bodies were competing in the border states (Maryland, West Virginia, Kentucky, Tennessee, and Missouri) and that the Northern Presbyterian Church was attempting to follow its own people as they moved into other areas for which the Southern Church alone could not adequately care (Texas, Arkansas, Oklahoma, Alabama, and Florida). Virginia, the Carolinas, and Georgia were not cultivated by the U.S.A. Assembly because here there was not the same need. There were U.S.A. Presbyterian churches in these states, but they were Negro churches gathered in their own presbyteries and synods. In the South proper the Presbyterian Church U.S.A. had four synods at the close of the century: Atlantic, with six presbyteries and 163 churches; Catawba, with four presbyteries and 156 churches; Tennessee, with three presbyteries, 48 ministers, 98 churches, and about 6,000 members; and Texas, with three presbyteries, 36 ministers, 52 churches, and 2,845 members. Atlantic and Catawba Synods were composed almost entirely of Negro churches and their pastors, representing largely the work of the old Freedman's Board. The Synod of Tennessee, which covered the eastern part of that state, western North Carolina, and northern Alabama, was in large part, and the Synod of Texas almost entirely, the outgrowth of work among Northern people who had moved southward since the war.

As a representative of the Northern board explained:

Our original idea of undertaking missionary work in Texas was to follow and help our own people, and people that were with the North in their sympathies on the one hand and help give the Gospel to the destitute on all hands. Northern people followed the railroad down into Texas . . . to find a milder climate . . . and they called back to us of the North, their old pastors, brethren and friends for the institutions of the Gospel. We could not refuse them.

But more than that; our church claims to be a National Church, and our Board a National Board. As we work for the destitute in the North, so we are ready to work for the same in the South . . . We have never intended to trench on rights of Southern Presbyterians . . . But we have no respect to any clamor or any claim of any church or any part who say ". . . hands off. We own this territory!" We claim the right to go anywhere, East, West, North or South where people are destitute of the Gospel . . . Meanwhile when the field is occupied we do not care to interfere . . .[1]

Some Southern Presbyterians resented this Northern "intrusion" into Texas. This was a Southern state, it was claimed, and therefore properly belonged to the Southern Church. Northern people and their ministers were indeed welcomed into the state, and no one disputed their right to organize their own distinctive churches. But this would not be for the best interests of Presbyterianism as a whole. "If they love us, let them come into our presbyteries and synods and labor with us to extend the Kingdom and the glory of Christ," urged the *Christian Observer*,[2] and continued: "Ministers of the gospel coming from the North by uniting with us can greatly strengthen our cause, by building up our churches and making them self-sustaining. By doing otherwise they will greatly divide and cripple our feeble congregations and organize a few weak and starving churches to be sustained by their Board of Missions for years to come."[3]

Northern papers pointed out in reply that the Southern Church did not have a sufficiency of either men or means to meet the rapidly increasing demands of its missionary fields (a charge readily acknowledged in the South), that many of the newcomers into the state desired the type of religious privileges to which they had been accustomed, and that the efforts of the U.S.A. Synod had been to occupy the newer portions of the state and to supplement rather than to compete with the work of the Southern Church.

Inevitably tensions arose, as in Abilene, where for a time there were both Northern and Southern churches, neither capable of self-support. A Northern editor charged that the Southern churches had come repeatedly into communities where Northern Presbyterians had organized churches and by means of political prejudices had divided the congregation and organized Southern churches. The Northern or National Church, he insisted, had repeatedly refused to enter fields where the Southern Church was organized. This rule, he claimed, had never been violated except in one instance, and here not designedly.[4]

There were those in the South, on the other hand, who held that "the spirit of unity had been marred by the course of Northern ministers or of the Northern Committee of Domestic Missions upon Southern soil. The feeling has prevailed among many of our people," declared the *Christian Observer*, "that the efforts of the Northern Church have been in hostility to ours, aiming to divide our churches, distract our councils, run away our ministers, and so forth."[5]

There was a growing recognition that there must be some rules of comity, that wasteful competition was a luxury that neither church could afford. Committees appointed by the two Texas synods drew up such rules in 1881. They provided that no presbytery should establish a church in a locality occupied by the other without its permission and that in towns where two churches were already organized under different assemblies and one or both were unable to sustain themselves the two churches should be organized under the banner of the one which had priority of occupation and maintenance of stated preaching.

The Southern Synod, in accordance with a General Assembly action of this same year, held that approval or disapproval of such comity principles must be left in the hands of the presbyteries. Western Texas proceeded to approve them and so informed its U.S.A. counterpart, the Presbytery of Austin.[6] The Presbytery of Paris, on the other hand, declared that it was unable to comply with the terms agreed upon by the Committee of Conference.[7] Central Texas went further. "This presbytery insists," it declared, "that Texas is not a region common to the two churches, but is territory which the advancement of Presbyterianism demands should be exclusively occupied by the Southern Church."[8] Cooperation, this same presbytery complained a few years later, is a thing which is used against us and for our injury. It affords an opportunity to scheming partisans, charged the *Southwestern Presbyterian*. "They are introduced to the confidence of our people under color of a mutual interest, and then proceed to betray the confidence of those who trusted them, and to rob them of their possession. Such is the idea emphatically presented by this presbytery, as a matter of personal experience; and hence they earnestly deprecate the idea of our church on its frontiers being exposed to similar destructive influences."[9]

In 1889, the General Assemblies of the two churches approved, as we have seen, for the first time general principles of comity and cooperation. Texas commissioners to the Southern Assembly, it may be noted, were divided regarding this limited cooperation with the sister church, six being in favor, with five opposed.

Despite the increasing goodwill, the comity rules which had been agreed upon, and the general desire to observe them, there continued to be misunderstandings, cases of thoughtlessness, unwise actions, frictions, needless duplication, and wasteful efforts, at times arousing bad feeling and other unchristian attitudes, including attempts at retaliation. Only a few years after the Assembly comity principles had been agreed upon, Rev. J. D. McLean, evangelist of Dallas Presbytery, charged that Trinity Presbytery U.S.A. had disregarded them and that therefore Dallas Presbytery was no longer bound.[10] The *Christian Observer* looked askance at the organization of U.S.A. churches in Galveston and Houston. To an onlooker, observed the editor, this action appears as a violation of the compact.[11] A little later the same paper reported a well-defined feeling in certain sections of our church, especially in Texas, that the agents of the Northern Church had paid but scant attention to the plan of cooperation. The result had been to check almost entirely in those actions any desire for closer relations with their brethren in the North.[12] Complaints of Northern interference with Southern work from the western presbyteries became so numerous that Dr. S. L. Morris termed the condition a chronic one.[13]

In 1907 the Southern General Assembly sent a formal complaint to the Northern Assembly, charging that in numerous instances after Southern evangelists had begun work with a view to organizing a new church and in some cases even after the church had been organized representatives of the Northern Church had induced them to change ecclesiastical connections, sometimes through the offer of financial aid. Evidence was offered to this effect. The U.S.A. Assembly replied that the evidence was too conflicting for any action to be taken, but urged all of its agents on the field to observe scrupulously the principles of Christian comity.[14] To the *Southwestern Presbyterian* it seemed that the Northern Church was spending money lavishly "on our territory, trying to oust us from Texas and Oklahoma and the Southwest generally."[15]

Union of the Cumberland and U.S.A. Presbyterian Churches in 1906 greatly augmented the strength of the so-called Northern (National) Church in the South and increased the possibility of friction. Relative strength of the three churches in 1904 at the beginning of union negotiations was as follows[16]:

	U.S.A.	Cumberland	U. S.
Kentucky	8,258	16,468	20,240
Missouri	23,809	28,342	12,818
Arkansas	very few	11,075	5,762

Alabama	1,000	7,855	14,096
Tennessee	7,232	41,923	18,994
Texas	3,379	30,908	21,213

A minority of the Cumberland Presbyterian Church bitterly opposed the union and declined to come into the Presbyterian Church U.S.A. The Stated Clerk of the continuing Cumberland Church, organized after the terms of union had been accepted, estimated the number of anti-unionist as follows[17]:

Alabama, 72 ministers	15 anti-unionists
Arkansas, 134 ministers	34 anti-unionists
Kentucky, 83 ministers	47 anti-unionists
Mississippi, 40 ministers	9 anti-unionists
Missouri, 164 ministers	48 anti-unionists
Tennessee, 173 ministers	124 anti-unionists
West Tennessee, 81 ministers	anti-unionists
Texas, 306 ministers	83 anti-unionists

When the smoke cleared away it was discovered that there had been leakage into other churches. In Texas, for example, it was estimated that about two-thirds of the preachers, but perhaps no more than one third of the membership, went into the Presbyterian Church U.S.A. Losses in membership to other denominations, as a result of the confusion attending the union disturbance and the lack of ministers to man the churches which might have been saved to the Cumberland cause, were almost as great as the number who went into the "union." Still in every Southern state where the Cumberland Church had any strength the comparative strength of the U.S.A. Church had been greatly increased.

In 1907, Texas Synod, continuing the original U.S.A. Synod, and Texas A Synod, representing the Cumberland contingent received, but as yet unmerged, reported as follows to the General Assembly:

Synods	Presbyteries	Ministers	Churches	Members
Texas	3	40	60	4,077
Texas A	21	245	580	24,373

The following year, when the merger had been completed, the single U.S.A. Synod and Southern Synod of Texas reported as follows:

Synods	Presbyteries	Ministers	Churches	Members
U.S.A.	12	263	461	21,884
U. S.	12	221	475	26,508

It will be observed that the two synods were now approximately the same size, with the same number of presbyteries, and with nearly the same boundaries. There were more ministers in the

U.S.A. Synod, but the U. S. Synod had the larger number of churches and more members. Each synod had its own college, Trinity (originally Cumberland Presbyterian) for the one, and Austin for the other. In Arkansas many Cumberland Presbyterians came into the Southern Church, rather than be carried into the National Church.[18]

The more aggressive Home Mission efforts of the U.S.A. Church in the states jointly occupied by the two major Presbyterian bodies following the Cumberland union multiplied the occasions of friction but also the calls for cooperation and union.

Three cases which aroused considerable feeling and remained live issues before the church for a number of years developed in New Orleans, Louisiana; Springdale, Arkansas; and El Paso, Texas.

In the New Orleans case, Rev. J. C. Barr, D.D., long-time pastor of Lafayette Church, broke with his presbytery and asked for a letter of dismission to Nashville Presbytery. Instead of presenting his letter to that presbytery, he took it to Jefferson Presbytery (U.S.A.), a small presbytery composed largely of ex-Cumberlanders, covering the whole state of Louisiana and a small portion of East Texas, and was received into its membership. In the meantime Lafayette Church renounced its allegiance to the Presbytery of New Orleans and declared itself an independent church. Immediately a call for the pastoral services of Dr. Barr was presented to Jefferson Presbytery and a commission was appointed to install him as pastor of this then independent church, which was afterward placed on the roll of Jefferson Presbytery.[19] The Presbytery of New Orleans claimed that Jefferson Presbytery had acted in an unfriendly and unconstitutional manner, and in disregard of the accepted laws of comity.

In Springdale, Arkansas, the Southern Church had maintained an organization for more than 30 years, nourished by Home Mission funds. Just when it was about to assume self-support the U.S.A. Church without consultation, so it was charged, entered the field so that instead of one Presbyterian church able to meet the needs of the community there were now two struggling churches.

In El Paso the Southern Church had undertaken a mission among the large number of Latin Americans congregated in that city. The Synod of Texas U.S.A., with superior resources, opened a better mission only a short distance away. All three of these cases were brought to the attention of the Northern Assembly. The Southern Church continued to press for meliorative action, but after six years accepted the recommendations of a joint committee on comity that settlement was barred by the "statute of limitations" and that further efforts be abandoned.[20]

It was agreed this same year that henceforth neither church would initiate foreign work in towns of less than 100,000 where the other church was at work. It has been previously agreed (1911) that there would be no duplication of Home Mission activity in towns of less than 5,000. Both Assemblies now urged their respective synods and presbyteries to make every effort to settle all cases of comity locally, before appeal was made to the Comity Committee of the Assemblies. In 1922 the Comity Committee was discharged, and all such problems referred to the respective Home Mission Boards.

Overlapping synods and presbyteries were coming now to a better understanding of their mutual mission responsibilities, though cases of friction would continue to arise and have done so down to the present time.

In the fall of 1889, carrying out the spirit of the Comity Agreement reached that year by the two General Assemblies, Lexington Presbytery in the Synod of Virginia and the West Virginia Presbytery in the Synod of Pennsylvania agreed that the first would undertake no new work north of the Parkersburg branch of the B & O Railroad and that the second would undertake no new work south of that line.[21] That agreement has been faithfully observed by successors of the original contracting parties to the present day.

The Committee on Comity reported in 1917 to the Synod of Texas (U. S.) that voluminous correspondence with the corresponding Committee of the U.S.A. Church convinced it that the latter did not intend to move beyond the sphere of friction and hurtful rivalry.[22] A decade later a subcommittee on comity reported to the synod that a fine spirited meeting had been held with the corresponding U.S.A. committee. A survey was being undertaken to discover the most serious cases of overlapping, and Presbyterial authorities were being consulted regarding overchurched towns in four different presbyteries. Exchange of churches was being planned. The synod called for unusual carefulness in keeping comity arrangements.[23]

The next year the Home Mission Committee reported: "We believe that it is possible to ultimately reach some agreements relative to our overlapping territory, and also to the allocation of unoccupied territories in Texas, that would be of large value to the harmony and efficiency of the working forces of Presbyterianism and the Lord's cause in our state."

The era of good feeling had finally arrived in this formerly strongly contested state.

In Kentucky, where once there had been so much bitterness, comity was giving way to cooperation. A joint educational work centering around Centre College and Louisville Seminary began, as we have seen, in 1901, to the distress of many who held that the Southern Church had distinctive principles which must not be compromised and feared that joint educational endeavors were an inevitable step toward union. A few years later the two synods approved a policy relating to the uniting of churches in the two denominations, where such union would be of value.[24] A still more advanced step was taken when the synod instructed its Home Mission Committee to hold joint meetings with the corresponding U.S.A. committee to arrange for a program of sustentation, evangelism, Sabbath school extension, and other kinds of advance work to eliminate competition or duplication of effort by these two bodies of Presbyterianism in Kentucky.[25]

Comity provisions and efforts at cooperation did not solve the problem of competing churches in the border synods. Almost inevitably there came repeated calls for what seemed the only adequate solution—the reunion of the two major branches of the church. Dr. James I. Vance, pastor of the First Church, Nashville, and a rising star in the Southern firmament, attracted attention, both North and South, by a sermon, preached on Christmas Day 1898, advocating efforts toward reunion. The *Christian Observer* deprecated all agitation of the question. "It is useless to ignore the issue," replied Dr. James Ferdinand Jacobs, editor of the *Southern Presbyterian*, now published in Clinton, S. C., "for it is one of the principle questions which has confronted the church for years, and will continue to confront it until the two churches drift so far apart as to make the thought of union absurd, or else come so close together as to consummate union."[26] Dr. Jacobs argued that the causes for separation had been removed, and that therefore the reasons for maintaining ecclesiastical divisions had disappeared. He even spoke disparagingly of "make-believe distinctive principles," thereby arousing the ire of his competitors.

Those who favored some form of closer relations with the Presbyterian Church U.S.A. (if only to end wasteful competition) but who opposed union, or who held that this was a step beyond hope of realization, now rallied around an alternative plan, which continued to be advocated by a number of Southern Presbyterians for the next generation and more—some form of federation. Dr. Stuart Robinson, one of the founding fathers of the Southern Church, had suggested some such plan a generation earlier. Dr. Alexander J.

McKelway, editor of the *Presbyterian Standard,* began to sponsor federation around the turn of the century. "The Southern Church," he wrote, "can never consent to a union under such conditions as that home-rule should be taken from her by a majority vote. She cannot see the interests to be forwarded by such union that would compensate for the interests threatened [the threat to Southern civilization involved in the relations between the two races]. But she nonetheless deplores the division of the Presbyterian host in America, and if any visible bond of unity can be established such as the Federation of Assemblies for the promotion of the common good and the equitable division of territory now occupied by rival churches while preserving the autonomy of the different Assemblies we believe that she will lend her voice and influence to the plan."[27]

The *Christian Observer* swung over to the support of this plan as the one best fitted to secure closer relations. Dr. C. R. Hemphill, Professor in Louisville Seminary, publicized this solution of the problem in an address delivered before a gathering of prominent Presbyterians in Chicago.[28]

The two Assemblies met a few weeks later. The Southern Assembly had before it a batch of overtures and memorials dealing with some form of closer relations between Presbyterians.

Before the Northern Assembly came a resolution to withdraw all aspersions and charges of any and every kind made by previous Assemblies against the Southern body, and to express a willingness to confer at any time with the Southern Assembly on the question of closer relations. There was a routine motion to refer. Some wished to know what was to be withdrawn. The mover, Dr. Tennis S. Hamlin, recalled that in 1882 all aspersions had been rescinded except those relating to disloyalty and rebellion. This restriction, Dr. Hamlin pleaded, ought now to be wiped out. He had no objection to it being referred but felt it would mean more if it were passed with spontaneous enthusiasm and without the appearance of calculating deliberation. His speech carried the day. There were a considerable number of votes for reference, but an overwhelming shout against it, and on the main question for adoption a whirlwind of ayes rose to the roof as over against one lonesome no. In an outburst of brotherly feeling the commissioners joined in singing "Blest Be the Tie That Binds."[29]

The telegram reporting the action of the Northern Assembly reached the Southern Assembly on the second day of its sessions. The proceedings had been uninteresting and the commissioners were weary. The Moderator announced that a telegraphic communication had been received from the Northern Assembly. As the Stated Clerk began to read, the hum which had been heard through the house instantly ceased, every eye was closely fixed, every ear intent, intense silence prevailed. "As the reading proceeded the excitement so plainly visible in all parts of the well-filled house steadily increased," reported the *Christian Observer,* "and at the moment that it closed, this staid conservative body, oblivious of the dignity that attaches to the proceedings of a General Assembly, forgetful that they were in a church, gave expression to their feelings of surprise and gratification in the most tumultuous applause ever heard in a meeting of our General Assembly. So loud and general was it that it drowned the sound of the Moderator's gavel as he rapped for order. It almost died away, and then once more rolled out in an unmistakeable evidence of the depth of feeling that had been evoked."[30]

A special committee to which the matter was referred recommended that a committee be appointed authorized to confer with similar committees representing other Presbyterian and Reformed bodies with a view to discovering: (1) the real sentiments of the churches on this subject; (2) the leading of God's Providence in the matter; (3) the obstacles that might stand in the way of closer relations; (4) whether and how such obstacles could be removed; and (5) what might be the nature and form of the relations which would best secure effective cooperation, whether it be by federation or otherwise. A long discussion followed. Opponents opposed the appointment of such a committee because it looked to organic union. Shades of the great men of the past were appealed to: Thornwell, Dabney, Palmer, Peck, Adger, Smyth, and the Wilsons. Differences between the two bodies were pointed out by Dr. Benjamin B. Palmer, nephew of Dr. B. M. Palmer, now deceased—the Negro question, the U.S.A. position in regard to the Scriptures, the U.S.A. Church's growing ritualism. The appointment of the committee, it was said, would mean the agitation for ten years of all these and other questions, the raking over of old grievances which had crippled the activities of the church. Dr. W. M. Morrison from Africa, speaking for the report, emphasized Christ's prayer for the unity of believers, the friction of the Home Mission work where there was overlapping, the uniting of the work on the foreign field prophetic of what would one day be done in the homeland.[31]

The recommendation to appoint the committee of conference was carried by a large majority—154 to 30. Some voted affirmatively because they thought it was the courteous thing to do; some, or so it was claimed, because they thought it was the best way to end talk of church union.

The action of the General Assembly did not meet with universal approval. James Power Smith, editor of the *Central Presbyterian* and a Civil War veteran, feared it would reopen the question of union; Central Texas Presbytery doubted that there was any strong desire for any closer relations than those already existing.

Greenbrier Presbytery (West Virginia), influenced by Dr. Eugene Daniel, a long-time opponent of union, adopted resolutions expressing its concern over appointment of the committee on conference, among other reasons, because of the doctrinal unrest of the day. The real issue, as it seemed to the presbytery, was the verbal, inerrant, plenary inspiration of the Bible. This was no time for the Southern Church to think of changes which might involve all its enterprises, all its agencies, all its property, all its public institutions, all its peculiar principles, all its most sacred sentiments, many of the holiest convictions of its noble women, the future of even its little children, and, above all, its as yet untouched standards of faith and its holy Bible.[32]

Dr. Jacobs, on the other hand, was jubilant. "Like the news of a sweet benediction comes the telegram out of the North," he wrote in the *Southern Presbyterian*. "It is the biggest thing that the Presbyterian Church in the United States of America has done since the days of the sad secession."[33] The trend of opinion, as he saw it, was steadily toward union. "It is coming, brethren," he wrote, "sooner or later, and we may as well line up behind the band-wagon. There is too much good feeling and real affectionate regard between the two branches of our church, and we have too many brethren who have crossed the line one way or the other for us to remain long apart."[34]

By 1906, after two years of deliberation, a joint committee representing the Presbyterian Church in the U.S.A., the Presbyterian Church in the U. S., the United Presbyterian Church, the Associate Reformed Presbyterian Church, the Reformed Church in the U. S., and the Reformed Church in America presented to their repective bodies a plan for a Council of the Reformed Churches in America holding the Presbyterian system.

This plan provided that every church entering into the agreement retained its distinct individuality, its own creed, government, and worship, as well as every power, jurisdiction, and right, which was not by these articles expressly and exclusively delegated to the body thereby constituted. It may be added, parenthetically, that no powers, jurisdictions, or rights were delegated at this time to the proposed Council, nor was there any serious move to do so at any later time. It was further provided that "the Council shall exercise only such powers as are conferred upon it by these articles, or such as may hereafter be conferred upon it by the constituent churches." But no powers were conferred upon it by the articles of agreement nor was it ever seriously suggested that such powers be conferred upon it later, except the power of advice, and even this power was seldom exercised. The articles of agreement provided further that "the Council shall promote the cooperation of the constituent churches in their Foreign Mission work, and also Home Mission work among the Colored People, Church Erection, Sabbath Schools, Publication and Education."[35] Unfortunately little or no progress was ever made toward achieving any one of these limited objectives.

These innocuous articles of agreement were viewed with alarm by leading ministers of the church. Venerable figures, like C. R. Vaughan of Lynchburg, R. K. Smoot of Texas, and James Power Smith, whose memories ran back to Civil War days, and also younger men, coming into their prime, like William M. McPheeters of Columbia Seminary and John M. Wells of Wilmington, North Carolina, opposed the Committee on Conference, and now the Article of Agreement on the familiar but all-sufficient grounds that to approve them would be a step toward union.

All the old arguments were revived. Memories of the Civil War were evoked: the Gardiner Spring Resolutions of 1861; the U.S.A. Assembly resolutions of 1865; the New School declaration that President Davis and General Lee should be executed as traitors to their country; the Walnut Street Case; the Gurley Ipso Facto Resolutions, leading to the virtual expulsion of the Synods of Kentucky and Missouri.

Southern Presbyterians were reminded again of their distinctive doctrine of the spirituality of the church. Our Northern brethren, wrote Rev. Edward E. Smith,

> believe the state is a great agency for morality, and that morality is conducive to spirituality. They believe on a righteousness which is by law . . . The great question between the two churches, Northern and Southern, lies just here. It is the old question whether men can be made righteous by law, and if they can, whether it is the duty of the church to so make them righteous . . . The one [church] holds that the kingdom of Christ is dependent on civil government. The other holds it to be independent. This difference in principle puts the Northern and Southern Presbyterian Churches as wide apart as the poles. The idea of the Northern Church is by no means a new one. It goes back beyond the sixties. It flares in the fires of Smithfield. It is bloody with

the butchery of Bartholomew . . . Against it the Southern Presbyterian
Church stands in protest from the beginning of her separate existence.
Her very existence proclaims to the world the independence of the church
of the Lord Jesus Christ, righteousness of the heart and life, which is not
by the law, but by faith in Jesus Christ . . .[36]

For Dr. John M. Wells the race question remained "the most
obvious and seemingly insurmountable difficulty of all." The situation
of the white people in the South, he explained, was unique in the
history of mankind. "We have an almost pure Anglo-Saxon people,
living in the same territory with a Negro race of almost equal numbers, and in some sections twenty times as numerous. This race . . .
is inferior and degraded. A large majority of its men are dishonest,
a large majority of its women are impure. Education has so far made
it more criminal . . . As a race it is retrograding . . . Were this race
thrown with Spaniards or Portuguese there would be no problem.
The white race would be amalgamated with the black, and a low
mongrel race having all the faults and few of the virtues of each
would result. With Anglo-Saxons of the type found in the South this
solution is unthinkable and abhorrent . . . we will die first." To make
this amalgamation impossible, Dr. Wells went on to argue, there
must be social separation of the races. For this reason meeting of the
races on the ground of social equality could not be tolerated by the
dominant race. The necessity of this position could not be understood
by those not similarly situated. It would be folly, therefore, to place
the settlement of these problems in their hands.[37]

Theological differences were not ignored. In the decade of the
1890's the Northern Church was rocked by a series of heresy trials
which attracted the attention of the nation. As a consequence three
of its most distinguished scholars—Professor Charles A. Briggs of Union
Theological Seminary in New York (1892), Professor Henry P. Smith
of Lane Seminary (1893), and Professor A. C. McGiffert of Union
(1899), all of whom had accepted the historical critical approach to
Scripture and rejected the doctrine of biblical inerrancy—were expelled or withdrew voluntarily from the church. The support manifested for their views in certain areas had disturbed the Southern
Church. It had also been concerned over efforts to revise the Standards
of the U.S.A. Church. In the end the revisions had been very slight
and to the open-minded in the South brought assurance of essential
soundness. Rev. Walter Lee Lingle, promising young pastor in Rock
Hill, South Carolina, confessed that he liked the revised U.S.A. Confession better than his own.[38] The *Southwestern Presbyterian* found
little objection to changes in the Confession but worried over "the

neutral tint" of the Brief Statement approved by the Assembly (though not adopted as a part of the Standards).[39] The *Central Presbyterian* feared that the spirit of inquiry which had prompted the present changes would in time require further progress and additional statements.[40] It finally persuaded itself that the slight modifications and additions to the Standards and the adoption of the Brief Statement of Doctrine represented "a serious yielding to the so-called liberal views and the advanced religious teaching of the day."[41]

But it was the U.S.A.–Cumberland Presbyterian Union, which most disturbed the Southern Church, a union made possible by the revision of the U.S.A. Standards. The Cumberland Church had originated in part because of its reaction to the alleged "fatalism" of the Westminster Confession. Its crucial attitude toward this aspect of the Confession had remained through the years. The Cumberland Church was regarded as an anti-Calvinistic body by many Southern Presbyterians. Their reception now into the U.S.A. Church was taken as indication of dangerous latitudinarianism. Dr. J. M. Wells insisted: "There are grave doctrinal objections to union. The Northern Presbyterian Church has modified its Calvinism to an extent that seems to many of our ablest thinkers vital. The Presbytery of Nassau has practically given up Calvinism. The Cumberland Presbyterian Church never had any Calvinism to modify. At least two of the constituent bodies are honeycombed with higher criticism . . . Subscription to the Standards with a majority is with mental reservations and a looseness that makes it well-nigh meaningless."[42]

Though opposition to the proposed Council of Reformed Churches was based largely on the fear that it was a step toward union, objection was also made to the articles of agreement. Dr. R. C. Reed of Columbia Seminary contended that if the Council were only an advisory body it was a superfluity, an expensive luxury, if nothing worse; if it were given real power it would become dangerous. Dr. G. B. Strickler of Union Seminary pointed out that the Council's advice might prove embarrassing. He was thinking particularly of Negro evangelization. "If we do our work ourselves, free from any obligations to outside parties," he pointed out, "we shall then be perfectly free to do it in our own way, consistently with those peculiar conditions that surround us."[43] Dr. C. R. Vaughan suggested that the Scriptural injunction to separate oneself from unbelievers prohibited federation with men who "teach otherwise" as fully as it did organic union.[44]

The *Presbyterian Standard* deplored the intemperate language of some opponents of cooperation or union—such as "they [i.e., North-

ern Presbyterians] are bent upon subduing us" or "It is safest not
trust these eager and rather unscrupulous gentlemen with any power
at all over our affairs."[45] A correspondent regretted that a carefully
prepared, though unsigned, pronouncement from "friends of the Independence and Autonomy of the Southern Presbyterian Church,"
addressed to "the Elders, Deacons, and thoughtful Laymen" of the
church, attempted to set laity against clergy.[46]

He recalled that, when the question of joining the Pan-Pres-
byterian Alliance was before the church, and, a little later, when
Fraternal Relations with the Northern Church was the burning
question, almost identical arguments were used by those opposed.
There were the same prophecies of speedy, organic union, the same
anticipation of dreadful results, the same charges of disloyalty to
the church and its peculiar mission, the same appeals to "contend
earnestly for the faith," the same recall of ugly charges made in
the past, the same dire predictions about the sure and speedy loss
of the autonomy and independence of the Southern Church.

To some the constant talk about the superior soundness of the
Southern Presbyterian Church, the insistence that it alone preserved
the spirituality of the church, smacked of Pharisaism.[47]

Rev. A. W. Pitzer, D.D., of Washington, insisted that obstacles
to reunion had disappeared. Rev. Newton Donaldson, pastor of the
First Church, Huntington, West Virginia, who had served ten years
in the Northern Church and now 11 years in the Southern Church,
recognized no serious differences between the two churches.[48] Dr.
C. R. Hemphill of Louisville Seminary favored the cooperative plan
among other reasons because it gave visible expression to the existing
unity of the Presbyterian and Reformed churches in the nation
and offered a means of deepening the consciousness of unity; also
because the cooperating churches would be able to use their resources more effectively and with less waste.[49] Dr. Francis R. Beattie,
also of Louisville Seminary, contended that in the changing situation,
with Northern people moving South, and with much of the Southern
territory opened by the Cumberland union to the Northern Church,
to follow a policy of isolation was neither wise nor safe.[50]

The charge of isolationism brought by Dr. Beattie and others was
deeply resented, but it was clear that two parties were emerging in
the church, the one more ecumenical, the other less. Dr. J. B. Mack,
who knew the mind of the church perhaps as well as anyone, insisted that "Organic Union" was the real question before the church.
And he predicted that it would come in time, but only in part. Perhaps 30 percent of our church, he estimated, are determined to have

the union; perhaps 30 percent are determined to maintain the autonomy of the Southern Presbyterian Church. The unionists, as he saw it, were mainly in the West, the anti-unionists mainly in the East. The time and the extent of the union, he held, would depend on the remaining 40 percent. Already, he insisted, we have a divided church. The only questions are when and where will the cleavage take place.[51]

In the 1905 General Assembly a crucial motion to drop the matter of the Council failed by a vote of 97 to 81. The following year the Assembly, unwilling to make a decision, by an even closer vote than before (89 to 84), sent the proposal down to the presbyteries for their consideration and advice. Fifty of the Presbyteries voted in favor of the Articles of Agreement; 28 (ten of which were in the Synod of Virginia) voted for their rejection. After prolonged debate extending over several days the 1907 Assembly approved the Articles of Agreement establishing a Presbyterian Council by a vote of 96 to 94. Opponents pointed out that the majority was obtained only through the votes of the four Negro commissioners and a "half breed Indian" who announced a change in his recorded vote after the roll call revealed a tie.[52]

The editor of the *Christian Observer* rejoiced: "The Southern Presbyterian Church," he wrote, now "enters upon a new epoch in its history with enlarged vision and prepared to occupy a much more influential position among the religious forces of this country." There were irreconcilables, on the other hand, who predicted that the consequences would be "disastrous in the extreme" and hinted darkly at the division of the church.[53]

In retrospect it seems much ado about nothing. Meetings of the Council were regularly held. Committees were appointed, good fellowship prevailed, resolutions were adopted, but nothing happened. The Council itself had no real power, and the governing bodies to which it reported took little note of its existence.

Erection of the Council under these circumstances did not halt the growth of union sentiment in the Southern Church—as some had hoped. Rather the contrary. The impotence of the Council called for other remedies. In addition a new generation was coming to the fore that longed to heal the divisions that crippled the work of the church. An expression of this point of view is found in the report of the simultaneous meetings of the U.S.A., the U. S., and the U. P. General Assemblies in Atlanta, Georgia, in May 1913, made by the Honorable A. M. Scales, Presbyterian Elder from Greensboro, North Carolina. Wrote Mr. Scales:

In our homes and from our political leaders, we who were born since the war, were taught to believe that every Yankee has a horn and a cloven hoof. Our Church papers were not to be outdone, and they adopted an attitude of suspicion and distrust of our Northern brethren; these papers hinted or openly taught that the Northern Church was unsound in faith and that we were sounder in the doctrines of Calvinism, and more loyal to our Lord and almost too good to associate with them, and we were always taught that if we should so far forget ourselves as to mix with them, that we must keep both eyes wide open for fear the goblins might get us. Our teachers believed this, and rather naturally, for it is so easy to attribute bad things to an enemy. Both the North and the South [continued Mr. Scales] have learned many things. We have intermarried with them, we have interchanged preachers freely, we have served on committees and councils with them, we have actually united with them in one or more educational institutions, and now we have rubbed up against them in Atlanta, and as far as the writer is concerned, he is about ready to admit that they are almost as good as he is.

Whether the Lord Christ intends by these and other signs to lead us into organic union, no one can tell. . . . It may be that the great Captain may want his Presbyterian regiments to fight under one blue flag in one great brigade, and if he does he will bring it to pass, and the Southern regiment will loyally and even joyfully obey orders . . .[54]

Overtures from four presbyteries asking for closer relations with other Presbyterian bodies were answered in the negative by the Atlanta Assembly on the ground that negotiations were underway for union with the United Presbyterian Church. The previous Assembly had unanimously appointed a committee of conference to explore the possibilities of union with this smaller but vital Presbyterian body, found in the Northern and Western states, and regarded as thoroughly conservative as the Southern Church. A suggested Basis of Union was agreed upon by the negotiating committee, accepted by the 1913 Assembly, and placed on the docket for consideration by the 1914 Assembly.[55] This body approved the plan and sent it down to the presbyteries for their adoption or rejection. The United Presbyterian Assembly, on the other hand, rejected the plan, in part because the boundaries of the two churches did not overlap, and in part because the U. P. Church felt that union would destroy its identity—i.e., that it would be swallowed up (an argument pressed by Southern Presbyterians when it was a question of union with the U.S.A. Church).[56]

To make it difficult to rush into any union, and particularly union with the Presbyterian Church–North, the 1914 General Assembly enacted an amendment to the Book of Church Order requiring a three-fourths vote of the presbyteries before the union could be consummated. The 1913 Atlanta General Assembly had proposed the amendment, 58 presbyteries had approved, 12 had disapproved, 15 had failed to vote. The barriers to union had been raised higher than that found in any other major denomination.

Sentiment in the Southern Church was now turning once again to some type of federation which would preserve the autonomy of the constituent bodies, but enable them to establish cooperative agencies that could do something more than the existing Council which had been given only advisory powers. As Dr. R. F. Campbell, pastor of the First Church, Asheville, North Carolina, saw it, closer relations were demanded by the entrance of the Northern Church into the South. This church was carrying on a vigorous work in the Asheville area. Organic union was out of the question. Federation was the answer.[57]

The *Presbyterian Standard*, edited now by Dr. J. R. Bridges, a thorough conservative, opted for federal union as the lesser of two evils. "For years," he wrote "we staved off the question [of union], aided by the appeals of the old men who bore the brunt of the fight. Now they are dead, and we, who were their children, are now the old men, and our appeals cannot touch the young and practical men, as our fathers' appeals touched us. The younger men are restless, and the time is rapidly coming when they will make their power known and felt." In support of his contention he quoted pastors from Mississippi, Kentucky, and Texas—all of whom had written that union was a necessity. The only question, as Dr. Bridges saw it, was what kind of union shall it be. And while he, with others of the "Old Guard," preferred things to remain as they were, federation, he held, was better than being swallowed up and losing denominational identity.[58]

As a step toward this end, the Assembly authorized the Presbyterian Council to formulate plans for a more effective federation, with provisions for administrative agencies in both home and foreign fields.

Three years later, while the Council was still seeking to perfect its plan of federal union, the question of organic union was again thrown in the lap of the Assembly. The invitation to consider such union came from the Northern Assembly in response to overtures from 195 of its presbyteries. Seven Southern presbyteries requested that invitation be accepted, three opposed the opening on the subject, and four asked that a study be made.

There was a minority in the Assembly (about 20) who favored union and voted that a committee be appointed to work toward that end; another minority, twice as large, who opposed organic union and thought it best to so indicate by declining to appoint a committee on conference; and a third group, the majority, who felt that courtesy demanded that a committee be appointed, but were determined that federal union, should be its objective rather than organic union. The final resolution, adopted by a vote of 141 to 42, read as follows: "While this Assembly does not regard organic union as practicable, yet it hereby appoints the Committee of Conference on Union asked for by the Assembly of the Presbyterian Church of the U.S.A. and recommends to the proposed Conference the consideration of a federation of all the Presbyterian Churches of our country upon some practical and effective basis."[59]

For the first time in its history the Presbyterian Church in the U. S., influenced somewhat it may be by the spirit of unity aroused by the great war, had appointed a committee free to consider union with the Presbyterian Church in the U.S.A. To that extent it was an important step forward, but that freedom was severely limited by the expressed preference for federation. The negotiations thus inaugurated continued for a period of five years and were finally wrecked over the difference in goals. Northern Presbyterians desired organic union. Southern Presbyterians as a whole were interested only in another federation, little if any stronger than the one already in existence.

From the outset the two committees found themselves at loggerheads. Neither would recede from its position; consequently two separate proposals came before the 1918 Assembly, one from the U.S.A. Committee, recommending organic union, with enlarged synodical powers, the other from the U. S. Committee, reporting its judgment that neither organic union nor federation was practical at the moment. Before the Assembly also came a revised plan of federal union approved at the recent meeting of the Council of Reformed Churches. The Assembly adopted a substitute motion offered by Dr. John M. Wells, which continued the committee as requested by the U.S.A. Church and added: "The Assembly goes on record as opposing Organic Union at this time, but as approving the idea of a Federal Union of all the Presbyterian and Reformed Churches in the United States."[60]

In closing the debate and arguing for his substitute motion, Dr. Wells emphasized the doctrinal differences, the differing attitude toward the Negroes ("We who love the Negro recognize that the social line is necessary for the preservation of both races"), and the continual political deliverances of the Northern Church. Organic union, he insisted, would rend the church.[61]

The conference committee, taking into account the action of the Southern Assembly, presented to the 1919 General Assemblies a plan for a federal union of all Presbyterian and Reformed Churches. The plan was rejected by the U.S.A. Assembly on the grounds that it did not differ materially from the plans already in operation (the Reformed Presbyterian Council); it was rejected also by the U. S. Assembly (by a vote of 134 to 100), apparently on the grounds that it went too far in some directions, and not far enough in others (leaving out Home Missions, "The very thing that calls for attention").[62]

The standing committee, in its carefully prepared report, pointed out that marked unrest existed in the Synods of West Virginia, Kentucky, Tennessee, and Missouri, and that there was an increasing desire for some form of closer relations with the Presbyterian Church in the U.S.A. and with other bodies of like faith and order in Arkansas, Texas, and Florida. The older and stronger synods, the Assembly was told, seemed to be content with conditions as they were.

The existence of these diverse currents of opinion and desire, the Assembly was advised, could not be safely or wisely ignored. Something needed to be done to remove friction and to prevent injury and waste.

Five courses of action, it was noted, had been proposed:

1. Complete organic union.

2. Organic union according to the so-called synodical plan.

3. Organic union on the basis of provincial assemblies, with one supreme national Assembly as the capstone of the system.

4. A federal body having only advisory powers, inspirational in its influence, serving as a kind of clearinghouse for the sentiments of fraternity and comradeship (the existing Council).

5. A federal union with clearly defined powers and responsibilities, which, at the same time, conserves the autonomy of the constituent churches in doctrine and discipline as well as in other matters of local interest, including the tenure of church property and other material assets.

In view of all the facts brought to its attention the committee was convinced that some form of closer relations was called for, and to this end it recommended that an ad interim committee continue its explorations in conjunction with similar committees from one or more of its sister churches.

From the floor came an amendment which read:

> In case the discussions of closer relations between this Church and any other Church shall contemplate organic union, the attention of the Ad Interim Committee is directed to past deliverances, and reports of this

Assembly, touching such matters, and it is advised that the Assembly and the Church would view with uneasiness any structure of union which failed to take into account and safeguard in the United Church the historic convictions and positions of this Church with respect to sound doctrine, just and effective discipline, the plenary inspiration and inerrancy of the Scriptures, the vicarious atonement, the spiritual mission of the church and its obligations to abstain from interference in matters purely of civil or political concern, its position as to its Negro constituency in the South, and other matters of like interest and importance.[63]

A keen observer noted that the older men tended to vote only for federal union, and the middle-aged and younger men were more ready to face the question of organic union, although probably most of the commissioners realized that such union was quite far away.[64]

A lively debate was carried on during the next year between those who favored organic union, particularly on the synodical plan, and those who preferred federal union. Against organic union were the traditional arguments which had come down from the past. On behalf of such union it was argued that continued division meant a waste of resources, that the division of the church was sectional (if politicians and soldiers could forgive, it was asked, why not the church?), that the condition of the border states made a real union imperative. An article in the *Presbyterian of the South* pointed out that Minutes of the General Assembly revealed duplication of efforts in at least 139 localities, most of these being in smaller towns and villages; in Ballinger, Texas, for example, there were Presbyterian churches U. S. and U.S.A. with 93 and 91 members, respectively. There was a similar overlapping in Sunday schools and in educational institutions, for example, Trinity University, Waxahatchie, Texas (U.S.A.), was but one hour's run from Texas Presbyterian College for Girls, at Milford, and about 85 miles from Austin College, Sherman, a U. S. coeducational institution.[65]

A later article pointed out that there were in the South ten synods with the same name, covering the same territory, with the same form of government, and the same confession of faith. Membership of these synods according to the official minutes of the Assembly[66] were:

Synod	U. S.	U.S.A.
Alabama	21,479	5,114
Arkansas	12,665	6,236
Florida	12,017	2,622
Kentucky	20,297	14,572
Missouri	17,334	52,532

Mississippi	21,268	2,323
Oklahoma	3,904	22,411
Tennessee	19,634	16,755
Texas	38,712	31,384
West Virginia	12,924	12,910

Not included were two synods, Appalachia in the Southern Church and East Tennessee in the U.S.A. Church, whose borders were not co-extensive.

The Joint Conference on Closer Relations presented to their respective judicatories in 1920 a basic plan for federation which would, it was stated, "evince and develop spiritual unity" and "promote closer relations and more effective administrative cooperation among these churches."[67] The Southern assembly, to the astonishment of everyone, adopted it without a dissenting vote. Other judicatories also approved the plan. It called for an Assembly to which work in various fields might be assigned. Since none was assigned, it did not actually go beyond the existing Council of Presbyterian Churches, which was already in operation, except for potentialities which remained to be spelled out. For those like Dr. John M. Wells, who desired cooperation among the various Presbyterian bodies but was adamantly opposed to organic union or any surrender of autonomy, such a plan represented the ideal compromise.[68]

Difficulties arose, however, when the various denominational committees sought to prepare the constitution for the proposed federation. What powers should be granted to the United Assembly? What work should be given to it? How should the laws of comity be enacted and enforced? These and other knotty questions were seemingly ironed out, but the day before the agreed-upon constitution was to be presented to the Southern Assembly the committee discovered that there were ambiguities that needed to be removed and asked that it be held over for another year.[69]

The Joint Conference held only one more meeting. The Southern Committee wished to amend the proposed constitution, drastically limiting the benevolent work which might be assigned the United Assembly (none was actually given), and giving it a larger role in enforcing the rules of comity which would have worked to the benefit of the South through the courts of the church. When this amended constitution proved unacceptable, the Southern Committee proposed four regional Assemblies, which would have meant absorption of all Presbyterian and Reformed churches in the South by the Southern Assembly which would in all important respects have preserved its complete autonomy. This plan, too, proved unacceptable.

The U.S.A. Committee indicated that its church would be interested in nothing less than full organic union, since the Council of Reformed Churches already in existence adequately covered the field of federal union. The Joint Conference adjourned without agreement regarding a constitution and never met again. Negotiations had extended over a period of four years, and as Dr. W. L. Lingle reported, "everybody was tired, and if there had ever been any enthusiasm for this plan, it had oozed away."[70]

The U. S. Committee, recognizing this to be the fact, recommended to the 1922 Assembly that the whole matter be dropped. One lone member, Dr. Thornton Whaling, President of Columbia Seminary, could not join in this recommendation, "It is an impeachment of the wisdom and statesmanship of these churches to conclude that nothing better than the maintenance of the 'status quo' is possible," he wrote. The status quo, he proceeded to point out, was marked by a minimum of cooperation and a maximum of competition. There was some cooperation in Foreign Missions and in the work of education as in Centre, Westminster, and Davis and Elkins Colleges (in Kentucky, Missouri, and West Virginia), and notably in Louisville Theological Seminary, but in most other realms there was ill-regulated and well-nigh unrestrained competition.[71] Dr. Whaling brought in a minority report recommending the selection of a new committee to take up the whole matter anew.

In lieu of both majority and minority recommendations the Assembly by a large majority adopted the amended constitution approved only by its own Conference Committee. It provided that the United Assembly of the Presbyterian and Reformed Churches of America was to become a reality whenever its constitution was approved by the General Assembly of the Presbyterian Church in the U.S.A. and one other Reformed or Presbyterian body.[72]

When informed of this action, the U.S.A. General Assembly reaffirmed its willingness to take any steps in the direction of actual union of Presbyterian and Reformed Churches. In its judgment, however, the proposed constitution secured no closer union than that made possible by the revised constitution of the General Council of the Reformed Churches already adopted by the majority of the Presbyterian and Reformed Churches and then in operation. "We therefore believe," continued the statement, "that for the present we should endeavor to promote that cooperation already made possible through the Council of the Reformed Churches and its amended articles of agreement [which had incorporated some of the ideas in the proposed constitution] until such time as the Presbyterian Church in the U. S. is willing to proceed further and adopt measures which will secure actual organic union."[73]

The following year the U.S.A. Assembly again reaffirmed its desire for organic union and its purpose to continue its efforts for the realization of one Presbyterian Reformed Church in America. The U. S. Assembly replied that the General Council of Presbyterian and Reformed Churches provided an agency for such genuine fellowship and effective cooperation that it did not feel that there was occasion for reopening the question of organic union.[74]*

So ended the longest sustained negotiations which the Southern Church had yet carried on regarding the question of closer relations with the Presbyterian Church in the U.S.A. The primary obstacle to organic union in the first two decades of the 20th century appeared to be the traditional view of the "spirituality" of the church. As President Thornton Whaling explained, "There is one Presbyterian church which holds the doctrine of the spirituality of the church as a supernatural and spiritual institute, estopping it from traveling the road of social, economic, industrial or moral reform. Other churches hold the view, quite intelligently and persistently, that the church has functions—civic, economic and social . . . Organic union would furnish the opportunity for dynamite explosions in controversial debate and throw lurid flames in the way of dissents and protests."[75] The racial issue had softened toward the end of the period because the Northern Church had in effect largely accommodated itself to the Southern point of view—Negro churches in their own presbyteries. The doctrinal issued remained but had lost much of its force.

But not for long. In 1910 the U.S.A. Assembly had entertained a complaint against the action of New York Presbytery in licensing and ordaining two candidates for the ministry who were not able to affirm positively their belief in the Virgin Birth. The Judicial Commission handling the complaint stated, "It is indubitable that this Church stands today as she has stood in all her history for the inspiration, integrity and authority of the Holy Scriptures, and confesses the Virgin Birth of our Lord and his actual bodily resurrection as component parts of the faith . . . No one who denies them or is in serious doubt concerning them should be either licensed or ordained

---

* The revised constitution provided for the appointment of administrative agencies, "as consented to by the supreme judicatories concerned." None were either suggested or consented to. In 1927 the Council was finally absorbed into the Western Alliance of the Reformed Churches Throughout the World Holding the Presbyterian System. For all practical purposes the Council simply went out of existence. The bright hopes which some had cherished for a meaningful federal union had completely faded.

as a minister." The complaint, however, was dismissed because the
record did not make it clear that the synod had erred in dismissing
the complaint against the presbytery. To make its own attitude perfectly plain the Assembly reaffirmed its adherence to the historic
Standards of the church and then proceeded to make a declaration
regarding "certain essential and necessary articles of the faith"—
namely, inerrant inspiration of the Scriptures, the Virgin Birth, penal
substitutionary atonement, the physical resurrection of Christ, and his
"mighty miracles." Following this declaration came a statement that
presbyteries were not to ordain candidates for the ministry unless
they accepted all the essential and necessary articles of the Confession, including by implication the five just named.

In 1916 a number of presbyteries sent up new overtures to the
U.S.A. Assembly complaining against recent actions of New York
Presbytery in ordaining men out of harmony with the Presbyterian
Standards. The Assembly in reply called all presbyteries' attention to
the deliverance of 1910, including the five "essentials" and enjoined
them not to license or ordain any candidates for the ministry not
in accord with this deliverance.

The Southern Church was disturbed by these evidences of liberalism in the Northern Church, but reassured by the Assembly's clear
affirmation of the fundamentals. This assurance was badly shaken
by developments in the early 1920's.

For about five years Dr. Harry Emerson Fosdick, a Baptist minister, had been preaching as guest minister in the pulpit of the First
Presbyterian Church and one sermon in particular—"Shall the
Fundamentalists Win?"—had at last called forth a mass of protest
against his preaching in a Presbyterian pulpit. The Assembly expressed its sorrow that doctrines contrary to the Standards of the
Church had been the cause of controversy and division in the
church, and directed the Presbytery of New York to take such action
as would require the preaching and teaching of the First Church,
New York, to conform to the system of doctrines taught in the Confession of Faith. It then proceeded to call the attention of the
presbyteries to the deliverance of the General Assembly of 1910
regarding the necessary and fundamental articles of the Confession,
"which deliverance," it said, "is hereby reaffirmed."

This action of the General Assembly called forth what became
known as the Auburn Affirmation.

In the opening paragraph the 150 ministers who signed the Affirmation (later 1,283 names including ministers and elders were added)
affirmed their "acceptance of the Westminster Confession of Faith

as we did at our ordination 'as containing the system of doctrine taught in the Holy Scriptures.'"

In the first main section it was pointed out that by its law and history the Presbyterian Church required its ministers to "receive and adopt the Confession of Faith as containing the system of doctrine taught in the Holy Scriptures." "Manifestly it does not require their assent to the very words of the Confession, or to all of its teachings, or to interpretations of the Confessions by individuals or church courts." The section ended with this significant paragraph:

> There is no assertion in the Scriptures that their writers were kept "from error." The Confession of Faith does not make this assertion; and it is significant that this assertion is not to be found in the Apostles' Creed or the Nicene Creed or in any of the Great Reformation Confessions. The doctrine of inerrancy, intended to enhance the authority of the Scriptures, in fact impairs their supreme authority for faith and life, and weakens the testimony of the Church to the power of God unto salvation through Jesus Christ. We hold that the General Assembly of 1923, in asserting that "the Holy Spirit did so inspire, guide and move the writers of Holy Scriptures as to keep them from error," spoke without warrant of the Scriptures, or the Confession of Faith. We hold rather to the words of the Confession of Faith, that the Scriptures are given by inspiration of God, to be the rule of faith and life.

In the second section it was maintained that while the General Assembly could "bear testimony against error in doctrine," it could not of itself alone determine that certain doctrines were essential doctrines of the Confession and impose its judgment upon the presbyteries. This would be to amend the Constitution, which could lawfully be done only by concurrent action of the General Assembly and the presbyteries.

Section IV of the Affirmation, the one about which most controversy was to rage, read as follows:

> The General Assembly of 1923 expresses the opinion concerning five doctrinal statements that each one "is an essential doctrine of the Word of God and our Standards." On the constitutional grounds, which we have before described, we are opposed to any attempt to elevate these five doctrinal statements, or any of them, to the position of tests of ordination, or for good standing in our Church. Furthermore, this opinion of the General Assembly attempts to commit our Church to certain theories concerning the inspiration of the Bible, and the Incarnation, the Atonement, the Resurrection, and the Continuing Life and Supernatural Power of our Lord Jesus Christ. We all hold most earnestly to these great facts and doctrines; we all believe from our hearts that the writers of the Bible were inspired of God; that Jesus Christ was God manifest in the flesh; that God was in Christ, reconciling the world unto Himself, and through Him, we have our redemption, that

having died for our sins, He rose from the dead and is our ever-living Savior; that in His earthly ministry He wrought many mighty works, and by His vicarious death and unfailing presence He is able to save to the uttermost. Some of us regard the particular theories contained in the deliverance of the General Assembly of 1923 as satisfactory explanations of these facts and doctrines. But we are united in believing that these are not the only theories allowed by the Scriptures and our Standards as explanations of these facts and doctrines of our religion, and that all who hold to these facts and doctrines, whatever theories they may employ to explain them, are worthy of all confidence and fellowship.

The following year (1924) New York Presbytery received again a number of candidates declared by a minority (because of their views regarding the Virgin Birth) to be out of harmony with the Presbyterian Standards. The 1925 Assembly upheld this contention and remanded the case to the presbytery for correction. Feelings ran high, and a possible schism was averted only by the Moderator's prompt appointment of a commission to study the spiritual condition of the church and the causes making for unrest. In its reports accepted by the Assembly of 1926-1927 it was pointed out that according to the constitution the licensure and ordination of candidates for the ministry were the exclusive functions of the presbytery; that once a candidate received ordination he could not against his will be deprived of his status except by prescribed constitutional procedure, which includes the preferring of specific charges, a formal trial, and a legal conviction. The Assembly recorded "its unshaken loyalty to the whole body of evangelical truth" and declared its purpose to uphold the constitution of the church and to maintain the integrity of its historic and corporate witness to the Lord Jesus Christ as he is represented in Scripture and to the system of doctrines set forth in the Westminster Confession of Faith. Efforts of "fundamentalists" to take punitive action against signers of the Auburn Affirmation failed. The faculty and board of Princeton Theological Seminary divided over the issue. Reorganization of the governing board by the General Assembly led to the resignation of three of the more conservative faculty members and the subsequent organization of an independent Presbyterian Seminary (Westminster) pledged to preserve the fundamentals of the faith, and finally of an independent Presbyterian Board of Foreign Missions. This in turn led to the ultimate withdrawal or expulsion of a small fundamentalist group from the Presbyterian Church in the U.S.A. and to the formation of a succession of small ultraconservative bodies—the Orthodox, the Bible, and the Covenant Presbyterian Churches.[76]

The growing desire for Presbyterian reunion in the Southern Church was not checked by these developments, but from this time on the theological objection became the one most frequently raised. The Auburn Affirmation would be cited again and again as certain proof that the Northern Church was fundamentally unsound in the faith.

XII

The Theological Rift

In the late 1890's—the decade in which pronounced theological differences first appeared in the Presbyterian Church in the U.S.A.—Professor Francis R. Beattie, originally from Canada, who had served as Professor of Apologetics in Columbia Theological Seminary and was now Professor of Systematic Theology in Louisville Presbyterian Seminary, described for Canadian Presbyterians essential features of the church into which he had thrown his lot. "The first feature of the Southern Presbyterian Church which has marked it from the outset," he wrote, "is its close adherence to the doctrinal system of its standards." It is a strict constructionist church. "Its type of doctrine is distinctly Old School. In its seminaries this has always been the type of doctrine taught without any toning down or explaining away. In other words, it adheres strongly to the Calvinism of its doctrinal symbols. The great majority of her pulpits are manned by men who preach the Gospel with doctrines after the manner of Calvin, of Knox, of Augustine, of Paul . . . In regard to the inspiration of the scriptures, the sovereignty of God, the lost estate of man in sin, the atonement of Christ, the necessity of grace to recover him, the security of the believer and similar doctrines of the Calvinistic system, there is almost no uncertain sound."[1]

Almost no uncertain sound! True; there were, however, some evidences of unrest—not yet to any noticeable degree in the theological seminaries, but in the pulpit. Thus, in 1892, the *Texas Presbyterian* referred to ministers in the church who could no longer accept all the teachings of the Confession of Faith. The revision of the Confession by the Northern Church, the paper indicated, had given them some hope that their "troubled consciences" might be relieved by similar action on the part of the Southern Assembly. "But our Church is so conservative," the editor assured his readers, "that such a proposition would be treated with hisses and the mover declared a heretic."[2]

A few months later the paper claimed to know at least one minister who repudiated "the doctrine of inspiration and inerrancy." "Men," he charged, "are beginning to think for themselves as they never did before. For some men this is a dangerous liberty . . ." Men who held erroneous opinions, the editor believed, could not honestly remain in the church. "The Presbyterian Church is scarce of ministers," he held, "but it can well afford to spare all who are not in full sympathy with its doctrine and polity."[3]

The following spring the paper noted that a difference of opinion has arisen in one of the Texas presbyteries as to whether or not the Westminster Standards required belief in verbal, inerrant inspiration. The editor argued that it did and insisted that this was the faith of the church.[4] This same year West Texas Presbytery divested Rev. B. D. D. Greer of his ministerial office on the grounds that he had expressed his abhorrence of doctrines taught in the Confession and catechisms of the church (his difficulty seemed to have been with the doctrine of eternal punishment).

There were other signs of ferment. Dr. J. R. Bridges, then editor of the *Trans-Mississippi Presbyterian*, detected a spirit of unrest, a spirit of inquiry, a spirit of protest against some of the generally accepted views of the church's Standards, which indicated to him that "even the conservative old Southern church" was beginning to be affected by the questions which were engaging the thoughts of their brethren of other denominations.[5]

In 1897 John M. Mecklin, a graduate of Southwestern, who had studied at Union in Virginia and who had only recently received his theological degree (from Princeton), abandoned the pastorate and with it any conception of the religious life whatever.

A few years later Rev. William Caldwell, a native of Mississippi, who had received his M.A. degree from Southwestern and a Ph.D. degree from the University of Chicago, came from Baltimore (Presbyterian Church U.S.A.) to Fort Worth, Texas, as pastor of the First Presbyterian Church of that city. The Presbytery of Fort Worth voted, by a bare majority, to receive him, but a complaint against this action was made on the grounds that Dr. Caldwell rejected the Mosaic authorship of the Pentateuch, the historicity of the early chapters of Genesis, and the penal substitutionary atonement.[6]

The synod, in view of the scanty record of the case, returned the case to the presbytery with instructions for a new hearing. The recorded questions and answers covering 17 pages of typewritten foolscap, included the following:

Q. Do you believe in the verbal plenary inspiration of the Bible in the original manuscript?

A. The Scriptures being the authoritative record of the Divine revelation, I believe in their plenary inspiration; as a guide to faith and practice they are wholly trustworthy and infallible.

[Questioned regarding the origin of the Pentateuch, Dr. Caldwell replied:] I believe the Pentateuch is a summation of laws, showing different strata of legislation. Moses did not write Deuteronomy in the form in which we hear it.

Q. Do you consider the account of Adam and Eve in the Garden of Eden historical or allegorical?

A. I do not regard the account of Adam and Eve in the Garden of Eden as scientific history . . . nor do I call it simply allegory . . . In a sense the story may be said to be both historical and allegorical. The great truth taught is that man, ideally in fellowship with God and free from sin, actually through his disobedience and transgression has fallen away from God.

According to Dr. Caldwell, Jonah was allegory. Asked about Daniel in the lion's den, he replied that it raises the general question "what is the style of literature presented to us in the Book of Daniel?" "There is today a growing concensus of opinion that the book belongs to the time of persecution under Antiochus Epiphanes . . . Its purpose is to strengthen the faith of men who through fear of suffering are in danger of falling away . . . A great injustice is done if the standard of strict historicity is applied."

In reply to other questions Dr. Caldwell stated unequivocally his belief in the miraculous conception of Christ, his divinity, the penal substitutionary sufferings of Christ, justification, sanctification and eternal punishment.[7]

The vote to sustain the examination and receive Dr. Caldwell were 14 in favor and 11 opposed. Opponents again filed notice of complaint. Synod sustained this complaint by a vote of 85 to 37, thereby annulling the action of Fort Worth Presbytery in receiving Dr. Caldwell, as well as the action by which he had been installed as pastor of the First Church of Fort Worth. A complaint regarding synod's action carried the matter to the General Assembly. The question here was a purely legal one—can a synod annul the reception of a minister by a presbytery or does its right extend only to an order instructing a presbytery to institute judicial process against a minister so received, looking to his ultimate removal? By a majority of one the General Assembly decided that the latter was the case. No mistake should be made as to the action of the General Assembly, the *Christian Observer* pointed out. Judgment was not passed one way or the other on the theological or critical opinions held by the brother. Not the slightest approval was put on the conclusions of higher criticism, nor was the door opened to men of unsound views desiring to enter the ministry of the Southern Church.[8]

Following the action of the 1906 General Assembly, the Synod of Texas instructed the Fort Worth Presbytery to investigate the doctrinal views of Dr. Caldwell, to decide whether or not he should be charged with heresy. Dr. Caldwell submitted a statement regarding his beliefs (which was accepted by the presbytery as satisfactory) but declined to affirm his belief in the historicity or literalness of the events recorded in the early chapters of Genesis. He claimed that these and similar inquiries belonged to the sphere of higher criticism and as such, whatever his views, did not affect his loyal adherence to the Standards of the Presbyterian Church.

The presbytery labeled this view as unsatisfactory, but declined to bring charges of heresy against Dr. Caldwell. A complaint brought the matter to presbytery once again, asking that presbytery make a full investigation and conclude the matter in a wise, just, and constitutional way.[9]

Presbytery saw nothing to gain by further investigation and requested that synod relieve it of further responsibility. This synod declined to do.[10] Presbytery then investigated the charges brought against Dr. Caldwell and reported that it found no evidence that afforded sufficient legal basis for an indictment for heresy; it had therefore voted that no further action be taken in the matter. The Synod of Texas, meeting in the fall of 1909, accepted this report as satisfactory and so the matter ended.[11]

Dr. Caldwell was a man respected for his scholarship and character, for his zeal and success as a pastor; Rev. F. E. Maddox, who, like Dr. Caldwell and Mr. Mecklin, had attended Southwestern University and had also for a time studied at the University of Chicago, who had organized and was now the pastor of the First Church, Texarkana, Arkansas, proved to be more of an irritant. In the spring of 1908 he preached a series of sermons on the passing of medievalism in religion, which were published for their news value in the *Daily Texarkanian* and aroused such interest that they were reprinted in book form. In his foreword Mr. Maddox wrote: "We live in an age of theological fermentation. Changes are taking place in religious thought not less radical than in the days of the Reformation and a process of reconstruction and readjustment is going on which is as wide-spread as it is revolutionary. We are moving away from some of the traditional positions of theology which for centuries have been regarded as bulwarks of evangelical faith, and both the pulpit and the pew of the present day are breaking with exploded theories and outgrown traditions . . . The break among the educated is not with the truth of the Bible, but medieval interpretations of it."[12]

The presbytery proceeded to charge and convict Mr. Maddox of heresy on the grounds that he rejected biblical inerrancy; that he taught that the Old Testament gives an inaccurate view of the character of God; that he thought salvation is not an instantaneous act but a regulated process, not an importation from without but a gradual revolution from within; that he denied the substitutionary atonement and taught that Christ was redeemer only as revealer.[13]

Mr. Maddox did not deny but rather boldly affirmed the charges brought against him. I think you will agree with me, he declared, that "there is a large number of preachers and a larger number of members of the Presbyterian church, who dissent from much that is in the Confession of Faith, but practically, do not say so. I avow myself, therefore, as being in harmony with that growing company of the younger men of the Presbyterian church, who interpret the Standards of the Presbyterian Church in line with results of scholarship, and who are preaching Calvinism as John Calvin would preach it if he were living in this day."[14] He insisted that the value of the Bible was not destroyed but enhanced by being accepted as partly human, and that nothing had proved a greater hindrance to religion than "this doctrine of the plenary inspiration of the scriptures."[15]

Suspended from the ministry by Ouachita Presbytery, Mr. Maddox withdrew from the Presbyterian Church, followed by a considerable number of the members of his congregation, who organized the first Congregational Church of Texarkana and called Mr. Maddox as their pastor.

The church suffered more serious loss through the defection of Dr. Henry M. Edmonds, pastor of the influential South Highlands Church in Birmingham, Alabama. In 1915 the session of this church requested North Alabama Presbytery to consider the soundness of their pastor's theological views. The presbytery held that Dr. Edmonds' views of the atonement were at variance with the doctrinal Standards of the church, but finding him sound in other respects, postponed further action until the next stated meeting of presbytery, hoping that further reflection would bring him into substantial agreement with the church's Standards.[16]

Dr. Edmonds did not wait for the presbytery to reconvene. Feeling that it was impossible for him to remain in his pulpit with any degree of self-respect, he renounced the jurisdiction of presbytery, followed by about 200 of the members of his congregation, who proceeded to organize themselves into the Independent Presbyterian Church of Birmingham (later received into the Presbyterian Church U.S.A.), of which Dr. Edmonds became the pastor.

It soon became plain that Dr. Edmonds and his congregation had other objections to the Calvinistic creed than those which had figured in the presbyterial examination. In justification of their withdrawal the officers of the Independent Church issued a stinging indictment not only of the North Alabama Presbytery, but of the Southern Church as a whole:

> The Presbytery of North Alabama [they charged] seems unwilling to accept the continued guidance of God, it closes its eyes to the new facts and new thoughts, it appears to think more of old statements of faith than it does of men, it is leading a pathetic but complacent hope against . . . other denominations who are meeting today's issues with today's light . . . The old intellectual leadership which the Southern Presbyterian Church once claimed is gone . . . She has been sadly outstripped in the field of education. Not one authoritative word has come from her ranks concerning the two great questions now before the church: religion and social service and the restatement of old truths in such a way that a new world may apprehend and appropriate. Her books are no longer on library shelves. In twenty-five years, so far as we know, she has written no book which has gained any acceptance outside the denomination and very few even for so narrow a reading.
>
> What is the matter? Many things, perhaps, but one thing certainly, a clinging to the mummified forms of dead leaders instead of advancing to the living spirit of those leaders. . . .[17]

The booklet went on to point out that starting with 189 members the Independent Church within little more than two months had increased its membership to nearly 500 and that congregations were numbering more than 2,000, many of them men and women who had been lost to the church.

Two years later Piedmont Presbytery reported that Rev. D. Witherspoon Dodge, a recent graduate of Union Seminary in Virginia, and pastor of the Central Church, Anderson, South Carolina, had been deposed from the ministry for "holding and teaching views of God's decrees, and of the punishment of the wicked, in conflict with the Scriptures as interpreted in the Confession of Faith.*

Presbyterian drumfire against the evolutionary theory, aroused by the Woodrow furor, we may observe, had never ceased. "Darwinism is rapidly declining under late scientific researches," announced the *Central Presbyterian* in 1903,[18] a claim

---

* Mr. Dodge entered the Congregational ministry and later became active as an organizer for the C.I.O.

which the church press would continue to advance for the next quarter of a century.

On the eve of the First World War, the *Presbyterian of the South* expressed great concern that this theory was being incorporated in textbooks taught in schools throughout the nation. "It is a crime against the home, against the state, against Christianity, against the immortal souls of our children to deliberately destroy their faith in their high origin, and their destiny as revealed in the Holy Scripture," protested the editor.[19]

When William Jennings Bryan, thrice-defeated candidate for the presidency, a Presbyterian elder, and a "staunch defender of the word of God," emerged after the war as leader of a crusade against evolution as destroyer of men's faith, there were many Southern Presbyterians who were prepared to follow.

Knowing that Mr. Bryan was deeply concerned over the aggressiveness of current skepticism and especially its inroads upon the faith of the college population, the faculty of Union Theological Seminary invited him to deliver its Sprunt Lectures for 1921. The faculty's hope, that he might "speak a reassuring word from the laymen's point of view to those who had been confused by the clamorous unbelief of the times," fitted in with a purpose which Mr. Bryan had long entertained.[20] He welcomed the opportunity and gave a series of lectures entitled "In His Image," because, he said, "God made us in His image, and placed us here to carry out a divine decree." The longest chapter in the published lectures and the one which attracted the most attention was headed "The Origin of Man." Darwin's theory is described in this chapter to be not only groundless and absurd, but also harmful to society. "In trying to show that it is absurd," Dr. Moore, the President of the seminary, wrote approvingly, "he uses the weapons of ridicule. But his tone deepens to indignation when he comes to speak of its harmful effects. He devotes about thirty pages to a description of its baneful influence, showing how it is being taught in our schools and colleges and how it is destroying the Christian faith of our young people, how through the teaching of Nietzsche it laid the foundation for Prussianism and the World War, how it enthrones selfishness and how it embitters the relations of capital and labor."[21]

The book was advertised by the Presbyterian Committee of Publication under boldface type: "BRYAN ANSWERS DARWIN." Four editions were issued within the first six months. Dr. J. D. Eggleston, President of Hampden-Sydney College, applauded Bryan's position.[22] The Synod of Mississippi passed resolutions commending "the stirring words of this distinguished man."[23]

The Great Commoner was now launched on what he declared to be his greatest crusade. Spurred on by his mighty eloquence, by a band of fiery evangelists and a host of fundamentalist preachers, three Southern states—Mississippi, Arkansas, and Tennessee—passed laws prohibiting the teaching of evolution in the public schools.

The tide was rising for similar legislation in other states. The *Richmond Times-Dispatch* claimed that the state of Tennessee was within its rights when it forbade the teaching of the so-called evolution theory in its schools—that in fact Tennessee had done nothing more than to say: "You shall not teach either religious or anti-religious doctrine in the schools of the state." Rather than leave the whole matter in the hands of youthful and radical or jaded and cynical teachers in the public schools, the *Times-Dispatch* would advocate the passage of just such a law in Virginia.[24]

The *Presbyterian of the South,* published in Richmond, maintained "that the people have a right to say what shall and what shall not be taught in the schools to which they send their children." This country in its sentiment and beliefs, the paper claimed, was distinctly Christian. "When any teacher undertakes in any way to undermine the faith of his students in the teaching of the Scriptures, the people certainly have the right to say that he must go elsewhere . . . The legislature of Tennessee had done the children of its State great service in decreeing that evolution shall not be taught in the schools of that state."[25]

Evolution, of course, was not the sole matter under discussion. Involved was the question of one's attitude toward Scripture, toward the critical study of Scripture, toward the inspiration of the Bible—in fact the whole range of differences between modernism and fundamentalism, then disturbing the churches both North and South.

In this struggle within the state of North Carolina the top leadership among Baptists and Methodists, the two largest denominations in the state, was divided. President William Louis Poteat of Wake Forest, a Baptist institution of higher education in the state, and William Preston Few, President of Duke, a Methodist University, took a strong stand on behalf of freedom in teaching in both denominational and state institutions and denied the fundamentalist contention that beliefs in evolution and Christianity were incompatible. In this stand they were supported by a large number of their loyal alumni. Presbyterian Davidson, on the other hand, took no forthright stand either on behalf of evolution or against the fundamentalist offensive in North Carolina, and it was the Presbyterian Church, the third largest denomination in the state, which gave the fundamentalists and anti-evolutionists their most solidly unified support. As Professor Willard B. Gatewood, Jr., has pointed out: "Among the most active fundamentalists in North Carolina were Presbyterians who occupied key posts in the church such as Synod Moderators and evangelists and influential figures within the Presbyteries. It was no accident therefore that the most concentrated fight on evolution emanated from Charlotte and Mecklenburg County, a stronghold of Presbyterianism 'of the blue-stocking variety,' that a Presbyterian governor [Cameron Morrison] banned evolution books from the public schools, that Presbyterians dominated the most active anti-evolutionist organization in the state and that a Presbyterian elder sponsored the bill to outlaw the teaching of evolution."[26]

Anti-evolutionists in North Carolina were strongly supported by the *Presbyterian Standard*, accepted voice of the North Carolina Synod, published in Charlotte. The editors, J. R. Bridges (former President of Presbyterian College for Women in Charlotte) and R. C. Reed (professor in Columbia Theological Seminary) proudly acknowledged that they were "mossback conservatives." In their judgment the two parties in the church differed basically in their view of the Bible. Fundamentalists viewed the Bible as the divinely inspired, "virtually inerrant," Word of God and only "infallible rule of faith and practice"; modernists, while believing that God revealed himself in the Bible, refused to believe that God spoke "throughout the whole Bible with an authoritative voice."[27]

As the controversy developed the *Standard* became increasingly harsh in its criticism of both evolution and modernism. It claimed that evolutionists reduced the Old Testament to the plane of naturalism, discarded Pauline theology, and skirted slyly around the figure of Christ, whom they hesitated to label as a product of evolution. But, said the *Standard*, if the modernists pursued a logical development of their own ideas, they would have to consider Christ a "descendant of the same Semian [sic] stock as the rest of us." This, the paper claimed, would invalidate the Christian religion.[28]

Anti-evolution sentiment in North Carolina was being whipped up meanwhile by popular evangelists—William A. (Billy) Sunday; Baxter F. McLendon, known professionally as "Cyclone Mack"; Mordecai F. Ham; and, above all, by the powerful voice of William Jennings Bryan, always a potent orator, and now turned newspaper columnist as well. The World's Christian Fundamentals Association, regarding North Carolina as a "pivotal" area, held annual Bible conferences at the Baptist Tabernacle in Raleigh.

In this same period Presbyterians became concerned about the character of the McNair Lectures delivered annually at the University of North Carolina. The lectureship had been established by John Calvin McNair, a conservative Presbyterian and graduate of the university in 1840, for the purpose of showing "the mutual bearing of science and theology upon each other." Charles Allen Dinsmore, Professor of Religion in Yale Divinity School, lecturing on "Religious Certitude in an Age of Science," sustained the conclusions of the higher criticism and upheld the principle of evolution. The *Presbyterian Standard* cried out in protest. The Dinsmore lectures, it charged, constituted a blatant perversion of the McNair Lectureship and provided a classic example of why "church people oppose state institutions."[29]

In January 1925 another university-sponsored project, the *Journal of Social Forces*, published two articles, both of which took the evolutionary philosophy for granted, one describing the gods as "products of the folk imagination," the other charging that the church derived its ethics from "an alleged sacred book" which in reality was a "product of the folkways and mores of the primitive Hebrews." Orange Presbytery, meeting in May, dispatched a strongly worded protest to the university trustees against the publication of such material; Fayetteville Presbytery protested the atheistical teaching of the articles in the *Journal of Social Forces* by a rising vote. The Presbytery of Mecklenburg, meanwhile, had overtured the General Assembly to reaffirm its 1886 (anti-Woodrow) deliverance, which stated that any evolutionary theory of creation was "a dangerous error, inasmuch as in the methods of interpreting Scripture it must demand, and in the consequences which by fair implication it will involve, it will lead to the denial of doctrines fundamental to the faith." The General Assembly obliged by unanimously reaffirming these convictions and publishing them "to the world."[30]

In this same year Albert S. Keister, Professor of Sociology at North Carolina College for Women in Greensboro, conducting a class for public school teachers in Charlotte, was asked "what a belief in evolution did to one who believed in the Bible." Professor Keister replied that evolution forced such a person to discard literal interpretations of portions of the Genesis account of creation and to view the account as an attempt by a people in a prescientific age to explain the origin of life. Present in the class was the wife of a prominent Presbyterian minister in the city. She informed her husband of what had been said and he laid the matter before the local ministerial association, which passed a "scorching resolution" rebuking Professor Keister for "teachings" which destroyed faith in the Bible and "sapped the very foundations of Christianity."[31] The Presbyterian Ministers' Association of Charlotte voiced its complaints against Keister in a strongly worded resolution dispatched directly to the Governor. The *Presbyterian Standard* charged that Keister, having "made short work of inspiration and reduced the Bible stories to mere legend," was only one example of many in state institutions who were instilling "their subtle poison into the minds of our young women, and thus touching the coming mothers of the future."[32]

The Keister incident, the announcement of President Poteat's election as McNair lecturer, and the publication of the bitterly resented articles in the *Journal of Social Forces* all helped to set the stage for the anti-evolutionary struggle that followed in the 1925 state legislature.

A bill to ban the teaching of evolution in state-supported institutions was introduced this year by Representative D. Scott Poole, a ruling elder in the Presbyterian Church, and a teacher of a Sunday school Bible class, who thereafter served as floor manager for the bill. It received strong support from other prominent Presbyterian legislators, among them Zebulon Vance Turlington of Iredell County, a Presbyterian elder and graduate of the University of North Carolina Law School, and Miss Julia Alexander of Mecklenburg County, a state university educated attorney, and the only woman member of the state legislature. Support came also from the Presbyterian Ministers' Association of Charlotte and from the *Presbyterian Standard*, which argued that Christian taxpayers had a right to say what should and should not be taught in the schools financed by their tax money.[33] The bill was finally killed by a vote of 70 to 41. Fifty-two percent of the Baptists, 45 percent of the Presbyterians, 40 percent of the Methodists, and 15 percent of the Episcopalians voted for the Poole measure "but in proportion to their total number in the House as well as the state as a whole," affirms Professor Gatewood, "the Presbyterians contributed the greatest support of the bill."[34]

Fundamentalists were not prepared to concede defeat. The *Presbyterian Standard* called upon all citizens who considered themselves Christians to select in the next general election only those legislators sympathetic with the moral traditions of "this Christian Commonwealth."[35]

The constitutionality of the Tennessee law was tested later this same year in the Scopes trial which both amazed and shamed a large part of the Christian world. Scopes, a young high school teacher, prosecuted by Bryan, was convicted and fined for his breach of the anti-evolution law, but the humiliation of Bryan by Clarence Darrow, brilliant criminal lawyer and agnostic, may have been a factor in Bryan's sudden death shortly thereafter. This tragic denouement spurred fundmentalist determination to carry his crusade on to final victory.

The *Presbyterian Standard* called upon all men, clergy and laity alike, to make their positions clear—to accept either evolution or Genesis, for there were no other alternatives. Certainly there was no room for theistic evolutionists, who, according to the *Standard,* were "cowardly souls trying to carry water on both shoulders." In effect, the Presbyterian paper issued a call for fundamentalists to close ranks in order to carry the fight begun by Bryan to a successful conclusion.[36]

Prominent Presbyterian pastors contributed their support. Dr. W. M. White, pastor of the First Church of Raleigh, took offense at some of the observations made in a religious forum discussing the conflict between science and religion. Rev. William P. McCorkle, a fundamentalist leader, continued the crusade against Keister, the *Journal of Social Forces,* and the "modernistic" McNair lectures. Other clergymen, such as Reverends W. I. Sinnott, Albert S. Johnson, and A. R. Shaw devoted their attention to the evil "fruits" of the evolution theory and repeatedly linked it to German militarism, the First World War, and Soviet Bolshevism.[37]

The North Carolina fundamentalists did not stand alone in the struggle against evolution. At the height of the struggle the Synod of Appalachia gave guarantees that no doctrine contrary to the deity of Christ and the Bible as the inspired Word of God would ever be taught in King College. Later a member of the synod congratulated the recently elected President of the Bryan Memorial University at Dayton, Tennessee, founded to reflect the Great Commoner's view regarding Scripture and evolution.[38] Thornwell Jacobs was convinced that his espousal of the evolutionary hypothesis had hurt his efforts to resurrect Oglethorpe College and build his cherished Presbyterian University.

Dr. Thomas Cary Johnson, Professor of Theology in Union Theological Seminary, published a little volume entitled *God's Answer to Evolution* (a resounding "No"), and Rev. P. B. Hill, pastor of the First Church, San Antonio, issued a volume entitled *The Truth about Evolution,* in which he quoted "leading scientists of the world" to prove that evolution could not be accepted as a fact. Both volumes were warmly commended by prominent ministers in the church. Dr. Henry B. Dosker, a venerable professor in Louisville Presbyterian Seminary, raised the question "Can a Christian be an evolutionist?"

and replied "If he is a true believer and firmly holds to the infallible authority of the Holy Scriptures he will plant himself squarely on the sure foundation that God is the Creator . . . The very minute we accept this position we virtually abandon the evolutionary hypothesis."[39]

The Synod of North Carolina, meeting in the fall of 1925, elected as its Moderator Rev. H. B. Searight, a strong opponent of evolution. Four ministers presented papers that condemned the prevalence of evolutionary and other "modernistic" teachings in tax-supported institutions. Finally adopted was a paper protesting "against rationalistic influences in our state schools" and appealing "for the adoption of proper remedial measures." The synod insisted that it was ready to welcome the findings of true science but declared that it was "uncompromisingly opposed to the teaching of the theory of evolution as a fact in our state supported institutions and also in our denominational schools." It also expressed emphatic opposition "to the publication or circulation of any paper or magazine by our state institutions which tends to lower moral standards and to discredit for the Scriptures as the inspired Word of God." Along with "the overwhelming majority of the people of North Carolina" it favored a more rigid censorship in the selection of textbooks to be used in state and public schools. "It is our profound conviction," said the synod, "that when the fact has been established that any official or teacher in any state or denominational school is inculcating theories which tend to destroy the faith of our young men and women in the Old and New Testaments as the inspired Word of God, that such officer or teacher should be promptly removed from his position." Ministers were urged to arouse the people to a sense of their civic responsibility, realizing that the remedy for the situation which obtained in state and denominational institutions was in their own hands. It was a clear invitation to elect legislators to the 1927 Assembly who would remedy the failure of the 1925 Assembly.[40]

To elect legislators who would support the anti-evolution crusade, a statewide Committee of One Hundred was formed, with Presbyterian fundamentalists (including Dr. Albert Sidney Johnson, pastor of the First Presbyterian Church of Charlotte, and W. E. Price, a well-known Presbyterian layman) playing leading roles. At an organizational meeting in Charlotte, Rev. William Black, general evangelist for the Synod of North Carolina, concluded a lengthy speech with the declaration: "Evolution is the blackest lie ever blasted out of Hell."[41] The "intolerance, bigotry and fanaticism" displayed by the Committee of One Hundred aroused opposition and led to the withdrawal of more responsible Presbyterian participants. Defeat of the anti-evolution candidates in the Democratic primary did not end the fundamentalist effort in North Carolina. The Committee of One Hundred, now known as the North Carolina Bible League, still under Presbyterian leadership, continued its activities, with its secretary, Julia Alexander, proclaiming confidently, "We are going to keep up the fight until we get control of the state and maybe the nation."[42] Included in its impressive roster of directors were outstanding Presbyterian laymen, such as Zebulon Vance Turlington, W. H. Sprunt of Wilmington, and W. H. Belk of Charlotte, along with influential clergymen, such as H. B. Searight of Washington and W. M. White of Raleigh.

A new Poole anti-evolution measure, introduced in the 1927 session of the Assembly, however, was roundly defeated and by the end of this year all hope of passing such legislation in North Carolina was ended. But fundamentalism in the Southern Presbyterian Church—in the Synod of North Carolina and elsewhere—was increasingly self-conscious and would soon turn against suspected liberal tendencies within its own denomination.[43]

Opposition to the anti-evolution movement had been rising now for some time in Presbyterian circles in North Carolina and elsewhere. Dr. Neal L. Anderson, Savannah pastor, had opposed Bryan's stand at the outset, insisting that "to attempt to make Scripture teach science" is a very dangerous thing.[44] Dunbar H. Ogden, pastor of the Government St. Church, Mobile, Alabama, had confessed his predilection for a doctrine of "creative, theistic evolution."[45]

Resistance to the fundamentalist crusade in the Synod of North Carolina was led by such men as David Scanlon, pastor of the First Church, Durham, and Rev. Murphy Williams, pastor in Greensboro. Rev. E. C. Murray of St. Paul's, published a tract entitled "Does the Bible Teach Natural Science?" It criticized anti-evolutionists for using the Bible as a textbook in science and for confusing the "scientific theory of evolution" with a "radical rationalistic philosophy of evolution."[46] Dr. Frazer Hood, Professor of Psychology in Davidson College, pointed out that the theory of evolution expressed the belief of an overwhelmingly large proportion of scientists, including those who were evangelical Christians. If evolution cannot be discounted as a fact, he said, we should attempt to show "that it is not subversive or contradictory to our belief in the Bible as the infallible rule of faith and practice." He rejoiced that there were a few brave souls leading such a movement, and that the influence of their efforts was telling.[47]

Young ministers (the author's generation) did not accept the anti-evolution views of their elders. One of my own earliest sermons (preached in 1922) was an attempt to prove that there was no incompatibility between belief in evolution and the first chapter of Genesis. Fundamentalism had in fact discredited itself, and a new generation, for whom the question held little interest, was coming to the fore. In retrospect, it becomes clear that the fundamentalist thrust of the 1920's was only the darkness that precedes the dawn.

Meanwhile, the struggle against "modernism within the church" had erupted on the Foreign Mission field, most strongly in China. The struggle here centered on two union institutions, the newly organized National Christian Council and the older, well-established, and influential Nanking Theological Seminary. The question was one of cooperation versus non-cooperation. Should the two Presbyterian missions enter the National Council of Churches and should they continue joint operation and control of the seminary—both of which, so it was charged, were now tainted with modernism?

Impetus for the organization of the National Christian Council had come from the International Missionary Conference held in Edinburgh in 1910, a historic meeting ushering in a new era in interchurch relations. From the conference came inspiration for the organization of the International Missionary Council (1921), the International Conferences of Life and Work (Stockholm, 1925; Oxford, 1937), the International Conferences on Faith and Order (Lausanne, 1927; Edinburgh, 1933), and ultimately the World Council of Churches (1943). One of the more immediate fruits of the Edinburgh Conference was a China Continuation Committee, a self-electing, non-representative body, seeking to promote more cooperation among the numerous missionary bodies operating in China. The Continuation Committee made arrangements for a National Conference to meet in May 1922 for the purpose of forming a permanent organization, a National Christian Council, composed of representatives duly elected by both missions and native churches.

Conservative missionaries, Presbyterian and others, meanwhile, had become alarmed over liberal views now appearing on the mission field. The faith of some of the Chinese students was being upset, complained Nelson Bell, M.D. "Books translated for use in the grammar and high schools were often permeated with the most advanced and modernistic teaching of the West, and in addition a message was at times being preached, not of salvation through Christ's atoning blood, but salvation through works, as a part of and the results of social service."[48]

In the summer of 1920, during a missionary conference held at Kuling, a small group, 18 in number, all, except two or three, Southern Presbyterians, had decided that the time had come "to make an open stand in defense of the faith once for all delivered to the saints."[49] Out of this gathering came The Bible Union of China, organized with 500 members, and soon—by 1922—totaling around 2,000. Some of this number, a minority so it was charged by some of its more moderate members, sought to turn this organization into a heresy hunting organization. Some held aloof because individual members of the union set themselves in violent and unalterable opposition to all union institutions and organizations for cooperative work among Christians in China.

From members of The Bible Union of China, prominent missionaries of the Southern Presbyterian Church, came violent opposition to the National Christian Council of China before and after its formal organization. Rev. Hugh W. White, veteran missionary and an ultra-conservative in his theology, charged that union movements in China had fallen under the leadership of the Continuation Committee of the Edinburgh Conference, a self-perpetuating body, dominated by radicals. Through its influences, he charged, theological seminaries were being radicalized, the Presbyterian seminary had been converted into an interdenominational seminary, and despite guarantees that it would stand firm for the fundamentals, radicals had been added to the faculty and radical texts were used in the classroom. Leaders of the National Christian Council, it was further charged, had fostered ecclesiastical union along the lines of compromise, and were now behind the movement to establish a National Council of Churches in China. In the Conference every effort was made to keep out all references to the redemptive Word of Christ. The Council itself had been "railroaded through." Dr. White proposed that instead of cooperating "in these amorphous union movements," the church align itself with the fundamentalist movement now developing on a world scale.[50]

Dr. Donald W. Richardson, a professor in Nanking Seminary, responding to Dr. White, acknowledged that there was modernism in China within the missionary body, and also within the native church. But the prevalence of modernism in China, he claimed, had been very much magnified. "Some men," wrote Dr. Richardson, "have got modernism on the brain. They go 'bughouse' on the subject."

Suggestions that The Bible Union of China, of which he had been a charter member, and that all evangelicals were opposed to the China Continuation Committee and the newly organized National

Christian Council, he claimed, were false. He himself had not championed the Continuation Committee because of its unrepresentative character. But the National Christian Council was a far finer effort to unite all the many bodies working in China in a great cooperative effort for more effective evangelism and for building up a self-supporting, self-governing Chinese Christian Church. The National Christian Conference called by the Continuation Committee was made up of approximately 1,200 delegates, practically all of whom were elected directly by the bodies which they represented and the overwhelming majority of whom, both Chinese and foreign, had been conservative evangelicals. It was this Conference which had elected the National Christian Council, composed of 100 members (half of whom were Chinese), most of them sound orthodox Christians. Rev. P. Frank Price, D.D., one of the Southern Presbyterian Church's most distinguished missionaries, had been elected vice president of the Council. A doctrinal statement drawn up by Chinese Christians, Dr. Richardson termed "a wonderfully thrilling statement of the fundaments of the Christian faith."[51]

The North Kiangsu Mission, of which Dr. White was a member, meeting in May 1922, voted 20 to 7 to request the General Assembly of the Southern Church not to recognize or finance the National Christian Council. Among the reasons given were:

1. Our church could not bear its proportion of the expense without either curtailing our own needy work or enlarging the debt.

2. The N.C.C. refused to give an unequivocal statement of its religious beliefs.

3. It was opposed by many influential Chinese pastors and church leaders.

4. The affiliation of most of its promoters was with modernism.

5. The National Council when finally established would become a super-government over all the churches and missions in China, wielding a power which it was unwise to put into the hands of any set of men, however good.[52]

Eleven members of the North Kiangsu Mission dispatched a long letter to the homeland explaining "Why some of the North Kiangsu Mission favor cooperation with the National Christian Council of China." It had no power, they explained, to make new creeds or to interfere with old ones. It was an advisory and representative body, without executive power, intended, among other things, to foster and express the fellowship and unity of the Christian Church in China; to watch and study the development of the church in self-support, self-government, and self-propagation; and to suggest methods and a course of action whereby the desired end might be more specially and completely gained. Few Chinese leaders opposed it. Of the more than 20 denominations of missions which had considered cooperation in the Council the North Kiangsu Mission was the only one to refuse cooperation. All Christian workers in China, whether native or foreign, must agree that some form of cooperative organization was desirable and necessary. The mission should cooperate because the Council and the Church of Christ in China needed the help that it could give and because the mission needed certain kinds of help which participation in such an organization could give to it. Some members of the mission were satisfied to profess desire for closer cooperation with missionaries of other denominations, to condemn the Council as modernistic, and to hold aloof in a spirit of provincial isolation. But such professions would not be accepted as genuine. "Our almost wholesale condemnation of all those who differ from us will be considered as dangerously close to thinking of ourselves more highly than we ought to think."[53] So said the North Kiangsu minority.

The Mid-China Mission meanwhile had postponed action on the N.C.C. for another year. Opinion in this mission pro and con was so divided that it was agreed by all to wait for more light. A correspondent explained that the divergent attitude of these two missions which would become more pronounced as time passed could be explained in part by their respective situations. The North Kiangsu Mission was engaged in extensive evangelistic work in a largely unoccupied field, with many villages and rural areas. The Mid-China Mission worked out from large cities and market towns, dividing the territory with other missions, with whom they had cooperated for many years, particularly in educational institutions, sorely needed, but too costly for any one mission or denomination to sustain alone. In doctrine the two missions were agreed; in policy they differed, as geography and economic conditions required.[54]

More serious than the attack of the North Kiangsu Mission on the National Christian Council was the charge of modernism brought by Dr. White against Nanking Theological Seminary. This institution had been founded by Northern and Southern Presbyterians early in the century. In 1911, one year after the Edinburgh Conference, it became interdenominational—Northern and Southern Methodist and Christian Churches joining in the venture. This cooperative enterprise became the largest and most influential theological seminary in China. In 1921 there were 158 students enrolled, and a faculty of ten, of whom three were Southern Presbyterians. White, with one other missionary, objected to the use of certain textbooks—specifically

Clark's *Outline of Theology* (a moderately liberal theological text, widely used in America at the time) and Hastings' *Bible Dictionary*, which accepted the critical approach to the Bible.

Dr. P. Frank Price and Dr. Donald W. Richardson, the latter a member of the faculty, in reply to Dr. White, denied that there were modernists on the faculty; admittedly some were more conservative, and others more liberal; but on the cardinal doctrines of evangelical Christian there was no divergence. For a handful of students one of the younger professors had made limited use of Clark's *Outline of Theology*, and when objection was raised, such use was discontinued. Hastings' *Bible Dictionary* had been used only as a reference. Errors in both volumes had been pointed out. It was further indicated that the two Presbyterian missions had a veto power over the election of any new faculty member and could likewise remove any professor from the faculty and preclude the use of any particular textbook. Two individuals, however, could not do this, and when they arrogated to themselves the functions and powers of the missions they met with no sympathy from those attempting to carry on the work of educating Chinese young men to the ministry of the church.[55]

A third issue came to the fore when the *Princeton Review* for October 1921 published an article by Dr. Griffith Thomas, "Modernism in China," in which Rev. J. Leighton Stuart, D.D., one of the Southern Church's most honored missionaries (later President of Peking University and American Ambassador to the Republic of China), was arraigned for giving utterance to unsound views on Scriptures and other matters. Dr. Stuart, home on furlough, requested a thorough examination by his presbytery (East Hanover); this was given, and Dr. Stuart was exonerated. A complaint by Dr. W. M. McPheeters carried the matter up to the Synod of Virginia—not once, but twice; complaints which the synod refused to sustain.[56]

Rumors regarding unsound teaching in some of the educational institutions on the mission fields led the 1921 General Assembly, in response to an overture from the Presbytery of Central Mississippi, to instruct its executive committee to investigate and report what action, if any, needed to be taken in the matter. The committee reported to the 1922 General Assembly that it had discovered nothing that would justify its withdrawing from any cooperative work upon which it had entered, but would continue its investigations.

A letter dispatched by the executive committee to the missions abroad recalled that use of Clark's *Theology* had led the Southern Church to withdraw from cooperative work with the Presbyterian Church U.S.A. in Japan and to establish its own theological seminary at Kobe; it urged the Board of Managers of Nanking Seminary now to make use of some other volume. At the same time the letter warned of the possible danger being done by individual missionaries writing letters to their friends in this country, or seeking to remedy what they might regard as evils on the mission fields by agitation of such matters in church papers and appealing to church courts with a view of bringing such questions before the General Assembly. Matters of such seriousness, it was urged, should be handled, if possible, by the missions as such; and if missionaries could not conscientiously accept the decision of their missions, appeal should be made from the mission to the executive committee, and from the executive committee, if necessary, to the General Assembly. The committee, it was added, had full confidence in its missionaries doctrinally and in every other way.[57]

A letter written by L. Nelson Bell, M.D., and given wide publicity in the church papers later this same year, added fuel to the flame. Dr. Bell, home on furlough, wrote in defense of the Bible Union. Modernism, he charged, was being insiduously and openly propagated in China. There were some—a few—who denied the fundamentals (the Virgin Birth, the blood atonement, the complete trustworthiness of Scripture) and who sought to substitute for this gospel the so-called social gospel; others, not denying the fundamentals, accepted the Bible only in part; still others, who themselves accepted the fundamentals, with false liberality felt that those who did not so believe should be accepted by the Foreign Mission Board and should not be molested even when upsetting the faith of others. He insisted that the Bible Union of China was not organized before it was needed. It was not against union. "It is pro-union . . . on the only basis we can accept."[58]

Dr. Bell's co-laborer, Rev. William F. Junkin, urged wide reading of Dr. Bell's article. "The contest is on," he wrote. "Modernism both open and insiduous has come to China."[59] William Ray Dobyns, pastor of the South Highland Church, Birmingham, added his commendation. "It isn't some 'narrow preacher', who is sounding the alarm," he warned, "but an 'M.D.', a sure enough doctor."*

Dr. Egbert W. Smith, Executive Secretary of Foreign Missions, pointed out that there was no reason to doubt the soundness of any missionary's faith; that investigation of union institutions with which the church was connected continued; that the two missions were not

---

* Dr. Bell, a skilled surgeon, gifted as writer and speaker, and versed in the Old Princetonian, Hodge-Warfield conservatism, has continued to carry the banner for orthodoxy down to the present.

connected with the National Christian Council of China and that there was no apparent prospect of such connection; and that the executive committee had declared itself to be in hearty sympathy with the purposes of the Bible Union and wished it Godspeed. The 1923 Assembly approved a report to this effect and urged that the church hold its judgment of individual missionaries or institutions in suspense and refrain from criticism until investigations had been completed and report made to the Assembly next year.

When the Assembly next met, the two missions had taken diverse actions regarding their relations to Nanking Seminary. The North Kiangsu Mission, by a majority of about two to one, had served notice on the Board of Managers of Nanking Seminary that they would sever their connections with the seminary, and the General Assembly was asked to approve this action. Among reasons assigned were the mission's failure to keep the institution free from the compromising influence of men of liberal views on the board, and its failure to secure satisfactory guarantees that future teaching in the seminary would be positively and definitely Christian, especially on the subject of biblical introduction and exegesis. The Mid-China Mission, in whose territory Nanking Seminary was located, on the other hand, had expressed its judgment almost unanimously in favor of continuing its connection with the seminary for at least the present, hoping that by patience and wise effort all reason for criticism might be removed. The Assembly permitted the Mid-China Mission to continue its connection with the seminary; the North Kiangsu Mission was permitted to withdraw, if after careful reconsideration, this remained its wish. The seminary authorities were warned that the church would withdraw "unless the instruction in the Seminary be kept in harmony with the historic, evangelical interpretation of the Bible." The same Assembly voted that in view of a division of opinion among our missionaries in Japan evangelistic work in that land be conducted for the present upon the plan hitherto used in the mission and not upon the cooperative plan proposed by the Church of Christ in Japan. Feelings in the Assembly over these issues had been very tense, and when a special committee brought in the report finally approved, the Assembly broke out spontaneously into the Doxology.

But the issue was not yet resolved. Dr. White, writing, he stated, at the request of a number of missionaries and in disregard of instructions of the executive committee that charges come through orderly channels, declared that there were modernists among the Southern Presbyterian missionary force, and that the issue "with us is as to indiscriminate unions in which Modernist manipulators are using Presbyterian men, Presbyterian money and Presbyterian influence to destroy faith in the Word." This, he charged, remained the situation in Nanking Seminary. The investigations ordered by the General Assembly, he insisted, had been inadequate and incomplete.[60]

For the second successive year Foreign Missions furnished the storm center of the Assembly.

Both China missions, meanwhile, had taken formal action, emphatically denying that modernism had invaded their ranks.

Debate in the Assembly raged around the so-called muzzling order of the executive committee, forbidding missionaries to broadcast changes against the beliefs or conduct of their fellow missionaries through the public press. In response to overtures, the General Assembly changed the resolution to read: "Missionaries who have what they consider well-founded charges affecting the conduct or orthodoxy of fellow missionaries or of institutions for whose management our church is responsible in whole or part should bring such charges first before the Mission directly concerned, or before the Executive Committee of Foreign Missions or before the proper Church Court in order that these charges might be thoroughly investigated in an orderly manner, and their truth or falsity determined, and appropriate action taken."[61]

The furor regarding the missionary enterprise gradually subsided; the missions remained divided in their attitude toward Nanking Seminary; neither mission supported the National Christian Council. In China, Japan, Korea, and other mission lands the question of cooperative Christianity would henceforth be a divisive one—as it was also on the home field.

The modernist-fundamentalist controversy was now raging in a number of the Northern churches, and with particular intensity in the Presbyterian Church U.S.A.

Southern Presbyterians followed these developments in their sister denomination with close attention, recognizing that they themselves could not remain entirely unaffected. Early in the struggle the *Presbyterian Standard* commented editorially: the Presbyterian Church U.S.A. lacks unity—you will find there higher critics and conservatives and ex-Cumberland Presbyterians. "Even in our own branch which is supposed to be more closely united than any other, there are varying elements—some intensely conservative, some standing close to the line of division, and some growing more radical as the years go by."[62]

The church, however, retained complete confidence in its theological seminaries. The *Presbyterian of the South* rejoiced that no breadth of heresy, no laxity of teaching, had ever come near them. "We send our young men to these schools of the prophets," it declared, without fear of damage.[63] Denominational colleges, too, were trusted, though the *Christian Observer* in 1923 commented that unbelief had become so common among college students generally that it presented a major problem to the churches.[64]

To guard against possible spread of the contamination in the Southern Church, spokesmen for the church by word and pen defended the doctrine of plenary (inerrant) inspiration, the doctrine which had been taught in the church from the beginning, the doctrine ably developed and maintained by Dr. B. B. Warfield of Princeton. Conclusions of historical criticism regarding the composition of the Old Testament Scriptures were generally rejected, and scholars of the church, occupants of Old Testament chairs in the various theological seminaries, assured their students and readers of church publications that the "destructive higher criticism: was on its way out." The editor of the *Presbyterian Standard* quoted scientists in defense of a literal interpretation of the story of Jonah and the whale. "Whether the modern man believes this story or not," he declared, "it is evident that our Lord did . . . If we refuse to believe it, then we can no longer believe in his . . . divinity." Nelson Bell, M.D., missionary from China, now returned to the United States, wrote in strong support of the fundamentalist point of view.[65] According to Rev. John M. Wells, D.D., President of Columbia Theological Seminary, modernism included pantheism, higher criticism (which rejected the Mosaic authorship of the Pentateuch), Unitarianism (which denied the deity of Christ), evolutionism, and Bolshevism, as one indivisible whole. "Those who hold some phases of it," he wrote, "may deny that they hold others. The philosopher of German monism and the cocksure higher critic may vehemently deny that they are Unitarians or Bolshevists, but they start from the same postulates; they use the same methods; they travel the same roads; they will ultimately land us in the same earthly hell."[66]

Among Southern Presbyterians generally the five "fundamentals," endorsed by the General Assembly of the Presbyterian Church in the U.S.A., were accepted without question. Militant fundamentalists as represented by the *Standard,* however, were becoming increasingly alarmed. "We have professors in our Seminaries, eloquent preachers in our pulpits and editors of the religious press," it complained, "insisting that a man's doctrine is of little moment, and that his life is everything. They pose as the prophets of peace and good will, and constantly by implication thank God that they are not as other men are, even these rigid fundamentalists . . . We love peace, but not peace at any price. The time is rapidly approaching when there must be raised the cry 'To your tents, O Israel'."[67]

This cry was heard more and more in the days that followed. Some will ridicule our fears, wrote Dr. Bridges, but "this paper will continue to warn the church that there is abroad an epidemic of heresy, not only in churches where it has shown itself at intervals in the past, but also it is incipient in our own ranks—and with the least encouragement it will break into open rebellion."[68]

The 1924 General Assembly had before it an ad interim report recommending extensive changes in the Book of Church Order. Dr. H. M. Moffett moved from the floor that the ordination vows of a minister be amended to require the candidate to signify his acceptance of half a dozen specific doctrines, fundamentals of the faith. In a brief recess that followed Dr. W. L. Lingle, chairman of the ad interim committee, pointed out to Dr. Moffett that this proposed amendment would change the Book of Church Order into a confession of faith and that in addition it was laying emphasis upon certain doctrines to the exclusion of others of equal importance. The two men then agreed upon a compromise proposal which required the candidate to promise that if at any time he found himself out of accord with any of the fundamentals of the system of doctrine set forth in the Confession of Faith he would on his own initiative make known to his presbytery the change which had taken place in his views since the assumption of his ordination vow. This proposal was accepted by the General Assembly and subsequently, according to prescribed constitutional procedure, by the church as a whole.

Dr. Lingle later recalled that within 24 hours he had come to regret his hasty and ill-considered acceptance of this amendment, in which subsequent events proved to have been an unnecessary concession.[69] This became clear when the Assembly, after prolonged and earnest discussion, declined to approve a ten-point doctrinal deliverance (including the inerrancy of Scriptures), as proposed by the Bills and Overtures Committee, and reaffirmed instead "its faith in the great fundamentals of our Church as set forth in our Confession of Faith and catechisms." No objection was made to the ten points in themselves. It was successfully argued that a doctrinal deliverance of the General Assembly would have no binding power; that it would inevitably, yet needlessly, divide the church; that if the Assembly selected ten points to be emphasized there would be a tendency to narrow down the church's creed to these points, thus obscuring other great doctrines; and, finally, that there was no need for such doctrinal deliverances because of the absence of any disposition to question the fundamental truths as set forth in the symbols of our faith.[70]

To the *Presbyterian Standard* and others this was a grievous mistake. Suspicions were arising regarding the orthodoxy of certain ministers, and Dr. Bridges charged that supposed leaders feared to divide the church. "They cried peace, when there is no peace, and can be none till the church does its duty and applies the test to all."[71]

Efforts to persuade the Assembly to make some deliverance regarding the fundamentals of the faith continued without success for a number of years. Meanwhile pressure from the mission field (China) induced Dr. Walter W. Moore, President of Union Theological Seminary, to withdraw an invitation to lecture extended to Dr. Harris E. Kirk, pastor of the Franklin Street Presbyterian Church in Baltimore, Maryland, and one of the church's most distinguished ministers and scholars.[72] Similar pressure from the home fields led to cancellation of invitations extended to Dr. George Buttrick and other eminent divines to lecture on the Montreat platform.

A more constructive effort to deal with the theological issues arising in the church was made in a series of conferences directed by Rev. Dr. D. Clay Lilly over a period of years in Reynolda, North Carolina. Annually a number of scholars were brought to Reynolda from various parts of the country to discuss what adequate defense could be offered by conservative scholarship against radical criticism, on the one hand, and materialistic theories in the realm of science and philosophy, on the other. "We are not reactionaries or obstructionists," stated Dr. Lilly in the opening conference. "We desire rather to confirm and illustrate faith by every fact established by science or criticism. We shall not be interested so much in proving others wrong as we shall be exhibiting the foundation of reality on which our faith rests." The conference, as Dr. Lilly saw it, was not concerned to prove evolution true or false—that was the task of science. The conference was to be concerned with its value or danger to the Christian faith and with what course of action would thereby be indicated. No formal conclusions were reached, but men, it was claimed, became acquainted with each other, and "differences seemed to grow less, as the frank, earnest, Christian talk proceeded."[73]

As the modernistic-fundamentalist controversy in the Northern Church ran its course, younger men, in the Southern Church began to find their voice. Rev. H. S. Turner, D.D., a young pastor in the

Valley of Virginia and an able Old Testament scholar, pointed out that critical conclusions regarding the Old Testament literature were now established in scholarly circles—a position still challenged in the Old Testament departments of the church's theological institutions. "Between the extreme form of radical criticism and the extreme form of narrow evangelicalism," Dr. Turner held, "no rapprochement is ever possible, but it ought not to be impossible to find a bridge between a sane and temperate criticism and a sane and liberal evangelicalism." "It is to such a position," he claimed, "that a study of the Old Testament Scriptures is moving today."[74] Dr. Turner's article was bitterly resented by his former mentor in Union Theological Seminary. Well founded hopes that he would be recommended to succeed Dr. Mack in the Old Testament chair at Union Theological Seminary suddenly vanished.[75]

Kenneth J. Foreman, Professor of Bible and Philosophy in Davidson College, wrote in support of Dr. Turner's position. The authority of Scripture, he indicated, did not depend on traditional views of inspiration. Poetry and folklore, legends, historical novels, midrashes, all, he added, may be utilized in the interests of religious truth. The minister should be protected from assaults on his orthodoxy while orienting himself to new viewpoints.[76]

Rev. Holmes Rolston, like Dr. Turner, a young pastor in the Valley of Virginia, also challenged the idea that an inerrant word is essential to religious certainty.[77] True scholarship, he wrote, requires that men approach their study with a mind open to new truth. "If a generation should arise which is able to apprehend more fully than our fathers have the meaning of the message which came through Christ," he further insisted, "then it will be the duty of the church to forsake her system and to fearlessly follow the truth."[78]

The author of this volume had come to Union Theological Seminary in Virginia in the fall of 1922 as Assistant Professor of English Bible (he was transferred three years later to the Department of Church History). Shortly thereafter he began to write a weekly exposition of the International Sunday School lessons in the *Presbyterian Standard* (continued later in the *Presbyterian of the South*). In these lessons an attempt was made to acquaint the reader with some of the more certain results of biblical criticism and also to apply the text meaningfully to some of the social conditions in the South, particularly the race issue—an approach which drew some fire. Within a few years he became Book Editor of the *Union Seminary Review* and in this position sought to encourage a wider reading of all significant books appearing in the theological realm. In a 1931 issue of the *Review*

appeared an article which he wrote, tracing theological developments in the Presbyterian Church U.S.A. and raising the question
"is the Northern Church theologically sound?" The answer was "that
our sister denomination is fundamentally sound in faith, and is just as
likely to remain so as our own . . . Differences of interpretation undoubtedly exist and some 'liberal' views. But they also exist in our own
church, and will always exist."[79]

The writer's own orthodoxy was immediately challenged by Dr.
J. M. Wells, a former Moderator of the church and, though acceptable
assurances were given to the interlocutor, the suspicion lingered that
a professor in the church's leading seminary who argued for the
soundness of the Northern Church was himself unsound in the faith.[80]

Older ministers, men of stature and standing in the church, were
now calling for greater freedom of expression within the church.
Dr. W. L. Lingle, President of the Assembly's Training School, applauded the Assembly's refusal to make a doctrinal deliverance on
the inspiration of Scripture, and took occasion to point out that the
Confession of Faith is not committed to a doctrine of inerrant inspiration.[81]

Rev. Robert F. Campbell, D.D., honored pastor of the First
Church, Asheville, North Carolina, delivered the annual Sprunt Lectures at Union Seminary on "Freedom and Restraint." He warned
against the danger of equating inspiration with inerrancy, and pled
for a larger freedom in the interpretation of Scripture and in the understanding of the minister's ordination vows[82]—to the open distress,
it may be added, of Dr. Thomas Cary Johnson, the senior member of
the faculty.

A few months later Dr. D. Clay Lilly, of Reynolda fame, now one
of the elder statesmen of the church, spoke to the students of Union
Theological Seminary on "The Coming Creative Period." "It is a
time to build," he challenged, and claimed that the church was facing
its greatest intellectual and spiritual opportunities. "A new domain
of fact and a new attitude of authority and a new method of education are bringing us to the place," he said, "where it will be necessary
for us to restate our fundamentals of religion. Anyone can see that
this restatement is sure to be made. But none of us knows just what
this restatement will be like. This is the important matter of the
next fifty years . . . We will need scholars, we will need thinkers, we
will need prophets . . . we will need martyrs."[83]

The following autumn there appeared a special issue of the Union
Seminary Review (one of the last edited by Eugene C. Caldwell)
with a number of articles bearing on "The Reformers and the Bible."

In one of the lead articles, Dr. Hugh Ross MacIntosh, eminent Scottish theologian, recognized that both Luther and Calvin held at times to the old notion of a verbally inspired Bible; that both, however, were compelled by facts to break away from the rigid dogma of verbal inspiration which they had inherited. John Oman, Moderator of the Presbyterian Church in England, was quoted as saying that infallibility as an external authority was an idea carried over from the sacerdotal idea of salvation and the hierarchical idea of the church which is not consistent with the conception of salvation as reconciliation through Jesus Christ by a gracious God.[84]

The alumni address at Austin Theological Seminary was delivered this same year by Rev. George L. Bitzer of Holly Springs, Mississippi, returning to his alma mater after 46 years in the ministry. We are living in a difficult time for the evangelical minister, declared Dr. Bitzer, a time of change and necessary readjustment. He claimed to be as orthodox as orthodox could be, but confessed that he felt the challenge of countless new facts in biology, psychology, and sociology. "I hold it to be the duty of the religious leader," he said, "to think his message through for himself in the light of all the facts . . . One difficulty is this, we have in our churches a host of good Christians who are afraid of new teachings, think them dangerous, and love to hear the shibboleths of the Gospel pronounced in just the same accents that their mothers said it. But beyond them are uncounted thousands of tempted, doubt-driven, sin-stained souls who have no Christ, and who question the old shibboleths. Why not forget the saints for a season," he asked, "and try to restate and re-emphasize the message to meet the needs of the questioners." It is impossible, he added, for our church to remain steady, and it is not steady; the church and the ministry, he insisted, were changing more than many realized.[85]

A series of test cases in the next few years revealed the growth of a more tolerant spirit in the church. The first of these test cases concerned Dr. Hay Watson Smith, pastor of the Second Church, Little Rock, Arkansas. Dr. Smith, whose father was a distinguished Presbyterian minister and one of whose brothers was Secretary of the Executive Committee of Foreign Missions, had studied at Union Theological Seminary in Virginia and then as a graduate student in the more stimulating atmosphere of Union in New York. After serving Congregational churches in the North for a number of years, he came to Little Rock. Applying for admission to Arkansas Presbytery he acknowledged openly his belief in the theory of organic evolution, his disbelief in the verbal inerrancy of the Bible, and his divergence in some respects from the Confession of Faith (its doctrine of total depravity, for example). The fact that Dr. Smith "openly flaunted" his dissent from the Presbyterian Standards led the Presbytery of Ouachita in the Synod of Arkansas to overture the 1924 General Assembly to adopt a series of doctrinal statements which would have laid Dr. Smith open to a charge of heresy[86]; efforts in this direction continued without success over the next five years. In 1928 the Assembly was explicitly asked for a deliverance on inspiration and evolution, and once again as heretofore declined to act.[87]

Then came the open attack—an overture from the Presbytery of Augusta asking the General Assembly to take some action regarding views of Dr. Smith set forth in a pamphlet entitled "Some Facts About Evolution," which, said the presbytery, assailed the truthfulness of the Bible, the intelligence of the ministers who held views in variance with those of the author, and the fairness and wisdom of the church papers which excluded articles from Dr. Smith's pen. The Assembly, responding to an earnest appeal by Dr. W. M. McPheeters, passed a resolution enjoining the Presbytery of Arkansas to investigate the rumors that were abroad regarding Dr. Smith's soundness in the faith. The issues were openly discussed in the church papers, particularly in an exchange of letters between Dr. Smith and his assailants. Dr. Smith acknowledged that he did not hold distinctive Calvinistic doctrines as set forth in the Standards and doubted whether a tithe of the ministers, elders, and deacons in the church did so either.[88]

The presbytery accepted its commission's report, which found that Dr. Smith's belief in theistic evolution, his rejection of inerrant inspiration, and his admitted divergence from the Confession of Faith were not of sufficient character to disqualify him as a minister of the church, nor was he sufficiently out of line not to be accepted as a minister in good standing in the church.[89]

The matter was carried by complaint to the synod and came again before the 1931 Assembly, which remanded the case to the Synod of Arkansas for a new hearing; synod in turn sent the matter back to presbytery, which again declined to indict Dr. Smith. This action was sustained by both synod and General Assembly and in 1934 the case was finally closed. The only investigation of Dr. Smith's orthodoxy was that made by the Presbytery of Arkansas; synod and General Assembly had been concerned only with procedural matters.

The second test case revealing a gradual shift in the church's position was that of Dr. Charles E. Diehl, President of Southwestern College, who had successfully led the movement relocating the old school in its promising new site at Memphis, Tennessee. In 1917, when

Dr. Diehl became President of Southwestern, there had been eight members on the faculty and 74 students, only 50 of whom were regular students. In June 1919 there were two candidates for the Bachelor's Degree and the total assets were little more than $300,000; the college had been dropped from the list of accredited colleges of the Association of Colleges and Secondary Schools of the Southern States. Now, 13 years later, there was a faculty of 25 and 440 students, including a graduate class of more than 50. The assets were more than two million dollars, and the school was fully accredited. The college had been relocated, and the beginnings of its fine new plant erected. But whispers regarding Dr. Diehl's orthodoxy had been spreading in the supporting synods for some time. More than whispers. Before his election as President of the school, a faculty member had circulated through the church reports regarding his lack of soundness in the faith. These reports had been carefully considered at Dr. Diehl's request and dismissed as groundless before he accepted the post of President. They continued to crop up during the course of the financial campaign which followed. Once more Dr. Diehl offered his resignation, and once again the board declined to accept it. On September 30, 1930, a letter containing specific charges against Dr. Diehl was circulated through the supporting synods by Dr. W. S. Lacy, who had served for seven years as Executive Secretary of the college. On October 10, 1930, a petition signed by 11 ministers, members of the Presbytery of Memphis, was lodged with the Secretary of the Board of Directors of the college. In this petition the signers stated that they had reason to believe:

1. That the president of the college is not what may be called "sound of faith", that he disbelieves in the full inspiration of the Scriptures, and does not adhere to many of the teachings of the Standards of the Presbyterian Church in the United States . . .

2. That the president of Southwestern is a reckless administrator in the handling of the funds belonging to the college.

3. That it is our belief that the Presbyterian Constituency of Memphis has lost confidence in the administration of the presidency of the college.

Dr. J. P. Robertson, spokesman for the 11 ministers, an ardent fundamentalist, stated that he and his associates were bringing no charges against Dr. Diehl, merely laying before the board what had been brought to their attention, most of which in substance had been a matter of conversation for years.

The board questioned Dr. Diehl regarding the various items in the indictment and heard his statement of faith. Dr. Diehl declined to commit himself to a doctrine of inerrant inspiration, but confessed his faith in Scriptures as "the only rule of faith and practice." After hearing Dr. Diehl, the board agreed unanimously that he adhered to all the essentials of the faith—"in other words, he does hold the system of doctrine contained in the Confession of Faith and Catechism of our Church; which is the utmost that the Presbyterian Church in the U. S. requires of any of its ordained ministers."[90]

Dr. Diehl was subsequently cleared of the charges against his orthodoxy by his own Presbytery (Nashville) whom he had invited to inquire into the matter.[91] Concern over the soundness of the instruction given at Southwestern continued, particularly in the Synod of Mississippi, but the other supporting synods maintained full confidence in the school; Dr. Diehl remained in good standing in the church and ten years later, in 1941, was elected Moderator of the General Assembly.

A somewhat different case with its implications not so clear, arose in 1933 when Rev. Donald H. Stewart, a gifted young minister, who had graduated at Louisville Presbyterian Seminary and continued his theological studies in Edinburgh, was called to become student pastor at the University of Virginia. "From the beginning of his examination for reception into West Hanover Presbytery," wrote Rev. Dwight M. Chalmers, pastor of the First Church, Charlottesville, "it was evident that something unusual was in store for us. The man was taking his examination seriously and honestly trying to tell us what he believed and why." He believed that the Scriptures were inspired of God and that Jesus was the incarnation of loving goodness, so intense and mighty that when we deal with him we deal with God. He was fully assured of the living presence of the risen Christ. On the other hand, he frankly stated that he believed that historical facts recorded in the Scripture, including the miracles, the Virgin Birth, and the accounts of the resurrection, should be subjected to careful examination, just as any other statements of supposed acts are investigated. Any other procedure he felt dishonoring to God. "Presbytery was surprised by his honesty, shocked by his failure to use familiar formulae and embarrassed by his frankness," wrote Dr. Chalmers.[92]

It was saddening and revealing, countered an older minister, to become aware of the extent to which modernism had crept into this "staid old and for the most part rural presbytery." Mr. Stewart was unable to accept statements of the Scripture as taught in the Standards of the church. They contradicted the testimony of his reason. This, for the minister in question—and others—was enough to decide the question.[93]

When the roll was finally called it showed 11 in favor of sustaining the examination as satisfactory and 22 opposed. Voting favorably were pastors of the two strongest churches in the presbytery; speaking in opposition was Dr. J. D. Eggleston, a ruling elder and President of Hampden-Sydney College. Rejected after a second examination before the same presbytery, Mr. Stewart was received by Granville Presbytery, where he served for six years as pastor of the Chapel Hill Church, which ministered to students and faculty of the University of North Carolina, after which he accepted a pastorate in the Presbyterian Church U.S.A.

The third revealing case, attracting Assembly-wide attention, developed a few years later. In January 1933 the writer of this volume became an associate editor of the *Presbyterian of the South,* responsible with a group of friends for a new department in the paper, in which representatives of various points of view were encouraged to write freely regarding all questions of interest to the church. A large number of ministers, some long prominent in the life of the church, others destined to play a larger role in the years to come, were enlisted in this effort. In the next few years articles appeared defending the critical study of both Old and New Testaments, challenging traditional views of inerrant inspiration, calling for reinterpretation of traditional doctrines, insisting that "truth is best served by free and open discussion."

One of the earlier contributions pointed out that there were in the Southern Presbyterian Church potential lines of cleavage. "Our younger ministers," it was claimed, "live in a different intellectual climate from that of the former generation."[94]

There was need, the article continued, for "sympathetic understanding between those in our church who prefer the old formulations of our Standards and those who are trying to make the teachings of our church vital in the life and experience of our students." For eight years the writer had worked among students in a Midwestern university. Many, he feared, did not understand what the church was up against "in this changing intellectual atmosphere."

In his first contribution, Rev. Kenneth J. Foreman, Professor of Bible in Davidson College, indicated that the church could be divided into two classes: those who believed that the 17th century had a final copyright on truth and those who didn't. He put himself distinctly in the latter class. "It must be frankly said," he concluded, that "if the church insists upon speaking to a dying world in a dead language, it only hastens the process of dissolution."[95]

In a subsequent article, Dr. Foreman called for reinterpretation
of the church's view of man, a rejection of the view that woman was
made from the rib of man, an acceptance of the evolutionary view
of man's origin, and a revision of the confessional statement that man
"is utterly indisposed, disabled and made opposite to all good and
wholly inclined to all evil." This, he charged, was a ghastly misrepre-
sentation of what the church actually believed. The church also
needed, he said, to reconsider its traditional doctrine of separation between church and state, a doctrine which once enabled it to dodge the
question of slavery, and now permitted its members to underpay
their employees, overcharge interest on loans to their tenants, oppose
child labor laws, and still maintain membership in good and regular
standing.[96]

Dr. Lewis J. Sherrill, Professor of Religious Education in Louisville Seminary, contributed an article on "The Need for Freedom
of Discussion among Presbyterians." "There are problems on which
the scholarship of the entire world is practically united and has been
for years," he wrote, "which cannot be introduced in some Presbyterian
circles, without risk of a head . . . Scholarship has laid at our doors
the results of years of scientific research, and yet a few pioneers who
wish to help us utilize these results in interpreting the Gospel to our
day have been hailed up for heresy . . . Happily," he went on to
point out, "the temper of the church is changing in this matter of
freedom of discussion . . . there are still places where patient or fearful men suffer a domination which they know should have been
broken long ago. But the tone of much published material, of many
debates, and especially of conversations, breathes a quiet, sane, declaration of freedom to think and to speak. . . ."[97]

A few months earlier, it may be observed, 200 ministers of the
church participated in a forum at Montreat, arranged by a committee
appointed by an informal group of ministers the preceding summer,
to discuss "The Practical Application of the Teachings of Jesus to the
Problems of the Day." Success of this gathering led to the organization
of a permanent forum, to which all ministers of the church were eligible. The purpose of the forum was to encourage the free discussion
of any problem bearing on the life and teachings of the Southern
Presbyterian Church. The forum continued to meet for a number of
years, with programs arranged by the ministers themselves, during
which time there was frank and open discussion of numerous problems, particularly in the field of theology and ethics. There were
also comparable forums at Kerrville in Texas and at Massanetta in
Virginia.[98]

From the columns of the *Presbyterian of the South* and through the ministers' forum came support for the establishment of Committees on Moral and Social Welfare in Assembly and synods—the beginning of a long and sustained but ultimately fruitless effort to bring about union with the Presbyterian Church in the United States of America—and efforts, only partially successful, to revise the Confession of Faith.

In the fall of 1937 continued illness of Rev. W. S. Campbell, D.D., editor of the *Presbyterian of the South,* compelled this writer to assume editorial responsibility for the paper as a whole. Indispensable assistance was rendered particularly by Rev. Holmes Rolston, Jr., Rev. Ansley C. Moore, Rev. Kenneth J. Foreman, Rev. Aubrey N. Brown, and Rev. Patrick H. Carmichael, the latter conducting a "Book Table" which sought to stimulate the church leadership to read more widely in the field of religious literature. The paper once a bulwark of conservatism and still open to all varieties of opinion had become a medium through which new points of view were finding expression.

Suggestions for change were coming now from all quarters and, of course, opposition—defense of plenary verbal inspiration; defense of rigid, unyielding Calvinism; opposition to the annual reports on Moral and Social Welfare presented to the General Assembly; bitter, intensely bitter, opposition to efforts being made for reunion of the two major branches of Presbyterianism.

One of the most earnest and able opponents of various new trends in the church was Tom Glasgow, businessman and elder in Charlotte, North Carolina. Mr. Glasgow, who frequently represented his church and presbytery in the higher courts, was a passionate defender of the older views of inspiration; he was strenuously opposed to any approaches to union with the Presbyterian Church in the U.S.A., he objected to the social deliverances of the church, and he earnestly advocated withdrawal from the Federal Council of Churches. In May 1940, he led a close but losing fight in the General Assembly to abolish the Assembly's Permanent Committee on Moral and Social Welfare, of which the author of this volume was a member. At this same Assembly he urged that the General Assembly appoint a committee to inquire into the teaching emanating from the seminaries— in particular regarding their views of the Bible. Dr. B. R. Lacy, President of Union Theological Seminary, opposed this effort, on constitutional grounds, arguing that any such investigation should be made either by the boards of the institutions or by the presbyteries to which individual members of the faculty were responsible.

In the fall of this same year Mr. Glasgow mailed to all ministers and all courts of the church a pamphlet entitled "Shall the Southern Presbyterian Church Abandon Its Historic Position? A Plea for Common Honesty. Exposing the Attack of Dr. Ernest Trice Thompson, of Union Theological Seminary, Upon the Standards of the Presbyterian Church in the United States." In the pamphlet Mr. Glasgow charged that Dr. Thompson "openly and actively supports doctrines and interpretations of Scripture which are foreign to our interpretation of the Faith." The emphasis seemed to be on the final words of the sentence "doctrines and interpretations *foreign to our interpretation of the Faith,*" for this idea was iterated and reiterated. As Mr. Glasgow wrote: "It is here contended as both basic and fundamental that Southern Presbyterian Theological Seminaries were created and are supported to produce preachers who hold and support the interpretations of Scripture and doctrine which this Church has historically held."

This historic position of the church, from which there must be no departure, he identified with the view of inspiration supported by Dr. Benjamin B. Warfield of Princeton, which he claimed with some justice had been held by the founders of the Southern Presbyterian Church and by all professors of theology in Union Seminary up to this time—a doctrine that "looks upon the Bible as an oracular Book, as the Word of God, in such a sense that whatever it says, God says—not a book, then, in which one may, by searching, find some word of God, but a Book which may be frankly appealed to at any point with the assurance that whatever it may be found to say, that is the Word of God."[99]

Mr. Glasgow brought together numerous quotations from Dr. Thompson's exposition of the Sunday school lesson over the years which, he claimed, contradicted this view of inspiration and departed from traditional Presbyterian doctrines.

The situation was more serious, as Mr. Glasgow saw it, because Dr. Thompson was a professor in a theological seminary, training young men for the ministry, and thus as it were, poisoning the spring at the source. He urged that Dr. Thompson be immediately retired from the faculty of Union Seminary "for the safety of the young men who go to this great Seminary and for the honor of the name of the Church." If this were not done, he prophesied, within five years, or, at the most ten, " 'Liberalism', 'Higher Criticism' and 'Modernism' will have become entrenched and in power."

Mr. Glasgow's pamphlet reached ministers on the eve of the assembly of two of the seminary's controlling synods. This timing produced some reaction—a rallying to the support of a beloved institution. The Synod of North Carolina elected as its Moderator Dr. W. Taliaferro Thompson, Professor of Christian Education in the seminary, and adopted resolutions deploring attacks on the character or orthodoxy of ministers and agencies of the church from pulpits or by pamphlets. It called upon those who had charges to pursue the orderly processes clearly set forth in the Book of Church Order. The Synod of Virginia adopted similar resolutions and as, a token of its confidence, elected the accused professor as its Moderator, even though he had held that office on a previous occasion, and no minister had been elected twice to this position for more than 100 years.

The Synod of West Virginia, by unanimous vote, disapproved the character of the attack and directed that a letter be sent to Dr. Thompson expressing the synod's confidence in him. The Synod of Appalachia, the seminary's fourth supporting synod, referred the pamphlet to the Seminary's Board of Trustees for appropriate consideration.

Since Mr. Glasgow declined to press charges before the presbytery of which Dr. Thompson was a member, claiming that there would be an inevitable whitewash, the latter asked the presbytery to make a thorough investigation of the charges. The examining committee reported that Mr. Glasgow's charges rested on five questionable assumptions: (1) that a theological professor must accept the interpretation placed upon the Standards of the church by his predecessors; (2) that a seminary professor had no right to hold or disseminate views which deviated, even in details from the official Standards of the church; (3) that there was but one allowable theory of the inspiration of the Bible; (4) that one might not accept the assured results of textual criticism without being disloyal to the Bible; (5) that there was but one allowable method of interpretation of Scripture. In the judgment of the committee the whole force of Mr. Glasgow's pamphlet was lost if these questionable assumptions were not granted. Specific charges advanced by Mr. Glasgow were considered and dismissed. It was the committee's judgment, accepted by the presbytery and later by the synod, that Mr. Glasgow has not established his contention that Dr. Thompson was disqualified for a place on the faculty of the seminary, and that the investigation had revealed no ground for a judicial trial.[100] An investigation by the Board of Trustees of the seminary likewise found no reason why the accused should be relieved of his position on the faculty of the seminary.[101] It was suggested, however, that he be a little more careful how he wrote.

The East Hanover Report, circulated through the church, led Mr. Glasgow to follow it with a second pamphlet entitled "Glasgow's Reply to the Report and Action of East Hanover Presbytery." The presbytery's conclusions were dismissed as the expected whitewash, and Mr. Glasgow again strongly urged that Dr. Thompson not "be continued as a Professor in our largest Seminary," disseminating his point of view to the future ministers of the church.

The matter came before the General Assembly of 1941 on overture, three presbyteries (Mecklenburg, Central Mississippi, and Roanoke) asking that a committee be appointed to investigate and report on Dr. Thompson's teaching; two presbyteries, Harmony and Knoxville, requesting that a committee be appointed to investigate the teachings of all the seminaries. Commissioners to the Assembly received from Mr. Glasgow a small booklet (48 pages) containing reprints of his previous pamphlets, the report of the committee as accepted by East Hanover Presbytery, and opposing judgments supporting Mr. Glasgow's conclusions.[102]

After extended debate the General Assembly narrowly defeated (101-94) a minority recommendation that the General Assembly appoint a committee to investigate the teachings of all the members of all the faculties in all the seminaries, and then adopted by overwhelming vote the majority recommendation that the various overtures be answered in the negative on the ground that, in accordance with the constitution of the church, charges against a minister should be brought before the presbytery of which he was a member and before the highest court of the church only by appeal or complaint. Supervision of the General Assembly over the seminaries of the church was exercised, it was further noted, through the owning and controlling synods.

It may be observed that this was the first charge of unsound teaching lodged against a professor in one of the theological seminaries since the days of Dr. James Woodrow, half a century earlier. Dr. Woodrow had been driven from his position by public pressure, on the grounds that his teaching was contrary to the traditional understanding of Scripture and Confession of Faith. The same sort of campaign on this occasion had failed to achieve its objective. Freedom from the dead hand of the past, from the assumptions which underlay Mr. Glasgow's charges and which others shared that a theological professor must not teach anything contrary to the Standards of the Church or the traditional interpretation of those Standards, had been upheld. But there were now two clearly defined groups in the church, two wings, two divergent points of view, two extremes, some would claim, both equally sincere, one holding that newer points of view threatened the very existence of the faith, the other that they were essential if the faith was to remain viable for modern man.

XIII

The Church and Its Worship

In the closing decades of the 19th and the opening decades of the 20th century, churches in town and city normally held three services of worship—two on Sunday, the third on Wednesday evening.

Attendance at the Sunday morning service seems to have held up well—"good," "gratifying," and "increasing" ran the reports (especially during World War I). In the early 1920's various synods estimated the proportion of their membership who attended morning service as follows: Arkansas, 75 percent; South Carolina from 70 to 80 percent; other synods between 60 and 65 percent; Florida was low with an estimated 58 percent. The estimates may have erred on the optimistic side, but it may be recalled that at this time the proportion of church members to total population was much lower than at present.

Attendance at the Sunday evening service was less gratifying. That there are tendencies in modern life undermining attendance on this service, commented the *Christian Observer* shortly after the turn of the century, is clear to every observant eye. Among these tendencies it mentioned, "the general religious indifference which we often so greatly lament"; the alarming custom of having dinners and social functions on the sacred day; the most undesirable custom of young women receiving company on the Sabbath evening; the terrible tendency to turn the holy day into a holiday with excursions, baseball games, and so forth; and also the fact that some good people honestly believe it is best for parents to spend the Sabbath evening at home with their families.[1]

The problem of maintaining the second service was far more difficult in the heat of the summer. Many of the city churches sought to solve the problem by abandoning evening services for one or two months. Around 1907 a new experiment—out-of-doors union services

—began to be tried and for a time with some success. But the problem of the regular evening service remained.

In 1921 synods estimated the proportion of members attending this service as ranging from a low of 25 percent (Florida) to a high of 50 percent (Georgia, Arkansas, Appalachia, and South Carolina), which to those of us of the present day seems a suspiciously high figure. Decline in attendance at the second service was precipitous after World War II (along with the growing popularity of television), and gradually it was dropped in the vast majority of Presbyterian churches. Compensation for its loss was found by many churches in increased attendance at the young people's meetings. Ministers claimed that attention given by them to such meetings was a more constructive use of their time than preparing a second sermon to a dwindling evening congregation.

Attendance at the midweek service, which for some reason was widely claimed to be the spiritual barometer of the church, was naturally less than at the two Sunday services, and here, too, the progress was steadily downward. Gypsy Smith, visiting the United States in 1907, recalled that on the occasion of his first visit, 18 years earlier, church members were expected to go to the weeknight prayer meetings and that large numbers went. It was no uncommon thing, said he, to see half, if not two thirds, of the church membership present.[2] There is nothing in the records of the Southern Presbyterian Church to indicate that attendance was ever quite so large, but there are numerous references to declining attendance, and in the early 1920's when most synods estimated average attendance on the three worship services of the church the estimate of attendance in proportion to church membership at the prayer meeting ranged from a high of 23 percent in Oklahoma to a low in Florida of 11 percent. Decline in attendance at this service after World War II was as marked as that indicated for the Sunday evening service. However, when we take into account the women's circles and the various other meetings of the church, it is quite likely that the total volume of social prayer was as large if not greater than before. Also, in many churches, large and small, the old-fashioned midweek service came to be replaced by a church or family night, beginning with the church supper, and ending with a brief program, devotional or otherwise, that attracted a larger number of church members than had attended the former type of service.

In every decade complaints were made that children did not attend church as they did in the good old days. Often this was blamed on the Sunday school. "Teacher," writing toward the close of the century, offered another explanation. In the "good old days," she recalled, children sat for long hours in school on uncomfortable seats in poorly ventilated or cold rooms every day. Consequently, it was not a difficult matter for them to sit quietly in church during a long sermon. Now children sit in seats adapted to their size, in pleasant rooms, and they never sit for more than 20 minutes at a time. The teacher keeps them interested in subjects they can understand, and the school hours seem short and pleasant. In church, on the other hand, the children sit on pews with their feet dangling between heaven and earth. Nothing in the service is arranged with them in mind, and "O, that second prayer. We have timed it when it was ten minutes long. There the little ones stand, trying to keep still . . . and to listen to petitions which they do not at all comprehend. We have often wondered why so many ministers make this prayer so long . . ." And the long sermon, 40 minutes. Hymns and choir renditions which the children cannot understand. Is it any wonder next Sunday the child teases Mama to be left at home, and that the mother feels tempted to relent?[3]

Actually there were times when the "long prayer" ran for 20 minutes. And there were those who continued to contend that all but the weak and infirm should stand for the prayers however long. "The most casual observer cannot fail to note that a great change has taken place in this matter during recent years," commented the *Christian Observer*. "Many of our old readers can remember when the whole congregation in unbroken rank stood reverently during the prayer in public services. This was true of Presbyterian churches, both in city and in country. But how matters have changed, especially in our town and city churches. Looking over one of our city congregations today, while the public prayer is being offered by the minister, what an irregular sight meets us. Some are standing, some bowing forward in the pew, and some sitting bolt upright, looking all about."[4]

This continued to be the picture until the older generation, accustomed to stand in prayer, gave in or died; for a little longer there were those who bowed with their head resting on the back of the pew in front of them; finally, the most pious did no more than close their eyes and slightly incline their heads.

How long should the sermon be? In the 1880's, 45 minutes was regarded as the orthodox level; in the 1890's, 40 minutes was the more accepted length; in the next decade the norm became 30 minutes, and so remained for another generation when in many pulpits it dropped to 25 and even 20 minutes. Not all approved. How the world grumbles over long sermons, exclaimed the editor of the *Southern Presbyterian*. The *Nashville Christian Advocate* asked why any minister should wish to preach 45 minutes on a hot day. Why should he not do so, retorted the editor of the *Southern Presbyterian*. "For more than forty-five minutes did Jesus suffer for us."[5]

Some topics can be more effectively treated in 15 minutes, some in 30; others cannot be treated adequately in less than 45 minutes or an hour, insisted the *Presbyterian Standard*, "and the preacher whose heart is on fire can afford to treat them at that length."[6]

The Directory of Worship, which had served the undivided church and which had been adopted by the Assembly of the Southern Presbyterian Church as a part of its official Standards in 1861, contained no order of service. It indicated that public worship should include some reading from the Scripture (a minimum of one chapter), prayer, Psalms or hymns, and a sermon. The proportion of time given to each of these major elements of the service was left to the minister, with the injunction to have regard "to the time, that neither reading, singing, praying, preaching, or any other ordinance, be disproportionate the one to the other; nor the whole rendered too short, or too tedious." It was suggested that public worship in the sanctuary begin with a short prayer, and that then after a Psalm or hymn had been sung there be a comprehensive prayer—"first, adoring the glory and perfections of God . . . Second, giving thanks to him for all his mercies . . . Third, making humble confession of sin, both original and actual . . . Fourth, making earnest supplication for the pardon of sin, and peace with God . . . Fifth, pleading . . . the glory of God in the comfort and happiness of his people . . . Sixth, intercession for others, including the whole world of mankind . . ."[7] After the sermon the minister was to pray, a Psalm was to be sung, and "a collection raised for the poor, or other purposes of the church."[8]

There were no forms provided for the observance of the sacraments or for marriage or funeral services.

This "formlessness" of Presbyterian worship, a departure from the original Reformed tradition, was due in part to the influence of the Puritan reaction against all liturgical elements in religion and in part to the influence of the revivalistic sects on the American frontier. About the middle of the 19th century there was an awakening of liturgical interest in American Presbyterianism, particularly in the North; it was given a setback in the Civil War period, but revived shortly thereafter. In 1882 Rev. Dr. A. A. Hodge, Professor of Theology in Princeton Theological Seminary and highly regarded in the Southern Church, issued a Manual of Forms, a private compilation designed for optional use in the Presbyterian Church U.S.A., which many ministers in the Southern Church also found of help.

Need for revision of the old Directory of Worship was increasingly felt. It had in fact almost become obsolete and was very little used. This was not only because of its style and because some of its expressions were those of another age, but also because of some important omissions—there were, for example, no provisions for the Sunday school, no mention of prayer meetings, and no indication that there should be a public profession of faith on the part of those admitted to full membership, except in the case of those not baptized in infancy. It had become the practice, however, for all persons making the required profession for admission to the communion to do it in the presence of the congregation.[9]

Revision of the Directory, contemplated as early as 1864 but delayed while the Assembly entered upon its long drawn-out efforts to revise its Form of Government and Rules of Discipline, was finally completed in 1893. New chapters were added, covering worship in the Sabbath school and at prayer meetings. One paragraph, about which there had been a division of opinion, was finally retained: "In time of public worship, let all the people attend with gravity and reverence, forbearing to read anything except what the minister is reading or citing: abstaining from all whispering, from salutation of persons present or coming in: and from gazing about, sleeping, smiling, and all other improper [in the earlier Directory it had read "indecent"] behavior."[10] Every pastor in town or country knows how pertinent and how important these admonitions are, argued one influential minister.[11] We could allow expressions such as this, explained Dr. Robert P. Kerr, "because of their noble origin," though we would not write such paragraphs at the present time.[12]

In a futile effort to arrest a mounting trend, there was added a statement, reading: "The standing position [in prayer] is sanctioned by Scripture, and is recommended by the practice of the primitive church, and by immemorial usage of Presbyterians." The revised Directory included questions which might be addressed to parents presenting their infant children for baptism and to adults being admitted to the Lord's Supper. Reminiscent of an earlier day was a paragraph, originally marked for excision but restored to its original place in response to objections, which read: "As it had been customary, in some parts of the church, to observe a fast before the Lord's Supper; to have a sermon on Saturday and Monday; and to invite two or three ministers on such occasions; and as these seasons have been blessed to many souls, and may tend to keep up a stricter union of ministers and congregations, we think it now proper that they who choose it may continue in this practice."[13] This had once been a common custom but there were few now, if any, who so chose.

The most important innovation was the inclusion of three optional forms in the appendix to the Directory—a marriage form, one for an adult funeral, and another for a child's funeral. Fifty years earlier this would have been impossible. The church was adamantly opposed to all forms. But ministers having come to the conclusion that funeral sermons were inexpedient had begun to use funeral services which they themselves had collated, or which had been prepared and published by some well-known divine. "At last the church has decided that forms for funerals are desirable and edifying," wrote Dr. Robert P. Kerr, "and that without curtailing the liberty of any man, it is well for the church to have a form of its own, carefully prepared, and recommended for use by ministers, containing not only the Scripture passages to be read, but also forms of prayers to be said, or used as models by him who officiates . . . In the matter of marriages it has become evident long ago that the church needed a service of its own. Ministers were often requested . . . to use the Episcopal form. How much better to have our own service."[14]

The revised Directory had been adopted by a very large majority, but the controversy over the conduct of public worship was by no means ended. As new aids to worship were introduced into other communions and began to find their way into Southern Presbyterian Churches, opposition to any liturgical concessions intensified.

All Protestant churches, even the strictest, were reflecting the silent influences of Rome, charged Dr. Robert L. Dabney. "A comparison of prevalent usages of today and of seventy years ago in the Methodist, Baptist, Congregational and Presbyterian Churches [except those of the Secession]," he continued, "would startle any thinking mind. Every one of them now admits usages which were then universally rejected by them, such as architectural pomps, pictured windows, floral decorations, instrumental and operatic music. One may say that these are matters of indifference which cannot be proved anti-scriptural; but every sensible man knows that they proceed from one impulse, the craving for more spectacular and ritualistic worship. That is precisely the impulse which brought about prelacy and popery in the patristic ages. The strictest Protestant communions are now moving upon the same inclined plane."[15]

Dr. Dabney expressed here the view that prevailed among the founders of the Southern Presbyterian Church, a group now passing from the center of the stage, but younger men coming into positions

of leadership retained the same point of view. So Thomas Cary
Johnson, now serving as Professor of Church History in Union Theological Seminary, insisted that the increasing emphasis on liturgy
was a return to medievalism. Pastors and congregations who introduced into their worship things against the nature and genius of the
Directory of Worship, he charged, violated the constitution and were
guilty of covenant-breaking.[16]

Dr. R. F. Campbell, pastor of the First Church, Asheville, N. C.,
addressing the graduating class at Union Theological Seminary, held
that they must choose between a worship based on revelation and
one based on symbolic rite. "There are many things creeping into
our own churches," he claimed, "especially in the large cities, whose
tendency is towards Rome . . ."

"Akin to [the] ritualistic movement (which means a return to
Rome), and tributary to it," he specified, "is the unregulated
aestheticism that has of late years entered so largely into the services
of the non-ritualistic churches. Like Symbolism it appeals to the
senses, but lacks the dignity of a well-ordered ritual. It manifests
itself in rich and expensive floral decorations to catch the eye, and
in musical programs, more or less elaborate, executed by soloists,
quartettes and choruses, for the delectation of the audience. The
tendency of this is to drive the gospel out or put it in a corner."[17]

The church papers kept up a steady drumfire of criticism against
ritualistic developments in the Anglican communion, and all traces
of this movement which they saw creeping into Presbyterian worship.

Most of the attempts "to enrich the service" appeared first in
the Northern churches. The *Presbyterian Standard* acknowledged that
there were some of the same experiments in the Southern churches,
but held that they were composed of such comparatively harmless
features as repeating the Lord's Prayer "in unintelligible unison," or
making a presentation of the contents of the basket to the Lord, with
the deacons grouped around the pulpit, in an effort to teach people
that the offering is worship. "And in the fashionable churches the
choirs can always be counted on to throw in a few extras not in the
Directory of Worship."[18]

The *Christian Observer* acknowledged that in former times the
devotional parts of the service had been largely subordinated to
the sermon. No less importance should be attached to the sermon,
the editor suggested, but more attention should be given to the
other parts of the service. In this direction, he thought, lay the
remedy, not in the use of liturgical elements.

In 1905 there appeared a complete book of forms called *The Book of Common Worship,* prepared by a committee of the U.S.A. Assembly, of which Dr. Henry Van Dyke was the chairman. In addition to orders for regular and special service of various sorts there was a Treasury of Prayers, a Psalter, and a collection of ancient hymns and canticles. It was approved by the Northern Assembly not as a substitute for the Directory of Worship but as a discretionary supplement to be used by churches and ministers at their own option. "For some years," commented the *Central Presbyterian,* "many Presbyterian churches in Northern cities . . . have been using forms of worship more or less approaching a liturgical service . . . It [is] hoped [by this book] to secure uniformity and to 'enrich' the services." The paper was sure that it would find no use in the Southern Church. Our church, said the editor, has stood so firmly for the spirituality of the church and the simplicity of its worship, that it will have no sympathy with the introduction of any liturgical forms.[19]

True, few, if any Southern Presbyterian ministers, made use of the orders offered for morning or evening worship, but increasing numbers made use of the forms provided for weddings, funerals, and other special occasions. And gradually elements permitting fuller participation on the part of church members made their way into the service—recitation of the Lord's Prayer and of the Apostles' Creed, responsive readings—little more than this for another generation.

Individual communion cups began to be used in the Lord's Supper about 1900. To the *Southwestern Presbyterian* this innovation, "a fruit of the microbe craze," was little short of sacrilegious.[20] But to the *Southern Presbyterian* and the church generally the individual cups or glasses were clean, hygienic, convenient, neat, conducive to quiet and deliberate partaking of the sacrament, and in every way as much superior to the use of goblets as a private silver cup is to the universal dirty tumbler in a railway car.[21]

The real debate was not over cups vs. goblet but over fermented or unfermented grape juice. Sentiment against alcoholic drinks was increasing rapidly throughout the nation as a part of the prohibition movement and with it sentiment against wine in the communion service. People strongly opposed to beverage alcohol in any form could not easily partake of the wine in the sacrament of the Lord's Supper. It was possible, they averred, that some would find the practice a step toward immoderate indulgence. Confronted with Jesus' example, some developed the "two-wine" theory, claiming that, in spite of the fact only one word for wine is used in the New Testament, the context reveals that there was a wine of blessing (unfermented) and a wine of cursing (fermented). It was the wine of blessing (unfermented grape juice) that Jesus provided at the marriage at Cana, and drank at the Last Supper. A few leading advocates of this theory did not hesitate to say that if they believed that the wine made by Jesus at the marriage feast in Cana was alcoholic wine, they would say, "Down with Christianity."[22]

The matter was brought to the Assembly, for the first time, in 1892. In response to an overture from Holston Presbytery, the General Assembly declared by a large majority vote that in its judgment the Scriptural element to be used in the Lord's Supper was fermented grape juice. This did not mean, however, that the use of unfermented grape juice as conscientiously practiced by some Presbyterian churches would necessarily vitiate the validity of this ordinance.[23]

It was this judgment, reaffirmed by the Assembly of 1893, that touched off the debate on the subject that continued a full generation. Many, if not most, deprecated the agitation, but extremists on both sides insisted that there were fundamental principles involved.

The General Assembly in 1911 reaffirmed previous deliverances, but refused to reopen the issue and left the question of the particular kind of bread and wine to be used to the discretion and judgment of each church.[24]

Debate coninued, and three years later the Assembly appointed an ad interim committee to answer the explicit question: is unfermented wine equally Scriptural with the fermented wine, and is the ordinance of the Lord's Supper equally valid when the unfermented wine is used as when the fermented wine is used? The 1916 Assembly answered, on recommendation of the ad interim committee, that actions of previous Assemblies met all the needs of the case, providing ample liberty for any session to be guided by its own interpretation of the Scripture in this matter.[25]

There the matter rested, in large part because the question had resolved itself. As Dr. R. F. Campbell wrote in 1915: "The use of wine at this sacred ordinance is becoming offensive to an increasing number of conscientious Christians, who decline to partake of it. Thus the Lord's Supper which was intended to be an occasion of Communion is in danger of becoming an occasion of disunion and strife. Shall one of the main purposes of the ordinance," he asked, "be sacrificed to a mere question of the elements to be used?"[26] He and his session had come to recognize that no question of principle was involved in the substitution of unfermented for fermented grape juice in the sacrament, and all were now able to partake in complete amity. So it happened with minor exceptions throughout the Assembly.

In my own boyhood it was customary for a large portion of the congregation to leave after the sermon, and only a portion of the congregation remain for the Communion service. Infant baptisms were frequently performed outside the regular church services. Both of these practices have long since ceased to be the case. The two sacraments—baptism and the Lord's Supper—have become not less, but more, meaningful elements of the church's public worship.

The growing interest in worship led in 1929 to a revision of the Southern Presbyterian Directory of Worship. Six of the 27 chapters of the new Directory were devoted to a description of the normal Sunday morning service and the Holy Communion. No fixed forms were given, and the suggestions offered allowed for considerable flexibility, leaving the minister as the final judge for the precise wording and order. The order naturally indicated, however, and the order which became normative in the church's worship, was as follows:

Doxology
Invocation
The Lord's Prayer (in unison)
Psalm or Hymn [The 1894 Directory made no references to musical instruments, to which there was still some opposition. In the Revised Directory it is stated that "the use of musical instruments should have an important part in public worship."]
Scripture Reading
Comprehensive prayer, embracing some or all of the following elements: adoration, confession of sin; supplication for pardon and peace with God through the atonement, with all the happy fruits thereof; pleading, intercession; and petition for the outpouring of the Holy Spirit on all flesh, for all classes and conditions of men, for private citizens and public officials and for whatever else may seem necessary or suitable for the occasion. [The recommendation of the standing posture in prayer was dropped in the Revised Directory, which merely recommended that the posture be reverent and as far as possible uniform.]
Offering and prayer of dedication at some time in the service
Sermon
Prayer relating to the subject treated in the sermon
Psalm or Hymn
Benediction

The committee working on the revision of the Directory had given some thought to revising the optional forms that might be used by ministers at baptism, weddings, and funerals. Instead, wisely, the committee recommended that the Assembly authorize an imprint edition of the Presbyterian U.S.A. *Book of Common Worship* then in process of revision with any alterations that might appear advisable.

In 1931 this revision, prepared with the invaluable assistance of 30 ministers in the active pastorate appeared—not a new book but "the older one made more useful, beautiful and . . . spirited." The following year the Southern Assembly issued an imprint edition of this revision, making only necessary changes, such as having its own name substituted for that of the U.S.A. Church. This book was now officially accepted as a supplement to the Directory of Worship to be used at the discretion of the minister. "Thus," commented Rev. Dr. Allen Cabaniss, "the Southern Church has officially returned to its heritage."[27]

The Assembly had finally at least given its blessings to the use of liturgy and to the fuller participation of the congregation in the worship service. In the years that followed there would be increasing experimentation in new worship forms on the part of various churches throughout the Assembly.

Hand in hand with the opposition to liturgical worship had gone opposition to recognition of the great days of the church year, especially Christmas and Easter, though here the battle was more quickly lost, popular pressure being too great for the church to resist.

There was no objection to Christmas as a time of festivity—a day when families reassembled and when tokens of friendship and love were exchanged—just so no religious significance was attached to it.

Gradually it became the custom to have editorials bearing on the significance of the birth of the Savior during the Christmas season in the church press, and in 1897 the *Southwestern Presbyterian* came out for the first time with an illustrated cover, in honor of the event.

The Sunday school children had enjoyed for some time illuminated Christmas trees, loaded with presents which were distributed to them by Santa Claus, and here and there a minister took advantage of the fact that all Christendom was turning its thoughts at Christmas to the Savior's birth to direct his meditation to the significance of the birth of Christ, even while he pointed out that there was no reason to believe that Christ was born on Christmas Day. In 1903, however, the *Southwestern Presbyterian* pointed out that no Southern General Assembly had ever suggested religious service on the 25th of December, and declared that it was not aware that any such service had ever been held in a Southern Presbyterian Church (special services on the Sabbath before Christmas were by this time commonplace in the Northern Presbyterian churches). The editor acknowledged at the same time that there was no harm in an observance of the anniversary by children, sometime in the Christmas season, so long as it was not considered strictly religious and obligatory. Indeed, admitted the editor, there seems to be something approaching fitness in children celebrating in lively songs that which for them has peculiar fascination, the birth of the wonderful babe, the Savior of men.[28]

Recognition of Easter as a holy day was opposed even more strenuously than Christmas. The editor of the *Texas Presbyterian* was amazed to learn that observance of Easter was being boldly advocated by some Presbyterian pulpits outside of the South. "As Presbyterians," he protested, "we have no more right to institute an Easter than we have to set up a golden calf in the sanctuary. The man who does not understand that lacks the essentials of a Presbyterian and should cease to call himself one."[29]

The editor of the *Southwestern Presbyterian* was similarly distressed. It is not Presbyterian, he insisted, to add to the New Testament ordinances such others as our fancy may dictate. If Christmas and Easter are adopted, he queried, where is the innovation to end?[30]

The Presbytery of Athens in 1899 asked the Assembly to make "a pronounced and explicit declaration" against the recognition of Christmas and Easter as religious days. The Assembly replied that there was no warrant in Scripture for observing either Christmas or Easter as holy days, rather the contrary (Gal. 4:9-11; Col. 2:16-21), and that such observance was contrary to the principles of the Reformed faith, conducive to "will-worship," and not in harmony with the simplicity of the gospel of Jesus Christ.[31] The deliverance was applauded by the various church papers. The time has come, declared the *Presbyterian Standard*, when the Presbyterian Church should present an undivided front against anything that looks like the observance of Easter.[32]

But the front could not be maintained. Only a few years later "a preacher" was perturbed by advertisements of Southern Presbyterian churches regarding "Easter music," special "floral decorations," Easter sermons, and so forth, such, he indicated, as one might expect to find in Episcopal or Roman Catholic, but not in Presbyterian churches.[33]

"The great Presbyterian churches which have so long stood as the bulwark of orthodoxy and simple worship have to all appearances abandoned the flight and are going over, piece by piece to liberalism and ritualism," lamented the *Christian Observer* a decade later.

"The occasion for this jeremiad was the fact that in a 'conservative Presbyterian church', which the editor had attended on the first Sabbath of April [1912] had been a celebration of Easter, a cross of flowers had occupied a central place on the pulpit, and a gowned choir of twenty-four voices had entered the church in stately procession and passed out [the phrase is his] singing the recessional hymn, while in other Presbyterian churches the Apostles creed was being recited."[34]

"What was happening to cause such consternation in the editor of the Christian Observer?" "First," comments Dr. Kenneth G. Phifer, "there was a recognition of Easter, a tentative step toward an acceptance of the church year. Secondly, the editor detected a symbol, a material symbol in the form of a cross of flowers . . . Further, there were symbolic garments in the form of a vested choir. There were symbolic actions in the processional and recessional. Lastly, there was the spectacle in other churches, if not in the one he attended on that first Sunday in April 1912, of a congregation engaging in the liturgical recitation of a creedal statement. Most of the elements of the liturgical revival of the Protestant Church of the Twentieth century were there in that conservative old Presbyterian church in Louisville, Kentucky."[35]

The opposition to such liturgical renewal was not quickly abandoned.

In 1913 the General Assembly renewed instructions, given in 1899 and 1903, that no Christmas and Easter lessons be published by the Committee on Christian Education for the Sunday schools, and again in 1916 discouraged in every respect the growing tendency of celebrating special days in the Sabbath school other than those recommended by the Assembly.

Every year, lamented the *Presbyterian Standard* in 1922, the churches troubled by the question of Easter observance grows less and less. The other churches observe the day; their Sunday schools lay great stress upon it; the papers, both secular and religious, are full of Easter stories and Easter pictures. "All these facts appeal with tremendous force to the young and the thoughtless, and the man who sets himself against the tide does so at the risk of personal popularity and its consequent loss of influence."[36]

The *Presbyterian Standard*, whose editor acknowledged that he was an old fogy, went down fighting Christmas pageants and Easter observance to the end, as did the *Central Presbyterian*. But the *Presbyterian of the South*, which had absorbed the *Central Presbyterian*, the *Southern Presbyterian*, and the *Southwestern Presbyterian* and was soon to absorb the *Presbyterian Standard* as well, had swung around to the support of what was now clearly the mood of the church. On March 25, 1920, it published a special Easter number, with an editorial commending special Easter services. Without any direction of the Assembly, with Christians of all other churches, declared the editor, we, as individuals, if not as churches, celebrate the birth of the Savior at Christmas. In the same spirit, we can at Easter turn our thoughts to the resurrection from the dead.[37]

The following year, the General Assembly declined to repeat its former injunction against religious exercises on Easter Sunday, and wisely referred the question to each session.[38]

Not until 1950 did the Assembly, in response to an overture from East Hanover Presbytery, positively endorse the religious observance of both Christmas and Easter. On this occasion, without debate, it voted to include not only those dates but also Pentecost in its annual religious calendar, which had included hitherto only Thanksgiving Day, Mother's Day, Reformation Sunday, Stewardship observances, and the like. The church at large took no notice, for both Christmas and Easter had long since received religious recognition by a generation who did not know that it had ever been otherwise; Pentecost Sunday, as before, received little or no recognition.

Choirs had become almost universal by the close of the century, though here and there precentors, paid or unpaid, were still to be found. Differences of opinion remained, however, regarding the function of choirs. Some maintained that their sole function was to lead the congregational singing, and that when they sang alone it was to acquaint the congregation with new hymns which in time the congregation, too, could sing. For others the choirs' "voluntaries" became an end in themselves. The *Southern Presbyterian* complained that many people now came to church for the sole purpose of hearing fine music. "The rest of the service is regarded as a bore and is submitted to only for the songs, solos, chants, and other *performances* of the ecclesiastical orchestra." God could not be pleased with such worship, declared the editor.[39] Some in the 1890's still opposed organs or any other musical instruments in the worship service. Rev. Dr. George A. Blackburn, a pupil and son-in-law of Dr. Girardeau, for 31 years pastor of the Arsenal Hill Church in Columbia, South Carolina, continued unyielding in his opposition until his death (1918). But Dr. Blackburn was the last of his kind, and his peculiarity, we are told, limited no little the extent of his ministerial activity. "There are not many churches," commented the *Presbyterian Standard*, "which would consent to part with an organ to secure a pastor."[40]

For a time it became fashionable for large city churches to hire professional singers, and the solos, duets, and quartettes which were featured gave some basis for the complaints that continued to be raised.

Gradually chorus choirs replaced the paid quartettes, and by 1926 some of these were becoming robed in sober black. "On first thought," wrote Dr. Walter L. Lingle in his popular column in the *Presbyterian of the South*, "they may look like returning to 'the rags of popery'; but on second thought we can see that it puts all members of the choir, rich and poor, on an equality. Besides these black gowns cover a great variety of millinery which might otherwise be distracting to the congregation. For these reasons I have come to look on caps and gowns with more favor than I used to do."[41] The minister, who in the 19th century had been garbed in a Prince Albert coat and a white tie, and in the opening decade of the 20th century in a smart cutaway, followed the example of his choir and also became robed, usually in a simple academic robe, without bands or hood.

For a few years the newly organized Southern Presbyterian Church had used the hymnbook *Psalms and Hymns*, approved by the Old School General Assembly in 1843. Part I contained one or more versions of all the Psalms; Part II included 680 hymns (some mere doggerels) and 16 doxologies. Separate tune books had been published, and the precentor selected from these the tunes to be used for any given Psalm or hymn. In 1867 the Assembly approved a revised edition of this hymnbook, retaining metrical versions of all the Psalms, and an even larger collection of hymns. It, too, was published in word edition only and tune books remained in use.

Hymns in books prepared for the Sunday schools, recalled the *Presbyterian Standard*, were mostly inane, on the supposition that children with less intelligence than grown people required more nonsense. And then suddenly everyone, old and young, began to sing, "Hold the Fort, for I Am Coming" and "The Gates Ajar for Me." The Moody and Sankey hymns became tremendously popular —printed on cheap paper, with catchy popular tunes. They soon superseded the children's books in the Sunday school, and then made their way into the prayer meeting, and the night services which were supposed to be less dignified and formal.[42]

Sentiment was rising now for a hymnbook with tunes matched to the words. In response to repeated overtures, the Assembly in 1882 authorized the Committee of Publication to place its imprint upon a book used by a number of Southern Presbyterian churches— *Psalms and Hymns and Spiritual Songs*, edited by Rev. Charles S. Robinson, a minister of the Presbyterian Church in the U.S.A. This book too began with metrical versions of all the Psalms followed by a large collection of hymns; all were set to music printed on the same page with the words. Among the new hymns contained in this book were "A Mighty Fortress Is Our God"; "He Leadeth Me: O Blessed Thought!"; "Holy, Holy, Holy! Lord God Almighty!"; "I Need Thee Every Hour"; "In the Cross of Christ I Glory"; "Lead, Kindly Light"; "Now Thank We All Our God"; "Onward, Christian Soldiers"; and many others. This book did not prove wholly satisfactory, however, and in 1893 the Assembly gave its approval to a third book, a collection of hymns compiled and edited by Rev. Dr. Robert P. Kerr, pastor of the First Church, Richmond, Virginia, and entitled *Hymns of the Ages*. The Assembly had now placed its imprimatur upon three hymnbooks, the old *Psalms and Hymns* (which had come out now in a musical edition) and the newer books by Robinson and Kerr, no one of which was able to establish itself as the hymnbook of the church. The abandonment of a single hymnbook for the church as a whole opened the way for other hymnbooks that were on the market, and "all sorts of books, the cheapest preferred, were introduced into the churches."[43] It was not uncommon to find in the same city as many different hymnbooks as there were Presbyterian churches in the city.[44]

Mounting dissatisfaction led to the appointment of an ad interim committee which secured the services of two expert musicians and after several years of labor brought forth in 1901 a new hymnbook also entitled *Psalms and Hymns*, which replaced the other three, at least in the larger city churches, and served the church for a full generation. The old name had been retained but fewer Psalms were published, and they were not labeled or separated from the hymns. Dr. J. W. Walden, chairman of the committee charged with preparing the hymnal, explained that the following canons among others had guided the committee: (1) To retain every old hymn of decided merit; (2) To retain a large number of the best versions of the Psalms; (3) To introduce the best of the modern hymns, giving preference to those that were direct inscriptions of praise; (4) To exclude hymns that were purely didactic, personally exaggerated, and highly wrought in sentiment, and all those that had made little or no impression on the mind and heart of the church.[45]

A little more than half of the hymns found in *Hymns of the Ages* were included in the new book; most of the others were more or less familiar as old hymns—about 80 were classed as new hymns. "The new book may be just a little ahead of the church in the class of music it has selected, where the new hymns and tunes are concerned," commented the *Presbyterian Standard*. "But this is a good fault like an oversized coat for a growing boy."[46]

Some were critical. The *Christian Observer* objected to two hymns by Whittier, particularly to the one beginning "Immortal Love, forever full . . ." with its final stanza beginning "O Lord and Master of us all . . ." Whittier, the editor complained, was known as a liberal of the liberals, drawing little distinction between the truths of evangelical religion and those of Unitarianism or Universalism.[47]

Another critic complained that of the 529 tunes nearly 400 were new, and most of these were "English, you know." This music, he acknowledged, was good, strong music, "but we are not educated up to it. It is not American."[48] "It is not to be expected that the same book will suit the fashionable city church and the country congregation," commented Professor James Lewis Howe. "I fear that in spite of all that we can do the largest proportion of our mission churches will continue to use Gospel Hymns."[49] And so they did.

To provide a more popular hymnbook for mission churches and others the Publication Committee issued in 1918 its *Life and Service Hymns*, which contained a large proportion of "classic" hymns along with numerous hymns of evangelistic character. Some of these were old gospel hymns; some new favorites introduced by popular evangelists of the day. *Premier Hymns*, issued in 1926, served the same general purpose, assembling, so it was claimed, a happy balance of the stately hymns of the church in all ages combined with familiar gospel hymns. So in Sunday school, young people's conferences, and the like, many of the cheaper hymns, which would not be heard in the larger city churches, continued to be sung.

In response to many requests from presbyteries and individuals, the General Assembly in May 1925 appointed a committee to prepare a more acceptable hymnbook for the church. Among other things, the Assembly directed that the many unused hymns and tunes in the older book be omitted, that new hymns of merit be included, that the words of all hymns be printed within the music score, that "Amen" should be added to each hymn (an innovation to which some strongly objected), and that Scripture reading for responsive reading should be included. This book, *The Presbyterian Hymnal*, appeared in 1927; it included 500 hymns, less than 300 of which were taken from the old book, which had carried a total of 700 hymns. A number of the new hymns were listed under two topics, hardly represented in the older books, which had more recently come to engage the interest of the church—"Service" and "Brotherhood." New hymns under the first topic included Washington Gladden's "O Master, Let Me Walk with Thee" and William Pierson Merrill's "Rise Up, O Men of God"; under "Brotherhood" were found "Teach Us, O Lord,

True Brotherhood," "In Christ There Is No East or West," and "The Light of God Is Falling." Phillips Brooks' familiar "O Little Town of Bethlehem" appeared for the first time in the church's hymnbook. Other welcome additions were "Lead On, O King Eternal," "O Beautiful for Spacious Skies," Kipling's Recessional (said to be a great favorite among the young people), and "O Master Workman of the Race." This book, which retained a number of the higher class gospel hymns, was a great advance over the previous hymnbooks of the church and served the church for another generation.

Throughout the period the exposition of the Word of God remained the central element in the church's worship. At the second service on the Sabbath, even when the time came that few were present but church members, it was apt to have more of an evangelical message. At the midweek service it became a sermonette, or a running exposition or devotional treatment of a particular passage of Scripture, but even if other features were introduced the Word remained at the heart of the service.

Charles L. King, the young pastor of Grace Covenant Church, Richmond, Virginia, preached the dedicatory sermon at the opening of the church's beautiful new auditorium. In his sermon he laid emphasis on the point that the pulpit of the new church was dedicated not to addresses on welfare movements or world reforms, but to the proclamation of the age-old and ever-new truth that the regeneration of the individual by the power of the Holy Spirit, living faith in the divine Savior of mankind, and conduct shaped according to the principles of the master teacher were the only solvents for the ills of the individual or society and of the world. This, in capsule form, had been the message of the Southern Presbyterian pulpit and would so remain. Dr. King himself was then and has remained to the present time a great expository preacher. This does not seem to have been true of the Southern Presbyterian pulpit as a whole. But the sermons were almost always biblical, and based on a text, which gave the preacher his theme for the occasion. Whatever the starting point, most sermons ended with a presentation of the gospel, God's redeeming love in Jesus Christ. The preacher pointed his hearers to Christ who forgives, heals, comforts, invites, strengthens, and gives eternal life. The final call was usually to acceptance or commitment.

Many lamented the decline of doctrinal preaching. "The preacher of today addresses an audience of a different temper than that of bygone days," explained the *Christian Observer* shortly after the turn of the century. "This makes a difference in two ways. As the congregation is not so spiritual the preacher feels tempted to preach on subjects that can be grasped without an effort, and he feels a lack of sympathy on doctrinal themes which would spur him to a higher flight." The change had begun, the editor suggested, about 30 years before, when the effort became almost general to win men to repentance by presenting the love of God to the exclusion of preaching sin and guilt.[50]

Doctrinal preaching may have declined, but it had not ceased, and sermons were still heard in defense of the peculiar Presbyterian tenets. There were frequent articles on Presbyterian beliefs in the church press.

Dr. Givens Brown Strickler (1840-1913), pastor of a large rural church in the Valley of Virginia, then of the important Central Presbyterian Church in Atlanta, and finally Professor of Systematic Theology in Union Seminary, regarded by many as the most powerful preacher in the Southern Presbyterian Church, was preeminently a preacher of doctrine—one who appealed to the most highly educated and also to those of little education. And the doctrine he preached was good old-fashioned Calvinism. The preaching of doctrine, however, was not for Dr. Strickler an end in itself; it emphasized rather the urgency of a decision for Christ. "He preached for the conversion of his hearers and constantly came back to the call for a decision. This was not always just a call to the unconverted, but often a plea for the Christian's decision for deeper commitment."[51]

One of the glaring omissions in Dr. Strickler's preaching, it has been pointed out, is the absence of ethical preaching, that is, applying his message to individual and community social issues. It is not "that he is blind to such. It was just that he chose to approach such indirectly, or as he states the matter, 'we are, in the most effective way, preaching (on matters of moral reform) all the time. We are seeking to bring them under the power of the Gospel; we are seeking to implant in them by regeneration the principles of righteousness and holiness, and if we can do that then moral reform in all the directions in which it is desired, in temperance, in politics, in business, will follow as the certain and inevitable result.' "[52]

Unfortunately the "glaring omission" in Dr. Strickler's preaching is present in Southern Presbyterian preaching as a whole through this period as it had been from the beginning. Dr. Strickler's mistaken assumption that moral reform is the automatic fruit of regeneration, belied by the evidence all about him, and the whole of Christian history, was shared by the vast majority of his contemporaries. Southern Presbyterian ministers preached the evangelical gospel convicting men of sin, pointing them to Christ, confirming them in the faith, comforting them in sorrow, strengthening them for the battles of life, setting before them high personal ideals, planting seeds which would bring forth "the fruit of the Spirit" (Gal. 5:22-23), but not a gospel which pricked the conscience regarding the deeply entrenched wrongs of Southern society or which inspired them to change in any serious way the social inequities of their day.

In 1896 the Publication Committee issued a collection of sermons by ministers of the Southern Presbyterian Church entitled *Southern Presbyterian Pulpit,* 33 sermons in all by as many leaders of the church's pulpit. Included were all the founding fathers still actively at work, B. M. Palmer, R. L. Dabney, Moses D. Hoge, Joseph R. Wilson, John L. Girardeau; leading pulpiteers of the second generation, such as G. B. Strickler, Robert P. Kerr, W. W. Moore, J. R. Howerton, and C. R. Hemphill; and a few of the younger men whose stars were rising above the horizon, like James I. Vance. The sermons deal helpfully with various aspects of personal religion, but there is no reference to the white man's obligation to the black man, no recognition in fact there was a racial question in the South, though lynchings continued to increase, and the Jim Crow mentality was becoming a part of the Southern way of life. In 1929 appeared another volume entitled *The Southern Presbyterian Pulpit*—it contained 24 sermons by men occupying the leading pulpits of the denomination. A war had been recently fought to make the world safe for democracy. Negroes were growing restless, and sensitive Southerners were giving consideration to a problem that now demanded attention. But in this new collection of sermons, as in the first, there is no reference to race (except in one fleeting instance). The burden of the sermons was rather what Charles L. Goodall in a foreword describes as "the eternal verities," "a dateless religion, one that is 'the same yesterday, today and forever.'" This was the type of sermon expected of a Southern Presbyterian minister; the long-accepted doctrine of the spirituality (nonsecular character) of the church would permit no other, unless it be in general, not specific, terms.

One sermon in the 1928 volume by Dr. D. Clay Lilly emphasized a theme that would be heard more frequently in the years ahead. "The attitude of the public toward the Church has changed very much in the last few decades," began Dr. Lilly. "What was once a feeling of appreciation and an attitude of deference has changed to a position of inquiry which challenges the worth of the Church, its place in life, and asks very frankly whether it is a worthwhile institution. There is a wide demand that the Church show its faith by its works. Students of social conditions call upon it to make good its claim of possessing the remedy for the ills of our common life, while less reverent voices speak of it as a cumberer of the ground or even as a parasite feeding, to no purpose, on the resources of a burdened humanity."[53]

To meet this charge Dr. Lilly went on to point out the church must be concerned not only with spiritual and moral issues, but also with social, industrial, economic, civic, and political questions of the day. "It is ours," he declared, "to take the truths of the Bible and apply them to: capital and labor, monopolies and profits, hours of work per day, child labor, strikes and lockouts, poverty and wealth ... The Church is interested in the questions of immigration, international relationships, international good will. It has a real message about racial unity. It has a high service to render in the prevention of war and in the preservation of world peace."[54]

On May 12, 1931, Dr. George L. Bitzer, pastor of the Presbyterian Church, Holly Springs, Mississippi, returned after 46 years in the ministry to deliver the annual alumni address at the commencement of Austin Theological Seminary. "We are living in a difficult time for the evangelical minister, a time of change and of necessary readjustments," he began and went on to point out that it was impossible for the Presbyterian Church to remain static in a changing world. Church and ministry, he noted, were in fact changing far more than many realized. Comparing the two volumes of sermons from Southern Presbyterian pulpits, the one in 1896, the other in 1929, Dr. Bitzer commented on some of the changes in the minister's message that were discernible. Among them the fact that the chief stress in preaching was no longer upon justification by faith alone; that equal stress was now placed upon sanctification, the subjective aspects of redemption; and again the fact that church and state were no longer regarded as so widely separated that ministers could not refer to social responsibilities. The old time Calvinism, Dr. Bitzer indicated, had lost its appeal. "Is there a personal God?" "If so, does he answer prayer?" "Is there a life beyond?" "Are we real personalities, or mere cogs in the World Wheel?" These, he stated, were questions that men in the street were now asking, and it was to such questions that sermons must now be directed. Dr. Bitzer urged young ministers to make use of the new scientific thought of the day. "I think the world never needed ministers more than now," he concluded, "ministers who do their own thinking, and speak with the power of personal conviction, and with the passion of a great love. Men who study the problems of the time, and bring to doubt-ridden men a Gospel message in terms of the thinking of today."[55]

Two years earlier, Dr. Harris E. Kirk, addressing the General Assembly as its retiring Moderator, declared:

> The weakness of the church at the close of the nineteenth century . . . was its acceptance of the ideal of comfortableness, in which religious peace was identified with middle class contentment. To such a temperament change of any kind is most disturbing. But the age of comfortableness is gone, for this generation, gone forever . . . The nineteenth century church accepted comfortableness because it was still living in undisturbed areas; but the church in the twentieth century faces change in all phases of society. The great inertias, like race and sex, are changing, and no one can predict the character of the world in the immediate future . . . [The church] must not fear alterations in the face of society . . . It must not be afraid of living thought; it must be generous in accepting truth from any quarter; it must never retreat towards any kind of shelter in the interest of living safely. It must wholeheartedly determine to live dangerously; keep in close contact with living generations and advance with the moving tide. . . .[56]

The tide was moving; and however slowly, however hesitatingly, the Presbyterian Church in the United States was beginning to move with it.

Part 2

INTO THE MAIN STREAM

XIV

Carrying the Program

In the 1870's and early 1880's the church became greatly agitated over a proposed program of retrenchment and reform. Older leaders of the church, recalling Thornwell's strictures against boards, had become concerned over the growing powers of the Executive Committees. Some went so far as to propose that all paid secretaries be abolished. Others urged that the Committee on Education operate without a paid executive—its one function being to receive funds from the stronger presbyteries for distribution to ministerial candidates in the weaker presbyteries—and that the Committee on Home Missions retain its secretary, but that each presbytery gather and expend its own funds. The single function of the Executive Committee on Home Missions would be to receive funds from the stronger presbyteries for distribution among weaker presbyteries on the frontier.

The program of retrenchment and reform offered to the General Assembly of 1881 failed of adoption, but fear of centralized authority as exercised by the Assembly's agencies lingered on. Inevitably, however, the Executive Committees expanded their functions, and the General Assembly and its agencies assumed a larger role in the life of the church.

These enlarged functions were made possible only by the increasing giving of the people—a giving that constantly fell short of what was desired and which therefore needed to be constantly stimulated.

Some continued to defend the older method of raising funds through church fairs and suppers as a supplementary measure. "The church festival," wrote an opponent of the practice, "has become an established and conspicuous factor in modern religious activity. At first much opposed in its various forms of suppers, bazaars, lectures, and theatricals, the opening century finds it adopted in almost the entire church, Catholic and Protestant."[1]

The 1916 General Assembly appointed an ad interim committee to study and report on the matter of church entertainments and kindred ways of raising money for the church. The committee recommended and the Assembly adopted a statement, "Whereas, It appears to have become quite common for our people to secure money for church purposes by concerts, suppers, etc., be it Resolved, that the General Assembly advise against all such means for securing money to be used in the Master's work. This advice is given because we believe that the Lord has ordained that giving should be an act of worship, and thus a means of grace."[2] This resolution was only a reaffirmation of a deliverance approved in 1888 and again in 1891; it expressed what had gradually become the general sentiment of the church.[3]

Pew renting was abandoned by many, though not all, of the large city churches, in the 1890's. It remained one of the easiest ways to raise money, but was said to discourage the general public from attending the worship services, to favor the rich at the expense of the poor, and to do nothing to cultivate the grace of giving.

Formerly in the cities, churches depended on pew rents and in the country on subscription lists, which placed the subscriber under not only a moral but a legal obligation to pay so much per annum for the maintenance of the church work, recalled the *Christian Observer*. "This money was collected by a collector, going from house to house. Then, in a better day for the church, the envelope system was devised. It relieves the necessity of having any 'collectors' to visit the people at their homes, for under it the members bring their contributions to church with them in an envelope and simply drop it into the collection basket. Under this plan the people have contributed quite as largely, in proportion to their means, and perhaps more largely than under the old plan. There has been much less friction, and more appreciation of the fact that giving to the Lord's cause is an *act of worship*."[4]

Under the envelope system, rapidly becoming universal, ordinary offerings went to the pastor's salary and for the contingent expenses of the local church. Offerings for the Assembly's benevolent causes were received on specially designated Sundays, usually the last day of the month, designated by the General Assembly for this particular cause. These benevolent offerings were supplemented by contributions made through missionary societies, Sabbath schools, and other sources.

Before 1889 the special collections for benevolences were received on the average about every two months; after this date there were collections every month. In other words, each month was assigned to one particular cause, and the Executive Committees through their secretaries and the pastors and boards of deacons in the local churches were expected to present the claims for each cause in its assigned period.

As time passed dissatisfaction with this procedure mounted. As a "village pastor" complained:

1. It necessitates in all of our churches an unceasing call for money. A pastor is required to present the cause of each month at the proper time, and it sometimes happens that there are two causes to be presented in a single month. A simple announcement is a sure means of inducing a small collection.

2. The number of the causes and the frequency of their presentation breeds confusion. Our three-headed home mission plan is a marvel of unnecessary complexity. The invalid fund is a sentimental misnomer which needs to be explained over and over again. Sustentation is an antiquated piece of bombast. Colored evangelization is a bugbear, which many of our pastors are afraid to speak of.

3. Important causes suffer because of the season of the year when the collection is taken. Our city churches do not give as much as they might to the invalid fund because many of the wealthier people are out of the city in July. Our country churches do not give as much as they ought to Foreign Missions because one collection is taken in May when farmers are at their busiest with little money to spare, and the other in October when cotton-picking is at its height. Or it may be the weather: a hard rain, a cold wave, or intense heat on a Sunday assigned for a particular cause may lead to a drop in the offering.[5]

Many churches made no contribution at all to one cause or another. Thus in 1901, 1,800 churches out of the 2,991 churches in the Assembly made no contribution to ministerial relief; 1,860 churches made no gift to the publication and colportage cause.[6]

By 1909 the number of special collections had increased to 16. The next year came the breakthrough, a change in method for which there had long been a clamor, the beginning of a period of rapid growth in the benevolent offerings of Southern Presbyterians.

The General Assembly that year (1910) adopted the report of an ad interim committee which provided (1) that the number of Executive Committees be reduced to four—Foreign Missions, Home Missions, Ministerial Education and Relief, and Publication and Sabbath Schools; (2) that the Assembly's Standing Committee on Systematic Beneficence be made a Permanent Committee with the responsibility of meeting with the Executive Secretaries of these committees annually to consider the total work of the church and of presenting to the General Assembly the annual reports and financial askings of the four Executive Committees with recommendations; and (3) that a new method for raising funds for the Assembly's causes be set in operation. This plan, drawn from the successful experience of other churches, notably the Presbyterian Church in the U.S.A., separated the stated beneficences of the church at large from current expenses and particular interests of the local church. Instead of depending on special Sabbath collections for the benevolent causes, there was to be an Every Member Canvass in which each member would be asked to subscribe an amount to be paid at stated periods, weekly if possible, through duplex envelopes or some other system approved by the session.[7]

Out of this initial proposal came the following year the church's benevolent budget. The plan provided for the Systematic Beneficence Committee to recommend to the General Assembly each year the minimum amount needed for the total benevolent program of the church, and to apportion and recommend to the synods the quota to be raised according to the relative strength of each. The synods were to apportion and recommend to the presbyteries the amount each was to raise for both the Assembly's and synod's benevolences, and the presbyteries, adding their own benevolences, were to do likewise for the local churches.[8]

The plan opposed at first by some as new, radical, revolutionary, and dangerous met with general approval, and with modifications remains the basis of the church's present organization and method.

Promotion of the Every Member Canvass was carried on by the four Executive Committees, in cooperation with the Laymen's Missionary Movement, through a special campaign committee on Evangelism and Stewardship (later the Campaign Committee on Stewardship). Rev. R. L. Walkup of Mississippi served as secretary of this committee from 1915 until his death in 1918 and was primarily responsible for the intensive educational campaign on "stewardship" carried on throughout the church during this period. "In only two or three brief periods of the Church's history," declared the committee, "namely: in the apostolic days, [not] again until about the middle of the nineteenth century for a very brief period, and then not again until just now, has the great question of stewardship ever been seriously studied."[9]

One question keenly debated throughout this period, for a full generation and more, was that regarding the tithe—whether or not it was a binding obligation on all Christians. In 1889 the General

Assembly asked the presbyteries for an expression of their opinion. Of the 68 presbyteries reporting, 51 held that the law of the tithe was not binding under the New Testament dispensation; ten regarded it as still binding; one was unclear; and six declined to express an opinion. The question continued to arise. In 1908 the Committee on Systematic Beneficence declared that the tithe was "God's ordained plan" for the raising of church money. This led to prolonged discussion and the appointment of an ad interim committee to report back to the following Assembly. This Assembly, "while encouraging and even enjoining the personal adoption of some definite proportion as a minimum," stated that it did not feel authorized to fix that proportion which, under the Gospel, had been left to the individual's enlightened conscience.[10]

By 1915, five years after the Every Member Canvass plan had been adopted, approximately one-third of the churches in the Assembly were making such a canvass. These churches contributed 65 percent of all the church's benevolences, though many of the largest and most generous churches in the Assembly had not yet accepted the plan. The number of churches attempting an Every Member Canvass increased thereafter year by year, and it was in these churches that the largest increase in giving occurred. In 1921 Dr. W. L. Lingle noted that the 1910 reorganization, as revised and improved from time to time, had "absolutely revolutionized" the financial aspects of the church's work. Figures illustrate the progress which had been made:

	1910	1921
Assembly's Foreign Missions	$420,602	$1,153,629
Assembly's Home Missions	$106,042	$536,836
Local Home Missions	$232,231	$900,000
Publications, Sabbath School	$20,113	$100,028
Total for All Causes	$3,855,913	$12,124,891

Capitalizing on the new energy released by World War I the church embarked on a new movement of advance. It was a day of "Forward Movements." The Northern Presbyterian Church had its "New Era Movement"; the Methodists, their "Centenary Movement"; the Baptists, their "$75,000,000 Campaign." The Stewardship Committee of the Southern Presbyterian Church launched its forward movement with a three million dollar campaign for benevolences in the year 1917. Encouraged by the church's response to this movement the committee the following year laid out for the Assembly's approval a three-year financial program for an aggregate of twelve million dollars beginning with three and a half million and increasing it by half a million for each of the two succeeding years. In addition to the financial goals the committee outlined an eight point plan of advance entitled the Presbyterian Progressive Program. The church's benevolent giving for the next three years surpassed all previous records; the per capita giving of Southern Presbyterians for benevolences now topped that of all larger Protestant bodies.

One grandiose enterprise in which the Presbyterian Church U. S. participated, the idea of which it had indeed originated, did not fare so well. The Interchurch World Movement, hailed by Dr. John R. Mott as one of the most significant movements of modern times, originated in the Executive Committee of Foreign Missions of the Southern Presbyterian Church, meeting one day after the great World War came to an end. It received quick and unanimous endorsement by influential Protestant leaders. Its purpose was to develop a plan whereby the evangelical churches of North America could cooperate in carrying out their educational, missionary, and benevolent programs. It called for a combined survey of the fields of need both at home and abroad, a combined educational campaign to make these needs known to the church, a combined financial campaign to secure the funds required, and a combined treasurer to distribute the funds received on a basis of approved estimates. Direction of the movement was entrusted to a council of 100 selected by the various boards of the participating denominations. An expensive survey was made. But the men of means who, it had been thought, would rather give to the general work of all the churches than to that of one denomination did not respond as anticipated. The project had to be abandoned for lack of funds. A heavy debt remained to be paid off gradually over a period of years.

"The Interchurch World Movement failed to reach its objectives," Dr. James I. Vance, chairman of the Executive Committee of World Missions, generally regarded as the father of the movement, commented, "but it did not fail. It carried the idea of a unified and coordinated Protestantism further than it had been carried before. It has attempted big things and partly accomplished them. Its surveys, while far from complete, are nevertheless, as they stand, the most valuable the church has ever secured. . . . The Movement has demonstrated that the churches must get together. . . . World conditions call for a church that can function at its best. . . . We cannot lie back and say, 'Every denomination for itself.' We must get together. Cooperation is the strategy of victory."[11] This was a new note to be sounded in the Southern Presbyterian Church.

For ten years and more there had been a steady, even "phenomenal" increase in the church's benevolent giving. Credit for this increase was commonly given to the instruction on stewardship given during this period; but, as pointed out by Dr. R. B. Woodworth, the church's increase in membership and wealth must also be taken into account. There was a growing feeling, however, that too much money was being spent on overhead; that there was unnecessary competition for funds—particularly in connection with designated gifts; that jealousy had arisen among the executive secretaries; that they were no longer able to work in harmony, on the contrary, that they were actually arrayed against each other. "There are too many people in our ministry and church membership," wrote Dr. J. Sprole Lyons, "who are partisans of special causes, they are *lop-sided* towards Home Missions or Foreign Missions, and are willing to let other causes get along as best they can."[12] The Assembly's call to raise an equipment fund of $500,000 a year for ten years failed to arouse the enthusiasm of the church and had to be modified. Many felt that the church had undertaken too ambitious a program, and this sentiment grew as a decline in the church's giving (an anticipation of the coming Depression) became apparent.

In response to numerous overtures, the General Assembly of 1926 appointed a survey committee to bring in recommendations. "Overlapping," "Efficiency," "Economy," and "Adjustment" were the prominent words in the overtures and in the General Assembly's action. Accepting the committee's report the following year, the Assembly set up a committee of 44 to be known as the Committee on the Assembly's Work, to whom was entrusted administration of the total benevolent work of the church. The responsibilities of the former executive and promotional committees were entrusted to subcommittees of the one great committee, which sought to give unity and effectiveness to the benevolent work of the Assembly as a whole. The unseemly competition among the executive agencies was ended, but the church had expected economies which could not be effected, and, when the great Depression hit and incomes were drastically reduced and heavy debts incurred, it became increasingly clear that the burden was too heavy for any single committee to shoulder. After a four-year trial the Committee on the Assembly's Work was abolished; the four Executive Committees—Foreign Missions, Home Missions, Religious Education, and Christian Education and Ministerial Relief—once more came into being, vested with full responsibility for the conduct of the work entrusted to them. The Assembly sought to retain the values of the former Committee on the Assembly's

Work by erecting a new Commitee on Stewardship and Finance, consisting of representatives from the four Executive Committees and other agencies—rather than representatives of the various synods as heretofore. The new Stewardship Committee was to assemble, review, and submit to the Assembly the annual budget for its committee and agencies and to handle all matters involving inter-committee cooperation in finance, education, and promotion.

On recommendation of this committee, the Assembly dropped what had now become an empty phrase—the Presbyterian Progressive Program—replacing it with the Church's Program. The name "Presbyterian Progressive Program," as Dr. J. M. Walker pointed out, suggested that the church was marching under a banner calling for progress. He recalled the increasing goals: $2,750,000; $3,000,000; $3,500,000; $4,000,000; $4,500,000. "Each year found us pressing on, new lands being taken for Christ, new missionaries being sent out . . . It is hardly conceivable that these things were hampering in our church less than ten years ago." What had happened? The general explanation was that because of "the Depression that is upon us, and which has been getting worse from year to year, our receipts have been falling off, so as to make it absolutely necessary that we curtail our work and reduce our expenditure. [This] has been going on now for so long a time that it is perfectly foolish to speak any longer about our church as a *Progressive* Program." It would be truer to the facts, said Dr. Walker, to call it "the Presbyterian Regressive Program."[13]

More and more emphasis was now placed upon the tithe as the minimum of Christian giving. "In no case," declared the 1924 General Assembly, "does the Bible name a smaller proportion than the tithe."[14] In 1934 ministers and church officers were urged to conduct an active campaign for tithers and proportionate givers as the only solution for the financial problems of the church.[15] In this year the Assembly endorsed what had come to be known as the Belmont Covenant Plan, in which church members covenanted to give a tithe for a definite period of time. It spread widely through the church and led many who tithed for a period to adopt this practice as a permanent principle. In 1943 the Assembly declared that the Bible taught that it was every man's duty to set aside a definite portion of his income, "beginning with one-tenth as belonging peculiarly to God . . ."[16] For many the tithe had come to be regarded as a means to material as well as spiritual enrichment (as suggested in Malachi 3:10). This the church officially denied, and likewise that it was a legal obligation. But it continued to teach that for the Christian the tithe should be accepted as a "divinely revealed" minimum[17]; and for a time a probationary "Prove God Period" was encouraged which suggested, to say the least, that tithing would be followed by some marked evidence of the divine favor.[18]

Gradually the executive agencies retired the indebtedness which had accrued during the Depression years; slowly the benevolent program gathered new momentum. Following World War II came the industrial development of the South, the growth of its cities, and a rapid gain in population. To meet the needs of the church the Assembly in 1947 gave hearty and unanimous endorsement to a new—five year—Program of Progress, covering a wide range of objectives, spiritual, educational, and financial, including a goal of $7,250,000, to be raised during the five-year period as a capital fund of the Assembly's causes over and above the regular budget. While the full hopes of the five-year effort were not realized, there were commendable gains: an increase in the church's membership of 105,000; 267 new churches organized, an average of more than one new church each week; a decided increase in Sunday school enrollment (from 470,000 in 1948 to 563,000 in 1952). Gifts in 1948 totaled more than 30 million dollars and in the church year 1951-1952 almost 48 million. Cash credited to the Program of Progress goals was more than five million dollars. The giving during the previous year had been, both as to total amount and in per capita giving, the highest in the history of the denomination.[19] "God is pouring out upon our people such a spirit of liberality as he poured out upon the churches of Macedonia," declared the Stewardship Committee.[20] It may be recalled that growth in church membership during the quarter century 1925-1950 had been 50 percent, only half that reported by Southern Baptists, but higher than that of most major Protestant denominations.

In 1910 the report of an ad interim committee on the coordination of Executive Committees had been adopted placing the Assembly's benevolent work in the hands of four major committees. Since that time new functions had been added, and the agencies of the church—21 executive and permanent committees in all—had multiplied. In 1947 the General Assembly recorded its conviction that the time had come for a careful and comprehensive study of the many executive, administrative, and promotional committees and agencies to the end that greater economy, foresight, and effectiveness might be achieved. An ad interim committee was appointed with this purpose in view.

The committee employed a management engineer to make a careful survey of all Assembly agencies and operations and after two years of careful study presented its report, drawn from a mass of accumulated material, in a printed booklet of 107 pages. To the surprise of everyone, the Assembly promptly adopted the report with only slight amendments, and by an overwhelming vote.

Among the important changes effected were the following:

1. Names were changed from Executive Committees to Boards. Dr. J. H. Thornwell, who more than any other had set the lines which the Southern Presbyterian Church followed for the next three generations, had opposed the semiautonomous Boards which were found at the time in the mother church; in lieu thereof the Southern Church had erected "Executive Committees" which the General Assembly kept under close surveillance. Irrational prejudice against the word "Board" continued long after the practical differences between Northern Boards and Southern Executive Committees had become erased. Now at last the more cumbersome word was dropped, and the Southern Assembly adopted the generally accepted nomenclature. A new generation had arisen to whom the disputes of yesterday were unknown.

2. The Boards—five in all—were authorized to divide their responsibilities into divisions and to appoint councils, composed of members of the Board and others qualified to render helpful service in particular areas of the division's responsibility. Board members, who heretofore for all practical purposes had held life tenure, were now restricted to three terms of three years each. Interim appointments, which had made the Executive Committees almost self-perpetuating, were forbidden. Executive secretaries, heretofore elected by the General Assembly and responsible to it, were now to be elected by and responsible to the Board. A Permanent Nominating Committee was set up to give careful thought to appointees to all Assembly agencies, and no person was to serve more than one agency at a time. These changes made for more democracy, for greater flexibility, and for more competent oversight of the church's work.

The Executive Committee of Foreign Missions now became the Board of World Missions, responsible also for overseas relief and rehabilitation.

A Board of Church Extension was erected, responsible for the work of Home Missions, Evangelism, Radio, Negro Work, and Christian Relations—each of which had previously been assigned to its own independent agency; it was also given responsibility for the Country Church, for Sunday School Extension, and for chaplains in the armed forces heretofore borne by the Committee of Religious Education; a new department of Urban Church was recommended.

The Board of Education (later renamed Christian Education) assumed responsibility for the church's total educational program—the old work of "Religious Education" (Sunday schools, young people's organizations, and publication) to which was added responsibility for Higher Education and for the student work heretofore carried by the Executive Committee on Christian Education.

The old Executive Committee of Christian Education, relieved now of its responsibility for Higher Education, became the Board of Annuities and Relief. It was expected to explore the possibility of group insurance for ministers and lay workers.

The Board of Women's Work, which to this time had received its financial support from the other Executive Agencies (reminiscent of its original purpose to promote the benevolent program of the church) now drew its support from a general fund of the church—a further recognition of its coordinate status with the other major Boards of the church.

The Office of the General Assembly was established, with expanded functions and duties lodged in its chief administrative officer, the Stated Clerk, who until this time had done little more than preserve the Assembly's records. This office now became directly responsible to a Permanent Committee on Assembly Operation rather than to the General Assembly itself. New rules were set up for the operation of the Assembly which added much to its efficiency. It was suggested that more use be made of the Assembly's Moderator—a "public relations man" of great potentialities for good in the life of the church—during his term of office.

The Permanent Committee on Cooperation and Union became the liaison agency between the church and other denominations and interdenominational agencies.

The Permanent Judicial Committee—soon to become the Permanent Judicial Commission—was strengthened and its powers extended.

A General Council was erected in place of the old Stewardship Committee and given additional responsibility for the total program of the church. For 40 years the church had been feeling its way toward a more unified operation. The first step in this direction had been taken in 1910 when a Permanent Committee on Systematic Beneficence was erected—with primary responsibility for drawing up an Assembly's budget—the germ at least of a program. Nine years later this committee was combined with the Campaign Committee on Evangelism and Stewardship, responsible for promotion of the church's program in these two important areas of the church's life. In 1927 this agency became a subcommittee within the Committee on Assembly's Work. Four years later it was again an independent agency, known first as the Committee on Stewardship and Finance, later as simply the Committee on Stewardship. The membership of this committee (drawn at times exclusively from the major agencies, at times altogether apart from the agencies, and at others in varying proportions from one and the other), along with its functions, had varied through the years. By the time of the reorganization its business, among other things, was to draw up the General Assembly budget, to promote stewardship, to coordinate the church's program, to handle the publicity of the General Assembly, to give technical supervision to the Program of Progress, and to make recommendations to the General Assembly regarding the total program of the church.[21]

It was, however, unable to discharge the full responsibility laid upon it; and it did not attempt to make recommendations to the General Assembly regarding the total program of the church. To meet these needs more adequately a General Council was now organized with larger representation from the church at large, and with its responsibilities distributed among four committees:

First, a Budget Committee. The need here was for a real budget, with percentages allotted on the basis of need. The previous practice, as the ad interim committee pointed out, made income depend largely on the energy, popularity, and appeals of the secretary and its staff; new causes and those without a staff were at a disadvantage.

Second, a Program Committee. There had been a planning committee composed of key employees of the major agencies which attempted to serve as a clearinghouse for these agencies and to coordinate their programs, but such a committee was not prepared for the long-range planning which was needed. The new Program Committee was composed of selected members of the General Council and additional ministers and laymen chosen, with this end in view, for their particular skills and qualifications.

Third, a Publicity Committee. The one staff member responsible for Assembly publicity had not been able to accomplish what was needed. The new committee was expected to coordinate the work of and to establish policies for the publicity phase of the General Assembly and of its various Boards and agencies.

Fourth, a Research Committee. "If the General Council is to give the church the guidance and counsel that it needs," said the ad interim committee, "it must have the services of men skilled in research and able to project themselves far into the future. There should be some group, freed from other responsibilities that will limit their vision, whose function will be to analyze present problems and trends in church and state, keep abreast of developments in other denominations, study the operations of our own agencies, and make long range plans for 5, 10, 25, 50 and even 100 years . . ." It recommended that a Research Committee be appointed with such ends in view, and that the General Council consider the advisability of electing a Director of Research.

In the years following the reorganization some changes in the overall organization have naturally been found desirable.

Of particular significance has been the development of and increasing attention given to Television, Radio, and Audio-Visuals. In 1943 an ad interim committee on radio, with Rev. John M. Alexander, D.D., as chairman, was established to study and report; three years later Dr. Alexander reported that the Southern Religious Radio Conference had been formed in cooperation with the Baptist and Methodist Churches (joined a little later by the Protestant Episcopal and the United Lutheran Church) and that the "Presbyterian Hour" was being heard through its facilities on a network of 39 stations from Baltimore to Corpus Christi. Six years later the Presbyterian Hour was being heard over 70 stations; a second program, "Presbyterian Laymen Speak," over 130 stations; and individual programs over more than 200 stations. The Presbyterian Hour network was said to offer the best coverage of any network religious broadcast in the South, and compared favorably with the largest non-commercial network acceptances in the nation. The Southern Religious Radio Conference was the first of its kind in the nation, and was widely hailed by leaders in radio broadcasting as a landmark in the field of interchurch cooperation.

In 1950, the year in which the Permanent Radio Committee became a division within the Board of Church Extension, a Protestant Radio Center, with Dr. Alexander as Director, opened with the finest broadcasting and transcription available, on the campus of Agnes Scott College. Three years later, under Dr. Alexander's guidance, a site had been secured, the money raised, and ground broken for the first and only interdenominationally owned Protestant Radio Center in the nation. When Dr. Alexander died in 1957 the Radio Center was his monument, one of which the church could well be proud. The next year the Division of Radio and Television was removed from the Board of Church Extension and set up as a Permanent Committee on Television, Radio, and Audio-Visuals (TRAV) responsible to the General Assembly.

The most popular radio preacher in the Southern Presbyterian Church was Dr. John A. Redhead, pastor of the First Presbyterian Church, Greensboro, North Carolina. Dr. Redhead appeared regularly, year after year, on a program produced at the Radio Center in Atlanta, but aired on the Protestant Hour, over a national hookup. From the number of requests received for his messages, he appeared to be the most popular preacher heard on this worldwide network. More than 22,000 copies of a single sermon had been distributed the preceding year, it was reported to the 1960 General Assembly, and the average number was three thousand. In view of the times Dr. Redhead had spoken over the Protestant Hour and the broad coverage of the network, including the Armed Forces Radio Service, the Greensboro minister was acclaimed as the most listened to Presbyterian minister of all times.[22]

From time to time the church had been troubled by what seemed to be an extravagant claim for "faith-healing." In 1954 the General Assembly received an overture from the Presbytery of Brazos which noted that the "teaching and practice of so-called 'faith-healing' or 'divine healing'" was not only the practice of many of the non-established and traditional churches, but also increasingly was drawing attention among many of "our constituency." An ad interim committee was appointed to make a thorough study of this matter and bring in a written report of its findings to the General Assembly.

The ad interim committee, composed of pastors, physicians, theologians, and men in the field of physical and mental therapy, brought in a long and careful report which stated that "God is concerned with the whole nature of man. . . . That desire for healing has led to some interpretations of faith which find no support in the scriptures. . . . That it places a false limitation upon the power of God to say that if healing is mediated through the ministry of a physician or surgeon or psychiatrist, it is therefore less from God than healing which comes through less visible means. . . . It is not unreasonable to believe, that prayer may be . . . one of the conditions through which God sends his healing. . . ."[23]

The committee was continued and became in time a permanent committee, working for better understanding between ministers and medical men, holding seminars, and reporting annually to the General Assembly on the subject of religion and health. In 1967 the committee was abolished and its responsibilities transferred to the old Board of Church Extension, renamed this year the Board of National Ministries.

An earlier responsibility assigned to the Board of Church Extension was that of Homes and Christian Welfare. The assignment grew out of the growing interest in homes for the aging. A few synods had erected such homes, and others were being planned. In response to an overture from Nashville Presbytery the 1956 General Assembly appointed an ad interim committee to study the needs for Presbyterian hospitals and homes, for children as well as the aging, the best type of home, and the responsibility of the General Assembly in this area.

The following year the Assembly unanimously approved as a Christian ministry the establishment of Presbyterian homes for the aging and increased activity in this field on the part of synods, presbyteries, and local church groups; it declined to adopt a policy of establishing Presbyterian hospitals, but endorsed the establishment of nursing homes by synods, presbyteries, and local church groups as a growing and needy field of Christian service; and it set up a division of homes and Christian welfare within the Board of Church Extension to counsel with the synods and presbyteries in all matters relating to policies and standards of children's homes, nursing homes, and homes for the aging.[24]

Children's homes existed at the time within the bounds of every synod. The oldest of them, Goodland Presbyterian Children's Home in Hugo, Oklahoma, had been opened in 1850 as a part of the Indian mission. More orphanages were established after the Civil War to care for the orphans of veterans who had been killed in battle. The Presbyterian Home in Talladega, Alabama, established for this purpose in 1864, had been in continuous operation since that time. One of the latest homes—for retarded children—was opened in the Synod of Virginia in 1966. The homes differed in the services provided: some provided only institutional care, others were multifunction agencies, providing also foster home care, in-home aid, adoptive placement, and other specialized services. One preferred orphans; others received "any normal child," destitute, neglected, deserted, or from homes in which there was a definite indication of need for Christian training or education. One worked exclusively with emotionally disturbed children; while others provided care and training for mentally retarded youth. One let it be publicly known that it received only white children; another gave preference to Indian children, but was one of a number which announced no restriction regarding race, color, or creed.[25]

In the 1940's the Synod of Florida protested a charter provision which excluded illegitimate children from Thornwell Orphanage;

the two other controlling synods—Georgia and South Carolina—declined to act in the matter. The ensuing debate aroused considerable heat but brought no change. "The policies of the orphanage must be right," declared the president of the institution, "for they have paid unique dividends . . . for seventy five years."[26] The policy of discrimination, it was announced to the 1971 General Assembly, had been abandoned.

Homes for the aging are a more recent phenomenon. The home owned and operated by the Synod of Georgia at Quitman was established in 1949; the North Carolina Home opened at High Point in 1952; Virginia's Home, opening at Massanetta in 1955, absorbed an earlier one for "old ladies" established in 1912. By 1965 there were 15 homes for the aging within the bounds of the Assembly. A few of these were owned or sponsored by local churches or by presbyteries; most were operated by synods. The church would soon have more homes for senior citizens than it had for children.

In the further development of both types of home the Board of National Ministries, through its Division of Homes and Welfare, could be expected to give direction and aid. Already manuals for volunteers and homes for senior citizens had been prepared. A scholarship program was maintained by the division as a means of helping to meet the increasing needs for trained professional staff in the church's welfare institutions. Much of the division's work was being done through the Presbyterian Association of Child Care Agencies and the Presbyterian Association of Homes for the Aging. Steps were being taken through these organizations to establish standards for "Presbyterian Homes" which might be expected to raise standards of excellence for the homes as similar standards had done for the educational institutions.

As functions of the various boards expanded and new responsibilities were assumed the need for oversight of the total program by the General Council increased.

The ad interim committee offering its recommedations for the Reorganization of the Assembly's agencies in 1949 had underlined the urgent need for the Assembly's budget to become a real budget, in which percentages allocated to the various causes of need by those who were in the best position to know should be actually adhered to. To meet this need an Equalization Fund was set up. It proved inadequate. Most Assembly agencies continued to receive a smaller percentage than the Assembly budget had approved, and the gross inequities in receipts continued. For 20 years the one effective solution—establishment of a Central Treasury instructed to distribute undesignated benevolences in such a way as to guarantee that the budgeted needs of all causes be met in like proportion—was repeatedly proposed and as often rejected. Some opposed the idea because they wanted designated gifts to increase the amount given to their favored cause (generally Foreign Missions) by just so much; others, because they wished—by withholding funds—to diminish the amount given to a cause of which they disapproved (generally the National Council of Churches) by just so much. They could not accept the idea that others might permit their undesignated gifts to be distributed so as to bring all causes up to their budgeted allotment. Continued pressure led to the appointment of an ad interim committee which finally convinced the General Assembly (in 1964) to set up a Central Treasury. The General Assembly and the church at large was at last agreed that "the successful fulfillment of the mission of each specific program area is bound up with the success of every other such area."[27] After 50 years of development and experimentation the budget of the Assembly had become a true budget.

An important step toward a coordinated program had been taken meanwhile by the establishment of the Inter-Agency Council, which operated as a subcommittee of the Committee of Planning in the General Council. Under its aegis, the former unilateral promotional approach of the various Boards was discontinued, and there developed a plan of worship and work for the guidance of the local church which enabled the Boards and agencies to offer their combined efforts and resources to aid local congregations in carrying out a program, developed from below rather than handed down from above.

Church publicity, a third area of responsibility assigned to the General Council, was now handled by an expanded Department of Information which had broadened its functions. Local churches were encouraged to make better use of the channels opened to them through religious news clinics held in cooperation with leading newspapers of the South in various localities. By 1965 there had been held a hundred such clinics.

For approximately 150 years evangelical denominations depended on independent church papers to supply their members with news of the Christian world and to afford a forum for an interchange of views. At the beginning of the new century five such papers continued to be published in the interests of the Southern Presbyterian Church—the *Central Presbyterian* (Richmond), the *Presbyterian Standard* (Charlotte), the *Southern Presbyterian* (Atlanta), the *Southwestern Presbyterian* (New Orleans), and the *Christian Observer* (Louisville). In the second quarter of the 20th century independent papers published in the interests of a single denomination passed rapidly from the scene; in their place came official magazines subsidized by the denomination itself. The Presbyterian Church in the United States took steps in 1952 to transform the *Presbyterian Survey,** heretofore a promotional agent for the church agencies, into a church magazine. It was freed from Board control, given its own Board of Directors, its own editorial staff, a sizable subsidy from the benevolences of the church; an "every family plan" encouraged sessions to see that a copy of the journal went into every Presbyterian home. As the paper, under the guidance of its editor, Ben Hartley, gradually developed its own policy, slightly left of center, subscriptions dropped, particularly after a cover featuring the flower-laden casket of the martyred Martin Luther King. Eighteen months later Mr. Hartley and his associate editor had been dismissed, and the future of the publication appeared uncertain.

Establishment of an official (monthly) denominational magazine made continuance of the independent (weekly) journals—now reduced to three, the *Christian Observer,* the *Presbyterian Outlook,* and the *Presbyterian Journal*—more uncertain, if the experience of other denominations could be taken as an example. The General Council in 1956 offered a statement regarding the value of the independent press and its service to the church which was approved by the General Assembly.

> It would be most unfortunate and foreboding [ran the statement] if the only avenues of information and opinion open to the church were avenues over which the church maintained control, and of which the church exercised that custodianship which is always given to ownership. The independent church press has a large, significant and continuing service to perform to our church and to the whole religious community. The Council is mindful of and grateful for the meaningful and constructive contribution which these three independent papers have made to the life of the church in supporting its endeavors, communicating news of its affairs, encouraging the enhancement of the devotional life of churchmen, and giving a forum for the frank expression of opinion and ambition in matters of the church's contemporary or prospective engagements.[28]

In four important areas, it had been pointed out in the 1949 Reorganization, the church must advance under the direction of its

---

* The General Assembly in 1911 called for a magazine which would combine the *Missionary,* published by the Foreign Missions Committee, and the *Home Mission Herald,* published by the Home Missions Committee, and in which the two other Executive Committees would have departments. The first issue of the new magazine, then called *The Missionary Survey,* appeared in the fall of this same year.

overall coordinating agency—budget, program, publicity, and research. This last area had been regarded as one of the most important, the area in which the church had been most deficient. A committee of research was established by the Council as it started its work, but it was starved for lack of funds, and without the director which the plan has envisaged, failed to get off the ground. Five years later the department was discontinued.

In 1966 Lawrence I. Stell, pastor of the First Church, St. Petersburg, Florida, succeeded James G. Patton as Executive Secretary of the General Council. Three years later the General Assembly appointed an ad interim committee to draw up a comprehensive plan of reorganization, looking to the restructuring of the General Assembly's Boards and agencies.

The proposed plan, providing for centralization of the denomination's benevolent work under a General Executive Board in Atlanta, was approved by the 1972 Assembly. Responsibility for providing leadership and material resources for program and mission will fall more directly on the seven enlarged synods as set up by the 1971-1972 Assemblies. Program priorities will be determined annually by the Assembly itself.

XV

The Women of the Church

Women have played an indispensable role in the life of the church from the beginning. By 1861, when the Southern Presbyterian Church began its independent existence, the majority of churches had some form of local women's organization and many had three or four. They aided the pastor in numberless ways, looked after the furnishing and equipment of the church building, helped in the care of the sick and the poor, searched out and visited new families, aided young men to make their way through college and seminary, and contributed to the mission work. It was in fact for this purpose that most of them were organized.

In 1868 a momentous appeal went out to the Christian women of the Presbyterian Church in the United States, signed by J. Leighton Wilson, Secretary of Sustentation and Foreign Missions, and E. T. Baird, Secretary of Education and Publication; these two represented now the combined benevolent work of the church. Attention of the women was called to the desperate plight of every phase of the church's work and the overwhelming need for funds. But what could the women do? Much, replied the secretaries, and they gave examples. Women in six or eight churches in South Carolina and Georgia had been invited to organize themselves into missionary associations for the purpose of aiding the cause of sustentation. At first it was thought they could accomplish very little. They went to work, however, "and by taxing certain resources that had never been called into service for the Lord before; by retrenching in some departments of their household arrangements; by soliciting contributions from their friends and acquaintances, and in various other ways, of which the mind of women is so suggestive—*they raised in every case more than twice as much as was given by the whole congregation, to which they belonged, to the object; and in two cases at least, their contributions were truly magnificent.*"[1] The secretaries were not urging that any new projects be undertaken, but that the women support enterprises authorized by the proper ecclesiastical bodies, and that they organize themselves into missionary associations for the purpose of raising funds for these objects of benevolence.

It was for this end, and in response to this and similar appeals from the various church courts, supported by the religious journals, that women's organizations now began to multiply, most of them, it may be observed, for the support of Foreign Missions. In hundreds of churches, where the men seemed as a rule indifferent, Dr. Egbert W. Smith later recalled, it was the women who kept this cause alive.[2] They raised funds in various ways. The Young Ladies Missionary Association in the First Presbyterian Church at Chattanooga, Tennessee, for example, adopted a threefold method: first, by dues— each member paying 25¢ a month; second, by admitting to membership gentlemen who paid the same dues, but did not attend the meetings; third, by giving literary sociables and holding bazaars. All kinds of fancy work were kept constantly on hand for sale.[3] By such means the Association was able to send to the Executive Committee something over $100 annually.

In 1875 the Assembly called attention to the "remarkable fact" that the gifts of the Sabbath schools and the "Women's Missionary Associations" during the last year had amounted to one-third of the entire sum contributed by the church to the cause of Foreign Missions.[4] Three years later the Assembly exhorted all congregations to form Ladies' Missionary Societies for the specific purpose of raising funds for this important cause.[5]

In response the number of missionary societies was greatly increased, but there was no uniformity of organization, no educational program, no mutual consultation or aid, no organization of any sort beyond the local level. Women in other denominations had organizations on the state and national levels, but the Southern Presbyterian Church remained strongly opposed to such organizations on principle. Local societies under the control of the session were acceptable—though there were some who opposed even these— but organizations on presbyterial, synodical, or Assembly level were rejected as unscriptural.

Unscriptural—perhaps; but certainly more efficient. Thus in the year 1876 the secretaries reported that a total of nearly $8,000 had been contributed by all the Ladies Missionary Associations throughout the Southern Assembly. In this same year Presbyterian women in New York City alone had given $30,000; those in Chicago,

$27,000; and those in Philadelphia, $87,000. The work of the women in the Northern Church had been organized, beginning about 1870, along different lines from that in the Southern Church; there were not only local organizations, but larger unions in presbytery, synod, and General Assembly. By 1884 Presbyterian women in the North were giving nearly $200,000 to the work of Foreign Missions; Southern women gave a little more than $12,000.

With the example of the Northern Presbyterian organization before them it was inevitable that a movement would arise for some larger organization for Southern Presbyterian women.

The first step in this direction came in 1884. A young woman, Miss Jennie Hanna of Kansas City, Missouri, had organized her girls' Sunday school class into a mission band. She felt the need for being associated with some larger organization that could provide information and direction. This she found in the Women's Board of the Presbyterian Church U.S.A. She thought for a time of going into the Northern Church just because of their women's work, but Dr. M. H. Houston, Secretary of Foreign Missions in the Southern Church, persuaded her to make the effort to arouse the Southern women to form a larger organization of their own. She proceeded to raise the question of forming presbyterial mission unions, such as the Northern women had had for years. The idea caught fire with an older woman, Mrs. Josiah Sibley of Augusta, Georgia. These two women, after some correspondence, wrote each church in the Assembly in an effort to secure the names of the missionary-minded women in their congregations. Many churches, of course, did not reply, but there were some which did.

Hundreds of letters were then written to the women whose names had been received, urging an organization of women on presbyterial lines. Dr. Houston had advised them not to mention their hopes for synodical and Assembly organization. Wisely, as events proved. For the suggestion of even presbyterial organization evoked a storm of "criticism, misconception and indignation" which they had not anticipated.[6] Ministers denounced the movement as "unscriptural, un-Presbyterian, unwomanly." Presbyteries began to overture the Assembly against it. On the other hand, letters of approbation and support came in from all parts of the Assembly. Two presbyterial organizations were formed almost at once—East Hanover in Virginia and Wilmington in North Carolina; both for Foreign Missions only.

The organization of these two presbyterial unions led Concord Presbytery to send an overture to the General Assembly calling at-

tention to certain dangers involved in the formation of missionary associations within the local church—for example, tendencies to dis-
place the organized church with societies without Scriptural
authority, to give undue prominence to one phase of church work to
the injury of others, and to obscure the unity of the church. The
Assembly was asked to give its judgment regarding the wisdom and
propriety of forming such distinct outside agencies as presbyterial
unions. Without expressing any judgment on the subject, the General Assembly sent the overture down to the presbyteries with the
direction that they patiently consider the whole subject of societies
within and without the church and return carefully formulated papers upon these points to the next General Assembly.[7] Sixty-eight
presbyteries replied to this request; 18 of these favored unions corresponding to all the church courts; one favored sessional and presbyterial societies only; 39 opposed anything beyond the local society
under the control of a session; and the rest held intermediate positions. The General Assembly recorded this response, adding no recommendation of its own.[8]

Leaders of this movement were disappointed at the presbyteries'
response, but not disheartened, and the number of presbyterial unions
gradually increased. Opposition also intensified. Some renewed the
old objections to all societies, male or female. "If we have societies
for foreign mission work, societies for home mission work, societies
for visiting the poor and sick, societies for interesting the young
people in prayer meetings, and societies for promoting temperance
and purity," asked W. S. Bean, the new editor of the *Southern Presbyterian,* "what will remain for those who do not happen to belong
to any of these organizations? Great care will have to be exercised
to keep the proper place of honor and authority the divinely organized church itself."[9]

Some took the opportunity to warn against the whole "Woman's
Movement" of which the presbyterial unions were a significant expression, for example, the Synod of Virginia, which in 1899 adopted
a lengthy report prepared by an ad interim committee on "the rights
and duties of woman in the church of God and in the home," a
report from which the "opposition" would continue to draw for
years to come.

According to this report "the woman was created out of and for the
man . . . The first law of human government is, 'Thy desire shall be
unto thy husband, and he shall rule over thee' . . . While thus made
subordinate to man, woman is not regarded nor to be treated as
inferior. While she is to be 'in subjection' . . . to 'submit' . . . 'be

obedient unto' her own husband, yet she is to receive honor, and to
be loved and cherished . . ." The "Woman's Movement" was said to
ignore or deny this subordination of women by divine appointment.

"The family, the home," continued the synod, "is by the Scriptures made the special sphere of woman . . . 'Wandering from house
to house' characterizes those on whom the censure of the Holy
Spirit falls heavily . . . The home and the family, the last and
strongest bulwark of society, of the state and of the church, the
'Woman's Movement' tends to undermine and destroy."

Against this background the synod moved on to consider the
Scriptural teaching as to woman's sphere and rights in the church.
The Scriptures, it was pointed out, forbid a woman to hold office
or bear rule in the church, this prohibition being based upon the
broad law, controlling the relation of the sexes in every sphere of
their intercourse, the subordination of woman to man. The Scriptures, it was argued at great length, do not permit a woman to
preach, exhort, or lead in prayer in a public assembly—rather, she
is commanded to keep silence in the church. She could, however,
teach in the privacy of the home and also in the Sunday school. It
was permissible for her to sing in the church. Nothing was found in
the principles laid down "to prevent concert for prayer by devout
women, nor anything to prevent the formation of aid and missionary
societies by women in their own church and under the control of
the session of that church," but the synod found it "questionable,
to say the least, whether under the polity of the Presbyterian
Church, founded as it is professed to be, upon the word of God,
union societies, presbyterial, synodical, or mixed denominational are
legitimate. . . . this doubt is strengthened by the strong and growing
tendency in such unions to assume to themselves the work of the
church, to throw this zeal and strength outside of authorized channels, and to put themselves beyond control, while they absorb the
time, energies, prayers and means of many of our best women . . . ."[10]

Despite such arguments the presbyterial unions quickly proved
their value for the church's benevolences, and their number continued to increase. By 1900 there were approximately 1,000 women's
societies within the church and 30 presbyterial unions, each formed
only after approval had been given by their respective presbyteries.

In 1904 came the second step—the formation of synodical
unions. The first of these was in Texas. Distances here were long, and
the annual visit of missionaries to presbyterials in this state were
time consuming and expensive. A synodical union was organized
to make more effective use of the visitors' time.[11] A little later in the

same year Virginia formed its synodical organization. Alabama followed in 1908, Missouri and Georgia in 1910. Unions were now found in 78 out of 84 presbyteries, and in five out of the 14 synods, but a general, Assembly-wide organization, of which the pioneers had dreamed, was apparently no nearer than before.

1910-1911 was a Jubilee year in which Women's Boards of various denominations celebrated 50 years of organized women's work for missions. Southern Presbyterian women were brought into contact with the leaders of organized women's work in other denominations. They were humiliated to discover how poorly the work of their scattered groups compared with the efficient work of other denominations; to find that theirs was the only important evangelical denomination in America with no department of women's work, and with no systematic promotion of the missionary program of the church among its women.

A busy housewife, with six children, in Kansas City, decided that the time had come to act. This woman, Mrs. W. C. Winsborough, wrote down her thoughts: "Some Reasons Why a General Secretary of Women's Missionary Work is Needed in the Presbyterian Church, U. S."; she sent her paper to Mrs. D. A. Macmillan, President of the Missouri Synodical, who put her in touch with Miss Jennie Hanna. The paper was then sent to the presidents of the other five synodicals and received their hearty approval. Out of this consultation came an overture from the Missouri Synodical to the General Assembly requesting the appointment of a woman secretary. It bore the endorsement of the five other synodicals, 41 presbyterial unions, the Synod of Missouri, and four presbyteries.

But strong opposition had also appeared. Dr. Thomas Cary Johnson of Union Seminary in Virginia wrote a long article for the church press in which he argued that appointment of a woman secretary would be unscriptural, unconstitutional, and unwise. "These noble women," he charged, "are unconsciously assuming the position of advisors of the Lord as to how he should have his people do their work; that God's revealed will is insufficient as a book of directions to his church."[12] One synod and six presbyteries expressed open disapproval. The Women's Missionary Society of the Waynesboro, Virginia, Church was confident that the great majority of Southern Presbyterian women were opposed.[13]

Ladies who supported the overture were described as "unwomanly." "A limited pope," "a woman bishop," "an ecclesiastical suffragette," were some of the mild and euphonious names given to the woman secretary, should she ever materialize. "A divided Church," "a woman's Church," "the camel's nose of a woman's Board," were terms used in the published opposition to the women's overture.[14]

But strong support for the overture came from well-known leaders of the church—laymen, ministers, former Moderators of the Assembly, Executive Secretaries of all important Boards and agencies of the church (all of whom recognized that they had much to gain from a more efficient organization of women's work in the church).

The debate grew more spirited as commissioners gathered for the Bristol Assembly. The women attending the Assembly were prepared for opposition; they expected speeches for and against. "When Dr. Grier read the report of the Committee on Church Societies," recalled Mrs. Winsborough, "we knew for the first time that he and his committee approved the overture. The Moderator D. T. S. Clyce called for . . . discussion. We gripped the edge of the seat and awaited the expected blasts of the opposition. To our amazement there was a great silence. No one rose to say 'yea' or 'nay'. No discussion whatever ensued. When the vote was taken, we heard no audible dissenting voice."[15]

The unexpected unanimity of the action, according to one astute observer, came from the wisdom of the committee which authorized the appointment not of a "woman secretary" (a title which appeared to threaten the male's prerogative) but simply "a woman possessing suitable gifts" to carry out "the assigned responsibility," which was to organize "synodical and presbyterial unions and local societies under control of synods, presbyteries and sessions respectively; coordinating women's and young people's societies as now organized; stimulating interest by gathering and disseminating needed information. . . ."[16]

Mrs. Winsborough, elected as first "superintendent" of the Auxiliary, proved a wise and able executive. She moved slowly, seeking to build a single Women's Auxiliary in every local church without destroying the existing organizations, encouraging the formation of presbyterial and synodical "Auxiliaries" where they did not exist.

Organization of the new department of women's work, as directed by the Assembly, was effected under the direction of a supervisory committee, composed of the four Executive Committees, in consultation with official representatives of the various synodical organizations. It was agreed that the official title would be the "Women's Auxiliary of the Presbyterian Church in the United States"; that the title of the salaried official (until this time the women had referred to "her" as "it") would be "Superintendent" (not until 1927 was there a "Secretary" of Women's Work, with a title comparable to that of the church's male executives); and that there should be an advisory council, composed of one representative from each synodical organization.

Plans for the "Auxiliary" were revolutionary, differing in a number of important aspects from those of any existing women's organization. The first annual report of the Auxiliary stated plainly the basis of the new plan in words which afterward became a slogan: "All the women of the Church working for, praying for and giving to all the Causes of the Church." Distinctive features of the plan were that (1) it was auxiliary; (2) it included all the women of the church; and (3) it embraced all the causes of the church.

Other denominations at this time had independent Women's Boards, carrying on certain phases of Home or Foreign Missions. The Auxiliary, as its name indicated, did not develop any independent benevolent work—it was formed rather to promote the benevolent work of the established agencies.

Earlier organizations had competed with other organizations for their membership among the women of the church; but all women became members of the Auxiliary by virtue of being members of the church.

Earlier organizations had been organized to support one or more phases of the church's work—Home Missions, or more likely Foreign Missions, or the work of the local church—ladies' aid societies. None of the existing societies were supporting the work then carried on by the Executive Committees of Christian Education and Ministerial Relief and the Executive Committee of Publication and Sunday School Extension. The purpose of the Auxiliary was to support all causes, the total program of the church.

To bring this about, it was recommended that there be elected a secretary of each cause in every society in the church; it was the business of each of these secretaries to promote the department which she was elected to represent and to serve as a channel through which each Assembly's committee could and would reach the women of the church. Not all at once, but gradually, this plan was put into effect throughout the Assembly, and the women of the church became far better informed regarding the church's work than the men, including most officers and many of the ministers of the church.

A fourth characteristic of the new plan for women's work was the "circle," which grew out of the successful experimentation of certain local churches, notably the North Avenue Church, Atlanta, Georgia, and the First Church, Tuscaloosa, Alabama. The Circle Plan, adopted in 1917, put each woman in a small circle, under its own leader, with membership and leader changed at regular intervals. It proved to be the most effective plan of women's church organization then in use, enlisting more women, providing a place of service for all willing to serve, developing leaders, promoting sociability, educating all the women in the work of the church, encouraging spiritual growth.

Opposition to the Auxiliary plan did not disappear overnight. It continued to come, as Mrs. Winsborough recalled, for some years, some of it from disapproving women, some from ministers—opposition "that was bitter, unfair, and, hardest of all, conscientious."[17] There were women indeed, as in the First Church, Staunton, and the Ginter Park Church, Richmond, who refused to disband old organizations or to countenance the new until a beloved pastor, conscientiously opposed to the new form of organization, had passed from the scene.

In less than a year, however, after Mrs. Winsborough's election, every presbytery and every synod had its organization of women, and local Auxiliaries were multiplying rapidly.

The first Colored Women's Conference, held under the auspices of the Auxiliary, met in 1916 at Stillman in Tuscaloosa, Alabama, though no Executive Committee sponsored it, and few advisers thought it was a wise thing to undertake. It was successful beyond all hopes and became an annual affair, leading to 12 other such conferences supported by synodicals in as many states.

Shortly after the conclusion of World War I, a Commission in Inter-racial Cooperation was set up in Atlanta, Georgia, representing all denominations and promoting a plan of cooperation between white and colored races in states, counties, and cities of the South. The Auxiliary became a member of the Women's Department which was established shortly thereafter and became active in its support, as was the case later with the Federal Council's Committee on Race Relations. Throughout its history the leadership of the Auxiliary has been fully abreast of the church in its efforts toward better racial understanding, and so in the whole area first defined as moral and social welfare, later Christian Relations, and still later as Church and Society.

In 1920 Mrs. Winsborough was sent on a trip to the Orient. Out of this trip came the White Cross Work of the Auxiliary, through which there has been made available to the church's medical missionaries needed supplies over and above what otherwise could be furnished them—and also a new impetus to mission study.

In 1921 the Woman's Auxiliary was asked by the Secretary of Stewardship to assume responsibility for raising a definite part of the Equipment Fund which had been approved by the General Assembly for use in securing sorely needed equipment in the Home and Foreign Mission fields. In mulling over the request Mrs. Winsborough conceived the plan of an annual birthday offering to be raised by the Auxiliary for specific projects in the Home and Foreign Mission field. No definite amount would be promised, the objective of the women's gift would be selected by the women themselves, and they would be left free to promote the offering as they thought best. The Auxiliary's offer was gratefully received, and, in 1922, on the tenth anniversary of the Auxiliary's founding, the first birthday offering was received—for Miss Annie Dowd's school for underprivileged girls in Japan, which Mrs. Winsborough had visited; a portion also was given to Montreat where the Auxiliary had been organized. The birthday offering has been taken each succeeding year, alternating between projects on the Home and Foreign Mission fields, the sums increasing year by year, until by 1959 the total of 38 birthday gift offerings was in excess of three and a half million dollars. The abiding value of these gifts, for a wide variety of projects, often imaginatively conceived, is beyond estimation.

In 1924 the Moderator of the Assembly appointed Mrs. Winsborough as an official to the Christian Conference on Faith and Work meeting at Stockholm, Sweden. It was the first time a woman had ever been appointed to serve as an official representative of the church. Mrs. Winsborough had previously represented the Committee on Women's Work on various interdenominational agencies. As the years have gone by the Auxiliary has had its representatives in attendance not only on the courts of the church, but also on a wide variety of international boards and meetings. So the leaders of the women's work have kept informed not only regarding the work of their denomination but of all important phases of ecumenical endeavor, and through their various educational and promotional channels, and within the limits set by the Assembly's actions, have participated in, learned from, contributed to, and kept the women of the church informed regarding all such enterprises.

In 1929 Mrs. Winsborough was compelled to relinquish her post because of ill health. The General Assembly of that year summed up the 17 years of her leadership of the Woman's Auxiliary in these words of tribute: "To Mrs. Winsborough, preeminently, is due the credit for organizing and perfecting the most effective piece of work, perhaps ever accomplished in any denomination. It has been her leadership, her far-reaching vision, and her indefatigable toil that have aroused to enthusiastic service the excellent women of the church."[18]

Reviewing Mrs. Winsborough's book, *Yesteryears,* Dr. W. L. Lingle, who knew the church in all its aspects as few other men, commented: "The organization and development of the women's work has been the most constructive piece of work done in our church during the past 25 years, or, I might well say, since the organization of our church as a separate denomination in 1861."[19] An overstatement it may be, but not altogether undeserved.

Mrs. Winsborough was succeeded as Secretary by Miss Janie W. McGaughey, who had served on the staff in the office of the Department of Women's Work as Director of Spiritual Life and later as Assistant Secretary. She served in this post for a period of 25 years. Miss Janie McCutchen, writing at the request of the Women's Board, noted that all the major emphases that were begun during the administration of the first Secretary continued to receive attention under Miss McGaughey's administration until there was some adequate reason in the natural course of events to introduce a change. The work of the Women of the Church (substituted for Women's Auxiliary in 1927) had become more efficient with the passing of the years, and has become more and more identified with the total work of the church. Miss McCutchen held that Miss McGaughey made her most signal contributions in four fields: first, in her emphasis on World Missions (mission study books were carefully planned; the Friendship Student plan was inaugurated; several Nationals representing women's work in our mission fields were brought to this country); second, in her emphasis on interdenominational work. "The work of the United Church Women was interpreted by Miss McGaughey as a part of the total program of the women of our Church. She saw in co-operative work an opportunity for Presbyterian U. S. women to go beyond themselves doing things with other Protestant Church women that they could not do alone. . . ."[20] Because of this emphasis it may be, certainly in part, because of their training in the Women of the Church, Southern Presbyterian women have played a prominent part in a variety of ecumenical endeavors. Mrs. Murdock McLeod on the staff of the Committee on Women's Work, for example, became Executive Secretary of the United Church Women; Mrs. C. S. Harrington was one of two women elected to serve on the Central Committee of the World Council of Churches.

A third emphasis in women's work during Miss McGaughey's administration was in the field of adult education. "She thought of the organized work of the women . . . as a specialized phase of education and was alert to know and use in the program new strategies in the education of adults."[21]

A fourth signal contribution made by Miss McGaughey to women's work, as seen by Miss McCutchen, was in the efforts made to deepen the spititual life of the women of the church.

Miss McCutchen thought it noteworthy that phases of the work initiated in the Committee, later the Board of Women's Work, under the leadership of Miss McGaughey moved into the total life of the church as a part of the adult educational program. As early as 1935 the Committee on Women's Work, under the inspiration and vision of its Secretary, proposed a special committee be set up representing men's work, adult Bible classes, and the women of the church to study adult education in the church and to plan for its further correlation. This beginning of cooperation in the adult program of the church was the forefunner of the Inter-Board Adult Council, erected to coordinate the work of all Boards and agencies of the Assembly in the total program of the church for adults.[22]

Along these lines the work of the Women of the Church has continued to move under the brief administration of Mrs. Rowena McCutchen and the quiet, but astute leadership of Miss Evelyn Green. Under the latter, in step with the General Assembly and its deliverances, has come increasing concern with the vital social issues that confront the South and the nation. And with this trend there has come from expected quarters the inevitable criticism.

There have also been changes in programming and structures, prompted in part by the fact that more women are gainfully employed and have less free time for the old style general meeting, along with other accustomed activities. More important is the fact that programs have become less Board-oriented and more woman-centered, and that women and women's work, aided by the gentle but increasingly persistent prodding of the Board of Women's Work are slowly becoming incorporated into the total life and work of the church.

The growth of women's work in the church has been accompanied necessarily by changes in women's status in the church.

The women's rights movement, arising in the North, seemed alien to the Southern tradition. Southern critics were confident that it would not penetrate the South, and least of all the church in the South. In 1879, however, Dr. James Woodrow confessed to a feeling of uneasiness on the subject. He wrote:

Until a comparatively late period, we congratulated ourselves on what seemed to be a sort of physical and moral impossibility that such a perversion of woman's influence should ever prevail in our own section. Our general conservatism and even our climate seemed to be against it . . . Male women, female lecturers, public speakers and preachers, and all "woman's rights" advocates, were the abomination of our people. . . .

But we seriously fear that a change for the worse has begun . . . What gives us the greatest uneasiness is that this new or at least imported spirit is seen very largely in the popular methods of female education. There is [a growing tendency] to thrust our girls before the public eye and ear. . . . To secure this, not only are our girls paraded before a crowd in concert and in "solo" performances, but they are taught and stimulated to declaim . . . exhibiting precisely as boys do who are expected to be lawyers, statesmen, and preachers of the future . . .[23]

Dr. Woodrow returned to the subject the following year. He was outraged that "the timid, shrinking girl" who entered college was expected before she left to read her own productions with the eyes of perhaps 500 men turned upon her unveiled face and form, and that she was neither dismayed or abashed. "There is no worse thing in our civilization," he cried. "It is a Trojan horse, introduced into the midst of us, which in twenty years will make the Southern woman as bold as her sisters in any part of the country. And when that feat has been accomplished, we say there will be no longer a South worth living for or worth dying for."[24]

Dr. Woodrow was old-fashioned on this, as on some other matters. But there was general agreement that a woman's voice should not be heard in a mixed audience within the church. Women claiming the right to preach were causing disturbance in some sections of the North; there were indications, as the *Texas Presbyterian* recognized, that "the evil will, by degrees, steal in upon us."[25]

Dr. R. L. Dabney lamented that "ministers of our own communion" were beginning to hesitate before the pressure of public opinion. To nip this movement in the bud, he published an article contending that the public preaching of women was an assault of infidelity on God's truth and Kingdom which should be withstood as any other assault.[26] Recognizing that some were being disturbed over the question, the Synod of North Carolina resolved "that public preaching by women, being opposed to the Word of God, is therefore opposed to the welfare of His people, and all our members are instructed to give it no countenance."[27] The Synod of Texas adopted also a statement discountenancing preaching by women and overtured the General Assembly to do likewise. The Assembly obliged by declaring that to introduce a woman into the pulpit for the purpose of publicly expounding God's Word was an irregularity not to be tolerated.[28]

Feeling the need for a more explicit declaration, the Presbytery of East Texas in 1891 overtured the General Assembly to "pronounce in express and Scriptural terms the conviction of our church that women are not permitted to speak in a public way in any of the meetings of the church, congregational or devotional, where men are present. . . ." Once again the Assembly obliged, adding, however, "We do not hold that Christian women are prohibited from holding meetings among themselves for mutual edification and comfort . . . or to devise ways and means to aid the general branches of church work, such as Home and Foreign Missions . . . or to teach a class in the Sabbath School."[29] The resolution passed with only two dissenting votes. One of these dissenters explained that he was in favor of women speaking in the small assemblies of the Christian Endeavor Societies; the other that he thought it proper for a returned female missionary to tell of her work to a general audience.[30]

But the women's movement in the nation as a whole was gaining momentum, and the South could not remain unaffected. "Even the conservative Presbyterian Church of the South is not altogether free from the incipient incursions of this radical movement," complained a contributor to the *Presbyterian Quarterly*. "The debate in the Assembly . . . last year revealed the fact that even a small portion of our ministry is somewhat infected with error on this subject. A few of the younger minds, who have caught the spirit of the times, declared themselves as being in favor of a revolutionary revision of the church's historic interpretation of Scripture concerning woman's part in the public exercise of worship."[31]

To strengthen the dikes, to hold back the threatening flood, a stream of arguments were published in the church press. "The great question at issue is, shall the authority of God or human wisdom prevail," wrote Dr. J. R. Howerton, D.D., who later was to become one of the pioneers for women's rights in the church.[32] "There is no more practical question before the church today," began a 40-page pamphlet entitled "Bible Studies on Woman's Position and Work in the Church."[33]

The movement to have women speak in the church, according to Dr. R. L. Dabney, was "part and parcel of French Jacobinism," that travesty of true republicanism, which caused the reign of terror in France, and which disorganizes every society which it invades.[34]

In 1897 the question came once again before the Assembly. After much debate the Assembly reaffirmed the ban on the historic position of the church, especially as set forth in the deliverance of 1832: "To teach and exhort, or lead in prayer in public and promiscuous assemblies, is clearly forbidden to women in the holy oracles."[35]

"It is to be hoped," commented Dr. W. McF. Alexander, "that those brethren—very few in number—who have been permitting women to talk in prayer meetings, and in young people's societies, to read missionary papers, etc. before mixed audiences, will take heed to this almost unanimous deliverance of the Assembly. The Assembly was in no mood to tolerate women speaking to mixed audiences under any circumstances."[36]

The Synod of Virginia, in the fall of this year, appointed a committee to report more fully on the Bible teaching regarding women's rights and sphere within the church. Two years later it adopted the comprehensive report previously summarized, supporting the church's traditional stand regarding woman's place in the church and questioning the propriety of unions for women beyond the congregational level.

Only a few years later a great furor was aroused in the church when Dr. J. R. Howerton of Charlotte, North Carolina (who acknowledged that his views on the subject had changed in the last five years), permitted a woman, Mrs. Howard Taylor, to make a missionary address in the First Church, of which he was pastor, in the presence of men and, what was worse, defended his views, insisting that under similar circumstances he would do it again. The permanent moral principle set forth in Scripture, Dr. Howerton argued, was the subordination of women, or the headship of man in the family and in the church. He had come to believe that it was neither the intention of Paul nor the mind of the Spirit to affirm that in all ages and among all people, despite changing social custom, women should be forbidden to speak in the presence of men, or that to do so involved a renunciation of womanly modesty and subjection.[37] There were a few who arose to defend Dr. Howerton, notably Dr. Egbert W. Smith, Executive Secretary of Foreign Missions, but the overwhelming preponderance of opinion was against him. Dr. A. J. McKelway, crusading editor of the *Presbyterian Standard,* acknowledged that he had heard no one make a better missionary address than Mrs. Hudson, excepting possibly "our Secretary of Foreign Missions and Robert E. Speer"; and he could see no objection to her making a missionary address to a mixed assembly so long as it was not in a church.[38] More agreed with Rev. R. A. Lapsley (a long-time editor of Sunday school literature in the Executive Committee of Christian Education), who held that on this question Calvinists could not compromise. "Logically," he wrote, "there is no safe spot on which to rest the sole of your foot between the old-time view of the woman question and all the abominations of womanism." Dr. Lapsley commended the lengthy study approved by the Synod of Virginia in 1899. He saw the ominous ripples of a rising tide which threatened to engulf all that men held dear. Womanly modesty, the sacredness of the marriage tie, biblical ideas of wifehood and motherhood, and with them reverence for the Bible as God's inspired Word were all in danger of disappearing beneath the incoming flood.[39]

In 1910 the General Assembly, in response to an overture, declared there had been no change in the settled policy of the church regarding the speaking of women before mixed assemblies.[40]

But the question would not remain down. Women were entering the business world; the suffrage, which prominent churchmen had opposed on biblical grounds, was being extended; with women's "rights" being recognized in other areas, the church could not remain unaffected. In addition, as some pointed out, the church's own actions had not been completely in harmony with its teaching on the subject. For some time the church had recognized the necessity for using women on the mission fields at home and abroad. Now, in response to this need, the Assembly's Training School had been established to prepare young women for mission service. Men—ministers and others—were dropping in on Auxiliary services; in some Presbyterials and Synodicals the men were not only invited, but urged, to attend. Some ministers encouraged their women to participate in the prayer meetings. Women were invited to address Sunday schools, with pastor, elders, and deacons in their audience.

Faced with this growing divergence in practice, the General Assembly in 1915 appointed an ad interim committee of five to make a careful study of Scripture on the subject of woman's position in the church. But there was no longer agreement on this point. Consideration of the committee's report—with majority and minority reports, and other divergencies—was the main business before the 1916 General Assembly. After a long and sometimes heated debate the Assembly by a vote of 132 to 80 finally reaffirmed the action of the 1880 Assembly forbidding women to preach but left all other services of Christian women to the discretion of the sessions and the enlightened consciences of the Christian women themselves. Specific attention was called to the fact that while women were excluded from the office of presbyter or elder, no such barrier was thrown around the diaconal ministry. Sessions were encouraged to utilize the services of godly women in such ministry (no provision was made to elect women to the office of deacon).[41] The Assembly further voted that, through its Training School in Richmond and other agencies, instruction and training be provided for women who desired to devote their lives to religious work as would fit them for efficient service in the Home or Foreign Mission fields.

Sixty or more commissioners filed a protest against this action of the Assembly on the grounds, among others, that it reversed the historic position of the Presbyterian Church U. S. on the subject without Scriptural warrant. It did indeed reverse the historic position of the church on the subject, bringing its theory more in line with what had become its practice. In answer to the Scriptural protest, the Assembly replied: "The Scriptures may have their authority discredited not merely by a violation of their precepts, but also by any attempt on the part of ecclesiastical courts to bind the consciences of God's people on matters of doubtful interpretation."[42]

A number of observers commented on the division between progressives and conservatives evident at the Assembly. The editor of the *Presbyterian Standard* was impressed with the fact that among the former there was "a spirit of rebellion against what they term 'the hide-bound conservatism' of the past . . ."[43] He was saddened to note that older men of the highest standing in the church voted with the majority on the question. "We do not question the motives of these brethren," added the editor. "We only lament that they have left the old paths."

The woman question in the church was by no means settled, but the church had taken a decisive step forward from which there would be no retreat. Involved, though not recognized at the time, was the beginning of a break from the literal, legalistic, *jure divino* interpretation of Scripture, which had retarded and confined the development of the church in other areas. Further steps inevitably followed. In 1917 the General Assembly elected two women as trustees of the Assembly's Training School, the first time the Assembly had ever elected a woman to any such position. In 1920 Mrs. Winsborough was permitted to address the Assembly, speaking on the work of the Women's Auxiliary. The Assembly voted to hear her again in 1923. This they did, commented Dr. R. C. Reed, who cast the lone dissenting vote, without thinking to take counsel of Paul.[44]

Before this same Assembly came a proposal that at least one woman be placed on each of the Executive Committees. After a long and serious debate the Assembly voted, 139 to 50, to add three women to each of the Executive Committees (an action taken in recognition of the magnificent work of the Auxiliary).

This action of the Assembly did not meet with the unanimous approval of the church. One synod—South Carolina—and five presbyteries overtured the 1924 Assembly that the action be rescinded. The overtures were decisively rejected, however, and the Assembly with practical unanimity reaffirmed the previous action. Mrs. Winsborough was elected this year as one of the church's representatives to the international Christian Conference on Faith and Work meeting the following year at Stockholm. The dam had broken and women would soon be appointed to serve on committees to nominate pastors and to report to the various courts of the church.

But the strict constructionist party was not yet ready to acknowledge defeat. In 1925, responding to an overture requesting a deliverance on the right of women to speak on the floor of church courts, the Assembly reaffirmed previous deliverances forbidding women to speak or pray in public gatherings of the church (overlooking or ignoring, in effect reversing, the more liberal deliverance of 1916), but added: "However, presenting a report to a church court of work done by Auxiliary or other associations is not to be construed as speaking or discussing if due care is taken that such reports when presented by women are not made the occasion of speaking by them, and ordinarily these reports ought to be presented through the advisory committee or some member of the court appointed for the purpose."[45]

The following year when the report of the Auxiliary was called for (at a night session) a motion that Mrs. Winsborough be allowed to read her own report was carried by a vote of 163 to 61. Objection was raised on a point of order. Motions and counter-motions followed. According to one scribe: "The moderator tried to agree with everybody, no matter how different he might be from everybody else; and so it went for probably thirty minutes, until someone made a motion to adjourn, which quickly prevailed. But what a session! I have witnessed many exciting and tense situations at church courts, but never one like that evening session."[46]

The next morning the Auxiliary report, on written request of Mrs. Winsborough, was read by Dr. Henry H. Sweets, chairman of the Auxiliary Supervisory Committee. The Assembly then reaffirmed by a large majority the 1916 deliverance, which left other services than preaching by Christian women to the discretion of the church courts, after which a resolution was introduced and carried which permitted the Superintendent of the Woman's Auxiliary, as an authorized and responsible agent of the Assembly the right to read her report to the Assembly.[47] From this time on the Secretary of the Auxiliary presented the organization's annual report to the Assembly

in person. For a number of years a few conscientious objectors
pointedly rose to their feet and withdrew in silent protest when
this was done, but at no time did they muster more than a corporal's
guard. The body of the church had moved on beyond them. In
1927 a woman (Mrs. E. L. Russell) gave a series of popular Bible
lectures at the Women's Conference at Montreat. Scores of men
attended. Dr. J. R. Bridges, conservative editor of the *Presbyterian
Standard,* who had opposed every step of the women's advance in
the church, acknowledged that she was a remarkable Bible teacher,
far above the ordinary. His one remaining hope now was that
Presbyterian women would not seek to enter the pulpit.[48] That
privilege, and the privilege of serving as elder and deacon in the
church, would have to wait for another generation.

XVI

The Thrust of the Church

In the second third of the present century the South experienced an unprecedented Depression, a Second World War, massive shifts of population, rapid industrialization, increasing urbanization, a racial revolution, and a search for new values.

The thrust of the Presbyterian Church in the U. S. during this period was inevitably affected by these factors in ways which paralleled roughly those of other denominations. The Depression years brought retrenchment in missions. No funds were available for expansion; many congregations were carrying debts for buildings erected in boom times of high prices, therefore benevolences were cut and all missionary support suffered radical reduction. The Executive Committee of Home Missions borrowed until its credit was exhausted, after which it was forced to go on a cash-and-carry basis. By the mid-1930's the worst of the Depression was over, but many church debts remained to be paid, and this fact continued as a hindrance to advance for some years.

Growth of the church during this period was slowed down. In 1931, indeed, total membership was less than it had been five years earlier, and gains for the next five years remained limited.

Southern industry had grown since 1900. Nonetheless, the South's total output in 1929 was only a fraction of that of the nation as a whole (six percent, compared to the Northeast's 40 percent), and in 1939 a presidential commission could with justice describe the South as the nation's number one economic problem.

With the coming of World War II industrial development in the South accelerated at a rapid pace. The *Manufacturer's Record* for February 1947 noted that the industrial progress of the region in the last ten years had been greater than that of the preceding 50 years, and was twice that of the nation as a whole. In the next ten years four Gulf states—Texas, Louisiana, Mississippi, and Alabama—accounted for one-sixth of the industrial growth of the nation. *Life* magazine described the South's economic advance as the "most dramatic regional transformation since the opening of the West or the War between the States."

Where factories created jobs, people followed. Soon many areas over the South were suffering acute growing pains. New communities began to spring up; towns grew into cities; larger cities became metropolitan centers. The churches of the South were facing a challenge comparable to that faced by the church in post-Revolutionary days when the great westward migration had begun.

Home Mission forces of the denomination were overwhelmed with opportunities to extend the church into these growing new communities, especially around the larger cities now beginning to spread over entire counties.

To meet the need the General Assembly in 1942 ordered a five-year campaign to raise a Home Mission Emergency Fund of $1,250,000. The money was to be used in paying off debts of Home Mission churches in areas of rapid growth and to provide ministers, manses, and church buildings in promising new communities. The amount requested was raised in full and became an important factor in launching the church on the greatest period of growth in its history. Within a five-year period, 196 new Presbyterian churches were organized, located in 66 different presbyteries. There were also 409 new Sunday schools, many of which subsequently became churches.

The Home Mission Emergency Fund was followed by the Program of Progress, a well-rounded program of advance, including Home Mission objectives, and laying great stress on stewardship. Under the stimulus of this movement the total giving of the church rose at a rapid rate, producing approximately one million dollars of additional money for the Board of Church Extension (so named after the Reorganization of 1949). Most of this amount was used for erecting new churches in areas of rapid growth. Of equal importance was the stimulus given to expansion efforts of synods and presbyteries.

The Program of Progress was followed in turn by a three-year program entitled "Forward with Christ." Four years later the Assembly approved a million dollar challenge fund for the building of new churches and the strengthening of existing ones. Each presbytery now was to retain 80 percent of the amount raised for its own needed work, and to forward 20 percent to the Assembly's Board. The fact that the larger proportion of the amount raised was to be spent in the home presbytery, where the needs could be seen, encouraged liberality; the 20 percent allotted to the Board of Church Extension enabled it to offer challenge funds in areas of greater growth potentiality.

In earlier periods of mission enthusiasm new churches had been erected in rural areas, and often in cities, where there was little opportunity for growth. As a consequence considerable mission funds on both local and Assembly level were tied up in sustentation needs, continued in many cases for successive generations—leaving so much less for planting churches in areas where they were now badly needed and where in a short time they could be expected to become self-supporting. To insure the best use of funds, particularly in the rapidly growing suburbs, the Board (in 1950) erected an Urban Church Department, later more appropriately named the Department of Survey and Church Location. Mr. Hal Hyde, a layman, especially trained for his new responsibility, was called to head this new department. The Board announced that he would be available to counsel with local churches or presbyteries concerning their expansion programs and to survey metropolitan areas with regard to the location of new churches or the relocation of existing ones. From the beginning the services of Mr. Hyde, as later those of his associate, Mr. James Earhart, were heavily in demand. Assistance was given to particular churches; surveys were made of cities, metropolitan areas, presbyteries, and even synods. Within a few years surveys had been made of all major cities within the bounds of the General Assembly, and in many of the smaller ones. It was an era of expansion. For 15 years an average of one new church a week was organized in the Southern Presbyterian Church. By 1956 one-eighth of the total membership of the denomination was said to be in new churches organized since the close of World War II.[1]

Throughout the period the church continued to put emphasis on evangelism. The year of 1933 was designated an evangelistic year and the Assembly urged that every synod, every presbytery, and each local church join in preparation for a church-wide program. The results were disappointing—fewer additions on confession of faith than in preceding years. Taking note of this fact and the further fact that "the obvious and real mission and business of our church is to show the way of eternal salvation through our Lord and Savior Jesus Christ to those who know him not," the 1933 General Assembly (the same Assembly which expunged from the record the fact that it had even attempted to establish a Permanent Committee on Moral and Social Welfare) "resolved that we humbly confess to our God our shortcomings and sins, our failures and lack of faith and courage and beg his forgiveness; that we earnestly pray that he place upon our hearts more than ever before the burden of unsaved souls . . ."[2] The Assembly then renewed its call to the church to put first things first, to think evangelism, to pray evangelism. To give effective direction to this call the Assembly established a three-year plan for special evangelistic effort throughout the church. "I do not see how a better plan could have been devised," commented Dr. Walter L. Lingle the following year.[3] But the longed-for revival did not materialize.

Disturbed by the comparatively few members brought into the church on profession of faith, the 1937 General Assembly took action which led to the appointment of a permanent committee on evangelism (previously a responsibility of the Executive Committee on Home Missions) with Dr. Donald W. Richardson of Union Theological Seminary in Virginia as its chairman. The first report of this committee stirred the Assembly as it had seldom been stirred before or since. Dr. John A. MacLean of Richmond set the stage by a moving account of how the preaching of an evangelist, the late Dr. William Black, led to the crisis of his life and brought him to a decision for Christ, and how another evangelist, Dr. J. Ernest Thacker, led him to turn from a promising career in the law to the gospel ministry. Dr. Richardson followed (the next morning) by recounting some "startling and humiliating facts"—the appalling paucity of accessions to the membership of the church on professions of faith for the four-year period 1935-1939 (compared with the members added in the period 1931-1934), and also the fact that during the past eight-year period there had been a steady decrease in the number enrolled in the Sunday schools. When it was discovered that due to the depleted state of the Assembly's treasury the Permanent Committee's request for a budget of $10,000 had been reduced to a paltry $1,500, protests arose from all over the Assembly, and in an unprecedented move the full amount originally requested was personally pledged by commissioners rising to their feet more rapidly than they could be recognized.

It was determined to plan not a spasm of evangelism, but a crusade which would be continuous, not for one month, three months, or a year, but year after year. There was to be no rented office, no office force, no salaries, and no superintendent.[4]

Synods and presbyteries responded readily to the Assembly's lead and moved to go forward in a great evangelistic effort. When news came that the church had received on confession during the evangelistic year 25,513 members, the largest number of additions by profession in many years and possibly the largest in the church's history, there was great elation. The standing committee reported: "Our church's life has been enriched. Its work has been extended. The spirit of evangelism in churches, auxiliaries, Sunday Schools and individuals has been greatly quickened."[5]

The Permanent Committee on Evangelism was continued with instructions that the evangelistic crusade be given primary emphasis in the work of the church for the second year. Then came the awakening. Belatedly it was discovered that the first evangelistic year had included two Easters, the time when young people having completed their instruction were normally received into the church. This year the additions on confession had been abnormally high. The second year, with no Easter in the church year, the figure was correspondingly low. The average for the two years was slightly less than normal. For a third year evangelism was kept in the forefront of the church's thinking and planning. Despite all the efforts to arouse the church to greater efforts, 8,902 fewer names were added to the church's membership than had been added the preceding year. Dr. Walter L. Lingle recalled the enthusiasm that swept over the Assembly three years earlier. The reports prepared by the committee had been inspiring; there were no finer reports available. And the committee had issued numbers of extraordinary able pamphlets on evangelism. But the records had been disappointing, and enthusiasm had faded.[6]

Evangelism continued, however, to be stressed before the General Assembly. As the standing committee reminded the 1944 General Assembly: "The greatest challenge before our church today is the winning of souls for Jesus Christ . . . The greatest migration of people that the nation has ever experienced is taking place before our own eyes. From all points of our country great multitudes of people are coming to the Training Camps, shipyards and manufacturing centers of the South. Now as never before we must emphasize evangelism . . ."[7]

Dr. H. H. Thompson, who had served the committee for a brief period as a field agent, on leave of absence from his church, was persuaded this year to accept a full-time position as secretary of evangelism. The following year, for the second successive year, there was a small increase in the number of additions to the church. Visitation evangelism was now the method being emphasized. The basic procedure was not new. It had in fact been employed for 25 years or more. But in the last three or four years it had come to be used more and more and with great success by a number of the leading denominations. According to the *Christian Observer* it was a simple, but well thought-out plan for utilizing the lay forces of the church. As described in one of its manuals: "Visitation evangelism trains carefully chosen laymen to call two by two in a friendly manner according to a special plan which includes instruction and experience. They meet for a series of instruction conferences. After each conference they accept assignments to interview prospects. By alternating periods of instruction and experience they become effective in their visitation, and go out to secure decisions for Christ and membership for the church."[8]

This was the method now stressed by Dr. Thompson. It proved to be the method for the time. "The amazing results of the Atlanta Home Visitation," wrote Dr. Stuart R. Oglesby, "have caused many, both in Atlanta and elsewhere, to believe . . . that we have at last found a true and effective evangelistic method . . . Last year the total number of additions by profession reported by Atlanta Presbytery was 602. In four days of visitation evangelism a larger number of people than that signed confession cards and many more were later received into church membership by profession, as a result of the spiritual momentum which has been generated during the campaign. It is significant also that these professions of faith came largely from adults hitherto untouched by the church, or at least uninfluenced by it."[9]

In April 1947, Dr. H. H. Thompson, Director of Evangelism, listed results from churches that had made thoughtful preparation. Among them[10]:

Warrington, Florida—135 members, 71 decisions
Montgomery, West Virginia—413 members, 63 decisions
Pryor Street, Atlanta—410 members, 89 decisions
Central Church, Little Rock—413 members, 60 decisions
Westminster Church, St. Louis—735 members, 101 decisions

Reports to the General Assembly this spring indicated the addition of 23,121 persons to the membership of the church on profession of faith and 40,127 on certificate, both figures being the largest since 1940, the combined figures said to be the largest in the history of the church. The following year accessions to the church from both sources was still greater. In its report to the General Assembly the Permanent Committee on Evangelism said in part: "Lay members have for the first time availed themselves of the high privilege of being used to win their fellow men to Christ and to his church. Many churches have seemed to rediscover the real purpose for which they have been brought into existence in being witnesses for him. Hundreds of individuals have had their faith vindicated by their visitation experiences of spiritual joy in a way different from anything they had ever known before. In fact, a great cross section of people have been reached by lay activity and have been encouraged themselves to do what had been done for them . . . Visitation evangelism has been carried on in hundreds of churches in the Assembly and at least thirty central places have been utilized in an appropriate way for inspiration and training."[11]

During the last five years of Dr. Thompson's tenure of office the Southern Presbyterian Church received more on profession of faith and had more net gains than in the previous 20 years combined.

Dr. William H. McCorkle succeeded Dr. H. H. Thompson as Secretary of the Division of Evangelism in January 1952. Visitation evangelism continued to be encouraged, but other methods, constituting a fully rounded program of evangelism, were recommended. Special efforts were made to encourage simultaneous campaigns of evangelism over large areas—an exchange of ministers, for example, in adjoining synods. A pre-assembly Conference on Evangelism, instituted in 1951, became a permanent feature.

As the decade of the 1950's drew to a close, there were evidences that the 20-year "revival" which had brought to the American churches one of their largest periods of growth was drawing to an end.

In a centennial study book, published in 1960, the author wrote:

> How long the present upsurge of religious interest will continue is uncertain. There is an ebb and flow in religion as in other fields of interest. The tide may turn tomorrow, in fact may already have begun to turn, or it may continue for years.
> Many feel that to the present time it has not run very deep; that it is characterized by a vague religiosity, lacking in content, what Martin E. Marty terms "religion-in-general", that it is group-oriented, arising in many cases out of a need for community rather than a need for redemption; a faith "observed more in rhetoric than in rubric", in word more than in practice; a religion which offers inward peace and outward fellowship; but does not commit one deeply to the cause of Christ—in fact to any cause.[12]

The Southern Presbyterian Church was at this time making the most thorough preparation in all of its history for a great evangelistic effort that was to constitute the major thrust of its centennial observance.

Rev. Albert E. Dimmock, who had succeeded Dr. McCorkle as Secretary of Evangelism, was seeking to give the movement greater depth, leading to the deeper commitment which so many felt to be

hitherto lacking. Traditional methods of evangelism were emphasized and expanded; new insights were added from the personality
sciences; evangelism was wedded to social action. The year-long
preparations included a pre-Assembly Evangelism Conference; pre-
synod conferences; summer courses in Christian witnessing in presbytery and synod conferences for men, women, and youth; fall emphases in meetings of presbyteries, presbyterials, and in rallies of
men and youth; calvacades in 80 cities led by outstanding teams of
leaders, moving across the Assembly; and self-examination by every
church.

But the concentrated evangelistic effort launched in the first
three months of 1961 proved a grievous disappointment. Instead of a
gain over the previous year there was a loss, both in numbers added
on profession of faith and otherwise. The ratio of additions to total
membership dropped and continued to do so in the years that followed, as it did also in other major denominations in America.

The church had made extensive gains, however,
during the first half of the 20th century. In the first quarter of the
century, membership had more than doubled, from 225,227 to 457,-
093; in the second quarter of century, 1925 to 1950, there had
been an approximate 50 percent increase, from 457,093 to 675,439.
This was a larger proportionate gain than the total population growth
of the area, a larger proportionate gain than that made by any
other major denomination represented in the National Council of
Churches. It was less rapid, however, than the Southern Baptist
Convention, the Roman Catholic Church, the Mormons, and many
of the newer sects.

The three largest synods in 1960 were in order: North Carolina,
Virginia, and Texas, as they had been three decades earlier. Synods
which during this period had made the largest proportionate gains
were in order: Florida (now the fourth largest synod in size), Geo-
gia, Texas, and Louisiana; synods which made the smallest proportionate gains were in decreasing order: Missouri, Oklahoma, Kentucky, and Arkansas. In general the greatest growth had taken place
in those areas which had grown most in population: churches
planted in the burgeoning suburbs had thrived; churches in the rural
areas had declined.*

---

* In a 30-year period (1920-1950) 215 churches were dissolved in the Synod
of Texas. Only one of these was in a town of more than 10,000; 94 percent were
in towns of less than 2,500 (PO [October 1951], p. 3).

A computerized profile of membership compiled in 1966 revealed that in Florida, Texas, the Carolinas, and Virginia, and in many large cities of other states, church membership like population was booming. In the cotton and coal areas—Alabama, Mississippi, Tennessee, Arkansas, and West Virginia—where population was being drained away by automation and other factors, it was otherwise. These five synods all showed a loss of membership, and in growth were at the bottom of the list.[13]

The South remained predominantly rural, as it had been throughout its history, up to the 1950's; there were at this time only four states in the territory of the Southern Presbyterian Church which were more urban than rural (a population of 10,000 being the dividing line). Two-thirds of the churches were in town and country, but less than a third of the total church membership, the lowest proportion of rural membership it was estimated of any major church represented in the area.[14] The largest number of rural churches were in those states and in those areas originally settled by the Scotch-Irish—Virginia and the two Carolinas.[15]

The trek from the farms set in after the Civil War, reached major proportions in the 1920's, declined during the 1930's (because of the great Depression), rose to a new and unprecedented height during the World War II years (between 1940 and 1945 the Southern farm population fell by 3,203,000 as compared with a decrease of only 1,876,000 for the rest of the nation), and has continued to the present.

The rural churches on the whole, therefore, faced a declining population. Many located in sites appropriate for horse and buggy days now found themselves poorly located in overchurched communities. They had failed to adopt their program to meet the rapidly changing environmental conditions. This was the judgment of experienced and interested observers who collaborated in studying the rural communities of the South under the auspices of the Board of Christian Education, as it had been the earlier judgment of President Hoover's Research Committee on Social Trends. S. H. Hobbs, Jr., wrote:

> Rural life conditions have undergone tremendous changes in the United States in the last few decades. Perhaps no institution has changed as little as the country church. Improved roads, the automobile, and other means of communication and transportation have annihilated distance. The mechanization of agriculture and agricultural education have transformed farming. The farm population has declined . . . Rural needs

have given us a type of community heretofore unknown, namely the village which is the service station to the farmer. The individualism of the American farmer has largely given way to cooperative effort. The consolidated school has largely replaced the one-teacher school. Everywhere in rural America horizons are enlarging. This applies to everything except the country church.[16]

The typical country church, the author went on to point out, had one or two rooms; a slowly declining constituency; a non-resident minister; a weak organization competing for new members with several other churches, some, if not all, aided in the struggle by Home Mission grants. This, said Mr. Hobbs, "described the average situation which practically all of the denominations cling to tenaciously and under which there can be no real religious progress."[17] The rural church seemingly found it hard to change its ways, despite the many changes which made the old ways increasingly inappropriate.

Thousands of rural churches are facing a difficult future, wrote Dr. James M. Carr, Secretary of the Town and Country Church Department of the Board of Church Extension, in 1956. He noted that 798 new churches had been established in the preceding 25 years; in the same period no less than 550 churches had been dissolved, the great majority of these in rural and village areas. In the preceding ten years 186 churches had been dissolved, and of this number 170 were rural. If the same ratio applied over the 25 year period, as was probably the case, 91 percent of the 550 dissolved churches, Dr. Carr pointed out, were in the town and country.[18]

Attention had been called to the disintegration and neglect of rural life by the Country Life Commission appointed by President Theodore Roosevelt in 1908. One consequence was the erection of Town and Country Church Departments in the various denominations. In PCUS this department was erected in 1925. Elected as director was Dr. Henry W. McLaughlin, pastor of a large country church in the Valley of Virginia. He was expected to offer courses on the country church in the various theological seminaries, to secure volunteers for country church work, to train young men for this form of service, to conduct conferences, to investigate rural church needs, and to execute the instructions of the Assembly for the promotion of the general welfare of the country church. All this he did with rare devotion and skill until his retirement in 1946. He was succeeded by Dr. James M. Carr, who continued to serve in this capacity until 1967, when the Department of Town and Country Church was finally merged into the newly created Department of Church and Community.

Much was done by both Dr. McLaughlin and his successor, Dr. Carr, to call attention to the needs of the town and country churches and to assist them in efforts to meet these needs. Notable were the Institutes for Town and Country Pastors held annually for many years at the four theological seminaries and at the Rural Ministers Conferences conducted with aid and assistance from the Town and Country Church Department at a number of state universities.

In the Valley of Virginia and the Piedmont of North and South Carolina, areas settled originally by the Scotch-Irish, there were a number of strong rural churches, able to maintain a resident pastor, modern facilities, and a well-rounded program. But a large number of country churches had small membership and limited financial strength and were unable to employ a full-time minister. To meet this situation several plans were developed. The most successful and the one advocated by the Town and Country Church Department was the larger parish plan. Louisville Theological Seminary was the first to put such a plan into operation, under the supervision of Dr. C. Morton Hannah, Professor in the Department on the Rural Church, followed by Union Theological Seminary under the direction of Dr. James Appleby, Director of Field Work. In 1946, Dr. R. G. Hutcheson became the pastor and director of the Old Providence Rural Parish in West Hanover Presbytery. The parish was composed of eight churches, all located either in a small town or village or in the open country. Dr. Hutcheson was assisted by students from Union Theological Seminary and the General Assembly's Training School. The churches in the parish were now able to have preaching every Sunday and to develop a rounded program such as had not been possible before. The parish gained quickly both in numbers and in financial strength.

At the heart of the larger parish plan was a council composed of representatives from each of the participating churches, which planned a cooperative program, utilizing the combined resources of the parish as a whole, for the benefit of all.[19]

Dr. J. M. Carr cited statistics to show that in a 25-year period (1930-1954) 315 new town and country churches had been organized and that during this period there had been an increase of approximately 53 percent in the rural church membership of PCUS (excluding from the count the loss of membership from the large number of rural churches closed during the same period), despite the fact that the average membership of the rural churches continued to decline. He pointed out that almost one-half of PCUS

churches in Texas—an urban state with declining rural population—
were in town and country areas, and that all of these except 20
were in towns or villages increasing in population.[20] He visited 25
of these churches in four days and was informed that every church
in the presbytery had either just completed a building program or
was in the midst of one or had made plans for one in the immediate
future. "Throughout rural America," declared Dr. Carr, "town and
country churches are tearing down the old and making place for the
new in sanctuaries, educational buildings, better recreational facilities, and more comfortable manses."[21] The larger parish plan, regarded as the hope of the town and country church, was still in its
infancy. To Dr. Carr, at least, the future for the rural church seemed
bright.[22]

        The cities, however, continued to grow at the ex-
pense of the rural areas. The earliest U. S. Census in 1790 revealed
that only five percent of the people lived in communities which had
a population of more than 2,500. In 1860 it was 20 percent; in 1890,
34 percent; in 1920, 51 percent; in 1960, more than 65 percent. In
the South the growth of cities was more tardy, but the trend was in
the same direction. Thus in 1790 only one and a fraction individuals
(1.2 percent) out of every 100 lived in communities with a population of 2,500 and over. In 1860 it was five percent; in 1890,
ten percent; in 1940, 38 percent; and, by 1960, approximately 50
percent.

The population movement was not only from rural to urban areas,
but from the center of the city to the circumference. Though every
city had its own pattern of growth and differed in some respects
from that of every other, all cities of any size came to possess a
downtown business area, slums, declining areas, stable areas (stable,
that is, for a time), growing residential sections, and suburbs—in
each of these the churched faced distinctive problems.

The task of the church in the city as a whole was made more
difficult by the excessive mobility of the population—approximately
one-fifth of the church's membership changing their residence every
year; by changing neighborhoods—in general, as one group of people moved out, another group of lower income and different religiously, culturally, and racially moved in; and by various other
problems growing out of the city's development, such as traffic
arteries and increase of apartment dwellers.

The prime concern of urban missions from the outset was to establish churches in areas of new or expected growth, usually in

middle-class neighborhoods where Presbyterianism could be expected to appeal. In an early period expansion came largely through congregational effort. Older churches sent out colonies, or established outpost Sunday schools, which in time grew into churches. In Charleston, West Virginia, and its environs—which by 1950 had come to possess the largest concentration of Presbyterians in proportion to population within the bounds of the Assembly[23]—there were 24 churches, the fruit of outposts established by the First Church and its eldest daughter, Bream Memorial.[24]

In Dallas, Texas, laymen played a leading role. The population of this city in 1920 was 158,976; in 1940, 294,734; and in 1950, 432,850, yet by 1947 no new Presbyterian church had been organized in the city for 20 years. In this year an extension committee was erected, composed of four laymen from each church, appointed by the session, plus the minister and the chairman of the Board of Deacons. This committee, working closely with the presbytery's Committee on Home Missions, purchased strategic sites and raised money for the erection of a building; presbytery's committee employed the personnel essential to the initiation of work and continued its aid until self-support was attained. This plan, based essentially on that developed in Jackson, Mississippi, and Corpus Christi, Texas, spread to other cities, including Atlanta, Memphis, and Nashville.[25]

Charlotte, North Carolina, in an area where Presbyterianism had been strong since the colonial period, had nine Presbyterian churches by 1912; in the next 29 years only two more were established. In 1941 the Home Mission Committee took on new life, a survey was made, an executive secretary (Rev. R. H. Stone) secured, and within a decade ten or more churches were organized. Expansion here was greatly aided by the generosity of a Presbyterian layman, Mr. W. H. Belk,[26] and by a fund established by his sons, to which every Belk-affiliated store made annual contributions.

In Norfolk, Virginia, one of the most rapidly growing cities in the Southeast, Presbytery's Church Committee, guided by Ruling Elder N. B. Ethridge, sought to secure a church site as soon as from 500 to 1,000 new homes were projected in any area.

In most cases now it was the presbytery, with an executive secretary working through a church extension committee, on which influential laymen were largely represented, which chose strategic sites for the erection of future churches. For a time normal procedure had been first a Sunday school, then a church; in the 1950's it became the more usual procedure to provide adequate facilities and to organize both church and Sunday school at the outset. Any church, built after proper survey in a rapidly growing area, could be expected to become self-supporting within a brief period of years. It was in such areas, in the better residential sections of the new metropolitan areas, that a large part, perhaps the chief part, of the church's growth took place.

Problems for churches in the older areas of the city, meanwhile, were becoming more pressing. The task of the downtown church was conditioned by the fact that its members moved increasingly to the outlying residential districts or suburbs. Many retained their membership in the central church but eventually they or their children were likely to join a church in their own neighborhood. The question then arose—should the church remain in its central location downtown or follow its members into the suburbs? Some did one and some the other. Some, like Central Church, Atlanta, found a way to attract people from the outlying areas back to the center of town and at the same time to reach out in a helpful ministry to their immediate neighborhood. Most churches in declining neighborhoods were fighting a losing battle. They found it difficult at best to relate to a lower income group replacing those in a higher income bracket, next to impossible when the newcomers, as was often the case, were members of another race.

Few churches were established in low income areas or in sections where industrial workers predominated. There were notable exceptions—the McAllister Memorial Church in Covington, Virginia; the West End Church in Hopewell, Virginia—but these were exceptions. "The Presbyterian Church in the United States remained predominantly a middle-class church, with a smaller percentage of its membership in the lower income brackets, and with a larger percentage of professional men and of college graduates among its members [except for the Episcopal Church] than any other denomination in the South."[27]

A Home Mission study book posed a question, "Shall we become increasingly a church of the comfortable middle-class, appealing to business men, professional men and independent farmers (in a few restricted areas), to executives and engineers and white collar workers, or shall we seek to win also those in the lower income brackets, sharecroppers as well as independent farmers, laborers as well as industrialists, the less privileged as well as the more privileged, those who labor with their hands as well as those who labor with their minds?"[28]

Such questions were now troubling the church. In 1958, 21 overtures were sent up to the General Assembly expressing the concern of the respective presbyteries over this issue and requesting that the Board of Church Extension develop a ministry to Southern industrial workers.

Out of this agitation, and the Board's own concern, came a new department of urban church headed by Rev. John Robert Smith, D.D. (the earlier department now becoming in name, as it had been in fact, the Department of Survey and Church Location). The attention of the church was drawn to its responsibility to the city as a whole.[29] Presbyteries experiencing rapid urban change were encouraged to support congregations which desired to stay and minister to a changing neighborhood, for which their own funds or leadership or moral support was insufficient; to help each urban and suburban congregation to understand its particular mission within the total Presbyterian mission to the city; and to formulate programs by which the congregation could best serve its own particular neighborhood.[30]

Lifted up for special consideration was the problem of the inner city. Churches that remained to serve in a declining neighborhood or which developed vital contacts with the lives and needs of people throughout their community (Seigle Avenue Presbyterian Church in Charlotte, Westminster Presbyterian Church in St. Louis, Northside Community Church in Kansas City) and great city churches that developed a vital downtown ministry (Central Presbyterian Church in Atlanta) were held up for emulation.[31]

Special training for ministers in urban situations was stressed and was being provided for now in theological seminaries, in special conferences, and in institutes and centers.

In 1965 the Board of National Ministries voted to make funds available not only for new churches in the growing suburbs and for struggling churches in the inner city, but also for a wide variety of experimental ministries in urban settings. The response of the presbyteries was gratifying, revealing a growing readiness to reach out in new and imaginative ways to develop ministries outside the accustomed parish activities. In some such cases the ministry of the Word was subordinated to the ministry of the deed—a ministry to human needs was carried on for its own sake, or rather to meet the need in question, whether or not it opened the way for an articulated witness to Christ. In a number of cities urban councils were erected, a city missionary was appointed, or a denominational or interdenominational agency was created to study the needs of the city as a whole and to draw upon the total resources of the churches to meet whatever needs were discovered.

In accord with this new approach to the problem of the city was a significant paper on the theology of evangelism approved by the Board of National Ministries. Mr. Albert E. Dimmock had resigned his post as Secretary of Evangelism in 1962. Four years passed before the Board secured his successor, in part because the church seemed uncertain regarding the character of the evangelism which the times demanded. A carefully planned self-study, calling on experts from within and without the church, provided no answer. A task force, appointed to study and report on a theology of evangelism, after several years of effort, brought in a report (approved by the Board) which recognized that tensions and differences regarding the character of the evangelistic enterprise remained within the church as within the task force itself. The report registered, nonetheless, a large body of agreement. Revealing was this statement:

> Evangelism must take account of the worldly structures and relationships in which men live . . . The evangelistic invitation . . . is a call to be Christ's men within those structures and responsibilities . . . in our evangelism we must demonstrate concretely that we are for our fellow human beings. We must show an active concern for their physical, intellectual, emotional and social welfare. Jesus showed just such an active concern for all men whom he encountered. This service of human need is a way of declaring God's love for all men. It is the Gospel in action and we should feel no uneasiness or guilt about giving our time to it. There will not in every instance be a direct combination of word and deed. At times the deed may be without the word. At other times the word may be without any concrete deed. It is the total style of the church's life that counts. A church which is not habitually engaged in selfless service to human need cannot expect a needy world to heed its words.[32]

In this statement was a new conception of evangelism, which had profound implications for the church and all of its agencies.

The older, traditional types of evangelism continued meanwhile to be employed, exemplified by an independently organized group, under the leadership of Rev. William E. Hill, Jr., known as the Presbyterian Evangelistic Fellowship Inc. Included in 1968 were ten full-time evangelists, who emphasized preaching of the old-time gospel as a means for reviving churches, changing individuals, and calling young men into full-time Christian service. Their services were sought almost exclusively in smaller churches throughout the Assembly.

The population movement that developed in the South after the First and Second World War affected Negroes as well as whites—it was a movement of the Negroes from the farms to the cities, and to the cities of the South as well as to those of the North. Despite the exodus of the Negroes from the South during the war years there were three percent more Negroes in the region in 1950 than there had been in 1940. The ratio of Negroes in the South's population had diminished from 23.8 percent to 21.6 percent. But the Negro population was much more thickly congregated in the cities. Large-scale housing developments for Negroes were under way in such cities as Memphis, Nashville, Atlanta, Orlando, Houston, and Louisville. In Richmond, Virginia, 24,000 dwelling units formerly owned by whites were taken over by Negroes within five years.

A second important movement among Negroes might be termed a cultural movement. The status of the urban Negro was improving—economically, socially, politically (to some extent), and above all, educationally. In almost every city a new class of Negro leadership was emerging, including artists, businessmen, dentists, editors, lawyers, physicians, social workers, and others. But comparatively few educated Negroes were entering the ministry. In 1955 less than 100 Negro ministers graduated from all seminaries with a B.D. degree to serve the Baptist, Methodist, and Pentecostal churches which among them enrolled most of the Negroes in America. The new generation of educated Negroes meanwhile was less willing to sit under the preaching of untrained ministers and less attracted by the emotional type of religion found in the typical Negro church. Many were being lost therefore to the church.

Southern Presbyterian ministers were beginning to recognize the inadequacy of their own denomination's approach to the Negroes.[33] There was a growing feeling that something was amiss. The 1944 General Assembly referred two overtures regarding Negro work to the Home Mission Council. Its report affirming that Negro work merited the fullest confidence of the church was dismissed as superficial, and the matter was turned over to a new ad interim committee which brought in a more realistic appraisal.

In 1891 when the General Assembly first created the Executive Committee of Colored Evangelization, the church was reminded by the ad interim committee, there had been 40 Negro ministers, 55 churches, and 1,300 members. In 1910 when the Negro work was transferred to the Home Missions Committee there were 43 Negro ministers, 70 churches and missions, and 2,355 members. In 1946 there were 56 Negro churches, only two of which were self-supporting; 46 Negro ministers, 12 of whom were inactive; and 3,368 members. "The growth of Negro membership in our church," commented the committee, "has been painfully slow." The majority of the ministers, it went on to point out, were inadequately trained for the gospel ministry. They were also poorly paid, with the result that most of them were compelled to take on another occupation in order to support their families. Stillman Institute, the denomination's only school for Negroes, was a struggling junior college which fell far short of the requirements of a first-class educational institution. It was conditionally accredited by the Southern Association of Schools and Colleges, but this partial recognition was in danger of being withdrawn. The theological department had almost ceased to function, with one student at the time and one course taught by a Methodist minister. The department of nurses' training, once the pride of the school, had lost its professional standing. There were evidences of serious unrest among the student body, verging from time to time on open rebellion. The indication was that Stillman had lost the confidence of the church's Negro constituency.[34]

It had lost the confidence of its Negro constituency, in large part, the committee had discovered, although it did not say so publicly, because too many in positions of responsibility retained the traditional attitude in the South for the Negro, a patronizing attitude which no longer permitted the "new" Negro to maintain his self-respect.[35]

The ad interim committee recommended that a permanent Committee on Negro Work be erected, with its own full-time secretary, that control of Stillman College (previously in the hands of the Executive Committee of Home Missions) be vested in a Board of Trustees chosen by the General Assembly, that plans be approved for "a great forward movement in Negro work" which would lift the imagination and challenge the loyalty of the church as a whole.

The vote of the General Assembly was overwhelmingly in favor of the ad interim committee's report.

The fact that a forward movement in the Negro work actually developed was due in large measure to the permanent committee's newly elected Secretary, Rev. Alex R. Batchelor. Mr. Batchelor had been born in Geneva, New York, to Scottish parents, recently arrived in America. Brought up in the bounds of the Southern Presbyterian Church, he had been rejected as a missionary to Africa because of the ill-health of his wife. Happy, enthusiastic, deeply committed, stressing the need for evangelism and education, he "made the Negro feel like a person," yet never lost the confidence of the whites. Under his inspiring leadership the church seemed to be awakening for the first time to its responsibility for giving the gospel to the Negro.

Most of the existing Negro churches were in rural areas where there was little opportunity for growth. The need, as Mr. Batchelor saw it, was for churches in the new housing communities, growing rapidly now in every Southern city. Within a few years a number of such churches had been organized—in Jackson, Mississippi; in Richmond, Virginia; in Birmingham, Alabama; in Memphis and Nashville, Tennessee; in Pine Bluff, Arkansas; in Houston, Texas. These churches, in contradistinction from the older churches gathered in their own widely scattered presbyteries, were received into the white presbyteries within whose bounds they were located, and on an unsegregated basis. For a generation and more Richmond Presbyterians had boasted of their Negro Sunday school, the 17th Street Mission, carried on in one of the poorer Negro sections in the city. But because of the racial complications that might arise no church had been organized—until now.

The new policy carried out in the border synods regarding Negro churches led Dr. Walter L. Lingle, President Emeritus of Davidson College, to propose dissolution of Snedecor Memorial Synod and its presbyteries and reception of the Negro ministers and churches into the so-called white presbyteries. "The time has come," he wrote, "when we will have to abolish the color line in our religious work if we wish to reach the present generation of Negroes . . . we will have to do our religious work among the Negroes of this generation on terms of Christian equality or not at all. We will have to remember that the ground around the cross is level."[36] The *Presbyterian Outlook* added its endorsement to the proposed policy. Five overtures requesting that this step be taken were referred to the Board of Church Extension, of which Negro work was now a division, for recommendation.

The Board in reply pointed out that the 11 churches and six ministers then members of white presbyteries were mostly in the border synods, and that the time was not yet ripe for the dissolution of the three Negro presbyteries (whose churches were all in the deep South). It proposed as an alternative that the synod be dissolved, and its three presbyteries be distributed among the synods of Georgia, Alabama, and Louisiana. Such a step, it was explained, would accomplish most of the benefits sought, particularly the fellowship between Negro and white ministers and leaders "which is so necessary for this day," and avoid many of the difficulties. Open the fellowship of the synod to our Negro brethren, it was suggested, and the presbyteries can follow later at the discretion of the synod and presbyteries involved.

Opposition to this limited step developed on the floor of the Assembly, and the outcome seemed uncertain, when Ruling Elder Francis Pickens Miller took the floor. "In the discussion so far," he said, "I have gotten the idea that the question was being considered on the basis of what is practical . . . The question we ought to face is, What do you mean by the church? . . . Is it a race thing? . . . God forbid. The Church of our Lord Jesus Christ is a community of all believers . . . The goal to which all of us are striving . . . in a world . . . that is challenging all our assumptions . . . is that the Church of Jesus Christ includes all the sons of God . . . the recommendation brought before us is a small and feeble step in the right direction and I pray that we can take that step." His statement produced thunderous applause, and the measure carried by unmistakable voice vote.[37]

The Synod of Georgia voted by approximately 3 to 1, and those of Alabama and Louisiana 2 to 1 in favor of the step recommended, and the favorable vote of Snedecor Memorial Synod followed. A note attached to the resolution adopted by the Synod of Alabama receiving Central Alabama Presbytery, with its 25 Negro churches, as one of its presbyteries (but not included in the minutes) called the issue "one of administrative policy." It stated that the new move did not affect the present practices in the matter of segregation in the Presbyterian Church in the United States.[38]

The following year a two million dollar campaign was launched— one million dollars to go to Stillman College, the other million dollars to go to the Committee on Negro Work to be used for the erection of new churches. Within two years the amount sought had been oversubscribed—the first time in the history of the church, it was said, that a large financial campaign was oversubscribed on time. The controversy over racial segregation that followed the Supreme Court's decision in 1954 led many to cancel their pledges and others to fall short in their payments. The campaign continued to be pressed, however, until practically the full amount was raised (a grand total of $1,930,000 by February 1, 1957).

The campaign stimulated local interest "beyond our highest hope" reported the Negro Work Committee in 1954. In the two years in which it had been under way surveys looking toward the establishment of Negro churches had been carried out in 40 cities in 12 or more states, and requests for surveys had come in from as many more. Ten new churches had been organized since 1950; and there were plans to begin work on 20 others.[39]

By the time Dr. Batchelor died, the following year, the future of Negro work in PCUS appeared bright—for the first time in its history. Additional churches were in process of formation. Stillman College, under the leadership of its new President, Rev. Sam Burney Hay, D.D., had become a four-year college. An able faculty (integrated) had been assembled and accreditation was on its way, new buildings were being erected, the student body was increasing, and the morale of students and faculty was high. The idea of a theological department fortunately had been abandoned, and graduates of the school were received into the established theological seminaries.

Progress continued to be made. New churches were organized (24 in the period 1950-1958), and a number achieved self-support. The vast majority of these were in predominantly white presbyteries. A number of the Negro churches were located near college campuses and effective efforts were being made in Campus Christian Life Work.

In a five-year period (1954-1959) growth of the Negro church was 40.8 percent, three times that of the church as a whole. The major part of this growth, it was reported, came from those churches which were members of geographical (predominantly white) rather than racial presbyteries; in the former it was 191.5 percent; in the latter, only 7.5 percent. In the five-year period giving in the Negro churches as a whole had doubled; in the churches in geographical presbyteries it had quadrupled.[40]

Many other communities hoped to establish Negro churches. But funds for buildings were no longer available, and the supply of Negro ministers was drying up. A number of the more promising Negro churches found themselves compelled to accept white ministers. The Negro churches, it may be noted, had been discouraged from involving themselves in local integration controversies, encouraged rather to remain centers of evangelization and religious instruction.[41] A number of the Negro ministers, however, at least in the upper South, had become involved in the struggle of their people for civil rights. "We are living in times that are difficult for all Negro churches which seek to be loyal parts of a predominantly white denomination," declared the Board.[42]

In 1963 attention was called to the fact that two formerly white presbyteries in the deep South without pressure from outside had voluntarily invited and received Negro churches located within their geographic bounds, and another was moving to do so. The following year the General Assembly adopted a resolution declaring that racial presbyteries were unconstitutional and instructing all presbyteries to receive Negro churches within their bounds. Slowly, in some cases, reluctantly, recalcitrant presbyteries yielded to the persistent pressure of the General Assembly.

"In more and more of our cities," reported the Board of Church

Extension, "some of our traditional, racially segregated congregations (of whatever race) are beginning to give way to a degree of racial incorporation. In some cases this is nothing more than the occasional, but completely accepted, presence of persons of other races in the worship service and teaching activities of the congregation. In other cases this racial integration is on the basis of full membership and ministry in the church."[43] There was one church at least, with both white and Negro ministers, appealing to a double constituency.

The Department of Negro Work, within the Division of Home Missions, Board of Church Extension, had (since 1964) ceased to exist. Theoretically at least the Board recognized no distinctions of race.

During the long course of its history, the responsibilities of the agency known variously as the Executive Committee of Sustentation, the Executive Committee of Home Missions, and the Board of Church Extension had taken on different dimensions. During the Civil War its ministry had been largely to the men in gray. In the Reconstruction era, its main task came to be that of sustentation— to keep alive churches impoverished by the war. As the South rose from the ashes, surplus funds were directed into the growing West, toward the frontiers of the church. With the growth of industry and the rise of the "New South" the Executive Committee channeled its funds to promising areas in the South as a whole. In 1951 reorganization of the Assembly's agencies took place, and the Board of Church Extension was erected, absorbing the Executive Committee on Home Missions, the Permanent Committees on Evangelism and Negro Work, responsibility for chaplains and military service, and for a time TRAV and Christian Relations. New departments were added: Survey and Church Location, Church Architecture, the Urban Church. A new Division of Homes and Social Welfare was created by the General Assembly. Synods had long operated homes for children in need; now homes for the aging were increasing. The Board through its new division was prepared to give needed help. The Permanent Committee on Religion and Health was absorbed. To more adequately describe the enlarged functions of the Board its name was changed (in 1967) to the Board of National Ministries. Under the dynamic leadership of its new secretary, Dr. John F. Anderson, the Board was seeking to provide aggressive leadership to the church as it faced the challenge of the new "secular city."

The increasing involvement of the Board in ecumenical endeavors and in interracial issues, its new understanding of evangelism, and its openness to fresh currents in worship and mission aroused inevitable opposition. The Board retained, however, the overwhelming support of the General Assembly,[44] and it seemed likely that the church would continue to move in directions that the Board had charted.

XVII

The Church Overseas

For half a century it was "Foreign" Missions, which, more than any other benevolent cause, caught and held the imagination of Southern Presbyterians. It became, as someone said, "the glory of the church." Support for this cause reached a peak in 1926. The church, with a membership of less than half a million, maintained at this time more than 500 missionaries in half a dozen foreign lands. For a few brief years support remained at this high level. Then came the Depression. Foreign Mission contributions dropped from $1,248,000 in 1926 to less than half this figure in 1934. Unable to afford replacements the mission forces declined from 516 to 395; scores of volunteers were turned back; salaries were reduced almost to the point of deprivation; schools were closed; native workers were dismissed.

Dr. C. Darby Fulton, a missionary son of missionary parents, who had served the Executive Committee of Foreign Missions for some years as its Field Secretary, succeeded Dr. Egbert W. Smith as Executive Secretary in 1932, when the Depression was at its height. The movement during the next quarter of a century when his hand was at the helm could be characterized as "Advance—Through Storm," actually a series of storms.

In 1936, when the church celebrated the 75th anniversary of its founding, conditions on the home front were improving, and the general outlook abroad was encouraging.

The period of expansion which had begun in the Congo in 1910 was continuing. Missionaries were looking forward to the gradual formation of an independent church of Christ in this area. The anticlerical policy of the revolutionary government in Mexico varied greatly from state to state. Permission for holding public meetings was readily given in some towns; summarily refused in others. The evangelical movement in Brazil had begun to gather momentum. In the vast interior a distinct attitude of friendliness and open-mindedness had developed rapidly in the last two or three years. Churches were well attended.

In China, so it was reported, "A great day of opportunity is here. All the hostility so frightfully demonstrated a few years ago [in the nationalist outbreak of 1927] has gone. The year just closed has been the most fruitful in the seventy years of our work in this land . . ."[1] Missionaries in Korea were brimming with optimism. The church was growing; the nation was moving into the modern world. The outstanding accomplishment of the mission in Japan, as seen by the Executive Committee, was the development of the Presbyterian Church in Japan, a church thoroughly indigenous, with its own well-trained leadership, the strongest Protestant group in the land, both in numbers and influence. There was, however, a small black cloud on the horizon—a recrudescence of nationalism, which, it was pointed out, affected every form of national thought and life. "The omnipresent evidence of this spirit," it was stated, "is a determination to have absolute equality in all matters, whether great or small with all other nations, or individuals of other races . . ." Christianity, it was added, "is not making a tremendous advance, in fact some churches and missionaries report a decline; but it is holding its own and gradually finding itself."[2]

This nationalistic spirit, on which the Executive Committee had commented, grew rapidly, and there were indications of approaching storm. Serious threat to the church's mission appeared first in Korea, then a Japanese dependency. Shintoism, a fusion of religion and patriotism, was the national religion. Worship at the Shinto shrines, involving a recognition of the Emperor as divine, was regarded as the basis of all patriotic education. Japanese authorities in Korea demanded that the Christian schools participate officially in the shrine worship. Southern Presbyterian missionaries in Korea refused, holding that shrine worship was inconsistent with Christian monotheism. They were sustained in this attitude by Dr. Fulton and the Executive Committee. As a consequence all schools supported by the mission were closed—a handicap to the work; it was a policy, however, which enhanced the prestige of the missionaries among the Koreans.

On August 13, 1937, the Japanese armies began their invasion of China. Pressure on Christians in both Korea and Japan to participate in the shrine worship now became more intense.

The war in its earlier stages was fought largely in the territory occupied by the Southern Presbyterian missions, and much of their property was destroyed. As many as possible of the missionaries remained at their posts; a few whose furloughs were due were brought home; others were evacuated to various areas. As the fighting moved farther west, most returned to their stations, and their work returned to something like normal basis. We are facing our greatest need and opportunity, reported the Executive Committee. "The openheartedness of the people toward the Gospel is striking."[3] In Japan the public services of the churches suffered from the nationalistic spirit; but missionaries continued to be sought out by individuals "seeking light and truth and salvation in Christ."[4]

On September 28, 1940, Japan announced her definite alignment with the Axis forces. In Korea scores of Christian pastors and leaders were jailed, mistreated, and even tortured; in Japan popular feeling was intense. The missions felt that arrangements should be made for the temporary withdrawal of the women and children, missionaries whose furloughs were approaching, those in impaired health, and others whose presence on the field did not seem essential at the moment. The Executive Committee reported to the 1941 General Assembly that 124 had returned home since October, leaving 69 missionaries on the field: five in Korea, six in Japan, 58 in China. Reasons for the withdrawal were summarized as follows:

1. The extraordinary pressure of the American consular authorities in the Far East.

2. The possibility of war and of internment in concentration camps.

3. In many localities, particularly in Korea, Christian work had been virtually stopped by the police.

4. More and more Christian activities were being made to conform to a national policy out of harmony with Christian principles.

5. Many missionaries, particularly in Japan, felt that because of the strong national animosities that existed, their presence as Americans had become for the time being a definite hindrance to the work.

6. The presence of the missionaries in many cases had become a source of danger and persecution to the native Christians.[5]

When the Japanese attack on Pearl Harbor (December 7, 1941) opened hostilities with America, 60 missionaries still remained in the Pacific area. Of these, two were in Free China, 36 in Occupied China, six in Japan, four in Korea, seven in the Philippines (attending language schools), and five in the Hawaiian Islands. All of these save the two in Free China and those in the Hawaiian Islands were in Japanese-occupied territory. Most of these latter had insisted on remaining at their stations even when given opportunity of going to places of safety. Eighteen months later the majority of these (about 40 in number) were repatriated, along with 1,451 other Americans, half of them missionaries, who came on the steamship Gripsholm, which arrived in New York on August 25, 1942. Eleven more were brought back the following year, leaving only six young missionaries interned in the Philippines; these suffered many deprivations and were not liberated until the closing days of the war.

With the war's end missionaries returned as quickly as possible to their posts in the Far East—58 of them within 18 months after the end of hostilities; most of them returned to China. They found in Japan, Korea, and China, property losses running into the millions —schools, hospitals, and churches standing with gaping windows and shattered walls; missionary homes had been divested of all furniture and disfigured by successive occupations.

In other fields unscarred by war there were also pressing needs, in the face of vast opportunities. The Depression years had cut the missionary forces, and the war following shortly thereafter had reduced the flow of reinforcement to a mere trickle; properties were in disrepair; missionaries, exhausted by long years of overwork, were discouraged and desperate.[6] Added to the other difficulties was the problem of a galloping post-war inflation.

The war, however, brought a new interest in world missions. Missionaries reported that they had never known the spirit of concern and inquiry to be so earnest, not only in the church, but also among the general public. "The American GI has brought back a new witness to Missions, the result of first-hand examination," said the Executive Committee. "There is a new recognition that the trouble with the world has been fundamentally spiritual and that only a spiritual solution will suffice . . . For the first time many have seen utterly the peril of material power without God."[7]

Relief came to the mission forces with the launching of a Program of Progress. Within two years two million dollars had been raised— over and above the regular benevolent budget—as a capital fund for building, equipment, and permanent improvement. For the first time, reported the Executive Committee, our missions are being equipped with the buildings and the tools that they need.[8] Within a few years regular contributions surpassed those given in the pre-Depression era. The number of missionaries also showed a steady increase. In 1949-1950, 48 new missionaries were sent out, the largest contingent ever appointed, up to this time, in the course of a single year. In 1965, after the third consecutive year of major increase in the number of new missionaries dispatched, the total number—567—finally topped (by 14) the high watermark reached in pre-Depression days, nearly 40 years earlier.

Missionaries returning to the Far East after the close of World War II met with a warm welcome on the part of the people, a surprisingly warm welcome, even in Occupied Japan.

In China, however, the respite was brief. Some missionaries had hailed Free China under Chiang Kai-Shek, himself a professing Christian, with many Christians in key positions, as the most strongly motivated Christian government in existence. Dr. Frank W. Price, who had followed the exiled government to the west, was an honored adviser and was the one foreigner who accompanied the Chinese delegation to San Francisco at the formation of the United Nations. Rev. J. Leighton Stuart, D.D., distinguished President of the prestigious Yenching University of Peking, was appointed American ambassador to the newly restored government. But corruption ran rampant in the Nationalist government after its return to power; and the well-disciplined Communist forces led by Mao Tse-tung grew in strength and soon swept all before them.

In 1949 the Executive Committee reported that about 30 missionaries had returned to America; about the same number had remained in China, convinced that Christianity must find a way to bear its witness even under a Communist regime. Their hopes, however, proved illusory, and two years later, only seven missionaries remained in the land; all of these had applied for exit permits and were awaiting favorable action by the authorities. The last of these, Dr. and Mrs. Frank W. Price, were finally permitted to leave in October 1952.

Dr. Price recalled that the Southern Presbyterian Church had sent its first missionary to China in August 1867. For 85 years, through civil wars, international wars, anti-foreign movements, revolutions, and political changes, the missionaries of PCUS had continued without a break in personnel to preach the gospel and serve the Chinese people. They had founded a dozen hospitals, a college, scores of schools, several theological seminaries, and a number of orphanages. They had planted churches that reached a membership of nearly 20,000 baptized Christians. At the peak of missionary activity just before the Sino-Japanese war about 200 men and women were on the roll of the China Mission. After the big drop during the war the number rose again after the peace to nearly 80. These, in turn, had been forced out gradually by the advancing Communist tide. It was, as Dr. Price remarked, the end of an era in Chinese missions; but he, with others, was confident that Christianity in China would continue to live.[9]

Most of the missionaries were compelled to withdraw temporarily from Korea—at the height of the Korean War—when it seemed for a moment as though the advancing Communist forces would occupy the whole of the peninsula, but they were soon back, in high favor with the Korean people, now freed from foreign domination.

It was six years before missionary forces in Japan were back to pre-Pearl Harbor strength. By this time the first enthusiastic rush toward Christianity had subsided perceptibly, but there was still a receptiveness to Christian truth, and a more favorable attitude than had existed in prewar days. A sizable number of missionaries withdrawn from China had followed the Nationalist forces to Taiwan, and a thriving work was soon in process. .

Missions in Africa, in Mexico, and in Brazil had continued through the war years without interruption. Growth of the Congo mission had been very rapid. But the war had brought changes. The simple Africa we knew a few years ago is no more, the Board reported in 1954. The Africa in which the missionary was accorded extraordinary prestige was gone. Missionaries had hoped that young people trained in the mission schools would return to their villages to propagate the Christian faith, but the lure of big cities and of good paying jobs was drawing them away. In Mexico the 1940's brought a gradual relaxation of the regulations which for a time handicapped missionary activities in that land. Formal school activities were not permitted, but evangelistic work was not seriously affected. In Brazil, Presbyterianism, along with Protestantism generally, had entered upon a period of unprecedented growth. In the post-war years cooperative undertakings were begun in a number of new fields: in Portugal (1945) with the Presbyterian Church in the United States of America and the Presbyterian Church in Brazil; in Ecuador (1946), with Northern Presbyterians, the Evangelical and Reformed Church, and the Evangelical and United Brethren Church; in Iraq (1956), with the U.S.A. Presbyterians, the Evangelical and Reformed Church, and the Reformed Church in America.

In spite of the recovery of the foreign missionary enterprise, the increased offering, the enlarging personnel, the encouraging growth on the field, all was not well with the missionary cause at home or abroad. The Board pointed out again and again that while missionary giving was reaching a new high, proportionate giving to Foreign Missions (now World Missions) was far less than it had been a generation earlier. Twice as many people (approximately) in 1960 were giving about the same amount of money (in actual purchasing power) as their fathers and mothers, half their number, had given 30 years earlier. In 1938, 10.5 percent of the church's total giving went to World Missions; in 1957 only 4.4 percent. This did not necessarily bespeak a loss of missionary interest. The church on the home field had necessarily undertaken new responsibilities which had not been recognized or did not exist in the simpler days of an earlier period.

But new questions were coming to the fore. One of these which troubled many in the home church for a number of years was regarding the attitude of the Mission Board toward the United Christian Church in Japan (popularly known as the Kyodan) and the Japan International Christian University.

Before World War II the Southern Presbyterian missions had been affiliated with the Church of Christ in Japan, which was basically Reformed in doctrine. It had about 75,000 members, of whom 20,000 came from churches founded by PCUS missions. During World War II there was formed under government pressure a federation of 11 church bodies. After the war some groups withdrew, but the Kyodan, now a voluntary union, retained about 150,000 church members, approximately two-thirds of the Protestant communicants in Japan.

Among those withdrawing from the Kyodan were a small number of fundamentalist ministers, strongly influenced by splinter Presbyterian denominations in America, who came together early in 1946 to form the Synod of the Reformed Church in Japan. Eight years later it had approximately 3,000 members. The small group of PCUS missionaries who returned to Japan shortly after the close of the war belonged to the more conservative wing of the church, and were not representative of the pre-war mission as a whole, or with the majority of Southern Presbyterians in the homeland. Under their lead the Japanese mission limited its relations largely to the newly organized Reformed Church in Japan rather than with the Kyodan, to which belonged the majority of the Christians formerly connected with the Southern Presbyterian mission. The mission also declined to enter the Japan Council of Churches.[10]

The Japan International Christian University (JICU) was an ambitious cooperative venture, growing out of a post-war suggestion—for a counter to the destruction by atomic bombs of the two Japanese cities, Hiroshima and Nagasaki—made originally by Dr. J. A. MacLean, pastor of the Ginter Park Presbyterian Church in Richmond, and taken up and supported generally by churches and churchmen related to the National Council of Churches. It gave hopes of becoming a first-class institution, the one outstanding educational institution under Christian auspices in Japan. It had the support of all major denominations carrying on missionary activity in Japan—with the exception of the Presbyterian Church in the United States. The Japan mission, with its post-war fundamentalist outlook, opposed support of the new undertaking on the ground that the basic Christian position of the institution was not sufficiently clear; that the foundation controlling the university was not responsible to any ecclesiastical body; that it had been formed for the "advancement of the Japanese people," rather than for the advancement of the Kingdom of Christ; and that it would be wiser policy to confine aid to institutions where responsibility and policy were clearly and definitely stated.[11]

The mission, it may be noted, prior to its consideration of JICU, had decided to establish a men's college of its own. This was opened in 1950, one year after the organization of the JICU, largely through the aid of funds received from the Program of Progress. The new college was closely identified with the fundamentalist Reformed Church in Japan. The mission also supported a small theological seminary, in cooperation with the Orthodox Presbyterian Church, one of the splinter groups breaking off from the Presbyterian Church in the U.S.A.

The Board reported to the General Assembly that it had declined to assume financial or administrative responsibility for the Japan University on the grounds that it was under pressure of assigning funds to work already established and to objects which appeared to have greater claims upon its resources and which had prospects of greater value to the missionary enterprise, and because, in accordance with the general policy, it had consulted with its mission on the field and they twice advised noncooperation. However, they wished the new institution well and prayed for its success.[12]

The *Presbyterian Outlook,* in editorials and contributed articles, questioned the wisdom of this policy, and a number of overtures to the General Assembly requested that the Board's decision be reversed. In support of these overtures, Dr. W. L. Carson of Richmond warned of the growing concern of a considerable element of the church regarding points of view advocated by some missionaries in some of the mission fields. He added: "I believe that this is going to be a day that our church will long regret when it goes down on record for posterity that we, the only major denomination that I know of working in Japan, felt compelled to decline to participate in any way in this great international, inter-denominational expression of Christian brotherhood and good-will." In response, Dr. Fulton, the Executive Secretary of the Board, made clear a point that the Board in its public statement had sought to avoid—that the real objection to participation in the proposed university was misgivings about the theological stance of the university. "On this," said Dr. Fulton, "I stand with the

Mission absolutely."[13] Here the lines were drawn. To one group, JICU had become a symbol of ecumenicity and a willingness to cooperate with other Christian bodies in Japan. To the other, it was a concrete illustration of a loose use of the term "Christian," without any indication as to the meaning of the term, and without any doctrinal safeguards. Dr. Fulton was an eloquent man, unrivaled in debate. On this occasion, as usual, he carried the day. The Assembly contrary to custom applauded his remarks and later stood in appreciation of his services. The Board's policy was approved with only a few scattered noes.

But the dissatisfaction remained. Many were outraged that the church followed an isolationist position in Japan that it had rejected on the home front and in many areas abroad. The Synod of Virginia called upon its churches to contribute generously to the support of JICU and overtured the General Assembly to reconsider its former action. The Synods of Kentucky and Texas took similar actions. In each case the action was unanimous or nearly so. A group of younger missionaries recently arrived in Japan indicated their support for the university. The Executive Secretary felt very strongly on the matter. Meeting with a standing committee of the General Assembly he stated that he would prefer for a Japanese student to attend one of the pagan universities in that land rather than JICU, for if he attended the latter he would very likely become infected with an inadequate Christianity which would be more difficult to overcome than outright paganism.[14] After hearing Dr. Fulton, the standing committee of the 1951 General Assembly recommended and the Assembly itself voted unanimously to reaffirm the action of the previous Assembly.

The following year the General Assembly heard Dr. J. A. MacLean present at some length the case for the Japanese International Christian University and then Dr. Fulton in rebuttal. Once more the Assembly upheld the policy of the Board. But the growing concern of a considerable group was revealed when the Assembly suspended its rules to permit introduction of a resolution calling for appointment of an ad interim committee to make a thorough study of the missionary obligation and strategy of the church in "today's world." The motion carried, despite opposition, by a vote of 105 to 69.

Some of the reflections which prompted this resolution were set forth in an article written shortly after the General Assembly by Dr. T. Watson Street in the pages of the *Presbyterian Outlook*. Dr. Street, Professor of Church History and Missions in Austin Presbyterian Theological Seminary, had spent a part of his Sabbatical leave in the Congo. A review of the church's missionary strategy, he argued, was urgently needed. This, he affirmed, was no condemnation of the present strategy, but a recognition that times and conditions were changing, and that the missions' methods must be constantly reviewed and revised. For example, since the work was first established in Africa, the Congo had become industrialized. Towns and cities were developing. Much of the work was poorly located with respect to these new centers. Work in the growing urban centers was pitifully small, and young Africans moving to these centers were largely lost to the church. Meanwhile the rural work was not as effective as formerly. There were also problems, he found, in the realm of missionary-African relationships, tensions likely to increase as a consequence of the rising nationalistic spirit.

He found three grievances in particular among the native Christians on the mission fields generally and especially in Africa. First, that they were not being treated as persons; that there were expressions of what the Africans regarded as race prejudice. "There is no doubt," commented Dr. Street, "that the predominant racial attitude and practice of our Mission is very conservative, akin to what one meets in conservative sections of the South. There is no doubt, either, that in our Mission there is a line of separation between the missionaries and the national Christians. Some of the separation is inevitable . . . but the line of separation is increasingly resented by many."

The second grievance voiced by the African leaders was they were not given a worthy role in the direction of the mission. This matter of self-government, Dr. Street noted, was an issue in almost every field. Self-government or approximations of it, he felt, were being granted too slowly, despite the standard response that responsibility was being shared as rapidly as the Africans proved themselves worthy of it.

The third grievance of the African leaders was on the subject of money. The government was setting a minimum wage. The mission had requested the government to exempt it from this requirement, and this the Africans could not understand. "What is the responsibility of the church as an employer of thousands for the economic life of its employees?" asked Dr. Street. This, he held, was an important question regarding missionary responsibility.

These same grievances, Dr. Street had found, were also basic issues in other mission fields.[15]

Rev. John Morrison, a veteran missionary in the Congo, wrote a series of articles in rebuttal, indicating that the criticisms lacked justification. Justified or not, Dr. Street replied, the grievances, as felt by the Africans, were real. The church awaited the report of its ad interim committee with deepened interest. It came two years later after conference with many leaders of the world mission enterprise. Attention was called to many of the factors affecting World Missions— among them, the development of the ecumenical movement; the younger churches' desire for more independence; the dangers of paternalism; the tensions in church-missions relations; the inadequate identification of missionaries with the life and needs of the peoples served; the problems related to mission property and its transfer to the national churches; the rapid spread of Communism and its exploitation of sore spots, such as hunger, unemployment, and social restlessness; political chaos; and anti-Westernism. Dr. Street also made specific suggestions regarding missionary policies in general and also in particular fields: that the Japan mission, for example, be asked to bring its program into harmony with the theological position and cooperative policy of the home church.

More rapid progress, the ad interim committee concluded, must be made toward an indigenous church on every mission field. Our kind of a world, said the committee, cannot wait for a leisurely evolution. "The tensions of the time demand that our missionaries undergo the additional discipline of learning how to fit themselves into the life and outreach of the indigenous church not as bosses and directors, but as counsellors and servants." The committee also stressed the need for greater cooperation between the various communions on the mission fields in order to produce the needed Christian literature, to present the claims of the gospel, to train professional and lay leadership. "Too long," it was asserted, "have we through our mission efforts perpetuated our denominational differences that stem from our cultural and historical backgrounds."[16]

The ad interim committee asked that its report be referred to the Board of World Missions for study and report, which was done unanimously and without debate. The Board's response to the ad interim report was made to the 1955 General Assembly. Exception was taken to certain factual statements; at points genuine differences in judgments were expressed; on the whole, there was expressed agreement. The Board stated that it was well aware of the conditions described in the report and seeking to meet them. A spirited defense was made of the policy being followed in Japan: no official relationship with the Japan International Christian University, and freedom of the missionaries to work with established churches in or out of the Kyodan. There was no indication that any change of mission policy could be expected from the ad interim report.[17] The Assembly commended the Board for the serious thought and careful attention it had given to the report, and so the matter rested—for the moment; nothing, it would seem, had been accomplished.

The ad interim committee, however, had recognized correctly that pertinent questions were being raised regarding current mission policy by a sizable minority in the church. Evidence of this fact arose in the Assembly which commended the Board for its careful consideration of the ad interim report. The Standing Committee of World Missions had taken the liberty of nominating, for membership on the Executive Committee, Dr. T. Watson Street, who more than any other had raised the questions which were now being asked regarding the Foreign Mission enterprise, in lieu of one of the nominees submitted by the Permanent Nominating Committee, a valid procedure but one rarely taken. A determined floor fight then developed to remove both Dr. Street and Dr. Harry M. Moffett—thought to be critical of certain Board policies—from the list of nominees submitted by the standing committee and to substitute for them men who, it was claimed, would support present policies and aims of the Board. After considerable debate and parliamentary maneuvering, the recommendations of the Standing Committee were accepted, and its two nominees became members of the Board.[18]

The following year the Board of World Missions stated that in line with previous decisions it had once more declined to accept any official responsibility for the Japan International Christian University. On motion from the floor the Assembly, by a vote of approximately two to one, requested the Board to reappraise its policy. The Japan mission, reinforced by a large number of younger missionaries, now reversed its former stand on both JICU and the National Christian Council in Japan, voting by a slight majority in favor of participation in both. With this information before it, the Board of World Missions reversed its earlier recommendations and the General Assembly adopted unanimously the statement "that we would favor our Board accepting membership in the J.I.C.U. Foundation in New York when it sees its way clear to put in its Constitution the doctrinal basis of the World Council of Churches, which affirms its acceptance of Jesus Christ as God and Savior." This the Foundation did, and so finally PCUS gave financial support and accepted responsibility for the further development of an important educational institution whose value for the Christian cause it had belatedly recognized—but, until now, had done nothing to promote.

In 1958, the General Assembly again rejected a nominee for the Board of World Missions proposed by the Permanent Nominating Committee and elected, on nomination from the floor, a layman,

General Joseph B. Fraser, thought to possess a more progressive point of view.

The ad interim report of 1954 had called attention to tensions aggravated by the growing nationalistic spirit arising in some areas between national church and missions from abroad. Alternative conceptions of missionary strategy were presented. The basic plan under which denominations generally had operated in the past, and under which many, including PCUS, continued to operate, was to establish in every land as rapidly as possible an indigenous church, which should be self-supporting, self-governing, and self-propagating. The mission, however, continued to operate alongside the indigenous church as an independent organization, responsible for its own operation under the general direction and oversight of its Board of World Missions, assuming responsibility for the evangelization of unreached areas (the important task of pioneer missions) and for the administration and maintenance of various missionary institutions, such as hospitals and schools. Whenever a new congregation was organized and became capable of self-support, it was immediately turned over to the indigenous church. Schools and hospitals were also turned over as soon as the national church was able to support them. To our own Board of World Missions, to a majority of the missionaries on the field, and to many of the nationals themselves this seemed a fair division of labor which enabled both mission and church to cooperate most effectively for the advancement of the gospel in a land where Protestants remained a tiny minority of the total population.

To an increasing number of missionary leaders, however, and to many national Christians, this traditional relationship of church and mission, under new world conditions, seemed no longer desirable, or in accordance with the New Testament conception of the church.

The newer conception of missionary strategy, as accepted, for example, by the Presbyterian Church in the U.S.A., called for the dissolution of the mission as a unit charged with the conduct of missionary operations and for placing responsibility for conducting the total mission of the overseas church (including the management of educational institutions and the evangelization of frontier regions) squarely upon the national church. Missionaries, to be sent so long as their presence was desired and needed by the younger churches, became "fraternal workers." They were placed at the disposal of the national church and were expected to identify themselves in every possible way with its life and work.[19]

The clash between these two contrasting strategies explains in part the restlessness appearing on the foreign fields, the questions troubling many on the home field. The issue was highlighted by a vigorous attack launched on traditional plans of missionary operation at the General Assembly of the Presbyterian Church in Mexico in the spring of 1960, a meeting which the Moderator of the Presbyterian Church in the United States had been strongly urged to attend. He, as well as veteran missionaries in attendance, was amazed at the strong resentment voiced by both ministers and elders at the tutelage in which they felt they were held, by what seemed to them a refusal by the aiding churches to recognize the Presbyterian Church in Mexico as a mature Christian body, a true church, in need of aid, but fully capable, and responsible for making ultimate decisions regarding the conduct of the Christian enterprise in Mexico. From this Assembly came a request to the General Assembly of PCUS: "That there be worked out with the Churches and ecclesiastical bodies in other countries which have relations with our Church through missionary work, an agreement by which they recognize this as a divinely instituted and properly organized Body . . ."[20]

The Board of World Missions in its report to the General Assembly this year recognized that the problem of church-mission relations was one which deserved the most careful study and attention. It stressed that it was not committed to any set pattern of church-mission relations; pointed out that in general the missionary program was determined by cooperative planning between church and mission; and laid down essential principles for the future conduct of the work which anticipated apparently the perpetuation of the mission as an operating unit.[21]

To this same Assembly came an overture from Central Texas Presbytery, indicating that unrest in the home field was not yet allayed. The General Assembly was asked to appoint an ad interim committee composed of persons other than executives and members of the Boards and agencies of the church to study and report on the philosophy and promotion of world missions in the light of the rapidly changing missionary situation around the world.[22] The Standing Committee recommended that this overture be answered in the negative. From the floor came a substitute, adopted after some debate by the Assembly, "That the Board of World Missions consider and report to the next General Assembly on the advisability of the Board itself appointing a committee, including personnel from overseas [not consulted in the 1954 study] and from other bodies than our own, which shall study and report on the philosophy and promotion of World Missions in the light of the rapidly changing missionary situation around the world . . ."[23] The mover recognized that any change in missionary policy must come from within, not from without, and that the Board in considering necessary changes in policy needed far broader information than it had hitherto received.

The Board was at the time seeking for a successor to Dr. Fulton, who was approaching retirement age. After others had declined the position, the Board turned to Dr. T. Watson Street as its new executive, and so it happened that the man who had done more than any other to awaken the church to the new day in missions arranged for the Consultation, which drew guidelines for the new administration to follow.

The Consultation, for which careful plans had been made, gathered at Montreat in the fall of 1962. Consultants on various phases of mission work had been invited by the Board of World Missions. All other participants had been chosen by the groups they were representing. There were missionaries from PCUS and other churches; national Christian leaders from many lands; distinguished personnel from inter-denominational missionary organizations; representatives of the Boards and agencies of PCUS; students from seminaries, colleges, and high schools; and average members of local churches. The Consultation participants represented varying theological emphases and differing views on missionary philosophy and practice. There were young and old, Christians from various races, countries, and economic conditions. There were Asians, Africans, Europeans, Latin Americans, and North Americans. Two hundred in all. The chief difference of opinion arose in regard to the church-mission relations—most of the nationals being on one side and most of the missionaries on the other. The recommendations in this area finally agreed upon represented something of a compromise, but with the balance tilted definitely on the side of the national churches. Thus in the section on the role of the missionary came the following statement: "Recognizing that a wide diversity of circumstances exist in our fields, and that the relationship between the missionary and the indigenous church must vary accordingly, this relationship should move in the following direction: the missionary should be willing to work in the framework of the national church. Work assignments should be made by the proper court of the national church."[24]

In the section of the role of the mission we read that the committee considered various types of structures, including complete integration, partial integration and a number of cooperative plans. No agreement as to an overall plan or policy seemed possible, but it was agreed that all structures should be determined in accordance with the following unanimous action of the committee: "That the structure of relationship of missionaries to a national church should be worked out by that national church in consultation with the Presbyterian Church in the United States."[25]

Five years after the Consultation, a landmark in PCUS World Missions, a Missionary Convocation was called by the Board to meet in the city of Memphis. Approximately one-third of the church's total mission force was in attendance. In his opening address, Dr. Street indicated that the Board, during the five preceding years, had been seeking to implement the recommendations of the Consultation in four particular ways:

1. To relate the missionary effort more closely to the church in each land. As a direct consequence of the Consultation, Dr. Street indicated, a shift had taken place, from a mission-based approach to a church-based approach. In every land where a national church had been established PCUS missionaries now worked in and through that church. The national church, explained Dr. Street, "becomes our partner and advises us as to our best contribution to the Christian World Mission in that place."[26] Inevitably this transition had brought difficulties, problems, and frustrations. It was in part to resolve the questions that had arisen that the Convocation of 1967 was called.

2. To move toward a fuller realization of the church's unity. The Consultation had echoed again and again the need for cooperative endeavors to reflect the unity and wholeness of God's people. Cooperative efforts, particularly with other Presbyterian and Reformed bodies, had been carried on in most missions from the beginning, and a number of new cooperative efforts had been launched in the years preceding the Consultation, but in the next five years giant new strides had been taken. Bonds had been strengthened with the mainstream ecumenical movement—with the Division of Overseas Ministries of the National Council of Churches and with the Division of World Mission and Evangelism of the World Council of Churches and with the churches in these ecumenical bodies. This new policy meant more joint action by the participating churches in support of programs drawn up by the national churches themselves rather than those on the outside.

3. To interpret the Christian message more broadly. Before 1962 the missionary obligation as defined again and again was evangelism, an effort to bring individuals to Christ through a proclamation of the gospel. Medical services and educational institutions were only means to this end. The attitude toward political, social, and economic reform was negative rather than positive. In 1957 the Board stated:

We need to remember that the kingdom of God is within us. It does not consist in outward world order. We are not here first to build a new world . . . Our primary interest is in the reign of our Lord Jesus Christ in the hearts of men . . . We need to confront this revolutionary world with the redemptive message of Christ as the world's Savior and Lord. The deep hurt of the world is spiritual, and nothing less than a spiritual remedy will suffice. It is easy to be tricked into treating symptoms instead of causes. We must make sure that we get down to the roots of humanity's trouble and that we do not spend our time dealing with minor, surface ailments that are but eruptions from poisons that lie deeper down. . . . "Let the Church be the Church"—not a political action committee or an economic conference, or a foreign policy association. Let her emphasize the great themes of sin and repentance and faith and salvation . . .[27]

After 1962 came a more positive note. The emphasis on evangelism did not cease, but evangelism was conceived in broader terms, and concern for justice in all human relations as an essential part of the gospel was far more in evidence. As stated by Dr. Street: "We have sought to reflect in program and literature something of the breadth and depth of the theological statement of the Consultation of 1962, with its emphasis on God as Creator and Ruler, on mission as witness to the saving power of the gospel, on the Lordship of Christ, on the imperative of ministry of service . . . on 'the application of the redemption of Christ to the whole of the life of the people among whom we serve'. It is not an accident therefore that we have emphasized our duty, as a part of mission and missions, to preach justification and justice . . . that we have emphasized that the mission is to the totality of human life."[28]

An illustration of the new attitude came when 250 missionaries expressed their concern openly "about the effect that the existence of various forms of racial segregation in the Church has on the work of Christ in other lands. Our witness is affected adversely . . . by the existence of segregation in America . . . we feel it is a contradiction of the Gospel to allow it to continue in the church." The Board not only approved this statement of its missionaries, but passed it on to the General Assembly, with a strong statement of its own, and a recommendation that the Assembly call upon all of its churches and members to look to their behavior less they constitute a hindrance to Christian witness in other countries.[29]

4. The fourth endeavor since 1962, as summarized by Dr. Street, was "to experiment, to be flexible, to be responsive."

Area secretaries were appointed shortly after Dr. Street took office. A more flexible personnel policy was introduced, with provision for limited terms of service, and for special assignments not demanding protracted residence abroad; long-range recruitment programs were developed; participation in seminars and involvement in work camps and in voluntary service projects were promoted; scholarships were awarded to students from abroad—future leaders of the churches in their lands—to come to America for study; a missionary couple was appointed to minister to the vast number of Africans flocking to our national capital. Financial aid was given to a powerful radio station in Addis Ababa, to challenging opportunities in Indonesia, Hong Kong, Vietnam, Belgium, Zambia, and Ghana—all "areas and enclaves of high potential for spreading the gospel." In 1926 PCUS was laboring in nine countries; in 1967 it had personnel in 15 nations.

There were of course questions regarding the new directions in which the world mission of the church was moving; objections to its broadening ecumenical relations, to its growing social concern, and to its new understanding of "evangelism" were not lacking. "The popular tide of 'mission' has shifted to activism, inclusivism and syncretism," complained the *Presbyterian Journal*. "Many," it pointed out, "would rejoice if the Presbyterian Church US would retake the lead in stressing those objectives in mission work which God had ordained and blessed down through the years."[30]

Continuing dissatisfaction on the part of the more conservative faction led (in 1971) to the formation of an Executive Commission on Overseas Evangelism (an offshoot of the Presbyterian Evangelistic Fellowship), which announced its purpose of supporting "evangelical, conservative missionaries," with a mission philosophy "somewhat different from the staff of the PCUS Board of World Missions."

It seemed certain, however, that the denomination's missionary policy would continue along the lines which the consultation of 1962 had mapped.

XVIII

The New Look in Education

Responsibility for the promotion of Sunday schools and young people's work had been vested, from the start, in the Executive Committee on Publication, later to become the Executive Committee of Publication and Religious Education. In 1929 the name of this committee was changed again, this time to Executive Committee of Religious Education and Publication—the change in order indicating the growing importance of the church's educational program.

Mr. R. E. Magill retired as Executive Secretary of this committee in 1934 and was succeeded by Mr. Edward D. Grant, like Mr. Magill, a layman, whose career to this time, however, had been spent in the service of the church. The 18 years of his brilliant and dynamic leadership witnessed vast changes in the work and program of the Board. During this period the business department was modernized, the Presbyterian building completely remodeled, the educational program broadened, new departments added, services to the church greatly expanded. The reorganization of 1949-1950 brought to this committee the responsibility for institutions of higher learning, formerly assigned to the Executive Committee of Christian Education and Ministerial Relief. The name, changed at this time to Board of Education, was shortly thereafter renamed the Board of Christian Education.

Dr. John L. Fairley, who retired as Secretary of the Division of Religious Education in 1956, summed up some of the important developments which had occurred in his particular field during the 27 years in which he had served the Board. In 1929 seven persons had been employed in the division; in 1955 there were 18. The program had developed in breadth, scope, and quality, and new age groups had been added—older groups and children under two. "It would be inaccurate," commented Dr. Fairley, "to say that the great social issues were ignored completely during the 1920s, but during the past twenty-five years they have been lifted up in a way to challenge the thought of the church. Today, the problems of our day and generation are so presented as to be of interest and concern to every age group." During this period the person and his needs moved into a place of prominence in the program. Children's material shifted to the informal method and was planned to lay more emphasis on bringing about certain changes in the lives of the individuals for whom it was prepared. This led to a long series of discussions on the place and use of the Bible in the teaching materials, the amount of Bible content needed, and the real purpose of Bible teaching. "Scarcely an Assembly passed during the early years of the period without overtures," recalled Dr. Fairley, "at times, as many as half a dozen, directed at the teaching materials. Since that time," he added, ". . . much greater understanding has come about in the field, and on the part of teachers and leaders." No doubt, but complaints still came from parents who wished for more Bible content, particularly in the lessons for little children, and objected to the disuse of the catechisms. A changed attitude toward the church's educational program, Dr. Fairley pointed out, was found in the amazing number of new buildings erected for the purpose. There was scarcely a church, large or small, but had erected or remodeled its educational building in recent years. Other indications were the increased demand for Directors of Christian Education, for specialized leaders such as Directors of Children's Work, and for ministers of education.[1]

The most important and far-reaching development in Dr. Grant's administration was the Religious Education Restudy for which authorization was asked in 1944. "War has introduced the Executive Committee of Religious Education to new and varied problems," ran the statement. "The area served by our General Assembly has, within the past 24 months, been transformed before our eyes. New populations, new cities, new industries, new social conditions, new home problems, have all confronted Presbyterian churches and Sunday schools and parents, and out of these have grown demands upon the Executive Committee which seem at the moment impossible of fulfillment . . ."

"In the light of tremendous difficulties confronting our religious educational program at this time, and anticipating additional problems as well as opportunities, which undoubtedly will emerge during the next ten years of national and international reconstruction," the Executive Committee requested approval of "a thorough and serious reexamination" of the church's program of religious education.[2]

This study, carried out in depth over the next four years, with help from the outside, including members of the Staff of the Institute for Research in Social Sciences of the University of North Carolina, gave the church a larger body of facts regarding its educational needs than had ever been presented to any American denomination.[3]

In his popular study, presenting results of the more technical study to the church, Dr. Lewis J. Sherrill, Dean and Professor of Religious Education in Louisville Presbyterian Seminary, gave three major impressions of the church's schools which emerged from the study. First, the loyalty of the volunteer workers, some 30,000 officers and teachers. Second, an impression of achievement against great odds. "Often, though not always, they work in inadequate buildings, with limited budgets, with insufficient backing from church officers, with indifferent support from parents, and at times even under a minister who cares for none of these things. Usually the workers themselves have had insufficient training for the job they are asked to perform. And always they work in a secularized culture, in the midst of spiritual illiteracy, where the most commonplace terms in the Bible and the most elemental ideas concerning the Kingdom of God sound strange even to otherwise well-educated adults."[4]

The third impression was that of an appalling amount of wasted effort, which the study had pinpointed in meticulous detail.

The average teacher in a PCUS Sunday school was found to be a woman, 45 years of age, married, with two children. She had had one year of college, and no teaching experience save in the Sunday school. She had taken no course in teacher training. In preparing for her Sunday school lesson she was accustomed to spend a little less than an hour a week, usually on Saturday night. She acknowledged that she was habitually late in coming to Sunday school and that she missed approximately one Sunday out of five. She felt that her work as a teacher was a success more often than a failure, and she attributed her success to her thorough and careful preparation.[5]

Attendance in the Sunday school was found to be poor, about 60 percent of the enrollment, two pupils out of five being absent every Sunday; a large part of the hour was taken up in opening exercises, in which all ages participated. There was little or nothing distinctive offered for either high school or college youth. "The picture suggests that as youth advance through the departments of [the] division, they listen longer and longer to lectures, with slight increase, if indeed any at all, in more active forms of participation. The custom of merely listening seems to be settling down upon them as they grow older in the church school, as it does in so many other phases of the church's life."[6]

An analysis of the curriculum material provided for children, youth, and adults revealed that there were practically no references to the great moral and social issues confronting the South in any of them. Referring to treatments of the Uniform Lesson topics for adults, the committee said: "The treatments of these lessons for adults could and should, we believe, point more forcibly to modern conditions. Especially do we urge that the writers of these lesson treatments be advised to stress any problem in modern life which has a moral or religious aspect. We are not advocating a 'social Gospel,' but we are pleading that in these lessons which so many adults use, the Gospel not be put in chains, but be allowed rather to penetrate into every phase of human life. These writers are not called upon to provide 'solutions' for every problem. That they cannot do. But we can fairly ask them to help us open our eyes more fully to ourselves and our world to the end that we may seek to view all with the mind of Christ."[7]

The Board of Education found the real meat of the report in the 34 specific recommendations, covering every phase of the church's educational program, with which the Restudy Report concluded.[8] The Board outlined 30 steps it had already taken to implement these recommendations. They continued to guide the Board in the years that followed and lay back of the great advances subsequently made in various aspects of its work. Among these advances were staff reorganizations; new attention given to the Daily Vacation Bible School Summer Program, to the training of elders and deacons, and to the preparation of new leadership materials; the development of a Teacher-Consultation-Training Center Plan and of Area Laboratory Schools, of an Audio-Visual Aid Department, of a Christian Family Training Department; of a Church Music Department, and of the Vocational Guidance Program; improvements in the total curriculum, particularly in the offerings for adults and youth, culminating in the new Covenant Life Curriculum, and including a new and growing concern for an application of the gospel to the vital issues of the day.

This latter development brought opposition, particularly from the deep South: on the one hand, there were overtures calling for more attention and closer conformity to the doctrinal Standards of the church (the Westminster Confession of Faith and the catechisms); on the other hand, there were criticisms of the literature dealing with the moral issues of the day, especially race—not only criticism, but in many cases, repudiation, rejection, and threatened and actual withholding of funds from the benevolences of the church.

"The Gospel is revolutionary in its nature," countered the Board. "It seeks to bring about change in character, conduct, ideals and relationships. Its purpose is to establish the Kingdom of God, the rule of God in the world. It is because the teachings of the Gospel are revolutionary in nature that man rebels against them. Some of the opposition to curriculum material arises from opposition to the revolutionary teaching of the Word of God. It is not pleasant to face those teachings, but it is profitable to do so."[9]

In 1958 the Division of Christian Teaching, under the leadership of its newly elected director, William P. Anderson, taking full note of the serious opposition that had arisen, presented a statement to guide its work toward a united staff position for the division on the segregation-integration issue. Four possible positions were recognized:

1. That the present pattern of segregation should be preserved as the will of God for Southern society. This position the division felt compelled to reject as out of harmony with the Bible and with the deliverances of the General Assembly.

2. That the issue should be avoided by elimination of any references to the crucial decisions concerning segregation which were being faced by members of the church. This position also the division could not accept. "We believe," it was stated, "that a Christian Education curriculum which has no relevance to the major decisions which our generation of Christians must make is not fulfilling its true function as being a bearer of the Word of God for our time."

3. That the division should embark upon a crusade for the elimination of segregation in the South. "This," it was felt, "would not serve the best interests of our church. We believe, at this time, that we must maintain balance and perspective . . . We should deal with the subject of segregation only when it is necessarily involved in the subject we are treating . . . We should seek to lead and guide our constituency and not to move so far in advance of them that we lose touch with them."

4. Finally there was the position recommended by the division, adopted by the Board, and approved by the General Assembly: "We believe it to be our responsibility to bring to bear on the Christian conscience the meaning of the Christian faith for the patterns of our contemporary society. In the effort to do this there are certain considerations by which we believe we should be guided." Among them that "we have no right intentionally to break Christian fellowship with those who continue to hold that the preservation of segregation patterns is for the best interests of Southern society." On the other hand, that "we must avoid substituting a religion of only form and ceremony for a religion which is deeply concerned with justice . . . We must see the New Testament vision of the Christian community

as a fellowship in which divisions based on the distinctions of the secular society are transcended . . ."[10]

The Young People's Council had been forcing consideration of the racial question on the Board of Christian Education and on the church at large for some time.

One of the first questions to arise after formation of the Council (in 1931) was concerning a representative from Snedecor Memorial— the Negro—Synod. On a point of order it was recognized that he was constitutionally entitled to attend; it was quickly agreed that he should be encouraged to do so. Meetings of the Young People's Council led to development of the Young People's Leadership School, held at Montreat, first as a part of the Adult Leadership School and subsequently as an independent school. The race question now became a more difficult one. A letter was written by the Council to the Montreat Program Committee expressing the hope that representatives from Snedecor Memorial Synod might be admitted to the 1936 school. The Montreat Committee replied that it would save embarrassment if attendance was limited to white delegates, and if a separate conference were established for Negro young people, following the precedent set by the Women's Auxiliary with the approval of the General Assembly. If, however, it seemed necessary to have representatives of the Young People's Council of Snedecor Memorial Synod in the Montreat Leadership School the Program Committee would provide separate meals for them as was done for the Negro commissioners to the General Assembly. There could of course be no social intermingling. The delayed communication to this effect, received after the Leadership Conference had gotten underway, with two Negro delegates in attendance, caused the Council great embarrassment. They canceled plans for a hike, supper, and vesper services on Saturday, since the Negro young people would be excluded by this ruling, and abandoned plans to bring future delegates from Snedecor Memorial Synod.[11] This, they informed the Montreat Program Committee, wrought serious injury to their work. They urged the Program Committee to reconsider its position, which this body declined to do. Queried about the possible entertainment of Ruth Steele, Snedecor Memorial Council President, Dr. William M. Anderson, President of the Mountain Retreat Association, replied that she could stay with the colored cook and maid at one of the lodges, or perhaps with the Negro employees in the colored quarters[12] of the institution. Unwilling to accept such arrangements, Miss Steele was not encouraged to attend the meeting of the Council.

A letter was now addressed to the Executive Committee of Religious Education explaining the handicap this policy of the Program Committee presented to their work, and requesting that since it was based on precedent set by the General Assembly it be called to the attention of that body. Dr. Edward Grant, Executive Secretary of the Board of Christian Education, replied the following year that the request of the Young People's Council had been referred to a Joint Conference Committee representing the three Boards particularly interested in Negro Work (Christian Education, Home Missions, and Women's Work) and that this Conference Committee was recommending to their appointing agencies that "It is expedient to organize the educational work, conferences and training schools of Snedecor Memorial Synod around Stillman Institute rather than to consolidate them with the work of the other synods." The matter would not be carried therefore to the General Assembly. The Young People's Council acquiesced unhappily in this decision, expressing strong disagreement with the Joint Committee's interpretation of Christian principles.[13] They requested that for a clearer comprehension of youth's attitude and convictions, one of their representatives be allowed to meet with the Executive Committee of Religious Education for a consideration of this policy.

This request led to a series of negotiations with the Montreat Program Committee, continuing over a period of years. The young people urged that representatives of Snedecor Memorial Synod be admitted to the Leadership School, and that they be provided with equal living quarters and the privilege of a private table in the common dining room. They were prepared on their part to forgo any recreation in which the Negro young people would not be permitted to participate. In 1949 for the first time young people from Snedecor Memorial Synod attended the Leadership School under this arrangement. The young people abided strictly by their agreement—there were no folk games, no mingling in the dining room or in the general meetings, and all went well.

The following year the Montreat authorities, pressed by the Board of Christian Education, announced a general policy regarding race for all Montreat Conferences, which members of the Board of Directors acknowledged to be a compromise. It was agreed that henceforth entertainment for all *adult* groups should be on a non-segregated basis—within carefully defined limits: Fellowship Hall and the cafeteria, but not Assembly Inn. The young people were not included in this limited degree of integration. Negro delegates (except to the Assembly's Youth Council) would not be entertained henceforth in the Young People's Conferences, owing, the Board of Directors explained, "to the multiplicity of problems involved." Pressure, it appeared, had been brought to bear on the Board of Directors by Montreat cottage owners. Because of the 1949 policy, also, one presbytery had voted to send no more delegates to Montreat and two others had threatened to withdraw financial aid.[14]

The Young People's Council was very much upset by this change of policy and there was strong sentiment for holding the Young People's Conference at some other place than Montreat. Representatives of the Board pointed out that they were demanding of Montreat standards (non-segregation) which their own communities did not recognize.[15]

The young people continued year after year to press for a return to the 1949 policy. In 1952 they reached back to the ultimate source of authority, to the Holders of and Trustees of Stock in the Mountain Retreat Association. "We fully appreciate the necessity for moving with caution," they declared in their petition, "yet we fear lest our normal trepidation . . . hinder the action which . . . obedience to our Lord's command compels . . . The church must play the role of a prophet . . ."[16]

The Board of Directors were not moved; they declined to change their policy even after the General Assembly itself—in 1954—called upon its various institutions and agencies to abandon the policy of segregation. Finally in 1959, 25 years after the young people had begun their agitation, the trustees, after sharp debate, voted to include the Westminster (college-age) Fellowship under the provision for adult conferences, but by a narrow margin declared that all programs for church young people and children should remain on an entirely segregated basis.[17] Present was the specter of Negro parents bringing their families to Montreat.

For a generation the Young People's Council had been one of the voices that pricked the conscience of the church. As Dr. Alston, Director of Young People's Work, 1935-1938, observed, after his return to the pastorate: "The Young People's Program of the Presbyterian Church in the United States has achieved a measure of social awareness that . . . ought to be preserved . . . his social concern has not come easily. The right of youth to face their real problems openly and honestly has been established with a good deal of difficulty because of an ultraconservatism in the church and also because of an attitude on the part of well-intentioned adults that would limit the concern of religion too narrowly . . . Basic to our young people's program is the assumption that Christ's Gospel touches life at every conceivable point and that his way is applicable to every sort of personal and social issue."[18]

Four years earlier the United Christian Youth Movement had been launched under the auspices of the International Council of Religious Education. Out of this movement, in which Southern Presbyterians were active participants, came a "common commission plan," accepted by more than 30 denominations, which called Senior High youth to consider and become involved in five comprehensive areas of the church's work (Christian faith, witness, outreach, citizenship, and fellowship). Beginning in 1937, with a Presbyterian Youth Convention on World Missions, the church held every four years thereafter its own denominational conference for young people. The program was quickly broadened to include the total work of the church, and there was increasing emphasis on social issues.

An important step in the development of the young people's program was taken in 1938 when the General Assembly approved a Regional Directors' Plan, in which a Director, approved by the Executive Committee, but under the supervision of Synod Committees on Education, took responsibility for developing the total program in every synod or group of synods.

Another important development in the field of religious education, gathering momentum in the 1950's, was the multiplication of camps and conferences. Montreat, increasing its resources and improving its facilities under the leadership of C. Grier Davis (elected President of the Mountain Retreat Association in 1959) remained the Assembly's Conference Grounds and frequent meeting place. Massanetta, likewise improving its facilities; pretentious Mo-Ranch, replacing the old Kerrville Encampment; and NaCoMe, more rustic in its setting, served their respective synods—Virginia, Texas, and Tennessee. But the trend now was toward the establishment of presbyterial camps, with wooded lands and a lake, equipped to serve various groups for a week or more through the summer and to entertain overnight and weekend "retreats" for every type of organization through the year. In 1957 the Board of Christian Education elected a Director of Camps and Conferences to give some guidance to this burgeoning movement.

In 1947 appeared the germ of a new idea, an experimental vocational counseling service undertaken by Lexington Presbytery under the assumption that all young people should make of their lifework a Christian calling; the following year there was established an experimental Vocational Guidance Center within the same presbytery; and a year later the Assembly gave its approval to a church-wide vocational counseling service. In 1951 the Department of Christian Vocation with full-time director was established within the Division of Higher Education in the Board of Christian Education. The program it set in motion began in the local church where young people were given information regarding the many kinds of useful work to be done in the modern world. Adult leaders, including trained "vocational aides," helped the young person to evaluate his own abilities and inclinations and to pray and seek the guidance of the Holy Spirit as he sought to determine his lifework. From the local church young people were encouraged to go to the nearest Presbyterian Guidance Center for testing and counseling by able Christian psychologists. As a consequence of such counseling, many young persons found their way into the full-time service of the church, though that was not the primary purpose of the Guidance Centers. By the end of the decade more than a third of the congregations had begun a program within their own bounds; ten centers had been established; a number of other denominations were following the pioneering venture of PCUS; the idea was being promoted through the National Council of Churches.

Religious work among students in state-supported institutions was initiated and for many years carried on primarily by the Y.M.C.A.; denominational efforts followed more tardily. Clarence Shedd, in his book *The Church Follows its Students*, credits the Presbyterian Church at Blacksburg, Virginia, under the leadership of its pastor, Rev. David J. Woods, with making the first organized efforts in this direction, in the year 1899. Dr. H. H. Sweets, who became Secretary of the Executive Committee on Christian Education and Ministerial Relief in 1904, took an active interest in student work from the outset. In 1908 he again called the Assembly's attention to the importance of ministering to the spiritual needs of students, and the General Assembly, at his suggestion, adopted resolutions urging synods to follow the good example of the synods of Alabama, North Carolina, South Carolina, and Virginia in making special provision for Presbyterian students in state institutions. The following year the first Presbyterian student groups were organized on the campuses of two state-supported institutions—Virginia Polytechnic Institute and the University of Texas. Many synods were now giving encouragement to work among college and university students, and many pastors in centers of higher education were undertaking a ministry to students. In 1923 the Executive Committee held the first of what was to become an annual conference of such pastors to share their findings and to plan more effectively for their work. Eighteen years later the Executive Committees of Christian Education and Religious Education erected a Joint Committee on Student Work, and elected Rev. J. M. Garrison, as the denomination's first Director of Student Work. In the reorganization of 1950 the Joint Committee on Student Work became the Department of Campus Christian Life of the Board of Christian Education. The change of name was intended to make clear that the church was concerned not only with the students on a campus but also with faculty and staff.[19]

By 1965 seven out of every ten Southern Presbyterian students were enrolled in public colleges and universities; and in these institutions were 8,000 Southern Presbyterian professors and administrators. The Department of Campus Christian Life sought in a variety of ways to aid synod's committee (which had final responsibility for the work), full- and part-time campus workers, and the local churches to carry on their work, for example, obtaining and training personnel, providing helpful material, cooperating with other denominational groups, and participating in the ecumenical student movement.

The key organization on the campus was the Westminster Fellowship (by 1960 organized on more than 200 Southern college campuses)—a student organization related to a neighboring church or group of churches. Local groups were represented in a Synod's Fellowship, and the presidents of these became members of the General Assembly's Youth Council which met annually to plan the overall youth program of the church. On the national level the denominational student work became an integral part of the National Student Christian Fellowship, which helped to coordinate all Protestant student work; and through this organization Presbyterian students participated, on the international level, as members of the World Student Christian Fellowship. For some time it had become apparent that to carry on a really effective ministry on a large university campus the ministry must become a cooperative one—no one denomination had sufficient resources to develop the complete ministry that was needed. In 1966 the Board of Christian Education, responding to a request from the Assembly's Westminster Fellowship Council, voted "full and enthusiastic support" of a joint campus ministry with denominations of the United Campus Christian Fellowship, i.e., with United Presbyterians, Disciples, Evangelical, United Brethren,

Moravians, and the United Church of Christ. The effort proved short-lived and organized young people's work on the higher levels in PCUS had ceased to exist.

The Presbyterian Church has been interested in higher education throughout its history. Up to the time of the Civil War it had done more to establish colleges in America than any other denomination. After the war the Southern Church was impoverished and over-extended. Presbyterians continued to educate their sons and also their daughters, but the denomination's own schools were permitted to languish.

In 1910, with the election of Dr. Henry H. Sweets as Executive Secretary of the Executive Committee of Christian Education and Ministerial Relief, there came signs of an awakening. The Presbyterian Educational Association was organized, and the Assembly's Advisory Committee on Christian Education was called into being. Standards for Presbyterian educational institutions were drawn up and approved. Successful financial campaigns were conducted in various synods.

In 1927 a complete survey of the educational work and responsibility of the church was undertaken by competent educators under the direction of Dr. B. Warren Brown, who had had large experience in such lines of work. The report indicated that some of the synods had assumed a load in the field of education too heavy for either the willingness or the ability of the Presbyterians in the area. A comparison with other bodies revealed that Southern Presbyterians had proportionately a much larger number of institutions of higher learning than other denominations in the nation. Some of the institutions which had rendered great service in the past had been closed or merged with other institutions (not to be regarded in every instance as a backward step). Some, however, which might have lived, had died from neglect. Surviving institutions were burdened with a heavy debt. All the evidence indicated that the church was facing a very serious situation with regard to its educational institutions.[20] The plight of these institutions was augmented by the growing resources of the state schools, made possible by the power of taxation, and by accrediting agencies which rate institutions according to equipment, size of the faculty, courses of study and the like. Efforts of the Assembly's Committee to improve the situation were handicapped by the fact that the colleges and seminaries were owned and controlled by the synods, and not by the General Assembly. Some of the recommendations growing out of the Brown report, were approved by the Presbyterian Educational Association and proved of great value.[21]

Changes and adaptations occurring in this period included the following:

Synodical College, Fulton, Missouri—closed; its debt assumed by the Synod.
Centre College and Kentucky College for Women, Danville—combined.
Silliman College, Clinton, Louisiana—closed.
Sayre College, Lexington, Kentucky—given over to private control.
Greenbrier College, Lewisburg, West Virginia—sold.
Texas Presbyterian College for Women, Milford—consolidated with Austin College at Sherman.
Daniel Baker College, Brownwood, Texas—turned over to an independent board.
Chicora College, Columbia, South Carolina—consolidated with Queens.
Stonewall Jackson College, Abingdon, Virginia—closed.

In May 1940 the General Assembly set aside the church years 1941-1943 as a period in which responsibility for Christian education should be laid, by a joint campaign of publicity, upon the heart and conscience of the church. In connection with this effort another comprehensive survey of the colleges and seminaries of the church was carried out under the direction of a trained and experienced educator, Dr. George A. Works of Chicago. Included in the survey were 13 Presbyterian colleges, two affiliated colleges, eight junior colleges, the four theological seminaries, and Stillman College.

With reference to the colleges, the report found that the church was supporting—and supporting inadequately—too many colleges, and that these colleges had not been planned with any statesmanlike understanding of the needs of the church and its capacity to support them. This was evidenced by the low level of effectiveness at which a number of the institutions were running. Only nine of the 24 colleges included in the study were fully accredited by the regional accrediting association covering the territory in which they were located— these colleges being Agnes Scott, Centre, Davidson, Hampden-Sydney, Mary Baldwin, Queens, Schreiner Institute (Junior College), Southwestern, and Westminster. In many cases libraries were inadequate. Faculty salaries were generally low. In a few instances there was evidence of a lack of appreciation on the part of the Administration and some slight evidence of a tendency to compensate for a lack of scholarship on the part of faculty members by emphasizing their Christian qualities.

Higher education, it was noted, was more expensive than it had been 50 years earlier. Yet, despite this, the gifts of the church for educational purposes had been steadily declining. In 1918, for example, the sum of $297,928 had been contributed by the church for its educational institutions. This amount increased, reaching a peak in 1925 of more than a million dollars; then fell in the Depression years to a low of $190,196. In 1941, the amount given was $15,000 less than it had been in 1918, 23 years earlier—and this despite a considerable increase in church membership. "Only by the increased support of the strongest of the colleges," declared the report, "will the Presbyterians be able to secure the continuance of these colleges in the face of the rapid expansion of publicly supported higher education." Because of these and other facts it was recommended that the church endeavor to solve its problems regarding the church-related colleges by regions larger than by synods alone. "If some action of this general nature is not taken the church related college is in danger of drifting into oblivion." In some cases the only solution seemed to be through merger, discontinuance, or cooperation. The senior colleges named in this connection were Arkansas, Austin, Belhaven, Davis and Elkins, King, and Westminster. Flora Macdonald College and Presbyterian College were put in a special category of wait and see. Maintenance of the junior colleges was not encouraged. In regard to the theological seminaries, the report recommended that the number be reduced to two, one in Richmond, the other in Nashville.[22]

The report, as was pointed out, had necessarily focused on the weaknesses in the church's educational system. It emphasized, in closing, that the stronger colleges in the group were outstanding institutions and that even the weakest ones had some elements of strength. It sought to bring home to the laymen of the church that the denomination's institutions of higher learning were inadequately supported and that only by adjusting themselves to economic and social changes could the church-related colleges keep a place in American higher education.[23]

No colleges were closed and there were no mergers as suggested in the Works Report, but the report did serve as nothing else had done to awaken the church to its educational responsibility. Two years later reports to the Presbyterian Educational Association revealed important changes in courses, improvements in library facilities, debts reduced, endowments increased, new equipment secured. Dr. Frank H. Caldwell, Chairman of the Advisory Committee on Christian Education, reported: "During this time, there has been much forthright institutional self-analysis. At least some synods and presbyteries have been reorganized in relation to their educational programs and procedures . . . Constructive and persistent programs of publicity have created and renewed interest in and concern about Christian Education. Administrators, faculty members, and pastors have been stimulated to re-think the philosophy of Christian Education at a peculiarly crucial and opportune time."[24]

The Executive Committee began this year to offer challenge funds to colleges and seminaries, stimulating them to move toward attainment of higher standards in education.[25] Many of the colleges, encouraged by the General Assembly, undertook successful financial campaigns to increase their resources. Among the more ambitious efforts were the campaign of Centre College for $1,250,000; Agnes Scott and Southwestern for two million dollars each; and Queens College in Charlotte, North Carolina, for $3,250,000.[26] Some observers discerned "at long last" the beginnings of a real education movement within the Southern Presbyterian Church. This new educational interest was stimulated by the rapid increase in student enrollments which followed the ending of World War II.

In 1950 Dr. Hunter B. Blakely, President of Queens College, accepted a call to become Secretary of the Division of Higher Education in the reorganized Board of Education in Richmond. Progress from this time was rapid. Synods, trustees, and administrators were encouraged to evaluate their educational programs and to enter upon a program of advance for all phases of higher education. North Carolina, whose presbyteries, singly or in groups, had supported and controlled six institutions of higher learning (including three junior colleges), emerged with three colleges, Davidson, for men, the best endowed of all the denomination's institutions; St. Andrews, a new co-educational college, growing out of the merger of Flora Macdonald and the Junior College for Men; and Queens, for women, in Charlotte —all now under synod's control. For the first time there was in the synod a truly unified program of higher education.*

PCUS and UPUSA Synods in Florida joined in the support of a new college (Florida Presbyterian—now Eckerd), which opened its doors in 1960 and quickly took its place among the leading educational institutions supported by the church.

A statistical study of the church's 28 educational institutions released in 1956 revealed that Presbyterians had done more for their schools in the past six years than in all the years prior to 1940. Endowment and plant valuation was placed at more than 81 million dollars, an increase of 26 million dollars (47%) since 1950, an increase of more than 53 million (188%) since 1940. Within the last five years the Presbyterian Church had more than doubled its direct support to

---

* Peace, a junior college for women, kept out of the merger by court action, remained an associated Presbyterian institution, controlled by the First Presbyterian Church of Raleigh.

these institutions for annual operating expenses. In 1940 the total invested in campuses, buildings, and equipment was only 29½ million dollars, a comparatively niggardly sum; in 1958 the total investment had risen to 116 million dollars.

"The most marked contrast of these 22 colleges in 1960 with the colleges of 1950," reported the Board, "is that these colleges now know where they are going and have laid their plans to go where they intend to go. . . ." Many signs of progress were noted: an increase in capital assets, in library holdings, in regular giving by the churches; and the development of cooperative enterprises involving the colleges in programs of mutual aid.

During Dr. Blakely's 12 years of service (1940-1962), the capital assets of the church's institutions increased from 60 million to 150 million dollars. He had, in addition, instigated a permanent program of soliciting bequests and deferred gifts which would undoubtedly add further millions in years to come. By the use of challenge funds, he had stimulated the colleges to add to their budgets at such crucial points as library purchases, to raise additional funds for endowment, to open up their campuses, and to overcome the tendency toward provincialism by vastly increased programs of outside speakers. When he assumed office, seven church colleges were still unaccredited; when he retired all were accredited.[27]

Under Dr. Blakely's direction the Presbyterian Guidance Program had been established to assist youth in making wise vocational decisions. In this effort PCUS led all other Protestant denominations. In 1950 the church had only a small department of student work, with fewer than 50 campus ministers, about half of them part-time. In 1950, under Dr. Blakely, this work was renamed; it became the Department of Campus Christian Life, operating under a new philosophy and with broader scope. By 1962 the Presbyterian campus ministry was conducted on 300 campuses throughout the region, with more than 100 workers, most of them full-time. Out of the seed planted by Dr. Blakely had come the faculty Christian Fellowship, sponsored officially by the National Council of Churches.

In the opening decades of the present century there was growing interest in adult Bible classes—men and women meeting separately, and listening, usually, to an exposition (often a lay sermonette) of the International Sunday School Lessons. Following fixed orders of worship, men's Bible classes, in particular, duplicated, though less formally, many features of the 11 o'clock service of worship. Emphasis was placed upon singing and music. At times there was a tendency for the Bible class to become a church within the church, with little vital connection with its parent church or with the denomination of which it was a part.

The interest of men in the larger program of the church was stimulated by the Laymen's Missionary Movement, which grew out of a vision caught by a businessman after visiting the mission fields of the world. In 1906—centenary of the "Haystack Prayer Meeting" which had launched the Foreign Mission enterprise in the United States—laymen of several denominations banded themselves together to arouse the churches to a deeper commitment to the missionary task. Their watchword was the popular slogan of the day— "The evangelization of the world in this generation." The contagion spread rapidly. The General Secretary of the movement reported in 1911 that the past five years had witnessed the most extensive and inspiring increase of missionary interest in modern times. Thousands of men had gathered in huge interdenominational meetings throughout the nation. The increase in mission giving was the greatest that the Protestant churches had experienced.

In 1907 a group of over 30 representative laymen met in Birmingham and organized the Laymen's Missionary Movement in the Presbyterian Church, U. S., the first denominational group to be so organized. Gatherings of men in the interest of Foreign Missions were held throughout the denomination. Educational material was mailed out. An effort was made to reach every layman in the church. More than 60 businessmen visited the church's mission fields at their own expense and returned to spread their enthusiasm with others. A Laymen's Missionary Convention, held in Birmingham in 1909 and attended by 1,131 delegates, was acclaimed by Dr. Walter L. Lingle as "the greatest gathering of any kind ever held in the Southern Presbyterian Church."[28]

The Second General Convention, held in Chattanooga in 1912, was attended by 1,535 delegates. "Many laymen's missionary conferences and conventions have been held in different parts of our country, but never has such a floodtide of enthusiasm been opened," reported the *Christian Observer*. "Many who were present could think of nothing else to which it could be compared than the day of Pentecost."[29] Excitement reached its highest peak when Rev. Motte Martin made a brief appeal setting forth the needs and opportunities in the Congo. Only 13 workers remained in the field, and Mr. Martin was appealing for reinforcements. Mr. J. Campbell White asked all who had volunteered or were willing to volunteer for Africa to come to the platform. "Twenty-five men and four women instantly and joyfully answered his request. The vast audience could no longer repress its joy, and cheer after cheer rang out, and men said one to another, 'We never saw such a sight as this'."[30] It had been no part of the plan for the convention to solicit offerings. But when Mr. White asked the audience what they planned to do when this large number of volunteers had offered to give themselves to the work, pledges for support and equipment were rapidly forthcoming. "It was a scene," reported the *Christian Observer* "never to be forgotten."[31] It was, perhaps, the peak of Foreign Mission interest in the Southern Presbyterian Church (at a time, it may be added, when little interest was shown in the needs of the Negro within the United States).

The third convention to be held under the leadership of the Laymen's Missionary Movement in the Southern Presbyterian Church met the following year in Memphis—this time in the interest of Home Missions. Personal work and personal consecration of time, talents, and money were keynotes of the convention. The fourth convention, held in Charlotte, North Carolina, two years later, was again in the interest of Foreign Missions and—with 3,367 registered delegates—was more largely attended than the great convention in Chattanooga. The next year twin conventions were held in Lexington, Kentucky, and in New Orleans, again in the interest of Home Missions.

The original purpose of the Laymen's Missionary Movement had been to create among men larger interest and more liberal support for Foreign Missions. But more than this was accomplished. New interest was developed in other phases of the church's work, notably in stewardship and in Home Missions.[32]

With the coming of World War I the activities of the Laymen's Missionary Movement were suspended in the interests of the ill-starred Interchurch World Movement. Attempts made after the war to revive the movement in the Southern Presbyterian Church met with little success, and it was gradually merged into the more comprehensive movement developed by the General Assembly's Permanent Committee on Men's Work.

The Assembly in 1922 had erected this committee with instructions to develop a men's organization in harmony with the Presbyterian Progressive Program (i.e., one prepared to support the total program of the church).* Dr. J. E. Purcell became the first Secretary of

---

* An earlier effort to establish Men's Brotherhoods had met with only limited success. At the peak of interest in 1917 there were 115 Brotherhoods enrolled with 2,910 members.

Men's Work and under his supervision and direction an organizational framework was developed under the name "Men of the Church." It provided that every male member of the local church, by virtue of that fact, be considered a member of the men's organization, as was the case with the women of the church. A number of local organizations were established (in 1931, 316 organizations were reported), and some on the presbyterial and synodical level. But the mortality rate was high, and in many areas "men's work" never got off the ground.

In 1932 the Permanent Committee on Men's Work was dissolved, and its responsibilities taken over by the Department of Adult Education in the Board of Religious Education. An effort was now made to teach men the history, the aims, the beliefs, and the work of the church, built upon a solid foundation of Bible study, and with a view to personal spiritual development.[33] At no time, now or earlier, did more than ten or 15 percent of the churches develop men's organizations. Dr. Purcell resigned in 1937 because of ill-health and was succeeded four years later by Mr. S. J. (Jap) Patterson, Jr., a layman, former football coach, serving when elected as Director of Religious Education in the Synods of Arkansas and Missouri.

Men's work was now reinterpreted to cover every relationship and activity of Presbyterian men wherever and however organized. Program aids continued to be offered, and every organization was urged to keep before its membership the whole educational and beneficent program of the church. An important step forward was taken in 1947 when the Department of Men's Work began to cooperate actively with the Committee on Women's Work. A Joint Committee was set up to guide the "together phase" of Adult Work and at the same time to help each agency discharge more effectively its particular responsibility. Emphasis was placed upon the training of elders and deacons for their important responsibilities. In 1949 a new series of Men's Conventions were instituted, the first being held this year in Atlanta; the seventh biennial convention, held in Dallas, was attended by approximately 8,000 men. Meanwhile an Assembly's Men's Council had been created, which provided material for Men's Conferences in synods and presbyteries. A division on Men's Work, set up in the Board of Christian Education, provided a practical working relationship between the Men's Council and the Board of Education. In 1952 the Division reported 1,039 men's clubs functioning on the local level, and the Men's Work fully organized on presbyterial, synodical, and Assembly levels.

Organized Men's Work, however, faced difficulties not found in the work for women and young people. A new decline in interest, particularly among younger men, led to one of the most thorough and far-reaching reappraisal of Men's Work ever carried out in any denomination (1966-1968). It became clear that earlier efforts to remain noncontroversial had had some unfortunate effects; vital issues had been left out of the program and men had not had opportunities to learn how to come to grips with the most pressing questions where there was likely to be differences of opinion. The study committee concluded, and the Board agreed, that men are called today to be equipped for mission, not only within the church, but also "out there in the world," "penetrating and influencing every aspect of the life of the world . . . witnessing to social issues and to the structures of society, and dealing with human needs wherever they appear."[34] It was in this direction that Men's Work hoped to move in the years ahead. Four years later there were few signs of progress. The future of organized Men's Work remained uncertain.

The Board of Christian Education, under the leadership of its Executive Secretary, Dr. Marshall C. Dendy, had launched in 1955 the program that eventuated eight years later in the introduction of the new Covenant Life Curriculum. The effort was undertaken in the belief "that the number of new developments and insights currently available in various areas which constitute the foundation disciplines for Christian education justify a major effort at this time to reexamine and, if appropriate, to reconstruct the philosophy of Christian Education upon which the educational work of the Presbyterian Church is carried forward." In undertaking this radical revision of its educational program, PCUS, learning from pioneer efforts of other bodies, was able to advance further along the trail blazed by other denominations, including the Presbyterian Church in the U.S.A.

Dr. Rachel Henderlite came to the Board as Director of Research in 1958; two years later she became Director of Curriculum Development and carried the project through to its final completion. The new curriculum provided systematic instruction, such as the denomination had never had before, in three areas, the Bible, the Church (its history and doctrine), and the Christian Life (particularly social ethics). It recognized that the aim of Christian education was not primarily to transmit a body of knowledge—though this was not neglected—and certainly not to furnish rules of conduct that would apply to every situation, but rather to bring the child, the youth, and the adult to the place where they might hear and respond through life to the God who continues to address them personally in Christ. The home was recognized as the primary agency of nurture, and the whole church and its program as the context of education. A new emphasis was placed on the education of adults. An improved methodology in harmony with modern educational practice and including full discussion of the vital issues in church and society was encouraged.

Some adults naturally persisted in the comfortable ways to which they had been accustomed; some objected to the abandonment of "pure" Bible study; some complained that the new materials were too difficult to comprehend or teach; some took violent exception to the new discussion method, in lieu of the traditional lecture, embracing problems on which there were pronounced differences of opinion; and some, following the *Presbyterian Journal*, registered dissatisfaction with the theological viewpoint of particular units. But the response of the church as a whole was gratifying. The educational theory and practice of the church had been brought to a higher level of maturity. The philosophy of the Covenent Life Curriculum, it was hoped, would influence the total program of the church.

As envisioned by Dr. Dendy:

> The Covenent Life Curriculum gives promise of bringing genuine renewal to the church. It presents a dynamic approach to study . . . that should lead men into a genuine confrontation with God. . . . Christians will be better informed concerning the contents of faith and the history of the church. Christians will be called upon to enter into the struggles of a society that cries out for justice, freedom, and dignity. The organized church will give less consideration to its institutional patterns of life and greater consideration to its relationships with God and man in the name of Christ . . . [It] will be more concerned about drawing into its fellowship, and into convenant relationship with God, all people, regardless of class, color, or condition, and less concerned about a form of church life that has become too much like the life of a secular world.[35]

After six years of trial, however, it was becoming clear that the CLC was no end product, but only a launching pad from which further creative effort would spring.[36]

As the 1960's drew to a close, a reexamination of the Board's total activities was called for. The squeeze between diminishing funds and rising costs (felt in other denominations as well) necessitated a 42 percent cut in personnel, with comparable reduction in services. New patterns of operation were in prospect—more joint activities with other denominations, a closer partnership between Assembly's Board and the middle judicatories. In accordance with the restructuring plans adopted by the 1972 General Assembly, the Board of Christian Education will cease to exist as an independent agency—its functions assumed by one or more of the divisions within the new General Executive Board.

XIX

The Minister and His Work

In 1926, Dr. Benjamin Rice Lacy, Jr., a Rhodes scholar
and an army chaplain cited for bravery in World War I, who had
served for some years as a Home Mission pastor and then as pastor
of an important downtown city church, succeeded Dr. Walter W.
Moore, as President of Union, in Virginia. In his inaugural address
Dr. Lacy stressed three points toward which he felt that theological
education in the Southern Presbyterian Church must move: first, that
church people must make it possible for theological seminaries to
advance equally with other professional schools, if the church itself
was not to lose ground; second, that the theological seminary must
prepare its students to meet the challenge of a new age, the problems
raised by critical students of the Scriptures, by philosophers, and
scientists, and particularly by the new psychologists. "In the face of
such conditions," said Dr. Lacy, "what is a theological seminary's task?
Our students can go out to a disquieted people and do one of three
things. They can dodge, or they can dogmatize or they can say 'Come
now and let us reason together.' They can take those disquieted men
or women, boys or girls, and lead them along paths which they themselves have trod, past the opposition of science falsely so called,
past the scare-heads of 'accepted scholarship' to the assurance of
those things verily believed. It means arduous work for them; it means
that we must give them here facilities to equip themselves to meet
these issues." In the third place, Dr. Lacy saw that the seminary must
render larger service to the church as a whole, including ministers in
the field. It must, in addition, produce more productive scholars. "We
have to admit," said he, "that for many a decade our beloved church
has produced few books of real learning and scholarship which
have affected the currents of religious thought outside of our own
communion."[1]

These were the directions in which theological education in PCUS was to move in the generation ahead. But did the denomination need four theological seminaries, and did it have the resources to equip adequately this number for the quality education which the times demanded? Shortly after Dr. Lacy spoke, this question became a vital one. The Great Depression followed by World War II led to a drop in student enrollment and to a call for retrenchment, rather than expansion. To the eminent authorities associated with Dr. George A. Works in the survey of the denomination's colleges and seminaries, the need for reduction in the number of the latter seemed evident. On the financial side, the argument was compelling: "Institutions of learning generally, as well as some of these seminaries, are having a desperate struggle to balance their budgets, not to speak of the sorely-needed expansions of their programs. Furthermore . . . the seminaries do not have the funds they need. Three of the four seminaries need either entirely new library buildings or expansion of present quarters. Increase in staff, with resultant increase in the annual budget, is essential if the separate institutions are all maintained. . . ."

On the educational side the argument for reduction seemed equally decisive. "Faculty and library are the most important factors in a seminary. The faculty is admittedly the more important of these two, and, unfortunately, the supply of good teachers in any one generation is more limited than the supply of good books. The candidate for the ministry deserves the finest teachers, but the most limited experience in seminary education is enough to demonstrate that the supply of first-rate teachers for seminary positions is very small . . . Once the good teacher has been found, he must not be overloaded with class hours and extra-curricular activity, but must be given time for continuing study. He must be provided with a first class library which will serve his need as well as those of the students. . . ."

In the light of these factors the report recommended that the number of seminaries be reduced to two, one in the East, serving the synods along the Atlantic Seaboard—Richmond, the site of the denomination's best equipped seminary, being the natural location; for the other, Nashville, in the center of the church's western constituency and a great educational center, was the recommended site.[2]

The Trustees of Louisville Seminary were willing to consider a merger with Austin and Columbia Seminaries in Nashville, but neither of the other two was prepared to leave its own site. After the failure of this merger effort, promising negotiations were carried on for a time between the Trustees of Louisville and Union Seminaries, but in the end these also failed. With the coming of the South's post-war prosperity, all thought of merger was forgotten, and each of the seminaries moved to improve its own resources.

Columbia Theological Seminary, which had only recently removed to Atlanta, for a time faced an uncertain future, but came through the Depression years, under the able leadership of its president, Dr. J. McDowell Richards, without a deficit. For years it carried on with small endowment and limited resources. Gradually it erected a modern plant and a successful financial campaign (for five million dollars) in 1959 eased its financial situation and left it with bright hopes for the future. Austin Seminary modernized its plant in the early 1960's. Louisville, a little later, erected handsome new buildings on a beautiful new campus in the Louisville suburbs. Union Seminary completed a successful Mid-Century Development Campaign in 1950 (the first financial campaign in which it had engaged for 40 years) and in 1967 a still more successful one (for more than seven million dollars), which enabled it to make extensive improvements in its somewhat antiquated plant. Continuing gifts of many generous donors over a period of years had seemingly disproved, for the time, the earlier conviction that the Southern Presbyterian Church could not or would not adequately support its four theological institutions. There were still needs, but all talk of merger had long since ceased.

The number of students studying for the ministry fluctuated, but the general trend was upward. Undergraduate enrollment in Union Seminary, for example, declined from 140 in 1925-1926 to a low of 85 in the Depression years 1935-1936; for another decade it rarely exceeded the century mark (there were only a few more than had attended the institution half a century earlier). As World War II drew to an end, however, student enrollment increased rapidly. In five years, 1946 through 1951, the number doubled from 99 to 198; for the next five years it hovered around 200, then rose to a peak of 245, after which came a sharp decline, and finally once more the beginning of an upward curve. The decline from the post-war high was accompanied, in fact preceded, by a marked drop in the number of candidates for the ministry in the church as a whole, and was similar to that experienced by other denominations in the same period. The greatest net gain of students in the period was registered by Columbia Theological Seminary. In its new location it seemed to have recovered entirely from the doldrums which set in after the Civil War. In the 1950's its enrollment became comparable with that of Union. The student body at Austin and Louisville also showed a healthy increase, though the majority of Louisville students were drawn from the Northern Church.

Particularly noticeable was the increase in the number of married students. There had always been some of those in the seminaries, but prior to World War II they were the exception rather than the rule, mostly older men who had come into the ministry from other occupations. For years the faculty sought to discourage students from marrying during their course of study. When it became evident after World War II that a change had indeed taken place on college and university campuses, as well as those of the theological seminaries, the faculty and Trustees quickly accepted the inevitable; the time came when apartments for married students outnumbered dormitories for single students.

Theological faculties displayed no prejudice against women in the classrooms. It was such instruction given to young women that led to the establishment of the General Assembly's Training School, later the Presbyterian School of Christian Education, and almost from the beginning classrooms in the seminary across the street were open to regularly matriculated students from that institution. The first B.D. was awarded to a woman almost by accident. A middle-aged Methodist woman, hoping to teach, took classes as a special student and won credits sufficient for graduation almost before the faculty was aware.[3] The "exceptional" case soon became a precedent, and in 1957 the Union Seminary Board approved the admission of women candidates for the B.D. degree without qualification. Once the ordination of women was permitted, the number of women students in all the seminaries began to climb.

For many years Union Theological Seminary enrolled Negro students in its graduate departments and opened its library and other facilities not only to these graduate students but also to undergraduates from the neighboring Virginia Union University (a Baptist institution). Union Theological Seminary, in fact, seems to have been the first educational institution in the South to drop the bars of segregation. For some time the only applicants or enrollees were graduate students. When properly qualified Negro students from the new Stillman began to apply—in the early 1950's—they were readily received by all four of the church's seminaries. For a time it seemed as though there might be a continuing stream—however small—of young Negro ministers, college trained, graduating from the theological seminaries, and going out to build up the Negro churches being received into the prevailing white presbyteries. But after a few years the stream began to dry up. Able young Negroes were graduating from Stillman College, but very few of them were entering the ministry. As explained to the General Assembly, "Both White and Negro young people have indicated

reluctance to consider the minister in a church whose practise is contrary to its claims to be the church of ALL whom Christ loves, for
whom he died and lives, and whom he invited into membership in his
body."[4] In 1969 Union Theological Seminary and P.S.C.E. entered
into an arrangement with the Theological Department of Virginia
Union University, whereby operations of the latter would be carried
out on the premises and using the facilities of the two former. It was
a decided step forward in interracial cooperation.

The student bodies of the four seminaries had always included
members of other denominations. After World War II all received a
limited number of foreign students who came to America for study.
It became an accepted custom for Union Seminary to accept each year
a student from the Reformed Seminary in Montpellier in France,
and to send one if its own students for a year to Montpellier in return.

From early days faculties complained periodically that presbyteries
insisted on sending men not intellectually qualified for seminary work.
To meet the needs of poorly prepared students, or the desires of those
unwilling to toil over the original languages, a special English course
without degree was offered. For a brief period only one of the two
Bible languages was required for graduation. But beginning around
the 1940's all of this was changed. There was more careful screening
of prospective students. Only college graduates or those who would
shortly receive their degree were accepted. Psychological tests were
applied. Quality credits were introduced, and penalties for failure
became more severe. More, not less, emphasis was put on the original
languages of Scriptures.

Dr. W. L. Lingle in an article, "Changes I Have Seen," described
some of the changes he had witnessed in theological education. When
I was a student, he wrote, there was a limited number of courses and
a limited number of subjects. Two years in Dabney's *Theology* constituted the backbone of our studies. There were no electives. We had
a very good library, but there were very few fresh books in it. The
library was open only a very few hours a day, and students used it very
little. It was a place to keep books. Our work consisted largely in
memorizing the textbooks and the professors' notes, which did not
develop much original thinking. There were very few lecturers or
preachers from the outside. Today the number of courses and subjects
taught is bewildering to an old-timer. The courses and the studies have
been multiplied; new subjects have been added, notably religious
education, missions, evangelism, social teachings of the Bible, worship, field work, public speaking, music, and others. There are numerous electives. There has also been a change in the methods of

teaching. The library has become the central workship. In addition to the old masters, new books are being constantly added. Students are now sent to the library to see what the leading scholars of America and Europe have to say on the subjects they are studying. They are encouraged to do their own thinking. Lectureships have been established. Leading theological students and churchmen in America, Scotland, England, and continental Europe are invited to speak to our students. Fellowships have been endowed for the purpose of enabling outstanding students to do graduate work at home or abroad. All of this has deepened the scholarship and widened the horizons of many of our thoughtful young ministers.[5]

Later came seminars, in which students were enabled to discover the joys of independent research. More students continued in graduate study, not only with fellowship aid, but also on their own. At first the majority of those who went abroad were drawn—largely for sentimental reasons—to Scotland, later more went to the Continent, especially to Switzerland and Germany; some had always been drawn to Princeton, larger numbers went now to Union in New York, to Harvard, and to Yale; a few ventured out to the West Coast. A still larger number enrolled in the graduate departments which had developed over the years in the denomination's own theological institutions.

For a long time faculties had numbered no more than six or seven members; an increase in numbers came not only because of the growing student bodies, but also because more courses needed to be offered, and more specialization was required. It is significant that in 1925 only one member of the Union Seminary faculty had an earned doctor's degree. Younger members of all the faculties came to have more thorough training in their particular specialties, a development which affected the total life of the seminary and, in time, that of the church.

The Bible Department continued to be the heart and center of the seminary's instruction. It absorbed most of the students' time and was the most adequately staffed.

Systematic theology, which provided the backbone of theological education, had devoted its whole time to the exposition and defense of scholastic Calvinism as set forth in the writings of Charles Hodge or Robert L. Dabney. The passing of "Dabney" in Union marked the end of an epoch. Dr. John Newton Thomas, who came to this seminary in 1940, required students to read more in modern theology, as well as in John Calvin, to whose writings, strangely enough, students in this seminary had not previously been introduced. One man continued to carry the course in theology—with some assistance from the history department, where courses in the history of doctrine had been introduced some years earlier—until 1951 when a Professor of Christian Ethics was elected. A chair of Historical Theology came in the 1960's.

Chairs of Missions were established in the late 1920's; there was no further specialization in the Department of History until the 1960's when Union Seminary added a chair of American Church History.

The greatest expansion in the faculties came in the Department of Pastoral Theology. When the writer was a student in Union there was a short course on Sunday school administration taught by the Professor of Church History. Pastoral theology, such as it was, was given a little attention by the Professor of English Bible in connection with an exegetical study of the pastoral Epistles; there was a course in homiletics—the entire faculty criticized the students' preaching and for one month every year instruction was given in the use of the voice —that was all. Gradually more courses were offered, and by men specially trained in their field—full-time professors of homiletics, specialists in the use of the voice, with the aid of audio-visuals, directors of field work, men trained in counseling. Austin Seminary, under the direction of Dr. Henry Quinius, pioneered by giving first-year men wider acquaintance with local problems and community service resources by riding patrol cars at night, cruising in taxicabs, observing in hospital emergency wards, and calling with social workers. In the late 1960's all the seminaries were reexamining and readjusting curriculums and teaching methods in the light of joint studies carried out under the auspices of the American Association of Theological Schools.

Libraries did not play a vital part in the seminaries' educational program, indeed could not do so, until full-time librarians were added to the staff—the first of them in 1930.[6] Now at last the library which had been opened for only a few hours a day remained open for a full working day, not eight, but fourteen, hours in all. Students and others were coaxed, stimulated, or enticed by one means or another to read; the library was integrated into the total curriculum; it became the nerve center of the seminary's instructional program.

Facilities of the libraries were made available to ministers of all denominations, to laymen, and to students in other institutions. A special responsibility was assumed for ministers in out-of-the-way places and ministers with budgets inadequate to purchase the books needed for their own intellectual and spiritual development. In every way possible ministers were encouraged to borrow from the seminary's collections. The Charles G. Reigner Recording Library, under the auspices of Union Seminary, provided a free-circulating library of magnetic tape recordings, including sermons, worship services, theological lectures, and religious radio programs by leading churchmen throughout the world, which circulated even more widely than the printed word.

Out of the libraries' expanding service came programs of continuing education for ministers on the field. Summer clinics and seminars were developed. Small groups of ministers were brought to the campus throughout the year. Participants in the program spent a major part of their time in independent study, but also conferred with members of the faculty regarding recent developments in the various theological disciplines; seminars were offered, led by visiting specialists. Opportunities were provided not only for resident study, but also for study courses, drawing upon the seminaries' resources to be followed in the minister's own home.

In 1966 the Board of Christian Education reported to the General Assembly: "Our study has revealed that our four theological seminaries have in recent years expanded their programs of continuing education and are among the leaders in American theological education in this development. . . . The programs . . . include: (1) advanced degree study opportunities; (2) annual lecture weeks to which ministers in the field are especially invited; (3) twelve day periods of resident studies; (4) directed home study courses; (5) library extension services; (6) special short courses and institutes during school terms and in the summer months; and (7) provision of published materials designed to keep leaders abreast of theological developments."[7]

In addition to its four theological seminaries, the church had one institution for the training of layworkers, the former Assembly's Training School, renamed the Presbyterian School of Christian Education. This institution passed through phases analogous to those experienced by the theological seminaries. Physical facilities and endowments were increased, the faculty was enlarged, offerings were improved, standards raised, a student body maintained, though not largely increased. As young women enrolled in the theological seminaries for the B.D. degrees, so men enrolled in what had been largely a school for young women; some ministers came seeking more training in religious education. Graduates of the school served the church in a wide variety of capacities—as foreign missionaries; home missionaries; directors of religious education in churches, presbyteries, and synods; choir leaders; teachers in mission schools; teachers of Bible in public schools and in colleges; writers and editors. Most of the young women married and became in the end voluntary workers in their local churches.

Presbyteries were beginning to exercise more care in their approval of candidates for the ministry. As a stimulus in this direction the 1954 General Assembly recommended that presbyteries in determining candidates' fitness make use of recognized intelligence tests, a vocational interest test, and one or more of the recognized personality tests, to be given or interpreted by psychologists or other competent persons.

The church had declined throughout its history to lower the educational qualifications required for ordination. Even ministers who acknowledged that they made little or no use of the original languages of Scripture voted, when polled, that both Hebrew and Greek continued to be required subjects for the B.D. degree. A candidate lacking such training (a graduate of Union Theological Seminary in New York, for example) could be received, however, as an "extraordinary case." From 1914 on presbyteries were permitted to accept college and seminary certificates in lieu of the presbyterial examinations formerly required on most academic subjects. From this time on the candidate was also permitted to write his presbyterial thesis in English as well as in Latin. The suggestion that it might be Latin, a choice never exercised, was not removed until the 1945 revision of the Book of Church Order.

In recent years, various amendments have been adopted making it more difficult for a presbytery to receive into its membership ministers lacking proper educational qualifications from its own or other denominations.

Always there had been times when ministers who desired to change their locations were unable to do so, or when churches seemed unable to find or lose a minister. The problem became more acute in the Depression years, when for a time movement of ministers almost ceased. Out of this situation came Presbyterial Commissions (later committees) on the Minister and His Work, supplemented by similar committees on the synod and Assembly levels. Presbyteries' committees aided churches to secure a pastor and counseled with minister or churches when there was need.

The Assembly's Committee made needed information on ministers and churches readily available. Working with committees on the presbyterial and synodical level the plight of ministers desiring a change was somewhat eased. But the problem of supplying vacant churches without prolonged delay and of enabling ministers to move when there was a desire or need to do so remained unsolved. Suggestions for more radical remedies continued to be heard from time to time, but no church or minister appeared ready to accept the episcopal authority which seemed necessary for a really efficient system.

One of the two earliest benevolences of the church (dating from the year 1719) was a fund to care for the widows and orphans of deceased ministers. Eight years after the organization of PCUS as a separate denomination, three years after the close of the Civil War, the General Assembly of the Presbyterian Church in the United States ordered an annual collection in all of its churches to be used for the relief of disabled ministers. Relief available from this source was meager. Year after year, reported the *Christian Observer* in 1901, the collections have been so small as to allow an average appropriation of less than $100 each, less than 26 cents a day, to furnish food, clothing, fuel, house rent, education, and miscellaneous expenses.

Some years earlier (1895) the Assembly had approved establishment of an endowment fund which, it was hoped, would permit an increase in benefits, but no systematic effort was made to build up this fund and the aid it afforded was insignificant.

Meanwhile, the General Assembly had assumed responsibility for a home and school operated in Fredericksburg, Virginia, particularly for the children of deceased home and foreign missionaries. In addition to primary and secondary education there was a collegiate department, which soon became an independent but closely related institution (Fredericksburg College). For a short time there was conducted also a training school for young women planning to go to the mission field. Missionaries returning from their fields were invited to make the home and school their headquarters. The widows of ministers and missionaries were encouraged to come to Fredericksburg and, if able, to purchase homes, in which children in the home could be boarded.

Realizing that more adequate provision needed to be made for needy ministers and their families, the General Assembly appointed an ad interim committee to study the whole matter and to collect information as to the methods used by other churches which enabled them to offer relief two, three, and even four times as much as the Southern Presbyterian Church.

The report of this committee led to the establishment (in 1901) of an Executive Committee of Ministerial Relief which three years later was joined with the Executive Committee on Education for the Ministry to form the Executive Committee of Ministerial Education and Relief.

In 1910 this committee, joined with the Executive Committee on Schools and Colleges to become the Executive Committee of Christian Education and Ministerial Relief, was given responsibility for the home and school at Fredericksburg. The Executive Committee soon afterward made other arrangements for the maintenance of the widows involved and for the education of their children and this particular form of ministerial relief came to an end. Such relief, it had been discovered, could be distributed more equitably (in relation to other families needing aid), at less cost, and in better ways than gathering widows and their children into a single community.

The Executive Committee had by now begun serious efforts to increase the endowment fund for ministerial relief. In 1906 the total on hand was a paltry $25,000. A series of new goals were set—and reached—first, $250,000, then $500,000, then a million, and then with the generous aid of a ruling elder, C. E. Graham, two and a half million dollars.

From time to time suggestions had been made for a supplemental pension plan, such as was to be found in a number of other denominations. Discouraged perhaps by an earlier contributory plan which had proved none too successful, such suggestions were declined. In 1922 the Assembly called attention to the annual report of the committee of that year which expressed serious doubt as to whether a pension plan for ministers could be justified on social, economic, or Christian grounds. Two years later, the Assembly finally agreed to follow the example of other churches and to put its work of ministerial relief on a contributory reserve basis, or pension plan, to be known as the Ministers' Annuity. To launch the plan it was necessary to raise an accrued liability fund of three million dollars. The campaign for this fund was launched in 1930. Its final success ten years later—in spite of the great Depression of the early 1930's, the lesser depression of 1937-1938, and the coming of World War II—was due to the indefatigable labors and the unruffled patience of Dr. Henry H. Sweets, Secretary of the Executive Committee of Christian Education and Ministerial Relief. "Already," wrote Dr. Dunbar H. Ogden, a few weeks later, "the Pension Plan has strengthened the morale of our church and in numerous cases has solved the problem of an aged pastor holding on to a work far beyond his strength. An increasing demand is at once created for capable young ministers."[8] Adoption of the annuity plan made it possible a little later to adopt an amendment to the Book of Church Order requiring compulsory retirement of all ministers at the age of 70 (with the possibility of annual reelection for five additional years). Adoption of the Ministers' Annuity Plan, supplemented later by the government's Social Security Plan, enabled the minister, whose salary was always modest compared with those offered in other professions, to look forward to his old age with far less anxiety than otherwise would have been the case.

In the reorganization of 1949 the Executive Committee of Christian Education and Ministerial Relief became the Board of Annuities and Relief, charged with this sole responsibility. In the years that followed, wise administration has enabled the Board to liberalize its benefits. In addition, an employees' annuity fund has been established, and group insurance protection of various types has been made available.

There had been a tendency over the years to give fuller recognition to the parity between ruling and teaching elders. Ruling elders were encouraged to exhort in vacant pulpits following the Civil War.[9] But this was an emergency measure. The Book of Church Order still provided that "ruling elders do not labor in word and doctrine," and in 1876 the Assembly ruled that the constitution did not permit a ruling elder to be elected as Moderator of a church court, because only a teaching elder could deliver the sermon by which such courts must be opened.[10] Ten years later an amendment was approved, permitting ruling elders to be elected as Moderators, but providing that "the preaching of the opening sermon, or any other official duty, the performance of which requires the exercise of functions pertaining only to the teaching elder, shall be remitted by him for execution to such minister of the Word, being a member of the court, as he may select."[11]

In another decade (1899) the Assembly approved over considerable opposition an amendment permitting ruling elders to deliver a charge to the congregation in an ordination or installation service of a minister. The opposition held that it would break down the distinction between the duty of ruling, which is shared by all elders, and the duty of preaching, which was done only by teaching elders or ministers. Many of the ruling elders shared the same hesitancy.[12]

With the same idea in mind the Assembly insisted in 1916 that the fundamental distinction between ruling and teaching elders must not be lost sight of in services of worship.[13] Three years later, however, when the United States was in the midst of another war and many ministers were necessarily absent from their pulpits, the Assembly once again urged that ruling elders be more widely used in conducting services in vacant churches.[14]

The statement that ruling elders do not labor in word and doctrine was dropped in the 1925 revision of the Book of Church Order and it was now declared that they should cultivate zealously their aptness to teach the Bible and should improve every opportunity to do so, to the end that destitute places, mission points, and churches without pastors, may be supplied with religious services. Ruling elders now as a matter of course, when called upon to serve as Moderator, opened presbytery, synod, and General Assembly with sermon or address.

Attempts were also made to enhance the office of the deacon. The matter came before the Assembly in 1919 on overture from the Presbytery of Central Texas, asking for the appointment of an ad interim committee to consider enlarging the work of this office, and coordinating it with the work of the minister and elders in the higher courts of the church. In 1922 amendments were adopted giving specifications for a Board of Deacons. Joint meetings with the session were recommended and other measures approved looking toward the wider use of the deacons in the courts of the church.

To remove all uncertainty the 1945 revision of the Book of Church Order stated explicitly that the session could void or amend any action of the Board of Deacons or return it to them for fuller consideration; also that "all organizations within the local church shall be subject to the review and control of the session." This had always been taken for granted, but never before explicitly stated.

The tendency in recent years has been toward more democracy in the government of the church. A decided step in this direction was taken in 1932 when the General Assembly adopted an amendment permitting elders and deacons to be elected for a limited term of office—a plan which permitted a rotation in office, hence commonly called the rotary system. The plan had been before the Assembly almost continuously for a full quarter of a century before it was finally approved. Arguments urged against adoption were, among others, that the rotary plan was unscriptural, belittling (it would rob the office of its dignity), and unwise (it would keep the church in continual unrest).[15]

Arguments advanced in favor of the plan included the following: it was in line with the representative government of the Presbyterian Church; it enabled men to retire honorably from the eldership or diaconate when they desired to do so; it permitted churches to rid themselves more easily of deadwood; it permitted the congregations to call more able men into their service; it was optional—no congregation needed to accept the plan unless it cared to do so. Fifteen years after the adoption of the new provision returns indicated that about one-tenth of the churches followed this plan in the election of one or both groups of officers. Ultimately most of the larger churches adopted the plan; some, especially in more conservative areas, continued to elect officers, both elders and deacons, for life.

The most significant step toward democratization of the church, and perhaps the most far-reaching change in its polity, was adoption of an amendment which permitted women to be elected and ordained as ministers, elders, and deacons. This step had been taken by various other Presbyterian and Reformed churches at home and abroad, and had been approved by the World Alliance of Reformed Churches Throughout the World Holding the Presbyterian System. Woman's status in the Southern Presbyterian Church had been discussed time and again, as we have seen. Slowly she was given more privileges. Women's work in the church grew rapidly, especially after 1912 when the Women's Auxiliary was formed. In 1955, the General Assembly, in response to overtures, appointed an ad interim committee to make a biblical study of the position of women in the church. "Without such study," stated the General Assembly, "we do not feel an opinion can be reached by the church." This committee, including representatives from the various theological faculties, brought in a report giving careful consideration to the biblical data leading to the statement:

> We believe that the Holy Spirit is *leading us today* into a new understanding of the place of women in the Church. As evidence of this guidance we mention a few of the steps which have been taken by our Church and blessed by God.
> (1) Women speak and vote in the congregational meetings of our Church.
> (2) Women serve as Church School teachers, Bible teachers, Directors of Christian Education, and as Professors in some of our Church Schools and the Assembly's Training School. In their work they teach both men and women students.
> (3) Women serve on many of the important committees of the local Church, presbytery and synod.
> (4) Women serve on all of the Boards of our Church. . . .
> (5) Women are in the *majority* in all of our Missions on our Mission fields. . . .[16]

The ad interim committee's recommendation that steps be taken to amend the Book of Church Order to provide for the eligibility of women to hold the offices of ruling elder and deacon was approved by the General Assembly. This action was significant, not only for the particular matter in hand, but because it marked a clear departure from the Thornwellian tradition, the legalistic static *jure divino* interpretation of Scripture which had for so long dominated the church's life; the acceptance of a more dynamic understanding of Scripture— as set forth by the ad interim committee, "From our study of the Bible we are led to believe that the Holy Spirit will progressively lead God's people into a new understanding of the practice of the will of God. This is the promise of Jesus (John 16:13-14)."[17]

The debate on the proposal in the church papers and within the presbyteries was frequently passionate. Opposition to the innovation was based in part on practical grounds, but in greater part on the Pauline injunctions which for so long had been regarded as God's final word on the matter. Women, for the most part, remained aloof from the debate. The vote revealed that the church was not yet ready for the change.

In 1962 the proposal was sent down for a second time to the presbyteries—this time in broader scope, permitting women to be ordained not only as elders and deacons, but also as ministers. In the five-year interim there had come another massive change of opinion. In this period at least two Moderators traveling about the church had spoken out strongly for the ordination of women. More significantly the Board of Women's Work and other outspoken women throughout the church gave the proposal their strong support. Emphasis this time was laid on the right of every member of the church to serve the church with all his (or her) power, in any position to which he might be called. On this occasion 53 presbyteries voted in favor of the amendment, with only 27 in opposition, and the change in the constitution was duly enacted.

Surprising was the rapidity with which churches in all parts of the Assembly proceeded to elect women to the office of both elder and deacon. In 1965 Dr. Rachel Henderlite, with a Ph.D. in religion from Yale Divinity School, who had taught in P.S.C.E., and had been the Director under whom the church's Covenant Life Curriculum had been developed, was ordained as the first woman minister in the church. Significantly the ordination service took place in All Souls Church in Richmond, Virginia, a church predominantly Negro, of which Dr. Henderlite had been a member. Both Negroes and whites took part in the ordination service, and the Associated Press photograph of the event was carried in papers throughout the nation.

A large proportion of Southern Presbyterian churches remained small in size. Thus as late as 1965 more than two out of every five had less than 100 members, and more than three out of five had less than 250 members. While rural churches declined, many urban churches grew larger than any Presbyterian churches had been in the past. In 1900 three churches (in Charlotte, Kansas City, and Atlanta) were approaching the 1,000 mark. Thirty years later there were 36 with more than 1,000 members and two had reached the 2,000 mark; in another 35 years there were 138 churches with more than 1,000 members, 17 with more than 2,000 members, four that had topped the 3,000 mark, one with more than 4,000 and one—the Highland Park Presbyterian Church in Dallas—with more than 6,000 members. In these larger churches there was a move toward a multiple ministry along with a greatly enlarged staff.

In the early 1930's the pastor of a city church, nearing the 1,000 mark, who carried the work alone, except for secretarial help, complained that the round of activities in the local church had become so burdensome as to make it almost impossible for the minister to do thorough work. The responsibility which he carried for two sermons on Sunday—morning and evening—with a mid-week service in addition, he noted, had originated in a simpler time when there were not so many outside activities and organizations. "Many things have been added to the original program of the church," said he, "and nothing has been subtracted. A sort of super-church has grown up, wheels within wheels. It has not been long since there were no church schools with their various departments; no auxiliary; no young people's leagues; no men-of-the-church; no summer conferences; no vacation Bible schools; no leadership training schools. . . . Added to which we have added Rotary, Kiwanis, DAR, UDC, myriads of women's organizations . . . all of which take time and money and strength. Inevitably," he wrote, "the minister feels the effects of such a program and shows it."

In addition to the ever-increasing quantity of his output, the writer observed, the preacher must improve its quality as well. This was caused primarily by the improved standards of education. But, in addition, the preacher could no longer simply accept and pass on the theological teachings of the past. He had to meet the intellectual demands of a questioning age. The "thus saith the Lord" of an earlier age no longer carried weight with the typical American citizen of the 20th century. And neither could religious truth be interpreted according to the experiences of a pre-war age.[18]

A generation later most churches had abandoned the evening service, and many no longer held a mid-week service. A goodly number of these substituted a church family night, which made less demands on the minister.

A 42-page document describing the activities of the First Presbyterian Church, Charleston, West Virginia, takes one's breath away,
wrote Dr. Walter L. Lingle in 1949. The church at this time had over
3,000 members and was the second largest church in the Assembly.
In three and a half years, its pastor, Dr. George Vick, had received
1,044 members, and the total contributions for the preceding year had
been $140,283. The employed working staff consisted of the pastor, a
minister of education, a minister of church extension, an assistant
minister, and a number of secretaries. A duplicate preaching service
on Sunday morning—becoming a necessity in many churches at this
time—was about to be added to the program. The document contained
a 16-page report by the minister of education describing the organization and work of the various departments of the Sunday school. The
minister of church extension told of the work that was being carried
on in the several chapels and outpost Sunday schools, for which the
church took responsibility. In addition to the regular work there were
a number of special meetings during the year: a three-day school of
missions, a visitation evangelism program, a school of instruction for
new officers in the church, a school of instruction for new members,
weekday Bible classes for instruction of prospective Sunday school
teachers and others. Then there were the activities of the women,
the men, and the young people. There were Boy Scouts and the well-
equipped gymnasium with its manifold activities. Dr. Lingle was
especially impressed with the family night dinners held in conjunction
with the mid-week worship service. Large numbers dropped in from
their employment downtown for dinner and the prayer service
before returning to their homes.[19] A number of other churches attracted
many of the same group to a noon luncheon program.

In the period of rapid growth following World War II
many new church edifices were built to house young, growing congregations or older congregations moving to a more favorable site. Most
of these churches followed the traditional style of architecture then
prevalent, Colonial (usual) or Georgian adaptations of a basic neo-
Gothic form. As one writer put it:

> The appeal of the Gothic style and the neo-medieval plan continued
> virtually unchallenged down to the middle of the 20th Century. For most
> Protestant ministers and congregations this plan and style have come
> to constitute the normative "idea of a church" and most of the churches
> that have been built in Canada and the United States since the close of
> the 1st World War have followed it. Characteristic is the long and
> rather narrow nave with a centre aisle leading to a recessed chancel.
> The addition of transepts at the crossing and a clerestory-side aisle ar-

rangement is frequently a feature of the larger and costlier buildings. The choir is invariably located in stalls on both sides of the chancel, the pulpit to one side or the other at the front of the chancel and the alter or communion table at the remote east end of the chancel, as far from the congregation as it can be put.[20]

In such churches the minister was accustomed to read the Scriptures from a reading stand and then cross over to the other side of the chancel and proclaim the Word of God from a pulpit, from which the Bible was usually conspicuously absent. As often as not there was no baptismal font. When needed an elder came forward with water in a silver bowl.

Around mid-century, however, came a new interest in the theological requirements of worship and renewed study of the original Reformed tradition of worship from which there had come such widespread departure. Churches began to build according to the modern conception in which form follows function. The table was brought forward so that it might be as near to the congregation as possible. The pulpit, from which the Word of God was read and expounded, the table, and the font were placed so as to fit more properly into the service. An effort was made to realize intimacy between people and the liturgy, and not just between pastor and people. Sanctuaries were planned on the basis of repetitive worship services, allowing for an average attendance of 50 percent with adjustments for local conditions. The largest congregations began thinking in terms of 500 or 600 seatings rather than in terms of the 1,000 or 1,200 figures of a generation earlier. Among the better examples of modern religious architecture cited by the consultants on church architecture in the Board of National Ministries (in 1969) were John Knox Church, Marietta, Georgia; St. Andrews, San Antonio, Texas; Key Biscayne, Miami, Florida; Westover Hills, Little Rock, Arkansas; First, Belmont, North Carolina; Westminster, Greenville, South Carolina; First, Gastonia, North Carolina; and First, Anniston, Alabama.

As air conditioning spread from stores, offices, and public building to homes, it became more and more a requisite in churches as well.

In 1951 Dr. Lingle wrote on changes which had occurred during his lifetime in worship. In his youth he noted that services were conducted with Puritan simplicity. All that went before the sermon was frequently referred to as the "preliminary exercises." Some churches were still opposed to instrumental music in the church. In many churches a paid church choir was looked upon as an abomination. Now, he noted, more emphasis was placed upon worship and maybe a little less on the sermon. Many of the newer churches were being constructed with a view to making the architecture an aid to worship. Members of the choir wore vestments, and many of the ministers were wearing the Genevan gown with tabs, which the Professor of Systematic Theology in his student days had contemptuously dismissed as "rags of popery." Church services had become more elaborate. Responsive readings, the Lord's prayer, and the Apostles' Creed had been brought into the services and there was more and better music. The people were given a larger part in the services.[21]

These and other trends continued in the decades that followed. In 1956 the General Assembly approved the preparation of a Joint Book of Worship with the United Presbyterian Church. The provisional forms of worship, released by the Joint Committee, returning to earlier ideals of Reformed worship and inviting larger participation on the part of the congregation, found greater acceptance than the older Book of Common Worship on which PCUS had placed an imprimatur. In 1965 the General Assembly answered affirmatively an overture that the four Sundays of Advent, Epiphany, and the beginning of Lent be added to the church calendar.[22] The church calendar now carried a general outline of the traditional Christian Year, together with colors appropriate to the season and special days, in addition to denominational emphases and special days and seasons, and here and there ministers were beginning to garb themselves in the appropriate colors—white, green, red, violet, purple, and black.

The *Presbyterian Hymnal* of 1927—"The Blue Book"—served the church for a generation, the average life-span of a hymnbook, but with less and less satisfaction. It contained an over-balance of gospel hymns—subjective rather than objective in their approach—and lacked a representative hymnody from all periods of the church's life. Many PCUS congregations preferred to use the older hymnbook of the Presbyterian Church in the U.S.A. The *Hymnal for Christian Worship*, published in 1940, under the musical editorship of James R. Sydnor, offered a judicious selection of hymns, but was intended mainly for Sunday schools and was too limited in size for a regular church hymnal. In 1955 came *The Hymnbook*, a joint project (initiated by PCUS) of five denominations in the Presbyterian and Reformed tradition. It contained some 600 hymns, Psalms, choral responses, and other selections, with a special selection of responsive readings. It too contained more of the gospel-type hymns than some would have preferred, but was far superior in choice of hymns and in general makeup and appearance to any hymnbook hitherto produced by the church. It is noticeable that many of the old favorites retained in the new book, hymns of an evangelistic and missionary character, tended to be sung less as time passed. A new hymnbook to accompany *Worship-book* is (1972) in preparation.

In the late 1960's experiments with newer (contemporary) forms of worship—including jazz, folk music, the idea of celebration, the use of lights and rapidly flashing pictures—began to appear in colleges and theological seminaries, in an occasional church service, in conferences at Montreat, and elsewhere. Some were shocked—to the *Presbyterian Journal* a communion service held in Montreat in the summer of 1968 was "blasphemy." Complaints were made to the General Assembly, which, after heated debate, commended its Boards for their "creative leadership in communicating the Gospel in our time" and recommended continued leadership in new forms of worship. The Boards were asked at the same time to be sensitive to the feelings of all and to hear dissent and different viewpoints.

Dr. Lingle—in 1951—recalled the days when preachers had clerical tones and delivered their sermons in declamatory style. Sometimes they shouted at the top of their voices. Now, he noted, they spoke with simplicity and in conversational tones. Their vocabulary was simpler. Broadly speaking the former generation had placed almost its whole emphasis upon beliefs; the present generation put more emphasis upon duties; the older generation engaged in more doctrinal preaching; the new generation did more ethical preaching.

In a study of contemporary preaching (1949-1950) William H. Kadel discovered that the preaching of PCUS ministers centered on the doctrine of redemption through Jesus as it had done through the history of the church. He also found that a large proportion of the sermons submitted—more than a quarter—dealt with the practical application of the gospel to everyday life, largely with personal ethics, but that ministers also were beginning to deal with social issues, including the race problem from a Christian perspective (others meanwhile preaching against the welfare state). Psychological preaching, addressed to the inner needs of men, was also becoming popular. Such preaching stressed faith as a bulwark in times of distress, a pillar of support "when life caves in."[23]

After the Supreme Court decision which declared segregation in the public schools to be unconstitutional, congregations, especially but by no means exclusively in the deep South, became extraordinarily sensitive to any references to race from the pulpit. Many ministers, aware of the possibilities and the impossibilities in this area, touched upon this issue in the pulpit very lightly, if at all. Many others spoke out, some cautiously, others boldly and even prophetically.[24] Of these not a few were forced out of their pulpit by bitter opposition within their congregation and communities, though often the real cause of opposition was camouflaged by a host of other rather transparent and evasive issues.

Articles in popular magazines had indicated that ministers under modern conditions were peculiarly liable to nervous breakdown. A careful investigation carried out under the auspices of the Permanent Committee on Christianity and Health found that this was not the case as far as ministers in PCUS were concerned. On the other hand, it was made clear that the minister was as subject to functional illnesses as was any other person and that a minister of the gospel had entered "one of the most exacting and stressful vocations open to human beings. . . . In fact fidelity to the Christian Gospel *guarantees* extraordinary stress in service."

It was further found that within "the past several decades, the Protestant ministry has changed, of necessity, as the social and cultural milieu of the nation has changed. Frequently, as a consequence, the contemporary minister's vocational gratifications have been relatively reduced as compared with those of his predecessor in an earlier generation. . . . suburban living patterns, parish dispersion and congregational transiency had added to the sheer work of the ministry . . . pastoral duties are inevitably more taxing and more frustrating . . . current pressures in society . . . increasingly demand that the minister take a public stand on one or the other side of grave social issues. The minister speaks out with a certainty that he will alienate some of his parishioners; the minister remains silent at the expense of a conflict of conscience . . ."[25]

In the light of these and other conditions outlined by the permanent committee it appeared surprising that the mental health of Presbyterian pastors and their wives was as good as it appeared.

While the tensions inherent in the minister's vocation increased, and the relationships of pastor and people were subjected to new strains, there had been gains of another sort. "When I was a lad," wrote Dr. Lingle, "the minister with his Prince Albert coat, his white tie and beard, seemed rather remote. We stood in awe of him . . . In my early ministry I heard people say frequently that they had just discovered that ministers are human . . . Little children no longer stand in awe of the minister. Boy Scouts feel that he is one of them."[26] The tendency marked by Dr. Lingle has continued. Ministry and laity, both young and old, tend to be on a first-name basis. The easy camaraderie of the service club has invaded the church. The ties between pastor and people on the whole remain firmly knit. Pastors still hope that their sons will follow them into the ministry, and this a large proportion of them continue to do.

XX

Toward Theological Maturity

In the 1920's the Southern Presbyterian Church remained predominantly conservative, adhering closely to the tradition of the fathers, including the doctrinal system of the Standards, strictly construed; a *jure divino* Presbyterianism, which demanded a "Thus saith the Lord" for any change in theology, polity, or worship; a rejection of "higher criticism" and evolution; an insistence on the spiritual or non-secular character of the church; and strong opposition to any union with the Presbyterian Church in the United States of America.

In the following decade, as we have seen, there came ferment, change, a growing desire to escape from the dead hand of the past.

As one acute observer saw it, there were two parallel movements developing in the church: on the one hand, a more liberal spirit, expressing itself in the desire for reunion with the Presbyterian church in the U.S.A., for continued membership in the Federal Council of Churches, for a more comprehensive theological point of view, for a readier acceptance of the critical results of Bible study, and for a greater concern with social issues; on the other hand, a movement of concern, of fear, of protest against all such departures from the past.[1]

Opposition to the newer tendencies in the church came in part from dispensationalists—to be distinguished from earlier premillenarians, who had existed peacefully along with postmillenarians and the more numerous amillenarians through most of the history of the church. Dispensationalists, with premillenarians generally, looked for the early return of Christ, who would set up his millennial reign on earth, but dispensationalists distinguished successive dispensations in biblical history, in each of which God has dealt with his people after a different fashion. The Bible thus interpreted becomes in many ways a radically different book. Those who accepted this point of view became a divisive force in the church as earlier premillenarians had never done.

The spread of dispensationalism in the church was stimulated by the wide popularity of the Scofield Bible. Dr. C. I. Scofield, editor of this Bible which bore his name, left a successful legal career to enter the ministry in his mid-thirties. His theological education was secured through private study under the guidance of a Presbyterian minister, Dr. James H. Brookes of Missouri. He was pastor for some years of a Congregational Church in Dallas, was closely associated for a time with Dwight L. Moody in Northfield, and became in later life (from 1913 to his death in 1921) a minister, without charge, in the Southern Presbyterian Church. It was in this latter period of his life that he prepared the notes and helps of the Scofield Reference Bible, which did much to spread the dispensational teaching among conservative groups in various evangelical denominations.

Dispensational teaching was also taught in various "Bible Colleges." Two of these whose influence was felt for a time in the Southern Presbyterian Church were the Columbia Bible College (founded 1923), whose President was Robert Crawford McQuilkin, and the Evangelical Theological College of Dallas (founded 1924), whose President was Lewis Sperry Chafer. Both Dr. McQuilkin and Dr. Chafer, like Dr. Scofield, came out of other denominational backgrounds into the ministry of the Southern Presbyterian Church.

The impetus given to Bible study on the part of laymen by these men and the graduates of their schools was at first welcomed by some Southern Presbyterian ministers, but the movement soon proved to be a divisive one. Dispensationalists tended to use their own literature and program. Bible teachers undermined the authority of their pastors. In 1939 Dr. Walter L. Lingle, the columnist of the *Christian Observer*, wrote "What Does Presbyterianism Stand For?" We might as well face the fact, he wrote, that there has been growing up in the Presbyterian churches teachings which are utterly foreign to those set forth in the Confession and catechisms of the church. He gave as examples cases he had personally encountered—church members who claimed that the Ten Commandments and the Lord's Prayer were not intended for the present age; church members who believed that Jesus came into the world to restore the Jewish kingdom and to preside over that kingdom in person. These views "may not seem of any great importance," said Dr. Lingle, "but they are. They affect to a large degree one's interpretation of the Bible from beginning to end, and one's conception of Christianity itself. They have been the source of bitter controversy and of some divisions in the church."[2]

A year earlier East Mississippi Presbytery had overtured the Assembly to prevent its seminaries, ministers, and Sunday school teachers from propagating dispensational teaching within the church. The General Assembly declined at this time to act but was led a little later by mounting concern to appoint an ad interim committee to consider whether dispensational teaching was in harmony with the Confession of Faith. This committee, composed of representatives from the theological seminaries, to whom a couple of old-fashioned premillenarians were later added, brought in a lengthy and carefully worded report, adopted practically without debate, which ended with the unanimous judgment of the committee that dispensationalism was "out of accord with the system of the doctrine set forth in the Confession of Faith, not primarily or simply in the field of eschatology, but because it attacks the very heart of the theology of our church. . . ."[3]

The Assembly did not recommend that any steps be taken against the teaching of dispensationalism, but some sessions, armed with the Assembly's statement, barred such teaching from their church schools, and one presbytery, at least, indicated that it would receive no more graduates from the Evangelical Theological College of Dallas into its membership. Within a few years dispensationalism had ceased to be a disturbing factor in the church.

Within the conservative wing generally a new type of leadership was coming to the fore. For two generations or more after the Civil War the church was largely of one mind. Theological professors, editors, and influential pastors championed the traditional point of view, while laymen, for the most part remained in the background. The new conservative leadership, lacking the same degree of ministerial support, depended more largely on zealous laymen, most of these ruling elders. A considerable portion of the ministerial leadership came into the Southern Church from without.

The *Christian Observer*, oldest religious journal serving the denomination, had become by now a family paper, taking no editorial stand on critical issues before the church. The *Presbyterian of the South*, which had absorbed other journals on the Eastern Seaboard (the *Central Presbyterian*, the *Southern Presbyterian*, the *Presbyterian Standard*, and also the *Southwestern Presbyterian* [New Orleans]), had ceased to be a conservative mouthpiece, and though it, like the *Observer*, remained open to opposing points of view, it had become increasingly the medium through which the more liberal point of view was presented.

The felt need for an organ through which the more conservative point of view could be advanced—heightened by the failure of the Glasgow pamphlet campaign in 1941—led the following year to the appearance of the *Southern Presbyterian Journal* (later simply the *Presbyterian Journal*). This paper, supported financially by a group of wealthy laymen, and edited by Rev. Henry B. Dendy (1942-1959), with strong support from Dr. Nelson Bell, returned missionary from China, quickly became and has since remained not only the voice but also the rallying point for the more conservative group within the denomination. In its opening issues the paper made clear its fundamental policy which has been continued to the present time—opposition to the more liberal theological trends within the church, to its growing ecumenical interest, to its increasing social concern.

In the opening issue explaining "Why the Journal at This Time?" the editor declared:

> The civilization of which we are a part is perched precariously on the edge of the abyss . . . The tragedy is that, in part, the Christian Church is to blame.
>
> It is to blame insofar as it has left its God-given task of preaching the Gospel of salvation from sin through the Lord Jesus Christ.
>
> It is to blame insofar as it has turned from faith in, and the preaching of, the Bible as truly and wholly the Word of God . . .
>
> It is to blame where it has substituted for the Gospel of redemption a programme of social reform.
>
> It is to blame to the extent to which it has stepped out of its spiritual role, to meddle, as the Church, in political and economic matters and affairs of state . . .[4]

The sole aim of the supporters of the venture, it was explained,

> is to call our Southern Presbyterian Church back to her original position, a position unequivocally loyal to the Word of God and the Standards of our Church . . . There are certain great basic principles which brought our Southern Presbyterian Church into being and we feel it is our duty and privilege to seek to reaffirm these truths and to keep them before the Church. The *Southern Presbyterian Journal* accepts without any reservation the standards of the Southern Presbyterian Church . . . It understands that these standards . . . teach the full inspiration of the Scriptures . . . the Virgin Birth of Christ . . . His substitutionary atonement; his bodily resurrection . . . his ascension into heaven; and that this same Christ is coming again to judge the quick and the dead. The *Southern Presbyterian Journal* believes that the mission of the Church is spiritual and redemptive; and that it should not be used to promote the political, economic and social teachings of any group or extra-church organization . . .[5]

The early issues of the *Journal* made it abundantly clear that calling the church "back to her original position" included unrelenting opposition not only to current trends in theological and biblical scholarship, and to the church's growing concern in social issues, but also to the church's continued membership in the Federal Council of Churches and to its growing interest in reunion with the Presbyterian Church in the U.S.A.

In 1943, one year after the appearance of the *Journal*, the *Presbyterian of the South*, which for some years had carried on with meager financial support and only a part-time editor, came under new control. Rev. Aubrey N. Brown, Jr., assumed editorial responsibility and the name of the paper was changed to the *Presbyterian Outlook*. Dr. Ernest T. Thompson remained nominally as editor-in-chief and then as co-editor and continued his regular contributions to the paper. The *Outlook* has remained the medium through which the more liberal voice of the denomination has found expression. It has reflected a more modern theological attitude and a larger acceptance of the results of biblical scholarship than the *Journal;* it has advocated reunion with the Presbyterian Church in the U.S.A., and has supported continued membership in the Federal, later the National and World, Council of Churches; it has called the church to an ever greater concern for social justice, particularly in the field of race.

In the years following the organization of the *Journal* and the reorganization of the *Outlook,* the Southern Presbyterian Church has remained theologically conservative, as it would be generally judged by an outside observer, but has moved away from the rigid Calvinism, the *jure divino,* "Thus saith the Lord" ecclesiasticism of the earlier period. It has remained biblically centered but has accepted by and large the critical approach to the Scriptures and no longer insists that its scholars be bound by the traditional interpretation of Scripture or creed.

An indication of this shifting point of view was seen in the partially successful effort to revise the Confession of Faith in the late 1930's.

This movement grew out of a widely publicized report made to East Hanover Presbytery at its spring meeting in 1935. The report called attention to some of the more extreme statements of the Confession to which objections might be validly raised and also to some important omissions—to the fact, for example, that there was no chapter on the Holy Spirit, on the love of God, on missions, on the ideal Christian character, on the character of Christian civilization, or on the responsibility of the Christian to labor for the estab-lishment of God's Kingdom on earth.[6]

As a consequence of this report a number of overtures came up to the 1935 Assembly requesting amendments to the Confession of one sort or another. The Assembly referred the whole matter of re-vision to an ad interim committee, made up of the Moderator and the professors of theology in the four theological seminaries. In 1938, after tentative approval had been given by the preceding Assembly, the committee brought in a lengthy report recommending changes in some 18 paragraphs of the Confession, the omission of three para-graphs, and the addition of two chapters on the subject "Of the Holy Spirit" and "Of the Gospel." It also recommended slight changes in the two catechisms, including the addition of "love" to the at-tributes enumerated in the famed definition of God (Q. 4).[7]

Some of the proposed changes were simply an attempt to mod-ernize the language, others to avoid expressions that were needlessly offensive (a reference to the pope as the antichrist, for example). Others sought to soften or eliminate some of the more extreme Cal-vinistic positions—among others, the statement that the number of the elect was "so certain and definite that it cannot be either increased or diminished" (Ch. III, Par. 4), and again the statement that man since the Fall of Adam was "utterly indisposed, disabled and *made opposite to all good,* and wholly inclined to all evil." Dr. J. B. Green, Professor of Systematic Theology in Columbia Theological Sem-inary and chairman of the ad interim committee, insisted that the statements which it was proposed to delete lacked Scriptural sup-port; that they contained nothing essential to the integrity of the doctrines in question; that they added nothing to the maturity of preaching; and that parts of the sections involved were not an aid to faith but a hindrance.[8] The Assembly approved the changes and sent them down to the presbyteries for their advice and consent. The matter of the two additional chapters was left in the hands of the committee.

The proposed amendments attracted strong support and aroused vigorous opposition. Greatest interest was aroused by the debate carried on in the church press between Dr. J. B. Green and Dr. William Childs Robinson, both on the faculty of Columbia Theolog-ical Seminary. Dr. Robinson charged that the amendments reflected a liberal, rationalistic trend and a movement away from essential Calvinism, charges which Dr. Green, known as a stalwart conser-vative, indignantly rejected. All of the 18 proposed changes were approved by an overwhelming vote of the presbyteries (more than two to one); three, however, fell short of the required three-fourths majority. Despite this vote the 1939 General Assembly declined to enact any of the more important amendments.[9] Dr. Robinson, present as a commissioner, spoke in opposition; there was no one of equal weight to uphold the affirmative, and the matter was decided practically without debate.

Before this same Assembly came a motion to amend the ordination vow of ministers as defined in the Book of Church Order by requiring adhesion to certain particular doctrines. Dr. Robinson offered as a substitute a declaration that the General Assembly "regards the acceptance of the infallible truth and divine authority of the Scriptures and of Christ as very and eternal God, who became man by being born of a virgin, who offered up himself a sacrifice to satisfy divine justice and reconcile us to God, who rose from the dead with the same body with which he suffered, and who will return again to judge the world as being involved in the ordination vows to which we subscribe."[10]

The substitute motion was quickly seconded by one of the more liberal-minded commissioners (to head off approval of the original motion), and accepted overwhelmingly by the Assembly. So the Assembly finally approved a list of fundamental doctrines said to be involved in the ordination vows, something which it had repeatedly declined to do in the past. The declaration was recognized to be an *in thesi* deliverance, and not necessarily binding on the conscience.[11]

Three years later the Assembly adopted and enacted, over the strenuous opposition of Dr. Robinson, the two proposed additional chapters to the Confession of Faith, "Of the Holy Spirit" and "Of the Gospel," identical with those which had been added to the Northern Presbyterian Confession a generation earlier.

One well-known minister in the church had pled: "Let us take down the picture of God which Calvinism has hung in [the Standards], presenting to our view a God who has unchangeably elected some men to eternal life and unchangeably ordained the rest of mankind to eternal death." This, he now felt, the addition of the two new chapters to the Confession had done. "Glory be to God! Amen! and Amen!" he exclaimed.[12]

True, the harsher statements of a polemic Calvinism remained, but since responsible professors in the four theological seminaries, two General Assemblies, and two-thirds or more of the presbyteries had voted for the elimination of these more difficult portions of the Confession they could hardly claim to reflect the mind of the church.

In the generation that followed ministers (and officers) have continued to accept the system of doctrine set forth in the Confession of Faith, but the General Assembly has interpreted this to mean only the essentials of the system,[13] and it has become quite clear that the essentials of the system are understood quite differently from what they were one or two generations earlier. Which indeed must be the case if there is not to be stagnation—and death.

Way to more rapid change was opened when the four theological seminaries established fellowships for graduate study which, unlike the earlier fellowships, permitted study in outside institutions. Young men who formerly would have completed an additional year of study in their own alma mater or perhaps at Princeton Theological Seminary (with much the same point of view) now went on to secure their doctorates from Edinburgh or Basel, from Yale Divinity School or Union in New York. Some, reacting from their exposure to a more liberal theology, returned more conservative, if not fundamentalist in their point of view. A few, reacting from their conservative background, became "modernists," and no longer felt at home in the church in which they had been nurtured. The great majority remained conservative evangelicals, but with a more moderate and open point of view. It was from this latter group that the church would increasingly find the scholars to teach in its theological seminaries, and also in the expanded departments of religion in its denominational colleges.

The decade of the 1940's was a pivotal one for the theological seminaries; faculties until this time had been largely ingrown, containing few men who had done graduate work outside of the South. As late as 1939 Union Theological Seminary in Virginia had on its faculty only one professor with an earned doctorate. The following year, when Dr. John Newton Thomas with a Ph.D. from the University of Edinburgh and John Bright with a doctorate from Johns Hopkins University joined the faculty, the pattern was broken. Only rarely from this time on would anyone be called to teach in any of the four theological seminaries who did not have, or who did not expect soon to receive, the highest graduate degree.

Dr. James Porter Smith, who succeeded Dr. Thomas Cary Johnson as Professor of Systematic Theology in 1931, had replaced Dabney's *Theology* as the basis of instruction with the theological works of Augustus H. Strong, a thoroughgoing Calvinist, sound in all respects save those concerning the distinctive beliefs of his own (Baptist) church. The passing of "Dabney" in Union and of "Hodge"— about the same time—in the other seminaries marked the end of an era. Dr. Thomas at Union and Dr. Felix B. Gear who came a few years later to Columbia Theological Seminary, in succession to Dr. Green, required students to read widely for the first time in modern theology as well as in John Calvin, to whose writings Southern Presbyterian students previously, strange as it may seem, had seldom been introduced. Prior to 1940 theological students in the Southern Presbyterian Church were carefully trained by professors of systematic theology in one system of theology only—old-line Calvinism. Since 1940 they have been made increasingly aware of the wider spectrum of theological thought.

"The church still believes that the Confession of Faith contains the system of doctrine taught in Holy Scripture," Dr. Walter L. Lingle had written in the 1950's, "but we no longer believe that it is final in all its statements."[14] The old battles between Calvinism and Arminianism by this time had long since ceased. The so-called five points of Calvinism were seldom proclaimed from the pulpits; they had ceased to be matters on which theological students were examined by their presbyteries. Theological faculties and students and ministers in their exposition of the gospel were concerned with the more vital issues of their own day.

Calvinism has remained the system of theology favored in the church's theological institutions but it is not the rigid, unyielding Calvinism of earlier years, a Reformed theology rather prepared to accept insights from Barth, Brunner, Bonhoeffer, Tillich, and others, all subject to revision in the light of a growing understanding of Scripture.

In the late 1950's a new effort arose to delete statements in the Confession indicating that God predistined some men to everlasting death. The Assembly finally adopted recommendation of an ad interim committee:

1. That no revision be made in chapter III of the Confession because it is an historic and integral statement. Any revision would destroy the unity of the creed without resolving the problem.

2. That the General Assembly declare that in its judgment the doctrine of fore-ordination to everlasting death as formulated in the Confession is not an adequate statement of Christian faith, because it implies, regardless of the intention of the authors, an eternal negative degree, and that the doctrine as stated in the Confession is not essential to Reformed theology as is indicated by its absence in this vigorous form in such authentic Reformed creeds as The Scots' Confession of 1560, the Second Helvetic Confession, and the Heidelberg Confession.

3. That the General Assembly recommend to presbyteries, sessions and members the study of God's sovereignty as it is taught in the Bible and as it has been understood in our Reformed tradition, that we may come to a deeper understanding of this great doctrine.

4. That the General Assembly emphasize the importance of studying the Confession in the context of the *total* Reformed tradition. . . .

5. That the General Assembly call attention to the importance of the following truths in the study of paragraphs 3, 4, and 7 [the paragraphs which it had been proposed to delete].

a. The God who elects is the God who has made himself known to us in Jesus Christ. Therefore his sovereignity involves his love as well as his power.

b. In Jesus Christ we find the meaning of our election and God's will concerning all mankind.

c. God always deals with us as men and not as sticks and stones. God's dealing with us is personal, not mechanical.

d. Election is to service, holiness and blessedness.

e. God "desires all men to be saved and to come to the knowledge of the truth". . . .[15]

The same year in which this statement was adopted, Dr. Felix B. Gear (Columbia Seminary) wrote a study book, *Basic Beliefs of the Reformed Faith*. Doctrines included were The Sovereignty of God; The Promise and Possibilities of Man; Christ: Son of God and Son of Man; Salvation: What the Gospel Offers Man; The Purpose of Predestination; and The Church of the New Testament.

Predestination, wrote Dr. Gear, is not intended to raise questions about who is and who is not saved. It brings assurance rather that "He will never let you down, He will never let anything get you down, and He will put down everything that stands in the way of His final purpose for you."[16] There was little, if anything, in the book which an evangelical Arminian, or in fact an evangelical of any persuasion, could not accept.

The following year the Assembly adopted a Brief Statement of Belief on which an ad interim committee had labored for a number of years to replace the earlier such statement adopted in 1913. In this latest Brief Statement the church sets forth its faith in six sections on God and Revelation, Christ and Salvation, the Church and the Means of Grace, Christian Life and Work (including a paragraph on Social Responsibility—a theme not included in the Confession of Faith or in the earlier Brief Statement), and Judgment and the Life to Come. Chapter III, "Of God's Eternal Decrees," in the Confession of Faith declares that "God from all eternity did . . . unchangeably ordain whatsoever comes to pass . . ." The Brief Statement of 1961 reads instead: "God has an eternal, inclusive purpose for his world, which embraces the free and responsible choices of man '. . . This purpose of God will surely be accomplished." In the Brief Statement there is no mention of predestination. It is a document which has aroused neither enthusiasm nor opposition.

The adult CLC study book for 1968-1969, *Christian Doctrine* written by Shirley C. Guthrie, Jr., Professor of Systematic Theology in Columbia Theological Seminary, was in the Reformed tradition, but with a pronounced Barthian slant and open to other points of view. It was a book attuned to modern man and the questions which naturally come to his mind. To Dr. Guthrie "the predestinating, electing God is the God who has gathered together a visible earthly 'family,' committed himself to it and invited all men to become a part of it." An assurance that we are among the chosen does not allow or require us "to judge whether any man or whether whole groups of people are finally saved or damned."[17]

The General Assembly in 1961 had recognized the need for a contemporary formulation of Reformed faith and expressed the hope that this might be undertaken by the world-wide Reformed Community.[18] Agreement to draw up a new Confession, "reflective of the whole of Reformed Thought and in full accord with the system of doctrine in our present standards," was included in the proposed plan of union with the Reformed Church in America. Rejection of the union by R.C.A. was followed by a decision of the Southern Assembly to begin such an undertaking on its own. An ad interim committee, appointed for this purpose, was instructed to prepare a new Confession of Faith, together with a Book of Confessions (such as had been adopted earlier by the United Presbyterian Church).

The decade of the 1940's witnessed the beginnings of a shift not only to a broader theological point of view but also to a wider acceptance of the results of the historical criticism of the Bible. Dr. Samuel A. Cartledge, Professor of New Testament in Columbia Theological Seminary, had authored in 1938 *A Conservative Introduction to the New Testament*, which underwent five editions in the next ten years and met with wide acclaim in conservative circles within and without the denomination. In 1943 Dr. Cartledge followed this earlier volume with *A Conservative Introduction to the Old Testament*, in which he presented fairly the opposing views held by scholars regarding the authorship and interpretation of the various Old Testament books, and concluded that "a conservative" who accepted the Bible as the Word of God was not bound to a belief in inerrant inspiration and that he was free to accept many of the conclusions of historical criticism, including the documentary theory of the Pentateuch, the two Isaiahs, the parabolic character of Jonah, and the non-historicity of the book of Daniel. *The Christian Century*, most influential liberal theological journal, published a favorable review of the book under the caption "Enlightened Conservatism." The author's openness as a conservative to critical conclusions of Old Testament scholarship was termed epoch-making. The *Southern Presbyterian Journal,* on the other hand, found in the book distressing evidence of the liberal philosophy of Scripture interpretation, whose influence was spreading through the church—more reason to regret the Assembly's failure to investigate unsound teaching in the theological seminaries, as had been requested two years earlier. The *Journal* believed that the majority of the ministers and the laymen of the church were still sound in the faith. It gravely questioned, however, whether some of the leadership of the church had not passed into other hands. It warned that, if trustees of seminaries failed to act, the control of the church courts would soon be taken over by young men influenced by their liberal teachers.[19]

John Bright, who had come to Union Theological Seminary as a professor in the Department of Old Testament three years before the publication of *A Conservative Introduction to the Old Testament,* had developed, meanwhile, a required course in Old Testament Introduction which faced squarely all of the critical problems of the Old Testament and sought to fit each book into its proper historical setting. Dr. Bright accepted the historical-critical method of Bible study, and many of its conclusions, but rejected the radical reinterpretation of Israel's history, which held that monotheism, the belief in one God, was a late development in Israel's history. The basic historical accuracy of the Old Testament was defended, on archaelogical grounds, among others, without reliance on any particular theory of biblical inspiration. Dr. Bright was convinced that there was "an evangelical and Bible-centered theology" which was not "ultra-fundamentalism and certainly not radical liberalism, which lies somewhere in between and seeks to preserve the virtues and avoid the excesses of both."[20]

Dr. Donald G. Miller and Dr. Balmer H. Kelly joined the Union faculty in 1943, the former in the New Testament Department, the latter teaching in both Old Testament and New Testament fields. From these three men—Bright, Miller, and Kelly—came a deepened interest in biblical theology and in biblical preaching, based on a reverent, yet critical, study of the text that had wide influence in the church.

In his inaugural address Dr. Miller declared that it was not likely that there would be any large-scale return to the wholly uncritical approach to the Scriptures. "The Scriptures raise problems," he asserted. "And these problems must be faced, frankly and honestly.

The day is happily gone when any considerable support can be summoned to an assertion that all Higher Criticism 'repudiates the truth of God's revelation to man, makes Almighty God a liar, and denies the testimony of the Holy Spirit' [as set forth in *The Christian Beacon*]." Dr. Miller insisted, however, that the critical approach to Scripture had not been adequate either to understand it or to release its power in life. In the body of his address he went on to suggest a few neglected emphases in biblical study, "which, if given due regard, might serve at least to supplement, if not to correct, both the method and the conclusions which have been widely current in critical circles." Among other things, he indicated that there had been "an unwholesome preoccupation with the environmental matrix out of which the Bible was born, rather than to a vivid sense of the elements in it which completely transcend environment and speak a 'timeless' Word of God to our souls."[21]

Responding to a student who insisted on biblical inerrancy, Dr. Miller pointed out that since the original autographs are nonexistent the existence of error in them can be neither proven nor disproven. But the only Bible we now have has errors—for example, Matthew 27:9, which attributes to Jeremiah a quotation from Zechariah. But the major heresy of fundamentalism, he charged, was its tendency to substitute doctrines for realities. "The Christian faith," he insisted, "does not stand or fall on 'the substitutionary' atonement and the physical resurrection of Christ. Neither 'substitutionary' nor 'physical' are biblical words but human attempts to explain inexplicable and transcendent realities. . . ."

"Many of us," he added, "who love the Bible and have risked our souls on a final trust in the fact that God has uniquely acted in Christ for the redemption of the world are incurably evangelical but not fundamentalist. . . ."[22]

In 1955 James Herbert Gailey, Jr., began to teach the required Old Testament Introduction courses at Columbia Seminary with full appreciation of critical research. At Austin the stimulus for a critical study of the Bible came from guest professors of biblical theology from Europe (1953-1959). The decisive turning point came in 1959 when Professor James Wharton commenced teaching a required course on Old Testament Introduction with "special emphasis upon the origins of biblical literature."[23]

The gradual acceptance of the critical approach to the study of Scripture in all four of the church's theological seminaries brought greater, not lesser, interest in Bible study in the theological seminaries—it was this field, for example, which proved most appealing to graduate students—and stimulated greater, not lesser, emphasis on biblical preaching.

One evidence of this increased interest in critical, yet constructive, study of the Bible was the appearance of *Interpretation*. For more than half a century students and faculty of Union Theological Seminary in Virginia published the *Union Seminary Review*, which had become the only quarterly theological publication within the bounds of the church. It encouraged Southern Presbyterian ministers to write, kept ministers and laymen informed of the progress of theological scholarship, and from time to time published articles of enduring worth; but its circulation was limited and did not reach to an appreciable extent beyond denominational borders. In 1946 the *Union Seminary Review* became *Interpretation: A Theological and Biblical Quarterly*, devoted particularly to biblical theology, a subject at this time of growing interest throughout Christendom. Eliciting the support of leading biblical scholars throughout the Protestant world, this quarterly soon established itself as one of the leading theological journals of the day. By 1960 there were subscribers in every state of the Union and over 30 different countries. Though most of its contributors came from other branches of the church, *Interpretation* was one medium through which the Southern Presbyterian Church was at last beginning to speak to the larger Christian world.

Some years earlier Louis J. Sherrill, Dean of Louisville Presbyterian Seminary, had written in the *Union Seminary Review* an article entitled "The Barrenness of the Southern Presbyterian Pen," which attracted a great deal of attention in the church. "The Southern Presbyterian pen has almost run dry," charged Dean Sherrill. It is a period, he reminded his readers in which "the world has been thinking on some of the weightiest of human problems. Books stream from the press. Magazines and journals of every description carry articles on religion. The radio pours its message out to some forty million people. Every conceivable viewpoint is represented . . . the world is in some sense being remade before our eyes. . . .[But] in all of this we are strangely silent . . . Take any line of theological or allied thinking and run it back—how long has it been since a vigorous original production appeared from a Southern Presbyterian minister?"[24]

The situation which Dr. Sherrill described could not be gainsaid. As a matter of fact the arraignment could have been more severe. Books had indeed come from the Southern Presbyterian pen, some of which were widely read, and greatly influential in the Southern

Presbyterian Church, but no book had appeared before 1861 or after, up to this time, which had been recognized beyond the denomination as a distinct contribution to theological literature.

Why had Southern Presbyterians not made a greater contribution to theological scholarship? Many ministers, Dr. Sherrill recognized, did not have the taste, nor the disposition for creative scholarship; others who might have become productive scholars lacked the leisure to master a particular field of study. It was the seminary professors who might be expected to have written. Why, asked Dr. Sherrill had they not done so? One reason, he replied, was the widespread assumption in the South that a professor should distinguish himself by his preaching rather than by his teaching. Another was the relatively limited library equipment that was available to him. A third was the demand (actually the economic necessity) that the professor spend a large part of his vacation in summer conferences and teaching. A fourth was the custom of so dividing the professor's time between many fields of teaching that he was left little opportunity for the mastery of one. A fifth was the lack of clerical and stenographic help for theological professors (not until 1955 was such help provided for faculty members at Union Seminary). Undoubtedly the reasons stressed by Dr. Sherrill helped to explain the situation which he now decried. But Dr. Sherrill found a still deeper reason in the fact that the method of teaching which had prevailed in the seminaries did not prepare students for an independent critical study of the sources. In the American Presbyterian educational history he noted there were two clearly discernible ideas: "one is that the purpose of education in religion is to produce in the 'learner' a complete adjustment to an unchanging heritage; the second is that education in religion should, along with familiarity with and allegiance to that heritage, induce the enlargement of it by new discovery and fresh achievement . . ."[25]

Only in the encouragement of this second conception of education did Dr. Sherrill see hope for productive scholarship in the Southern Presbyterian Church. If such scholarship did not appear, what then? "If we become a non-productive group, living merely upon our past," replied Dr. Sherrill, "leadership in spiritual affairs in the present will not come into our hands as a denomination. If we resist outside influences we can hardly hope for more than our own static persistence in the backwater while the main currents flow on regardless of us."[26]

It was just here that Cecil V. Crabb, one of the church's more scholarly pastors, found a part of the difficulty. "We are perfectly willing to dig in and hold our cherished traditions and principles forever," said he.[27] "The theological atmosphere of our church has not been conducive to creative effort," Dr. C. L. King added, a few years later. "We have been too suspicious and critical toward that which was new or different from the fare to which we have been accustomed. Such an attitude does not encourage men who for years have studied biblical and theological subjects to venture forth to tell us the conclusions of their thinking."[28]

Fortunately, even as Dr. Sherrill initiated the discussion, the road to improvement was opening. Winds of freedom were beginning to blow, and the type of scholarship for which Dr. Sherrill was pleading was being encouraged. At the time of this writing (the late 1960's) it remains true as Dr. King pointed out a generation earlier: "The books used by the students in the seminaries are largely the products of minds outside the church. The books being purchased by the ministers out in the field are from minds outside our church. A few volumes from our writers have received wide acclaim . . . But the number of books produced by our church compared with that of other denominations . . . seems pathetically small."[29] Yet books by Southern Presbyterian ministers are appearing in increasing numbers, and they are receiving a far wider circulation. And a few of the church's scholars have produced volumes which have received acclaim on both sides of the Atlantic and are finding their way into the classrooms. Among them would be listed writings of Dr. Lewis J. Sherrill himself (in the field of religious psychology), the writings of John Bright in the Old Testament field, and those of Dr. James M. Robinson* in the area of New Testament research and interpretation. Among the newer additions to the faculties of the four seminaries are able young scholars who have produced works of genuine merit and of whom the church may expect much in the years that lie ahead.

Further encouragement to creative scholarship came with the organization of John Knox Press. The Board of Christian Education, through its Division of Publication, had published a few books, a very few, from year to year—none of which circulated very widely, if at all, outside the denomination. A step forward was taken in 1955 when John Knox Press was instituted as the publishing house, and the number of books published greatly increased, with authors drawn from home and abroad; a reputation for publishing worthwhile re-

---

* Dr. Robinson, teaching now without the bounds of PCUS, has transferred his membership to the United Presbyterian Church in the U.S.A.

ligious books was established and for the first time books published
under the auspices of the Southern Presbyterian Church circulated
widely beyond its own borders. Of particular significance was the
encouragement given to scholarly writing by the quiet dropping
of hampering restrictions intended to preserve the ancient shibboleths.

A worthy contribution to biblical scholarship was made through
publication of the Layman's Bible Commentary, a series of 24 small
volumes covering both the Old and New Testaments, written by
competent scholars, a number of whom came from the Presbyterian
Church in the United States. Circulation of the series has been extensive both in the United States and in Great Britain. Publication of
these volumes by John Knox Press, its reception by the church,
its endorsement by the General Assembly after a series of attacks
in the columns of the *Presbyterian Journal*, indicated that the transition had taken place—not only were the scholars of the church free
to write, but the church membership was prepared to accept informed, yet reverent, expositions of the Word of God, based on
sound principles of historical criticism.

One of the foundation papers prepared in 1960 for the Covenant
Life Curriculum, prepared under the auspices of the Board of
Christian Education, contained statements which summarized what
had come to be the mainstream position of the Presbyterian Church
in the United States: "The documents which are preserved in our
Bible are human writings. We have every responsibility to try to
understand the way in which they were written. We do not need to
fear the critical approach of those who stand reverently within
the believing community of those who acknowledge Jesus as Lord."[30]

One of the clearest statements setting forth the attitude of the
church's theological institutions in regard to the Bible came from the
faculty of Union Theological Seminary in response to a direct question regarding the infallibility of Scripture addressed to it by Central
Mississippi Presbytery. The seminary faculty, with approval of the
Board of Trustees, replied unanimously as follows:

    1. "Infallibility" as a term associated with Biblical and theological
perspectives has had varied meanings in the history of the whole church.
In order to be as clear as possible in our use of the word we affirm:
        a. That Union Seminary believes and teaches the "infallibility" of
the Scriptures" in the sense that the Bible, illuminated by the Holy
Spirit, is definitive and authoritative for the church's faith and life.
        b. That since the Bible is God's gracious gift to the church to
communicate knowledge of himself, to elicit the response of faith
from the believer, and to manifest those procedures by which the

redemption wrought by Christ has been established, we teach and believe that all of the Scripture must be in the light of the sovereign purpose for which it has been provided and employed by the Holy Ghost.

c. That in some matters of history, science and nature not related to the Bible's controlling message, the literal accuracy of the Scriptures is not necessary for that purpose.

2. Union Seminary is committed to the careful, critical, historical and linguistic study of the Scriptures, employing every tool and skill of reverent scholarship, as being the duty of those who are convinced that the Holy Spirit employs such means to make plain what Christ has said and would say to the church of which he is the head.

3. Union Seminary deliberately and decisively has given to the study of the Bible the central place in its curriculum, under the conviction that the "Teaching Elder", for whose preparation the Seminary exists, is encouraged thereby to believe the Scriptures, to love them, to search them, to submit to them, and to proclaim them.[31]

Instruction in the church's other theological institutions was based on the same general point of view.

Reaction to trends described in this chapter led in 1964 to the formation of an independent theological seminary in Jackson, Mississippi. Listed among its "distinctives" were a commitment to the "plenary, verbal inspiration" of the Bible and "its absolute inerrancy as the divinely revealed and authoritative Word of God"; to "the sovereignty of God as a central tenet of Biblical faith, along with the related doctrines of absolute predestination and unconditional election"; and to "strict creedal subscription to the whole Reformed faith."[32] Three years after the founding of the institution there were 33 students enrolled, the majority of them being graduates of Belhaven College, also located in Jackson.

The more conservative wing of the church now had its paper (the *Presbyterian Journal*), its organization (The Concerned Presbyterians), with a sizable budget and agents crisscrossing the Assembly, and a seminary, for the training of its ministers—all obsessed with the idea that the authorized leaders, the scholars in the church's own institutions, had rejected fundamental truth and so betrayed the gospel. Back of the theological differences there were others —differences regarding the mission of the church (involving the attitude toward race and other social issues) and irreconcilable differences regarding cooperation and union with other religious bodies.

XXI

"Spirituality" Reinterpreted

Southern Presbyterians continued to emphasize their "distinctive" doctrine of the spirituality of the church through the early decades of the present century. It was not that the church, its ministers, and its members were indifferent to the social needs of the time. Blind to particular evils in their own area, yes, but not unconcerned for the pressing problems of the day. The silence of the church regarding such matters was justified on the ground that proclamation of the gospel struck at the root of all social evils and that reconciliation of man with God inevitably led to reconciliation with his fellowman in all the complex relations of life. So Dr. Harris E. Kirk, the Southern Church's most distinguished pulpiteer, solemnly announced that the social evils of the day were the effects of well-defined secondary causes. Injustice, for example, was the result of covetousness. But such secondary causes were themselves effects of primary causes, and the most powerful primary cause was sin, the sin of alienation from God. "Reconcile man to God," explained Dr. Kirk, "and you remove the primary cause of human evils; both the secondary causes and their surface effects will disappear . . ."[1]

This was the widely accepted view, and it defined the church's mission. It was, however, beginning to be challenged. In the 1890's Dr. A. J. McKelway, crusading editor of the *Presbyterian Standard,* had insisted that the doctrine of the spirituality of the church was carried too far when it forbade the church to speak against the abuses of child labor in Southern mills. Dr. Walter Lee Lingle, whose voice as preacher, teacher, columnist, and director of the "Montreat Platform" was heard through the church, acknowledged the new insights which had come to him from reading Walter Rauschenbusch's epochal volume, *Christianity and the Social Crisis* (1907). Shortly thereafter he began to teach a course in Union Theological

Seminary on "The Social Teachings of the Bible," which helped to shape the mind of a new generation of theological students.

It was reaction to World War I, however, which led to the first significant breach in the church's long-defended position. The traditional position of the church had deterred the Assembly from any strong endorsement of the war and its aims, but ministers had been caught up in the moral fervor of the times, confident that a war to make the world "safe for democracy" had the divine blessing. In the aftermath of the war came inevitable reaction, disillusionment, a growing conviction that the church of Jesus Christ must never again be used as an instrument for the promotion of war. Various declarations were adopted to this effect. A wave of near-pacifism swept over the church.

A second question on which churchmen found it increasingly difficult to remain silent was the race question, greatly intensified by the war. Some denied that a problem existed. Thus one of the more influential ministers of the church, Dr. A. A. Little, long-time pastor of the First Presbyterian Church in Meridian, Mississippi, denied "in toto" the assumption that the Negro was a downtrodden race, or that in some areas he was denied the rights that God had given him. Anglo-Saxons in the South had indeed chosen, and would continue to choose, not to permit intermarriage between the races, but this Dr. Little insisted was clearly within their rights, as were the various methods adopted to insure this end—separate schools, coaches on trains, hotel accommodations, sections of cities where the different races could live. All this, as Dr. Little saw it, only led to good order and peace. True, there were occasional lynchings, and this was to be regretted, but in the courts, Dr. Little insisted, even-handed justice was handed out to white and Negro alike.[2]

Others, however, saw the situation differently. Christian men met in Atlanta after the war to devise means by which misunderstandings between the two races might be removed and justice insured. Out of this movement came the Southern Inter-racial Commission, whose interlocking committees spread through the South. The General Assembly in 1920 and again in 1921 commended these efforts and recommended that Southern Presbyterians give them full support.[3] Presbyteries and synods added their endorsement, and appointed committees on interracial affairs. Addresses were heard, resolutions adopted, sermons preached calling for justice to the Negroes, and in 1929 the General Assembly approved an article which the Federal Council proposed adding to its social creed, reading: "That the churches stand for the removal of discriminations which prevent equal opportunity of development of all races, and for the equal sharing of rights and privileges."[4]

A few in the Southern Church were beginning to speak out boldly against the mistreatment of the Negro, among them Rev. William Crowe, Jr., then a young pastor in Bluefield, West Virginia, who spelled out the backwardness of their education, their disfranchisement at the polls, the irrational prejudices held by white people in the South. He quoted severe criticisms leveled at the church for its interracial attitudes by Dr. W. E. B. Du Bois and acknowledged that they were just.[5]

The third stimulus to social concern and perhaps the catalyst that brought the various influences to a head was the Depression and its effects. Ten million men were out of work. There were bread lines and hunger marches; army veterans marched on Washington. The number of destitute on relief rolls in the South was three times that of the country as a whole. The textile mills, the region's leading industry, had been in a chronic depression for most of the preceding decade. Pay cuts and introduction of the stretch-out during the Depression years produced unrest, strikes, and violence. Communism was gathering support, and with it came signs of incipient revolution. "The optimism of the post-war years was gone; the very world itself seemed to have jumped the track, and people were ready and looking for a change. The hoped for change [came] in 1933 with the inauguration of Franklin Delano Roosevelt and the beginning of the New Deal. America was entering a new era. A government with a new sense of social responsibility was in power, setting out with high hopes on a course directed to the changing of the social and economic practises of America that the needs of all her citizens might be met."

Rev. William Crowe, Jr., one of the more articulate spokesmen for the church's changing point of view, in a personal letter to the author, recalls the situation:

> The spiritual climate into which we younger ministers entered as we started on our careers was deeply permeated with a restlessness over social conditions. World War I had stirred an idealistic feeling in the American churches . . . but when it was over the idealism faded and the dreamers of a better society were aware of a vast frustration. There swept over our nation a demand that social institutions must be made to reflect the mind of Jesus. The *Christian Century* became a popular periodical among Presbyterians. Books poured from the press that were pleading for social improvement . . . World War I, the aggressive claims of pacifism, the emergence of the labor movement, the stock market debacle, the great depression, and the rise of FDR and the new doctrine of government, gave tremendous impetus to the spread of acceptance of the social implications of the Gospel.

Instead of an isolated voice here and there, there was now a chorus. Dr. W. L. Carson, pastor of the First Presbyterian Church in Richmond, Virginia, spoke for a new generation of ministers when he said, "to speak of saving individuals without attempting to reform society is a contradiction in terms."[6]

"The time has passed when it is possible to hold the attention of a great many people simply by talking about the salvation of . . . souls," wrote Dr. John A. MacLean, "The social and economic problems are so acute and so pressing, the issues involved so far-reaching and the results of injustice and confusion so terrible and crushing that people are eagerly seeking some means of establishing a better world, here and now . . . Unless the Southern Presbyterian Church," he added, "takes cognizance of present conditions and acts accordingly we stand to lose a large part of the enthusiasm and loyalty of many of our members, especially the young."[7]

In January 1933, the *Presbyterian of the South* opened its new Round Table Department, with a distinguished group of contributing editors, committed to a frank and open discussion of the vital issues before the church. Six months later, one of the contributing editors, Rev. Chris Matheson of Shawnee, Oklahoma, noted that practically all the articles appearing in the paper since the appointment of the contributing editors dealt with some phase of the social mission of the church.[8]

The Synod of Virginia the previous year had transformed its committee on interracial relations into a committee on moral and social welfare, stating: "it shall be the duty of this committee to secure and to present to Synod pertinent information regarding inter-racial relations, and also information regarding other moral and social issues that may be of interest or concern to the Synod and to suggest any action that it may deem wise for the Synod to take."[9]

The following spring the General Assembly, by a standing vote of 134 to 39, voted to appoint a similar committee, but the next morning after a lengthy debate voted to reconsider its hasty action of the preceding day. A ruling elder, Judge Samuel M. Wilson, stamped the proposal as un-Presbyterian, "a new and unwarranted departure from our historic practices." He urged that all reference to the matter be expunged from the records, that no trace remain of the Assembly's momentary departure from its traditional view of the church and its mission, and this the Assembly did by a vote of 137 to 99.[10]

But the tide of social concern was rising and could not be so easily checked. A group of ministers persuaded the Montreat authorities to attempt a new type of Pastor's Conference for the summer of 1933. Dr. Walter L. Lingle, who had done more than any other man to awaken the church to its responsibility in this area, gave a series of popular Bible addresses bearing on the pressing issues of the day. Following each address there was an open forum for ministers with free discussion of the problems involved. Before the week was out a continuing organization—The Ministers' Forum —was organized to promote similar inquiry and discussion in the future.[11]

A few weeks later the Synod of Virginia heard the first report of its Committee on Moral and Social Welfare, presented by its chairman, Dr. John A. MacLean of Richmond. Reluctance of the church to cut loose from its old shibboleths was given as a possible reason why its message of salvation had not been heard or heeded by more than a few of the suppressed classes and underprivileged citizens of the nation, such as the white tenant, the day laborer, the isolated and impoverished mountaineer, and the Negro. In Russia, once a deeply religious land, Christianity was now regarded as the opiate of the people. America should take warning. There followed sections on interracial relations, on temperance, on war and peace, on the church and economic order, on Christianity and crime, with appropriate resolutions in each of these areas. "The Christian message," it was stated, "is a message not only of personal regeneration, but of social redemption, and . . . in Jesus Christ and His Gospel we have resources which are adequate not only for the spiritual needs of mankind, but for the satisfactory solution of the ethical, social and moral problems of the world." It was the privilege and duty of the church of Christ, he continued, to teach, interpret, and apply these principles to such problems.[12]

This report, the most passionate and soul-searching on the subject yet to be heard in a Presbyterian court, stirred the synod profoundly and was adopted almost unanimously. Printed in pamphlet form and widely distributed through the church it did more to stir the church to action than anything else which had been done.[13]

The Synod of Alabama, meeting a little later, spent an hour and a half on two different mornings discussing the general topic "The Church and the Secular World."

At the conclusion of the discussion the synod declared its determination "To lay more emphasis upon Christ's message for the practical affairs of life" and appointed a permanent committee to study social relations and to report its recommendations to synod.[14] Four other synods—Georgia, Louisiana, North Carolina, and West Virginia—appointed that fall committees on moral and social welfare, as did a number of presbyteries. Two synods—Virginia and West Virginia—overtured the General Assembly to do likewise.

Many opposed such action. Some argued that the discussion of social and moral questions would destroy the "worshipful" nature of church courts and remove men's thoughts from "holy" matters. Representative of this group was Rev. R. A. White of Mooresville, North Carolina, who held that it would "open the floodgates to all sorts of questions that will come in to try our souls and take our minds from more spiritual matters." He feared especially its effect upon the evangelistic efforts of the church.[15]

Others based their opposition on the historic principle of the spirituality of the church. One of the ablest representatives of this viewpoint was Judge Samuel M. Wilson of Kentucky, who wrote an article for the *Union Seminary Review* in which he defended his thesis: "The proposed Assembly's Committee on Social and Moral Questions is inexpedient, unwise and unconstitutional."[16]

Disregarding such objections, the 1934 General Assembly voted to establish the requested committee by a vote of 163 to 103, observing that the desire for the help which it could give was widespread and increasing. Responsibility of the committee for the first year was limited to defining its own scope and function for the approval of the 1935 General Assembly.

Three conferences on religion and social issues held in the summer of 1934—at Montreat, Massanetta, and Kerrville—revealed a growing wave of interest in the topic.[17] The Montreat Conference (Ministers' Forum) drew men from all parts of the church and continued to meet annually for a number of years. Rev. D. P. McGeachy, D.D., pastor of the First Church, Decatur, Georgia, first chairman of the forum, provided its early dynamic; participating in the forum were many of the emerging leaders of the church.

Three additional synods—Kentucky, Oklahoma, and Texas—appointed committees on moral and social welfare in the fall of 1934. The first report of the Assembly's Permanent Committee on Moral and Social Welfare was adopted the following May without debate by the General Assembly. It constituted in effect a reinterpretation or reversal of the church's traditional view of the spirituality (or non-secular mission) of the church.

Said the Assembly:

> It is the historic position of the Presbyterian Church in the United States that the power of the church is exclusively spiritual, that the provinces of Church and State are perfectly distinct, and the one has no right to usurp the jurisdiction of the other . . .
> We believe, however, that the Church in fulfillment of its spiritual function must interpret and present Christ's ideal for the individual and for society, must warn men of the presence of sin and of its effects in the

individual life and in the social life, must offer Christ to the individual
and to society as the only Revealer of God and the only Redeemer of
mankind, must seek with the spiritual weapons at its disposal to establish His Lordship in the hearts of all men, and over every area of human
life. . . .

It cannot discharge this part of its responsibility unless it deals
with those actual evils in the individual life, and in the social order which
threaten man's moral and spiritual development, which hinder the progress of God's Kingdom here on earth, and which produce needless suffering and distress among . . . men; unless in some definite and concrete
fashion it encourages and stimulates its members to realize the ideals of
Christ in their individual lives, in the life of each group of which they
are participants and in the total life of the nation.[18]

The following year the newly erected committee brought in its
first report, a lengthy one, dealing with a variety of issues then confronting the nation and particularly the South—the problems of
alcohol and gambling, the threat of war, the need of economic
justice, the call for racial justice. The 1937 report went more fully
into the economic situation then acute in the South, and dealt with
unemployment, child labor, the plight of the sharecropper, and
the whole question of poverty. In 1936 there was a motion, handily
defeated, to abolish the Committee on Moral and Social Welfare;
in 1937 the opposition was more vocal, and after adoption of the
report's recommendations there was a strong protest signed by 23
commissioners on the grounds, among others, that the wide range
of action contemplated and the character of the remedies proposed
were inconsistent with the historic position of the founders of the
church.[19]

Two years later there was a more determined effort to abolish
the Committee on Moral and Social Welfare, led by ruling elder
Tom Glasgow from Charlotte, North Carolina (the report this year
stressed the social implications of the Ten Commandments). The efforts failed by a vote of 132 to 104. Evangelism was the main concern of the following Assembly, and the committee's report dealt
with evangelism and morals, insisting that vital evangelism could
not be divorced from moral and social concern. Opposition developed
this year not to the report itself, but to a recommendation that material from the annual reports of the Committee on Moral and Social Welfare be used in the preparation of the lesson and program
material of the church. After long debate came the vote, a thunder
of approval for the proposal, which one observer described as a
rout, rather than a defeat of the opponents of the permanent committee.[20]

The Assembly votes in these two years (1939-1940) marks a turning of the tide. Reports on moral and social welfare for the next half-dozen years (1941-1946) dealt with problems of the war and post-war world and aroused little opposition. In 1945 the Assembly gave the permanent committee permission to speak to the church in its own name and not simply report recommendations to the General Assembly, and the following year it was given for the first time a salaried secretary or director; the name was changed at this time to the Council on Christian Relations.

The question of race relations was now becoming acute and the recommendations on this question presented to and adopted by the General Assembly, particularly after the Supreme Court's decision (1954) regarding segregation in the public schools, aroused new opposition.

The Council on Christian Relations had become in 1949 a division within the newly organized Board of Church Extension. Five years later, to prevent continuing embarrassment to the Board, a new independent agency (permanent committee) was appointed to report directly to the Assembly; the Division of Christian Relations with its director, charged now with implementing the actions of the Assembly in this area, was transferred to the Board of Christian Education. In 1966 the recently organized permanent committee and its functions were absorbed by a reorganized Division of Church and Society within the Board of Christian Education.

The General Assembly adopted this year a paper entitled "Theological Basis for Christian Social Action," in which it was claimed that the responsibility of church and individual Christians to concern themselves with the political, social, economic, and cultural life of the world was rooted in the Scripture's revelation of God as Creator, Judge, Savior, and Lord. The church's earlier doctrine of the "purely spiritual" character of the church's mission, proclaimed to the world in 1861, reinterpreted in 1935, had by now been completely transformed.[21]

In the decades following the Depression, the Assembly had spoken on a wide variety of issues weighing on the minds and hearts of Southern churchmen.

The use and abuse of alcoholic beverages had remained a matter of concern. The successful battle for the establishment of national prohibition had been waged in the South largely by Baptists and Methodists. Presbyterians enlisted in the struggle as individuals, but strongly held views regarding the non-secular mission of the church prevented the church courts from adopting resolutions on the subject.*

Ministers generally had not supported the amendment from their pulpits; the church periodicals, however, had not hesitated to do so.

Once the amendment was enacted, ministers who had hesitated to bring "politics" into the pulpit felt free, with biblical authority, to urge obedience to the law of the land. Influential ministers, despite the difficulties with enforcement, insisted to the very end that benefits of prohibition outweighed its evils. "It is our unanimous opinion," declared the Presbyterian ministers of Atlanta, "that no great moral undertaking has ever had a more gratifying history than has the cause of temperance in America . . . We believe that temperance progress has been made beyond calculation in the last few years. Not only is it true that a generation is growing up that has never seen a saloon—it is also true that a generation is growing up that does not know the taste of alcoholic liquors."[22]

The church papers, meanwhile, urged passage of more effective legislation to secure enforcement of the law and opposed the growing efforts at repeal. "Restoration of the liquor traffic in our national life," declared the *Christian Observer,* "will be the greatest step backwards that civilization has taken in all its history."[23]

The General Assembly laid upon the conscience of its members "the peculiarly urgent duty to be true in life and in testimony in the supreme effort now being made to deliver our land from the age-long curse of alcohol and its attendant evils," but did not openly oppose repeal.

After repeal had taken place the Assembly repeatedly called attention to evils attending overindulgence in alcoholic beverages and deplored the wide advertising of beer and liquor through the channel of radio, newspapers, magazines, and later television. It urged its churches to become more active in their programs of alcohol education and the rehabilitation of alcoholics. It continued to reaffirm voluntary total abstinence as the Christian ideal toward which church members should strive.

It gradually became clear, however, that total abstinence was no longer accepted, as it once was, as the ideal by the average church member, by officers of the church, and even by ministers. Indicative of the changed attitude is a report made to Hanover Presbytery by

---

* Exceptions to this rule were the Presbytery of North Alabama in 1909 and the General Assembly itself in 1914.

its Committee on Christian Relations in 1963. Returns from more than half the churches in the presbytery—some small, some medium, some larger in size, from rural, urban, and suburban churches, a fair sample of the presbytery as a whole—indicated that moderate drinking was the general custom among both men and women, young men and young women, youth in both high school and college, in homes, in society, at dances, and at athletic contests. "All of this," stated the report, "is what might have been expected from any study of social drinking within the bounds of our Presbytery. For it is clear to all careful observers that there has been a silent revolution in this area in recent years—that drinking habits which once prevailed among those in the lower and upper economic brackets have become increasingly those in the more restrained middle class as well; that drinking has become more general among women and young people than formerly; that it is found more frequently in homes; that it is now taken for granted in numerous gatherings both public and private." Churches in the presbytery did not seem to be grappling with the problems arising from this increased use of alcoholic beverages. Occasional sermons; active support in some cases of Alcoholics Anonymous; the conscientious efforts, it might be assumed, of numerous parents and Sunday school teachers; and the ideal of abstinence still widely prevalent in Presbyterian churches was about the extent of it. The presbytery, accepting the report, urged consideration of total abstinence as desirable Christian practice, but recognized that there were devoted Christians who maintained that temperance, rather than abstinence, was the true Christian ideal. "Each Christian," the presbytery pointed out, "must determine his own position in the matter."[24]

Seven years later the General Assembly approved a paper prepared by its Council on Church and Society which declared that reaffirmation of "voluntary total abstinence as the Christian ideal had not provided helpful guidance for decision making by individuals, nor had it given the church an adequate framework for dealing with the alcohol problem of individuals and society. Whether, where, when and under what circumstances drinking is appropriate," stated the Assembly, "is a personal decision of the individual Christian."[25] Significantly, the changed attitude received little attention and aroused no particular opposition.

The old Puritan ideal for the Sabbath was retained theoretically long after it had been abandoned in practice. Thus in 1934 the Assembly declared that God in Scripture demanded that on the Sabbath there be a "complete separation from the distracting demands of material things, whether of toil or pleasure."[26]

In 1942, after the outbreak of the Second World War, the Assembly instructed its Stated Clerk to send a communication to the President of the United States, informing him of the church's view that the Fourth Commandment "involves the preservation of one day in seven as the divine right of man for worship and for rest from all works except such as are involved in deeds of necessity and mercy." The present national emergency, said the Assembly, "demands an economic efficiency and a moral security, neither of which can be fully had apart from an observance of the Sabbath in accordance with the divine purposes for which it was given for the good of man and the glory of Almighty God."[27]

For 16 years the General Assembly issued no further statements on Sabbath observance; then in 1958 came a long ad interim committee report, adopted by the Assembly, which for the first time took into account the realities of modern life. A legalistic interpretation of the Scriptural teaching was avoided. "Anything that detracts from the public worship of God or leaves us less than our best when we come into his presence" was deplored. But it was the positive that was accentuated, not the negative. The Sabbath is intended to be a day for the worship of God, for instruction, for rededication, a family day (but not an occasion of dreary discipline: "The reading of good books, playing games, listening to great music, even the serving of special refreshments," it was said, "can be a glad part of the family's day of rest and renewal"), a day of rest (but not necessarily of physical inactivity: "For many exercise can be a means of rest"), a day of Christian service, a day of rejoicing.[28]

The following year the Assembly adopted a supplemental report growing out of the Seventh Day Adventists' attack on all special recognition or observance of the first day of the week. Included was a statement that "Our Church does not feel that civil legislation protecting Sunday as a day of rest for the majority of the American people is sectarian legislation, or that laws providing for Sunday as a universal day of rest from business activity, except for necessary services, are religious laws."[29] The church had long since ceased to contend for the passage of any such legislation, though individual Christians it may be assumed continued to support legislation for the limiting of trade on Sunday on religious as well as humanitarian grounds.

In 1930, as we have seen, the Assembly finally turned away from indiscriminate condemnation of the so-called

worldly amusements as unbecoming in a Christian and left the decision to "the scripturally enlightened conscience" of the individual
member under the guidance of the Holy Spirit. Responding to an
overture from the Presbytery of Abingdon, which had requested reaffirmation of a 1900 deliverance in which the dance was spoken of as
"conforming to the world," the Assembly in 1945 replied (1) that it
would be quite impossible to condemn dancing per se from the
teaching of the Scripture; (2) lascivious dancing, forbidden in the
Larger Catechism, was already universally condemned by all right-
thinking Christians; (3) the amusements usually listed as "worldly"
—dancing, theater-going, and card playing—were not inherently
evil, nor did they always lead to evil. To condemn them therefore as
"worldly amusements" would be to give young people and others a
false and distorted view of the Christian life; it would be better
for the church to warn against overindulgence and abuse of these
and other amusements and to encourage positively all wholesome
recreation and fun.

Instead of condemning amusements which may be innocent, the
Assembly continued, "we should rather condemn the evil motives
which sometimes pervert them. . . . 'The principles and practises that
mar Christian character and influence' have their roots in the heart
and may be, and often are, manifested as dangerously in business,
politics, race relations, and in national selfishness and isolationism,
as in amusements." The statement concluded: "If a Christian finds
that his amusements, his business, his politics, or his position with
reference to the great and unsolved problems of the world are taking
him away from Christ, it is his duty to give them up, or to bring
them into conformity with the Christian ideal . . ."[30]

This statement remains the Assembly's final statement on the
subject. The *Presbyterian Outlook* took this as an occasion to poll
200 ministers and their wives on the subject of dancing. Responses
indicated that a third of the ministers and half of the wives had
danced before marriage and that none of these regretted having done
so. Forty-three percent of the ministers said that from 90 to 100
percent of the young people in their congregation danced; and 23
percent said, from 75 to 89 percent; children of the church officers
danced in approximately the same proportions. Almost nine out of
ten of the ministers' children danced or were expected to dance when
they became old enough.[31]

Liquor, Sabbath observance, worldly amusements
—these were the moral issues to which the church had devoted most

of its attention before 1935. On all three there had come a radical
change of attitude. During this same period there had also come
a changed attitude on the vexed questions of divorce and remarriage and planned parenthood.

The Westminster Confession of Faith recognized only two legitimate (i.e., Scriptural) grounds for divorce—adultery and "such willful desertion as can no way be remedied by the Church or civil
magistrate." The General Assembly interpreted this to mean that
remarriage was permitted only to the innocent party in either case.
The decision as to whether or not remarriage was justified was left
in the hands of the minister, who was subject to the censure of his
presbytery for any improper course of conduct.[32] Such censure,
however, was never attempted, and the minister followed his own conscience in the matter without help or hindrance from either session
or presbytery unless he himself chose to seek their advice. Occasionally this was done. Those who conscientiously sought to follow the law of the church found it exceedingly difficult, if not impossible, to determine when desertion was willful and irremediable or
who was the innocent party in a divorce case. Some under these
circumstances avoided responsibility by refusing to marry any divorced person; some declined to act only "when they knew about it";
some recognized other grounds for divorce than the two named in
the Confession; some were prepared to marry those who seemed sin-
cerely desirous of building a Christian home, regardless of past failures.

An early effort to escape from the legalism of the Confession
came in 1929 when Dr. Charles E. Diehl, President of Southwestern
in Memphis, offered a minority recommendation to the General Assembly, which read: "We recognize the violation of the Seventh
Commandment or its moral equivalent as the only ground for divorce. In our judgment brutality, willful and prolonged desertion,
sex perversion, and perhaps some other causes constitute what
may be termed 'moral equivalent', but the merits of each case must
be determined by well-established evidence and by the peculiar
circumstances in each individual case."[33] This idea of adultery or its
moral equivalent would gain increasing acceptance in the church,
but its time was not yet. In 1938 the Permanent Committee on Social and Moral Welfare devoted its entire report to the subject of
divorce and remarriage, but no new ground was broken. The General Assembly voted on its recommendation that each presbytery
erect a permanent advisory committee on divorce and remarriage
whose duty it would be to decide concerning cases submitted to it

whether or not the proposed remarriage was within the law of the church.[34] The thinking was still in the area of Scriptural legalities— two justifiable grounds of divorce and no others.

The first indication that the church was prepared to reconsider its traditional viewpoint came in 1946, shortly after the close of World War II. The Permanent Committee on Moral and Social Welfare, which had been requested to study and report on the laws of the church regarding divorce, expressed the opinion that there were cases where remarriage should be allowed to divorced persons who had not followed the law of the church but who were truly penitent and who desired to enter into a new marriage bond with a Christian understanding of that sacred relationship. It asked time for further study which was granted.[35]

Four years later the permanent committee, now the Council on Christian Relations, made a preliminary report, in which it called attention to the wide variety of practices being followed by ministers in regard to the remarriage of divorced persons, each in effect a law unto himself. The Council suggested that primary consideration should be given to the people involved rather than to the rule legalistically interpreted and that the church should work constructively to build Christian homes rather than to weep impotent tears at the increasing break-up of homes. "It is a bit strange," commented the *Presbyterian Outlook*, "that the church has to be reminded in this connection or in any other, of its gospel of forgiveness for the repentant sinner."[36]

The Assembly approved this new approach to the question, and, three years after the study had been ordered, the Council brought in its recommendations for a constitutional change breaking with the legalistic principle of the Confession. The heart of the proposed changes were found in the following paragraphs:

> 5. The weakness of one or both parties in marriage may lead to such gross and persistent unfaithfulness, physical or spiritual, that marriage dies at the heart, and to one or both parties the union becomes intolerable; yet only in cases of extreme, repeated or unrepented infidelity; should separation or divorce be regarded as unavoidable.
>
> 6. The remarriage of divorced persons may be sanctioned by the church in keeping with the redemptive gospel of Christ, when sufficient penitence for sin and failure is evident, and a firm purpose of and endeavor after Christian marriage is manifest.[37]

The proposed change was debated at length before the Assembly. Opponents took their stand on the traditional interpretation of the Scripture texts, and proponents argued that the proposed re-

vision was Scriptural because it made forgiveness real and because its
concern was not only with what man had been, but with what he
might become with the help of Jesus Christ. It was in line with the
experience and the growing Christian insight of other denominations
which had a high ideal for marriage. They were in accord with the
growing spiritual insight, the sensitized conscience, and the habitual
practice of the majority of the ministers of the church.[38]

The General Assembly, in agreement with this line of thought,
gave the proposed amendment its overwhelming approval, but the
continued opposition of respected leaders of the church led a majority of the presbyteries to vote otherwise.

The question was thereupon put in the hands of a new committee, chaired by the biblical theologian (Dr. Donald G. Miller)
who had led the opposition to the earlier proposal. The new ad
interim committee, under his guidance, concluded that Jesus had
permitted divorce under no circumstances (since the clause "except for fornication" was not a part of the original text). The Committee recommended deletion of all material permitting divorce and
remarriage, leaving only a witness to the biblical intention that marriage was indissoluble except by death. The chairman explained that
the committee had attempted to follow strictly the Bible teaching,
where they could find no justification for divorce on any grounds.
The Assembly approved this recommendation without debate and
sent it to the presbyteries for their approval. The continuing debate
made it clear that the dilemma of the clergy, and the plight of
estranged couples under such constitutional arrangement, would be
more difficult than before. The vote rejecting the proposal was
greater than in the previous case.

The Assembly now put the matter into the hands of a third committee, dominated by another school of biblical theologians. The new
committee renewed the key recommendations of the first committee
(the Council on Christian Relations), recognizing the admissibility
of divorce under extreme circumstances and of the remarriage of
even the non-innocent party when there was "sufficient penitence
for sin and failure" and "a firm purpose of an endeavor after Christian marriage," but placed them more firmly within the total biblical
revelation, with its emphasis on sin as destructive of the divine intent and on redemptive love as the divine way of dealing with man's
failure in marriage, as in all other relations of life.[39]

Once again the proposal was sent down to the presbyteries for
their approval, which on this occasion was overwhelming, 69 to 13.
The 1959 General Assembly then ratified their decision. So after 14

years of discussion and debate, the church reached general agreement on a subject which had long perplexed them—an agreement which put it in line with the trend in other evangelical denominations.

The following year the Assembly received and ordered printed a statement, drawn up by a joint committee appointed by the Moderators of the two Presbyterian General Assemblies, which stated that the sexual relation within the marital bond is to be regarded not merely as a means of bringing children into the world but also as a divine provision for the mutual fulfillment of husband and wife, and further that "if a man and wife are not to be denied mutual fulfillment in the sexual relation, and if society is not to be penalized by the unplanned and irresponsible production of children, it will follow that access to information regarding the best methods of birth control is the right of all married couples, and the provision of this information is a duty of a responsible society."[40] This represented a considerable change in Presbyterian sentiment, since the time when a guarded recommendation of birth control under some circumstances had led the Assembly to withdraw from the Federal Council of Churches; as did the General Assembly's subsequent declaration (in 1970) that the willful termination of pregnancy by medical means on the considered decision of a pregnant woman may on occasion be morally justifiable.[41]

Sex, war, industry, race—these were the four great moral issues with which the Christian churches generally were concerned during the second third of the 20th century, and which in one form or another were often before the Assembly.

The wave of near pacifism (committed pacifists were few) which developed after World War I continued its growth in the church until the outbreak of World War II when it largely disappeared. In the Ministers' Forum of 1934, war and preparedness for war were the main topics of discussion. Strong sentiment had developed against the R.O.T.C. or any military training in the curriculum of a Christian college.[42] Anti-war sentiment found expression in church periodicals and on college campuses, as well as among groups of young people in Christian Endeavor Societies, in summer retreats, and other gatherings.

By 1936 Germany, under the direction of Adolf Hitler, had withdrawn from the League of Nations and set about the open rebuilding of the German armed forces; Mussolini had invaded Ethiopia; civil war had begun in Spain, leading to the involvement of fascist forces on the one side and of Communist Russia on the other. In this year the General Assembly warned against propaganda which sought to arouse suspicion of and hatred for other people, "who perhaps have as much reason to be afraid of our increasing armaments as we have to fear theirs." The Assembly was insistent that America must remain neutral in case there was another world conflict, and to this end favored the adoption of "protective neutrality legislation."[43] The Synod of Tennessee expressed opposition to the "tremendous increase in armaments on the part of our national government."[44]

Early in 1938 the Germans marched into Austria, forcibly uniting this German state with their own; the build-up against Czechoslovakia had begun. This year an effort was made to alter the Confessional statement which permitted the government to wage war upon "just and necessary occasion" so as to permit only defensive wars upon just and necessary occasions. The effort failed, but by a close vote, 138 to 164.[45]

Even after Germany had seized Czechoslovakia, invaded Poland, and launched its attack against France by way of the Low Countries, voices were heard insisting that it was not the function of the church to arouse anger, bitterness, or hatred against individuals or nations, insisting that the church maintain its ecumenical character and decline to be used as an instrument for propaganda in the hands of the state. But as the Western democracies reeled before the rapid German advance, other voices were heard, calling for all possible aid to Great Britain.[46]

After Pearl Harbor all but a handful of convinced pacifists accepted the inevitability of war, but in no vindictive spirit. "In our righteous wrath at the way in which we are attacked," wrote Holmes Rolston, "we in America should not close our eyes to our guilt in bringing about the world situation which has resulted in this terrible conflict. America's refusal to enter the League of Nations was the first step. America's immigration laws, America's barriers to free world trade have played their parts. We should realize that the attack upon America by the Axis powers has come as the inevitable result of the [post-war] foreign policy of the United States." "The evils upon us are in part the fruit of our own selfishness," agreed Kenneth J. Foreman.[47] Writing a few months after Pearl Harbor, Dr. Walter M. Buchanan, who had spent many years as a missionary in Japan, sought to explain the reaction which had developed in Japan against the West. It was due, he indicated, to (1) disappointments in their contacts with Western civilization; (2) disgust with the ugly, bitter spirit that prevailed in the Versailles Conference; (3) resentment that the Versailles Peace Conference had declined to recognize the principle of racial equality and that America again in 1924 through its immigration act had made the same discrimination; (4) opposition to the domination of China's economic development by Britain and America; (5) a deep feeling of outrage at the superior and sometimes arrogant air of the white race toward the Asiatics.[48]

The church did however "bless" the war, as it had said repeatedly after World War I it would never again do. "Christian civilization is challenged today as it has not been challenged in a thousand years," wrote Dr. Henry Wade DuBose, a contributing editor of the *Christian Observer*. "We who believe in God and the sanctity of human rights are bound to resist this threat to freedom and justice with all the means at our disposal . . ."[49]

A few weeks later these same sentiments were expressed by the General Assembly. "It is difficult for us to escape the conclusion," said the highest court of the church, "that our hopes for a just world order, the continuance of the democratic way of life, and the very freedom of the church to continue her world mission are definitely at stake in this conflict. Under such circumstances our duty appears to be clear. Whatever the service which the Christian may be called upon to perform in loyalty to his earthly government, it may rightly be expected of him that he will do more, rather than less, than his fellow citizens who owe no allegiance to Christ."[50]

At the same time the Assembly reminded its members that the church must continually strive to promote a spirit of love and goodwill rather than of hatred and bitterness. Even in the midst of conflict, it urged that it be borne constantly in mind that the spirit of war was not the spirit of Christ.[51]

The *Christian Observer* approved the "Statement of Purpose" adopted by the First Presbyterian Church of Lafayette, Louisiana, of which the Rev. Jack B. McMichael was the pastor. "The Christian Church," declared the church, "is dedicated to a mission and a message which is universal, spiritual and eternal, rather than national, temporal or temporary." It pledged itself to preach the sovereignty and love of God primarily and to the exclusion of matters directly pertaining to the war, to work toward brotherly love among all men and especially for a just peace with the defeated nations, and to minister in every way possible to the suffering bodies, tormented minds, and sin-sick souls of men everywhere. They agreed that no attempts would be made to use the pulpits, bulletins, or other channels of the church as mediums for announcements of any type of propaganda not essentially related to the mission of the church.[52]

Dr. W. L. Lingle, in his widely read column, *Talks on Timely Topics,* commended the example of his pastor, Rev. Carl Pritchett, who had written in his bulletin: "I have resolved that I will not identify the victory of our nation with the will of God . . . I have resolved that I will not contribute to the ugly racial and national hatred which is engulfing our country. . . . I have resolved to remind you that there is a bond between us and some of our nation's enemies which is more spiritual and enduring than those which bind us to our own race and nation. The bond is the union between us and our Christian brethren in Japan, Germany and Italy. . . ."[53]

To a very large extent these utterances reflected the spirit and the attitude of the church as a whole.

The General Assembly, along with the lower courts and the church-at-large, recognized from the start that it had a responsibility for the men in the armed services. The Moderator of the Assembly, without waiting for the court to meet, had appointed a defense service council to coordinate and direct the church's efforts. Rev. D. T. Caldwell, pastor of the Second Presbyterian Church, Petersburg, served as director throughout the war years and until after the war forces had been demobilized.

All possible assistance was given to the chaplains serving the church at home and abroad—throughout the war Southern Presbyterian chaplains served in excess of assigned quotas. Local churches were encouraged to keep in touch with their men in the armed forces and to minister, as they were able, to men in the camps and enjoying leisure in their communities, "providing health giving and edifying opportunities for worship, fellowship and recreation."[54]

From the outset the Committee on Moral and Social Welfare led the Assembly, and through the Assembly the church, to consider the needs of the post-war world. If the various dangers are to be overcome and a just and durable peace established, it warned that it would be necessary for the United Nations and particularly America to exercise statesmanship of the highest order and to exhibit an enlightened conscience not hitherto made effective in international affairs. The church, it was insisted, must continue to combat the growth of hatred and to strengthen the hands of leaders in planning for a great ministry of mercy to all mankind to follow immediately upon the cessation of hostilities.[55]

The Southern Presbyterian Church, in company with other Protestant Churches included in the Federal Council of Churches, gave much attention during the war years and afterward to the character of the peace that was to be made.

In 1943 and again in 1944 the General Assembly endorsed the six principles underlying "a just and durable peace," which had grown out of a study conference held at Delaware, Ohio, in 1942, under the auspices of a Commission of the Federal Council of Churches, headed by John Foster Dulles, later to become President Eisenhower's Secretary of State. In 1944 the Assembly summed up the obligations resting on the church and the Christian in the new world order as follows: "The church at the close of the present war should raise her voice once more in behalf of peace, a righteous peace that will endure. The church should preach the duty that we owe to foreign peoples as well as to our own, especially in the matter of feeding the hungry and helping the weak. To ourselves we owe it to take steps that the moral let down which followed World War I shall not recur, nor shall a spirit of cynicism and disillusionment become prevalent. While proclaiming our faith in democracy, Christians of America should practice justice and fairness to all races, including the Negroes. Only by following such lines of action shall we further peace on earth, good will among men."[56]

In January 1945 the second national study conference on "The Church and a Just and Durable Peace" was held in Cleveland, Ohio. The Southern Church was fully represented in this conference and supplied the chairman of one of the important sections. The General Assembly that spring commended the message of the Cleveland conference and urged the churches to observe the month of September as World Order Study Month, basing their study on a booklet, entitled *Bases of World Order,* which had grown out of a seminar held during the summer at Montreat. The study book included chapters on the spiritual, political, economic, and social bases for Christian world order, and drew on the findings of many of the important church conferences held on this subject in recent years.[57]

In the fall of that year came the explosion of the first atomic bomb, and the sudden surrender of Japan. The Assembly's Committee on Christian Relations for the first time addressed the church directly, emphasizing the necessity of some international control of atomic power and expressing confidence in the United Nations recently organized in San Francisco.[58] The General Assembly from time to time affirmed and reaffirmed its support of this world organization.

Facing the problems of the post-war world the church spoke repeatedly on behalf of world order (the bases of a just and durable peace), including the extension of economic aid (the Point 4 Program), human rights ("The rising recognition of the rights of all men, without regard to race or class, must be accepted as one of the mandates of a virile, realistic Christian faith"),[59] and the admittance of a substantial number of displaced persons to the United States.[60]

Voices had been raised in the church for ultimate reconciliation with the people of Japan even while the war raged; such voices were increased with the war's end. In January 1946 Rev. John A. Mac-Lean, D.D., pastor of the Ginter Park Church in Richmond, Virginia, suggested that a movement be started to raise funds for a hospital or some other appropriate memorial in the atom-bombed cities of Hiroshima and Nagasaki—something that would contribute to the relief of human suffering and "to allay the evil spirit of suspicion, hatred and revenge now so prevalent in the world."[61] The movement grew, was taken over by the Federal Council of Churches, and eventuated in the establishment of the International Japanese Christian University, now one of the important educational institutions in that land.

The General Assembly continued to speak out against exploitation and colonialism ("America ought to be careful lest she identify herself with the reactionary elements in distant lands and thereby lend aid in perpetuating systems which have no place in the new order struggling to be born"[62]); against militant Communism; against hysterical anti-Communism ("the appeal to fear and the hysteria campaigns . . . to label as Communist those who espouse constructive change or to smear the character and bemean the motives of political opponents are perversions of personal freedom. Character assassination is serious . . ."[63]).

The Assembly returned to this subject again and again. In 1957, for example, it pointed out:

> The fear of Communism has bred suspicion and distrust which is injurious not only in arresting creative thinking but in bringing our nation into disrepute among the free nations. The consequences of this fear are still seen in many areas of life whenever the stigma of Communism is put on anyone who dares vary from the customary pattern of society. It may occur in politics, in business, in education or in the Church. A congressman is not re-elected, a school teacher faces investigation, a health officer is dismissed, a journalist is forced to leave the community, a man suddenly loses his credit and a minister loses his congregation— all because they exercised their right to speak freely. We would reaffirm our condemnation of Communism as a system and deplore the use of its evil methods against our own citizens by our own citizens.[64]

In 1961, at a time when widespread and undocumented charges of Communism among the clergy were being aired in the public press, "raising doubts in the minds of the uninformed and throwing suspicions on many," the Assembly insisted that the time had come to name names and to deliver evidence, and if this could not be done to remain silent. The reference was to blanket charges, without basis in fact, brought against PCUS ministers and others connected with the National Council of Churches.[65]

The Assembly had little to say on the hydrogen bomb. Indeed, on one occasion (1950), it declared that it was unqualified to speak on the subject. In 1960 the Permanent Committee on Christian Relations presented a paper, "Christian Faith and the Contemporary Problem of War," which recognized that with the advent of atomic weapons a new era in warfare had dawned. Christians were urged to pray for the abolition of all means of warfare involving mass destruction, but no resolutions were offered. In 1964 the Assembly went a step further, urging its members to do all within their power to support the efforts of the nation's leaders as they worked toward the goal of multilateral banning of all nuclear weapons tests and for the establishment of international controls over all aspects of the nuclear arms race. As a further step toward world order, Christians were urged to give themselves with renewed vigor to the solution of the social, economic, and political problems which existed in the international as well as in the national and local communities.[66]

The Assembly was slow in taking a stand on the undeclared war in Vietnam. Finally (in 1966) it approved the policy statement on Vietnam which had been drawn up and adopted by the General Board of the National Council of Churches, a statement which recognized a difference of Christian viewpoint on the war, and put its stamp of approval upon a course of action which it hoped would help to bring peace and growing justice and freedom to the territories of Vietnam.[67]

In 1967 the Assembly raised a series of questions regarding the war which, if taken seriously, would have made continued support of the war decidedly problematic. The following Assembly, after extended debate, narrowly defeated a resolution favoring government recognition of selective conscientious objectors to a particular war. A vigorous protest against this action by 46 commissioners, along with an unprecedented declaration of deep disappointment signed by the majority of the pages present (representative of the four theological seminaries), reflected the strong feeling on this issue and regarding the war in general, particularly among younger groups in the church. A year later this decision was reversed, and selective conscientious objection was approved by a wide margin (260-165). In 1970 the General Assembly urged the government to continue and, as far as possible, to accelerate the orderly withdrawal of all American troops from Southeastern Asia.[68] "The continuation of this war cannot be morally justified," it declared the following year. "The killing must be stopped."

The great Depression and its aftermath led to a rising chorus of demands that Christian principles find fuller expression in the nation's economic life. "Much of the suffering of our time is traceable to . . . a pagan conception of property," declared the Synod of Alabama. "The unequal distribution of wealth, the unfair discrimination against labor in favor of invested capital, the failure of business leaders to protect employees, are essentially results of the pagan philosophy which has directed our economic policies. We, therefore, call upon Christian leaders to reveal the implications of the Gospel of love as they relate to economic policies."[69] The inadequacy of the old order is now obvious to everyone, declared Dr. W. L. Carson, pastor of the First Presbyterian Church, Richmond, Virginia. The world is willing and eager to try something new. "If the Christian Church can show the modern world that in the applications of the principles of Christ is found the real solution of the problems of the economic life of the world, it can lead humanity to embrace the Christian religion with eagerness and enthusiasm."[70]

Such expressions, typical of many others both in their earnestness and also in their easy generalities, indicated a definite change of direction in the church's attitude toward economic issues, heretofore largely a forbidden area. Southern Presbyterian ministers did not turn to socialism as the answer, as did many church leaders in other bodies, nor did they at any time cease to emphasize the need of individual regeneration if a Christian order of society was to be instituted. But there was criticism of some of the ways in which the capitalistic system had operated in America; a repudiation of the status quo; support for the ideals of the New Deal; insistence that "the church should give reiterated emphasis to the truth that one has no right to enjoy wealth and luxury at the cost of poverty and privation to others"; along with reminders that greater justice in the economic order remained the most effective antidote to Communism. At times voices were even raised on behalf of labor unions, to which Southern industrialists on the whole were bitterly opposed.[71]

Said the Synod of Tennessee, "We feel that the church must come face to face with the appalling fact, namely, that many laboring people in this country have come to feel, rightly or wrongly, that organized Christianity is unfriendly to organized labor. . . . We believe that it is the responsibility of the church to close the gap that has been created and to face frankly and fearlessly our duty and responsibility in this matter . . . The right of labor to organize and to bargain collectively with employers is clearly an inalienable right in a democracy and has so been recognized by our government."[72]

There was, of course, opposition to this essay into the economic realm. "It appears to me," wrote Ruling Elder W. Calvin Wells, "that in our religious journals or papers we see nothing except a denunciation of the economic system under which we live in the United States and of the horrible oppression of the rich against the poor, and how we should ditch our present economic system and political form of government and get some new untried system."[73] A gross exaggeration of course, Some objected because the church had no right to speak on economic issues; some because it turned the church aside from its true mission—the saving of souls. "Far from short-circuiting our evangelistic or spiritual power," replied Dr. J. H. Marion, then pastor of the First Presbyterian Church, Durham, North Carolina, "a gospel of economic salvation, drawn straight from the life and teachings of Christ, is indispensable to the preservation of that power. Fairer dealings among men, better collective organization, more humane social and economic systems—we must plead for these with intelligence and patience, not for the sake of some vague and humanitarian ideal, but that men and women and children like ourselves, now stifled in soul by grinding want and debasing environments, may have a better chance to believe in God and live in goodness."[74]

The first comprehensive report presented to the General Assembly by the newly created Committee on Moral and Social Welfare contained a section on economic justice which offered what might be considered as a Christian economic creed. Here it was affirmed, among other things, that human rights must have precedence over property rights; that provision should be made for every person incapable of self-support; that adequate security should be provided against the accidents of life, illness, unemployment, and old age; that all business should be considered a cooperative enterprise for the common good, in which capital, management, labor, and society have rights that must be protected.[75]

The report for the following year contained a section dealing with child labor, unemployment, sharecroppers, and poverty. This section was sharply attacked. The Assembly declined to delete the section, but in the end voted to receive the report as information and to adopt only the recommendation that members of the church study their individual responsibility for the achievement of the important ends, including the abolition of child labor, mentioned in the report.[76]

Sections dealing with economic issues were included in many succeeding reports, and approved by the General Assembly.

In 1957, some years before the Federal government opened its warfare against poverty, the Assembly adopted a report on "Freedom—the Christian Concept" which contained a section on "Freedom From Want," emphasizing Christians' responsibilities for seeking to relieve poverty at home and abroad.[77]

The following year the Assembly recommended that its theological seminaries and other educational institutions seek increasingly to acquaint students with the problems of industry and labor, and to relate them to the Christian ethic.[78] The theological seminaries were already moving hesitatingly in this direction, but instruction in social ethics remained one of the most neglected elements in the seminary curriculum.

In 1959 the Assembly observed that the PCUS church was manifesting an increasing zeal to involve itself through evangelism and church extension in industrial neighborhoods and that there was need for the church to study seriously the means within its ministry to effect just and redemptive relationships between management and labor. "Labor, as a militant force, should be reminded that its purpose is to rectify inequality and unfairness to people—not to destroy industry by condoning less for more. Management, as a governing force, should be called upon to manage fairly for all concerned, to stockholders, customers and employees alike . . ."[79] The church still tended to speak in generalities, but it was speaking.

A few years later, after the Johnson Administration opened its "war on poverty," the Assembly approved a statement which dealt with the extent of this problem in the United States, its human costs, and the motives for alleviating it,[80] a study completed the following year by a complementary report on work and leisure.[81]

In company with other churches holding membership in the National Council of Churches, the Southern Presbyterian Church called upon its member churches to engage in a special study of "Affluence and Poverty" during the church year 1966-1967. The denominational study book emphasized the role of the church in preaching (i.e., in speaking for the needy), in teaching, in serving, and in identifying itself with the poor.[82]

The 1969 Assembly approved a report which emphasized that there could be no law and order (for which there was a rising demand) without justice. It also declared that the problem of world hunger was to be recognized as a top priority concern and that all possible resources of the church were to be focused for the next five years at least on ways and means of dealing with this problem.[83] A task force drawn from the various Boards and agencies of the church was set up for this purpose.

The General Assembly had seldom approved concrete measures in the economic field; its statements had served to remind its members that the economic realm was one to which Christian principles needed to be applied.

XXII

Toward Ethical Maturity

The major issue before the South in the second third of the century, as it had been for the past 100 years and more, was the race question.

This, as we have seen, was one of the major issues stressed from the beginning by those who led in the social awakening in the Southern Presbyterian Church. The first full report of the newly erected Committee on Moral and Social Welfare (1936) recognized that Negroes in the South were economically handicapped and politically disfranchised, had inadequate housing, educational, and recreational facilities, and frequently failed to secure equal justice in the courts. The higher infant mortality rates among Negroes, the larger number of deaths from tuberculosis, the wider prevalence of crime were due, in large measure, it was stated, to living conditions for which the white people in the South were chiefly responsible.[1]

A number of the lower church courts were now beginning to adopt similar reports. But a poll conducted by Rev. William Crowe, Jr., indicated, to no one's surprise, that the subject of race relations was seldom discussed in the pulpit. As a leading pastor explained, "Making it an open question gives opportunity to those who are out of sympathy with the cause to become belligerent." Mr. Crowe found however "some evidence" of "a slight awakening in the church to this tragic racial situation." A few years back, he noted the traditional view seemed to be held by all Southern Presbyterians. Now there was an increasing divergence of opinions. Ministers were agreed that race relationships in the South were far from satisfactory.[2]

Actually the viewpoint of the church's leaders was changing more rapidly than Mr. Crowe was aware. A number of factors compelled ministers to reassess their obligations in this area—a second war in which Negroes fought for a country which denied them first-class citizenship, the mood of the returning soldiers, the FEPC (Fair Employment Practice Commission) of the war years, the drive for Civil Rights in the post-war years, the stepped-up activity of the NAACP, a series of court decisions admitting Negroes to institutions of higher learning and threatening segregated education in the public schools.

The *Presbyterian Outlook* (continuing the *Presbyterian of the South*), now edited by Rev. Aubrey Brown, gave over a large portion of its news columns to reporting developments in this area, to editorial comment thereon, and to articles concerned with Christian attitudes toward race. In answer to occasional complaints that too much attention was being given to this single issue, the editors explained: "The daily press is full of news items which have to do with this problem; editorials and articles in many magazines are coming to grips with it. If this paper does anything like an honest job in keeping its readers informed as to what Christians are thinking and doing about the most delicate problem in our land, then it must give such news items and it must print the deliberations of Christian leaders who are desperately concerned to see the church measure up to its challenge. Our people are concerned to see and follow the Christian way in this area. They want courageous Christian leadership, and it is the purpose of the editors of this paper to encourage men and women to write along this line in order that our church may face frankly and intelligently this important demand upon it . . . When one news item or article dealing with this situation appears in print, our friends will understand that five or ten others were held back."[3]

The church's changing attitude was reflected in successive deliverances of the General Assembly. In 1943 the Assembly pointed out that Christians who condemned the Nazi persecution of non-Aryans must "combat with all earnestness and power racial prejudice against Negroes in the South."[4] The following year it pointed out that thousands of Negroes were now in the army and navy, exposed to equal dangers with white men, and enjoying privileges that were not theirs in civilian life either in the North or in the South. Negro leaders were demanding equal rights with white people under the law. And such rights in the administration of the law, in the courts, in public accommodations, in educational facilities, and in equal chances of public health could no longer be denied them.[5]

As the war drew to its end, the Assembly gave renewed attention to the church's responsibility to Negroes who had fought for freedom and justice abroad and might rightly expect to receive a larger share of these on their return. The Assembly said:

The pattern of our society will not be altered over night, and a separateness of the races in some spheres of life may well be maintained for the good of each. Discrimination against Negroes in employment and in the use of the ballot, unequal educational, housing, and health advantages, and a failure to enforce the law with an even hand are different matters . . . It is highly important that contact be maintained between Christians of both races and that these should consult and cooperate with one another in the reduction of racial friction and in the encouragement of mutual understanding and helpfulness. In most communities we believe that the establishment by all the churches of inter-racial committees which could function in this area would be exceedingly helpful. Opportunities for worship in which members of both races will participate should also be arranged. . . .[6]

Such resolutions did not arouse any great emotional response—chiefly, it may be, because the South's familiar pattern of life was not yet seriously threatened. The emotional atmosphere however rapidly altered when the Truman administration threw its full weight into the fight for civil rights.

In 1949, when the issue had become a vital one, the General Assembly commanded a study paper, "States Rights and Human Rights," drawn up by its permanent committee on Christian Relations. Five points were emphasized:

1. The South's insistence on states' rights in opposition to federally enforced civil rights has deep and tenacious roots in Southern history and Southern feelings.

2. The present-day claims of American minorities to full civil rights have a sound moral and historical basis.

3. The South has made commendable progress in extending and protecting the civil rights of its minority peoples, but these rights are still widely denied or restricted by unequal treatment in many places.

4. Any sound program for safeguarding human rights must recognize the role of both education and legislation.

5. The Southern churches have a large unfinished task in the fields of education concerning human rights.

The report concluded: "A church that tries to be neutral by keeping silent, or a church that resorts to compromise to save itself, will to that extent forfeit its redemptive power and influence among men. Only a church that heeds the summons of principle above all else, and that dares in deed and spirit to defend the rights of all men without fear or favor, will gain the abiding respect of the world and the full blessing of God."[7]

Various synods also wrestled with the problem. The Synod of South Carolina adopted the section in its Christian Relations Report referring to civil rights by a narrow margin, after deleting a number of expressions, one referring to the report of President Truman's Commission on Civil Rights, which a prominent minister declared "contains the rankest communist doctrine I ever read." Another wondered why racial issues should be brought into the report when they didn't have a thing to do with the saving of souls.[8]

The Synod of North Carolina featured a panel discussion on the civil rights report, in which Dr. Holmes Rolston, Charlotte pastor, stressed the importance of the Negro securing the right to vote. Facts reveal that the Negro does not have equality of opportunity to health, education, living conditions, and economic status, he declared, and the vote is the key to all the rest.[9]

A basic value in the struggle, now coming to the fore, was the question of enforced segregation, and it was this question which churchmen were at last compelled to face. Earlier spokesmen for racial justice in the church did not anticipate the social mingling of the races. Dr. J. McDowell Richards, President of Columbia Theological Seminary, in the heart of the South, spoke often and powerfully for justice to our "brother in black," but iterated and reiterated, if I were a Negro, "I should wish the integrity of my race to be respected and preserved. To that end, I should approve the preservation of the separateness of the races insofar as social matters are concerned while desiring equal opportunity and equal justice in all respects."[10]

The General Assembly in 1944, pleading for justice for the returning Negro servicemen, was convinced that few Negroes or white men desired the abrogation of all racial distinctions, and denied that it was the province of the church to bring this about. "Certain social customs of long standing and universal recognition have drawn sharp lines between the two races," declared the Assembly, "with the avowed purpose of preserving the identity of each. We have not forgotten the chaos that arose in the sixties and seventies from ill-advised efforts to destroy such customs. We should not desire a repetition of that mistake even under the very different conditions now prevailing."[11]

But even as the Assembly spoke the practice of segregation was being challenged by Negroes and white, in both church and state. This very year there appeared the most searching study yet to appear on the race situation in America: *An American Dilemma— The Negroes' Freedom and Modern Democracy*, by the Swedish sociologist Gunnar Myrdal. In this book segregation was made to appear as a major block to all substantial progress in the field of Negroes' rights. Within a few years after the publication of this book, however it may be explained, the Southern Presbyterian ministry as a whole had become convinced that enforced segregation was not compatible with the Christian faith.

In July 1945 the *Presbyterian Outlook* published an article by Lillian Smith, a lifetime resident of Clayton, Georgia, widely known as writer, speaker, and editor of *The South Today*. "In our attempts to segregate ourselves from our own conscience," wrote Miss Smith, "we have segregated not only other human beings from us, but have segregated ourselves from the heart of religion."[12] It was perhaps the first suggestion to appear in any of the church's periodicals that segregation was a denial of the Christian gospel.

A few years later a brief was filed in the United States Supreme Court by the Federal Council of Churches supporting the petition of Herman Marion Sweatt, Texas Negro, for review of a case in which he had been denied admission to the University of Texas. The brief noted that one denomination—the Presbyterian Church in the United States—disassociated itself from the action by vote of its representatives on the Council's Executive Committee. There followed an interchange of letters between Dr. J. McDowell Richards, one of the church's two representatives, and Dr. John Marion, Director of the Assembly's Council on Christian Relations, in which the latter rejected segregation as utterly wrong in principle and pernicious in practice. Dr. Marion declared:

> We white Southerners have lived with segregation so long that we tend to accept it as something handed down from Sinai. Actually, its cost is so high and its fruits so bitter that it might better be looked on as a monster sprung from Hades. What does compulsory segregation do? Basically it sets up a caste system with a viciously unspiritual scale of values . . . It inflicts on Negroes a deep and terrible psychological hurt . . . On the political level [it] flouts and often nullifies the basic principles of democracy . . . It hurts the white man . . . far worse, quite often, than it hurts [the Negro] . . . Can such a system be Christian? I tried for a long time to think it wasn't so unchristian, but I've quit trying. I am now convinced that, no matter how fine and Christian individual Christian white people seek to be within the confines of segregation, the pattern itself will stand as a grievous affront to human personality . . .[13]

Dr. Richards, clarifying his own position, admitted that he could not reconcile enforced segregation with the teachings of Christ and therefore felt that ultimately it must go, but was of the opinion that for some years it might be the lesser of two evils in the deep South. He could not believe, therefore, that the immediate abolition of segregation would be the wisest or most Christian solution of the problem for either race.[14]

The fact that two such respected leaders were agreed that one of the most widely spread and deeply entrenched customs of the South was positively unchristian seemed to the *Presbyterian Outlook* deeply significant. "Too many of us," it added, "have for too long told ourselves or others in effect that after all segregation was for the best, it must be according to the will of God. Now we see a new courage in saying for all the world to hear that this is in violent opposition to the will of God and that the sooner we square our practices with our professed principle the better it will be for us and for all."[15]

In the fall of this year the Synod of Alabama adopted a challenging report from its Christian Relations Committee which declared: "We are faced with two inevitables, the federal constitution and the Christian conscience. Both dictate that legal segregation shall not last forever. Therefore we may as well admit the removal of legal segregation to be the end toward which we work. Segregation is living on borrowed time."[16]

This report, adopted by a vote of more than two to one, and from a synod in the deep South, was significant. It points, said the *Presbyterian Outlook*, to the fact that men's minds and attitudes are in ferment. "We are coming to grips with the demands of the Christian conscience as we scarcely would have believed possible a few years ago."[17]

The Christian conscience, now becoming aroused against legal segregation in society, had become increasingly aroused also against de facto segregation in the church.

In 1916, as we have seen, the Assembly formally and of necessity abandoned—for the time—its announced purpose of establishing an independent Negro Presbyterian Church. The weak, struggling Negro churches which had been organized were gathered into four presbyteries, organized into their own synod (Snedecor Memorial), which was a part of, and yet largely apart from, the life of the church as a whole. Commissioners from the Negro presbyteries attended the meeting of the General Assembly, but were quartered apart from the white commissioners (at Montreat, the church's own conference grounds, in little green cottages, where the servants were lodged) and of course ate by themselves (at Montreat, on one occasion, at least, in an anteroom off from the kitchen, where the chickens were killed and dressed). In the Assembly itself they sat by themselves at the rear of the building or in a corner; they were spectators, permitted to vote, but with no other part in the proceedings.

The first indication of a changing attitude, recalled by Dr. Walter Lee Lingle was at the Assembly meeting in New Orleans in 1919. On this occasion a table was set for the Negro commissioners, and the cultured Christian women of New Orleans served them just as they did the white ones. But this set no precedent and did not alter the prevailing pattern.[18]

In writing his account of the 1933 Assembly, Rev. George C. Bellingrath thought it worthy of note that two commissioners had gone over deliberately to the far side of the auditorium where the business sessions were held and sat in the section recognized by all as reserved for colored people. In a few moments he noted the small group of colored commissioners were so surrounded by white men that they ceased to be a group part, but merged into and became a part of the Assembly body. Later, he learned, that some of the white commissioners had taken it upon themselves to eat at the same table with the colored men in their corner of the dining room.[19] A small gesture, indeed, and yet the breaking of a firmly established tradition, what might be termed the cracking of the shell.

Ten years later, in the early days of World War II, at a time when civil rights were beginning to become a serious issue, ministerial associations in many Southern cities were broadened to include Negro ministers as well as whites; state councils of churches, with Presbyterian leadership strongly in evidence, were organized in some Southern states, notably in Virginia and North Carolina, completely integrated from the outset. A Negro commissioner, for the first time, was appointed chairman of a standing committee of the General Assembly. As such he was expected to make the report of the committee to the Assembly. But when the time came he was not on hand. Not until later was it learned that the standing committee had declined to permit the report to be given by its Negro chairman—and that he had returned, grievously disappointed, to his home—and that all the Negro commissioners had withdrawn from the Assembly in silent protest at the indignity. Publicity given to this incident aroused intense indignation from commissioners to the Assembly and throughout the church at large. The following year another Negro commissioner was appointed chairman of a standing committee of the Assembly, and this time he made his report without incident. This same Assembly adopted a resolution to the effect that henceforth there should be no distinction in the treatment of commissioners to the General Assembly on grounds of race or color.[20] Unfortunately, however, this was not put into immediate effect. Two years later the *Presbyterian Outlook* noted that Negro commissioners were still quartered in the little green cabins (the servants' quarters), below the Assembly Inn, and that they still entered the dining room of the Assembly Inn through a back door and sat at a far corner table distinctly separated from the rest of the guests.[21]

But dissatisfaction was mounting. An ad interim committee, as we have seen, recommended that the 1946 General Assembly take Negro work out of the hands of the Executive Committee of Home Missions, thus repudiating the paternalistic policy it had hitherto followed, and place it in the hands of an independent Negro Work Committee. Opponents recognized what was at stake. As Rev. W. H. McIntosh of Hattiesburg, Mississippi, stated: "The report proposes the most momentous action taken by the Southern Presbyterian Church in many years. There is a great deal more in it than a casual reading of it would indicate. It commits us to a program that involves the whole policy of the church . . . [It] has much to do with social and political and economic aims . . . It involves a complete repudiation of the work of home missions that we have been trying to do all these years."[22]

Dr. Price Henderson Gwynn, Jr., in supporting the recommendation, agreed that the Assembly was called to make a momentous decision. "This is a clarion call to a new day in the work among the Negroes in the South for whose salvation we are responsible . . . In reports of the Home Mission Committee across the years I do not find a philosophy that is adequate for our needs in this work . . ." Arch B. Taylor, a Winston-Salem elder and a member of the ad interim committee, was even more plain-spoken. "What we have done for the Negro," he said, "has been for the most part benevolent; seldom has it been fraternal; frequently it has been brutal . . . We have had no desire to see the Negro achieve . . . We've had too much paternalism."[23] In his judgment a new committee, with a new attitude toward the Negro, was imperative.

The vote, when taken, was overwhelmingly in favor of the appointment of a new committee as recommended by the ad interim committee. This new committee, under the inspired leadership of Dr. Alex R. Batchelor, would move step by step to integrate the Negro work into the full life of the church, with the Negro for the first time a fully accepted member of the church. At Stillman there was a new policy—an integrated faculty—the student respected as a person. New churches organized among the Negroes in the border synods would be received into the white presbyteries on an equal basis.

The church had begun its work in Tuscaloosa with the prime intention of educating Negroes for the ministry—the ad interim committee of 1946 still looked toward the establishment of an adequate department of theological education at Stillman. The church soon recognized that this was not the wisest move. The 1946 Assembly instructed the Assembly's Committee on Negro Work to "explore the possibility of sending the [Negro] students to our own seminaries." These institutions were prepared to receive those with proper qualifications, and faculties and students were ready to welcome them.[24] Union Theological Seminary had, in fact, received students into its graduate department on an unsegregated basis since 1935 (it seems to have been the first educational institution in the South to do so).[25] Presbyterian ministerial candidates from Stillman could not be received into the B.D. programs, however, until it had become an accredited four-year college. But the direction was now set, and it was along this line the church would move.

Meanwhile, there had come a change of administration at Montreat, where the Assembly ordinarily held its sessions, and with it a change of policy. Now for the first time Negro commissioners to the General Assembly were not subjected to the humiliation of being assigned to the green shacks where the servants were quartered. For the first time they were assigned to one of the buildings where white commissioners were assigned, and for the first time they entered the dining room of Assembly Inn through the main entrance.[26]

In 1950 the Assembly met at Massanetta, the Synod of Virginia's conference grounds, and here for the first time Negro commissioners were treated on a complete equality with all other commissioners. "There was no segregation in living quarters or in the dining room and no particular notice of the phenomenon. New commissioners evidently thought it had always been done that way."[27] The arrangement was accepted by all as a matter of course. The Montreat Board of Directors meanwhile had adopted a new policy—the residence halls and the cafeteria would henceforth be opened to both Negroes and whites attending adult conferences, including the General Assembly itself. "Owing to the multiplicity of problems involved," however, the Board of Directors decided that it could entertain no Negro delegates to young people's conferences except to the Assembly's Youth Council.[28]

The same question was now coming to the fore for the first time at Massanetta. Heretofore—with no Negro churches in the synod— the question had not been raised. Now, however, under the new program of Negro work several churches had been organized and received into the white presbyteries. The question as to whether these churches could send representatives to the various Massanetta Conferences came before the 1953 synod, and the synod took unanimous action directing the Board of Trustees to permit unsegregated conferences (for adults) at Massanetta.[29] This policy was later extended to all conferences.

The General Assembly adopted this year (1953) a very general and therefore innocuous recommendation: "That the Church practice no discrimination . . ." A young minister, Rev. Jack Ewart of Radford, Virginia, sought to put some teeth into this resolution by offering an amendment: "That the General Assembly in carrying out the implication of this action shall direct the trustees of all its institutions of higher education to open its doors to all races. That the General Assembly strongly recommends the same action to synods and presbyteries. That the local churches be directed to practise no discrimination within [their] fellowship or outreach."[30]

The Assembly, only too ready to shift responsibility for answering this resolution to other shoulders, voted to refer this resolution to the Council of Christian Relations for report to the following Assembly.

The Council seized the opportunity to grapple with the whole issue of segregation. There could have been no more opportune time. The Supreme Court of the United States had before it the question of segregation in the public schools, and a decision might be expected within the not too distant future.

The Council drew up two comprehensive papers, seeking to prepare the church for the acceptance of integration in both church and society, and offering the following recommendations:

> 1. That the General Assembly affirm that enforced segregation of the races is discrimination which is out of harmony with Christian theology and ethics . . .
> 2. That the General Assembly . . . urge
>   1. That the trustees of institutions of higher education belonging to the General Assembly adopt a policy of opening the doors of these institutions to all races.
>   2. That the synods consider earnestly the adoption of a similar recommendation to trustees of institutions under their control.
>   3. That the governing bodies of the various conferences held throughout the Church consider the adoption of a similar policy.
>   4. That the sessions of local churches admit persons to membership and fellowship in the local church on the Scriptural basis of faith in the Lord Jesus Christ without reference to race. . . .[31]

This report, with its recommendations, declared by the nondenominational *Christian Century* to be "superior to anything of comparable character on the subject by any religious group," was drawn up prior to the decision of the Supreme Court, rendered on May 17, 1954, that segregated schools were by their nature infringements on personal rights. The General Assembly, meeting on May 27, adopted its committee's recommendations by a vote of 239 to 169. Added was a brief recommendation that the Assembly commend the principle of the Supreme Court's decision and urge its members to aid those charged with its implementation. Later a specific resolution was adopted urging the trustees of Montreat to conform to the announced policy of the Assembly in all of its gatherings.

It so happened that the Southern Presbyterian Assembly was the first major church court to meet after the rendering of the Supreme Court's decision—it became the first therefore to endorse the decision and to urge its people to aid in its implementation. The Assembly had not permitted a civil court to determine its position as some charged. It is quite clear that the Assembly would have condemned enforced segregation as recommended by its Permanent Committee, whether or not the Court had spoken.

Naturally there were those who disapproved of what the Assembly had said. A number of commissioners who had voted for the resolutions received protests from their home churches while they were at the Assembly, others immediately upon their return. A few were forced out of their pulpits. A number of sessions—in Jackson, Mississippi; Birmingham, Alabama; Goldsboro and Fayetteville, North Carolina, for example—were quick to announce their dissent from the Assembly's action. The vote in the Jackson First Church and the South Highlands Church, Birmingham, was unanimous; in Goldsboro, Rev. James M. McChesney had his vote recorded on the negative against the solid vote of his elders, the vote in the Fayetteville First session was 13 to 3, with the pastor, Walter Healy, recorded as dissenting.[32] Two synods, South Carolina and Mississippi, also recorded their disapproval. Dr. Guy T. Gillespie, former President of Belhaven College, presenting the report adopted by the Synod of Mississippi, termed segregation "one of nature's universal laws," defensible on biblical grounds, and a "well-considered and time-tested American policy." His statement was elaborated, printed, and widely distributed through the South.[33]

Two years after the Assembly had approved the Supreme Court's decision, supporters of the *Presbyterian Journal* held their annual meeting in Weaverville, North Carolina. From the meeting came a formal statement affirming that "voluntary segregation in churches, schools and other social relations is for the highest interest of the races and is not un-Christian." "Racial integrity," continued the statement, "is something to be fostered, not to be broken down, and those who would force a program countenancing and looking to the amalgamation of the races are doing great harm to the finding of the ultimate solution."[34]

But there was also widespread support for the Assembly's deliverances on segregation. Prominent pastors publicly endorsed the Assembly's action, as did former Moderators of the Assembly. A number of presbyteries promptly recorded their approval; six synods—Arkansas, Kentucky, Missouri, Texas, Virginia, and West Virginia—did likewise. The synods of Appalachia, Florida, and North Carolina added their endorsement the following year. The Synod of Virginia adopted resolutions similar to those approved by the Assembly and, in addition, appointed representatives to urge compliance with the Supreme Court's decision by the State legislature.

An attempt to reverse the 1954 statement was defeated in the 1955 General Assembly by a vote of 293 to 109. The margin of victory was greater than it had been the preceding year.

A battle was now being waged throughout the South to save the public schools. In 1957 Arkansas Governor Orval Faubus created a turmoil by calling out the Arkansas National Guard to prevent the integration of Central High School in Little Rock. Presbyterian ministers joined other groups in protesting Governor Faubus' action. Ten Presbyterian ministers meeting in Huntsville, the Governor's hometown, sent him a telegram stating "we deplore your recent shameful conduct . . ." Presbyterian ministers of the Clarksville area told the Governor, "We believe that the program of integration of the schools should continue and . . . not be thwarted by political pressure."[35] Rev. Marion A. Boggs, D.D., pastor of the Second Church, Little Rock, and Rev. Richard B. Hardie, pastor of the Westover Hills Church, gave strong support to the integration cause. Rev. Dunbar H. Ogden, Jr., pastor of the Central Church and President of the Greater Little Rock Ministerial Association, played a leading role in the effort to save the situation. On the opening morning of the school session, he and his son, along with several other ministers, accompanied the seven Negro students who presented themselves for admission to Central High School only to be turned away by troops placed there by the order of the Governor. Later Mr. Ogden reported the affair over the Voice of America, which translated his remarks into 12 or more languages and broadcast them around the world. Mr. Ogden did not have the full support of his congregation, and in the end was forced to accept another pastorate.

The lesson of Little Rock was not lost on other Southern states, but for some time it remained an open question, in various communities, whether public schools should be maintained.

In December 1958, 300 Atlanta ministers, including most of the Presbyterian ministers in the city, issued the second of a series of statements dealing with the interracial situation. The statement included the following points: "It is clearer now than ever before that at all costs freedom of speech must be preserved . . . that we must obey the law . . . that the public school system must be preserved . . . that hatred and scorn for those of another race, or for those who hold a position different from our own can never be justified . . . that communication between responsible leaders of the races must be maintained."[36] In Virginia ministers, laymen, presbyteries, and the synod all entered the struggle, whose outcome for a time seemed quite uncertain.

The 1958 General Assembly, in response to a number of overtures, recorded its opposition to the use of any facilities owned by any of its churches for the establishment of schools, public or private, supported in whole or in part by state or community funds for the purpose of evading the decrees of the courts of the United States regarding segregation.[37]

A leader in this anti-integration effort, ruling elder R. B. Crawford of Prince Edward County, Virginia (where public schools were to be closed down for more than a decade), indignantly declared, "The worst obstacle we face in the fight to preserve segregated schools in the South is the white preacher."[38] Thomas Pettigrew, Assistant Professor of Social Psychology in Harvard University, and Ernest Campbell, Assistant Professor of Sociology at the University of North Carolina, in a paper presented to the American Psychological Association, asserted that "the Christian ministry in the South is the only significant group throughout the area willing to stand up for integration." Lawrence Rogin, education director of the Textile Workers' Union of America, bore similar testimony. The churches in the Southern States, he averred, were "the greatest social force" toward achieving acceptance of the Supreme Court decision outlawing racial segregation in public schools.[39] A survey conducted about the same time by the *Pulpit Digest,* a nondenominational journal for the ministry, indicated that a majority of Protestant ministers in the 17 Southern states favored compliance with the Supreme Court's orders for the racial integration in the public schools. Of the 765 ministers who answered the *Digest* questionnaire, four out of five expressed sentiment favoring integration. The ratio varied from a high of 89 percent in Kentucky to a low of 50 percent in South Carolina. Southern Presbyterian ministers supported integration efforts certainly as strongly and perhaps more strongly than any other white religious group. The *Presbyterian Outlook* gave them unwavering support.

New tensions arose in the South as a result of the sit-ins, the demonstrations, the efforts to pass civil rights legislation. One of the earliest Presbyterian ministers to support such efforts was the Rev. Charles M. Jones, pastor of the Presbyterian Church in Chapel Hill,

North Carolina. Regarded by his congregation as something of a "saint," with unusual sympathy for any who were in need, Mr. Jones was little concerned with the niceties of Presbyterian belief and practice. Many in presbytery and synod, and some in the congregation, felt that the church would be better served in this university community by one who was a more "orthodox" in his views. Dissatisfaction mounted when Mr. Jones took into his home two Negroes and two whites who were threatened with physical violence after their test of the Jim Crow laws in Chapel Hill. "Charlie makes many mistakes," admitted Dr. Frank Graham, President of the university and a ruling elder in the congregation, and added, "Here's why it hurts. He disturbs the social order of our times. And for anybody who does that, there has got to be fault finding."[40] A commission of Orange Presbytery, appointed to look into the situation, finally dissolved the pastoral relations between Mr. Jones and the church, on the grounds that "the interests of religion imperatively demanded it," and relieved the elders and deacons who had consistently supported him from their posts. But no charges had been brought against Mr. Jones, and many in the church and out of it believed that it was his racial stand which determined the outcome. The *Presbyterian Outlook* vigorously championed Mr. Jones right to an open hearing. The General Assembly, to whom the matter finally came on appeal, agreed that Orange Presbytery must grant Mr. Jones a formal trial if he so desired. When the presbytery refused a change of venue, Mr. Jones, claiming that an unprejudiced trial before this court was out of the question, withdrew from the church.

As protests and sit-ins against segregated lunch counters and other services spread across the South, various church and ministerial groups, including Presbyterians in their numbers, openly manifested their sympathy. In Raleigh, North Carolina, some 30 Protestant clergymen offered to support any chain store agreeing to end racial segregation at its lunch counter. In Greensboro, North Carolina, the Ministers' Fellowship called for equal treatment of all customers by businesses serving members of both races. In Chapel Hill, North Carolina, all of the clergymen signed a statement supporting the picketing there taking place. In Richmond, Virginia, on an Inter-Faith radio broadcast, an interpretation was given of the basic objectives represented by these demonstrations and strong support was expressed for this movement to attain personal dignity. Those voicing their support included Dr. James W. Clarke, pastor of the aristocratic Second Presbyterian Church. A few days later in Richmond a number of students from Union Theological Seminary joined Negro

students on the picket line around one of the leading department
stores in the city to protest segregated eating facilities there—one of
the earliest occasions when Presbyterian students had openly participated in such movements. The students carried signs emphasizing
religious reasons for their concern. To the press they explained,
"As Christians we see segregation based on race as evil, and are
bound to do everything we can to eliminate it."[41]

A major demonstration was planned for Washington, D.C., in the
summer of 1964. It was designed to give massive support to the
limping Civil Rights Bill, long stalled in the United States Senate.
It had the endorsement of leading religious bodies, Roman Catholic,
Protestant, and Jewish, including the National Council of Churches.
The General Assembly that spring approved a pastoral letter, addressed to the local sessions of its churches, dealing with the social
revolution, which was proving so painful to the South and "especially
to its churches." The various kinds of demonstrations employed by
the Negroes—marching, picketing, boycotting, and sit-ins, which,
it was remarked, had been remarkably peaceful—were termed by
the Assembly amoral means to a moral end. It recognized that
ministers had been forced out of their pulpits or subject to various
types of harassment because they had complied with the expressed
views of the Assembly. It urged sessions to support and defend their
pastors as they proclaimed the Word of God even if it ran counter
to community mores and traditions.[42]

The Assembly declined, however, to adopt a resolution endorsing
the march on Washington, and just a few days before the march
was scheduled to occur a statement was released, signed by a number
of the church's leaders, explaining why denominational support had
not been forthcoming. To some it appeared that the Presbyterian
Church in the U. S. was the one major religious body in the nation
that opposed a march which proved to be remarkably orderly and
which played an important part in rallying necessary support for the
final passage of the Civil Rights Bill. The unfavorable image that
this gave the church led a number of younger ministers, some of
whom had participated in the march, to form a Fellowship of Concern, open to all ministers and laymen in the Presbyterian Church
in the U. S., who shared "a desire to see the Presbyterian Church in the
United States more relevantly related in program and service to the
critical issues of the twentieth century." The declared purpose of
the Fellowship was:

> To interpret the Reformed Doctrine of the sovereignty of God in its
> authentic application to all of life.

> To seek for our Church a more vital role in the struggle for social justice and the search for Christian unity. . . .
>
> To help the church to assert moral leadership in the changing patterns of racial and cultural revolution.
>
> To support those who have been put under extreme pressure because of their faithfulness to the Church's social witness.

The Fellowship secured signatures from all of the 16 synods to a memorial urging the passage of the Civil Rights Bill. Representatives of the movement were present at the memorial services for Rev. James Reeb, who had been brutally beaten to death in Selma, Alabama, a service attended by perhaps the largest outpouring of clergy of all faiths from all parts of the nation ever seen on the continent; some of the Fellowship remained to participate in the memorable march from Selma to Montgomery, which aided in the passage of the second Civil Rights Bill.

In the spring of this year, the General Assembly adopted a paper presented by its Permanent Committee on Christian Relations, "The Civil Rights Movement in the Light of Christian Teaching," which endorsed peaceful demonstrations and expressed guarded approval under extreme circumstances of civil disobedience, defined as the open, non-violent, and conscientious refusal to obey a law or laws as a means of appeal to a higher law, combined with the willing acceptance of the penalty.[43] Many laymen were profoundly disturbed by this action, particularly as it was reported in the public press.

The next Assembly declined to rescind its former action but defined its position more exactly. It pointed out that there were instances when those charged with administering the law had enforced it inconsistently within their communities, with the result that not only had there been occasions of injustice, but also that this injustice had had the quiet sanction of the law. "In these sorrowful instances," said the Assembly, "some of those more sensitive to injustice who have been deprived of the full benefits of the law have frequently been unable to secure the redress of their rights through the exercise of the law. The same circumstances that deprived these individuals of their rights have served to deny or frustrate their lawful petitions for the redress of those rights, depriving them also of that ultimate means of redress within our system, a free ballot. Under this situation an appeal was made by some to the larger community through the practice of civil disobedience as a final resort, other peaceful means having been deprived them. In these acts, those who were civilly disobedient accepted the consequences of the law imposed upon them for its violation. Only under such sorrowful circumstances can civil disobedience be countenanced. . . ."[44]

Increasing pressure meanwhile had been brought to bear on the Montreat authorities by ministers, by the women of the church, and by the young people to liberalize its policies, to admit Negroes to all its facilities and to all its conferences. The Trustees, after sharp debate, in 1959 voted to include the Westminster (college-age) Fellowship under the provisions for adult conferences, but by a narrow margin declared that all programs for younger ages should be on an entirely segregated basis. Negro young people attending a regional Westminster Fellowship Conference this summer were still not permitted to swim in Lake Susan. The conference, as a result, requested none of its delegates to use the lake and voted to meet the next year in a site where everyone might have an opportunity to participate in all phases of the conference program.

The General Assembly in May of this year reiterated its earlier recommendations regarding desegregation policies for all Presbyterian institutions, regretting that many had not acted in the matter and that some had taken contrary action.

Institutions of higher learning gradually adopted the open door policy, colleges in the border states—West Virginia, Kentucky, and Missouri—very quickly; others, like Davidson in North Carolina and Hampden-Sydney in Virginia more slowly, the last only after considerable prodding from the synod. Florida Presbyterian College, an ambitious new institution, adopted an integration policy from the start (as did St. Andrews in North Carolina) even though it meant the loss of greatly needed gifts. By 1963, 11 of the 23 junior and senior colleges had indicated publicly their readiness to receive Negro students. The remaining institutions, Belhaven in Mississippi being the last (1966), gradually fell into line. Some, it must be admitted, accepted Federal guidelines only in order that they might become eligible for Federal funds. Montreat had now become fully integrated, as had Massanetta some time earlier. So with most of the women's conferences.

Hanover Presbytery purchased land and raised funds to establish an all-year-round camp and conference ground in 1956-1957. The question of policy—whether or not children, young people, and adults from the three Negro churches in the presbytery were to be admitted on the same terms as those from the white churches—was fully and frankly faced. The policy agreed upon was complete integration, and this policy was followed consistently from the start, though a few churches for a time would not permit their young people to attend. Conference and camping ground were also integrated in other presbyteries; in some, where the effort was made, the danger of violence proved too great, and efforts had to be abandoned. The Synod of Louisiana was finally compelled to sell its synodical conference grounds—the old Silliman College—because over a period of years public officials steadfastly refused to promise protection, and threats of violence could not be discounted.

Snedecor Memorial Synod had been dissolved, and its presbyteries distributed among the white synods in 1951. In 1964 the General Assembly took steps to dissolve the Negro presbyteries and instructed the white presbyteries to receive the Negro churches within their bounds. Questions were raised regarding the constitutionality of this action—the bypassing of synod. Tuscaloosa Presbytery also pointed out some of the difficulties it and other presbyteries faced in carrying out such instruction and requested the General Assembly to reconsider its action and to consider using only the appeal of love rather than a resort to methods of constraint. The 1965 General Assembly in response requested, "with all Christian compassion and understanding," that presbyteries having Negro churches within their bounds take immediate action to receive said churches into their membership if this had not already been accomplished.[45]

A year later some presbyteries still had not acted. The General Assembly, its purpose unaltered, but moving slowly and constitutionally, instructed all synods having Negro churches within their bounds to report to the next Assembly what action had been taken by their presbyteries to receive the Negro churches within their bounds and by what date they could expect the synods to take action to see that all Negro churches were included within the bounds of presbyteries in which they were located.[46] Finally, in 1968, the last Negro church was so received.

The most stubborn resistance to the desegregation ideal of the Assembly was found in local churches. Not in all by any means. Some expressed their willingness almost immediately to seat worshipers of any color without discrimination and also to receive Negroes into the membership of the church. A small number of Negro members were so received. In the vast majority of churches no question arose. A few had been quick to record their disagreement with the Assembly's position. And in a very large number of churches, particularly in the deep South but in other states as well, the minister must be very cautious indeed in what he said about race if he did not wish to terminate his pastorate. In numerous cases pastorates were terminated, some rudely, after threats of violence and other forms of harassment, some more obliquely, with secondary causes brought forward to obscure the real ones behind the break.

The case attracting widest attention probably was that of Rev. Robert B. McNeill, pastor of the First Church, Columbus, Georgia. A Commission of Southwest Georgia Presbytery, invited by the pastor to look into the trouble which had arisen between the congregation and himself over a period of years, concluded that the trouble had stemmed from Mr. McNeill's efforts to relate the gospel to the current racial problem in the South. The unrest had reached a peak following publication of what seemed to most a mild and conciliatory article by Mr. McNeill in *Look* magazine in May 1957. Finding the differences irreconcilable the Commission finally suggested that Mr. McNeill resign and seek another pastorate; when he declined to do so, the Commission dissolved the pastoral relation claiming that "The time has now come when what has been the voice of the pulpit should also become the voice of the people . . ." The chairman of the commission explained this unfortunate statement to mean that "the pulpit and the congregation should be more or less united in proclaiming the divine mission of the church." The action of the Commission received wide publicity, reaching to mission lands overseas. Church officers insisted other factors were involved, but the *Columbus Ledger* editorialized, "No one could seriously doubt that Mr. McNeill's views on the racial conflict were the underlying cause of his removal."[47] To many it now seemed clear that a minister holding views approved by the General Assembly but unacceptable to an important group in his congregation could not expect to be supported in his position by the higher courts of the church. There were many similar cases. The number will never be known, but almost any minister could name a dozen or more which had come to his own personal attention.

Ralph McGill, crusading editor of the *Atlanta Constitution*, taking the McNeill case as his text, wrote understandingly on "The Agony of the Southern Minister." He "is pressed between his conscience, which dictates racial tolerance, and members of his congregation, who have set their faces even against token integration." A minister was quoted as saying, "It is uncomfortable to see successful business and professional men, who have been old friends and strong financial props suddenly become cold and aloof because one voices the opinion that a colored person is a child of God and has a right to worship in any of God's houses." "A sense of shame and self-accusation is especially noticeable among younger ministers encountering for the first time the harshness of some older men whom they had regarded as great Christian lay leaders," wrote Mr. McGill; "they have stories to tell which, while sometimes wryly, are always sad with disillusionment. . . . Many a minister today," he concludes, "is holding on in a Southern Church, developing a technique of survival, merely because he does not want to desert those in the congregation who depend on him and need him. Still others remain, believing that time and God are working together in their behalf."[48] *

As indeed they were. Some congregations, along with their ministers, remained obdurate, justifying their refusal to seat Negroes on the ground that they came with no sincere desire to worship, but the climate of the church was changing. Some ministers had supported the Assembly's position openly from the outset, with the sympathy or at least the sufferance of their officers and congregations. In 1962-1963, 1,178 churches replied to a questionnaire sent to them by the Permanent Committee on Christian Relations. Of these churches, 623 replied that Negroes were welcomed in the worship of the church; 295 indicated that they were not. Twenty-eight stated that Negroes had been received into the membership of the church; 513 stated that they had not.

The following year the Assembly said that in its opinion the constitution of the church as interpreted from 1865 on precluded any exclusion of persons from participation in public worship solely on the basis of race or color. To make this position unmistakably clear, it recommended that the Directory of Worship be amended by adding a sentence to read: "No one shall be excluded from participation in public worship in the Lord's house on the grounds of race, color, or class." This amendment, favored by 69 of the presbyteries, with 11 opposed, was enacted into law the following year.[49]

The General Assembly had expected to meet this year as guests of the Second Presbyterian Church in Memphis— with the assurance which had been required for some years past that all facilities would be completely integrated. When it came to the attention of the church at large that the host church was unwilling to receive Negro worshipers at its own services a storm of protest arose. When the Moderator, all other resorts having failed, finally took the unprecedented step of changing the place of meeting, he acted with the full support of the church. Shortly thereafter sentiment in the Second Church, Memphis, had become so manifest that the intransigent elders responsible for the segregation policy withdrew, with a small band of followers, to form their own "independent" Presbyterian

---

* For a sample of sermons on the racial issue preached by Southern Presbyterian ministers during this period, see *The Unsilent South*, ed. by Donald W. Shriver, Jr. (Richmond, Va.: John Knox Press, 1965).

church. A new invitation for the Assembly to meet in the Second Church, Memphis, at a future date, was extended and accepted.

During the year 1967-1968, all the great Boards of the church (World Missions, National Ministries, Christian Education, and Women's Work) became actively engaged in various cooperative efforts to ease the racial tensions which gripped the nation. Vigorous protests against such involvement in what was termed "The Crisis of the Nation" was voiced by the *Presbyterian Journal* and by the Concerned Presbyterians; a number of overtures brought the issue before the General Assembly. The Assembly not only declined to rebuke its various Boards for their involvement in secular affairs but adopted a resolution which declared:

> Whereas, the critical racial situation in the United States challenges the Church of Jesus Christ not only to say but also to show where it stands; and
>
> Whereas the 106th General Assembly . . . in adopting the paper, "The Theological Basis for Christian Social Action," expressed its belief that "the God to whom we bear witness is a God who is interested and actively involved in men's social, political, economic and cultural life as well as in their religious life" and its conviction that commitment to Him "makes the church's and the individual Christian's involvement in secular, social, economic and political affairs both an inescapable necessity and a great privilege," and
>
> Whereas, the Boards . . . and their executive secretaries have given leadership to the denomination by responding to the crisis . . .
>
> Therefore, Be It Resolved that the 108th General Assembly . . .
>
> Commends these boards and their executive secretaries . . . and
>
> Calls upon all members . . . to support their assembly-elected leaders . . . and to commit themselves anew in their own situations to seeking justice for all men, proclaiming the gospel of salvation and reconciliation, and doing God's will *on earth* as it is done in heaven.[50]

In response to the Assembly's questionnaire (1967) all but two synods had replied (by 1971) that no discriminatory policies or practices, so far as known, were carried on by institutions or agencies or, in the case of most synods, by individual congregations within their bounds. The two remaining synods, South Carolina and Florida, were again instructed to reply by the following year. It seemed clear that Assembly pressure would continue until recognized cases of racial discrimination had ceased throughout the church, as they had already in the General Assembly and its agencies.

For 50 years after the Civil War, Southern Presbyterians shared the common conviction of their region that the Negroes were an inferior race, not to be trusted with the ballot, and that amalgamation of the races was to be avoided at all costs. Churchmen apparently had unlimited confidence in the good intentions of the white man to act for the best interests of the black man, and were strangely blind to the many injustices which had developed. Segregation and disfranchisement were accepted as the Southern, and a fully Christian, way of life.

The viewpoint of the church began to change after World War I and the ensuing struggle first for elementary justice and then for full civil rights. It is not true that the church, particularly the Presbyterian Church in the South, lagged behind other institutions in the fight for human rights. There was a cutting, growing edge in the church, composed of ministers, laymen, women, and young people, that remained well abreast of other (white) pioneers in this area and far in advance of public opinion generally, and especially of its political leadership. Slowly, but surely, the church as a whole was responding to its own leadership, and in this movement there was hope—for the South and also for the church.

XXIII

Toward Greater Ecumenicity

For a time—in the 1930's—it seemed as though the Presbyterian Church in the United States was moving toward a new isolationism.

The General Assembly, as we have seen, withdrew in 1931 from the Federal Council of Churches, the cooperative agency of more than 20 of the major denominations in America, by a decisive vote of 179 to 79. The question of re-entry continued to arise, however, and in 1937 the Assembly referred the question to the presbyteries for their advice, which led to the most intense debate on the issue which the church had yet known.

Advocates of re-entry pointed out that the Federal Council was the only organization which represented the united Protestant forces of America—the only organization that could speak or act for the Protestant Churches of America. There were some things the individual denominations could not do so well, other things they could not do at all, except through this cooperative body. To say that the faith of Southern Presbyterians was too pure to belong to the one organization which represented the evangelical forces of the nation smacked of spiritual arrogance. By entering, the Southern Church played a constructive part in making it an effective organization. Theological objections had long since ceased to be an issue. The charges of Communism made against the Council had been discredited. The Council, since the withdrawal of the Southern Church, had been reorganized, making it more responsible to the constituent denominations. The commissions whose independent utterances had been objected to had been abolished.[1] So claimed proponents of re-entry.

Opponents insisted that the church remain out of the Council because the Council was controlled by modernists and indifferentists. We must heed the Scriptural injunction "Be not unequally yoked together with unbelievers." We can accomplish more for the Kingdom by doing our own work than by duplicating the activities of this and other "social agencies." We are not called of God to accomplish his aims by organization but by preaching the gospel. The Council is using the radio to set forth doctrines opposed to our Confession of Faith. It is moving in the direction of merging the denominations on an anticreedal basis. By joining the Council we will be led, as a church, away from our spiritual mission to secular matters. The literature of the Council reveals that its interests lie largely in the fields of humanism. The religion of the Council is largely a religion without theology. In supporting the Council financially we would compel those who oppose it to violate their conscience.[2] Re-entry into the Council would run the risk of dividing the church. So the arguments ran.

To the *Christian Observer* the church seemed to be hopelessly divided on the issue. Those who favored affiliation did so largely as a matter of more effective Christian statesmanship, that the church might present a united front to the forces of evil in the world. Those who opposed it looked upon the step as unfaithfulness to Christ and his cause, as a lowering of the church's standards, as infidelity to the Scriptures, and as the negation of the church's historical belief in the spirituality of the church.[3] A polarity in the church had indeed developed over this and other issues which it seemed that nothing could heal.

The vote of the presbyterics this year was 48 against re-entry into the Council, 38 in favor of re-entry. In the light of this vote the Assembly voted unanimously to drop the idea.

But the wave of fear and resentment which had swept the church out of the Council gradually ebbed, and in 1941 the issue was once more before the Assembly. Those who favored re-entry at this time argued that the state of the world demanded cooperation on the part of all Protestant forces, that the differences which naturally existed should not prevent the church from associating and working with other evangelical denominations, that we should not stand on the sidelines and criticize. Those who opposed re-entrance took the isolationist point of view, that we would work as effectively for the advancement of the Kingdom alone as in cooperation, that our differences from the Council in doctrine and attitude on moral and political questions indicated that this was the proper decision to make. After thorough debate the Assembly voted to re-enter the Council by a majority of 154 to 101.[4]

The following year there came the inevitable effort to reverse this decision. It was defeated by a decisive vote of 190 to 60. The question in one form or another would come before nearly every subsequent

Assembly, with dwindling hope of success. Not that the Assembly approved all that the Council did. Far from it. But regardless of agreement or disagreement with some particular deliverance or some particular activity the Assembly, it appeared, was committed to the continuance of cooperative effort with its sister denominations through the Federal, later the National, Council of Churches.

Recognizing that the clergy were now overwhelmingly in favor of the cooperative movement as embodied in the FCC, opponents appealed more directly to the laity—as they were now doing in their opposition to church union—and began to put more emphasis on economic factors than on theological ones.

This new attack was launched in the 1947 General Assembly. Chalmers W. Alexander, a Jackson, Mississippi, lawyer, declared that the FCC favored "fair employment" legislation, a non-segregated church in a non-segregated society, increase of minimum wage rates, full employment guaranteed by the government, labor's right to strike, special planning and control of the credit and monetary systems, and pacifism. John M. Ward, on the staff of the Alabama State Chamber of Commerce, referred to his close contact with business and industrial leaders of many sections. These laymen, he said, were questioning the church's participation in the FCC. They think they know something about economic relations, labor relations, meeting payrolls, and the like, even though they may not know much about theology. Many of them believed that the FCC was using the church to undermine the capitalistic system, along with the social structure of the South. J. P. McCallie, ruling elder from Chattanooga, Tennessee, said: "I detect a definite feeling on the part of laymen that our ministers are leading us down the river. Many of them will not put another penny into the causes of the church until they have assurance about our relationships to this organization."[5]

Since the majority of the presbyteries had voted in 1937 to remain out of the Council, opponents demanded that it be submitted to their judgment again, and to this the Assembly finally agreed. For a full year this remained the chief issue before the church. The Continuing Church Committee and other groups organized to fight union with the Presbyterian Church in the U.S.A. were equally opposed to continued membership in the Federal Council. They circulated their literature widely through the church and held public meetings designed particularly to arouse the laity in opposition. To counter their efforts more than 200 laymen organized a church-wide Committee on Protestant Cooperation to keep the Southern Presbyterian Church fully affiliated with the Council and to provide the church with factual information on its services to the church.

In our sorely divided and discordant world [declared their opening statement], we are driven to the conviction that our first duty is to make evident to the world our unity in Christ as something far greater than our differences of interpretation . . .

We repudiate as a dangerous error the supposition that our Presbyterian Church can make its way in isolation from our Christian brethren . . .

We therefore call upon our fellow Christians to hold high the banner of our historic Presbyterian spirit, which involved the acknowledgement as brethren in Christ of all who profess faith in him, and the duty of laboring with them in Christian fellowship for the honor of Christ and the advancement of his kingdom.[6]

A poll conducted by the committee to discover how the church's leaders felt about the Federal Council revealed favorable sentiment as follows[7]:

Moderators of the Assembly, 11 to 0
College presidents, 15 to 2
Seminary and ATS presidents, 5 to 0
Chairmen of the Assembly's Committees, 15 to 0
Secretaries and Directors of Assembly's Committees, 8 to 0
Current Moderators of synods, 14 to 0
Synodical Auxiliary presidents, 9 to 1
Synod's men's councils, 12 to 1
Presidents of synods' young people, 6 to 0

The church as a whole, it turned out, supported its leadership, and the vote of the presbyteries—61 in favor of the Council, 24 opposed —only underlined the strong commitment of the church to continued cooperation with its brethren.

Unwilling to accept the verdict of the presbyteries, to which they had appealed, opponents of the Council renewed their fight before the 1948 General Assembly. There followed the fullest debate on the subject which the Assembly had ever heard—each side being given an hour to present its case, through carefully chosen representatives. The case against the Council was presented largely by laymen, who emphasized the theological aberrations and pacifistic tendencies of its leaders (Dr. H. B. Dendy, editor of the *Presbyterian Journal*, suggested that the leaders of the FCC were partly responsible for the disaster of Pearl Harbor),[8] but especially its dangerous economic leanings. L. E. Faulkner of Hattiesburg, Mississippi, who had circularized commissioners through the years with a dozen or more mimeographed letters, termed the Federal Council one of the most powerful enemies of the business and professional men because so many of their objectives were contrary to the competitive enterprise system. He charged the Council and other groups as being identified with Communist-front organizations. According to the Rev. C. G.

McClure, the Federal Council was the greatest enemy of the Protestant faith then existing. Pro-Council speakers acknowledged that some criticism of the Council was justified but insisted that much of it was distorted, mistaken, imagined, or untrue. All the criticism together, it was pointed out, affected only a small part of the Council's work; only three of the Council's 20 departments were involved, and only a small portion of these. The question as they saw it was: "Shall we continue to cooperate with other great denominations in America or withdraw into isolationism?" Follow this latter course, said Dr. Charles L. King, and we might well become the sanctifier of all re-actionary interests and influences in the realm of race and of economics and of politics. "I am not willing," he said, "for my denomination to be a tool in the hand of reactionary forces who seek to preserve the *status quo* in a changing world."[9]

The vote to remain in the Council this year was more than two to one, 274 to 108.

Two years later eight major organizations, including the Federal Council of Churches, responsible among them for the highly de-veloped cooperative work of the Protestant Church in most all of its varied aspects, came together to form the National Council of Churches. Criticism by Southern Presbyterians was muted for a time, but only for a time. In 1956 the Permanent Committee on Interchurch Re-lations was asked to investigate specific charges which had been brought against the National and World Council of Churches. The majority report signed by ten of the 14 members weighed the charges brought against both organizations and concluded that "to withdraw from either would be a regrettable step which we cannot believe our church desired to take."[10] The Assembly sustained this conclusion by a vote of more than two to one.

In 1958-1959 a new wave of criticism was unleashed against the Council by a resolution adopted by a World Order Study Conference held at Cleveland, Ohio, under the sponsorship of the Council, looking toward ultimate recognition of Red China by the United States Government. The General Assembly disproved the resolution, but up-held the right of the study conference to express a judgment on it. A key vote revealed 341 votes in basic support of the Council, with 116 opposed.[11]

Resentment against Council activities was building now because of its participation in the struggle for civil rights. The Assembly con-tinued from time to time, as it had done from the beginning, to caution the Council, but the size of its supporting majority remained unchanged. Up to this time the Southern Church had remained in the Council despite the social deliverances, which it did not seek to defend. Gradually the defensive stance altered. The 1959 Assembly affirmed "the right and duty of Conferences of Christians—laymen and ministers—to give free, prayerful, and thoughtful consideration to moral and spiritual problems inherent in world relations."[12] The following year, it declared:

> We feel that the Council's prophetic voice is very much needed in our day . . . We interpet [the Confession of Faith, chapter 33, paragraph 4] as giving Christians both as individuals and in groups, a mandate for speaking, in the spirit of the prophets and in the spirit of our Lord, on any issues that concern the life of man under God.
>
> The National Council of Churches is certainly not perfect. There is much about it that can and should be improved. But we deplore the unmerited attacks made on the National Council which result inevitably in a distrust and weakening of the Christian witness in our land and throughout the world. We regard our united work with other Christians as being of paramount importance in today's world and we urge our representatives on the National Council to support, encourage, and sustain this vital effort.[13]

The Assembly this same year instructed its representatives to the NCC to investigate and report concerning recent charges reflecting on the patriotism and indicating Communistic leanings on the part of certain church leaders associated with the National Council made in the U. S. Air Force Manual and repeated in publications and voiced by persons critical of the Council. These charges, later withdrawn, it was discovered, had been inserted into the manual by certain fundamentalist right-wingers. No evidence was found to justify the charges; other investigations, it was noted, had reached similar conclusions. "Such an indirect attack upon the NCC," said the Committee speaking unanimously, "using as its vehicle an attack upon persons related to the NCC is improper and should not be countenanced by member churches of the NCC . . . Many of the men accused have only sought to strengthen the social consciousness of the Church in seeking to remove evils and strive for justice, righteousness and peace . . . The technique of making false accusations, sowing distrust, creating suspicion, circulating slanders, manipulating words and using quotations out of context, and other distortion of facts is adopting the very methods of communism . . ."[14]

A later Assembly acknowledged that it had not made sufficient effort to acquaint the church with the positive value of the Council and its activities and adopted resolutions looking to this end.[15] One consequence of this resolution was a special edition of *Presbyterian Survey*, answering current charges brought against the Council and

giving an account of its manifold activities.[16] The Board of Christian
Education issued a pamphlet setting forth reasons why it supported
the National Council of Churches. In 1966 the General Assembly
further requested the Permanent Committee on Interchurch Relations
to develop ways and means of informing church courts and congregations about the purposes, policies, and programs of the National
Council.[17]

The Presbytery of Tuscaloosa, which brought undocumented
charges against the NCC, including a statement that it was "in revolt
against the basic ideas of Christianity" as taught by the Presbyterian
Church, was answered by reference to the report made in answer to the
Communistic charges contained in the Air Force Manual.[18] The Assembly also adopted a resolution that future overtures containing
charges against the NCC be specifically documented and that such
overtures be referred to the Permanent Committee on Interchurch
Relations for study and report to the General Assembly.

Feeling against the Council had never been more intense than it
was in the mid 1960's. The struggle over civil rights and reflections
on the Council and its activities appearing in the daily papers and over
certain radio and television stations in the South inflamed public
opinion and led at times to frenzied denunciation. It had become a
source of friction not only in the church courts, but also in many
local congregations and between a pastor and his people. It did not
seem likely however that the Assembly would cease to cooperate with
its sister denominations in this cooperative enterprise. As the decade
drew to its close, opposition to the National Council was overshadowed
by the old specter of more positive relations with the Northern Presbyterians—now the United Presbyterian Church in the U.S.A.—and of an
even wider union under the auspices of the Consultation on Church
Union.

For 60 years and more the Presbyterian Church in the U. S.
steadfastly refused to consider reunion with the mother church from
which it had separated at the outbreak of the Civil War. The one
serious conversation held during this period on "closer relations" was
broken off in 1922 by the refusal of the Southern Church to entertain
the possibility of anything beyond a meaningless "federal union"
which the Northern Church rightly insisted did not go beyond the
Council of Reformed and Presbyterian Churches already in existence.

Seven years later, in 1929, came a surprising development. The
Assembly approved a plan of union drawn up after a year's conversation with the United Presbyterian Church (a union which the latter
only a little later declined to approve). But it did more. In response

to overtures from a number of its presbyteries, it appointed a committee "to confer with and take active steps toward organic union of all Presbyterian bodies in the United States." For the first time in its history the Southern Assembly had taken the initiative and approved organic union with other Presbyterian bodies, including the Presbyterian Church in the U.S.A. The vote was overwhelmingly lopsided, 125 to 19.

How could this unexpected action be explained? As one commentator observed, "Church union is in the air,"[19] and so it was in the major denominations generally, and Southern Presbyterians could not remain unaffected. The wasteful competition in the border synods, if nothing else, kept the issue alive. Older men, it soon appeared, were thinking in terms of regional assemblies, permitting a large degree of local autonomy, with a General Assembly meeting every four or five years. Younger men meanwhile were coming to the fore, eager for reunion whether it be by regional assemblies or otherwise. The 1929 Assembly, some claimed, was a young man's assembly, and the young men, it was suggested, had gotten out of hand. The *Presbyterian Standard*, mixing its figures but reading the situation aright, reminded the advocates of union that "it is a long way to Tipperary" and that future Assemblies would probably have in their personnel more men who "knew Joseph" and remember what we owe to him.[20] So it happened, but the 1929 vote was token and sign of a changing tide, whose rise would soon be apparent.

The discussions, initiated by the 1929 U. S. Assembly, got off to a happy start. Representatives of the five leading Reformed and Presbyterian Churches in the nation—the Presbyterian Church in the U.S.A., the Presbyterian Church in the U. S., the United Presbyterian Church, the Reformed Church in America, and the Reformed Church in the United States—met in Philadelphia. After full and frank discussions, committees of the first four of these churches approved unanimously "Organic union with other Presbyterian and Reformed Churches on the basis of their existing Standards." On the U. S. committee were five ex-Moderators of the church. Opposition, however, was not slow in coming. All the old charges were refurbished and pressed —the Northern Church was doctrinally unsound (the Auburn Affirmation was cited as proof), and it held erroneous ideas regarding the "spirituality of the church" and unscriptural views regarding the place of women in the church (having recently voted to ordain women elders and deacons). The race question was injected as usual. Much emphasis was laid on the inevitable loss of property, if church union proved unwise and individual congregations later wished to withdraw.

On the other hand, influential pastors were now prepared to argue that the two churches were practically one in essentials, that union was vital for Presbyterianism in the border synods, and was the only thing that would satisfy the Lord's prayer that "they all may be one" (John 17:21).[21]

Continuance or discontinuance of the union negotiations was the chief matter of interest before the 1930 Assembly. After a long and acrimonious debate, in the course of which one of the venerable and revered ministers of the church insisted that there could never be union with a church which had voted to hang Jeff Davis, the Assembly agreed to continue the discussions, but in effect withdrew the previous Assembly's endorsement of organic union.

The following Assembly (1931) voted that all negotiations and conferences looking to organic union should cease but ordered that the ad interim committee be continued with directions to draft either singly or jointly a definite, complete, and detailed plan for "A Federal Union of our Church with any or all Presbyterian or Reformed bodies, and present the same to the next General Assembly for its consideration."[22]

The ad interim committee reported in 1932 that no other Presbyterian or Reformed Church had manifested the slightest interest in any additional plan of federal union. The committee proceeded, nevertheless, to offer its own plan, which the Assembly warmly approved. As was the case in 1920 it provided for federal union only in name. Each church, according to the plan, preserved as before its full autonomy; the United Assembly offered merely a forum for discussion—a forum already provided in the Western Section of the Alliance of Reformed and Presbyterian Churches Throughout the World, into which the Council of Reformed and Presbyterian Churches had now been merged.[23]

The ad interim committee, composed of one representative from each synod and manifestly opposed to any real scheme of organic union, was continued "with the primary purpose" of effecting the organization of a United Assembly which had no power and for which outside of PCUS there was no interest. The committee was also given power, not to initiate any action but to receive, consider, and report on proposals of Presbyterians or Reformed Churches looking toward well-recognized forms of church union. By this last action the Assembly removed the restrictions placed on its ad interim committee the preceding year and relieved itself of the charge of refusing to talk about any other forms of union than federal union. As one report indicated, the Assembly opened the door "a wee crack"[24] if important proposals for other forms of union were presented by any other Reformed or Presbyterian bodies. But it was only a very "wee crack." The Committee on Cooperation and Union served not to advance union but to bar as far as possible consideration of any plan for real, substantial union.

It is not surprising under the circumstances that no proposals of union from other denominations were received. A proposal from the U.S.A. Assembly that the constitution of the two denominations be amended so that ministers of union churches might belong simultaneously to two presbyteries, one in the Northern Church and the other in the Southern Church, was approved by the 1935 Assembly, but overwhelmingly rejected by vote of the presbyteries. Overtures, one from the Presbytery of Ebenezer (1934), another from the Synod of Kentucky (1935), that reunion discussions with the Presbyterian Church in the U.S.A. be re-opened were answered in the negative, "as we have an ad interim committee in whose hands these matters are left."[25]

The year of 1935 was a "Jubilee" year, in which the denomination celebrated the 75th anniversary of its founding. The Presbytery of Kanawha overtured the Assembly of this year to celebrate the occasion by inviting all of the Presbyterian and Reformed bodies to join with it in efforts to form one united Presbyterian church. Overtures looking to union came from three additional presbyteries. To avoid "what promised to become an extended and heated, and probably useless debate that might overshadow the important plans for the observance of the Jubilee"[26] the Assembly referred the various overtures and proposals to the ad interim committee for report to the 1937 Assembly.

This committee proceeded to recommend that "No action be taken touching any plan of union, since the plan of federal union advocated by our General Assembly has not met with acceptance on the part of our sister churches, and since they have not proposed any substitute therefore."[27] It expressed the conviction that in the present state of the world agitation of the union question would divert attention from the church's great task of preaching the gospel.

From the floor came a substitute motion that a Permanent Committee on Cooperation be erected, consisting of nine men appointed by the Moderator (to replace the old committee composed of representatives from the various synods, a committee which had become a graveyard for all union proposals), with instructions "to explore the possibilities of cooperation or union with the other Presbyterian bodies and to report each year its progress to the General Assembly."[28]

The substitute motion was promptly seconded and to the amazement of its proponents was passed, without discussion or debate.
For the second time in its history a General Assembly of the Southern Presbyterian Church had approved, in principle, the idea of
organic union with other Presbyterian bodies, and in 1937 as in 1929
it had taken the initiative in calling union negotiations into being.

The new committee proposed to the following Assembly a plan
of union which would give to the synods enlarged powers by reducing
correspondingly the powers of the General Assembly so as amply to
assure local self-government. The plan also contemplated the possible
enlargement of the territorial boundaries of the synods so that they
would become what might be termed "provincial synods." "The
members of the U.S.A. committee," it was stated, are "explicit and
emphatic in asserting that they would be quite ready and glad for
all powers possible, consistent with maintaining the integrity of the
reunited Church, to be taken from the Assembly and given to the
Synods." The committee asked that the General Assembly instruct it
"to continue its explorations along the lines indicated in this report."[29]

After a bitter discussion, in which personal charges were leveled
against leading advocates of union, the committee was dissolved and
dismissed with the thanks of the Assembly. The Assembly ordered,
however, that a new Committee on Cooperation and Union be
erected, with members being elected as originally by the respective
synods and with the same powers of exploration as the former committee. Opponents of union presumably assumed that a committee
so elected would bury all union proposals as earlier committees had
done.

But the new committee, reflecting a massive change of opinion on
the synodical level, continued its negotiations along the same line as
its predecessor. It reported to the 1939 General Assembly that the
Department of Cooperation and Union of the Presbyterian Church
U.S.A. looked with favor upon a plan of reunion including the following principles: the standards of the two churches to be the basis of
the reunion; provision to be made for local self-government by the
erection of reorganized regional synods; the unity of the church to be
maintained through a General Assembly which would administer
the general interests of the reunited church; Negro congregations,
presbyteries, and synods to be continued as they were, except where
they might be combined. "While commending to all of its members
devoted loyalty to the Nation and maintaining its duty of moral
leadership," it was stated, "the reunited Church will continue to recognize the principle of the separation of Church and State, as first

announced by the General Synod of the Church in 1729, and should maintain the spiritual character of the Church as separated from the kingdom of this world and having no other head than the Lord Jesus Christ."[30]

After pointing out the lines on which further exploration needed to be made, the committee asked for the instructions of the General Assembly as to whether it should carry on its exploration along the foregoing lines.

The Assembly refused to give the requested instructions but, instead, referred the whole report to the presbyteries without expression of opinion, asking that before the next General Assembly each of the presbyteries give its advice as to the whole question of union.

In response 29 presbyteries asked that the permanent committee be dismissed; ten that it be continued as a committee of cooperation only; 45, a majority of all the presbyteries, desired a continuation of the permanent committee as it was. Sentiment for continuation of the committee prevailed in the border synods, in the western synods, in some of the weakest and in the three of the strongest synods—North Carolina, Virginia, and Texas—altogether in 11 out of the 17 synods. Sentiment against continuation of union negotiations prevailed in the synods of Appalachia, Florida, Georgia, Mississippi, and South Carolina. In this vote, the first time that a majority of the presbyteries had approved the continuation of union negotiations, there was a clear indication of the massive shift in sentiment which within a few years had occurred in the Assembly, and of which the action of the "young ministers' Assembly" of 1929 had been an anticipation.

In the light of the presbyteries' vote the Standing Committee recommended unanimously that the Committee on Cooperation and Union be continued with two purposes: (1) to stress cooperation with other Presbyterian bodies, and (2) to continue to explore suitable ways and means of bringing into one body all branches of the Presbyterian family. Dr. B. R. Lacy, chairman of the committee, explained that the recommendations looked first to cooperation and later, if the way be clear, to union. It was recognized by all that the requisite vote for union (three-fourths of the presbyteries) was then not available.

Proponents of union accepted an amendment offered by opponents which instructed the committee "to safeguard the purity of doctrine, the properties of the church and endowments, the theological seminaries and other educational institutions, the administration of home missions, the direction of Foreign Missions supported by the respective synods, and the content of Sunday School literature, so that the synods, whether as present constituted or enlarged, will be the final authority in such matters."[31]

The resolution as thus amended was adopted by an overwhelming vote of the Assembly.

Dr. T. W. Currie, President of Austin Theological Seminary and Chairman of the Permanent Committee, explained to the following Assembly that the committee was proceeding cautiously with no thought of immediate union and that the Northern committee had been informed that no union could be consummated unless the Southern Church could be assured regarding the maintenance of doctrinal soundness, the safeguarding of property rights, and other matters. From the U.S.A. Assembly came a telegram expressing the hope that the two great branches of the Presbyterian Church might once more be organically united and reaffirming the fidelity of the church and its officers to its doctrinal standards. The Southern Assembly voted overwhelmingly with only a few scattered negatives to continue its committee and returned a telegram asking for "God's blessing upon the efforts of the joint committee to find a way for the organic union of our two churches." It adopted a resolution instructing the Executive Committees Home Missions, Foreign Missions, Christian Education, and Religious Education and Publication to confer with their counterparts in the U.S.A. Church regarding ways in which the missionary and educational work of the church could be more effectively coordinated and "where possible unified."[32]

In 1943 the Permanent Committee presented the first draft of a proposed plan of union drawn up by subcommittees representing the two churches. The following year the General Assembly requested its committee to seek for ways of bringing into one body all branches of the Presbyterian family, with specific reference to the Associate Reformed and United Presbyterian bodies, while continuing its consideration of union with the U.S.A. Church.

The next year a group of reunion opponents, backers of the *Presbyterian Journal,* drew up a statement calling for early submission of the proposed plan of reunion and appointing a continuing committee to project a vigorous campaign throughout the church in opposition to reunion. The tide toward union, as they recognized, was now rising rapidly, and some leaders of the opposition acknowledged that ultimate reunion was inevitable. Their purpose, it was frankly avowed, was to do everything possible to develop a continuing church and to secure for it as many of the tangible assets of the present church as was possible.[33]

A number of efforts had been made and continued to be made to amend the Book of Church Order so that in case of union churches might withdraw with their property intact. Decisions of the civil courts, following the Walnut Street Case of 1867, had regularly held that in cases of secession the true congregation retaining possession of the property was that group, whether a majority or a minority of the original congregation, which remained in the denominational structure. In 1932, after the first proposal emanating from the General Assembly to explore the possibilities of union had been beaten back, an amendment to the Book of Church Order was sent down to the presbyteries designed to permit one-fourth of a congregation (and so of a presbytery or synod) to withdraw in case of union with the whole or its property. The amendment was rejected by vote of the presbyteries 51 to 38.

Six years later, after negotiations regarding union had been resumed, the Assembly approved a seemingly innocuous amendment which it later became clear would have permitted a majority of a congregation to withdraw from the denomination with its property. After the disruptive effects of this amendment had been pointed out, the amendment was overwhelmingly rejected by vote of the presbyteries.

In 1942 the General Assembly rejected another effort to amend the Book of Church Order with the same end in view. Another such amendment came before the 1946 General Assembly. This Assembly approved with only a few scattered noes the report of the Permanent Committee on Cooperation and Union expressing its purpose and intention to present the revised and completed plan of union to the following Assembly—also a proposal to invite the United Presbyterian Church to enter the union discussions. The Assembly revealed itself as once again unwilling to amend its Book of Church Order in regard to the ownership of property; the Permanent Committee on Cooperation and Union, however, was asked to consider ways in which property rights of congregations wishing to remain out of the union might be recognized in the plan of union.[34]

A postcard poll sent out this year to all ministers in the church, to students in the four seminaries, and to hundreds of elders (1,901 replies being received out of a possible 3,500) revealed that 34 percent of the respondents favored union as soon as practicable, 34 percent favored reunion, but not while there was any considerable protesting minority; 29 percent remained unalterably opposed.[35]

The 1947 General Assembly voted unanimously to send the tentative plan of union submitted by the Permanent Committee on Cooperation and Union down to the presbyteries for their additional suggestions. The plan, extensively revised, in the light of numerous suggestions, carried with it a provision which would permit three-fourths of a congregation voting not to go into the reunited church to withdraw with its property within a year after the union was consummated.

In August of this year the Continuing Church Committee adopted a campaign budget of $25,000, including provision for a field secretary's salary and expense, and laid their plans for an intensive effort in the next nine months in opposition to Southern Presbyterian membership in the Federal Council of Churches (which question the General Assembly had submitted to a vote of the presbyteries) and the reunion of American Presbyterianism. The 1948 Assembly, it was clear, would be a crucial one, providing a clear test of strength between the two opposing points of view. The presbyteries this year by a substantial majority expressed themselves as being in favor of remaining within the Federal Council of Churches, and the General Assembly by a large majority sustained this position. It was clear that approximately the same majority would vote in favor of the plan of reunion. The vote of the presbyteries on the Federal Council suggested, however, that it would not be possible to secure the three-fourths vote required for reunion.

The recommendation of the Permanent Committee on Cooperation and Union was that the revised plan of union be received by the General Assembly and placed upon the docket of the 1949 Assembly, and that meanwhile the Permanent Committee be permitted to make further revisions in the plan as might seem desirable. The majority of the standing committee, favoring ultimate reunion, recommended an affirmative answer to this request. The minority of the committee, favoring rejection, recommended that it be sent down at once to the presbyteries for their vote. Ruling Elder L. Nelson Bell, a leading opponent of union, offered as a substitute that the question of union with the U.S.A. Church be held in abeyance for a period of five years. He urged adoption as a step toward stopping controversy and centering efforts on the great forward work of the church. Debate on this substitute was interrupted by the order of the day, the daily devotional service.

In the interim, friends of union, recognizing that favorable action by three-fourths of the presbyteries could not at the time be secured and confident that time worked in their favor, prepared their own motion which read: "That for a period of five years the entire plan of reunion with the Presbyterian Church U.S.A. be held in abeyance, and that during this time the committee confine its activities to exploring avenues of acquaintance and cooperation only, except that the committee shall complete the plan by March 1, 1949, and have the same printed in sufficient number to supply any request."[36]

This alternative proposal of the friends of reunion was accepted by Dr. Bell and others opposed, and also by Dr. Dunbar Ogden, chairman of the permanent committee. When the motion, thus supported, was put, it was adopted unanimously by the Assembly, whereupon the Assembly arose and sang the doxology. Dr. Nelson Bell then announced that there would be no meeting of the Continuing Church Committee for the next five years. It seemed for a moment as though an era of good feeling might be at hand.

Unfortunately, as soon became clear, the substitute motion, as adopted, was understood differently by the two parties. Friends of union had prepared the motion and supported it because it allowed the permanent committee during the so-called moratorium "to explore avenues of acquaintance and cooperation." To hold the plan of union in abeyance while this procedure was followed, thus creating a more favorable climate for the ultimate vote, had been the policy advocated for some time by the *Presbyterian Outlook*. Opponents of reunion, however, interpreted the motion in the light of their own original substitute. They assumed that there would be no steps either toward union or toward further cooperation and acquaintance.[37]

When the permanent committee in midwinter made public its report to the forthcoming General Assembly, recommending more than 20 "avenues of acquaintance and cooperation," there was an immediate outcry. Two members of the committee (out of 17) issued a minority report declaring that the proposed program would be "an all-out program of intensive cultivation and fraternization between the two denominations" and "open the door for immediate resumption of agitation with the whole question of union . . . on an intensified basis."[38]

An amendment which would have put aside the proposed program of cooperation, thus accepting the minority's interpretation of the moratorium, was defeated by a vote of 237 to 70, after which the main motion to adopt the program was passed by an even larger vote. The opponents of reunion now felt that they were free to campaign openly against the plan of reunion, which the friends of reunion had not expected to advocate, explain, or urge for the next five years.[39] The General Assembly, meanwhile, had enlarged the scope of the permanent committee, authorizing and instructing it to take advantage of the present five-year period when the plan of union was held in abeyance to explore avenues of acquaintance and cooperation, not only with the U.S.A. Church, but also with the ARP, the UP, the Reformed Church in America, and the Cumberland Presbyterian Church. The committee was instructed to extend invitations to these bodies, and to seek a basis for promoting the larger objective for which the committee was originally constituted: "To bring into one body all members of the Presbyterian family."[40]

One month after the 1949 Assembly meeting, opponents of reunion met in Montreat, declaring that the first matter of business was to reactivate the Continuing Church Committee. Once again the threat of a secession in case of reunion was raised.[41]

To prepare for such an eventuality, new efforts were made to obviate the well-established ruling of the civil courts which made it impossible for members of a local congregation to withdraw from the church along with its property, this time by changes in the charter of local churches. Matters were brought to a head when Atlanta Presbytery asked the General Assembly for counsel and advice regarding the action of one of its churches (Westminster) in changing its charter so as to give the congregation possession of its property "without any right, title, interest or estate, legal or equitable, existing in favor of any denomination, presbytery or other ecclesiastical body whatever."[42] The presbytery was advised to direct the church to take such action as may be required to have its charter altered so as to conform to the requirements of the Book of Church Order. The incident led to efforts to define more exactly the ownership of property by a local church which culminated in the adoption of a declaratory statement which read in part: "A beneficial ownership for the property of a particular church in the Presbyterian Church in the United States is in the congregation . . . the congregation, with respect to such property, may properly exercise any privilege of ownership possessed by property owners in such jurisdiction . . . Disposition of the property of a particular church rests in the will of the congregation of that church. The congregation is that body of persons recognized as members of that particular church by the respective courts of the church."[43]

To the 1951 General Assembly came a moving statement drawn up by Harrison Ray Anderson, Moderator, and approved by the U.S.A. General Assembly expressing regret and asking forgiveness for words spoken, articles written, charges made, and resolutions adopted in 1861 and later which had been unworthy of the Savior and which had wounded their Southern brethren. The Southern Assembly replied in the same spirit of forgiveness and reconciliation, all but a few rising for the standing vote.[44] What was usually one of the liveliest reports before the General Assembly—the report of the

Interchurch Relations Committee, occasioned this year only a minimum of discussion. The full list of recommended avenues of cooperation and acquaintance proposed by the Permanent Committee was approved. "No one in the Assembly," reported the *Presbyterian Outlook*, "could fail to sense what seemed to be the tides of the Spirit moving on toward the Presbyterian reunion which has been the object of countless prayers for generations."[45]

Entrance of the United Presbyterian Church into the negotiations this same year seemed to increase the possibility of ultimate success. The Southern Church had been ready to unite with this body in 1929 and a threeway union of U.S.A., U. S. and U.P. Churches seemed definitely more appealing than the former two-way union. Committees of the three churches which met in the spring of 1952 to draw up plans for union departed from the meeting optimistic for the future.[46]

Issues relating to union were to the fore in the 1952 Assembly. New recommendations for "acquaintance and cooperation" were adopted by a top-heavy vote, as were new comity proposals and the plans for a joint Presbyterian hymnal. The Permanent Committee was instructed to complete a plan of union and to make such recommendations regarding it to the 1953 General Assembly as the committee might deem wise.

Meanwhile, representatives of three unofficial groups within the church announced plans for a central office to fight the proposed merger. These groups were the Board of Directors of the *Southern Presbyterian Journal*; the Executive Board of the Continuing Church Committee; and a recently organized group centering in Memphis, Tennessee, calling itself the Association for the Preservation of the Southern Presbyterian Church. At a subsequent meeting of representatives of these various groups in Weaverville, North Carolina (the home of the *Southern Presbyterian Journal*), a campaign was projected and a $35,000 budget was accepted. A traveling agent was employed, and efforts were made to organize the opponents of union, especially the elders, presbytery by presbytery, and church by church.

Early in January the broadened plan for Presbyterian union began to be distributed throughout the three denominations.[47] The new plan, like the old one, permitted local congregations (in the U. S. and U.P. Churches) to withdraw with their property by a three-fourths vote within a year following the final approval of the plan of union.

The barrage of propaganda led many to fear that the Assembly of 1953 would prove to be a stormy one. The Standing Committee, however, brought in a resolution supported by both proponents and

opponents of union providing that the plan of union be received
and transmitted to the presbyteries and, as revised in the light of
further study, be docketed for consideration by the 1954 General
Assembly. The recommendations were approved unanimously without debate. The tension had been great, and now "the Assembly
stood and with tears in many eyes and voices breaking now and then
the commissioners and visitors sang together, 'Praise God from Whom
all blessings flow.' Many agreed with the Moderator when he stated,
'The fears of a split within the church have been much reduced.' "[48]
Hopes that a serious split might be averted even if union was approved
were increased in the following months when some of the leading
opponents of union indicated their intention of remaining in the
church whatever the outcome.

Threats of a continuing Presbyterian Church in case of reunion
continued, however, and the debate, carried on now for more than a
decade, increased in intensity—with the negative supported by articles
in the *Southern Presbyterian Journal* and by numerous pamphlets
issued by the Continuing Church Committee, and the affirmative
supported by articles in the *Presbyterian Outlook* and by pamphlets
issued under the auspices of the Sponsoring Committee for Presbyterian Union. There were articles pro and con in the *Christian Observer,* and formal debates in a number of centers by selected
champions of the two points of view.

The arguments against union iterated and reiterated over the 17-
year period when the topic was before the church may be grouped
under seven heads. First, regarding doctrine. Many, if not most, opponents of union gave first place to the supposed declension from the
faith on the part of the Northern Church, chief evidence for which
was found in the Auburn Affirmation, which had been signed by
more than 1,000 ministers and elders in the 1920's. Dr. W. C. Robinson defined the issue very simply: "Shall we stand . . . for the faith or
shall we surrender our corporate testimony by uniting with Auburn
Affirmationists in a body that does not regard such matters as the
Virgin Birth, the substitutionary atonement and the resurrection of
Christ as essential to ministerial ordination?"[49]

Second, regarding polity. Opponents charged that power was too
greatly centralized in the Northern Church, also they charged that
elders were downgraded, because (in accordance with the general
Reformed Church practice) they did not participate in the ordination
of ministers; the deacons likewise, because in the Northern body
the care of financial affairs was frequently put in the hands of trustees.

There was also objection to the ordination of women as elders and deacons as permitted in the Northern Church.

Third, regarding the "spirituality" of the church—the unwillingness of the Northern Church "to abstain from interference in matters purely of civil or political concern." "It may startle some of us to be informed that the Presbyterian Church U.S.A. . . . has given strong support and backing to every one of the controversial items called for in Mr. Truman's message on civil rights," declared Rev. James E. Cousar, D.D.[50]

Fourth, in regard to race. "We remind you of our situation in the South in regard to the race question," wrote prominent elders in an open letter to their fellow elders in the Presbyterian Church of the United States. "We must keep our hands free to settle it as our judgment here on the ground deems wise and best and right."[51]

Fifth, the "common sense" argument. Ruling Elder Kenneth Keyes, one of the most vigorous opponents among the laymen, developed charts which purported to show that the U.S.A. Church in recent years had regularly fallen below the U. S. Church in membership growth, Sunday school enrollment, and per capita gifts. To unite with the Northern Church under these circumstances, he argued, would not be in accord with sound business practices, especially since the Southern Church would become a minority stockholder in the merged operations (all of which led the *Presbyterian Outlook* to point out that the same logic would point to the liquidation of some of the weaker synods in the Southern Church, for example, Missouri, Mississippi, and Alabama).[52] A number of others played on variations of this theme.

Sixth, the property issue. In case of merger, it was claimed, the property of the local congregation would be endangered; in other words, there would be less opportunity for a local church to withdraw with its property from the denomination.

Seventh, a loss of identity. The Southern Church, with its noble heritage and distinctive principle (the spirituality of the church), would be submerged by the larger church, so it was claimed. Dr. George Summey made an extreme statement of this position when he charged, "Our church would be simply swallowed up, our principles buried, our testimony discounted and made ridiculous, our ministers and even courts disqualified by *ipso facto* methods without judicial procedure, our property become the property of the Assembly at the top of the system, the rights and properties of minorities ignored."[53]

Proponents of union countered these arguments, and developed in a variety of ways the case for union. Leading arguments were that

(1) union would help to answer the Lord's prayer "that they all may be one . . . that the world may believe . . ." (2) That Presbyterians North and South were one people, with a common heritage (for 150 years an undivided church), a common organization (only minor differences), a common doctrine (the same Standards, and no greater latitude of belief in the North than in the South), and a common worship; with a constant passage of members from one church to the other. (3) Union would enable the church to bear a broader witness (at home and abroad) and a more effective ministry. (4) It would enable the church to carry on the Lord's work with greater economy, with less duplication and waste, in an age when funds were always insufficient, when therefore waste became more and more inexcusable. The situation in the border states, with its extensive overlapping, was given as a case in point.

As time drew near for the decisive 1954 General Assembly, it became clear that most of the recognized leaders of the church were backing the union movement. It was noted, for example, that for 16 years the Committee on Cooperation and Union had been composed of representatives elected by their respective synods, one man from each, with the issues fully recognized by all. During this time they had consistently voted 15 to 2 in favor of union.[54] A straw poll taken by the *Presbyterian Outlook* prior to the 1954 Assembly revealed for union: former Moderators of the Assembly, 8 to 1; college presidents, 11 to 4; seminary and Assembly's Training School Presbyterians, 4 to 0; seminary faculty members, 27 to 0; Board and division secretaries, 18 to 1; presidents of the Synods' Men of the Church 8 to 7; presidents of the Synods' Westminster Fellowship, 12 to 1; past presidents of Assembly's Men's Council 3 to 0; Regional Directors of Christian Education, 8 to 0.[55] The Assembly's Youth Council expressed themselves in favor of union by a vote of 33 to 2.[56] Polls conducted in the Presbyterian theological seminaries and the Assembly's Training School revealed that the future leaders of the church favored union by a preponderance of more than six to one.[57]

A pre-Assembly poll (cards being sent to all ministers and all clerks of sessions) showed 49 presbyteries favoring union and 35 opposed; the ministers voted for union by a majority of 1,145 to 499; the clerks of sessions against union by a majority of 949 to 556.[58]

Union strength was particularly strong in the border states. The Synod of Kentucky adopted resolutions which it directed should be sent to every presbytery in the General Assembly, pointing out that cooperation, carried out in almost every area of the church's life, did not solve the problem of overlapping. "We feel most keenly," declared the synod, "that we are paying far too high a price, in time, energy, property and money in needless duplications. We desperately need the efficiency of union to do a better kingdom work."[59]

This same year the Synod of Missouri by a vote of 65 to 4 adopted an open letter, which stated, "In Missouri we are poignantly aware of the sad results of duplicating our efforts and doing inequitably what could be done with great effectiveness if we were united . . . Our plea to you is urgent . . . Help us to be one with these our brothers who also witness for Christ."[60]

The Synod of Texas heard "with sympathy, concern and understanding" the message of its sister synods and added: "We in Texas earnestly desire, desperately need, and humbly urge that we Presbyterians become one in concrete reality as already are in heart."[61] The vote for this statement was 270 to 31.

Anti-unionists, recognizing that ministers were more strongly committed to union than the elders, addressed their arguments largely to the latter, often in ways inclined to set the elders against their ministers. The charge had been openly made on the floor of the 1947 Assembly that ministers had sold the elders down the river. Chalmers W. Alexander, a ruling elder from Mississippi, defended the remark, declaring that it was a statement of plain fact. "It has been remarked," he said, "that such statements as these tend to drive a wedge between the ministers and the laymen. Such a remark I do not believe to be true . . . If a wedge has been driven, it has not been driven between the ministers as a whole and the laymen, but rather only between a small organized group of influential ministers and the large body of laymen of our denomination."[62]

The Assembly, however, had grown in grace. According to the interdenominational *Christian Century* the debate in the 1954 Assembly over the question as to whether or not the plan of union should be approved and sent to the presbyteries for their advice and consent had had "few equals and no superiors in recent American history. In relevancy and cogency of argument, and sensitivity to the historic importance of the issue being decided, in loftiness of spirit, it measured up to the highest Christian standard. Presbyterians can never forget this momentous Assembly, and they will recall it more thankfully because its public discussion was not marred by a single imputation of bad faith or one bitter personal reference."[63]

The vote to approve the plan of union and submit it to the presbyteries was decisive, 283 to 169, but not large enough to give more than a slight hope for the required three-fourths vote of the presbyteries.

Opponents of reunion now redoubled their efforts. The 13th

annual meeting of the groups opposed to Presbyterian union—now termed "The Association for the Preservation and Continuation of the Southern Presbyterian Church"—reported 600 persons present, representing 48 of the 50 presbyteries in 17 states.[64]

In a communication sent out to party workers from Reidsville, North Carolina, party workers were advised to concentrate on the elders, organize presbytery committees, subdivide into districts for every-elder solicitation, try to get anti-union majorities from the churches into the fall and winter meetings of presbytery, send the *Southern Presbyterian Journal* to every elder, and finally to treat the whole matter as a spiritual crusade.[65]

Advocates of union had realized from the start that it would not be easy to get a favorable vote from three-fourths of the presbyteries. The five-year moratorium, which leaders of the U.S.A. Church found it hard to understand, had been arranged because the tide toward union was running strong, increasing each year through the new batch of ministers coming in from the seminaries. For a time it seemed to be a wise strategy. What could not be foreseen was the fact that, only a few months before the 1954 General Assembly met, the Supreme Court of the United States would give out its decision outlawing segregation in the public schools. The reaction of the South to this decision was quick—massive resistance became the keyword, and rationality was submerged in a wave of emotionalism. The issue was not often raised in the continuing debates on reunion, but there can be little doubt but that it influenced the final vote. It is doubtful if a three-fourths vote for union could have been secured at any time. But the fact that the final vote stood 43 opposed to 42 in favor—in light of the favorable vote cast by 17 successive Assemblies—would indicate that a new factor had come into the situation, and that it was the race issue which proved to be the decisive one.

This conclusion is supported by a research project carried on under the auspices of the Laboratory of Social Relations of Harvard University. Two distinct methods were employed in studying the Southern Presbyterian rejection of the proposed union. The first, a content analysis of 40 published documents opposing union, most of it published under the aegis of the Association for the Preservation and Continuation of the Southern Presbyterian Church or by the *Southern Presbyterian Journal,* suggested that doctrinal differences were basic and current social issues of minor importance. The second approach, however, an ecological analysis of the vote by presbyteries, led to the conclusion that the segregation controversy was the major source of the opposition vote. This conclusion was strengthened by personal interviews carried out by the authors of the study. Various members of the Joint Committee were convinced that the segregation issue was the major obstacle in the attempt to negotiate a merger. No member of the committee expressed a contrary view.[66]

As soon as it became apparent that the union proposal would not carry, steps were taken to heal the scars of conflict. Twenty-five or more presbyteries sent overtures on the subject to the 1955 General Assembly.

A large Standing Committee on Interchurch Relations worked many hours to adjust the many differences on the subject and finally brought in a unanimous report, which recommended:

1. The dissolution of the Permanent Committee on Cooperation and Union, with the Assembly's thanks.

2. An expression of appreciation to the General Assemblies of the U.S.A. and the United Presbyterian Churches for their response to the invitation of our Assembly and for their willingness to enter into a union with our church.

3. A directive that the two Assemblies be informed that the rejection of the plan of union was not to be interpreted as a lack of confidence in their churches, but was due "to the conviction of a constitutional majority of our presbyteries that the interests of Christ could best be served by the continued existence of the Presbyterian Church US as an independent body."

Hope was expressed that the cooperative effort between the three bodies which had developed through the years might be continued and extended.

In place of the Permanent Committee on Cooperation and Union there was created a Permanent Committee on Interchurch Relations composed predominantly of representatives nominated by the various synods. This committee was to consider and report on relations with all other denominations and interdenominational agencies.[67]

For the next few years, the church, as the South generally, was largely concerned with problems created by the racial revolution in the South. It was not a time to raise again the question of union with the Northern Church. The church had spoken, and there was no hope of obtaining a reversal so long as emotions remained so deeply stirred. Then, too, some of those who had borne the heat of the day had grown weary of conflict, and were opposed to any steps that would endanger the peace of the church. Further obstacles arose when the United Presbyterian Church in the U.S.A. (resulting from the merger of the U.S.A. and U.P. Churches) entered into the Consultation on Church Union looking toward ultimate union with a number of denominations including the Protestant Episcopal, the Methodist, and the United Church of Christ. Still another obstacle came when the negotiations on union suddenly arose between the PCUS and the Reformed Church in America (originally the Dutch Reformed Church). There had been talk of union between these two churches back in 1874, but discussions ended when both denominations became members of the World Alliance of Reformed Churches, which was formed that year. Proponents felt the WARC would fulfill most of the aims of a cooperative alliance.

In more recent years the two churches had worked together for more than a decade in close cooperation in the field of Christian Education, especially in the development of the Covenant Life Curriculum.

The Reformed Church's General Synod in 1961 received several overtures asking for union conversations with the Presbyterian Church in the U.S.A. or with the Presbyterian Church in the U. S.

After meeting with representatives of both denominations an R.C.A. subcommittee recommended that the full Executive Committee meet with the Presbyterian U. S. Committee on Interchurch Relations "for the purpose of discussing the possibility of closer cooperative relationships." Out of this conference came a joint resolution adopted without dissent in 1962 by the two ranking judicatories which affirmed "the common purpose of the two churches, as branches of the holy catholic Church, to seek together a fuller expression of unity in faith and action . . ."

Responsibility for conducting further exploration of the possible relations between these two churches was put in the hands of a Joint Committee of Twenty-Four. In reporting to the judicatories in 1963 the committee noted "a broad meeting-ground in theology and church government," and the courts again affirmed "readiness to be led into whatever forms of church life and work are revealed as God's will for us." The following year, having found "no major differences" in the areas of theology, polity, and worship, the two judicatories officially affirmed that "we envision the union of our two churches," and the next year the same courts authorized the drafting of a plan of union.

Union negotiations with the R.C.A. Church, in marked distinction from those with the UPUSA Church, proceeded—with little open discussion and with no expressed opposition—until terms for the final vote. The R.C.A., one-fourth the size of the U. S. body, had churches in every state of the Union outside of the South (there was no overlapping to speak of) but real strength only in the New York–New Jersey, and Michigan–Iowa areas. The two denominations united would become in some sense, a national church, though in most states outside the

South its strength would remain very small. The question which haunted many of the ecumenists in the Southern Church was the bearing of the R.C.A. union on the ultimate union with the UPUSA Church, which in their judgment must remain the major goal.

Pressure for renewed negotiations with this latter church was again building up. It came especially, as it had for the previous half-century, from presbyteries and synods where the two churches found themselves in competition and where increasing cooperation led to a desire for the larger fruits of real union, and from a younger generation of ministers and laymen who recognized no ground for remaining apart.

One attempt to relieve tensions in the border synods had been the establishment of a number of union or federated churches. The General Assembly of 1957, agreed with a joint committee appointed to work out procedures that it was better that such churches become identified with one denomination or another, and approved arrangements whereby constitutionally this might be done (revised in 1962). Recognizing that not all uniting congregations saw their way clear to choose between denominations, the 1959 General Assembly proposed and the 1960 General Assembly approved an amendment to the Book of Church Order which provided for union churches, whose ministers should be members of both presbyteries of jurisdiction and whose benevolences were to be divided equally between the two Assemblies.[68]

The church was now preparing to celebrate the centenary of its birth—an event which excited little enthusiasm. Too many asked: why celebrate a divorce? With the coming celebration in mind the 1960 Assembly adopted resolutions which reopened the whole question of closer relations. It read:

> In this 100th year of the organization of our church and with the approaching centennial celebration of its founding, we are saddened that the division which came to our American Presbyterian family with a divided nation 100 years ago has not been healed even though the nation has long since been made one.
>
> We reaffirm the hope and prayer often expressed by previous Assemblies for the greatest possible unity in our Presbyterian family.
>
> We commend and encourage congregations, presbyteries, synods and agencies at all levels that are finding appropriate ways and means to increase Presbyterian cooperation and united efforts in their respective areas.
>
> At the Assembly level the Committee on Inter-church Relations is instructed to confer with the corresponding body in the United Presbyterian Church in the U.S.A. and other Presbyterian bodies as to ways in which present tensions, where they exist, may be eased, where coop-

eration may be extended and made more fruitful, and to arrange, where
advisable, for meetings of representation of our boards and agencies for
further exploration of ways and means of a greater united effort.[69]

Two years later identical overtures from three Missouri presbyteries
requested the Assembly to take the initiative in aiding synods and
presbyteries with the problems of church relationships, which in their
case, it was said, were becoming increasingly acute. The General
Assembly in response instructed its Permanent Committee to enter
into conversations with its U.S.A. counterpart "so that a common
approach to problems may be developed and possible solutions proposed . . ."

In 1960 one overture looking toward the resumption of union
negotiations was received, the first since the collapse of the 17-year
effort six years earlier. Each year thereafter there were overtures looking toward the same objective, in some years as many as nine to ten,
including overtures from the synods of Virginia, West Virginia,
Missouri, Kentucky, and Texas.

In 1961 and 1962 these overtures and a comparable invitation
from UPUSA were declined on the ground that the latter was engaged
in a consultation looking toward possible merger with churches of
different dogma and polity and that "only the most limited benefits
could be expected at this time from any explorations dedicated to
devising a plan of union with the UPUSA Church."[70]

In 1963 the Assembly responded by instructing its Permanent
Committee to continue its conversations with the UPUSA and other
Presbyterian and Reformed bodies toward reaching an understanding
of the similarities and differences of the several churches in order
that the Presbyterian Church U. S. might better equip itself for negotiations toward union with any or all churches committed to the Reformed
faith.[71]

It also expressed the conviction that ultimately the Presbyterian
and Reformed communions in the United States should present a
united life and witness according to the Reformed faith and Presbyterian order.[72]

In 1966 the Presbytery of Central Texas dispatched a long overture to the General Assembly in which it emphasized the value of
the cooperative work carried on between it and the U.S.A. Presbytery
of Brazos (occupying the same territory) and then went on to add:

> Whereas, conditions similar to this, where two denominational
> branches of Presbyterianism overlap, are prevalent in other areas of our
> denominations where the division of presbyterial oversight and jurisdic-
> tion over neighboring congregations and communities is frequently con-

fusing to our people and the general public, often detrimental to good order, likely to divide the Reformed witness, and certainly conducive to competitive and wasteful administrative, plenary and financial effort at the local level unless extreme care in communication and planning is exercised; and

Whereas the experience of these aforementioned presbyteries over the period of the past six years in undertaking joint administrative and financial adventures, notably in Christian Education and Church Extension, and in dealing with problems of overlapping work, have been successful and profitable . . .

Therefore, it was requested, that a new chapter be added to the Book of Church Order permitting the erection of union presbyteries with the Presbyterian Church U.S.A. or the Reformed Church in America along the same general lines as the chapter providing for the establishment of union churches.[73]

Similar overtures came from presbyteries in Kentucky and Missouri requesting that provision be made not only for union presbyteries but also union synods. The overtures, according to the rules of the Assembly, were referred to the Permanent Judicial Commission for study and report to the 1967 Assembly. Quite evidently new pressure was building up for some relief for the problems of the border synod.

The 1966 General Assembly had before it for immediate consideration a communication for the UPUSA Assembly reaffirming the "yearning" of that body "for a united Reformed and Presbyterian family" and proposing the establishment of a panel to objectively analyze the problems in such an undertaking. Support for this proposal came from ten overtures, four of which came from the synods of Kentucky, Missouri, Texas, and West Virginia. The Assembly in response directed its Permanent Committee "to explore intensely and thoroughly the problems and possibilities of our future relationships and report the status of exploration to the next Assembly." The Reformed Church in America was invited to participate in such explorations.[74]

The most surprising action of this Assembly was adoption by a large majority of a resolution, offered by a group of commissioners on the opening day of the Assembly, expressing the Assembly's desire to become a full participant in the Consultation on Church Union and authorizing the appointment of appropriate representatives to the Consultation. Previous overtures to this effect had been declined on the questionable ground that constitutional provisions forbade negotiations regarding organic union with churches not conforming to Presbyterian doctrine and order. The Assembly had, however, approved the attendance of Southern Presbyterian observers. Par-

ticipating in the Consultation, whose goal was a church truly reformed, truly evangelical, and truly catholic, were official representatives of the United Presbyterian Church in the U.S.A., the Methodist
Church, the Protestant Episcopal Church, the United Church of
Christ, and others.

The size of the favorable vote for full participation in the Consultation surprised even its advocates. Was this a freak Assembly,
not representative of the church at large, or had there been again a
silent but massive change of sentiment in the church? The fact that
five synods, meeting shortly thereafter, approved the Assembly's action;
four of these, including the three largest synods in the church (North
Carolina, Texas, and Virginia) by unanimous or near-unanimous
votes, suggested that it was the latter. It certainly did not mean,
however, that three-fourths of the presbyteries were prepared to vote
for any union proposal that might grow out of the Consultation.

The action proved very upsetting to the anti-ecumenical forces in
the church. The Concerned Presbyterians, successor body to the
old Continuing Church Committee of the 1940's, which had since
undergone several changes of names, were stirred to even more intensive action. Wealthy laymen busied themselves as aforetime to
organize laymen in every congregation and in every presbytery to
oppose not only COCU but the National Council of Churches and
the church's growing concern with social issues.

The *Presbyterian Journal*, giving open support to the Concerned
Presbyterians and serving as its editorial voice, took the COCU
decision as the final evidence that no reconciliation of the opposing
factions in the church was possible. Ultimate separation, the editor
reiterated over and over again, was inevitable—and to be welcomed.
Withdrawal of individuals and of local congregations was opposed
on the grounds that this meant fragmentation of upholders of the old
faith. The hope—the goal—was a continuing Southern Presbyterian
Church with its property intact, or a union of the conservative Reformed and Presbyterians drawn together from the various denominations, but without the loss of their property which would inevitably
follow open secession.

The 1967 General Assembly declined by a decisive vote to withdraw from COCU, indicating that its decision to remain in the Consultation was a firm one. This General Assembly also approved in
principle a proposal for union presbyteries and synods with other
Reformed and Presbyterian churches—a proposal which had strong
backing in the Western portion of the church, where competition

between Presbyterian bodies constituted a more serious problem than in the East. A properly drawn amendment to the Book of Church Order permitting such union judicatories was approved the following year by a sizable majority and sent down to the presbyteries for their advice and consent. Sent down also was the final draft of a plan for union with the R.C.A. There was opposition to this union on the part of some ecumenists, who felt that it was a backward step and from some anti-ecumenists who feared that it opened the door to still wider union, but little concerted opposition from either wing of the church—the vote to approve the Union in the General Assembly was well-nigh unanimous.

The Concerned Presbyterians, meanwhile, with larger financial backing and a paid staff, were extending their organization into every presbytery, and as far as possible into every congregation, bending their energies above all to defeat the proposal for union presbyteries and synods. Approval of this "backdoor" approach to union with the United Presbyterian Church in the U.S.A., they warned again, would lead to the inevitable split in the church, as would entrance into union with any new church growing out of COCU. The R.C.A. union was acceptable because of the "escape clause," which permitted local congregations to withdraw from their denomination with their property within a year after this or any subsequent union.

The threat of division proved no deterrent. A constitutional change permitting the formation of union presbyteries (but not union synods) was approved by a large majority of the presbyteries and enacted into law by the 1969 General Assembly. R.C.A. union was approved by the requisite three-fourths vote of the presbyteries; it failed, however, to secure the necessary two-thirds vote of the R.C.A. classes. Ecumenists in the Southern Church who had labored for this cause regretted this negative outcome of their efforts, but rejoiced that so many of their own presbyteries had been willing to enter a union that would take their branch of the church beyond the South into the nation as a whole. The General Assembly this year, in line with tendencies which had grown stronger through the years, reaffirmed the denomination's full participation in the Consultation on Church Union (whose committee appointed to draft the plan of union was now chaired by Rev. William A. Benfield, D.D., pastor of the First Church, Charleston, West Virginia) and instructed its Moderator (Rev. Matthew Lynn, D.D., of Midland, Texas) to appoint a committee to open immediate negotiations for union with the United Presbyterian Church in the U.S.A.

The formation of additional union presbyteries with UPUSA

(particularly in the Western synods), increased cooperation with this and other denominations on all levels of the church's life, and consideration of organic union with its sister denomination and with any larger body emerging from COCU were in prospect as the Presbyterian Church in the U. S. came into the 1970's. It had entered and was moving ever more fully into the mainstream of the nation's religious life. Opposition, meanwhile, had intensified, and there were organized bodies anticipating, some of them committed to, a final division of the church.

Notes and Acknowledgments

Notes and Acknowledgments

ABBREVIATIONS

I. The "New" South

1. John Samuel Ezell, *The South Since 1865* (New York: Macmillan and Co., 1963), p. 118.
2. Material in this section has been revised and adapted from E. T. Thompson, *The Changing South* (Richmond, Va.: John Knox Press, 1950), chapter 7.
3. Rupert B. Vance, *Human Geography of the South: A Study in Regional Resources and Human Geography* (Chapel Hill, N. C.: The University of North Carolina Press, 1932), p. 275.
4. Francis Butler Simkins, *The South: Old and New* (New York: Alfred A. Knopf, 1947), p. 240.
5. Benjamin Burk Kendrick and Alexander Matthews Arnett, *The South Looks at its Past* (Chapel Hill: The University of North Carolina Press, 1936), p. 127.
6. Ezell, *op. cit.*, p. 148.
7. SWP (July 30, 1896), p. 4.
8. Simkins, *op. cit.*, p. 370.
9. *Ibid.*, pp. 386-387.
10. *Ibid.*, p. 392.
11. Ezell, *op. cit.*, p. 153.
12. Paul H. Buck, *The Road to Reunion, 1865-1900* (Boston: Little and Brown, 1937), p. 287, quoted in *ibid.*, p. 181.
13. Ezell, *op. cit.*, p. 185.
14. *Ibid.*, p. 196.
15. *Ibid.*, p. 197.

II. The Growth of the Church

1. Report of Executive Committee on Home Missions, 1889, pp. 11-12.
2. *Ibid.*, 1892, pp. 13-15.
3. Egbert W. Smith, "Home Missions: An Address," USMg, Vol. VI, No. 1 (November-December 1894), p. 143.
4. "Changing Religious Problems for the South," CO (May 30, 1906).
5. Herman N. Morse, ed., *Home Missions: Today and Tomorrow* (New York: Home Missions Council, 1934), p. 238.
6. Abstract of the Annual Report of the

Executive Committee on Home Missions, GAM, 1910, p. 84.
7. SWP (February 3, 1904), p. 5.
8. Minutes, Synod of Virginia, 1918, p. 356.
9. SWP (March 20, 1884), p. 4.
10. Minutes, Synod of Nashville, 1886, p. 32.
11. Minutes, Synod of Georgia, 1912, p. 46.
12. "Revivals," CP (February 28, 1894), p. 4.
13. CP (April 4, 1894), p. 4.
14. Ibid. (July 30, 1890), p. 4; (August 13, 1890), p. 4.
15. "Revivals," ibid. (February 28, 1894), p. 4.
16. SP (May 26, 1898), p. 4.
17. "The Present Revival," CO (February 8, 1905), p. 2.
18. "Sane Evangelism," PSt (April 14, 1915), p. 2.
19. "An Evangelist Running Amuck," CO (June 10, 1908), p. 3.
20. "The Sunday Campaign," POS (March 12, 1919), p. 2.
21. Melton Clark, "The Message and the Method of Revival Preaching," USMg, Vol. XXIV (February-March 1913), p. 267.
22. C. R. Nisbet, "The Need of Revivals," USMg, Vol. XXIV (February-March 1913), pp. 258-259.
23. A. A. Little, "The Old Fashioned Protracted Meeting," POS (November 6, 1912), p. 10.
24. Report of the Executive Committee on Home Missions, 1897, p. 8.
25. Ibid., 1898, p. 7.
26. "A Few Observations on Texas Home Missionaries," USMg, Vol. VIII (September-October 1896), p. 45.
27. Report of Executive Committee on Home Missions, 1912, p. 8.
28. Ibid., 1921, p. 11.
29. The Missionary (June 1888), p. 211.
30. "The Assembly's Home Missions," CO (December 11, 1901), p. 4.
31. GAM, 1901, p. 42.
32. "The Assembly's Home Missions," CO (December 11, 1901), p. 4.
33. Report of the Executive Committee on Home Missions, 1907, p. 6.
34. Ibid., 1889, p. 11.
35. S. G. Miller, "Home Missions in Arkansas," SP (August 31, 1905), p. 15.
36. Report of the Executive Committee on Home Missions, 1915, p. 8.

37. Ibid., 1925, p. 13.
38. Ibid., 1926, p. 11.
39. S. L. Morris, At Our Door (Richmond, Va.: Executive Committee on Publication, 1904), p. 20.
40. NCP (September 16, 1897), pp. 4-5.
41. Thomas H. Law, "Presbyterianism in South Carolina," SLP (August 13, 1896), pp. 1, 3.
42. F. D. Jones and W. H. Mills, eds., History of the Presbyterian Church in South Carolina Since 1850 (Columbia, S. C.: The Synod of South Carolina, 1926), p. 323.
43. Ibid., p. 324.
44. James Stacy, A History of the Presbyterian Church in Georgia (Elberton, Ga.: 1912), p. 260.
45. SP (January 31, 1901), pp. 6-7, quoting from a letter printed in the Atlanta Journal (January 12, 1901).
46. William C. McElroy, Jr., "The Slow Growth of Presbyterianism in Kentucky," CO (January 19, 1910), p. 6.
47. Edward Marshall Craig, Highways and Byways (Kingsport, Tenn.: Kingsport Press, 1927), p. 6.
48. POS (December 1, 1909).
49. Penrose St. Amant, A History of the Presbyterian Church in Louisiana (Synod of Louisiana, 1961), p. 234. See B. Charles Bell, ed., Presbyterianism in North Louisiana to 1929 (Synod of Louisiana, 1930).
50. "The Growth of the Southern Presbyterian Church," CO (January 22, 1919), p. 3.
51. J. S. Watkins, "Our Country Churches," CO (March 14, 1894), p. 7.
52. "The City as a Home Mission Field," SWP (February 7, 1901), p. 3.
53. J. M. Spencer, "City Evangelization," SLP (July 14, 1893), p. 1.
54. Joseph A. Vance, "City Missions," USMg, Vol. IX, No. 3 (January-February 1898), pp. 203-212.
55. R. Q. Mallard, "The Institutional Church: A Candid Critique," PQ, Vol. X, No. 37 (July 1896), pp. 366-368.
56. Editorial, SWP (February 3, 1898), p. 4.
57. "Religious Workers in Our Great Cities," CO (September 23, 1903), p. 2.
58. Editorial, CO (December 21, 1904), p. 3.
59. S. B. McLean, "The Institutional Church," PSt (August 11, 1926), pp. 2-3, 6.

III. Wards of the South

1. For earlier chapters in this history, see Presbyterians in the South, Vol I, pp. 189-203, 444-448.
2. William B. Morrison, "The Red Man's Trail" (Richmond, Va.: Presbyterian Committee on Publication, 1932), p. 82.
3. Ibid., p. 103.
4. Ibid., p. 105.
5. Herman N. Morse, Home Missions: Today and Tomorrow (New York: Home Mission Council, 1934), p. 112.
6. T. C. Johnson, "Brief Sketch of the

Missions of the Southern Presbyterian Church," USMg, Vol. VII, No. 1 (September-October 1895), p. 81.
7. Home Missions Council, quoted in 59th Annual Report of the Executive Committee on Home Missions, 1925, p. 31.
8. George Warren Hinman, The American Indian and Christian Missions (New York: Fleming H. Revell Company, 1933), p. 134.
9. Report of the Executive Committee on Home Missions, 1924, p. 27.

10. Report of the Board of Church Extension, 1957, p. 16.
11. *Ibid.*, 1955, p. 23.
12. Thornton Whaling, "Our Duty toward the Negro," PQ, Vol. XVI (April 1903), p. 516.
13. Mrs. James G. Snedecor, "James George Snedecor, Sketches of His Life," typed Ms., Montreat.
14. J. G. Snedecor, Executive Committee of Colored Evangelization—Reports of the Secretary, 1903-1906, Ms., 1906, Montreat.
15. Minutes, Synod of Louisiana, 1903, p. 84.
16. O. B. Wilson, "Records of Visits to Churches, with the Services held, observations made and so forth, for the years 1896-1900," Ms. copy, Montreat, pp. 67-68.
17. R. R. Howison, "Our Church and Our Negroes," CP (October 17, 1894), p. 2.
18. "As to the Close Vote," CP (June 19, 1907), p. 9.
19. 1st Annual Report of the Executive Committee on Colored Evangelization, p. 4; 2nd Annual Report, p. 17.
20. 7th Annual Report of the Executive Committee on Colored Evangelization, 1898, p. 12.
21. 14th Annual Report of the Executive Committee on Colored Evangelization, 1904-1905, p. 9.

22. Abstract, 15th Annual Report of the Executive Committee on Colored Evangelization, Executive Committee, GAM, 1906, p. 92.
23. 19th Annual Report of the Executive Committee on Colored Evangelization, 1910, p. 104.
24. S. L. Morris, *The Romance of Home Missions* (Richmond, Va.: Presbyterian Committee of Publication, 1924), pp. 148-149.
25. 4th Annual Report of the Executive Committee on Colored Evangelization, 1895, p. 21.
26. Mrs. Snedecor, *op. cit.*
27. R. C. Reed, Editorial, PSt (August 2, 1905), p. 7.
28. "Closer Relations which Ought to Be," PSt (July 25, 1905), p. 5.
29. R. C. Reed, "What We Started Out to Say," PSt (August 9, 1905), p. 6; R. C. Reed, "Finally, Brethren," PSt (August 16, 1905), p. 9; R. C. Reed, "Secretary Snedecor Has his Say," PSt (August 25, 1905), p. 9.
30. "The Colored Sunday School," CP (November 11, 1903), p. 33.
31. 13th Annual Report of the Executive Committee on Colored Evangelization, 1903, p. 4.
32. 14th Annual Report of the Executive Committee on Colored Evangelization, 1905, p. 6.

IV. New Responsibilities of the South

1. E. R. Hooker, *Religion in the Highlands* (New York: Home Mission Council, 1932), p. 26.
2. E. A. Ross, "Pocketed Americans," *New Republic*, Vol. XXXVII.
3. R. F. Campbell, "Mission Work among the Mountain Whites in Asheville Presbytery, North Carolina," Asheville, 1899.
4. Hooker, *op. cit.*, p. 34.
5. *Ibid.*, pp. 35-36.
6. Drawn from material in *ibid.*
7. Quoted by J. Gray McAllister and Grace Owings Guerrant, *Edward O. Guerrant, Apostle to the Southern Highlands* (Richmond, Va.: John Knox Press, 1950), p. 90.

8. *Ibid.*, p. 91. S. L. Morris, *The Romance of Home Missions* (Richmond, Va.: Presbyterian Committee of Publication, 1924), p. 62.
9. Quoted by S. L. Morris, *The Task that Challenges* (Richmond, Va.: Presbyterian Committee of Publication, 1917), pp. 157-158.
10. Hooker, *op. cit.*, p. 201.
11. Robert F. Campbell, "Work among the Mountain Whites," CO (April 12, 1899), p. 6.
12. GAM, 1833, p. 92.
13. 66th Annual Report of the Executive Committee on Home Missions, 1932, p. 14.

V. Expanding Overseas

1. GAM, 1885, pp. 396-397.
2. Stillman to Houston, in application file of Rev. William M. Morrison, archives of the Board of World Missions, PCUS, cited by Stanley Shaloff, *Reform in Leopold's Congo* (Richmond, Va.: John Knox Press, 1970), p. 18.
3. S. H. Chester in *The Missionary* (September, 1895), p. 398, cited by Shaloff, *op. cit.*, p. 39.
4. Chester to Root, July 7, 1909. Root Papers, Library of Congress, cited by Shaloff, *op. cit.*, p. 48.
5. GAM, 1876, p. 300.
6. Samuel H. Chester, *Behind the Scenes: An Administrative History of the For-*

eign Mission Work of the Presbyterian Church in the United States (Austin: Von Boeckmann-Jones Press, 1928), p. 134; see also pp. 1-21.
7. *Ibid.*, pp. 18-21.
8. *Ibid.*, pp. 24-25.
9. *Ibid.*, pp. 24-26; CP (January 5, 1898), p. 8; (January 12, 1898), p. 8; CO (April 13, 1898; November 10, 1897; December 22, 1896); SWP (November 4, 1897; October 7, 1897; October 18, 1900).
10. Chester, *Behind the Scenes*, *op. cit.*, p. 34.
11. S. H. Chester, "Thirty Years in a Secretary's Office" (Address delivered at the

General Assembly, May 1925) (Nashville, Executive Board of Foreign Missions, PCUS), p. 24. Chester, *Behind the Scenes, op. cit.*, pp. 94-105; S. H. Chester, *Memories of Four-Score Years —An Autobiography*, Richmond, Va.: Presbyterian Committee of Publication, 1934), p. 181.

12. Chester, *Behind the Scenes, op. cit.*, p. 104.
13. Chester, *Memories of Four-Score Years —An Autobiography, op. cit.*, p. 178.
14. GAM, 1908, p. 65.
15. For this discussion, see Chester, *Behind the Scenes, op. cit.*, pp. 68-74.
16. This account is drawn largely from Palmer C. Dubose, "The Anti-Opium Movement in China: The Work of Rev. Hampden C. Dubose," a pamphlet issued by the Foreign Mission Committee, abridged in CO (July 31, 1918), pp. 5-6. See also *For the Glory of God, Memoirs of Dr. and Mrs. H. C. Dubose of Soochow, China*, compiled by Mrs. Nettie Dubose Junkin, n.d.
17. Chester, *Behind the Scenes, op. cit.*, p. 79.
18. W. H. Sheppard, L. C. Vass, and W. M. Morrison, "Situation in the Congo Free State," CP (January 4, 1905), p. 2.
19. T. C. Vinson, *William McCutchen Morrison: Twenty Years in Central Africa* (Richmond, Va.: Presbyterian Committee of Publication, 1921), p. 75.
20. "Proceedings of the General Assembly," CO (May 26, 1909), p. 14.
21. Chester, *Memories of Four-Score Years —An Autobiography, op. cit.*, pp. 175-176. The complete account is drawn largely from Chester, *Behind the Scenes, op. cit.*; Chester, *Memories of Four-Score Years—An Autobiography, op. cit.*; L. W. Irwin, "Rev. William McCutchen Morrison, An Address" (Lexington, Va.:

Washington and Lee Univ., 1926); Vinson, *William McCutchen Morrison: Twenty Years in Central Africa, op. cit.*; Shaloff, *Reform in Leopold's Congo, op. cit.*
22. Shaloff, *Reform in Leopold's Congo, op. cit.*, p. 178.
23. *Ibid.*, pp. 54-55; Stephen Neill, *A History of Christian Missions* (Grand Rapids: Wm. B. Eerdmans, 1965), p. 381.
24. Shaloff, *op. cit.*, p. 72.
25. Stanley Shaloff, "The American Presbyterian Congo Mission: A Study in Conflict, 1890-1921," Ph.D. Thesis, Northwestern University, 1967, p. 118; Vinson, *op. cit.*, p. 136.
26. Chester, "Thirty Years in a Secretary's Office," *op. cit.*, p. 27.
27. *Ibid.*
28. Donald W. Richardson, "A Great Heritage," USR, Vol. 47, No. 2 (January 1936), pp. 90-91.
29. *Our Church Faces Foreign Missions: A Comprehensive Study by the Southern Presbyterian Church of her own Foreign Mission Problems and Responsibilities*" (Nashville: Executive Committee of Foreign Missions, Presbyterian Church in the U. S., n.d.). Report of Commission II, "Surveying our Foreign Field," p. 57.
30. *Ibid.*, Report of Commission I, "Our Missionary Message and Obligation," p. 24.
31. *Ibid.*, pp. 37-38, 40.
32. *Ibid.*, p. 55.
33. *Ibid.*, Report of Commission II, "Surveying Our Foreign Field," p. 101.
34. *Ibid.*, p. 105.
35. *Ibid.*, pp. 106-107.
36. *Ibid.*, p. 107.
37. *Ibid.*, p. 121.

VI. *Advances in Religious Education*

1. R. C. Reed, "Forward Movement in the Publication Work," CO (January 31, 1906), p. 7.
2. GAM, 1888, p. 419.
3. T. P. Law, SP (March 19, 1896), p. 1.
4. T. D. Witherspoon, "The Sunday School, Its Present Peril," PQ, Vol. XI, No. 40 (April 1897), pp. 175-189.
5. Editorial, "The New Sunday School Movement," USMg, Vol. 13 (1901-1902), pp. 225-227.
6. R. E. Magill, "A Noble Servant Called Home," PSt (March 17, 1915), p. 5.
7. M. C. Dendy, *Changing Patterns in Christian Education* (Richmond, Va.: John Knox Press, 1964), p. 66.
8. CO (May 29, 1912; July 29, 1914); Dendy, *op. cit.*, p. 68.
9. Dendy, *op. cit.*, p. 69.
10. PSt (March 7, 1915).
11. R. E. Magill, *ibid.* (March 17, 1915).
12. Gilbert Glass, "Recent Outstanding Developments in Religious Education," CO (September 21, 1921), p. 6.

13. Minutes, Synod of Mississippi, 1920, pp. 33-40.
14. "The Society of Christian Endeavor," CO (August 24, 1887), p. 4.
15. R. Q. Mallard, "Christian Endeavor Societies," SWP (February 26, 1891), p. 4.
16. "Christian Endeavor Societies," SLP (July 3, 1891), p. 4.
17. GAM, 1892, p. 435.
18. *Ibid.*, 1893, Appendix, p. 74.
19. As finally adopted in *ibid.*, 1894, p. 238.
20. Hallie Paxon Winsborough, *Yesteryears* (Atlanta: Assembly's Committee of Women's Work, 1937), pp. 57-58.
21. Report of Executive Committee of Publication, 1917, p. 25.
22. GAM, 1917, p. 36.
23. CO (August 23, 1922).
24. Clarence P. Shedd, *Two Centuries of Student Christian Movements* (New York: Association Press, 1934), p. 252.
25. D. Clay Lilly, "The Young People's Conference," CO (March 15, 1905).

26. See Robert M. McGehee, "The Working of the Young People's Conference," Th.M. Thesis, UTS; Wallace M. Alston, "A History of Young People's Work in the Presbyterian Church in the United States, 1861-1938," Th.D. Thesis, UTS, p. 208.
27. Minutes, Synod of Texas, 1917, p. 393; Alston, *op. cit.*, p. 208.
28. CO (June 29, 1921), p. 1.
29. *Ibid.* (August 1, 1900).
30. J. R. Howerton, "Montreat—A Presbyterian Chautauqua," SP (March 1, 1906), p. 23.
31. CO (August 14, 1907), pp. 22-23.
32. GAM, 1922, p. 76.
33. Minutes, Synod of Texas, 1920, p. 547; 1932, p. 149.
34. Minutes, Synod of Virginia, 1922, p. 29;

1923, p. 130; 1926, p. 85; 1930, pp. 585-587; 1935, pp. 479-481.
35. GAM, 1916, p. 45; Alston, *op. cit.*, p. 176.
36. Alston, *op. cit.*, pp. 242-243.
37. *Ibid.*, pp. 258-259, 264-265.
38. "Findings of the Young People's Conference, Montreat, 1926," quoted in *ibid.*, pp. 272-289.
39. The letter of Mr. McGill to Dr. Getty is quoted in full in *ibid.*, pp. 289-293.
40. Quoted in *ibid.*, pp. 298-299.
41. *Ibid.*, pp. 311-312.
42. See especially W. Arnett Gamble, "Where is the Southern Presbyterian Church Going in Young People's Work," CO (July 24, 1929), pp. 8-9; reproduced in *ibid.*, pp. 328-337.

VII. *Toward a Sound Educational System*

1. Minutes, Synod of North Carolina, 1888, quoted by Luther L. Gobbel, *Church-State Relationships in Education in North Carolina Since 1775* (Durham, N. C.: Duke University Press, 1938), p. 195.
2. Report of Committee on the Church and Christian Education, Minutes, Synod of North Carolina, 1895, pp. 405-406. NCP (November 14, 1895), p. 4; SP (March 19, 1896).
3. Minutes, Synod of North Carolina, 1895, p. 406.
4. NCP (September 19, 1895); quoted by Gobbel, *op. cit.*, p. 6. See also "Parochial Schools," NCP (October 3, 1895), p. 1.
5. Minutes, Synod of Memphis, 1892, pp. 12-13.
6. *Ibid.*, 1893, p. 29.
7. R. P. Kerr, "The Religious Element in Education-Parochial Schools," PQ, Vol. XII, No. 4 (April 1898), pp. 216, 218, 222.
8. R. R. Howison, "The Overture Asking for Reunion of Church and State by Means of Parochial Schools," CO (May 11, 1898), p. 8.
9. A. J. McKelway, "The Southern Assembly," PQ, Vol. XIII, No. 49 (July 1899), pp. 553-557; see also, SWP (June 1, 1899), p. 4.
10. GAM, 1899, pp. 411-412.
11. J. L. Blair Buck, *The Development of Public Schools in Virginia 1607-1952* (Richmond: State Board of Education, 1952), pp. 121-122.
12. *Ibid.*, pp. 123-124.
13. Gobbel, *op. cit.*, p. 203.
14. Quoted by Buck, *op. cit.*, p. 155, from "The Record of Hampden-Sydney Alumni Association" (July 1941), p. 7.
15. SP (December 21, 1899), pp. 4-5.
16. GAM, 1900, p. 639.
17. "Important Matter," SP (May 31, 1900), p. 4.
18. H. B. Arbuckle, "The Presbyterian University, Our Church's Great Opportunity," SWP (April 23, 1903), p. 4.

19. GAM, 1907, p. 59.
20. W. L. Lingle, Editorial, USMg, Vol. XXV, No. 3 (February-March 1914).
21. Report of the Executive Committee of Christian Education and Ministerial Relief, 1923, p. 16.
22. Report of the Executive Committee on Christian Education and Ministerial Relief to the General Assembly, 1925, pp. 19-21.
23. *Ibid.*, 1926, p. 16.
24. Minutes, Synod of Virginia, 1913, p. 278.
25. Richard McIlwaine, *Memories of Three Score Years and Ten* (New York: The Neale Publishing Co., 1908), p. 351.
26. "Report of the President," Minutes, Synod of Virginia, 1929, pp. 457-458.
27. See Mary Watters, *The History of Mary Baldwin College, 1842-1942* (Staunton, Va.: Mary Baldwin College, 1942).
28. Quoted by Cornelia Rebekah Shaw, *Davidson College* (New York: Fleming H. Revell Press, 1923), p. 150.
29. Walter Lee Lingle, *Memories of Davidson College* (Richmond: John Knox Press, 1947), p. 24.
30. *Ibid.*, pp. 69-70.
31. *Ibid.*, p. 118.
32. Minutes, Synod of South Carolina, 1928, p. 53.
33. Minutes, Synod of Georgia, 1916, p. 45.
34. GAM, 1917, p. 33.
35. Thornwell Jacobs, *Step Down, Dr. Jacobs* (Atlanta: Westminster Publishers, 1945), pp. 287-288. For a brief account of the 30-year effort of Dr. Jacobs to build Oglethorpe University, see a review of the above volume by Dr. W. L. Lingle in PO (November 11, 1946).
36. PSt (May 30, 1917), p. 3.
37. GAM, 1917, pp. 34-35.
38. "Oglethorpe Policy and Campaign," PSt (June 6, 1917), p. 8.
39. Jacobs, *op. cit.*, p. 288.
40. *Ibid.*, p. 370.
41. CO (July 1, 1891).
42. *Ibid.*

43. "The Agnes Scott Institute," SWP (December 5, 1895), p. 4.
44. Waller Raymond Cooper, *Southwestern at Memphis 1848-1948* (Richmond: John Knox Press, 1949), p. 119.
45. *Ibid.*, pp. 133-136.
46. Quoted in *ibid.*, pp. 132-133.
47. Minutes, Synod of Arkansas, 1895, p. 23.
48. Minutes, Synod of Texas, 1913, p. 114.
49. *Ibid.*, 1928, pp. 470-475; adjourned meeting, pp. 518-525.
50. *Ibid.*, 1934, p. 291.
51. Minutes, Synod of Oklahoma, 1933, p. 3.
52. *Ibid.*, 1934, p. 5.
53. "Consolidation of the Presbyterian Institutions in Kentucky," CO (April 17, 1901), p. 2.
54. Report of Joint Commission on Schools and Colleges, Minutes, Synod of Kentucky, 1921, p. 15.
55. Minutes, Synod of South Carolina, 1928, pp. 50-51.
56. Editorial, "The Christian Schools," CO (February 24, 1909).
57. Minutes, Synod of Texas, 1915, pp. 244-257.
58. CO (November 1, 1905), p. 11.
59. Daniel A. Penick, "The Church's Opportunity among Students at State Institutions," USMg, Vol. XXII, No. 3 (February-March, 1911), pp. 171-180. Minutes, Synod of Texas, 1912, pp. 16-20.
60. R. B. Willis, "The Association of Presbyterian Church Workers in State Schools," CO (August 11, 1915), p. 15. Report of Executive Committee of Christian Education and Ministerial Relief, 1914, p. 8.

61. Minutes, Synod of Missouri, 1928, pp. 43-48.
62. SP (November 1, 1894), p. 2; Minutes, Synod of South Carolina, 1894, p. 22.
63. CO (May 14, 1902), p. 11.
64. GAM, 1904, p. 38; CO (August 31, 1904).
65. See Minutes, Synod of Oklahoma, 1909, p. 40; Minutes, Synod of Texas, 1923, pp. 190-192.
66. Minutes, Synod of Kentucky, 1913, p. 51.
67. "The Bible in the Schools," PSt (March 4, 1908), p. 2.
68. See Buck, *op. cit.*, pp. 174-177. Also Sadie Bell, *The Church, the State and Education in Virginia* (Philadelphia: The Science Press, 1930), pp. 491-492, 500, 510-525.
69. PSt (February 2, 1910), p. 3; (December 28, 1910), p. 3; (July 12, 1911), p. 2; (December 4, 1912), p. 21; (December 15, 1920); p. 3. The *Presbyterian Standard* was one of the most avid champions of Bible study in the public schools. See PSt (December 15, 1920), p. 3; (April 21, 1920), p. 3; (January 25, 1922), p. 2. In the post-World War I period it led a spirited attack on "the godless education" provided by state schools. See PSt (December 15, 1920), p. 3; (January 2, 1924), p. 2.
70. Gobbel, *op. cit.*, p. 211.
71. CO (October 26, 1910), p. 12. See also, Editorial, "Our Schools and Religion," CO (September 13, 1911), p. 2. Minutes, Synod of Texas, 1910, p. 286; 1911, p. 392.
72. Minutes, Synod of Alabama, 1917, p. 411.
73. Editorial, "An Alarming Exposure," POS (May 19, 1909).

VIII. *Maintaining the Faith*

1. I. J. Long, CO (August 27, 1884), p. 4.
2. C. H. Dobbs, "Austin Theological School," SWP (June 16, 1887), p. 2.
3. Thomas White Currie, "A History of Austin Presbyterian Theological Seminary, Austin, Texas, 1884-1943," transcript, Th.D. Thesis, UTS, p. 35.
4. GAM, 1894, p. 242.
5. "Combinations in Kentucky," CP (April 10, 1901), p. 3.
6. "The Kentucky Schism," *ibid.* (May 15, 1901).
7. SWP (May 30, 1901); (June 6, 1901); PSt (May 29, 1901), pp. 12-13; CP (May 29, 1901), pp. 3-4; CO (May 29, 1901), pp. 26-28.
8. SWP (May 29, 1902), pp. 1-2, 14-15.
9. Quoted by James A. Appleby in *The Days of Our Years* (Richmond, Va.: Union Theological Seminary, 1962), p. 61.
10. *Ibid.*, p. 62.
11. R. L. Dabney, "Do Not Remove the Seminary," CP (September 8, 1895), pp. 2-3.
12. W. H. Pratt, "The Synod of South

Carolina," CO (November 7, 1923), p. 8; Bulletin, Columbia Theological Seminary, Vol. 24, No. 2; "Report of the Theological Seminary," Minutes, Synod of South Carolina, 1923, pp. 57-61.
13. Louis LaMotte, *Colored Light: The Story of the Influence of Columbia Theological Seminary, 1828-1936* (Richmond, Va.: Presbyterian Committee of Publication, 1937), pp. 218-219.
14. CO (March 17, 1900), p. 1.
15. For the continuing debate on this question, see Russell Cecil, "The General Assembly of 1902," PQ, Vol. XVI, No. 60 (October 1902), pp. 235-236; W. A. Alexander, "Expunging the Latin Thesis," PQ, Vol. XVI, No. 62 (April 1903), pp. 536-540; T. W. Lingle, "Education of Ministerial Students, Again," USMg, Vol. X (1898-1899), p. 220; A. A. McGeachy, "The Latin Thesis—Let It Stand," CO (February 5, 1902); Hampden C. DuBose, "The Latin Thesis," CO (September 3, 1902), p. 10; Walter L. Lingle, "The Latin Thesis," CO

(January 22, 1902), p. 8; and USMg, Vol. XIII (October-November, 1901), pp. 98-101; R. R. Howison, "The Latin Thesis," CO (January 22, 1902), p. 9.

16. Herman Bavinck, quoted in Morton H. Smith, *Studies in Southern Presbyterian Theology* (Amsterdam: 1962), p. 69.

17. Ms. sermon on II Tim. 3:16, Peck collection at Montreat, quoted by Morton Smith, *op. cit.*, p. 270.

18. Ms. sermon on Isaiah 45:7, quoted by Morton Smith, *op. cit.*, p. 272.

19. "Death of Dr. Peck," SLP (October 13, 1893), p. 13.

20. T. C. Johnson, *Inspiration* (n.p.: n.d.), p. 2, quoted by Morton Smith, *op. cit.*, p. 310.

21. T. C. Johnson, "The Tenet of Jure Divino Presbyterian Polity," PQ, Vol. VII, No. 26 (October 1895), p. 528.

22. Thomas Cary Johnson, *A History of the Southern Presbyterian Church*, Vol. XI, American Church History Series (New York: 1894), p. 375.

23. CP (October 17, 1894), p. 4.

24. SWP (October 25, 1894), p. 4.

25. W. McF. Alexander, "Prof. Johnson's History of the Southern Presbyterian Church," PQ, Vol. VIII, No. 40 (October 1894), p. 600.

26. J. H. Thornwell, *Collected Works*, Vol. IV, p. 246, quoted by Morton Smith, *op. cit.*, p. 175.

27. John L. Girardeau, *Discussions of Theological Questions*, p. 289, quoted by Morton Smith, *op. cit.*, p. 241.

28. T. E. Peck, "Review of Calvinism and Evangelical Arminianism: Compared as to Election, Reprobation, Justification and Related Doctrines, by John L. Girardeau," PQ, Vol. IV, No. 14 (October 1890), pp. 629-634.

29. J. L. Girardeau, *Evolution in Columbia Theological Seminary*, pp. 22, 31, 32, summarized by W. C. Robinson, *Columbia Theological Seminary and the Southern Presbyterian Church 1831-1931*. Copyright by the author 1931, p. 210.

30. See "Inaugural Address of Whaling," *Columbia Seminary Bulletin* (July 1912).

31. See Morton Smith, *op. cit.*, pp. 254-264; Robinson, *Columbia Theological Seminary and the Southern Presbyterian Church 1831-1931*, *op. cit.*, p. 209.

32. R. A. Webb, reviewing Francis H. Beattie, *The Presbyterian Standards: an Exposition of the Westminster Confession of Faith and Catechisms*, PQ, Vol. II, No. 39 (January 1897), p. 99.

33. R. A. Webb, "Closed Questions," PQ, Vol. V, No. 18 (October 1891), pp. 610-615.

34. Samuel A. King, *The System of Doctrines of the Westminster Standards*, p. 7, quoted by Currie, *op. cit.*, p. 74.

35. Currie, *op. cit.*, p. 184.

36. W. M. McPheeters, reviewing Washington Gladden's *Who Wrote the Bible?* PQ, Vol. VI, No. 14 (January 1892), p. 143.

37. "Criticisms and Reviews," USMg, Vol. V, No. 3 (January-February 1894), p. 223.

38. W. W. Moore, reviewing Thomas Kelly Cheyne's *The Origin and Content of the Psalter*, in PQ, Vol. VI, No. 21 (July 1892), p. 454.

39. Walter W. Moore, "The Great Fish of Jonah," USMg, Vol. VII, No. 1 (September-October 1895), pp. 24-35.

40. W. W. Moore, "The Period of the Israelites' Sojourn in Egypt, in the Light of Archaeological Research," PQ, Vol. XIII, No. 47 (January 1899), pp. 24-43.

41. W. W. Moore, "Facts versus Fancies," USMg, Vol. II, No. 4 (March-April 1891), pp. 241-250.

42. W. W. Moore, reviewing S. R. Driver's *Introduction to the Old Testament*, USMg, Vol. XXII, No. 3 (February-March 1911), p. 244.

43. R. C. Reed, "A Modern Jehu," PQ, Vol. VI, No. 4 (October 1892), pp. 540, 552, 554-555, 558.

44. *Columbia Seminary Bulletin* (January 1926).

45. W. M. McPheeters, "Dr. Briggs' 'Higher Criticism of the Hexateuch,'" PQ, Vol. IX, No. 34 (October 1895), p. 528.

46. W. M. McPheeters, reviewing *Current Discussions in Theology*, PQ, Vol. V, No. 15 (January 1891), p. 126.

47. *Columbia Seminary Bulletin* (July 1936).

48. USMg, Vol. VII, No. 1 (September-October 1895), p. 73.

49. Francis R. Beattie, "The Higher Criticism," CO (January 3 September 5, 1894). E. C. Gordon, review of "The Higher Criticism" in SLP (May 2, 1895), p. 18.

50. CO (February 28, 1894), p. 3.

51. Currie, *op. cit.*, p. 207.

52. G. R. M. Montgomery, Jr., "A Historical Study of the Changing Attitudes toward Higher Criticism and a Theological Evaluation of this change in the Presbyterian Church of the United States 1879-1960, with particular emphasis on the creation account of Genesis Chapters one and two." A Thesis submitted to the Presbytery of Red River, June 4, 1962.

53. SWP (April 14, 1898), p. 1.

54. CO (January 1, 1890), p. 4.

55. "The New vs. the Old," CP (January 29, 1890), p. 4.

56. Eugene Daniel, "The Attitude of the Presbyterian Church, South, toward Modern 'Regenerated' Theology," PQ, Vol. XIII, No. 49 (April 1899), p. 496.

57. Henry C. Alexander, reviewing John DeWitt's *What is Inspiration?* PQ, Vol. VIII, No. 29 (July 1894), p. 467.

58. "Is our Bible Inerrant?" CO (September 30, 1891), p. 4.

59. George D. Armstrong, "The Word of God versus 'The Bible of the Modern Scientific Theology,'" PQ, Vol. II, No.

2 (April 1888), p. 58; cf. "Evolution," CO (November 8, 1899), p. 2; "Man and Evolution" (March 25, 1908), p. 3.

60. George D. Armstrong, "The Pentateuchal Story of Creation," PQ, Vol. II, No. 3 (October 1888), pp. 344-368.

61. NCP (January 19, 1893), p. 1.

62. W. McF. Alexander, "The Southern General Assembly," PQ, Vol. XI, No. 4 (July 1897), p. 392.

63. W. McF. Alexander, "The General Assembly–New Orleans–1898," PQ, Vol. XII, No. 46 (October 1898), pp. 576-577.

64. "The Assembly's Pastoral Letter," CP (November 30, 1898), pp. 2-3.

65. "The New Theology," PSt (August 28, 1907), p. 3.

66. CP (June 3, 1908), p. 4.

67. Editorial, "Our Assembly and Doctrine," PSt (May 26, 1909).

68. GAM, 1900, pp. 614, 643.

69. See, for example, SP (October 18, 1900), p. 3.

70. GAM, 1901, p. 59.

71. Ibid., 1902, p. 265.

72. "General Assembly Report," CO (May 29, 1912), p. 3.

73. PSt (June 5, 1912).

74. Ibid., p. 2; see also PSt (May 29, 1912), p. 3.

75. Minutes, Synod of Missouri, 1901, p. 340.

76. McIlwaine, Memories of Three Score Years and Ten, op. cit., p. 319.

77. Editorial, "Our Doctrinal Drift," CO (July 7, 1909), p. 2.

78. G. A. Blackburn, review of "Predestination" a sermon by James I. Vance, PQ, Vol. XII, No. 44 (October 1898), pp. 653-656.

79. PSt (August 21, 1918), p. 3.

80. "Our Assembly's Letter," CP (May 30, 1906), p. 344.

81. POS (June 3, 1914), p. 11.

IX. *What Does the Lord Require?*

1. Minutes, Synod of South Carolina, 1897, pp. 21-22.

2. Minutes, Synod of Virginia, 1908, p. 303.

3. "Report of the Committee on Sabbath Observances," Minutes, Synod of Texas, 1906, pp. 31-32.

4. GAM, 1890, p. 49.

5. "Sunday Amusements for Children," SWP (October 6, 1898), p. 2.

6. Minutes, Synod of Oklahoma, 1909, p. 44.

7. Ibid., 1920, p. 13.

8. GAM, 1920, pp. 77-78.

9. Ibid., 1934, pp. 90-91.

10. Ibid., 1912, p. 69.

11. Ibid., 1889, p. 621.

12. Ibid., 1894, p. 429.

13. "Sunday Laws and Sabbath Observances," CP (April 11, 1900), p. 8.

14. GAM, 1893, p. 73.

15. Minutes, Synod of Tennessee, 1906, p. 21.

16. GAM, 1921, pp. 60-61.

17. Ibid., 1958, pp. 45, 182-188.

18. See Presbyterians in the South, Vol. II, p. 396.

19. CO (May 14, 1900), p. 1.

20. Ibid. (May 31, 1899), p. 1.

21. GAM, 1900, p. 626.

22. CO (December 27, 1911), p. 11. See also, GAM, 1911, p. 44; 1912, p. 19.

23. "A Sermon that is Needed," PSt (March 8, 1916), p. 2.

24. POS (March 31, 1920), p. 1.

25. "Worldly Amusements," PSt (August 30, 1911), p. 2.

26. GAM, 1921, p. 65.

27. Ibid., 1930, p. 83.

28. Ibid., 1945, pp. 151ff.

29. SWP (May 7, 1891), p. 4.

30. SP (October 29, 1891), p. 2. SWP (May 21, 1891), p. 1; (October 22, 1891), p. 1.

31. Minutes, Synod of Mississippi, 1889, pp. 7-8.

32. GAM, 1890, p. 33.

33. For an account of the anti-lottery struggle, see Thomas Cary Johnson, The Life and Letters of Benjamin Morgan Palmer (Richmond: Presbyterian Committee of Publication, 1906), pp. 547-563, and issues of SWP 1887-1895.

34. J. W. Stagg, in a sermon, preached in Charlotte, N. C. See Editorial, PSt (February 3, 1901), p. 4; (April 25, 1966), p. 7.

35. Minutes, Synod of Mississippi, 1907, pp. 286-292.

36. Minutes, Synod of Kentucky, 1921, p. 30; 1922, p. 31; 1923, p. 9; 1924, p. 40; 1925, p. 54; 1927, p. 65.

37. GAM, 1936, pp. 36, 101.

38. Ibid., 1891, p. 244.

39. CP (February 1, 1905), p. 2.

40. "Why Preachers Oppose the Saloons," ibid. (February 26, 1908), p. 4.

41. GAM, 1897, pp. 17, 19; CO (June 2, 1897), p. 1.

42. Minutes, Synod of Missouri, 1907, pp. 27-28.

43. CO (November 21, 1906), p. 25; Minutes, Synod of Alabama, 1906, p. 271.

44. CO (November 6, 1907), p. 11.

45. "Proceedings of Fayetteville Presbytery," PSt (April 29, 1908), p. 7.

46. GAM, 1910, pp. 25, 43-45.

47. Ibid., 1911, p. 33.

48. Ibid., 1914, p. 71.

49. Professor James Lewis Howe, "The Assembly's Utterances," POS (July 29, 1914), p. 17.

50. For example, see Minutes, Presbytery of Arkansas (November 7, 1932), pp. 7-8; Pastoral Letter on Temperance and Law Enforcement, Minutes, Synod of Mississippi, 1933, pp. 246-248; Minutes, Synod of Florida, 1933, p. 15.

51. "How Are the Mighty Fallen," PSt (September 11, 1901), p. 4.

52. "Rights of the Strikers and Rights of

Those Who Do Not Strike," SWP (September 6, 1877), p. 2.

53. "The Tendency of Strikes," *ibid.* (November 19, 1885), p. 4.

54. "The Labor Movement," *ibid.* (April 1, 1886), p. 4.

55. "Men and Things," *ibid.* (July 14, 1892), p. 1; "Strikes and their Remedies," *ibid.* (September 29, 1892), p. 4.

56. "Lynchings and Strikes," *ibid.* (August 10, 1899), p. 2.

57. Editorial, "The Irrepressible Conflict," *ibid.* (July 11, 1901), p. 1.

58. R. L. Dabney, "The Gospel of Wealth," CP (December 31, 1890), p. 2.

59. A. C. Houston, "The Church and the Industrial Movement," CO (August 1, 1894), p. 10.

60. A. Bernstoff, "The Laboring Class and the Church," *ibid.* (July 8, 1896), p. 14.

61. "Murder for Gain," PSt (September 28, 1899), p. 10.

62. *Ibid.* (January 9, 1901), p. 1.

63. A. J. McKelway, "God and Money," *ibid.* (April 26, 1906), pp. 12-15.

64. "Rev. A. J. McKelway," *ibid.* (May 1, 1918), p. 2.

65. Editorial, "The Church and Socialism," CO (November 21, 1906), p. 2.

66. "Socialism," CP (August 5, 1908), p. 4.

67. "Socialism and the Church," CO (November 27, 1907), p. 3.

68. "The Rights of the Poor," *ibid.* (January 30, 1907), p. 2.

69. "A Question," CP (August 5, 1908), p. 4.

70. PSt (September 3, 1902).

71. *Ibid.* (February 22, 1905).

72. GAM, 1908, p. 19.

73. *Ibid.*, 1890, pp. 18-19.

74. CO (January 11, 1899), p. 22; NCP (February 5, 1897), p. 8; GAM, 1890, pp. 18-20; CO (February 10, 1897), p. 2.

75. W. A. Alexander, "The General Assembly–New Orleans–1898," PQ, Vol. XII, p. 579; GAM, 1898, p. 221.

76. SP (February 17, 1898).

77. *Ibid.* (May 5, 1898).

78. "The Great Victory at Manila," SWP (May 19, 1898), p. 2. Cf. CO (July 20, 1898); CP (July 27, 1898), p. 1.

79. NCP (July 14, 1898), p. 8.

80. CP (August 17, 1898), p. 1.

81. "The Prospects of Peace," CO (August 10, 1898), p. 1.

82. "The Loss of the Philippines," SP (June 16, 1898), p. 43.

83. *Ibid.* (June 23, 1898), p. 3.

84. *Ibid.* (April 21, 1899).

85. CP (July 23, 1898).

86. "Peace," PSt (January 10, 1917), p. 3.

87. "Critical Times," *ibid.* (March 7, 1917), p. 3.

88. "This War a Crusade," *ibid.* (November 13, 1918), p. 26.

89. GAM, 1917, p. 23.

90. *Ibid.*, p. 49.

91. *Ibid.*, 1918, p. 13.

92. Minutes, Synod of Florida, 1917, p. 10.

93. Minutes, Synod of Texas, 1917, p. 366.

94. Edward G. Leyburn, "The Church and the War," CO (July 11, 1917), p. 5.

95. "Liberty Bonds as a Means of Grace," PSt (May 1, 1918), p. 3.

96. GAM, 1918, p. 17; 1919, p. 38; 1920, p. 80b.

97. *Ibid.*, 1921, p. 15.

98. *Ibid.*, 1927, p. 40.

99. *Ibid.*, 1929, p. 80; 1931, p. 41.

X. The Church and Its Mission

1. See Ezell, *op. cit.*, pp. 112-114, 174-178.

2. See *ibid.*, pp. 184-187; and C. Vann Woodward, *The Strange Career of Jim Crow* (New York: Oxford University Press, 1935).

3. Ezell, *op. cit.*, p. 185.

4. Neal L. Anderson, "The Montgomery Conference on Race Problems at the South," PQ, Vol. XIV, No. 54 (October 1900), pp. 565-573.

5. "The Best Welfare of the Negro," CO (November 13, 1901), pp. 1-2.

6. "General Assembly Proceedings," SP (May 28, 1908), p. 19.

7. "Suffrage Limitation," CP (September 10, 1902), p. 8.

8. "The North, the South, and the Negro," PSt (May 1, 1901), p. 4.

9. "The Race Conflict in the South," CP (November 23, 1898), p. 9.

10. D. Clay Lilly, "The Attitude of the South to the Colored People," USMg, Vol. XVI (1904-1905), p. 271.

11. In an address at Montreat on behalf of Negro evangelization.

12. SWP (May 4, 1899), p. 1.

13. "Lynchings," *ibid.* (April 20, 1899), p. 1.

14. PQ, Vol. XIV, No. 53 (July 1900), p. 317.

15. SP (February 15, 1894).

16. "The Race Problem North and South," SWP (June 29, 1899), p. 1.

17. D. O. Davies, "The Man in Black," CO (April 11, 1888), p. 1.

18. "Another Horror," SP (May 4, 1899), p. 3; "The Wave of Crime," pp. 4-5.

19. John W. Stagg, "Race Problem in the South," PQ, Vol. XIV, No. 53 (July 1900), p. 342.

20. "As to the Colored People," CP (November 6, 1901), p. 9; (April 30, 1902), p. 8. See also "Booker Washington and the Negro Race," PSt (August 30, 1905), p. 5.

21. "The Race Problem," PSt (September 4, 1918), p. 8.

22. Neal L. Anderson, "The Montgomery Conference on Race Problems at the South," PQ, Vol. XIV, No. 54 (October 1900), pp. 565-573.

23. CP (May 30, 1900), p. 1.

24. D. Clay Lilly, "The Attitude of the South to the Colored People," USMg, Vol. XVI (1904-1905), pp. 271-287.

25. George Brown Tindall, *The Emergence*

of the New South (Baton Rouge: Louisiana State University Press, 1967), p. 177.

26. GAM, 1920, p. 45; 1921, p. 80.
27. "The Negro Problem—How to Solve It," PSt (January 19, 1921), p. 3.
28. CO (January 2, 1924), p. 15.
29. PSt (November 6, 1929), p. 8.
30. William Crowe, Jr., "Facing the Color Question," USR, Vol. 43, No. 3 (April 1932), pp. 317-328.
31. A. J. McKelway, "Labor's Judgment on the Church," *ibid.*, Vol. 41, No. 1 (October 1929), pp. 66-68.
32. SLP (August 31, 1888), p. 4.
33. C. R. Vaughan, "The Non-Secular Character of the Church," PQ, Vol. II, No. 3 (October 1888), p. 431.
34. CO (September 17, 1890), p. 6.
35. Dr. W. M. McPheeters, "The Independence and Spirituality of the Church Historically Considered," CP (April 12, 1905).
36. A. J. McKelway, "Dr. Reed and His Distinction," PSt (August 25, 1915), p. 5; R. C. Reed, "A Confession of Defeat," PSt (September 1, 1915), p. 6.
37. "Proceedings of the General Assembly," SP (June 2, 1898), pp. 3-4.
38. Editorial, "Dr. Parkhurst's Work in New York," USMg, Vol. VI, No. 3 (January-February 1895), pp. 200-201.
39. A. C. Houston, "The Church and the Industrial Movement," CO (August 1, 1894), p. 10.
40. "The Spirituality of the Church," SP (November 25, 1897), p. 8.
41. J. R. H., Editorial, "Scope of the Pulpit—Politics and the Pulpit," PSt (July 27, 1899), pp. 10-11.
42. "Charlotte," PSt (April 12, 1905), p. 7.
43. *Ibid.* (August 30, 1905), p. 7.
44. A. J. McKelway, "Social Service and Expert Knowledge," *ibid.* (August 13, 1913), p. 5.
45. W. L. Lingle, reviewing Rauschenbush's book in USMg, Vol. 23, No. 4 (April-May 1912), pp. 356-357.
46. A. W. McAlister, "Address as Retiring Moderator," POS (June 3, 1914), p. 23; (June 10, 1914), p. 3.
47. Stonewall J. McMurray, "An Address

Delivered to the Alumni of Austin Seminary, May 13, 1914" (Austin: 1914).
48. A. M. Scales, "The Atlanta Assembly," USMg, Vol. XXV, No. 1 (October-November 1913), p. 19.
49. "Social Service," PSt (September 8, 1912), p. 3.
50. James R. Howerton, *The Church and Social Reform* (New York: Fleming H. Revell Co., 1913), pp. 82-83.
51. "Us Four and No More," PSt (November 29, 1905), p. 5.
52. "The Interchurch Conference," SWP (October 18, 1905), p. 2.
53. W. M. McPheeters, "Has the Church a Right to Have a Social Program of Any Kind?" CO (March 10, 1909), pp. 7-8. Cf. PSt (December 13, 1905), p. 4; POS (February 17, 1909), p. 7.
54. PSt (November 30, 1910), p. 3.
55. GAM, 1911, p. 56.
56. "Apparent Isolation of the Church," PSt (February 14, 1912), p. 2.
57. "Proceedings of the General Assembly," CO (May 29, 1912), p. 26.
58. R. C. Reed, PSt (June 10, 1914), p. 2; USR, Vol. 26 (1914-1915), pp. 15-18.
59. GAM, 1915, p. 39; 1916, p. 76.
60. "The Federal Program," POS (August 7, 1912), p. 11.
61. A. W. Pitzer, "Sixteen Principles of the Federal Council," *ibid.* (January 14, 1914).
62. W. M. McPheeters, "An Unprecedented Action," PSt (March 15, 1922), p. 4.
63. POS (February 26, 1913), p. 9.
64. GAM, 1920, pp. 66ff.
65. *Ibid.*, 1922, p. 33.
66. CO Supplement (May 28, 1924), p. 544.
67. A. M. Scales, "The Other Side of the Federal Council Question," PSt (February 12, 1913), p. 3; A. W. McAlister, "Cooperative Christianity," PSt (April 23, 1913), pp. 6-7.
68. W. L. Lingle, "The General Assembly of 1929," USR, Vol. 40, No. 4 (July 1929), pp. 385-387.
69. PSt (April 29, 1931).
70. "Proceedings of the General Assembly," CO (June 8, 1932), p. 13.

XI. *Presbyterians North and South*

1. A letter sent to Dr. Matthews, chairman of the Committee of the U.S.A. Synod of Texas to confer with a committee from the U. S. Synod by H. Kendall, representing the Board of Home Missions of the Presbyterian Church in the U.S.A., published in TP (January 7, 1881), p. 4.
2. CO (April 24, 1872), p. 1.
3. *Ibid.* (May 15, 1872), p. 3. See also TP (September 21, 1883), p. 2; "An Error in Missions," CO (August 29, 1883), p. 4.
4. J. W. Allen in the *St. Louis Evangelist,* as quoted by D. Y. T., "Who

Plays Innocent," TP (January 21, 1881), p. 1.
5. CO (February 22, 1882), p. 4.
6. TP (April 21, 1882), p. 1.
7. *Ibid.* (April 29, 1881), p. 1.
8. *Ibid.* (April 18, 1884), p. 4.
9. "Working Cooperation," SWP (October 11, 1888), p. 4.
10. TP (June 9, 1892), p. 3.
11. CO (February 24, 1897), p. 1.
12. "The Reunion of the Churches, North and South," *ibid.* (May 3, 1899), p. 2.
13. S. L. Morris, "So Conflicting," CP (June 5, 1907), p. 4.
14. GAM, 1907, pp. 16, 20, and 54.
15. "Possessing the Southwest," SWP (June

24, 1908), p. 4; cf. CP (June 12, 1907), p. 5.
16. CO (February 30, 1904).
17. *Ibid.* (January 9, 1907), p. 2.
18. Minutes, Synod of Arkansas, 1907, p. 23.
19. "The New Orleans Case," POS (May 24, 1916), p. 2. "The Northern Synod of Texas" (Statement of Facts Concerning the Reception of Ministers into Churches in the City of New Orleans and South Louisiana by the Presbytery of Jefferson, U.S.A., January 18, 1915), POS (November 17, 1915), p. 2; see also Penrose St. Amant, "History of Louisiana," pp. 175ff, 196.
20. GAM, 1915, pp. 21, 30, 41, 76; 1916, pp. 19-23; 1917, p. 53; 1919, pp. 52, 69; 1920, pp. 24, 80c, 166-170; 1922, pp. 186-192.
21. "Cooperation with the Northern Church," CP (May 8, 1907), p. 7. Ms. Minutes, Lexington Presbytery, fall meeting 1899, pp. 304-305.
22. Minutes, Synod of Texas, 1917, p. 373.
23. *Ibid.*, 1928, p. 461.
24. CO (October 22, 1919), p. 11.
25. Minutes, Synod of Kentucky, 1922, p. 29.
26. "Reunion," SP (February 9, 1899), p. 4.
27. "Organic Union," PSt (May 18, 1899), pp. 10-11.
28. CP (May 18, 1904), p. 312.
29. As reported in *The Interior,* quoted in CP (June 8, 1904), p. 361.
30. "An Unprecedented Incident," CO (May 25, 1904), p. 1; SWP (May 25, 1904), p. 11.
31. SWP (June 1, 1904), pp. 5 7; CP (May 25, 1904), pp. 324-325; (June 1, 1904), pp. 340-341, 345; GAM, 1894, pp. 12, 18, 19, 32.
32. "Presbytery of Greenbrier and Closer Relations," SWP (September 7, 1904), p. 6; see Minutes, Greenbrier Presbytery, 1904.
33. SP (May 26, 1904), p. 8.
34. *Ibid.*, p. 5.
35. GAM, 1906, pp. 62-65.
36. Edward E. Smith, "The Northern Church at Winona," SWP (August 9, 1905), pp. 5-6.
37. "Federation," SP (March 8, 1906), p. 10.
38. USMg, Vol. XVI (December 1904–January 1905).
39. Editoral, "Revision in the Northern Church," SWP (May 21, 1903), p. 4.
40. "The Progress of Revision in the South," CP (April 22, 1903), p. 251.
41. "A Letter and an Answer," *ibid.* (September 23, 1903), p. 646.
42. J. M. Wells, "Federation," SP (March 8, 1906), p. 9.
43. G. B. Strickler, "The Articles of Agreement," PSt (January 30, 1907), p. 11.
44. C. R. Vaughan, "The Proposed Alliance," CP (February 15, 1905), p. 100.
45. Editorial, "An Intemperate Address," PSt (September 12, 1906), p. 7.
46. G.L.L., "The Real Question," *ibid.*

(September 27, 1906), pp. 13-14.
47. A. J. McKelway, Editorial, *ibid.* (March 14, 1906), p. 6.
48. CO (August 24, 1904), p. 6.
49. "Federation of the Presbyterian and Reformed Churches," SP (March 3, 1905), p. 22.
50. CP (May 9, 1906), p. 290.
51. J. B. Mack, "The Union Question," PSt (September 26, 1906), p. 14.
52. CP (May 9, 1907), p. 9; "Last Echoes from the Assembly," PSt (June 12, 1907), p. 2.
53. CO (May 29, 1907), Supplement, p. 547; "What Is to Be Done?" PSt (August 7, 1907), p. 4.
54. A. M. Scales, "The Atlanta Assembly," USMg, Vol. XXV, No. 1 (October-November 1913), pp. 16-17.
55. GAM, 1913, pp. 23-27.
56. R. C. Reed, USR, Vol. 26 (1914-1915), pp. 13-15.
57. R. F. Campbell, "The General Assembly of 1915," *ibid.*, pp. 301-304.
58. Editorial, "The Union of the Churches —Shall it be Organic or Federal?" PSt (September 23, 1914), p. 2.
59. GAM, 1917, p. 53.
60. *Ibid.*, 1918, p. 27.
61. CO Supplement, GA Report (May 28, 1918), pp. 17-18, 20-21; POS (May 29, 1918), pp. 4-5, 8, 17, 20; "Proceedings of the General Assembly," POS (June 5, 1918), p. 6.
62. POS (May 28, 1919), pp. 8, 17, 20; W. L. Lingle, "A Review of the New Orleans Assembly 1919," USR, Vol. 30, No. 4 (July 1919), pp. 287-294.
63. GAM, 1919, pp. 46-49, 157-165.
64. John R. Herndon, "The 'Aye and Nay' Vote," CO (June 11, 1919), p. 22.
65. Horace M. Cunningham, "Overlapping in Border Synods," POS (May 5, 1920), p. 5.
66. John C. Williams, "Overlapping Synods," *ibid.* (January 4, 1922), p. 6.
67. GAM, 1920, pp. 184-191.
68. J. M. Wells, "The Plan of Union," POS (July 28, 1920), pp. 2-3.
69. GAM, 1921, pp. 11, 25, 27, 33, 178.
70. W. L. Lingle, "The Charleston Assembly, 1922," USR, Vol. 33, No. 4 (July 1922), pp. 273-277.
71. Thornton Whaling, "Closer Relations," CO (February 1, 1922).
72. GAM, 1922, pp. 24-25, 172-175.
73. *Ibid.*, pp. 31, 34.
74. *Ibid.*, 1923, pp. 41, 55.
75. Thornton Whaling, "Unity and Union," USR, Vol. 32, No. 2 (January 1921), p. 146.
76. For a fuller account, see Leffert A. Loetcher, *The Broadening Church—A Study of Theological Issues in the Presbyterian Church since 1869* (Philadelphia: University of Pennsylvania Press, 1954). For a brief contemporary discussion, see E. T. Thompson, "Is the Northern Church Theologically Sound?" USR, Vol. XLII, No. 2 (January 1931), pp. 109-134.

XII. *The Theological Rift*

1. "Some Features of the Southern Presbyterian Church," *Canadian Presbyterian*, quoted in SLP (December 31, 1896), pp. 1, 3.
2. "Ordination Vows," TP (April 7, 1892), p. 4.
3. "Will They Obey," *ibid.* (July 7, 1892), p. 4.
4. "Inspiration," *ibid.* (June 1, 1893), p. 7.
5. Quoted in SWP (December 9, 1897), p. 240.
6. Minutes, Synod of Texas, 1904, pp. 235, 248.
7. "The Record of Fort Worth Presbytery," an abstract from the Minutes, n.d., p. 353.
8. CO (May 30, 1906), p. 540; GAM, 1906, pp. 12, 38, 44-45, 58.
9. Minutes, Synod of Texas, 1907, pp. 119, 129.
10. *Ibid.*, 1908, pp. 175-176.
11. *Ibid.*, 1909, pp. 214, 229-230.
12. F. E. Maddox, "The Passing of Medievalism in Religion" (Texarkana, Tex.: 1908).
13. F. E. Maddox, *Indictment of Presbyterian Church versus Rev. F. E. Maddox* (Texarkana, Ark.: 1908); "The Case of Rev. F. E. Maddox," SP (November 12, 1908), p. 3.
14. Maddox, *Indictment of Presbyterian Church versus Rev. F. E. Maddox, op. cit.*, p. 2.
15. *Ibid.*, p. 6.
16. "A review and an Exposition of the Case of Dr. H. M. Edmonds and the Presbytery of North Alabama," prepared and published by the Southern Presbyterian Ministers of Birmingham, n.d.
17. "The Other Side of the Recent Case of Dr. Henry Edmonds in the North Alabama Presbytery," prepared and published by the officers of the Independent Presbyterian Church of Birmingham, n.d.
18. CP (April 1, 1903), p. 1.
19. "Evolution in Text Books," POS (October 7, 1914), p. 10.
20. W. W. Moore, "In His Image—a Review," USR, Vol. XXXIII, No. 3 (April 1922), p. 180.
21. *Ibid.*, p. 186.
22. Minutes, Synod of Virginia, 1921, p. 44.
23. Minutes, Synod of Mississippi, 1921, p. 28.
24. *Richmond Times-Dispatch*, as quoted in Editorial, "Tennessee's Evolution Case," POS (June 17, 1925), p. 3.
25. POS (June 24, 1925), p. 1.
26. Willard B. Gatewood, Jr., *Preachers, Pedagogues and Politicians: The Evolution Controversy in North Carolina, 1920-1927* (Chapel Hill: University of North Carolina Press, 1966), p. 88. The following paragraphs draw largely from Gatewood's detailed account.
27. "Fundamentalists and Modernists," PSt
(January 2, 1924); see also Editorials, PSt (January 16, 1924); (January 30, 1924); (February 20, 1924).
28. Quoted by Gatewood, *op. cit.*
29. *Ibid.*, p. 112; PSt (October 8, 1924).
30. GAM, 1924, p. 64.
31. Gatewood, *op. cit.*, p. 120.
32. *Ibid.*, p. 122.
33. "Freedom of Speech," PSt (February 18, 1925), p. 1; Gatewood, *op. cit.*, p. 140.
34. Gatewood, *op. cit.*, p. 146.
35. "The Poole Bill and Our Legislature," PSt (March 4, 1925), pp. 2-3; Gatewood, *op. cit.*, p. 148.
36. Gatewood, *op. cit.*, p. 164.
37. *Ibid.*, p. 165.
38. Minutes, Synod of Appalachia, 1926, p. 31; 1930, p. 20.
39. "The Present Stage of the Evolutionary Hypothesis," CO (July 27, 1927), p. 2.
40. Minutes, Synod of North Carolina, 1925, pp. 490-492.
41. Quoted by Gatewood, *op. cit.*, p. 187.
42. *Statesville Landmark* (December 30, 1926); *News and Observer* (December 31, 1926), as quoted by Gatewood, *op. cit.*, p. 217.
43. See "The Bible League is Dead," PSt (February 23, 1927), p. 1.
44. Neal L. Anderson, "Evolution as a Science and a Philosophy," USR, Vol. 33, No. 4 (July 1922), pp. 288-298.
45. Dunbar H. Ogden, "The Bible and Evolution," *ibid.*, Vol. 35, No. 3 (April 1924), pp. 253-261.
46. E. C. Murray, "Does the Bible Teach Natural Science?" (Lumberton, N. C.: n.d.); Gatewood, *op. cit.*, p. 207.
47. Frazer Hood, "The Challenge of Science," USR, Vol. 36, No. 4 (July 1925), p. 328.
48. Nelson Bell, "The Bible Union of China," CO (November 22, 1922), p. 18.
49. *Ibid.*
50. "Orthodoxy in Nanking's Theological Seminary," PSt (June 21, 1922), pp. 4-5; "Union and Orthodoxy," PSt (June 14, 1922), p. 3.
51. Donald W. Richardson, "Modernism on the Church Mission Field," POS (August 30, 1922), pp. 2-3; (September 6, 1922), pp. 2-3. See also Rev. Warren Stuart in PSt (June 28, 1922), p. 3; POS (June 28, 1922), p. 2; Dr. James Mercer Blain in POS (July 5, 1922); P. Frank Price, "Orthodoxy in Nanking Theological Seminary," POS (August 16, 1922), p. 3; "The National Christian Conference in China," POS (August 23, 1922), p. 2.
52. CO (October 4, 1922), p. 23; "Why the North Kiangsu Mission Declined to Approve of a National Christian Council of China," POS (December 13, 1922), pp. 3-4.
53. POS (May 16, 1923), pp. 9-13; "Why Some of the North Kiangsu Mission Favor Cooperation," CO (April 23, 1923), pp. 5-7, 15.

54. W. H. Hudson in PSt (January 3, 1923), p. 5.

55. P. Frank Price, POS (August 16, 1922); D. W. Richardson, POS (August 16, 1922) and (September 6, 1922).

56. *Ibid.* (September 29, 1926), pp. 1-4; CO (May 17, 1922), p. 15; Minutes, Synod of Virginia, 1926, p. 27.

57. "A Letter Addressed to the China Missions on the Subject of Orthodoxy by the Executive Committee on Foreign Missions," CO (July 26, 1922), p. 4.

58. L. Nelson Bell: "The Bible Union of China," PSt (October 25, 1922).

59. *Ibid.*

60. Hugh W. White, "Our Mission Schools," PSt (April 29, 1925), p. 6.

61. GAM, 1925, p. 64.

62. "The Kind of Unity We Need," PSt (March 8, 1916).

63. "Our Seminaries;" POS (March 16, 1921), p. 2.

64. CO (August 22, 1923), p. 2.

65. "Jonah and the Whale," PSt (June 27, 1928), p. 2; (August 22, 1928), p. 6.

66. John M. Wells, "What is Modernism," USR, Vol. 34, No. 2 (January 1923), p. 98.

67. "Take Heed unto the Doctrine," PSt (February 21, 1923), p. 2.

68. "The Boldness of Liberalism," PSt (July 25, 1923), pp. 1-2.

69. Walter L. Lingle, "A Bit of Church History," CO (June 5, 1946), p. 3.

70. W. L. Lingle, "The San Antonio Assembly, 1924," USR, Vol. 35, No. 4 (July 1924), pp. 292-298; GAM, 1924, p. 63; CO, Supplement (May 28, 1924), p. 523.

71. "The Story of the General Assembly," PSt (June 4, 1924), p. 1.

72. See personal letters written by Dr. Moore to Dr. Kirk in files of Union Theological Seminary.

73. "The Church Today and Her Problem," PSt (June 25, 1924), p. 3; POS (November 14, 1923), p. 2; (July 2, 1924), p. 2; (July 14, 1926), p. 2; (July 6, 1926), p. 7.

74. H. S. Turner, "Old Testament Criticism," USR, Vol. 41, No. 1 (October 1929), p. 15. See also, Edward Mack, "The Present State of Old Testament Criticism," USR, Vol. 40, No. 1 (October 1928), pp. 12-32.

75. Personal correspondence from Dr. Mack to Dr. Turner, in possession of the author.

76. Kenneth J. Foreman, "The Composition of Scripture," USR, Vol. 41, No. 3 (April 1930), pp. 279-292.

77. Holmes Rolston, Jr., "The Source of Religious Certainty," USR, Vol. 41, No. 2 (January 1930), pp. 113-125.

78. "Is the Church Founded to Seek Truth or to Defend a System?" PSt (May 6, 1931), pp. 4-5.

79. Thompson, "Is the Northern Church Theologically Sound?" *op. cit.*, p. 134.

80. POS (May 13, 1931), p. 2; PSt (February 11, 1931), p. 2; (February 18, 1932), p. 12; (March 25, 1931), pp. 3, 18.

81. W. L. Lingle, "The General Assembly 1928," USR, Vol. 39, No. 4 (July 1928), pp. 383-384.

82. Robert F. Campbell, *Freedom and Restraint* (New York: Fleming H. Revell Co., 1930), Chs. 1, 2, 3.

83. D. Clay Lilly, "The Coming Creative Period," PSt (July 16, 1930), pp. 4, 5, 9; USR, Vol. 41, No. 4 (July 1930), p. 359.

84. Hugh Ross MacIntosh, "The Reformers' View of Scriptures"; John Oman, "The Westminster Confession of Faith," USR, Vol. 43, No. 1 (October 1931), pp. 7-11; 35-42.

85. George L. Bitzer, "The Gospel in the Changing World," delivered to Austin Seminary, May 12, 1931; "Rethinking for Today," the Annual Alumni Address at the Closing Exercises of the 46th Year of Austin Presbyterian Theological Seminary, May 12, 1931, pamphlet.

86. PSt (June 4, 1924), p. 1; (May 29, 1929), p. 3. See also PSt (April 25, 1900), p. 1; (May 16, 1900), p. 10.

87. USR, Vol. 39, No. 4 (July 1923), pp. 383-384.

88. PSt (January 15, 1930), p. 3.

89. CO (April 30, 1930), pp. 1, 2, 9; PSt (March 30, 1930), pp. 1-2; Minutes, Presbytery of Arkansas, 1930, pp. 21-31.

90. Extra *Southwestern Bulletin* (March 1931); see Hay Watson Smith, *Prestige and Perquisites* (Little Rock, Ark.: 1930).

91. Minutes, Presbytery of Nashville, Fall Session, 1931, pp. 8, 17-20.

92. POS (October 25, 1933), p. 6.

93. *Ibid.* (December 20, 1933).

94. John M. Alexander, "A Plea for Sympathetic Understanding," *ibid.* (January 25, 1933).

95. Kenneth J. Foreman, "Can the Voice of Yesterday Speak to the Need of Today?" *ibid.* (February 15, 1933).

96. Kenneth J. Foreman, "Re-Thinking Issues," *ibid.* (March 1, 1933).

97. Lewis J. Sherrill, "The Need for Freedom of Discussion among Presbyterians," *ibid.* (May 10, 1933).

98. See *ibid.* (September 6, 1932); (October 11, 1933); (July 18, 1934); (September 11, 1935); (August 5, 1936); (September 16, 1936).

99. Quoted by Tom Glasgow from Benjamin B. Warfield, "The Inspiration of the Bible," p. 4.

100. Minutes, East Hanover Presbytery, November 25, 1940, pp. 43-51.

101. POS (February 26, 1941), p. 7; Minutes, Board of Trustees, Union Theological Seminary, May 9, 1933.

102. Tom Glasgow, "A Statement for and Against Dr. Thompson in One Pamphlet for the Convenience of the Church in the Consideration of This Vital Issue."

XIII. *The Church and Its Worship*

1. "The Evening Service," CO (November 23, 1904), p. 2.
2. "Our Church Life in America," SP (March 28, 1907), p. 2.
3. "Little Children and Church Attendance," CO (August 18, 1897), p. 10.
4. "Posture in Public Prayer," *ibid.* (December 8, 1897).
5. SP (September 21, 1905), p. 1.
6. "How Long Should the Sermon Be?" PSt (January 21, 1914), p. 2.
7. The Directory for the Worship of God (1861), Ch. V, par. 2.
8. *Ibid.*, Ch. VI, par. 5.
9. Robert P. Kerr, "The Revised Directory for Worship," PQ, Vol. VI, No. 19 (January 1892), p. 116.
10. The Directory for the Worship of God (1894), Ch. II, par. 2.
11. R. R. Howison, "Shall the Presbyteries Approve," CO (March 22, 1892), p. 6.
12. Kerr, "The Revised Directory for Worship," *op. cit.*, pp. 115, 155.
13. The Directory for the Worship of God (1894), Ch. II, par. 8.
14. Robert P. Kerr, "Additional Forms," PQ, Vol. VIII, No. 28 (April 1894), pp. 269-270.
15. R. K. Dabney, "The Attractions of Popery," *ibid.*, p. 173.
16. T. C. Johnson, "The Oxford Movement in the Southern Presbyterian Church," USMg, Vol. VIII, No. 3 (January-February 1897), pp. 145-155.
17. R. F. Campbell, "Dangers Threatening the Purity of the Church," *ibid.*, Vol. XII, No. 1 (October-November 1900), pp. 12-13.
18. "Evangelism vs. Ritualism," PSt (June 17, 1903), p. 5.
19. CP (June 13, 1906).
20. SWP (April 20, 1899), p. 1.
21. SP (November 1, 1900), p. 4.
22. T. D. Witherspoon, "The General Assembly of 1892," PQ, Vol. VI, No. 21 (July 1892), pp. 435-437.
23. GAM, 1892, p. 451.
24. *Ibid.*, 1911, p. 29.
25. *Ibid.*, 1916, p. 26.
26. R. F. Campbell, "The General Assembly of 1915," USR, Vol. 26 (July 1915), p. 309.
27. Allen Cabaniss, "Liturgy in the Southern Presbyterian Church," *ibid.*, Vol. 54, No. 1 (November 1942), p. 19.
28. "Christmas Greeting," SWP (December 24, 1903), p. 4.

29. "Presbyterians and Easter," TP (May 4, 1893), p. 7.
30. "Easter Celebration," SWP (April 25, 1895), p. 4.
31. GAM, 1899, p. 430.
32. Editorial, "Easter," PSt (March 30, 1899), p. 1.
33. SWP (April 24, 1902).
34. Arthur Carl Piepkorn, "The Protestant Worship Revival and the Lutheran Liturgical Movement," in *The Liturgical Renewal of the Church*, ed. by Massey Hamilton Shepherd, Jr. (Oxford: Oxford University Press, 1960), pp. 66-67. Quoted by Kenneth G. Phifer, *A Protestant Case for Liturgical Renewal* (Philadelphia: The Westminster Press, 1965), p. 119.
35. Phifer, *op. cit.*, pp. 119-220.
36. "Shall We Observe Easter?" PSt (March 29, 1922), p. 1; "The Celebration of Easter," PSt (April 5, 1922), p. 1.
37. POS (March 25, 1920).
38. GAM, 1921, p. 73.
39. "Entertainment vs. Edification," SP (June 16, 1892), p. 2.
40. PSt (June 5, 1918), p. 3.
41. POS (June 16, 1926).
42. "Hymnbooks and Hymns," PSt (February 5, 1902), p. 2.
43. *Ibid.*
44. PQ, Vol. XVI, No. 50 (July 1902), p. 96.
45. SWP (May 31, 1900), p. 11.
46. PSt (February 5, 1902), p. 2.
47. CO (August 22, 1900), pp. 1-2.
48. *Ibid.* (August 29, 1900), p. 9.
49. *Ibid.*, p. 11.
50. *Ibid.* (March 19, 1902), pp. 1-2.
51. Walter T. Johnson, "Models of Great Preachers," Th.M. Thesis, 1966, UTS, p. 85.
52. *Ibid.*, p. 89; quotation from Givens Brown Strickler, "The Minister: His Character and Work" (unpublished lectures), p. 20.
53. D. Clay Lilly, "Christianity Full-Grown," in *The Southern Presbyterian Pulpit*, ed. by Charles Haddon Nabers (New York: Fleming H. Revell Co., 1929), p. 167.
54. *Ibid.*, pp. 172-173.
55. George L. Bitzer, "The Changeless Gospel in the Changing World," USR, Vol. 42 (July 1931), p. 421.
56. Harris E. Kirk, "The Presbyterian Mind," CO (May 22, 1929), pp. 3-5.

XIV. *Carrying the Program*

1. George W. Lawson, "Merchandise Methods in the Church, or Church Festivals and Scripture," PQ, Vol. XVI, No.1 (July 1902), p. 103.
2. GAM, 1916, p. 19.
3. In 1953 the question was again raised and the earlier resolutions reaffirmed. See GAM, 1953, p. 60.

4. "The Simple Envelope Plan," CO (December 18, 1895), p. 2.
5. *Ibid.* (August 8, 1900), p. 9.
6. CP (January 22, 1902).
7. GAM, 1910, pp. 21-22; CO (May 25, 1910).
8. GAM, 1911, pp. 70ff.
9. *Ibid.*, 1917, p. 66.
10. *Ibid.*, 1909, p. 128.

11. "The Interchurch World Movement," CO (July 21, 1920), p. 2.
12. J. Sprole Lyons, "The Pensacola Assembly," USR, Vol. 37 (1925-1926), pp. 320-323.
13. J. M. Walker, "The Passing of the Presbyterian Progressive Program," POS (September 28, 1932), p. 3.
14. GAM, 1924, p. 67.
15. Ibid., 1934, p. 52.
16. Ibid., 1943, p. 62.
17. See, for example, ibid., 1961, pp. 126-132.
18. See 18th Annual Report of the Committee on Stewardship, 1949, pp. 4-5.
19. "Program of Progress Results," CO (July 9, 1952).
20. 17th Annual Report of the Committee on Stewardship, 1948, p. 3.

21. For a brief sketch of this development, see 13th Annual Report of the Committee on Stewardship, 1944, pp. 23-27; "Report of the Ad Interim Committee to the General Assembly," GAM, 1949, pp. 158ff.
22. GAM, 1960, pp. 176-178.
23. Ibid., 1955, pp. 134ff.
24. Ibid., 1947, pp. 151-154.
25. See "Directory of Homes, related to the Presbyterian Church in the United States Division of Christian Homes and Christian Welfare, Board of Church Extension, Atlanta, Ga.," n.d.
26. PO (July 11, 1949); (October 3, 1949); (October 10, 1949); (October 17, 1949).
27. GAM, 1964, p. 120.
28. Ibid., 1956, p. 8.

XV. *The Women of the Church*

1. CP (December 16, 1885).
2. Egbert W. Smith, "Origin and Growth of the Organized Women's Work of the Southern Presbyterian Church," USR, Vol. 40 (1928-1929), pp. 23-34.
3. CP (June 12, 1878).
4. GAM, 1875, pp. 37-38.
5. Ibid., 1878, p. 619.
6. Mary D. Irvine and Alice L. Eastwood, Pioneer Women of the Presbyterian Church, United States (Richmond, Va.: Presbyterian Committee of Publication, 1923), pp. 41-46; Janie W. McGaughey, On the Crest of the Present (Atlanta: Board of Women's Work, 1961), pp. 7-9.
7. GAM, 1889, pp. 605-607.
8. Ibid., 1890, p. 39.
9. SP (April 20, 1893), p. 2.
10. "Report on the Sphere and Rights of Women in the Church," Minutes, Synod of Virginia, 1899, pp. 121-134.
11. "The First Synodical in the General Assembly," CO (November 26, 1941), p. 11.
12. Ibid. (April 3, 1912), p. 11.
13. Ibid. (April 10, 1912), p. 11.
14. Winsborough, op. cit., pp. 26-27.
15. Ibid., pp. 36-41.
16. A. B. Currie, "The Bristol Assembly," USMg, Vol. XXIV, No. 2 (January 1913), p. 182.
17. Winsborough, op. cit., p. 43.
18. GAM, 1929, p. 40.
19. Walter L. Lingle, "Yesteryears," CO (August 11, 1937), p. 3.
20. Jane McCutchen in McGaughey, op. cit., p. 185.
21. Ibid., p. 186.
22. Ibid., pp. 187-188.
23. "Woman's Work and Influence," SP (July 17, 1879), p. 2.
24. "Female College Commencements," ibid. (August 5, 1880), p. 2.
25. TP (November 21, 1879).
26. R. L. Dabney, "The Public Preaching of Women," SPR, Vol. XXX, No. 4 (October 1879), pp. 689-713.
27. NCP (November 7, 1879), p. 1; Ms.

Minutes, Synod of Texas, 1879, p. 136; Minutes, Synod of North Carolina, p. 84.
28. GAM, 1880, p. 186; Minutes, Synod of Texas, 1879, p. 136.
29. GAM, 1891, pp. 260-261.
30. Peyton H. Hoge, "The General Assembly of 1891," PQ, Vol. V, No. 17 (July 1891), p. 424.
31. Julius W. Walden, "Womanism in the South," PQ, Vol. VIII, No. 28 (April 1894), pp. 261-262.
32. J. R. Howerton, "May Woman Speak in Public Religious Assemblies?" SWP (July 27, 1893), p. 4.
33. James D. McLean, Bible Studies on Woman's Position and Work in the Church (Richmond, Va.: Whittet and Shepperson, 1893); SWP (October 26, 1893), p. 4.
34. R. L. Dabney, "Let Women Keep Silence in the Church," CO (October 7, 1891), p. 1.
35. GAM, 1897, p. 16; W. McF. Alexander, "The Southern General Assembly 1897," PQ, Vol. XI, No. 41 (July 1897), pp. 386-387.
36. Alexander, op. cit.
37. PSt (February 19, 1902), pp. 11-13.
38. R. A. Lapsley, "The Old Paths," ibid. (February 26, 1902), pp. 2-5.
39. Ibid. (March 5, 1902).
40. GAM, 1910, p. 67.
41. Ibid., 1916, pp. 47-49; Ernest Thompson, "The General Assembly of 1916 at Orlando," USR, Vol. 27, No. 4 (July 1916), pp. 289-293; CO (May 31, 1916), p. 523.
42. GAM, 1916, pp. 76, 80A.
43. "The Story of the Assembly," PSt (May 31, 1916), pp. 2-3.
44. Editorial, "Women Speaking," ibid. (August 1, 1923), p. 15; Russel Cecil, "The Montreat General Assembly," USR, Vol. 34, No. 4 (July 1923), pp. 317-320; "Woman on Executive Committees," PSt (August 15, 1923), p. 1.
45. GAM, 1925, p. 67.

46. D. Sprole Lyons, "The Pensacola Assembly," USR, Vol. 37, No. 4 (July 1926), p. 318.
47. GAM, 1926, pp. 43-52; CO (June 2,

1926), pp. 1-2; McGaughey, *op. cit.*, pp. 52-53. Winsborough, *op. cit.*, pp. 71-74.
48. PSt (August 5, 1927), p. 121.

XVI. *The Thrust of the Church*

1. GAM, 1957, p. 76.
2. *Ibid.*, 1933, p. 60.
3. Walter L. Lingle, "Revival by Resolution," CO (April 25, 1934), p. 3.
4. See CO (June 28, 1939), p. 3; Walter L. Lingle, "Notes on the General Assembly," CO (June 7, 1939), p. 4; Ernest Thompson, "The Presbyterian Evangelistic Crusade," USR, Vol. 51, No. 2 (January 1940), pp. 97-105.
5. GAM, 1940, p. 50.
6. Walter L. Lingle, "Three Years Ago," CO (March 3, 1943), p. 3.
7. GAM, 1944, pp. 46-47.
8. Editorial, "The 1945 General Assembly," CO (June 13, 1945), p. 2.
9. Stuart R. Oglesby, "The Atlanta Campaign—Two Months Later," *ibid.* (April 2, 1947), p. 3.
10. H. H. Thompson, "Visitation Evangelism," *ibid.* (April 23, 1947), p. 3.
11. GAM, 1948, pp. 137-138; CO (June 16, 1948), p. 2.
12. Ernest T. Thompson, *Tomorrow's Church/Tomorrow's World* (Richmond, Va.: John Knox Press, 1960), p. 25.
13. PO (September 19, 1966), pp. 3-4.
14. J. M. Carr, *Bright Future* (Richmond, Va.: John Knox Press, 1956), pp. 17, 19.
15. *Ibid.*, p. 74.
16. Gordon W. Blackwell, Lee M. Brooks, and S. H. Hobbs, Jr., *Church and Community in the South* (Richmond, Va.: John Knox Press, 1949), p. 45.
17. *Ibid.*, pp. 45-46.
18. Carr, *op. cit.*, p. 29.
19. See J. M. Carr, "The Larger Parish and the Presbyterian Church in the United States," 1952; *Working Together in the Larger Parish* (Atlanta: Church and Community Press, 1960).
20. Carr, *Bright Future, op. cit.*, pp. 60, 75.
21. *Ibid.*, p. 55.
22. *Ibid.*, p. 57.
23. Thomas W. Currie, *Our Cities for Christ* (Richmond, Va.: John Knox Press, 1954), p. 20.

24. Charles W. Gibbony, *By Faith* (Atlanta: Board of Church Extension, 1951), p. 152.
25. *Ibid.*, pp. 137-148.
26. W. E. Price, "The Charlotte Story," in *ibid.*, pp. 158-169.
27. Liston Pope, "Religion and the Class Structure," *The Annals of the American Academy of Political and Social Science* (March 1948), pp. 84-91.
28. Ernest T. Thompson, *The Changing South and the Presbyterian Church U. S.* (Richmond, Va.: John Knox Press, 1950).
29. See John Robert Smith, *The Presbyterian Task in an Urban South* (Richmond, Va.: John Knox Press, 1964).
30. GAM, 1964, p. 92.
31. Smith, *op. cit.*, pp. 25-45.
32. Annual Report, Board of National Ministries, 1968.
33. William Crowe, Jr., "Our Church and the Negro in the South," USR, Vol. 51, No. 4 (July 1940), pp. 329-340.
34. GAM, 1946, pp. 134-140.
35. As revealed to the author of this volume by members of the ad interim committee.
36. As reported in PO (April 10, 1950).
37. GAM, 1951, pp. 79-85; PO (June 25, 1952).
38. CO (October 17, 1951), p. 10; Minutes, Synod of Alabama, 1951, p. 28.
39. GAM, 1954, p. 86.
40. Annual Report, Board of Church Extension, 1959, p. 20.
41. P. D. Miller, ed., *Building the Church* (Atlanta: Board of Church Extension, 1958), p. 40.
42. Annual Report of the Board of Church Extension, 1959, p. 23.
43. Annual Report, Board of Church Extension, 1966, p. 10.
44. GAM, 1969, pp. 79-82; 1970, pp. 95-96; 1971, pp. 95-96.

XVII. *The Church Overseas*

1. Annual Report, Executive Committee on Foreign Missions, 1936, p. 10.
2. *Ibid.*, pp. 49-50.
3. *Ibid.*, 1938, p. 7.
4. *Ibid.*, 1940, p. 7.
5. *Ibid.*, 1941, pp. 7-9.
6. *Ibid.*, 1948.
7. *Ibid.*, 1946, p. 5.
8. *Ibid.*, 1949, p. 17.
9. Frank W. Price, "The End of an Era in China Missions," PO (December 8, 1952), p. 5.
10. Report of Ad Interim Committee on World Missions, GAM, 1954, p. 159.

11. Report of Subcommittee on Fields to Board of World Missions, as reported in "Why the Japan Mission Objects," PO (September 4, 1950), p. 8.
12. GAM, 1950, p. 65.
13. PO (June 26, 1950), pp. 7-10.
14. In a committee hearing attended by the author.
15. T. Watson Street, "Missionary Strategy and Our African Work," PO (August 11, 1952), pp. 5-7.
16. For the full report, see *ibid.* (April 19, 1954); Blue Book of the 94th General

Assembly of the Presbyterian Church in the U. S., pp. 9-27.
17. Report of the Board of World Missions on Its Study of the Report of the General Assembly's Ad Interim Committee on World Missions, in Blue Book of the 95th General Assembly of the Presbyterian Church in the U. S., pp. 100-128.
18. See PO (June 21, 1954), pp. 7-8.
19. See Thompson, *Tomorrow's Church/ Tomorrow's World, op. cit.*, pp. 103-111; T. Watson Street, *On the Growing Edge of the Church* (Richmond, Va.: John Knox Press, 1965), pp. 53-59.
20. GAM, 1960, pp. 71-72.
21. Annual Report, Board of World Missions, 1960, p. 7.

22. GAM, 1960, p. 30.
23. *Ibid.*, p. 72.
24. "Recommendations: Consultation on World Missions" (Nashville: Board of World Missions, Presbyterian Church in the United States, 1962), p. 16.
25. *Ibid.*, p. 19.
26. T. Watson Street, "The Road from Consultation 1962 to Convocation 1967" (typed copy).
27. "The Church in a Revolutionary Age," Annual Report, Board of World Missions, 1957, p. 7.
28. Street, "The Road from Consultation 1962 to Convocation 1967," *op. cit.*
29. GAM, 1964, pp. 93, 95-96.
30. Editorial, "Students in 'Mission,'" PJ (March 2, 1966), p. 12.

XVIII. *The New Look in Education*

1. Annual Report, Board of Christian Education, 1956, pp. 14-19.
2. Annual Report, Executive Committee of Religious Education and Publication, 1944, pp. 5, 9.
3. See Lewis J. Sherrill, *Lift Up Your Eyes: A Report to the Churches on the Religious Education Re-Study* (Richmond, Va.: John Knox Press, 1949); Lewis J. Sherrill, *A Restudy of Religious Education* (Richmond, Va.: John Knox Press, 1948); Hobbs, *et al.*, *Church and Community in the South, op. cit.*
4. Sherrill, *Lift Up Your Eyes*, p. 69.
5. *Ibid.*, pp. 132-133.
6. *Ibid.*, p. 81.
7. *Ibid.*, pp. 120-121.
8. Sherrill, *A Restudy of Religious Education, op. cit.*, pp. 92-97; Annual Report, Executive Committee of Religious Education, 1949, pp. 22-26.
9. Annual Report, Board of Christian Education, 1956, p. 6.
10. *Ibid.*, 1958, pp. 14-16.
11. Minutes of the General Assembly's Young People's Council, 1936, pp. 15, 20.
12. Alston, *op. cit.*, pp. 461-462.
13. *Ibid.*, pp. 480-481; Minutes of the General Assembly's Young People's Council, 1938, pp. 17-20.
14. Minutes of the General Assembly's Young People's Council, 1950, pp. 40-41.
15. *Ibid.*, p. 8.
16. *Ibid.*, 1952, pp. 41-42.
17. Frank W. Price, "Montreat's Race Relations Policy," PO (August 24, 1959), p. 8.
18. Alston, *op. cit.*, pp. 488-489.

19. Malcolm C. McIver, "Campus Christian Life" in *Church and Campus*, ed. by DeWitt C. Reddick (Richmond, Va.: John Knox Press, 1956), p. 124.
20. George A. Works (Director), *Report of a Survey of the Colleges and Theological Seminaries of the Presbyterian Church in the United States* (Louisville, Ky.: Board of Christian Education, 1942), p. 12; See Annual Report, Executive Committee of Religious Education, 1943, pp. 69-70.
21. Report of Executive Committee of Religious Education, 1936, p. 81.
22. Works, *op. cit.*, pp. 7, 10.
23. *Ibid.*, p. 50.
24. CO (July 19, 1944).
25. GAM, 1944, p. 88.
26. PO (July 30, 1945), pp. 3 4.
27. Annual Report, Board of Christian Education, 1963, p. 4.
28. W. L. Lingle, "The Birmingham Convention," POS (February 24, 1909), pp. 6-7.
29. CO (February 14, 1912), p. 2.
30. *Ibid.*
31. *Ibid.*
32. See Annual Report, Board of Education, 1950, p. 37.
33. *Ibid.*, pp. 37-39.
34. "The Future Involvement of Men in the Presbyterian Church in the United States" (report by a special study committee to the Board of Christian Education and the actions of the Board), 1968.
35. Dendy, *op. cit.*, pp. 92-93.
36. See Rachel Henderlite, "We Can't Go Home Again," *Austin Seminary Bulletin* (April 1967).

XIX. *The Minister and His Work*

1. B. R. Lacy, "Inaugural Address," POS (May 25, 1927), pp. 1-4.
2. Works, *op. cit.*, pp. 13-16.
3. Lacy, *Days of Our Years, op. cit.*, p. 77.
4. GAM, 1963, p. 87.
5. W. L. Lingle, "Changes I Have Seen," PO (February 19, 1951).

6. See Lacy, *Days of Our Years, op. cit.*, pp. 79-80.
7. 105th Annual Report, Board of Christian Education, 1966, pp. 64-65.
8. Dunbar H. Ogden, "Our 1940 General Assembly," USR, Vol. 51, No. 4 (July 1940), p. 321.

9. GAM, 1866, p. 37; 1868, p. 148.
10. *Ibid.*, 1876, p. 238; 1878, pp. 625-626.
11. *Ibid.*, 1887, pp. 196-197; 1878, p. 424.
12. CO (May 31, 1899), p. 1.
13. GAM, 1916, p. 71.
14. *Ibid.*, 1919, p. 51; 1943, p. 76.
15. A. M. Fraser, "Electing Officers for a Limited Term," POS (October 5, 1921), p. 4; R. C. Reed, "The General Assembly," USR, Vol. 26, No. 1 (October 1914), p. 10.
16. "Report of the Ad Interim Committee on a Biblical Study of the Position of Women in the Church," GAM, 1956, pp. 138-142.
17. *Ibid.*, p. 141.
18. J. A. Maclean, "The Program of the Local Church," USR, Vol. 42, No. 1 (October 1930), pp. 36-44.

19. CO (October 12, 1949).
20. Victor Fiddes, *The Architectural Requirements of Protestant Worship* (Toronto: The Ryerson Press, 1961), pp. 53, 90-91.
21. PO (February 19, 1951).
22. GAM, 1965, pp. 3-4, 76.
23. William H. Kadel, "Contemporary Preaching in the Presbyterian Church in the United States," Th.M. Thesis, typescript, Union Theological Seminary, 1950, pp. 1294ff.
24. See Donald W. Shriver, *The Unsilent South* (Richmond, Va.: John Knox Press, 1965).
25. Annual Report of the Permanent Committee on Christianity and Health, 1966, pp. 132, 137-138.
26. Lingle, "Changes I Have Seen," *op. cit.*

XX. *Toward Theological Maturity*

1. Lawrence I. Stell, in POS (July 27, 1938).
2. W. L. Lingle, "What Does Presbyterianism Stand For?" CO (May 10, 1939), pp. 3, 7.
3. GAM, 1944, pp. 123-127.
4. Editorial, "Why the Journal at This Time?" *Southern Presbyterian Journal*, Vol. I, No. 1 (May 1942), pp. 2-3.
5. *Ibid.*, Vol. I, No. 10 (February 1943), p. 2.
6. Minutes, East Hanover Presbytery, Adjourned Meeting (May 21, 1935), pp. 131-136.
7. GAM, 1938, pp. 128-136.
8. J. B. Green, "Regarding the Revision of the Confession of Faith and the Catechism," POS (June 15, 1938), p. 13.
9. GAM, 1939, pp. 68-71.
10. *Ibid.*, 1939, pp. 37, 71; POS (June 7, 1939), p. 9; CO (June 7, 1939), p. 14.
11. See GAM, 1879, pp. 23-25; 1880, pp. 201-202; 1881, p. 383; 1898, p. 223; 1936, p. 35.
12. Robert Ware Jopling, *Studies in the Confession of Faith and the Five Points of Calvinism Examined* (Clinton, S. C.: Jacobs Press, 1942); W. L. Lingle, "The Five Points Examined," CO (September 1, 1943), p. 3.
13. GAM, 1898, p. 223; 1928, p. 45; 1934, p. 32.
14. PO (February 5, 1951), p. 5.
15. GAM, 1961, pp. 39, 132-139.
16. Felix B. Gear, *Basic Beliefs of the Reformed Faith* (Richmond, Va.: John Knox Press, 1960), p. 55.
17. Shirley C. Guthrie, Jr., *Christian Doctrine* (Richmond, Va.: CLC Press, 1968), pp. 144, 140.
18. GAM, 1961, p. 139.
19. Editorial, "A Sacred Trust," *Southern*

Presbyterian Journal, Vol. II, No. 5 (September 1942), pp. 2-3.
20. John Bright, reviewing Oswald T. Allis, *The Unity of Isaiah*, in PO (May 21, 1951), p. 15.
21. Donald G. Miller, "Neglected Emphases in Biblical Criticism," USR, Vol. LVI, No. 4 (August 1945), pp. 328-329, 322, 336.
22. PO (May 18, 1953), p. 4.
23. G. Robert M. Montgomery, Jr., "A Historical Study of the Changing Attitude toward Higher Criticism and a Theological Evaluation of this change in the Presbyterian Church of the United States 1879-1960," typed thesis submitted to Red River Presbytery June 4, 1962. (The author has been helped by this thesis in the writing of the preceding paragraphs.)
24. Lewis J. Sherrill, "The Barrenness of the Southern Presbyterian Pen," USR, Vol. 42, No. 3 (April 1931), pp. 278-279.
25. *Ibid.*, p. 283.
26. *Ibid.*, pp. 285-286.
27. Cecil V. Crabb, "Creative Thought in the Southern Church," USR, Vol. 43, No. 4 (July 1932), p. 422.
28. Charles L. King, "The Prosperity and the Enlargement of the Church," PO (June 4, 1945), p. 4.
29. *Ibid.*
30. "The Nature of the Bible and Its Interpretation and Use in the Educational Work of the Church," Foundation Paper I, p. 8, quoted by Montgomery, *op. cit.*, p. 78.
31. Faculty Minutes, Union Theological Seminary, May 15, 1964, pp. 1133-1134.
32. Catalogue, Reformed Theological Seminary (1968-1969), pp. 7-8.

XXI. *"Spirituality" Reinterpreted*

1. Harris E. Kirk, "Christ and the Secular Temper," USMg, Vol. XXII, No. 2 (December 1910–January 1911), p. 116.

See also William Crowe, "A Divine Answer to a Human Digest," CO (June 1, 1932), p. 57.

2. Dr. A. A. Little, "The Peace Conference and the Negro," POS (January 29, 1919), p. 2.
3. GAM, 1920, p. 45; 1921, pp. 80-81; POS (June 2, 1920), p. 16.
4. GAM, 1929, p. 79; CO (May 29, 1929), p. 19.
5. William Crowe, "Fixing the Color Question," USR, Vol. 43, No. 3 (April 1932), pp. 317-328.
6. W. L. Carson, "The Social Tasks of the Church," ibid., Vol. 43, No. 4 (July 1932), p. 411.
7. John A. Maclean, "Can Christ Save Society?" ibid., Vol. 45, No. 3 (April 1934), pp. 183-185.
8. Chris Matheson, "The Mission of the Church," POS (June 21, 1933).
9. Minutes, Synod of Virginia, 1932, p. 156; J. J. Murray, "Evangelism and Social Welfare in the Synod of Virginia," USR, Vol. 44, No. 2 (January 1933), pp. 139-143.
10. See "General Assembly Proceedings" CO (June 7, 1933), p. 14; E. B. Paisley, "General Assembly and Social Questions," POS (July 12, 1933); S. R. Oglesby, "Committee on Moral and Social Questions," POS (June 14, 1933), pp. 4-5; USR, Vol. 44, No. 4 (July 1933), p. 341; W. D. Blanks, "The Southern Presbyterian View of the Mission of the Church," Th.M. Thesis, UTS (May 1958), pp. 36-40.
11. Henry Dubose, "Social Ethics at Montreat," CO (October 18, 1933).
12. Report of the Committee on Moral and Social Welfare, Minutes, Synod of Virginia, 1933, pp. 272-280; Blanks, op. cit., pp. 40-45.
13. Minutes, Synod of Virginia, 1933, pp. 283-290; W. L. Lingle, "Another Presbyterian Manifesto," CO (October 4, 1933), pp. 4-5; POS (September 20, 1933); Blanks, op. cit., pp. 40-45.
14. Minutes, Synod of Alabama, 1933, pp. 11-15; POS (November 1, 1933).
15. R. A. White, "The Church and Moral and Social Problems: A Panacea?" POS (January 24, 1934), citation from Blanks, op. cit., pp. 47-48.
16. Samuel M. Wilson, "The Proposed Assembly's Committee . . . ," USR, Vol. 45, No. 3 (April 1934), pp. 188-198; Blanks, op. cit., pp. 47-48.
17. Blanks, op cit., pp. 51-52; W. L. Lingle, "An Unusual Week at Massanetta," CO (July 1, 1934); USR, Vol. 46, No. 2 (January 1935).
18. GAM, 1935, pp. 93-95.
19. Ibid., 1937, pp. 37, 53-60, 75; POS (June 16, 1937), pp. 14-15.
20. Dunbar H. Ogden, "Our 1940 General Assembly," USR, Vol. 51, No. 4 (July 1940), pp. 323-324.
21. GAM, 1966, pp. 160-165.
22. PSt (February 5, 1930), pp. 1-2.
23. "Prohibition Repeal," CO (March 15, 1933), p. 2.
24. "Report on Social Drinking," Minutes,

Hanover Presbytery, winter meeting, 1963, pp. 16-23.
25. GAM, 1970, pp. 119-124.
26. Ibid., 1934, p. 91.
27. Ibid., 1942, pp. 84, 93-94, 139-140.
28. "Report of the Ad Interim Committee to Study the Biblical Teaching and the Proper Use of the Lord's Day," ibid., 1958, pp. 45, 182-187.
29. Ibid., 1959, pp. 43, 131-135.
30. Ibid., 1945, pp. 86, 151-152.
31 PO (April 30, 1945), pp. 208-209.
32. GAM, 1935, p. 43.
33. Charles E. Diehl, "Minority Report on Divorce," CO (May 8, 1929), p. 7.
34. Ibid. (April 27, 1938), pp. 5-7; "Social and Moral Welfare: Report of Permanent Committee," GAM, 1946, pp. 107-114.
35. "Moral and Social Welfare: Report of Permanent Committee," CO (April 17, 1946), p. 11, 164.
36. "The Report on Divorce," PO (May 22, 1950), p. 9.
37. GAM, 1953, pp. 89-92; PO (June 29, 1953), pp. 9-10; (July 13, 1953), pp. 4-6.
38. PO (June 29, 1953), pp. 9-10; (July 13, 1952), pp. 4-6.
39. GAM, 1958, pp. 188-191.
40. "A Message to the Nation," GAM, 1960, p. 43.
41. Ibid., 1970, pp. 124-126.
42. See, for example, Monroe Taylor Gilmour, "Christ or War," POS (January 8, 1936), pp. 3-4.
43. GAM, 1936, pp. 36, 96-97; 1937, pp. 37, 107-108.
44. POS (September 1, 1937), pp. 3-4.
45. Ibid. (June 1, 1938), p. 5.
46. W. L. Lingle, in CO (August 16, 1939), p. 3; Dr. John Cunningham, "Christ and the Present Crisis," CO (July 26, 1939), p. 4; GAM, 1941, pp. 65, 163; See Holmes Rolston, "A Policy for America," POS (September 11, 1940), p. 2; A. C. Moore, "Seven Spurious Shibboleths," POS (August 13, 1941), p. 3.
47. Kenneth J. Foreman, "If in the Far East," POS (December 24, 1941), p. 2.
48. Walter S. Buchanan, "Understanding Japan," ibid. (March 18, 1942), pp. 5-6.
49. Henry Wade DuBose, "Christian and the War Crisis," CO (April 1, 1942), p. 2.
50. "Report of Permanent Committee on Social and Moral Welfare," GAM, 1942, pp. 134-138.
51. Ibid.
52. CO (April 29, 1942).
53. W. L. Lingle, "My Minister and the War," CO (January 28, 1942), p. 3.
54. GAM, 1941, pp. 163-166.
55. Ibid., 1943, pp. 146-148.
56. Ibid., 1944, p. 151; "The Church and the Christian in the New World Order," CO (April 5, 1944), pp. 6, 8.
57. Bases of World Order, ed. by E. T. Thompson, et al. (Richmond, Va.: John Knox Press, 1945).
58. PO (November 5, 1945), pp. 5-6.

59. Annual Report, Board of Church Extension, 1951, p. 94; "Report of the Permanent Committee on Moral and Social Welfare," GAM, 1948, pp. 156-164; PO (May 7, 1951), pp. 5-6.
60. GAM, 1947, pp. 163-164; 1948, p. 89.
61. PO (January 28, 1946), p. 3.
62. "National Security and the Christian Message," Report of Division of Christian Relations, Board of Church Extension to 1951 General Assembly, pp. 93-94.
63. Ibid., pp. 90-91. See also "The Christian Faith and Communism," GAM, 1954, pp. 197-198.
64. "Freedom, the Christian Concept," GAM, 1957, p. 194.
65. Ibid., 1961, pp. 40, 69.
66. Ibid., 1964, pp. 152-153.
67. Ibid., 1966, pp. 171-173.
68. Ibid., 1970, pp. 124-126.
69. Minutes, Synod of Alabama, 1933, p. 1115; "The Synod of Alabama," CO (November 1, 1933), p. 11.
70. "The Church in the First and Twentieth Centuries," ibid. (May 16, 1934), p. 10.
71. Minutes, Synod of Alabama, 1938, p. 180; Minutes, Synod of Tennessee, 1943, pp. 15-16; David Park, "Synod of Alabama," CO (November 9, 1938), p. 9.
72. "Synod of Tennessee Endorses Organized Labor," POS (October 20, 1943), p. 7.
73. Ibid. (January 14, 1942).
74. J. H. Marion, Jr., "Southern Economic Needs Challenge the Church," USR, Vol. 51, No. 3 (April 1940), p. 247.
75. GAM, 1936, pp. 36, 98-99.
76. Ibid., 1937, pp. 37, 105ff.; CO (June 2, 1937).
77. GAM, 1957, p. 195.
78. Ibid., 1958, pp. 88, 226.
79. Ibid., 1959, p. 180.
80. "Poverty in the Light of the Christian Faith," ibid., 1965, pp. 161-162.
81. Ibid., 1966, pp. 167-171.
82. Ernest Trice Thompson, Plenty and Want: The Responsibility of the Church (Nashville, Tenn.: Board of World Missions, 1966).
83. GAM, 1969, pp. 100-105.

XXII. *Toward Ethical Maturity*

1. GAM, 1936, pp. 99-100.
2. William Crowe, Jr., "Our Church and the Negro in the South," USR, Vol. 51, No. 3 (April 1940), pp. 248-263; USR, Vol. 51, No. 4 (July 1940), pp. 329-340.
3. "Too Much Discussion of Race," PO (August 23, 1944).
4. GAM, 1943, p. 144.
5. Ibid., 1944, pp. 150-151.
6. Ibid., 1945, p. 147.
7. Ibid., 1949, pp. 100, 177-192.
8. PO (October 11, 1948), p. 3.
9. Ibid. (September 20, 1948), p. 4.
10. J. McDowell Richards, "The Golden Rule and Racial Relationships" (Address to Synod of Alabama); CO (February 25, 1948), pp. 8-9.
11. GAM, 1944, p. 151.
12. Lillian Smith, "The White Christian and His Conscience," PO (July 23, 1945), pp. 4-6.
13. John H. Marion, "Let's Face the Basic Issue," ibid. (January 16, 1950), pp. 5-6.
14. Ibid. (January 30, 1950), p. 2.
15. Ibid., p. 8.
16. Minutes, Synod of Alabama, 1950, p. 38; "Communism, Roman Catholicism, and the Negro People," PO (October 16, 1950), p. 6.
17. PO (October 16, 1950), p. 8.
18. W. L. Lingle, "On our Conscience," CO (September 4, 1946), p. 3.
19. George C. Bellingrath, "Impressions of our Recent General Assembly," USR, Vol. 45, No. 4 (July 1934), pp. 328-329.
20. GAM, 1943, p. 74.
21. PO (June 11, 1945), pp. 9-10.
22. As reported in PO (June 10, 1946), p. 8.
23. Ibid., pp. 9-10.
24. See "Seminary Students' Attitudes," ibid. (July 30, 1951), p. 2; "Columbia Students for Non-Segregation," ibid. (October 22, 1951), p. 2.
25. Ibid. (March 17, 1947), p. 3.
26. Ibid. (June 20, 1949), p. 8.
27. Ibid. (June 26, 1950), pp. 10-11.
28. Ibid., p. 11.
29. Ibid. (September 21, 1953), p. 3; CO (September 30, 1953), p. 14; Minutes, Synod of Virginia, p. 133.
30. GAM, 1953, p. 81.
31. "The Church and Segregation," A Statement to Southern Christians, GAM, 1954, pp. 187-198.
32. PO (June 28, 1954), p. 3; (July 19, 1954), p. 11.
33. See G. T. Gillespie, "Defence of the Principle of Racial Segregation," ibid. (March 14, 1955), pp. 5-9.
34. Ibid. (September 2, 1957), p. 4.
35. Ibid. (September 23, 1957), p. 10.
36. CO (December 10, 1958), p. 12; PO (December 8, 1958), pp. 65-66.
37. GAM, 1958, pp. 89-90.
38. PO (June 13, 1955), p. 6.
39. "Labor Leader Lauds Southern Churches," ibid. (March 28, 1955), p. 10.
40. Ibid. (February 2, 1953), p. 3.
41. Ibid. (March 21, 1960), pp. 3-4; (April 11, 1960), p. 6.
42. GAM, 1964, pp. 153-155.
43. Ibid., 1956, pp. 158-161.
44. Ibid., 1966, pp. 90-91.
45. Ibid., 1965, p. 94.
46. Ibid., 1966, p. 102.
47. PO (June 29, 1959), pp. 4, 10.

48. Quoted in *ibid.* (October 12, 1959) from an editorial by Ralph McGill in the *Atlanta Constitution* in an article, "The Agony of the Southern Minister,"

for the *New York Times Magazine* (September 27, 1959).
49. GAM, 1964, p. 79.
50. *Ibid.*, 1968, p. 133.

XXIII. *Toward Greater Ecumenicity*

1. "Our Church's Relation to the Federal Council," CO (May 4, 1938), p. 2; Walter Lingle, "More About the Federal Council," CO (September 15, 1937), p. 3.
2. *Ibid.* (May 4, 1938), p. 2.
3. *Ibid.*
4. POS (June 4, 1941), pp. 9, 13; CO (June 4, 1941), pp. 4, 15.
5. PO (June 16, 1947), pp. 6-8; CO (June 18, 1947), pp. 2, 10-11.
6. PO (August 27, 1947); (August 18, 1947).
7. *Ibid.* (August 18, 1947), pp. 3-4.
8. POS (June 10, 1942), p. 13.
9. PO (June 14, 1948), pp. 5-8; CO (June 16, 1948), pp. 9-10.
10. GAM, 1947, pp. 65, 162-169; CO (April 3, 1947), p. 2; (May 15, 1947), p. 3; PO (May 13, 1957), pp. 7-9.
11. GAM, 1959, p. 73; CO (February 11, 1959), pp. 2, 7; (February 25, 1959), p. 2; PO (May 11, 1959), pp. 8-10; CO (May 13, 1959), pp. 4-5.
12. GAM, 1959, p. 73.
13. *Ibid.*, 1960, p. 79.
14. *Ibid.*, 1961, pp. 107-108.
15. GAM, 1964, pp. 83-84.
16. "The Truth about the National Council of Churches," *Presbyterian Survey* (December 1964), pp. 33-47.
17. GAM, 1966, p. 96.
18. *Ibid.*, pp. 37, 95.
19. W. L. Lingle, "The General Assembly of 1929," USR, Vol. 40, No. 4 (July 1929), p. 384.
20. PSt (May 29, 1929), p. 7.
21. See articles by James I. Vance, J. L. Sherrod, and J. M. Wells in CO (March 26, 1930), pp. 6-7; and articles by W. L. Lingle and Addison Hogue in POS (February 26, 1930), p. 2, and (March 26, 1930), p. 4.
22. GAM, 1931, p. 68.
23. *Ibid.*, 1932, pp. 47, 137ff.
24. E. B. Paisley, "The General Assembly of 1932," USR, Vol. 43, No. 4 (July 1932), p. 457.
25. GAM, 1934, p. 34.
26. *Ibid.*, 1936, pp. 54-55.
27. "Proceedings of the General Assembly," CO (May 19, 1937), pp. 2, 5; (June 2, 1937), p. 13.
28. GAM, 1937, pp. 39, 123. "Proceedings of the General Assembly," CO (June 2, 1937), p. 13.
29. GAM, 1938, pp. 96-97.
30. CO (April 5, 1939), pp. 2, 5; GAM, 1939, pp. 102-103.
31. GAM, 1940, pp. 66-67; PO (May 29, 1940), pp. 12-13.

32. GAM, 1941, pp. 62-63, 76; PO (June 4, 1941), p. 9.
33. In a personal conversation with the author.
34. GAM, 1946, pp. 32-33, 69; PO (June 10, 1946), pp. 5-6.
35. "Toward Presbyterian Reunion," PO (May 13, 1946), p. 8.
36. GAM, 1948, p. 63; PO (June 14, 1938), pp. 9-10. The author of this volume was one of the small group which drew up this resolution.
37. See CO (June 16, 1948), pp. 10-11; PO (June 14, 1948), pp. 9-10; (June 21, 1948), pp. 8-9.
38. Blue Book of the 39th General Assembly, pp. 22-23.
39. "Proceedings of the General Assembly," PO (June 13, 1949), pp. 7-9.
40. GAM, 1949, p. 76; PO (June 13, 1949).
41. "Reunion Opponents Meet," PO (June 18, 1949), p. 3.
42. *Ibid.* (September 12, 1949), p. 10; (June 25, 1951), p. 4; (June 26, 1950), p. 6; (November 6, 1950), p. 10; CO (June 28, 1950), p. 28; (June 27, 1951), p. 4.
43. GAM, 1953, pp. 42, 143; PO (June 22, 1953), pp. 4-6; (July 6, 1953), p. 8.
44. PO (June 18, 1951), pp. 7, 15; (June 25, 1951), p. 9.
45. *Ibid.* (July 2, 1951), p. 8.
46. *Ibid.* (March 24, 1952), p. 3.
47. *Ibid.* (January 12, 1953), pp. 3-4.
48. *Ibid.* (June 22, 1953), p. 3; GAM, 1953, pp. 106-108.
49. W. C. Robinson, "Reunion of the Presbyterian Churches USA and US," CO (January 24, 1940), pp. 11, 22.
50. *Ibid.* (April 21, 1948), p. 10.
51. *Ibid.* (February 28, 1940), pp. 15, 22.
52. "Then Shall We Liquidate Missouri, Mississippi and Alabama?" PO (April 22, 1946), p. 8; CO (April 3, 1946), pp. 10-12.
53. *Ibid.* (April 17, 1940), p. 11.
54. PO (November 23, 1953), p. 2.
55. *Ibid.* (April 26, 1954), p. 1.
56. *Ibid.* (September 6, 1954), p. 3.
57. *Ibid.* (December 27, 1954), p. 10.
58. *Ibid.* (May 31, 1954), p. 7.
59. CO (September 1, 1954), p. 7.
60. *Ibid.* (August 18, 1954), pp. 5-6; PO (July 5, 1954).
61. PO (October 4, 1954), p. 3.
62. "Driving a Wedge," CO (October 22, 1947), p. 11.
63. Reported in PO (July 5, 1954), p. 4.
64. *Ibid.* (September 6, 1954), p. 3.
65. *Ibid.* (July 26, 1954), pp. 3-4.
66. Sanford M. Dornbusch and Roger D.

Irle, "The Failure of Presbyterian
Union," *Journal of Sociology*, reprinted
in *ibid*. (February 23, 1959), pp. 5-6.
67. GAM, 1955, p. 70; PO (June 20, 1955),
p. 5.
68. GAM, 1960, pp. 31, 59.

69. *Ibid*., p. 77.
70. *Ibid*., 1961, p. 72.
71. *Ibid*., 1963, p. 93.
72. *Ibid*., p. 94.
73. *Ibid*., 1966, pp. 43-48.
74. *Ibid*., p. 94.

Bibliography

Bibliography

Records

Minutes of the General Assembly of the Presbyterian Church in the United States.
Minutes of presbyteries and synods of the Presbyterian Church in the United States.
Reports of the Boards, Executive Committees, and Agencies of the Presbyterian Church in the United States.
Alexander, W. A. *A Digest of the Acts and Proceedings of the General Assembly of the Presbyterian Church in the United States.* Richmond, Va.: Presbyterian Committee of Publication, 1888. Revised Edition by W. A. Alexander and G. F. Nicolassen, 1911. Second Revised Edition by G. F. Nicolassen, 1923.
A Digest of the Acts and Proceedings of the General Assembly of the Presbyterian Church in the United States, 1861-1944. Edited and prepared by James A. Millard. Richmond, Va.: Presbyterian Committee of Publication, 1945. Based on materials gathered by James A. Millard, authorized and supplemented by E. C. Scott, Stated Clerk, 1945. Revised, James A. Millard, Jr., Stated Clerk, 1965. Supplementary Index, 1969.
Ministerial Directory of the Presbyterian Church U. S., 1861-1941. Compiled by E. C. Scott. Published by order of the General Assembly, 1942. Revised, 1951. Revised and supplemented, by E. D. Witherspoon, Jr., 1967.
Ms. Minutes of the General Assembly's Young People's Council, Presbyterian Church in the U. S., 1932-1961.

Periodicals*

* Files of most weekly publications incomplete.

Central Presbyterian. 1861-1908. (Merged with *Presbyterian of the South,* 1908.)
Christian Observer. 1861-1971.
Concerned Presbyterian. 1965-1971.
Home Mission Herald. 1908-1911. (Merged with *Presbyterian Survey,* 1911.)
The Missionary. 1868-1911. (Merged with *Presbyterian Survey,* 1911.)
North Carolina Presbyterian. 1861-1899. (Renamed *Presbyterian Standard,* 1899.)
Presbyterian Journal. 1942-1971. (Originally *Southern Presbyterian Journal.*)
Presbyterian of the South (combining the *Central Presbyterian,* the *Southern Presbyterian,* the *Southwestern Presbyterian*). 1909-1942. (Renamed *Presbyterian Outlook,* 1942.)
Presbyterian Outlook, 1942-1971. (Continuing the *Presbyterian of the South,* 1942, and the *Presbyterian Tribune,* 1955.)
Presbyterian Quarterly. 1877-1904.
Presbyterian Standard. 1899-1931. (Incorporated into the *Presbyterian of the South,* 1931.)
Presbyterian Survey. 1911-1971.
Southern Presbyterian. 1861-1908. (Incorporated into the *Presbyterian of the South,* 1909.)
Southwestern Presbyterian. 1869-1908. (Incorporated into the *Presbyterian of the South,* 1909.)
Texas Presbyterian. 1876-1885, 1892-1896, 1960-1971. (Consolidated with *St. Louis Presbyterian,* 1885; resumed publication in 1892; continued as *Trans-Mississippi Presbyterian and Presbyterian Record,* 1895-1902, when absorbed by *Southwestern Presbyterian;* renewed publication, 1960.)
Union Seminary Review. 1888-1945. (Published originally as *Union Seminary Magazine;* succeeded by *Interpretation.*)

Selected Articles

Anderson, Neal L. "The Montgomery Conference on Race Relations at the South." PQ, Vol. 14, No. 54 (October 1900).

Armstrong, George A. "The Pentateuchal Story of Creation." PQ, Vol. 2, No. 3 (October 1888).

Beattie, Francis R. "The Higher Criticism." Series of articles in CO (January 3 through September 5, 1895).

Bitzer, George L. "The Changeless Gospel in the Changing World." USR, Vol. 42, No. 4 (July 1931).

Cabaniss, Allen. "Liturgy in the Southern Presbyterian Church." USR, Vol. 54, No. 1 (November 1942).

Campbell, R. F. "Dangers Threatening the Purity of the Church." USMg, Vol. 12, No. 1 (October 1900).

Carson, Walter L. "The Social Task of the Church." USR, Vol. 43, No. 4 (July 1932).

Clark, Melton. "The Message and the Method of Revival Preaching." USMg, Vol. 24, No. 3 (February-March 1903).

Crabb, Cecil V. "Creative Thought in the Southern Church." USR, Vol. 43, No. 4 (July 1932).

Crowe, William, Jr. "Facing the Color Question." USR, Vol. 43, No. 3 (April 1932).

————. "Our Church and the Negro in the South." USR, Vol. 51, No. 4 (July 1940).

Daniel, Eugene. "The Attitude of the Presbyterian Church South toward Modern 'Regeneration' Theology." PQ, Vol. 13, No. 49 (April 1899).

Dornbusch, Sanford M., and Roger D. Irle. "The Failure of Presbyterian Union." American Journal of Sociology. Reprinted in PO (February 23, 1959).

Foreman, Kenneth J. "The Composition of Scripture." USR, Vol. 41, No. 3 (April 1930).

Kirk, Harris E. "Christ and the Secular Temper." USMg, Vol. 22, No. 2 (December 1910–January 1911).

Lacy, Benjamin R. "Inaugural Address." POS (May 25, 1927).

Lilly, D. Clay. "The Attitude of the South to the Colored People." USMg, Vol. 16, No. 3 (February-March 1905).

————. "The Coming Creative Period." USR, Vol. 41, No. 4 (July 1930).

MacLean, John A. "Can Christ Save Society?" USR, Vol. 44, No. 2 (January 1933).

————. "The Program of the Local Church." USR, Vol. 42, No. 1 (October 1930).

Mack, Edward. "The Present State of Old Testament Criticism." USR, Vol. 42, No. 1 (October 1930).

McKelway, A. J. "Labor's Judgment on the South." USR, Vol. 41, No. 1 (October 1929).

Marion, John H., Jr. "Southern Economic Needs Challenge the Church." USR, Vol. 51, No. 3 (April 1940).

Rolston, Holmes, Jr. "The Source of Religious Certainty." USR, Vol. 41, No. 2 (January 1930).

Sherrill, Lewis Joseph. "The Barrenness of the Southern Presbyterian Pen." USR, Vol. 42, No. 3 (April 1931).

Sisk, Glenn H. "Churches in the Alabama Black Belt." Church History, Vol. 28 (1954).

Smith, Egbert W. "Origin and Growth of the Organized Women's Work of the Southern Presbyterian Church." USR, Vol. 40, No. 1 (October 1928).

Stagg, John W. "Race Problem in the South." PQ, Vol. 14, No. 58 (July 1900).

Thompson, Ernest T. "Is the Northern Church Theologically Sound?" USR, Vol. 42, No. 2 (January 1931).

Turner, Herbert Snipes. "Old Testament Criticism." USR, Vol. 41, No. 1 (October 1929).

Welden, Julius W. "Womanism in the South." PQ, Vol. 8, No. 28 (April 1894).

Wilson, Samuel M. "The Proposed Assembly's Committee." USR, Vol. 45, No. 3 (April 1934).

Pamphlets and Papers

Anderson, R. C. "The Sunday Newspaper, An Address." Gastonia, N. C.: 1910.

Beard, Rudy, and Robert Morgan. "The Board of Church Extension 1950-1967." A term paper presented to the Department of Church History, Austin Presbyterian Theological Seminary. Austin, Tex.: 1967.

Blanks, W. Davidson. "Presbyterian Worship and Work in the 19th Century." Austin Seminary Bulletin (April 1965).

Board of Christian Education. "The Future Involvement of Men in the Presbyterian Church in the United States." Report by a Special Study Committee to the Board of Christian Education and the Actions of the Board, June 1968, Vols. I-II. Richmond, Va.: Board of Christian Education, 1968.

Board of World Missions. "Recommendations—Consultation on World Missions." Montreat, N. C.: 1962.

Campbell, Robert F. "The Last Fifty Years—The Presbyterian Church an Evangelistic Agency." A Centennial Address. Synod of South Carolina: 1913.
————. "Mission Work among the Mountain Whites in Asheville Presbytery, North Carolina." Asheville, N. C.: 1897. Revised, 1899.
————. "Some Aspects of the Race Problem in the South." Asheville, N. C.: 1899.
Central Mississippi Presbytery. "Report of a Special Committee appointed 1940 to investigate alleged erroneous teachings of Dr. Ernest Trice Thompson." Vicksburg, Miss.: April 9, 1941.
Columbia Theological Seminary. Bulletins:
"In Memoriam: Rev. Henry Alexander White." Vol. 21, No. 1 (October 1927).
"In Memoriam: Richard Clark Reed, 1861-1925." Vol. 20, No. 3 (January 1926).
"The Reverend Richard Turner Gillespie, 1879-1930." Vol. 24, No. 2 (November 1930).
"The Rev. William Marcellus McPheeters, 1854-1935." Vol. 29, No. 4 (July 1936).
Eagleton, Davis F. "A Tribute to the Memory of Rev. W. J. B. Lloyd, Missionary to the Choctaw Indians, 1870-1916." Richmond, Va.: 1916.
East Hanover Presbytery. "Report of Committee on Mr. Tom Glasgow's Pamphlet to East Hanover Presbytery and adopted November 25, 1940." Richmond, Va.: 1940.
Executive Committee of Foreign Missions. "Our Church Faces Foreign Missions: A Comprehensive Study of the Southern Presbyterian Church of her own Foreign Missions Problems and Responsibilities." Nashville, Tenn.: n.d.
Faulkner, L. E., "Rededication to our Forefathers' Ideals: An Address delivered before Kiwanis, Lions, Optimist Clubs of Hattiesburg, Mississippi, 1951." Hattiesburg, Miss.: n.d.
Flinn, Richard Orme. "Frankly Facing Facts: Address before Convention of Laymen's Missionary Movement, Charlotte, N. C., February 18, 1915." Athens, Ga.: n.d.
Fort Worth Presbytery. "The Record of an Abstract from the Minutes of Fort Worth Presbytery." (Examination of William Caldwell.) N.d.
Glasgow, Thomas M. "Shall the Southern Presbyterian Church Abandon its Historic Past: A Plea for Common Honesty. Exposing the Attack of Dr. Ernest Trice Thompson of Union Theological Seminary upon the Standards of the Presbyterian Church in the United States." Charlotte, N. C.: n.d.
————. "A Statement for and Against Dr. Thompson; In one Pamphlet for the Convenience of the Church in the Consideration of this Vital Issue." Charlotte, N. C.: n.d.
Henderlite, Rachel. "We Can't Go Home Again." Austin Seminary Bulletin (April 1967).
Jefferson Presbytery. "A Statement of Facts Concerning the Reception of Ministers in the Churches of the City of New Orleans and Southern Louisiana by the Presbytery of Jefferson U. S. A." New Orleans: 1915.
Johnson, W. Walter. "The New Direction of the New Directory." Austin Seminary Bulletin (April 1965).
Lanham, Sam. "Church Property Disputes in the Presbyterian Church U.S." Seminar Paper, Department of Church History, Austin Presbyterian Theological Seminary. Austin, Tex.: 1967.
Little, John L. "The Presbyterian Colored Mission." Louisville, Ky.: 1909.
McMurray, Stonewall J. "Social Service." Alumni Address at the Austin Presbyterian Theological Seminary, Austin, Texas, May 13, 1914. Austin, Tex.: 1914.
McNeilly, J. H. "50th Anniversary Sermon." Nashville, Tenn.: 1910.
Morris, Samuel L., editor. "Home Missions: Needs and Prospects." Atlanta: 1901.
Murray, E. C. "Does the Bible Teach Natural Science?" Lumberton, N. C.: n.d.
Nichols, Robert Hastings. "Fundamentalism in the Presbyterian Church." Reprinted from the Journal of Religion, Vol. 5, No. 1 (January 1925).
Officers of the Independent Church of Birmingham. "The Other Side of the Recent Case of Dr. H. M. Edmonds and the Presbytery of North Alabama." Birmingham: n.d.
Phillips, A. L. "The Presbyterian Church in the United States and the Colored People." Birmingham, Ala.: 1891.
Presbyterian Ministers' Association, Charlotte, N. C. "Religion and Science: A Protest against Dogmatism in Both." Richmond, Va.: n.d.
Richards, James McDowell. "Inaugural Address." Columbia Theological Seminary Bulletin, Vol. 27, No. 3 (July 1934).
Robertson, J. P. "Christian Philosophy and its Foes." Annual Alumni Address, Austin Theological Seminary, May 1928. Austin: 1928.
Shepherd, William H. "Presbyterian Pioneers in the Congo." Richmond, Va.: n.d.
Smith, Egbert W. "A Protest against Prejudice." N.p.: 1909.
Southern Presbyterian Ministers of Birmingham. "A Review and Exposition of the Case of Dr. H. M. Edmonds and the Presbytery of North Alabama." Birmingham: n.d.
Southwestern at Memphis. "The Official Report of the Hearing of the Charges Preferred by Eleven Presbyterian Ministers against President Charles E. Diehl, Held on Tuesday, February 3, 1931, by the Board of Directors of Southwestern." Extra Southwestern Bulletin, Vol. 14 (New Series), No. 2 (1931).

Union Theological Seminary Bulletin, No. I (July 1923). "The 1923 Anniversary: Union Theological Seminary."
United States Bureau of Education. *Report of the Commissioner of Education 1900-1901.* Article: "Dr. William Henry Ruffner and his Great Work for Popular Education." Reprinted from the *Virginia School Journal* (May 1, 1902).
University of South Carolina. "In Memoriam: Davison McDowell Douglass, 1869-1931." Columbia, S. C.: 1932.
World Missions, Board of. "Recommendations: Consultation on World Missions, Presbyterian Church in the United States." Nashville, Tenn.: 1962.

Autobiography, Correspondence, Journals, Memoirs

Bridges, J. B. Collected papers—not sorted. (Montreat.)
Chester, Samuel Hall. *Behind the Scenes: An Administrative History of the Foreign Work of the Presbyterian Church in the United States.* Austin, Tex.: Boeckman-Jones Co., 1928.
————. "Thirty Years in a Secretary's Office." Address delivered at the General Assembly, 1925. Nashville: 1925.
————. *Memories of Four-Score Years—An Autobiography.* Richmond, Va.: Presbyterian Committee of Publication, 1934.
Dodge, D. Witherspoon. *Southern Rebels in Reverse, The Autobiography of an Idol-Shaker.* New York: The American Press, 1961.
DuBose, H. C. *For the Glory of God, Memoirs of Dr. and Mrs. H. C. DuBose of Soochow, China.* Compiled by Mrs. Nettie DuBose Junkin. Lewisburg, W. Va.: n.d.
Glasgow, Tom. Personal correspondence, copies of letters regarding the E. T. Thompson case. (James A. Jones File, Richmond, Va.)
Jacobs, Thornwell, editor. *The Diary of William Plumer Jacobs.* Atlanta, Ga.: Oglethorpe University, 1937.
————. *Step Down, Dr. Jacobs: The Autobiography of an Autocrat.* Atlanta, Ga.: The Westminster Publishers, 1945.
Jones, James A. Correspondence with Tom Glasgow, regarding the E. T. Thompson case. (James A. Jones File, Richmond, Va.)
Law, William H. Letter of Dr. James Anderson, Feb. 14, 1921. (UTS File.)
Lingle, Walter L. Correspondence. (Lingle File, Montreat, N. C.)
McIlwaine, Richard. *Memories of Three Score Years and Ten.* New York: The Neale Publishing Company, 1908.
Moore, Walter W. Personal correspondence with Dr. Harris E. Kirk. (Files, Union Theological Seminary, Richmond, Va.)
Morris, Samuel Leslie. *S. L. Morris, An Autobiography.* Richmond, Va.: Presbyterian Committee of Publication, 1932.
Smith, Hay Watson. "Prestige and Perquisites." Little Rock: 1930.
Turner, Herbert Snipes. Personal correspondence with letters from Dr. Edward Mack.
Wallace, Addison A. "Memoirs and a Gospel Testimony." Nutley, N. J.: 1945.

Books—Biographical

Carr, James McLeod. *Glorious Ride: The Story of Henry Woods McLaughlin.* Atlanta: Church and Community Press, 1958.
Chester, Samuel H. *Hampden C. DuBose.* Nashville: n.d.
DuBose, Palmer C. *The Anti-Opium Movement in China: The Work of Rev. Hampden C. DuBose.* Nashville, Tenn.: 1918.
Eagleton, D. P. *A Tribute to the Memory of Rev. W. J. B. Lloyd, Missionary to the Choctaw Indians 1870-1916.* Richmond, Va.: Presbyterian Committee of Publication, 1916.
Ervin, Samuel J., Jr. *William Henry Belk (1862-1952): Merchant of the South.* New York: 1958.
Gist, Margaret Adams. *Presbyterian Women of South Carolina.* Woman's Auxiliary of the Synod of South Carolina, 1928.
Irvine, Mary D., and Alice L. Eastwood. *Pioneer Women of the Presbyterian Church, United States.* Richmond, Va.: Presbyterian Committee of Publication, 1923.
Irwin, L. W. *Rev. William McCutcheon Morrison.* An Address, delivered at Washington and Lee University, 1926. Lexington, Va.: 1926.
Jacobs, William P. "Memorial Issue: Rev. William P. Jacobs, 1842-1917." *Our Monthly,* Vol. 54 (September 1917). Clinton, S. C.: Thornwell Orphanage, 1917.
Lacy, Benjamin R. *George W. Watts: The Seminary's Great Benefactor—A Memorial Address.* Richmond, Va.: Union Theological Seminary, 1937.
Levine, Lawrence W. *Defender of the Faith: William Jennings Bryan, The Last Decade, 1915-1925.* New York: Oxford University Press, 1950.

McAllister, James Gray, *The Life and Letters of Walter W. Moore: Second Founder and First President of Union Theological Seminary*. Richmond, Va.: Presbyterian Committee of Publication, 1939.
————, and Grace Owens Guerrant. *Edward C. Guerrant, Apostle to the Southern Highlands*. Richmond, Va.: Presbyterian Committee of Publication, 1950.
Moore, Walter W. *Appreciations and Historical Addresses*. N.d.
Noble, J. Phillips. *Four Presbyterian Pioneers of the Congo*. Richmond, Va.: Presbyterian Committee of Publication, 1893.
Snedecor, Emily Estes. *Sketch of Rev. James George Snedecor*. Typed Ms., 1931.
Vinson, T. C. *William McCutcheon Morrison*. Richmond, Va.: Presbyterian Committee of Publication, 1921.
Wells, John M. *Presbyterian Worthies*. Richmond, Va.: Presbyterian Committee of Publication, 1936.
White, M. A. *Southern Presbyterian Leaders*. New York: The Neale Publishing Company, 1911.
Woods, Henry M. *Rev. Hampden C. DuBose: Missionary to China, 1872-1910.* 1953.

Books—Historical

Alston, Wallace McPherson. *A History of the Young People's Work in the Presbyterian Church in the United States (1861-1938)*. Unpublished Th.D. Thesis, Union Theological Seminary in Virginia, 1938.
Amant, Penrose S. T. *A History of the Presbyterian Church in Louisiana*. Richmond, Va.: Whittet and Shepperson, 1961.
Armstrong, Maurice W.; Lefferts A. Loetscher; Charles A. Anderson. *The Presbyterian Enterprise: Sources of American Presbyterian History*. Philadelphia: The Westminister Press, 1956.
Bailey, Kenneth K. *Southern White Protestantism in the 20th Century*. New York: Harper and Row, 1964.
Batchelor, Alex R. *Jacob's Ladder: Negro Work in the Presbyterian Church in the United States*. Atlanta, Ga.: Bowen Press, 1953.
Bear, James E. *The Mission Work of the Presbyterian Church in the United States in Southern Brazil, 1869-1958*. Vol. I. Typed Ms., Union Theological Seminary in Virginia.
Bell, Sadie. *The Church, the State and Education in Virginia*. Philadelphia: The Science Press Printing Co., 1930.
Blanks, William Davidson. *Ideal and Practice: A Study of the Conception of the Christian Life Prevailing in the Presbyterian Churches of the South during the 19th Century*. Unpublished Doctor's Thesis, Union Theological Seminary in Virginia, 1960.
————. *The Southern Presbyterian View of the Mission of the Church, 1932-1947. A Study in Historical Development*. Unpublished Master's Thesis, Union Theological Seminary in Virginia, 1958.
Blanton, Wyndham. *The History of a Downtown Church, the History of the 2nd Presbyterian Church*. Richmond, Va.: John Knox Press, 1945.
Brimm, Henry, and W. M. E. Rachal, editors. *Yesterday and Tomorrow in the Synod of Virginia*. Richmond, Va.: The Synod of Virginia, 1962.
Buck, Carlos S. *A Study of the History of the Mexican-American Presbyterian Church in Texas*. Unpublished Th.M. Thesis, Austin Presbyterian Theological Seminary, Austin, Texas, 1969.
Campbell, Robert F. "The Last Fifty Years: The Presbyterian Church an Evangelistic Agency," in *Centennial Addresses, Synod of North Carolina*. Greensboro, N. C.: Joseph J. Stone & Co., 1913.
————. *Mission Work among the Mountain Whites in Asheville Presbytery, North Carolina*. Asheville, N. C.: 1897. Second edition, slightly revised, 1899.
Clark, Thomas D. *The Emerging South*. New York: Oxford University Press, 1961.
Cooper, Waller Raymond. *Southwestern at Memphis, 1848-1948*. Richmond, Va.: John Knox Press, 1949.
Coulter, E. Merton. *The South During Reconstruction*. Baton Rouge: Louisiana State University Press, 1947.
Courtney, Lloyd McF. *The Church in the Western Waters: A History of Greenbrier Presbytery*. Richmond, Va.: Whittet and Shepperson, 1940.
Craig, D. L. *A History of the Development of the Presbyterian Church in North Carolina and of Synodical Home Missions together with Evangelistic Addresses by James I. Vance and others*. Richmond, Va.: Whittet and Shepperson, 1907.
Currie, Thomas White, Jr. *A History of Austin Presbyterian Theological Seminary, Austin, Texas, 1884-1943*. Unpublished Th.D. Thesis, Union Theological Seminary in Virginia, 1958.
Dabney, Charles William. *Universal Education in the South*. Two volumes. Chapel Hill: University of North Carolina Press, 1936.

Dendy, Marshall C. *Changing Patterns in Christian Education.* Richmond, Va.: John Knox Press, 1964.
Drury, Clifford Merrill. *Presbyterian Panorama.* Philadelphia: Board of Christian Education, 1952.
Ezell, John Samuel. *The South Since 1895.* New York: Macmillan and Co., 1963.
Fain, Abba Kilpatrick. *Texas Indians: The Story of Indian Village and the Alabama Indians in Polk County, Texas, on the Alabama-Coshetta Reservation.* Livingston, Tex.: 1960.
Garth, John G. *Sixty Years of Home Missions in the Presbyterian Synod of North Carolina.* Charlotte, N. C.: Standard Publishing Co., 1948.
Gatewood, Willard E., Jr. *Preachers, Pedagogues and Politicians: The Evolution Controversy in North Carolina, 1920-1927.* Chapel Hill: University of North Carolina Press, 1966.
Gist, Margaret Adams. *Presbyterian Women of South Carolina.* Published by Woman's Auxiliary of the Synod of South Carolina, 1929.
Gobbel, Luther L. *Church-State Relationships in Education in North Carolina since 1776.* Durham, N. C.: Duke University Press, 1938.
Grafton, C. W. *A Ms. History of the Synod of Mississippi.* Prepared under the auspices of a committee appointed by the Synod of Mississippi of which C. W. Grafton was chairman. Typed, 1927.
Hacker, Luis M., and Benjamin B. Kendrick. *The United States since 1865.* New York: F. S. Crofts and Co., 1953.
Hesseltine, William B., and David L. Smiley. *The South in American History.* Second Edition. Englewood Cliffs, N. J.: Prentice-Hall, Inc., 1960.
Hinman, George Warren. *The American Indian and Christian Missions.* New York: Fleming H. Revell Co., 1933.
Hunt, I. Cochrane. *Presbyterian Home Missions in Kentucky.* Lexington, Ky.: Transylvania Printing Co., 1914.
Jones, F. D., and W. H. Mills. *A History of the Presbyterian Church in South Carolina since 1850.* Columbia, S. C.: Synod of South Carolina, 1925.
Kendrick, Benjamin B., and Alexander Arnett. *The South Looks at its Past.* Chapel Hill: University of North Carolina, 1935.
Lacy, Benjamin R. *Revivals in the Midst of the Years.* Richmond, Va.: John Knox Press, 1945.
LaMotte, Louis C. *Colored Light: The Story of the Influence of Columbia Theological Seminary, 1828-1936.* Richmond, Va.: Presbyterian Committee of Publication, 1937.
Lapsley, S. D., compiler. *From the Past to the Present—A Handbook on Assembly's Home Missions.* Atlanta, Ga.: Executive Committee on Home Missions, 1947.
Lingle, Walter L. *Memories of Davidson College.* Richmond, Va.: John Knox Press, 1947.
Loetscher, Leffert A. *The Broadening Church—A Study of Theological Issues in the Presbyterian Church since 1869.* Philadelphia: University of Pennsylvania, 1950.
McGaughey, Janie W. *On the Crest of the Present: A History of Women's Work, Presbyterian Church in the United States.* Atlanta, Ga.: Board of Women's Work, 1961.
McGeachy, Neill R. *A History of the Sugaw Creek Presbyterian Church, Mecklenburg Presbytery, Charlotte, North Carolina.* Rock Hill, S. C.: Record Printing Co., 1954.
McGehee, Robert W. *The Working of the Young People's Conference.* Unpublished Th.M. Thesis, Union Theological Seminary in Virginia, 1934.
Mackorell, Virginia L. *An Historical Survey of the Hymnbooks of the Presbyterian Church in the United States.* Unpublished Th.M. Thesis, Presbyterian School of Christian Education, Richmond, Va., 1942.
Melton, Julius. *Presbyterian Worship in America.* Richmond, Va.: John Knox Press, 1967.
Morrison, William N. *The Red Man's Trail.* Richmond, Va.: Presbyterian Committee of Publication, 1932.
Morse, H. N. *Home Missions—Today and Tomorrow: A Review and a Forecast.* New York: Home Mission Council, 1934.
Morton, D. Blair, editor. *History of the Presbytery of Kanawha 1895-1956.* Charleston, W. Va.: Jarrett Publishing Co., 1956.
Murray, Andrew E. *Presbyterians and the Negro: A History.* Philadelphia: Presbyterian Historical Society, 1966.
Paschal, George H., Jr. *The History of the U.S.A. Presbyterian Church in Texas and Louisiana.* Unpublished Ph.D. Thesis, Louisiana State University, 1967.
Red, William Stuart. *A History of the Presbyterian Church in Texas.* N.d.
Robinson, William Childs. *Columbia Theological Seminary and the Southern Presbyterian Church, 1831-1931.* Atlanta, Ga.: Dennis Lindsey Publishing Co., 1931.
Schlesinger, Arthur Meier. *A Critical Period in American Religion, 1875-1900.* Philadelphia: Fortress Press, 1967.
Shaloff, Stanley. *The American Presbyterian Congo Mission: A Study in Conflict, 1890-1921.* Unpublished Ph.D. Thesis, Northwestern University, 1967.
————. *Reform in Leopold's Congo* (published form of the above). Richmond, Va.: John Knox Press, 1970.

Shaw, Cornelia Rebekah. *Davidson College.* New York: Fleming H. Revell, 1923.
Shedd, Clarence P. *Two Centuries of Student Christian Movements.* New York: Association Press, 1934.
Sheppard, William H. *Presbyterian Pioneers in the Congo.* Richmond, Va.: Presbyterian Committee of Publication, n.d.
Sherrill, Lewis Joseph. *Presbyterian Parochial Schools, 1846-1870.* New Haven: Yale University Press, 1932.
Simkins, Francis Butler. *The South: Old and New.* New York: Alfred A. Knopf, 1947.
Smith, Charles Lee. *The History of Education in North Carolina.* Washington, D. C.: Government Printing Office, 1888.
Smith, Elwyn A. *The Presbyterian Ministry in American Culture.* Philadelphia: The Westminster Press, 1962.
Smith, Morton H. *Studies in Southern Presbyterian Theology.* Amsterdam, Holland: 1962.
Snedecor, Mrs. J. G. *The Story of Colored Evangelization.* 1909.
Stacy, James. *A History of the Presbyterian Church in Georgia.* Elberton, Ga.: Press of the State, 1912.
Stoltzfus, Grant F. "Survey of the History and Present Publishing Program of the Presbyterian Church of the United States." Term paper, Union Theological Seminary in Virginia, 1955.
Street, T. Watson. *On the Growing Edge of the Church.* Richmond, Va.: John Knox Press, 1965.
————. "The Road from Consultation, 1962, to Convocation, 1967." Address, Ms. copy. Montreat: 1967.
————. *The Story of Southern Presbyterians.* Richmond, Va.: John Knox Press, 1960.
Thompson, Ernest Trice. *The Changing South and the Presbyterian Church in the United States.* Richmond, Va.: John Knox Press, 1950.
————. *Presbyterian Missions in the Southern United States.* Richmond, Va.: Presbyterian Committee of Publication, 1934.
————. *The Spirituality of the Church.* Richmond, Va.: John Knox Press, 1961.
————. "The Synod and Moral Issues" in *Yesterday and Tomorrow in the Synod of Virginia,* ed. by Henry Brimm and W. M. E. Rachal. Richmond, Va.: The Synod of Virginia, 1962.
Tindell, George Brown. *The Emergence of the New South.* Baton Rouge: Louisiana State University Press, 1967.
Topping, Leonard Wesley. *A History of Hampden-Sydney College in Virginia 1771-1883.* Unpublished Th.M. Thesis, Union Theological Seminary in Virginia, 1950.
Union Theological Seminary in Virginia. *The Days of our Years, 1812-1962.* Chapters by James Appleby, Frank B. Lewis, and Ernest T. Thompson. Richmond, Va.: Union Theological Seminary. 1962.
Watters, Mary. *The History of Mary Baldwin College, 1842-1942.* Staunton: 1942.
Winsborough, Hallie Paxson. *The Women's Auxiliary.* Richmond, Va.: Presbyterian Committee of Publication, 1927.
———— (as told to Rosa Gibbons). *Yesteryears.* Atlanta: Assembly's Committee of Women's Work, 1937.
Woodson, C. G. *The History of the Negro Church.* Washington, D. C.: Associated Publishers, 1921.
Woodward, C. Vann. *The Strange Case of Jim Crow.* New York: Oxford University Press, 1955.

Books—Miscellaneous

Annals of the American Academy of Political and Social Sciences. March 1948: *Religion in the United States.*
————. November 1960: *Religion in American Society.*
Best, Harry. *Of our Own Household—Tasks of the Presbyterian Church in Kentucky.* 1927.
Blackwell, Gordon; Lee M. Brooks; and S. H. Hobbs, Jr. *Church and Community in the South.* Richmond, Va.: John Knox Press, 1949.
Bowen, Trevor. *Divine White Right.* New York: Harper and Sons, 1935.
Campbell, Robert F. *Freedom and Restraint.* New York: Fleming H. Revell Co., 1930.
Carr, James McLeod. *Bright Future—A New Day for the Town and Country Church.* Richmond, Va.: John Knox Press, 1956.
————. *The Larger Parish and the Presbyterian Church in the United States.* Atlanta, Ga.: Board of Church Extension, 1952.
————. *Working Together in the Larger Parish.* Atlanta, Ga.: Board of Church Extension, 1960.
Cartledge, Samuel A. *A Conservative Introduction to the Old Testament.* Grand Rapids: Zondervan Publishing House, 1943.
Centennial Addresses, Synod of North Carolina. Greensboro, N. C.: Joseph J. Stone & Co., 1913.

Couch, W. T., editor. *Culture in the South.* Chapel Hill: University of North Carolina Press, 1934.

Craig, Edward Marshall. *Highways and Byways of Appalachia—A Study of the work of the Synod of Appalachia of the Presbyterian Church in the United States.* Kingsport, Tenn.: Kingsport Press, 1927.

Currie, Thomas White. *Our Cities for Christ.* Atlanta, Ga.: Board of Church Extension, 1954.

Dabbs, James McBride. *Who Speaks for the South?* New York: Funk and Wagnalls, 1964.

Diehl, Charles E., editor. *The Story of a Vineyard—The Work of the Presbyterian Church U. S. in the Synod of Tennessee.* Memphis, Tenn.: Davis Printing Co., 1927.

Ficklen, J. B. *The Task of the Presbyterian Church in Georgia.* 1927.

Gear, Felix B. *Basic Beliefs of the Reformation Faith: A Biblical Study of Presbyterian Doctrine.* Richmond, Va.: John Knox Press, 1960.

Gibboney, Charles H. *By Faith.* Atlanta, Ga.: Board of Church Extension, 1951.

Graves, Fred R. *The Presbyterian Work in Mississippi.* 1927.

Guthrie, Shirley C., Jr. *Christian Doctrine.* Richmond, Va.: CLC Press, 1968.

Hazen, James H., compiler. *The Southern Presbyterian Pulpit—A Collection of Sermons by Ministers of the Southern Presbyterian Church.* Richmond, Va.: Presbyterian Committee of Publication, 1896.

Hood, Frazer, editor. *If Ye Know These Things: The Presbyterian Task in North Carolina.* Charlotte: Presbyterian Standard Co., 1927.

Hooker, Elizabeth R. *Religion in the Highlands—Native Churches and Missionary Enterprises in the Southern Appalachians Area.* New York: Home Mission Council, 1933.

Howerton, James R. *The Church And Social Reform.* New York: Fleming H. Revell, 1913.

Hudson, William E. *The Least of These: The Beneficences of the Synod of Virginia.* Richmond, Va.: Presbyterian Committee of Publication, 1926.

Hunt, I. Cochrane. *Presbyterian Home Missions in Kentucky.* Lexington, Ky.: Transylvania Printing Co., 1914.

Johnson, William Walter. *Models of Great Preaching.* Unpublished Th.M. Thesis, Union Theological Seminary in Virginia, 1959.

Kadel, William Howard. *Contemporary Preaching in the Presbyterian Church U. S. and the Presbyterian Church U.S.A. in the Light of Preachers of History.* Unpublished Th.D. Thesis, Union Theological Seminary in Virginia, 1951.

Lapsley, Robert A., Jr. *Home Mission Investments.* Richmond, Va.: John Knox Press, 1946.

Lingle, Walter L. *The Bible and Social Problems.* New York: Fleming H. Revell, 1929.

Liston, Robert T. L. *The Neglected Educational Heritage of Southern Presbyterians.* Bristol, Tenn.: 1956.

Love, Herbert A., editor. *Opportunities-Responsibilities, The Work of the Presbyterian Church U. S. in Florida.* 1927.

McGehee, Robert M. *The Working of the Young People's Conference.* Unpublished Th.M. Thesis, Union Theological Seminary in Virginia, 1934.

McLean, James D. *Bible Studies on Women's Position and Work in the Church.* Richmond, Va.: Presbyterian Committee of Publication, 1893.

McLeod, William A., editor. *Presbyterian Expansion in the Synod of Texas of the Presbyterian Church U. S.* 1927.

McMillan, Homer. *Near Neighbors.* Richmond, Va.: Presbyterian Committee of Publication, 1930.

————. *Unfinished Tasks of the Southern Presbyterian Church.* Richmond, Va.: Presbyterian Committee of Publication, 1922.

Maddox, F. E. *Indictment of Presbyterian Church vs. F. E. Maddox.* Texarkana, Ark.: 1908.

————. *The Passing of Medievalism in Religion.* Texarkana, Ark.: 1908.

Memorial Volume of the Semi-Centennial of the Theological Seminary at Columbia, South Carolina. Columbia, S. C.: Presbyterian Publishing Co., 1884.

Miller, Patrick D., editor. *Building the Church.* Atlanta, Ga.: Board of Church Extension, 1958.

Moore, John D. *The South Today.* New York: Missionary Education Movement, 1916.

Morris, Samuel Leslie. *At our own Doors.* New York: Fleming H. Revell, 1904.

————. *Christianizing Christendom.* Richmond, Va.: Presbyterian Committee of Publication, Richmond, 1919.

————. *Home Missions: Needs and Prospects.* Atlanta, Ga.: Presbyterian Committee of Home Missions, 1901.

————. *The Task that Challenges.* Richmond, Va.: Presbyterian Committee of Publication, 1917.

Nabers, Charles Haddon, editor. *The Southern Presbyterian Pulpit.* New York: Fleming H. Revell Co., 1928.

Phifer, Kenneth G. *A Protestant Case for Liturgical Renewal.* Philadelphia: The Westminster Press, 1865.

Phillips, A. L. *The Call of the Home Land, A Study on Home Missions.* Richmond, Va.: Presbyterian Committee of Publication, 1906.

Raine, James Watt. *The Land of the Saddle Bags—A Study of the Mountain People of Appalachia*. Richmond, Va.: Presbyterian Committee of Publication, 1924.

Reddick, DeWitt C., editor. *Church and Campus*. Richmond, Va.: John Knox Press, 1956.

Sherrill, Lewis J. *Lift Up Your Eyes: A Report to the Churches on the Religious Education Restudy*. Richmond, Va.: John Knox Press, 1948.

—————. *A Study of Religious Education—Final Report of the Committee on Religious Education Restudy to the Executive Committee of Religious Education and Publication of PCUS*. Richmond, Va.: John Knox Press, 1948.

Shriver, Donald W., editor. *The Unsilent South*. Richmond, Va.: John Knox Press, 1965.

Silver, James W. *Mississippi: The Closed Society*. New York: Harcourt Brace and World, Inc., 1964.

Skinner, J. W. *Out of the Wilderness*. Richmond, Va.: Presbyterian Committee of Publication, 1925.

Smith, John Robert. *The Presbyterian Task in an Urban South*. Atlanta, Ga.: Board of Church Extension, 1964.

Swallow, I. F. *Show Me: Presbyterian Study Book, Synod of Missouri, Presbyterian Church U. S.* Kansas City, Mo.: 1927.

Thompson, Ernest Trice. *Tomorrow's Church/Tomorrow's World*. Richmond, Va.: John Knox Press, 1961.

Vance, Rupert B. *Human Geography of the South*. Chapel Hill: University of North Carolina Press, 1932.

Williams, Henry F. *In Seven Countries: A Sketch of the Foreign Mission Fields of the Presbyterian Church, U. S.* Nashville: Committee of Foreign Missions, n.d.

Works, George A., director. *Report of a Survey of the Colleges and Seminaries of the Presbyterian Church in the United States*. Louisville, Ky.: Presbyterian Committee of Christian Education, 1942.

Index

Index

PICKETT'S
CHARGE

PICKETT'S CHARGE

A NEW LOOK AT GETTYSBURG'S FINAL ATTACK

Phillip Thomas Tucker, PhD

Skyhorse Publishing

Visit our website at www.skyhorsepublishing.com.

10 9 8 7 6 5 4 3

Library of Congress Cataloging-in-Publication Data is available on file.

Cover design by Rain Saukas

Cover art courtesy of the Gettysburg Foundation. Detail of "The Battle of Gettysburg," Paul Dominique Philippoteaux, located at the Gettysburg Visitor Center and Museum, Gettysburg National Military Park, Gettysburg, Pennsylvania.

Print ISBN: 978-1-63450-796-7

Ebook ISBN: 978-1-63450-802-5

Printed in the United States of America

Dedication

To the good people at Skyhorse Publishing, especially
Bill Wolfsthal and Mike Lewis.

Contents

Gettysburg Time Line:
Leading up to Pickett's Charge

June 28, 1863
- General Robert E. Lee and Lieutenant General James Longstreet, in Chambersburg, Pennsylvania, receive word that the Federal Army of the Potomac is heading into Pennsylvania.

June 30
- Two brigades from John Buford's Union cavalry division scout ahead and enter Gettysburg. Finding signs of Confederates nearby to the northwest, Buford sends word to Major General John Reynolds in Emmitsburg, Maryland, to bring his infantry as soon as possible.

July 1
- 5:00 a.m. Major General Henry Heth's division, and Lieutenant General Ambrose Powell Hill's 3rd Corps, Army of Northern Virginia, depart Cashtown, Pennsylvania, and march for Gettysburg.
- 7:00 a.m. Advance elements of Heth's division are spied by a Federal signal corps officer from the cupola of the Lutheran Seminary on Seminary Ridge.
- 7:30 a.m. First shot fired three miles NW of Gettysburg at intersection of Knoxlyn Road and Chambersburg Pike by Lieutenant Marcellus Jones of the 8th Illinois Calvary, Buford's cavalry division, against Major General Henry Heth's division of A.P. Hill's corps.
- 8:00 a.m. Buford begins to deploy his cavalry units in a main line on McPherson's Ridge, west of Gettysburg, and on Herr's Ridge just west of McPherson's Ridge. With his troopers dismounted and in good defensive positions, Buford's vital mission is to hold firm as long as possible to buy time for the arrival of the 1st Corps, and keep the Confederates from gaining the defensive high-ground.

- 9:30 a.m. Heth's troops are unleashed, attacking the lengthy lines of Buford's cavalry division.
- 10:15 a.m. Advance elements of the 1st Corps, under Major General Reynolds, arrive on the field and reinforce Buford's division.
- 10:30 a.m. Reynolds and two brigades of the Union 1st Corps infantry arrive and join the line along McPherson Ridge. One is the Iron Brigade, the other is the PA Bucktail Brigade. A bullet through the base of his skull kills Reynolds. Major General Abner Doubleday takes command of the Union 1st Corps.
- 11:00 a.m. Two divisions of the Union 11th Corps arrive and take positions north of town. Lee and staff reach Cashtown and hear the heavy firing. Having been convinced that the Army of the Potomac was still in Maryland below the Pennsylvania line, Lee is shocked by the sounds of heavy fighting because he had ordered his commanders to avoid a major confrontation. Despite his best efforts, Lee cannot gain intelligence about what is happening.
- 11:15 a.m. Major General George G. Meade, the Army of the Potomac's new commander, dispatches additional units north to Gettysburg from his Taneytown, Maryland, headquarters.
- 12:15 p.m. Units of the 11th Corps take possession of the strategic high-ground of Cemetery Hill (at the northern end of Cemetery Ridge). Reynolds is now determined to keep this strategic position out of Rebel hands at all costs.
- 1:00 p.m. Major General Winfield Scott Hancock is dispatched by Meade to ascertain if good ground exists to fight a major battle. Hancock—now in command of all Union forces at Gettysburg because Meade was not yet on the field—orders hard-hit Federal units to retire to Cemetery Hill. Hancock decides to defend Cemetery Hill and Culp's Hill, establishing a solid anchor for a defensive stand.
- 2:00 p.m. One of one-legged Confederate Lieutenant General Richard Ewell's divisions arrives from the north and unleashes a powerful blow, engaging the right flank of the Union 1st Corps.
- 2:10 p.m. General Robert E. Lee arrives to find Heth preparing for a new attack. Forced by circumstances to commit to a full-scale battle that he had never desired, Lee orders an advance all along the line to exploit the favorable tactical gains achieved by Ewell, Heth, and Pender.

- 2:15 p.m. Another division of Ewell's attacks the 11th Corps position.
- 3:00 p.m. Where the Eternal Light Peace Memorial now stands, Confederate Major General Robert Rhode's division launches an attack. With five brigades, it's the largest division in either army.
- 4:00 p.m. Jubal Early's division of Ewell's corps arrives from the northeast on Harrisburg Road and causes the right flank of the 11th Corps, two small divisions known as the Dutch Corps (mainly German-Americans), to buckle. This sets off a chain reaction down the two-mile Union line. The 1st and 11th Corps retreat through town to Cemetery Hill and Culp's Hill. Major General Oliver Otis Howard, one-armed commander of the 11th, had reserved a third smaller division to fortify Cemetery Hill in case of retreat.
- 4:15 p.m. Hill orders Pender's division to advance from Herr's Ridge and attack toward Gettysburg.
- 5:00 p.m. Confederates appear to have won, but to complete the job, Lee tells Ewell, whose 3rd Division is arriving, to attack Cemetery Hill "if practicable." Ewell decides against it.
- 5:45 p.m. After finally receiving intelligence from Hancock, Meade commits himself to fighting a major battle at Gettysburg. Federal troops hold the key high-ground and thus a decided advantage. Three corps, the 3rd, 5th, and 12th, now march for Gettysburg to reinforce the battered 1st and 11th Corps.
- After midnight, Meade arrives.

July 2

- Before dawn. The Rebel Army of Northern Virginia reaches Gettysburg except Major General Jeb Stuart's cavalry and, from Longstreet's corps, Major General George Pickett's division and Brigadier General Evander Law's brigade. They arrive during the day after marching all night.
- 4:00 p.m. After a long march to avoid observation, Longstreet's troops attack, led by Evander Law's brigade. The army's chief of engineers, Brigadier General Gouverneur K. Warren, spots them coming, and Brigadier General Strong Vincent leads his men into position on Little Round Top. The 20th Maine, commanded by Colonel Joshua Lawrence Chamberlain (and made famous in the novel *The Killer Angels* and in the movie *Gettysburg*), is positioned on the left. Major General

Daniel E. Sickles had ordered his 3rd Corps to advance west from Meade's main Cemetery Ridge Line, extending south from Cemetery Hill, to take a defensive position on the higher ground of the Peach Orchard and the Emmitsburg Road ridge. Over the next three hours, battle rages across the Wheatfield. Confederates take Rose farm, the Peach Orchard, the Wheatfield, Trostle farm, and Devil's Den. The troops of Major General John Bell Hood's division, 1st Corps, attack Meade's far left at Little Round Top and then strike Union positions at the Devil's Den and Houck's Ridge, just northwest of Little Round Top. Sickles has a leg shot off, which he later has preserved in formaldehyde.

- 5:30 p.m. to 7:00 p.m. General William Barksdale's charge overwhelms Sickles's Peach Orchard salient. The steamrolling attack of the Mississippi brigade then continues east and all the way to Cemetery Ridge.

- 7:00 p.m. From a desperate defensive position on Little Round Top, Chamberlain gives the order—"Bayonet!"—and the Union men charge down the hill.

- 8:00 p.m. The Confederates still hold the Peach Orchard, the Wheatfield, Trostle farm, and Devil's Den. They will control Spangler's Spring overnight. Fighting between Brigadier General George S. Greene's brigade and Major General Edward Johnson's division with two brigades of Early's division becomes intense across Cemetery Hill and Culp's Hill; as dusk approaches Early's troops make significant gains, until pushed off the strategic hill by the Union counterattack.

- Overnight. Frequent firing is heard. On the Confederate side, Pickett's division and Stuart's three cavalry brigades arrive. On the Union side, Major General John Sedgwick's 6th Corps arrive. In Meade's headquarters, he takes a vote from his generals and they decide to stay and fight.

July 3

- 4:30 a.m. Union troops renew the fight at Culp's Hill. Federal troops atop the hill launch assaults down the slopes to catch the Confederates by surprise. Attacks and counterattacks continue for nearly seven hours.

- 5:00 a.m. Stuart leads the troopers of his cavalry division east from Gettysburg, beginning the attempt to gain the Army of the Potomac's rear.

- 7:30 a.m. Skirmishing opens on the Bill Bliss Farm between the lines before Cemetery Ridge.

- 8:30 a.m. Sniper fire between Confederate troops barricaded in town and Union troops on Cemetery Hill continues throughout the day. Twenty-year-old Mary Virginia "Jenny" Wade is shot by a stray bullet in her sister's kitchen on Baltimore Street as she makes biscuits for Union soldiers. She is the only civilian casualty of the battle.
- 9:00 a.m. Pickett's division reaches Seminary Ridge—the Confederate army's last fresh division to arrive on the battlefield.
- 1:00 p.m. Stuart leads his Confederate calvary around to confront the Union rear, including Brigadier General George Armstrong Custer, along Cemetery Ridge.
- 1:07 p.m. Two cannon shots fire from Seminary Ridge, the signal for Confederates to harden the attack near the now-famous copse of trees on Cemetery Ridge. The massive Confederate bombardment has begun in preparation for the launching of Pickett's Charge. The Union side retaliates. There are almost two hours of rapid fire from 250 cannons. It is reportedly heard in Pittsburgh, 150 miles west, but not in Chambersburg, only fifteen miles west.
- Between 2:00 p.m. and 3:00 p.m. The Confederate batteries run low on ammunition. Pickett asks Longstreet, "General, shall I advance?" and receives a nod to carry out the now-famous Pickett's Charge.

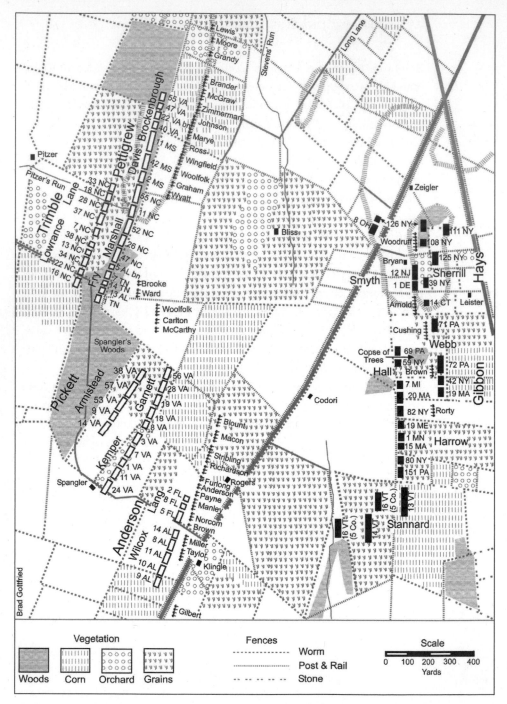

Tactical situation in preparation for the unleashing of Pickett's Charge, around 1:30 p.m. (*Courtesy of Bradley M. Gottfried, PhD.*)

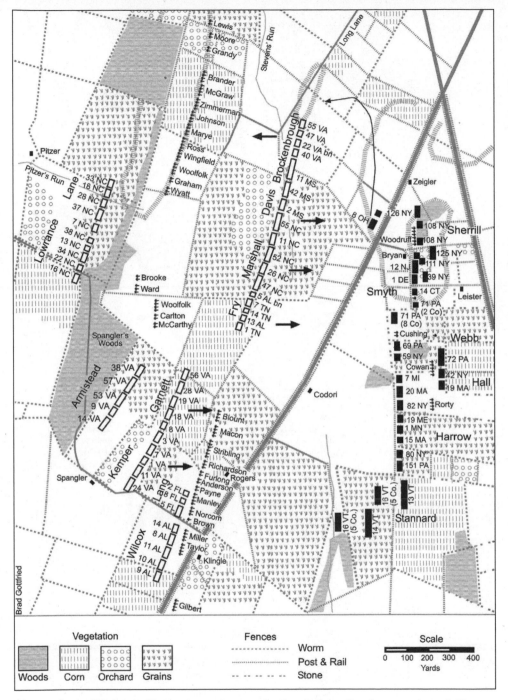

The attackers of Pickett's Charge descending on the Emmitsburg Road sector, about 2:30 p.m. *(Courtesy of Bradley M. Gottfried, PhD.)*

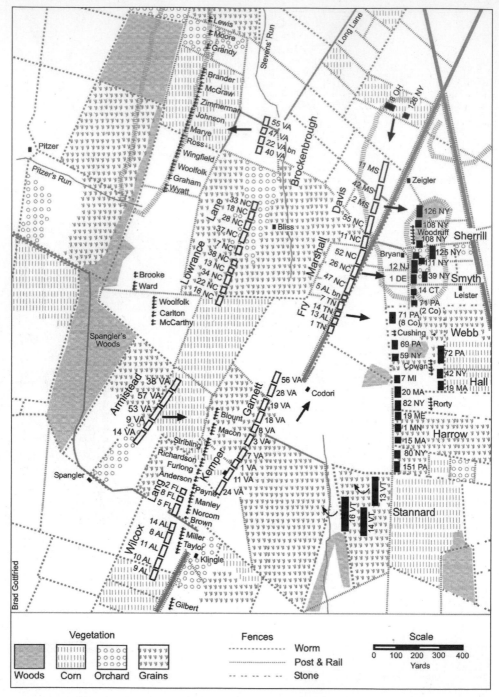

Garnett's and Kemper's brigades shifting north in a maneuver to gain the right of Pettigrew's division, about 2:30 p.m. *(Courtesy of Bradley M. Gottfried, PhD.)*

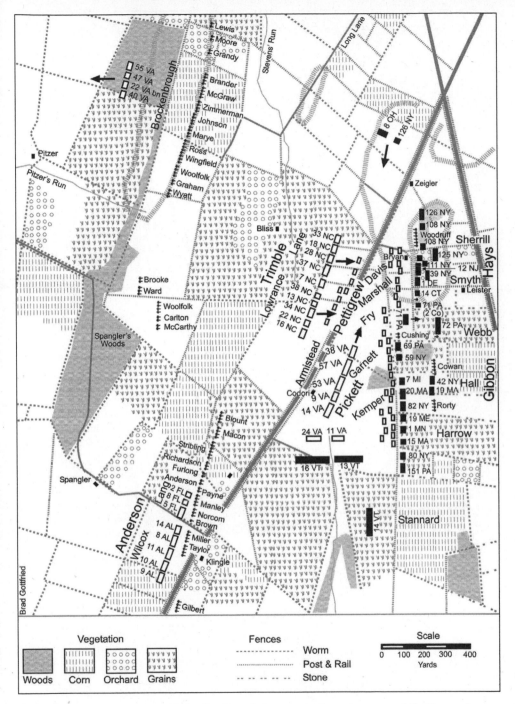

Pickett's troops surging toward the Angle and the copse of trees sectors, while Kemper's men on the far right face the flank threat posed by encroaching Vermont regiments on the south, about 2:40 p.m. (*Courtesy of Bradley M. Gottfried, PhD.*)